Mental Retardation

An Introduction to Intellectual Disabilities

Seventh Edition

Mary Beirne-Smith
University of Alabama

James R. Patton

Shannon H. Kim
Baddour Center
Senatobia, Mississippi

PEARSON

Merrill
Prentice Hall

Upper Saddle River, New Jersey
Columbus, Ohio

Library of Congress Cataloging-in-Publication Data

Beirne-Smith, Mary.
  Mental retardation: an introduction to intellectual disabilities/Mary Beirne-Smith, James R. Patton, Shannon H. Kim.—7th ed.
     p. cm.
  Includes bibliographical references and index.
  ISBN 0-13-118189-0
  1. Mental retardation. I. Patton, James R. II. Kim, Shannon H. III. Title.
  RC570.B45 2006
  362.3–dc22   2005003472

Vice President and Executive Publisher: Jeffery W. Johnston
Senior Editor: Allyson P. Sharp
Development Editor: Heather Doyle Fraser
Editorial Assistant: Kathleen S. Burk
Production Editor: Sheryl Glicker Langner
Production Coordination: Thistle Hill Publishing Services, LLC
Photo Coordinator: Sandy Schaefer
Design Coordinator: Diane C. Lorenzo
Cover Designer: Bryan Huber
Cover Image: Corbis
Production Manager: Laura Messerly
Director of Marketing: Ann Castel Davis
Marketing Manager: Autumn Purdy
Marketing Coordinator: Brian Mounts

This book was set in Usherwood Book by Carlisle Communications, Ltd. It was printed and bound by R.R. Donnelley & Sons Company. The cover was printed by The Lehigh Press, Inc.

Photo Credits: Ohio Historical Society, p. 2; Human Policy Press, p. 11; Edgar A. Doll, p. 19; Anthony Magnacca/Merrill, pp. 38, 312, 402; Anne Vega/Merrill, pp. 41, 150, 243, 256; Todd Yarrington/Merrill, pp. 65, 363; Robin Nelson/PhotoEdit, p. 84; Scott Cunningham/Merrill, pp. 93, 105, 160, 228, 239, 254, 273, 292, 316, 320, 412, 436; Stephen Ferry/Getty Images, Inc.—Liaison, p. 122; Tom Watson/Merrill, p. 136; Laura Dwight/Laura Dwight Photography, pp. 166, 377, 410; Barbara Schwartz/Merrill, pp. 175, 451; Brady/PH College, p. 180; Doug Martin/Merrill, p. 184; Steve Allen/Getty Images, Inc.—Image Bank, p. 219; Shirley Zeiberg/PH College, p. 235; Dr. Kenneth Salyer, Dallas, Texas, pp. 282, 283; Richard Hutchings/PhotoEdit, p. 341; Jeff Greenberg/Omni-Photo Communications, Inc., p. 350; Will and Deni McIntyre/Photo Researchers, Inc., p. 432.

Pearson Education Ltd.   Pearson Education Australia Pty. Limited
Pearson Education Singapore Pte. Ltd.   Pearson Education North Asia Ltd.
Pearson Education Canada, Ltd.   Pearson Educación de Mexico, S.A. de C.V.
Pearson Education—Japan   Pearson Education Malaysia Pte. Ltd.

10 9 8 7 6 5 4
ISBN: 0-13-118189-0

Dedicated to our families—
Michele, Harold, Jenny, Andrew, Alison
Joy, Kimi
Sammy, Landis

Educator Learning Center:
An Invaluable Online Resource

Merrill Education and the Association for Supervision and Curriculum Development (ASCD) invite you to take advantage of a new online resource, one that provides access to the top research and proven strategies associated with ASCD and Merrill—the Educator Learning Center. At www.educatorlearningcenter.com, you will find resources that will enhance your students' understanding of course topics and of current educational issues, in addition to being invaluable for further research.

HOW THE EDUCATOR LEARNING CENTER WILL HELP YOUR STUDENTS BECOME BETTER TEACHERS

With the combined resources of Merrill Education and ASCD, you and your students will find a wealth of tools and materials to better prepare them for the classroom.

Research
- More than 600 articles from the ASCD journal *Educational Leadership* discuss everyday issues faced by practicing teachers.
- A direct link on the site to Research Navigator™ gives students access to many of the leading education journals, as well as extensive content detailing the research process.
- Excerpts from Merrill Education texts give your students insights on important topics of instructional methods, diverse populations, assessment, classroom management, technology, and refining classroom practice.

Classroom Practice
- Hundreds of lesson plans and teaching strategies are categorized by content area and age range.
- Case studies and classroom video footage provide virtual field experience for student reflection.
- Computer simulations and other electronic tools keep your students abreast of today's classrooms and current technologies.

LOOK INTO THE VALUE OF EDUCATOR LEARNING CENTER YOURSELF

A four-month subscription to Educator Learning Center is $25 but is **FREE** when packaged with any Merrill Education text. In order for your students to have access to this site, you must use this special value-pack ISBN number **WHEN** placing your textbook order with the bookstore: 0-13-155986-9. Your students will then receive a copy of the text packaged with a free ASCD pincode. To preview the value of this website to you and your students, please go to www.educatorlearningcenter.com and click on "Demo."

Over time, a considerable body of knowledge has been compiled about individuals who have intellectual disabilities: how they learn, how and what to teach them, and how society treats them. The recent movements of inclusion and empowerment of individuals who are disabled into society in general are changing the way individuals with intellectual disabilities live, work, learn, and recreate. Recent developments in the fields of psychology, education, law, and medicine have made critical the need for informed, educated professionals in the field of mental retardation.

The first edition of this book was published in 1981 and subsequent editions have been published approximately every 4 years since that time. The first edition of this book was a derivative of a book entitled *Mental Retardation: Introduction and Personal Perspectives,* edited by James Kauffman and James Payne, that was published by Charles E. Merrill Publishing Company in 1975. The most current edition of this book owes much to its predecessors.

Our main purpose in writing the seventh edition of this text, as has been the intent of earlier editions, is to provide professionals with timely information about the many facets of mental retardation from a life-cycle perspective. We have tried to integrate the literature and ongoing work in the field of mental retardation with what we have learned from our own experiences. It is exciting and fulfilling to be involved in the area of mental retardation. We hope that our interest in this field and our enthusiasm about individuals who have intellectual disabilities, their families, their friends, their coworkers, others with whom they come in contact, and the society in which they live come through in this book.

As is the case with any revision of a book like this one, our challenge was to retain what was valuable from previous editions, add what is current to this edition, provide some new ways to organize and present information, and integrate it all into a meaningful whole. Throughout the revision process, we have been mindful of our goal of producing a text that is useful for a variety of professionals who work with individuals who have intellectual disabilities. As is true in previous editions of this text, we attempt to show relationships between theory and practice; we decode the terminology used in the literature on mental retardation, particularly that associated with causes of intellectual disabilities; and we relate these terms to the reality of the classroom, the world of work, life of the community, and life at home. In addition, we point out many valuable resources in the field of special education and the area of mental retardation.

FEATURES OF THE SEVENTH EDITION

We have retained the features of previous editions for which we received positive feedback from reviewers and users. We begin each chapter with a list of key terms and learning objectives. Each key term is defined in the chapter and included in the glossary for easy reference. Each chapter ends with bulleted summary statements. Finally, we have continued to use short features in each chapter to broaden the coverage of topics.

A book about mental retardation must address key concepts and topics that are germane to this field of study. We have maintained the general organization of the book, as we feel that the chapter selection addresses the major issues in the field. We did combine the chapters on school years and transition years. Critical new information has been introduced to all of the chapters, including up-to-date information on the reauthorization in fall 2004 of the Individuals with Disabilities Education Act (IDEA). Each chapter has been substantially revised, and, where appropriate, we have increased the focus on developmental disabilities and diversity considerations.

ORGANIZATION OF THE TEXT

We organized the text in four parts. In part 1, we concentrate on basic concepts about intellectual disabilities. In this section, we have chapters on historical perspectives, definition and terminology, assessment practices, and individual rights and legal issues. In part 2, we focus on the biology, psychology, and sociology of mental retardation. In this section, we have chapters on psychosocial aspects of mental retardation, biological causes and preventive efforts, and family considerations. Characteristics of individuals with milder forms of mental retardation and characteristics of individuals with more significant forms of mental retardation make up part 3. Finally, in part 4, we look at programming and intervention issues across the life span of individuals who have intellectual disabilities. In this section, we have chapters about infancy and early childhood years, school years, adult years, and assistive technology applications.

SUPPLEMENTS

The seventh edition has an enhanced supplement support package, including a Companion Website, an online version of the text for students, an online Instructor's Manual with Test Items, and online PowerPoint Transparencies.

COMPANION WEBSITE

Located at **http://www.prenhall.com/beirne-smith,** the Companion Website for this text includes a wealth of resources for both professors and students. The Syllabus Manager™ enables professors to create and maintain the class syllabus online while also allowing the student access to the syllabus at any time from any computer on the Internet. The student portion of the website helps students gauge their understanding of chapter content through the use of online chapter reviews, resources, interactive self-assessments, and video cases for interpretation and reflection.

Online Instructor's Manual with Test Items

The Instructor's Manual is available online at the Instructor Resource Center, described below. It is organized by chapter and contains chapter outlines, key terms, objectives, in-class activities, discussion questions, projects, presentations, and additional text resources. The manual also includes multiple choice, true/false, and essay test items for each chapter.

PowerPoint Transparencies

The transparencies—available in PowerPoint slide format at the Instructor Resource Center, described below—highlight key concepts, summarize content, and illustrate figures and charts from the text.

Instructor Resource Center

The Instructor Resource Center at **www.prenhall.com** has a variety of print and media resources available in downloadable, digital format—all in one location. As a registered faculty member, you can access and download pass-code protected resource files, course management content, and other premium online content directly to your computer.

Digital resources available for *Mental Retardation: An Introduction to Intellectual Disabilities,* Seventh Edition, include:

- Text-specific PowerPoint lectures
- An online version of the Instructor's Manual with Test Items

To access these items online, go to **www.prenhall.com** and click on the Instructor Support button and then go to the Download Supplements section. Here you will be able to log in or complete a one-time registration for a user name and password. If you have any questions regarding this process or the materials available online, please contact your local Prentice Hall sales representative.

SafariX Textbook Online: Where the Web Meets Textbooks for Student Savings!

SafariX Textbooks Online™ is an exciting new choice for students looking to save money. As an alternative to purchasing the print textbook, students can subscribe to the same content online and save up to 50% off the suggested list price of the print text. With a SafariX WebBook, students can search the text, make notes online, print out reading assignments that incorporate lecture notes, and bookmark important passages for later review. For more information, or to subscribe to the SafariX WebBook, visit **http://www.safarix.com.**

ACKNOWLEDGMENTS

In revising this text, we were inspired by many individuals. Without question, Jim Payne's mentorship and vision for this text is the pragmatic reason this book ever came to be. If not for Jim's philosophy of collaboration, none of us who have been or currently are coauthors of this most recent edition would be part of the party.

Our families and friends offered unconditional love and the support we needed to complete the task. Without these virtues shown to us, projects such as this one would not come to fruition.

We are indebted to those who contributed their time, energies, and expertise to previous editions: Diane M. Browder, Frances E. Butera, Gary Clark, Lawrence J. Coleman, Jill C. Dardig, Robert M. Davis, Dan Ezell, Keith Hume, Cynthia Jackson, Fay and David Jackson, Eric D. Jones, Allen K. Miller, John A. Nietupski, Jerry Nunnally, Ruth Ann Payne, Greg A. Robinson, Tommy Russell, H. Monroe Snider, Charlotte Sonnier-York, Janis Spiers, Carol Thomas, Thomas J. Zirpoli, and Vicki Knight.

We are especially appreciative of the contributions of Rick Ittenbach, who was a coauthor on the fourth through sixth editions. His work and efforts are much appreciated and his influence is still felt in this edition of the book.

We are grateful to our colleagues who contributed to this edition of the text: Edward Polloway, J. David Smith, Audrey Trainor, and Sylvia Dietrich. Their willingness to participate, the expertise they brought to the project, and the excellent work they produced are appreciated.

We wish to express our appreciation to Lynette Lacey-Godfrey, who devoted innumerable hours to developing our Instructor's Manual. We are also grateful to many individuals who contributed in various ways to the research and development of this edition.

We also want to thank the following reviewers for their guidance and feedback: Pam Gent, Clarion University; Ann Cranston-Gingras, University of South Florida; Tes Mehring, Emporia State University; Cliff Baker, University of Northern Colorado; and Carrie Ann Blackaller, California State University–Dominguez Hills.

Finally, we wish to express our sincere appreciation to the individuals at Merrill/Prentice Hall who encouraged and supported our efforts. Their *patience,* understanding, and professionalism are unequaled. We want to express our sincere gratitude to Heather Fraser, Allyson Sharp, and Kathy Burk, who hung in there with us through the development phase and Sheryl Langner and Sandy Schaefer at Merrill/Prentice Hall, along with Amanda Hosey at Thistle Hill Publishing Services, who took our manuscript and put it into print.

—MBS

—JRP

—SHK

Brief Contents

Contents

PART II
Biology, Psychology, and Sociology of Mental Retardation

PART III
Characteristics of Mental Retardation

PART IV
Programming and Issues Across the Life Span

Note: Every effort has been made to provide accurate and current Internet information in this book. However, the Internet and information posted on it are constantly changing, so it is inevitable that some of the Internet addresses listed in this textbook will change.

Mary Beirne-Smith

Mary Beirne-Smith, Ed.D., is an Associate Professor of Special Education at the University of Alabama. Her previous experience includes general and special education classroom teaching and administration. Her research interests center around collaboration, co-teaching, and accommodations and modifications for students with mild disabilities who are included in general education classrooms. She has written books, chapters, and articles in the area of special education and presented at numerous national and international professional conferences. Mary received her M.Ed. and Ed.D. from the University of Virginia.

James R. Patton

Jim Patton, Ed.D., currently is an independent consultant and Adjunct Associate Professor in the Department of Special Education at the University of Texas at Austin. He formerly was a special education teacher, having taught students with special needs at the elementary, secondary, and postsecondary levels. He has written books, chapters, articles, and tests in the area of special education. Jim's current areas of professional interest are the assessment of the transition strengths and needs of students, the infusion of real-life content into existing curricula, study skills instruction, behavioral intervention planning, and the accommodation of students with special needs in inclusive settings. He is also working as a mental retardation forensic specialist in regard to death penalty cases in Texas and other parts of the country. Jim received his B.S. from the University of Notre Dame and his M.Ed. and Ed.D. from the University of Virginia.

Shannon Hill Kim

Shannon Hill Kim, Ph.D., is currently serving as Director of Education and Research for the Baddour Center, a private nonprofit organization that provides residential and vocational services to adults with mental retardation. She also serves as Adjunct Professor of Counselor Education for the University of Mississippi. Shannon has served people with mental retardation in a variety of capacities, including direct care, vocational education, and behavior intervention. Her publications have been in the areas of mental health services to persons with mental retardation, behavioral supports, and deinstitutionalization outcomes. She received her Ph.D. in educational psychology from the University of Mississippi in 2000.

Sylvia L. Dietrich

Sylvia L. Dietrich, Ph.D., serves as Assistant Professor of Special Education at the University of Alabama in the Early Childhood Special Education program. She earned both her baccalaureate and M.S. degrees from Eastern Kentucky University. She was awarded her doctorate from the University of Tennessee. Her professional experience includes work as a special education teacher, disability specialist with Head Start, and assistant professor. Sylvia has made numerous presentations to national and international audiences on issues related to the education of young children with disabilities. She contributes to the literature on special education, human services, and teacher education through articles in scholarly and professional journals. Sylvia's research interests include relationships of young children with disabilities, the development and shaping of attitudes toward children with disabilities, and the collaboration of professionals and service providers in delivering quality services to young children and their families.

Edward A. Polloway

Edward A. Polloway, Ed.D., is Vice President for Community Advancement and Dean of Graduate Studies at Lynchburg College, where he has served as a special education faculty member and administrator since 1976. His undergraduate degree is from Dickinson College and his graduate degrees are from the University of Virginia. Ed is the author of a number of special education textbooks, including *Strategies for Teaching Learners with Special Needs* (now in its eighth edition), *Teaching Students with Special Needs in Inclusive Settings* (fourth edition), and *Language Instruction for Exceptional Learners* (third edition). He served two terms as President of the Division on Mental Retardation and Development Disabilities of the Council for Exceptional Children and is the recipient of its Burton Blatt Humanitarian Award. He also was a former member of the Board of the Trustees of the Council for Learning Disabilities (CLD). In 2001, he was invited to present CLD's 14th Annual Distinguished Lecture. Ed is the author or coauthor of approximately 100 articles in special education and related fields and served as the senior editor of the journal *Remedial and Special Education*.

J. David Smith

J. David Smith, Ed.D., serves as Professor of Special Education at The University of North Carolina at Greensboro. He earned both baccalaureate and M.S. degrees from Virginia Commonwealth University. He was awarded a second master's degree and his doctorate from Columbia University. His professional experience includes work as a special education teacher, counselor, professor, department chair, dean, and provost. Dave has made numerous invited presentations to national and international audiences. He regularly contributes to the literature on education, human services, and public policy through articles in scholarly and professional journals. Dave is the author of 11 books. One of the integrating themes of his research and writing is a concern for the rights and dignity of people with disabilities. He also has a particular interest in the history of mental retardation.

Audrey A. Trainor

Audrey A. Trainor, Ph.D., is an Assistant Professor in the Department of Rehabilitation Psychology and Special Education at the University of Wisconsin at Madison. Her interests include multicultural special education issues, postsecondary transition planning for students with learning disabilities, self-determination and adolescent development, family and student participation in special education, and English language learners diagnosed with disabilities. She received her Ph.D. in special education from the University of Texas at Austin in May 2003.

1

Historical Perspectives

OBJECTIVES

After reading this chapter, the student should be able to:

- Discuss the underlying dynamics that affect the history of the study of intellectual disability
- Identify major historical eras associated with certain dominant trends
- Discuss the contributions of persons who have had a significant effect on the development of the field
- Explain how various sociopolitical events have affected the treatment of people who are mentally retarded
- Trace the evolutionary development of contemporary issues

KEY TERMS

eugenics movement	mental test	right to education
homme sauvage	metabolic disturbance	sociopolitical forces
humanism	normalization	sterilization
inclusive environments	pedigree studies	

T he field of intellectual disability is rich with history and fascinating to study. Many events and people have influenced the field, and a look at some of them is worthwhile. From a survey of the history of the field, we can gain a better understanding of the factors that have led to the present state of affairs. In many disciplines, however, such study has been sacrificed in recent times in preference to other topics deemed more important. This slighting of history is unfortunate, because professionals in a variety of disciplines associated with intellectual disability need to know the contexts that have shaped this field.

A complete online glossary is available on the Companion Website, which may be accessed at www.prenhall.com/ beirne-smith

While much of the progress made in the field of intellectual disabilities has been due to the unending and dedicated efforts of individuals, strong **sociopolitical forces** have also been at work to influence its development. When studying history, we must appreciate the social climate of a given time. In the past, as in the present, much of what has happened to people with intellectual disabilities has been determined largely by social and political factors. Sociopolitical elements have shaped policy, practice, and treatment of individuals with intellectual disabilities.

Scholars such as Blatt and Sarason have paid much attention to the sociological implications of intellectual disability and conclude that intellectual disability is very much a social phenomenon. Blatt (1987) states: "Mental retardation is a concept that developed with history. It has changed through time in its nature and in its significance" (p. 9). Sarason (1985) suggests that mental retardation cannot be understood fully unless one examines the society, culture, and history within which it occurs.

In discussing the historical background of intellectual disability, we attempt to establish a case for what we call a "recycling phenomenon"—certain issues have resurfaced on different occasions over the course of history. Throughout this chapter, we mention issues that were discussed and debated long ago. You may feel dismayed by the fact that some long-standing issues still remain just that—issues, with "solutions" still forthcoming. The essence of this phenomenon is captured in the following quote:

> Many people also think that the issues facing special education today are completely new. But if you read the historical literature of special education, you will see that today's issues and problems are remarkably similar to those of long ago. Issues, problems, and ideas arise, flower, go to seed, and reappear when the conditions are again right for their growth. (Patton, Blackbourn, & Fad, 1996, p. 305)

This chapter has three primary objectives. First, as already mentioned, we focus on the historical context of intellectual disabilities, giving you a glimpse of both the sociopolitical influences that have determined where we are today and some recurrent themes expressed throughout the short documented history of the field. Second, we present the content of that history—that is, the names, dates, places, and events typically associated with it. Third, we introduce you to the complexities of human services as they relate to programming for people with intellectual disabilities.

HISTORICAL OVERVIEW

While attitudes toward and treatment of persons with intellectual disabilities can actually be traced back to ancient civilizations (including Egypt, Sparta, Rome, China, and the early Christian world), a documented history relating to intellectual disability is rather brief, spanning only about the last 300 years. Accordingly, this chapter focuses on the more recent history with some attention given to earlier times. For the sake of organization, we have divided history into five rather arbitrary time periods, based on an examination of trends in the field of intellectual disability (Polloway, Smith, Patton, & Smith, 1996). The reader is encouraged to accept these periods of time for their organizational value, not their exactness. The five eras are as follows:

1. Antiquity: Prior to 1700
2. Emergence and Early Disillusionment of a Field: 1700–1890
3. Facilities-Based Orientation: 1890–1960
4. Services-Based Orientation: 1960–1985
5. Supports-Based Orientation: 1985–Present

Before we proceed through the various periods, we must address terminology. For the most part throughout this chapter, language we use will be in accordance with current systems. While this usage will help us maintain a consistent standard, we would be remiss if we did not mention that, historically, various terms have been used officially to describe these individuals. (These terms are discussed in the next chapter on definitions.) Today, however, many professionals find such terms as *fool, moron, imbecile, idiot, feebleminded, mental defective,* and *retardate* (among others) to be historically accurate but personally offensive. It should be noted, however, that instances do occur in the chapter where historical terms are used to maintain historical accuracy.

For a more thorough review of intellectual disability in antiquity, refer to Scheerenberger (1983).

ANTIQUITY: PRIOR TO 1700

Before the 18th century, the concept of intellectual disability, regardless of the term used to describe it, was enigmatic to a world that did not have a sophisticated knowledge base with which to understand it. As a result, people around the world held a variety of attitudes and perceptions toward people whose mental abilities and adaptive behaviors varied from the norm.

Basically, there was no consensus among Western societies as to who these people were, why they acted the way they did, and how they should be treated. Different societies' responses to these questions ranged from treating these individuals as buffoons and court jesters to perceiving them as demons or as persons capable of receiving divine revelations. As a result, throughout ancient history different patterns of treatment and interaction developed.

Throughout this early history and continuing until the early 1900s, when we refer to persons with mental limitations, we are speaking specifically of individuals with more severe involvement. Milder forms of intellectual disability as we perceive them today were neither defined nor recognized. During times when physical skills were most important and when few individuals could read or write, most individuals with mild intellectual disabilities whose social competence was acceptable blended into society without too much difficulty. Not until the early part of the 20th century did mild intellectual disability become a describable condition.

Before 1700, certain developments resulting from the Renaissance of the 15th and 16th centuries created a new social climate that would eventually have direct implications for persons with intellectual disabilities. Although the Renaissance was important to the world in many ways, the fact that it "increased man's willingness to look at himself and his environment more openly, naturally, and empirically (i.e., scientifically)" (Maloney & Ward, 1978, pp. 21–22) is particularly noteworthy. The prevailing social forces tended to refocus people's concepts of themselves and the world. The ultimate effects of these changes were reflected in the development of a climate conducive to the philosophy of humanism and the revolutionary fervor of the 18th century.

Before 1700, if any service (using the word loosely) was provided to individuals with special needs, it was protective in nature (i.e., providing housing and sustenance) and often offered in monasteries. Little evidence exists that systematic programs of training or service delivery were available. Although obvious changes were occurring in the world, not much was altering for the 17th century person with intellectual disability.

In America at this time, the family unit was of primary importance, and it assumed much of the responsibility in caring for any exceptional member. This nature of care can be seen in many developing countries throughout the world today. Following European precedents, the colonies enacted laws that "provided for" many individuals who could not care for themselves, by creating almshouses and workhouses. Although looked upon as financial burdens, these individuals, some of whom must have been intellectually disabled, were at least taken care of by colonial society.

EMERGENCE AND EARLY DISILLUSIONMENT OF A FIELD: 1700–1890

Arguably the most significant features of the 18th century were the advent of "sensationalism" and the revolutionary changes in both Europe and America. Through the efforts of various philosophers, most notably John Locke (1632–1704) and Jean-Jacques Rousseau (1712–1778), new ideas stressing the importance of the senses in human development began to take hold. These ideas provided new ways of perceiving the nature of the human mind and ultimately influenced educational reform.

As mentioned earlier, Renaissance thinking encouraged a philosophy of **humanism,** principally concerned with people's worth as human beings and freedom to develop. The idea that all were created equal and had inalienable rights to life, liberty, and the pursuit of happiness was popular. Eventually, these notions came into conflict with the existing philosophies and policies of some established nations, and both Europeans and Americans reacted to these needs for freedom through revolution.

One might wonder what effect these historical events had on people with intellectual disabilities. We believe that they had two major implications. First, a new social attitude was established. It held that all "men," even those who had disabilities, had rights. Although this attitude was not always evidenced, it helped lead to a climate that would support efforts to assist these individuals. Second, the times were right for idealistic individuals to put the philosophy of humanism and the ideas of Locke and Rousseau into practice.

The first part of the 19th century can be described as a time of enthusiasm for working with people who had various disabilities, an enthusiasm displayed by a number of devoted individuals. Influenced by the events of the previous century, these pioneers were willing to attempt something that had never been tried before: to help less fortunate people through bona fide treatment programs. Special education and systematic services for individuals with disabilities thus were born in Europe in the early 1800s.

Itard and the Homme Sauvage

The field of special education was dramatically influenced by Jean-Marc Itard (1775–1838). Early in his career, Itard, a medical doctor who initially was concerned with diseases of the ear and the needs of the deaf, became quite interested in a feral child who was found in a wooded area near Aveyron, France, in 1799. Intrigued by this boy, whom he named Victor, Itard felt that he could transform this **homme sauvage** from a state of wildness to one of civilized behavior (Humphrey & Humphrey, 1962). Believing that Victor's skill deficiencies were fundamentally due to environmental limitations, Itard thought Victor could develop the skills that were absent by training with a systematic program.

Although Itard worked with Victor for 5 years, he was disappointed because he felt that Victor had not progressed as much as he had planned, particularly in expressive language, and he subsequently terminated the program. Although Itard felt he personally had failed in his efforts with Victor, he nevertheless received accolades from the French Academy of Science in recognition of his work. Itard's importance rests not so much in his success or failure but rather in the precedent that he set by developing and implementing a systematic program of intervention and achieving gains with a child who was considered severely limited. The influence he had on others clearly distinguishes him as one of the most significant pioneers in the field of education using specialized techniques. As Blatt (1987) remarks, "It [Itard's work] was the first of its kind, and all 'firsts' of important movements are especially important" (p. 34).

Itard's work with Victor will be discussed more thoroughly in chapter 5.

Seguin's Moral and Physiological Training Methods

One person who was affected by Itard's work was Edouard Seguin (1812–1880). Encouraged by Itard to get involved in the treatment of "idiocy," Seguin was motivated by a strong religious influence to help the less fortunate. Like Itard, Seguin also chose to undertake the education of an *enfant idiot*. After 18 months of intensive work with an "idiot" boy, Seguin could demonstrate that the boy had learned a number of skills. He extended his methods to other children, and in 1837 he established a program for "educating the feebleminded" at the Salpetrière in Paris.

Seguin's methods and educational programs, which were even more systematic than Itard's, stressed physiological and moral education. This methodology, as Seguin developed it, incorporated a general training program that integrated muscular, imitative, nervous, and reflective physiological functions (Seguin, 1846). Elements of the programs developed by Seguin—such as individualized instruction and behavior management—can be found in current practice.

Seguin emigrated to the United States in 1848, principally because of the political unrest in Paris at that time. While he lived in the United States, individuals often sought his advice and expertise on programming in institutional settings. In 1866, he published a book titled *Idiocy and Its Treatment by Physiological Methods,* which became a major reference work for educating individuals with intellectual disabilities in the latter part of the 19th century. Seguin also served as the first president of the Association of Medical Officers of American Institutions for Idiotic and Feeble-minded Persons. Hervey Wilbur (1880/1976), in his eulogy to Seguin, perhaps best summarized the impact this man had on the field: "He entered upon the work with enthusiasm. There he toiled, till there he grew, little by little, a system—principles and methods—which has been the guide of all later labors in the same direction, the world over" (p. 186).

Guggenbühl and His Abendberg

Another individual who figured significantly during this time in providing intellectual disability services was Johann Guggenbühl (1816–1863). Guggenbühl has been acknowledged as establishing, in 1841, the first residential facility designed to provide comprehensive treatment for individuals with intellectual disabilities, with reentry to normal living as the ultimate goal. Called the Abendberg, this facility was located in the mountains of Switzerland.

Well publicized through the efforts of Guggenbühl himself, the Abendberg drew the attention of many prominent people. The real significance of Guggenbühl's facility rests in its impact on the visitors it attracted, many of whom were interested in establishing similar facilities. As Kanner (1964) notes, "The Abendberg became the destination of pilgrimages made by physicians, philanthropists, and writers from many lands, who promptly published glowing reports when they went back home" (p. 25).

Unfortunately, the glowing reviews and accolades accorded the Abendberg were short-lived, and eventually the facility came under severe criticism. Although forced to close because of mismanagement and the resulting intolerable conditions, in its heyday the Abendberg served as a model of institutional programming that many other facilities in other parts of the world adopted. It also illustrates a program that achieved recognition but was unable to maintain it. Notwithstanding the problems, Guggenbühl created a prototype for institutional care, the effects of which dominated services in the early 20th century and can still be felt today.

American Pioneers: Dix, Howe, and Wilbur

Although the discipline of special education was conceived and born in Europe, the field also prospered from the work of important people and from events that occurred in the United States during the mid-1800s. Three individuals who had much to do with promoting the welfare of and developing services for persons with intellectual disability in this country were Dorothea Dix, Samuel Howe, and Hervey Wilbur.

During the early 1840s, Dorothea Dix (1802–1887) zealously campaigned for better treatment of the less fortunate who were housed in asylums, almshouses, poorhouses, and country homes. At that time, no other options were available for such people. Her efforts are reflected in her own words, directed toward the Massachusetts legislature in 1843:

> I come to present the strong claims of suffering humanity. I come to place before the Legislature of Massachusetts the condition of the miserable, the desolate, the outcast. I come as the advocate of helpless, forgotten, insane, and idiotic men and women; of beings sunk to a condition from which the most unconcerned would start with real horror; of beings wretched in our prisons, and more wretched in our almshouses. And I cannot suppose it needful to employ earnest persuasion, or stubborn argument, in order to arrest and fix attention upon a subject only the more strongly pressing in its claims because it is revolting and disgusting in its details. (Dix, 1843/1976, p. 5)

Obviously, Dix dramatized what advocacy is all about, and through her efforts she was able to focus much attention on those whom she called "suffering humanity" and for whom there were few advocates. A similar plea could be made today for the large number of homeless people in this country who also lack a strong advocacy base.

Samuel Howe (1801–1876) contributed greatly to providing services for people with intellectual disability through his efforts to establish public support for their training. In 1848, after visiting Guggenbühl's Abendberg and convincing the Massachusetts legislature to appropriate $2,500 per year for his cause, Howe established the first public setting for training individuals with intellectual disabilities. This new program was located in a wing of Boston's Perkins Institution for the Blind, of which Howe was the director. A few months earlier, Hervey Wilbur (1820–1883) had founded the first private setting for treating individuals with intellectual disability at his home in Barre, Massachusetts.

From Optimism to Disillusionment

What, then, was the result of the work of pioneers such as Itard, Seguin, Guggenbühl, Howe, Dix, and Wilbur? First, an atmosphere of optimism developed. Many individuals with intellectual disability, it was thought, could be trained, "cured," and reintegrated into the community as productive citizens. Second, based on this very same hope and enthusiasm, many promises were made, reflected in the lofty goals that were set. Ironically, it was precisely the enthusiasm prevalent at the time that would be partially responsible for the backlash that was to come.

As any student of U.S. history knows quite well, the 1860s were a time of national disharmony, inflamed by years of growing sectional conflict. Prior to the Civil War, America was basically an agrarian society characterized by small farms and towns. After the war, the country began to experience a dramatic change toward urbanization and industrialization. These and other developments had a strong effect on the treatment of persons with intellectual disabilities.

This national metamorphosis precipitated many problems, some of which accompanied the increased growth of cities. Correlates of urban life such as crime, poverty, and health issues were later to be associated with mental retardation. In addition, while industrialization provided vocational opportunities for many people, the skills required were not a good match for many persons with significant limitations.

What happened to the enthusiasm of the mid-1800s? Basically, a critical shift in attitude occurred. This change resulted from consideration of how realistic it was to reintegrate those with intellectual disabilities into the community. After initially accepting the grandiose claims of many individuals who suggested that those less fortunate could be "cured," critics began to realize that these goals, while laudable, were unrealistic. A pronounced climate of pessimism developed. We know today that those individuals who were considered capable of being cured in the 1800s were indeed capable of skill acquisition—but for most of them, attainment of "normalcy" was not possible. That individuals who were more severely disabled had not changed enough to be able to move back into community settings resulted in a negative perception of this group that pervaded many different areas.

Several problems contributed to this era's disillusionment, but four factors seem to be salient. First, as already mentioned, the population being addressed was not capable of being transformed into totally normal-functioning members of society. Second, community reintegration demands more than merely providing training and placement. If successful reintegration requires community preparation and development, as we think it does, then we should not be surprised that the neglect of this issue in the 1800s led to failure in attempts at reintegration. Sadly, even today the provision of community services and supports is glaringly inadequate in many cases. Third, after an atmosphere of hope and excitement had been created, many individuals with intellectual disabilities were pitied, resulting in two important developments: (1) a dilution of services to individuals who needed systematic, intensive programming, and (2) the establishment of more institutions. These developments were to have a tragic effect in the late 1800s. Fourth, the previously mentioned demands of an increasingly more complex society created by postwar urbanization and industrialization worked against those with limited intellectual skills and social competence.

Obviously, these were formidable obstacles to reaching the goals championed by the idealistic pioneers of the early and mid-1800s. While it is easy now to reproach those enthusiasts for creating a no-win situation that ultimately resulted in many regressive developments for those whom they wanted to help, we need to understand that these early advocates (however naive) were most sincere in their zeal, hopes, and efforts. Unfortunately, those individuals on whom the great expectations were based were now being perceived as untreatable. It was bad enough that the early enthusiasm had waned, but even more discouraging was the fact that the worst was yet to come.

FACILITIES-BASED ORIENTATION: 1890–1960

For more about the use of institutions to meet changing social definitions of intellectual disability, see Trent (1994).

As the 19th century came to a close, disillusionment began to take on a more reactionary tone. A change from concern for caring about individuals who had special needs to concern for protecting society from them was evident. Institutions originally designed to serve as training facilities from which individuals would leave to return to community settings now began to assume a custodial role.

During this period of alarm, a number of events caused a dramatic change in social attitudes, weakening most movements favorable to the needs of this group.

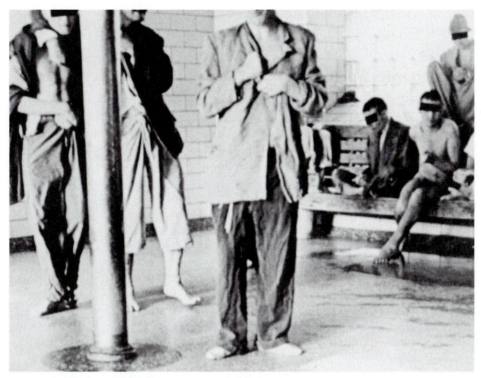

The idea that institutions are not appropriate for most persons with mental retardation is not new.

Many citizens were now afraid that these people were dangerous to society. Kanner (1964) describes the prevailing perceptions during this time:

> The mental defectives were viewed as a menace to civilization, incorrigible at home, burdens to the school, sexually promiscuous, breeders of feebleminded offspring, victims and spreaders of poverty, degeneracy, crime, and disease. Consequently, there was a cry for the segregation of all mental defectives, with the aim of purifying society, of erecting a solid wall between it and its contaminators. (p. 85)

It did not take long for society to develop ways to control people who were "mentally defective." The principal means for doing this included various forms of segregation, an extreme example of which was **sterilization.** A committee of the American Breeder's Association, formed in 1911, concluded that "segregation for life or at least during the reproductive years must, in the opinion of the committee, be the principal agent used by society in cutting off its supply of defectives" (cited in Kanner, 1964, p. 136). As an added measure of control, institutions strictly segregated men and women to eliminate their chances of producing offspring who would possibly be "feebleminded."

Many contributing factors precipitated repressive events in the late 1800s and early 1900s. Three factors in particular seem to have had a pronounced effect on the creation of this backlash: the eugenics scare, the influx of immigrants to the United States, and the mental test movement.

The Eugenics Scare

The **eugenics movement** was a scientific movement designed to improve the human race by manipulating breeding. Although the thrust of the eugenics movement was not felt until the late 1800s and early 1900s, its antecedents can be traced to earlier times. One of the key interests of this movement was to control the number of "feebleminded" persons through selective breeding.

Influenced by the ideas of Charles Darwin, Sir Francis Galton extended Darwin's concept of evolution to humans. In 1869, Galton published *Hereditary Genius,* which espoused the notion that individual traits, most notably genius, were inherited. Galton's work seemed to catalyze the eugenics movement, which advocated the genetic control of mental defectives. What Galton established was a theoretical basis for the inheritance of mental defectiveness. Gregor Mendel's discovery of the laws of inheritance in the latter part of the 19th century lent scientific support to Galton's ideas.

Two publications reinforced society's attitude that intellectual disability had genetic implications: *The Jukes: A Study of Crime, Pauperism, Disease and Heredity* (Dugdale, 1877) and *The Kallikak Family* (Goddard, 1912). Each of these works traced the genetic relationships of the families under study. Dugdale's original work actually focused on criminality and its correlates, and only later was the added correlate of intellectual disability inferred. Goddard's work, however, had as its central theme the notion that feeblemindedness was inherited; elaborate **pedigree studies** (through five generations) were presented as evidence. Goddard's work was very powerful and, along with other related events, fueled the movement to control the menace of feeblemindedness genetically. But many years later, Goddard's research on Martin Kallikak's two distinct family lines was called into question. The details of the social myth perpetuated by Goddard are described in J. D. Smith's (1985) book *Minds Made Feeble* (see Box 1.1).

Strong evidence that eugenics was being taken seriously can be found in the enactment of sterilization laws during the early 1900s. Indiana holds the dubious distinction of enacting the first such law in 1907. Within 20 years, similar legislation was on the books in 23 states. The constitutionality of these laws was challenged in several states and ultimately upheld by the Supreme Court in the famous case of *Buck v. Bell* (1927). As Smith (1987) highlights, this case "became the precedent for the right of state governments to intervene in the reproductive practices of those citizens deemed defective in some way" (p. 148). The case is noteworthy, not only for the precedent it set but also for two other reasons. First, Carrie Buck, the woman used to test Virginia's compulsory sterilization law, probably was not mentally retarded. Second, the prevailing attitude of the time was clearly expressed in the majority opinion given by Justice Oliver Wendell Holmes:

> We have seen more than once that the public welfare may call upon the best citizens for their lives. It would be strange if it could not call upon those who already sap the strength of the State for these lesser sacrifices, often felt to be much by those con-

Box 1.1 ✲ Minds Made Feeble

In 1912, Henry Goddard reported the results of his study of the inheritance of feeblemindedness. His book, *The Kallikak Family: A Study on the History of Feeble-Mindedness,* was influential because it underscored the perceived threat of feeblemindedness to society and helped fuel the eugenics movement. The book was very popular, and to this day the Kallikak story is regularly retold in discussions of mental retardation.

The effects of the study are described well by J. David Smith (1985) in *Minds Made Feeble:*

> Goddard's book on the Kallikak family was received with acclaim by the public and by much of the scientific community. . . . Only gradually was criticism forthcoming which questioned the methods used in the study and the implications and conclusions drawn from the data collected. Even in the light of substantive and knowledgeable criticism, however, the essential message of the Kallikak study persisted for years. Even today its influence, in convoluted forms, continues to have a social and political impact. That message is simple, yet powerful. Ignorance, poverty, and social pathology are in the blood—in the seed. It is not the environment in which people are born and develop that makes the critical difference in human lives. People are born either favored or beyond help.

It was this message and the social myth that accompanied it that compelled Smith to investigate and report the complete story of the Kallikak family and of Goddard's study. A few highlights of Smith's findings are presented here:

- Serious questions arise as to whether Deborah Kallikak, the woman with whom Goddard came into contact and whose ancestors are studied, was actually feebleminded.
- Goddard's professional acquaintance with influential eugenic leaders seems to have had a great influence on his work.
- The methodology used to study the Kallikak family and the skills of those who collected the information are once again questioned.
- The "real" Kallikaks were not as abhorrent as they were described by Goddard. Smith comments: "The truth of their lives was sacrificed to the effort to prove a point. The Kallikak study is fiction draped in the social science of its time."
- The implications of the study proved to be a very potent indictment against the poor, the uneducated, racial minorities, the foreign born, and those classified as mentally retarded or mentally ill, resulting in such social policies as compulsory sterilization, restricted immigration, and institutionalization, which adversely and unfairly affected these groups.
- Through painstaking investigation, Smith determined the real name of the family Goddard studied (Kallikak was a pseudonym). However, he does not reveal the name.

One of Smith's major contributions is his admonition to be aware of the significance and power of social myths: "Social myths are constantly in the making, compelling in their simplicity, and alluring because we want to believe them. Perhaps understanding the Kallikak story will help in recognizing and resisting them."

cerned, in order to prevent our being swamped with incompetence. It is better for all the world, if instead of waiting to execute degenerate offspring for crime, or to let them starve for their imbecility, society can prevent those who are manifestly unfit from continuing their kind. The principle that sustains compulsory vaccination is broad enough to cover cutting the Fallopian tubes. . . . Three generations of imbeciles are enough. (*Buck v. Bell,* 1927, p. 50)

Immigration

During the second half of the 19th century, the United States experienced a great increase in the number of immigrants, mostly from southern and eastern Europe. As most of these immigrants flocked to the growing urban centers, many problems emerged. Americans of northern and western European origin looked upon these immigrants as inferior; this stance was supported by another study conducted by Goddard (1917), which concluded that many of these foreigners were "feeble-minded." One outcome of this generalized concern was enactment of the Immigration Restriction Act in 1924. This legislation restricted the flow of Italians, Russians, Hungarians, and Jews into the United States until 1965.

The Testing Movement

A third major trend contributing to the alarmist climate of the early 1900s was the introduction of the **mental test.** In 1905, Alfred Binet and Theodore Simon developed an instrument for use in French schools to screen those students who were not benefiting from the regular classroom experience and might need special services. This intent mirrors the basic tenets of special education that would arise later in the century.

Interestingly, Binet himself was concerned that the instrument that he helped develop might be misused. As Gould (1981) notes, Binet "greatly feared that his practical device . . . could be perverted and used as an indelible label, rather than as a guide for identifying children who needed help" (p. 151). As we know, the mental test has had a lasting effect on the fields of psychology and education. In essence, in the mental scale of intelligence, Binet and Simon created a mechanism for identifying milder forms of intellectual disability that are more noticeable in academic settings. Before this time, people whose intellectual disability was recognized were more severely involved—but now, since individuals with less severe intellectual disability could be identified, new alarms were being sounded about the magnitude of the problem.

Although Binet and Simon introduced their test in France, before long it was brought to the United States. In 1911, Henry Goddard translated the Binet-Simon scales into English, and in 1916 Lewis Terman of Stanford University refined the mental scales into the instrument known as the Stanford-Binet. (W. Stern, a German psychologist, is given credit for developing the conceptual basis for determining IQ [intelligence quotient].)

Although the first special class for students with intellectual disability in the United States was established in Providence, Rhode Island, in 1896—predating the testing movement—the development and ultimate translation of the mental scales would have a great effect on education. Separate special classes for these students developed and grew in number. Another event of significance was New Jersey's enactment, in 1911, of legislation mandating education for this type of student. With the beginning of World War I, the military services needed a way to obtain information relatively quickly on large groups of people for use in assigning personnel. Thus, the first group intelligence scales (the alpha and beta tests) were developed and implemented. The results of this testing fed alarmist tendencies by suggesting that mild intellectual disability was more widespread than anyone had previously believed. Robert Yerkes's 1921 work on the intellectual capacities of World War I soldiers supported this assumption, further exacerbating negative feelings about intellectual disabilities.

An alarm had indeed been sounded. Society was frightened by the "menace" of intellectual disability. With the recognition of mental retardation's greater prevalence, its seeming inheritability, and its correlation with crime, poverty, incorrigibility, and disease, it is not difficult to understand how restrictive and segregationist attitudes and practices could develop and dominate. Quite strong by the end of the 1920s, this aura of fear would begin to fade in the ensuing years, but its impact would be long-lasting.

Related Sociopolitical Influences

Social attitudes toward individuals with disabilities changed somewhat after World War I. As a part of all warfare, many individuals were wounded and returned to their homes with lasting medical conditions. In 1920, the Vocational Rehabilitation Act (P.L. 66-236) was enacted to allow civilians to benefit from vocational rehabilitation. Important from the time it was introduced, this legislation has endured as one of the most significant laws created to provide training opportunities and protect the rights of individuals with disabilities. With the end of the war, the need for providing services to wounded veterans had been acknowledged. Now these services were being extended to others who needed them, too.

Another sociopolitical event that caused lifestyles to change—quickly—was the stock market crash of 1929 and the Great Depression that followed. The Great Depression was not a pleasant experience; however, some outcomes were beneficial. For example, the Depression caused the average person, who had been unaware of or uninterested in the problems of human need, to appreciate them, for almost everyone at that time was needy.

Visit the Companion Website at www.prenhall.com/beirne-smith and select Chapter 1, Web Destinations for links to the CEC and other organizations of historical significance.

Special education as a bona fide professional field took a tremendous step in 1922, when Elizabeth Farrell established the International Council for the Education of Exceptional Children. Prior to this time, the field had had no unifying organizational structure on a national level. Farrell served as the first president of this new organization, now known as the Council for Exceptional Children (CEC), and it became a new institutional force in the field of special education.

Thus, following a period of great concern about the social menace of mental retardation in the early 20th century, some movement toward greater enlightenment was evident, as Maloney and Ward (1978) state:

1. The view of mental retardation as a unitary, recessive, inherited trait began to fade as the science of genetics grew in scope and precision.
2. New clinical studies demonstrated the significance of other, nonhereditary, sources of mental retardation, such as trauma, infection, and endocrine disturbance.
3. The methodological flaws and biased interpretations of the pedigree studies were becoming more and more apparent.
4. Other surveys of institutional populations indicated that over one-half of them had intellectually normal parents, further weakening the singular heredity view and associated calls for eugenic solutions.

5. The older research studies that had linked mental retardation with every conceivable social ill were critically reanalyzed and found wanting.
6. Newer, better controlled, and more objective studies failed to reveal the dramatic links of the previous era. (p. 57)

During the early 1930s, the United States was trying to regain stability both economically and socially. One notable event occurred when President Herbert Hoover convened the first White House Conference on Child Health and Protection in 1930, drawing national attention, albeit briefly, to the needs of individuals with disabilities. Another important trend was the number of classes for special students, which kept increasing.

After the presidential election of 1932, the United States went through many changes. The new president, Franklin D. Roosevelt, influenced the country's attitudes toward the welfare of all its citizens. Roosevelt's New Deal philosophy was responsible for much social change through legislation and the formulation of new programs. One such piece of legislation that affected individuals with special needs was the Social Security Act of 1935. In a nutshell, during the 1930s, two major trends emerged in the treatment of individuals with disabilities: (1) the generation of a new attitude supportive of a public welfare system, and (2) the affirmation of responsibility to those in need.

With the direct involvement of the United States in World War II, the nation's attention and actions were refocused once again. We can see certain similarities between World War I and World War II vis-à-vis the field of intellectual disability. As in World War I, screening of soldiers in the 1940s readjusted the perceived extent of mild retardation. One source that contributed to this changed thinking was a study conducted by Ginzberg and Bray, as described in their book *The Uneducated* (1953). They studied two groups of men being considered for military service. Their primary group consisted of men who were rejected on the basis of mental deficiency; the other group included men who were accepted for service but who experienced major problems in academic skill areas (i.e., literacy).

World War II created increased employment opportunities in war-related industries for individuals with intellectual disabilities. When the war was over, the nation as a whole, and many families in particular, felt the realities of disability as wounded soldiers came home. A heightened sensitivity to the needs of disabled veterans thus developed.

As the 1950s began, the field of special education went through changes that would have notable effects in subsequent years. Foremost among these changes was a new national policy concerned with the problems of special groups of people.

In the years following World War II, the United States experienced a period of renewed prosperity. This created a climate in which "the demands of parents, the enthusiasm of professionals, and federal, state and private funding gave new impetus to progress in the area of mental retardation" (Hewett & Forness, 1977). These three forces, augmented by other factors, highlighted this turning point in the history of special education. Although institutional changes were beginning to occur, these events could be classified at best as only a "quiet revolution." Individuals were still being institutionalized at an alarming rate; tragically, many persons who should not have been placed in these settings found themselves there. Furthermore, too many had already suffered sterilization—a personal indignity and a violation of their civil rights. By 1938, compulsory sterilizations had been performed on more than 27,000 people in the United States (cited in Smith, 1987).

Certainly an important event during this time was the formation in 1950 of the National Association of Parents and Friends of Mentally Retarded Children—later known as the National Association of Retarded Children, and now known as the Arc of the United States. This organization, composed mostly of parents of children with intellectual disabilities, became an important advocate for these children and a source of support for families. Functioning as lobbyist, service provider, and promoter of research, this parent organization had a key effect on the development, expansion, and refinement of services for individuals with intellectual disability and their families (Braddock, Hemp, Parish, & Westrich, 1998). Most important, the organization provided a vehicle for its members to express their attitudes, beliefs, concerns, and desires in politically effective and coordinated ways. The eight original purposes of the organization are as follows:

- To promote the general welfare of mentally retarded children of all ages everywhere
- To further the advancement of all study, ameliorative, and preventive research and therapy in the field of mental retardation
- To develop a better understanding of the problems of mental retardation by the public and cooperate with all public, private, and religious agencies, and international federal, state, and local departments of education, health, and institutions
- To further the training and education of personnel for work in the field of mental retardation
- To encourage the formation of parent groups; to advise and aid parents in the solution of their problems; and to coordinate the efforts and activities of these groups
- To further the implementation of legislation in behalf of the mentally retarded
- To serve as a clearinghouse for gathering and disseminating information regarding the mentally retarded, and to foster the development of integrated programs in their behalf
- To solicit and receive funds for the accomplishment of the above purposes (National Association of Parents and Friends of Mentally Retarded Children, 1950)

By the early 1950s, the United States was beginning to adopt a national policy committed to the needs of those with intellectual disabilities and a policy willing to give financial support to endeavors that addressed these needs. Over the years, social attitudes toward people with intellectual disabilities had changed from fear and revulsion to tolerance and compassion. Whether sparked by the troubled times of the 1930s and 1940s that the nation as a whole had endured or influenced by purely economic motives during the 1950s, the financial backing required to develop more and better programs was provided. If only for economic reasons, the importance of maximizing the potential of persons who were disabled was beginning to be acknowledged, as was stated by President Dwight D. Eisenhower in a 1954 message to Congress:

> We are spending three times as much in public assistance to care for nonproductive disabled people as it would cost to make them self-sufficient and taxpaying members

of their communities. Rehabilitated people as a group pay back in federal income taxes many times the cost of their rehabilitation.

By 1952, 46 of the 48 states had enacted legislation for educating students with mental retardation. This legislation, however, did not provide programming for all students with intellectual disabilities. Many children in the moderate range and most children in the severe range were still excluded from receiving educational services in public settings. Abeson and Davis (2000) note that in 1949 no state had mandated education for children with IQs below 50.

Not until 1975 and the passage of the Education for All Handicapped Children Act (P.L. 94-142) was the issue of educating all students with intellectual disabilities formally addressed on a national level. But 1954 is also notable because in that year Congress passed the Cooperative Research Act (P.L. 83-531), which provided money for research that would focus on intellectual disabilities. In 1958, P.L. 85-926 was enacted, offering incentives to various organizations (state educational agencies and institutions of higher education) in the form of grants to encourage the preparation of teachers of this group of students. Thus, if we look at federal legislation as an index of national commitment to a cause, then we can see that policy supportive of the needs of people with intellectual disability was emerging in the 1950s.

As the decade came to a close, three forces were beginning to shape events. First, a new philosophical view of intellectual disability was forming, as reflected in the 1958 publication of *Mental Subnormality,* published by Masland, Sarason, and Gladwin. These authors stressed that certain social and cultural variables have a strong correlation with intellectual disability. The influence of this point of view on the field can be observed in the 1959 definition of mental retardation promoted by the American Association on Mental Deficiency (Heber, 1959). This definition associated intellectual deficits with "impairment in one or more of the following: (1) maturation, (2) learning, and (3) social adjustment" (Heber, 1959, p. 3).

Second, educators and advocates became concerned about the segregation in special classes of students with intellectual disabilities. Existing research tended to support the special class setting. Nevertheless, this issue would continue to be debated, resulting in some major changes in the 1970s. In addition, the Supreme Court decision in the *Brown v. Board of Education* (1954) desegregation case also affected thinking and policy making for individuals with intellectual disabilities.

Third, when the Soviet Union launched *Sputnik* in 1957, the United States responded dramatically; shocked by the event, the country made a commitment to technological development unparalleled in history. The nation's overwhelming desire to grow technologically would focus very sharply on the institution of education. Changes were evidently needed, and many did come about. Both regular and special education were affected by the vigor of the times. The nation was primed for the tumultuous 1960s.

Research and Programmatic Influences

During the period of facilities-based orientation many important developments took place in both social and physical sciences. In 1934, Ivar Asbjörn Fölling, a Norwegian physician, explained the biochemical mechanics related to the **metabolic**

Edgar A. Doll constructed the Vineland Social Maturity Scale, one of the first attempts to measure what we now call "adaptive behavior."

disturbance referred to as PKU (phenylketonuria)—a known cause of intellectual disability. The importance of this discovery goes beyond this single event:

> This contribution, termed "one of the great discoveries in medical history" by Clemens E. Bonda, at long last made the issue of mental deficiency appear respectable as a legitimate field of research in the biological sciences. Slowly and at first reluctantly, the medical profession began to take an interest. (Kanner, 1964, p. 141)

Two assessment instruments of major importance were developed during this period. In 1935, Edgar Doll published his *Vineland Social Maturity Scale* (VSMS). Use of this scale allowed professionals to gain additional information about a person's "social competence." In 1949, David Wechsler published another intelligence scale, the *Wechsler Intelligence Scale for Children* (WISC). Like the VSMS, this device became very popular. Ever since their publication, these instruments and their subsequent revisions have had a pronounced effect on the identification and classification of many individuals suspected of having intellectual disability.

Another influence on the public perception of intellectual disability was a number of studies that seemed to stress the importance of environment as a cause of mental retardation. Certain studies, most notably those performed by Harold Skeels and his colleagues, questioned the notion that IQ was biologically determined. Skeels and Dye (1939) inferred that environmental factors have a critical effect on IQ or, if you will, one's classification as mentally retarded.

The work of Skeels and Dye will be discussed in chapter 5.

SERVICES-BASED ORIENTATION: 1960–1985

In the 1960s, a new paradigm was emerging, as described by Polloway et al. (1996):

> On the heels of the facility-based period came a profound shift toward a "services-based paradigm." Through this model, there was again an attempt to provide special

services to individuals, as a preparation for their subsequent integration into society. Consequently, programs most typically included self-contained special education classes in regular schools, resource or pull-out programs, transitional [sheltered] workshops, related training programs, and the like. . . . In the services model, the assumption was made that appropriate programming for individuals with disabilities would be followed by successful integrated placement. (p. 5)

Sociopolitical Influences

If asked to reflect on the 1960s, one would probably think of the many tragic episodes in a time of rather extreme social change. The violent deaths of national leaders and the widespread opposition and reaction to the Vietnam War are vivid recollections of the 1960s. The early part of this decade, however, was characterized by a generalized enthusiasm, and this mood was quite evident in the area of special education. For many reasons, special education was on center stage during the 1960s.

 The Kennedy family continues to be a major force in the politics of intellectual disability. Visit the Companion Website at www.prenhall.com/beirne-smith and select Chapter 1, Read and Respond to find out more on this topic.

When President John F. Kennedy assumed office in 1961, he symbolized the energy of the country at that time. Kennedy, who had a sister with mental retardation, once again brought national attention to the needs of this group. At the beginning of his administration, he established the President's Panel on Mental Retardation (PPMR), now known as the President's Committee on Intellectual Disabilities, which was to serve as a guide and source for national policy formation. Under the direction of Leonard Mayo, this group published *A Proposed Program for National Action to Combat Mental Retardation* (Mayo, 1962), which set the tone for policy decisions for the next decade. Many of the principal recommendations found in the report relate to the goals of the National Association of Parents and Friends of Mentally Retarded Children and also have a contemporary flavor:

1. Research in the causes of retardation and in methods of care, rehabilitation, and learning.
2. Preventive health measures, including (a) a greatly strengthened program of maternal and infant care directed first at the centers of population where prematurity and the rate of "damaged" children are high; (b) protection against such known hazards to pregnancy as radiation and harmful drugs; and (c) extended diagnostic and screening services.
3. Strengthened educational programs generally and extended and enriched programs of special education in public and private schools closely coordinated with vocational guidance, vocational rehabilitation, and specific training and preparation for employment; education for the adult mentally retarded, and workshops geared to their needs.
4. More comprehensive and improved clinical and social services.
5. Improved methods and facilities for care, with emphasis on the development of a wide range of local community facilities.
6. A new legal, as well as social, concept of the retarded, including protection of their civil rights; life guardianship provisions when needed; an enlightened attitude on the part of the law and the courts; and clarification of the theory of responsibility in criminal acts.
7. Helping overcome the serious problems of manpower as they affect the entire field of science and every type of service through extended programs of re-

cruiting with fellowships; and increased opportunities for graduate students, and those preparing for the professions to observe and learn at first hand about the phenomenon of retardation. Because there will never be a fully adequate supply of personnel in this field and for other cogent reasons, the panel has emphasized the need for more volunteers in health, recreation, and welfare activities, and for a domestic Peace Corps to stimulate voluntary service.

8. Programs of education and information to increase public awareness of the problem of mental retardation. (Mayo, 1962, pp. 14–15)

Other recommendations, not unlike some proposed in the 1990s, included the following:

1. That programs for the retarded, including modern day care, recreation, residential services, and ample educational and vocational opportunities, be comprehensive.
2. That they operate in or close to the communities where the retarded live—that is, that they be community centered.
3. That services be so organized as to provide a central or fixed point for the guidance, assistance, and protection of retarded persons if and when needed, and to assure a sufficient array of continuum of services to meet different types of need.
4. That private agencies as well as public agencies at the local, state, and federal levels continue to provide resources and to increase them for this worthy purpose. While the federal government can assist, the principal responsibility for financing and improving services for the mentally retarded must continue to be borne by states and local communities. (Mayo, 1962, pp. 14–15)

Federal legislation relevant to the field of intellectual disability continued to be enacted during the 1960s. In 1963, Congress passed the Mental Retardation Facilities and Mental Health Centers Construction Act, which provided monies for the construction of Mental Retardation Research Centers (MRRCs). These centers conducted organized multidisciplinary research on various complex facets of intellectual disability. In 1965, the Elementary and Secondary Education Act (ESEA) (P.L. 89-10) was passed. Part of this legislation focused attention on the needs of disadvantaged students. In 1966, ESEA was amended, and as a result, the Bureau of Education for the Handicapped (BEH), a subcomponent of the Office of Education (OE), was created.

National policy directed to the needs of the disadvantaged reached its pinnacle with President Lyndon B. Johnson's War on Poverty. With the growing interest in social and cultural determinants of behavior, it is not surprising that much attention was given to environmental causes of intellectual disability. Project Head Start did just that. The concept that early intervention could ameliorate some of the negative effects of unfavorable situations was fashionable and encouraged during the mid-1960s.

If nothing else can be said of the 1960s, certainly it was a time responsive to personal and civil rights. The civil rights movement was consummated by passage of the Civil Rights Act of 1964; however, this law did not deal directly with people with disabilities. Nevertheless, the achievements and impetus provided by the civil rights movement and the resulting legislation would be realized and extended to people with disabilities in the 1970s through today.

Most notably, the early 1970s were litigious times. A new tactic for ensuring services was beginning to emerge. Previously, courts had been used as a last resort, but now they were used frequently and strategically. Rights afforded the regular citizenry had been denied to many individuals with intellectual disability, and the courtroom became the forum in which these rights were secured. This policy was supported by parent groups and at least tolerated by a society responsive to human rights infringements, and many issues were brought to the courtroom. Chief among them were rights to education and proper treatment.

The **right to education** issue was sparked in 1971 by a celebrated class action suit, *Pennsylvania Association for Retarded Children* [PARC] *v. Commonwealth of Pennsylvania.* This litigation resulted in an agreement that established the right to free, appropriate public school education for all children with mental retardation within the jurisdiction of this federal court district. However, the impact of the court-ordered agreement extended beyond eastern Pennsylvania, as similar suits dealing with the same issue were filed in many other states in the months following the decision.

Although *PARC v. Pennsylvania* was specifically concerned with the exclusion from public education of children whose primary descriptor was intellectual disabilities, other students with disabilities were soon to enjoy the same right. In that same year, a suit on behalf of all students with special educational needs, regardless of type and severity, was filed in federal district court in Washington, D.C. This case, *Mills v. Board of Education of the District of Columbia* (1972), was decided in favor of the plaintiffs, extending the right to education to all children with disabilities.

During this same period, many individuals living in institutions were receiving very little in the way of services beyond custodial care. In 1971, in the case *Wyatt v. Stickney,* the lack of appropriate treatment provided residents at an institution for people with mental retardation in Alabama was contested. The original decision declared that the residents of Partlow State School and Hospital were entitled to receive treatment, not just custodial care. The judge enumerated the steps to be taken to comply with this decision.

As can be seen, the courts began to shape certain practices during this time. What may seem strange to the casual observer—yet eminently significant to the special education professional—is the critical and influential roles that judges, lawyers, and expert witnesses played during the litigious early 1970s. To professionals in the field of intellectual disability, it seemed that policy was being formed by experts in other fields. Although to a certain extent this is true, knowledgeable parents and special educators were the ones who had realized that rights had not been secured or guaranteed through committee or panel action and that, as a result, legal procedures had become necessary.

The judicial activity of the early 1970s culminated in federal legislation that affected individuals with disabilities. Two pieces of legislation stood unparalleled in history at that time for what they mandated. In 1973, amendments to the Vocational Rehabilitation Act (P.L. 93-112) were passed. Serving as a bill of rights for people with disabilities, Section 504 of this act ensured that "the handicapped of America should have access to education and jobs, and should not be denied anything that any other citizen is entitled to or already receives" (LaVor, 1977, p. 249). Two years later, the landmark Education for All Handicapped Children Act (EHA) (P.L. 94-142) was signed into law. The major provisions of this legislation were as follows:

- Every child with a disability between the ages of 3 and 21 is entitled to a free, appropriate public education in the least restrictive environment.
- Due process is ensured to protect the rights of students and their parents.

- Students are entitled to special and related services, which are determined as necessary.
- Every student will have a written Individualized Educational Program (IEP) that parents and school personnel agree upon.
- First priority is given to students previously excluded from educational services and second priority to those whose programs were inappropriate.
- No eligible child is to be rejected from receiving services.

EHA has been revised several times and now exists as the Individuals with Disabilities Education Improvement Act (IDEA). Table 1.1 summarizes the major changes in the evolution of this law.

TABLE 1.1
Major Iterations of IDEA

Year of Enactment	Title	Major Provisions
1975	P. L. 94-142 Education for All Handicapped Children Act	Mandated a free appropriate education for all children with disabilities Ensured due process rights Mandated individualized education plans and instruction in the least restrictive environment
1986	P. L. 99-457 Education for All Handicapped Children Act	Extended services to children aged birth–5
1990	P. L. 101-476 Individuals with Disabilities Education Act	Clarified the definition of a child with disability Broadened the scope of related educational services Expanded early childhood services Emphasized community involvement as a goal for transition services
1997	P. L. 105-17 Individuals with Disabilities Education Act	Strengthened the provisions for inclusion Mandated participation in state and district assessments Established policies for discipline and mandated functional behavior assessments
2004	P. L. 108-446 Individuals with Disabilities Education Improvement Act	Defined "highly qualified teacher" Strengthened the transition planning process Restructured due process system Aligned assessment components with NCLB Eliminated the requirement for short-term objectives for most students

Another federal law that had an impact on persons with intellectual disability was the Developmental Disabilities Assistance and Bill of Rights Act of 1978 (P.L. 95-602). This legislation provided a functional way of conceptualizing developmental disabilities as well as funding to assist persons who demonstrate problems in major life function areas.

A major change in the Medicaid program, for which many individuals with intellectual disability qualify, occurred in 1981. The optional Home and Community Based Services (HCBS) waiver was created, allowing states to use Medicaid funds for a wider variety of community services. Over time, more states chose to use this option (Abeson & Davis, 2000).

Many important court cases took place in the 1980s, three of which are featured here. The case of *Larry P. v. Riles* (1972) was heard in the Ninth Circuit Court of Appeals. This court upheld a lower court ruling prohibiting California schools from using intelligence tests to place African American students in EMR classes. In *Pennhurst State School v. Halderman* (1981), the Supreme Court reversed the decision of the Third Circuit Court of Appeals, which had affirmed the right of the residents of Pennhurst State School and Hospital to adequate habilitation under the Developmentally Disabled Assistance and Bill of Rights Act. The Supreme Court made it clear that this act did not create any substantive rights to adequate treatment. The third litigative action was the first case relating to P.L. 94-142 heard by the Supreme Court. At issue in this case, *Board of Education of the Hendrick Hudson Central School District v. Rowley* (1982), was whether a female student with a hearing impairment was entitled to interpreter service to provide her with an appropriate education. Although acknowledging the procedural safeguards and need for individual education programs, the Supreme Court determined that states did not have to provide more than a minimal level of the services designated appropriate. As a result of this decision, schools do not have to be concerned with providing optimal educational programs for students with special needs. This has significant implications in terms of programs for students with intellectual disability.

During the mid-1980s, a dominant theme in both general and special education was the growing number of people "at risk" for any number of pejorative outcomes. At the school level, this includes students who are at risk for school failure (potential dropouts, substance abusers, pregnant teenagers). At the adult level, it includes people who are homeless, those who are unemployed or underemployed, and those who are not able to deal successfully with the demands of daily living. Individuals with intellectual disability can be found in all these groups.

Trends in Service Delivery

With continuing support from state and federal governments, programs and services for individuals with intellectual disability proliferated almost exponentially during the period of services-based orientation. But the spotlight was soon to flicker, if not dim. Lloyd Dunn's 1968 questioning of the efficacy of placing students with mild intellectual disability in special classes symbolized some of the reexamination occurring in the late 1960s and early 1970s.

A new philosophical theme was beginning to take hold. The concept of **normalization,** which originated during the 1950s in Scandinavia, was finding much support in the United States. N. E. Bank-Mikkelsen and Bengt Nirje were eminently responsible for the development and dissemination of this principle in Scandinavia, while Wolf Wolfensberger was instrumental in championing it in the United States.

To a great extent, the emergence of this philosophy was due to a single publication that had a great impact on professionals in the United States. Titled *Changing Patterns in Residential Services for the Mentally Retarded,* this work included a discussion of the principle of normalization by Nirje (1969), sparking a movement in this country that epitomized the next decade. Nirje defined *normalization* as "making available to the mentally retarded patterns and conditions of everyday life which are as close as possible to the norms and patterns of the mainstream of society" (p. 181).

As more professionals recognized the needs of people with intellectual disability a new emphasis was placed on community-based services. This trend has continued. To some degree, attention to community issues was a result of parental concern about their now adult children.

During the 1960s, the nature–nurture issue, which had been brewing for many years, seemed to be best answered by those arguing the importance of interaction between heredity and environment. Although supporters of this orientation acknowledged both hereditary and environmental determinants of many types of mild mental retardation, they felt that environmental factors were more influential. In 1969, much attention was drawn to this issue by Arthur Jensen. Jensen (1969) published an article in the *Harvard Educational Review,* titled "How Much Can We Boost IQ and Scholastic Achievement?" He argued that genetic factors are more important than environmental factors in determining IQ (i.e., the high inheritability of intelligence). Where Jensen's article received the most criticism was in his implication that social class and racial variations in intelligence are attributable to genetic differences.

In the changing social climate of the late 1960s, characterized by many forms of reactionary behavior, services to and certain concepts of those with intellectual disability were being challenged. The revolutionary fervor of the 1960s would wane as the 1970s progressed. For exceptional individuals and those working with them, however, the early 1970s was reminiscent of the turbulent prior decade in many ways.

In the entire history of services to persons with intellectual disability, there had been no period with more visible gains than the early 1970s. Without a doubt, the pioneers of the early 19th century had made great steps in initiating intervention; however, events of the 1970s were of similar significance. At long last, it was established that Americans with intellectual disabilities had certain personal and civil rights guaranteeing services and protection. As can be seen from Figure 1.1, the number of students receiving special education greatly increased during the 1960s and 1970s. (That this number began decreasing toward the end of the 1970s is discussed later.)

During the late 1960s and 1970s, special education for many students with mental retardation, when it did occur, typically took place in segregated settings. The resource room model, in which students would spend less than half of their school day in a special education setting (i.e., primarily for reading and math instruction), became very popular during this time. However, other academic issues remained, as

FIGURE 1.1
Enrollment of Students with
Mental Retardation in Special
Education

Source: Data from the U.S.
Department of the Census and the
U.S. Department of Education, Office
of Special Education.

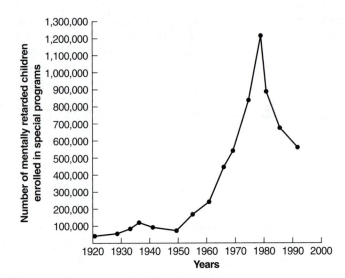

these students were in general education, usually without any accommodations, during subjects such as science and social studies.

The concept of "mainstreaming" students into general education became fashionable. Although the intent of educating students with intellectual disabilities along with their nondisabled peers was acceptable, this practice was mostly a physical integration without the elements needed for successful inclusion, as is advocated today.

The preparation for the realities of adulthood were often addressed through various vocational training programs. Patton, Polloway, and Smith (2000) describe one common type of program:

> Many students with mild mental retardation participated in work-study programs that were set up in high schools. In this arrangement, the student spent half of the instructional day at a specific job in the community and the other half of the day at school taking classes. In their often-cited book, *A High School Work Study Program for Mentally Subnormal Students,* Kolstoe and Frey (1965) described the job performance skills as well as the academic, personal, and social skills that are essential for meaningful outcomes. (p. 83)

SUPPORTS-BASED ORIENTATION: 1985–PRESENT

Significant changes have occurred in the field of intellectual disability in recent years. Polloway and colleagues (1996) suggest that the 1990s were particularly momentous for the field of intellectual disability:

> Changes in public attitudes toward persons with disabilities, and the resulting development and provision of services and supports, have been truly phenomenal. Consequently, the 1990s have become an exciting time to be participating in and/or adapting to the changing perspectives on mental retardation and developmental disabilities. One of the most challenging aspects in the field has been the mixed feelings that accompany these changes as we seek to understand new directions and consider their implications. (p. 3)

This supports-based perspective promotes as a basic tenet the notion of maintaining individuals with intellectual disabilities in inclusive settings along with appropriate supports to be used only when needed.

Sociopolitical Influences

Beginning in the 1980s and continuing into the 1990s, the data indicate that the number of school-age students qualifying for special education due to intellectual disability under IDEA has changed dramatically. The total number of students identified as mentally retarded has decreased substantially since the late 1970s (refer to Figure 1.1). Polloway and Smith (1983) have suggested several factors to account for this decrease including: (1) definitional changes and changes in professional thinking, which have encouraged caution and conservatism about identification and misdiagnosis, and (2) the effects of early intervention efforts in preventing some cases of mild intellectual disability.

The impact that the various educational reforms, such as the increasing attention on standards-based education, will have on students with intellectual disabilities is difficult to predict. For instance, the six National Education Goals (see Figure 1.2) put forth in the America 2000 strategy (issued in 1991 and, by the way, not all reached by 2000) portend positive as well as negative scenarios for students with intellectual disabilities. As an example, the intent of goal 5—for all adults to be literate and have the skills necessary to participate in a global economy and exercise full citizenship—is a worthy one for the country in general. However, for students who may need to concentrate on mastering the skills needed to be successful in their local communities, the part related to competing in a global economy may not hold the same level of importance as it might for others.

FIGURE 1.2
America 2000: The National Education Goals

By the year 2000:

1. All children in America will start school ready to learn.

2. The high school graduation rate will increase to at least 90%.

3. American students will leave grades 4, 8, and 12 having demonstrated competency in challenging subject matter including English, mathematics, science, history, and geography; and every school in America will ensure that all students learn to use their minds well, so they may be prepared for responsible citizenship, further learning, and productive employment in our modern economy.

4. U.S. students will be first in the world in science and mathematics achievement.

5. Every adult American will be literate and will possess the knowledge and skills necessary to compete in a global economy and exercise the rights and responsibilities of citizenship.

6. Every school in America will be free of drugs and violence and will offer a disciplined environment conducive to learning.

Another example of the supports-based, inclusion paradigm is reflected in the 1992 and 2002 definitions of mental retardation approved by the American Association on Mental Retardation (AAMR, 2002; Luckasson et al., 1992a, 1992b). Its emphasis on levels of support across various domains of functioning underscores this supports-based theme.

The importance of supports can be found throughout the literature, as the concept is used frequently, in relation to a variety of topics related to individuals with intellectual disabilities: inclusion, transition, living arrangements, employment, and family. At its most fundamental level, the concept of supports is a very common phenomenon, as Patton and Dunn (1998) point out:

> We are all, as Condeluci (1995) noted, interdependent beings. It is very natural to use supports that exist in our everyday environments. We ask co-workers for rides to work when our cars are in the shop. We drop off our children at their grandparents' houses when we need to be away from home. We pay folks to cut our grass, pick up our garbage, dry clean our clothes—we use community services regularly. None of us find anything wrong with it. With this in mind, it is essential that professionals convey to youth with special needs that the use of supports and services is acceptable and useful. (p. 17)

One of the most significant pieces of legislation for persons with intellectual disabilities was passed in 1990: the Americans with Disabilities Act (ADA) (P.L. 101-336). It has been referred to as the most important action related to civil rights since the Civil Rights Act of 1964 (Hardman, Drew, Egan, & Wolf, 1993). ADA aims to provide civil rights protections for and opportunities to individuals who are disabled. It covers both public and private settings and affects employment, public services, transportation, public accommodations (e.g., restaurants, shopping centers), and telecommunications (e.g., relay services). Even though this legislation is not specifically targeted toward persons with intellectual disabilities, its impact on this group is noteworthy.

In a similar vein, the Developmental Disabilities Assistance and Bill of Rights Act (DDA) was revised in 1994. The stated purpose was:

> . . . to assure that individuals with developmental disabilities and their families participate in the design of and have access to culturally competent services, supports, and other assistance and opportunities that promote independence, productivity, and integration and inclusion into the community . . . (42 U.S.C. 6000, § 101b)

A summary of the rights afforded to people with developmental disabilities under the DDA is presented in Figure 1.3.

FIGURE 1.3

Rights of Individuals with Developmental Disabilities Under DDA

- Appropriate treatment, services, and habilitation
- Services in the least restrictive environment
- Publicly funded services that meet rigorous minimum standards, including nourishing meals, appropriate medical and dental services, freedom from undue physical or chemical restraint, access to family, and compliance with safety standards
- Services designed for optimal outcomes

The Individuals with Disabilities Education Act (IDEA) was reauthorized in 1997, and again as the Individuals with Disabilities Education Improvement Act of 2004. While reaffirming the basic tenets of the law passed in 1975, the most recent law includes extensive provisions that have implications for students with intellectual disability and their families. Six key components of IDEA are described in Box 1.2.

Additionally, the Elementary and Secondary Education Act (ESEA) was again amended in 2002 as P.L. 107-110, and renamed the No Child Left Behind Act (NCLB)—a significant piece of legislation that has been met with mixed response. The goal of the law is to have "all children" performing at grade level by the year 2014. As you can imagine, this presents some problem for people with intellectual

---

Box 1.2 ⚜ Six Key Components of IDEA

Free, Appropriate Public Education

School districts must provide special education and related services necessary to meet the needs of students with special learning requirements. These services are available to all students, regardless of severity of disability, and are provided at no cost to the family. The schools must also furnish related services, such as speech therapy, parent training, or psychological services when deemed necessary to ensure an appropriate education.

Appropriate Evaluation

Prior to a student receiving special education for the first time, a "full and individual initial evaluation" must be conducted. The law requires the following safeguards: parental consent, nondiscriminatory evaluation practices, evaluation by a team, use of more than one procedure, testing in the student's native language, and reevaluations conducted when necessary. Also, students with disabilities must participate in state- and district-wide assessments to the greatest extent possible. Allowances for accommodations and alternative versions of these tests were included in the regulations.

Individualized Education Program (IEP)

An individualized education program is a written document summarizing a student's learning program, and it is required for every student who qualifies as having a disability. The IEP lists learning goals and educational services for an individual child, and

serves to enhance communication among parents and other professionals about a student's program.

Least Restrictive Environment

Schools must educate children to as great an extent as possible—in general education settings with their nondisabled peers.

Parent and Student Participation in Decision Making

Parents are primary members of the IEP team. Parental consent must accompany every decision affecting a child or youth who is disabled, including evaluation, service determination, and educational placement. In addition, parents have the right to obtain an independent educational evaluation (IEE) of their child. Lastly, parents have the right to challenge or appeal any decision related to any aspect of the special education process.

Procedural Safeguards

Parents are guaranteed the following rights: to obtain all educational records, to secure an IEE, to request a due process hearing, to appeal decisions, and to initiate civil action when appealing a final hearing decision. New disciplinary language and procedural safeguards—particularly in relation to change of placement due to violation of school rule or code of conduct, weapons, and illegal drugs—were added to the 1997 and 2004 amendments.

disabilities. A closer look at the tenets however, reveals that the term "all" is defined as 95% of the school population. States have been instructed to assess children at regular intervals and to use research-based teaching methods and curriculum. Students with intellectual disabilities are expected to participate in the assessments, but accommodations or alternate assessments are options.

Another area that is very much affected by sociopolitical influences is the institutionalization of individuals with intellectual disabilities. As you will learn in chapter 12, America has made great strides toward deinstitutionalizing people with intellectual disabilities. This movement was both affirmed and checked in the landmark case *Olmstead v. L. C.* (1999). The *Olmstead* decision compels states to ensure that community services are provided to people deemed eligible for them. However, it also states that the wishes of people with intellectual disabilities and their families should be considered in determining placement. For that reason, *Olmstead* is viewed as being supportive of the concept of a continuum of services.

Atkins v. Virginia and the other legislation and litigation introduced here will be discussed in more detail in chapter 4.

In a very different case, the courts moved away from the subject of where people with intellectual disabilities should live and on to the question of whether some should live at all. In *Atkins v. Virginia* (2002), the U.S. Supreme Court was charged with determining whether people with mental retardation convicted of capital crimes should be eligible for capital punishment. The ruling stated that people with mental retardation should not be executed because of a variety of cognitive, behavioral, and lifestyle factors that are commonly associated with intellectual disabilities. The ruling has brought issues of diagnosis and assessment to the fore in a very real, vitally important way.

Psychological, Medical, and Health Care Developments

The last 15 years have seen some astonishing developments in the fields of psychology, medicine, and health care. Many of these discoveries of science and research are having a significant impact on persons with intellectual disabilities. Some of the recent developments are described here.

Behavioral Interventions.   The application of behavioral analysis techniques to various problematic situations, particularly social ones, is the essence of positive behavioral support. Positive behavioral support focuses on the reasons for challenging behavior. Environmental events are restructured to decrease the frequency of problem behaviors. At the same time, the trainer attempts to teach skills that will eliminate the need for the challenging behavior.

Behavior interventions are discussed again in chapter 9.

Genetics.   Research of the last several years has brought us to the point where we are now on the brink of knowing the cause of genetically related disorders, many of which are associated with intellectual disability. Currently, ongoing research is looking into the genetic abnormalities that cause specific disorders. Other researchers are developing various methodologies such as gene replacement therapy for addressing these issues.

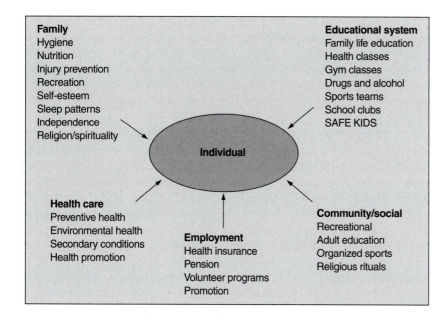

FIGURE 1.4

Model for Individual Health Promotion

Source: From "Health Promotion and Disability Prevention: The Case for Personal Responsibility and Independence," by D. E. Cohen, in M. L. Wehmeyer and J. R. Patton (Eds.), Mental Retardation In the 21st Century (pp. 251–264), 2000, Austin, TX: PRO-ED. Copyright © by PRO-ED. Reprinted by permission.

Moser (2000) identifies four technological advances that have been refined in recent years that will continue to have an impact on the field of intellectual disabilities: (1) refined biochemical and enzymatic assays (i.e., diagnostic techniques); (2) advances in neuroimaging (e.g., magnetic resonance imaging); (3) advances in neuroscience (e.g., neuronal activity); and (4) the U.S. Human Genome Project (i.e., development of genetic and physical maps).

Health Care.   During the 1990s, health care became a major concern in the United States, and a small but growing amount of attention was given specifically to the health care needs of persons with mental retardation. Cohen (2000) provides a model of health care promotion for individuals with intellectual disabilities that incorporates the notion of support from different entities (see Figure 1.4).

The importance of health care is unassailable, yet its availability to large numbers of folks who desperately need it is still a problem. As Crocker (2000) states, "Access to quality health care remains in our ethos as a natural right (although not literally an entitlement), yet many individuals are still left out of present coverage, or tumble out of it" (p. 277).

Trends in Service Delivery

The supports-based theme has influenced the delivery of service across the life span. The overall theme is that decisions about service delivery should involve the individual to the greatest extent possible and that appropriate services should be provided in inclusive settings.

A trend that emerged in the latter part of the 1990s is the notion of *empowerment*. The idea of creating situations in which individuals are more active participants in various aspects of their own lives is a logical outgrowth of a supports-based climate. Polloway and colleagues (1996) note that empowerment includes ideas around which professionals within the field of developmental disabilities "finally can rally because it can embrace considerations related to inclusion, curricular needs, and transitions" (p. 8).

Learn more about the philosophical shift from services to supports by visiting the Companion Website at www.prenhall.com/beirne-smith and selecting Chapter 1, Video Case Studies.

An important element of empowerment is *self-determination,* a topic that, although not new, began receiving broad professional attention in the 1990s. Wehmeyer (1993) offers the following explanation of self-determination: "Self-determination refers to the attitudes and abilities necessary to act as the primary causal agent in one's life, and to make choices and decisions regarding one's quality of life free from undue external influence or interference" (p. 16). Individuals who are afforded the freedom of choice and are more involved in making decisions associated with this choice are likely to enjoy a better quality of life because they have had a say in the way it should go.

Early Intervention.   Infants and toddlers with intellectual disabilities are being provided needed services in their natural environments. One of the most important changes in the nature of services for very young children is placing families at the center of the early intervention system (Guralnick, 2000). A major characteristic of early childhood intervention is the desire to provide families with the supports to assist them in carrying out the key pieces of the individual family service plan (IFSP) in which they can be involved.

The goal of services at the preschool age (i.e., ages 3 through 5) is to provide an appropriate education in settings with other children who are not disabled. For the most part, this goal has not been achieved, in great part because publicly supported preschool does not exist in the United States. As a result, the options for similar age inclusion are in the private sector. Some inclusion of older preschoolers can occur with kindergarten kids. Nevertheless, the development of effective preschool programs throughout the United States has been remarkable.

Education.   Efforts to teach students with intellectual disabilities in **inclusive environments** increased in the 1990s. Although data suggest many students with intellectual disabilities are still receiving the bulk of their education in separate classes (U.S. Department of Education, 2002), efforts to increase the opportunities for inclusion are intensifying, as are wonderful examples of effective inclusionary practices. When inclusion has been successful, the following features are typically present in the classroom: sense of community and social acceptance, appreciation of student diversity, attention to the student's curricular needs, evidence of effective management and instructional practices, and appropriate supports (Smith, Polloway, Patton, & Dowdy, 2001).

Another development that has affected the education of students with intellectual disabilities is the use of technology. Technology has short-term (i.e., assistance with immediate school-related challenges) as well as long-term applications (i.e., useful in a lifelong perspective) for individuals with intellectual disabilities. Technology is changing so fast that we cannot even envision what might be possible 10 years from now.

Adult Issues.   At the adult level, the supports-based theme can be easily recognized in a number of current initiatives. One of the most successful models of employment training is *supported employment*—sometimes referred to as *workplace supports*. In this arrangement, a job coach or employment specialist works with the individual on-site, providing training and addressing other support needs. The number of individuals who participate in supported employment increased dramatically during the 1990s (Wehman, Revell, & Kregel, 1997).

Even with the substantial increase in the number of people involved in various competitive employment settings, a number of adults are still engaged in sheltered employment settings. The reality is that many more individuals could be working in competitive employment settings, especially in times of low unemployment when workers are desperately needed.

Also on the rise is the creation of housing arrangements where staff is available as necessary to assist individuals with intellectual disabilities (supported living) who live in these settings. For older individuals, specialized approaches have been developed (supported retirement).

The adult years will be explored in chapter 12.

FINAL REFLECTIONS

An important concept that applies to all individuals with intellectual disabilities and should guide all research, intervention, and all other aspects of this field is consideration of quality of life. Although professional debate exists as to the validity of this concept and whether it can be measured, the fundamental essence of quality of life can be understood in the context of the eight core quality-of-life dimensions identified by Schalock (1996): emotional well-being, interpersonal relationships, material well-being, personal development, physical well-being, self-determination, social inclusion, and rights. Table 1.2 highlights the comprehensiveness of these dimensions and their relevance to the lives of persons with intellectual disabilities.

Other issues associated with intellectual disabilities have emerged and are still unresolved. Some of these include a host of ethical considerations (e.g., withholding treatment) and the continuing effects of poverty. These and other issues must still be addressed. Cutbacks and restrictions may result from economic problems or policy shifts. If a positive national policy supportive of people with special needs is not carefully maintained, society will be guilty of social neglect, and people who need help will not receive it. Blatt (1987) poignantly captured the gravity of the situation: "If the business of government isn't charity, and we aren't our brothers' keepers, then some needy people will die before their time, and many needy people will suffer" (p. 83). We must move through this new century with guarded optimism, because what can be done for people needing assistance has been, and will continue to be, grounded in vagaries of the sociopolitical context.

 To check your understanding of this chapter, go to the Companion Website at www.prenhall.com/beirne -smith and select Chapter 1. From there, you can access the Self-Test and Essay modules.

TABLE 1.2
Quality-of-Life Indicators

Dimension	Exemplary Indicators	
Emotional well-being	Safety	Freedom from stress
	Spirituality	Self-concept
	Happiness	Contentment
Interpersonal relationships	Intimacy	Interactions
	Affection	Friendships
	Family	Supports
Material well-being	Ownership	Employment
	Financial	Possessions
	Security	Socioeconomic status
	Food	Shelter
Personal development	Education	Personal competence
	Skills	Purposeful activity
	Fulfillment	Advancement
Physical well-being	Health	Health care
	Nutrition	Health Insurance
	Recreation	Leisure
	Mobility	Activities of daily living
Self-determination	Autonomy	Personal control
	Choices	Self-direction
	Decision	Personal goals/value
Social inclusion	Acceptance	Community activities
	Status	Roles
	Supports	Volunteer activities
	Work environment	Residential environment
Rights	Privacy	Due process
	Voting	Ownership
	Access	Civic responsibilities

Source: From Schalock (2000).

Summary

General

- Significant sociopolitical factors have contributed to the evolution of the field of intellectual disability.
- Intellectual disability is very much a social phenomenon.
- Many contemporary issues are not new.

Antiquity: Prior to 1700
- Before 1700, intellectual disability was misunderstood and treated in a variety of mysterious ways.
- Milder forms of intellectual disability were not recognizable.
- Custodial care was provided in certain settings.

Emergence and Early Disillusionment of a Field: 1700–1890
- Itard worked with Victor (the Wild Boy).
- Seguin developed instructional methodologies and programs—elements of which are still used today.
- In the United States, key individuals such as Dix, Howe, and Wilbur pioneered care for individuals with special needs.
- Toward the end of the 19th century, important social forces (urbanization and industrialization) were occurring that would have effects on those with cognitive limitations.
- Pessimism about what could be done for persons with intellectual disabilities developed.

Facilities-Based Orientation: 1890–1960
- Institutions became custodial in nature.
- The eugenics movement began, affecting many persons with intellectual disabilities through sterilization, segregation, and limitations on immigration.
- The mental test was developed, and milder forms of intellectual disabilities were now recognizable.
- A major professional organization for special education teachers (now known as the Council for Exceptional Children) was founded.
- Standardized scales for measuring social maturity and intelligence were introduced.
- The largest and most powerful parent organization advocating for people with intellectual disability (now called the Arc of the United States) was formed.
- Most states enacted legislation for educating some students with intellectual disability; many of those with more significant cognitive impairments were still excluded.

Services-Based Orientation: 1960–1985
- President Kennedy established a national agenda for mental retardation.
- The War on Poverty was initiated.
- The principle of normalization began to take hold.
- A series of major court cases began to force important changes.
- The Vocational Rehabilitation Act reauthorization of 1973 became a landmark piece of legislation.

- A free, appropriate public education became available to all students with disabilities with the passage of the Education for All Handicapped Children Act of 1975.
- Community services and placement were championed by advocates.

Supports-Based Orientation: 1985–Present
- The placement of children, youth, and adults into inclusive settings is advocated by parents and professionals.
- The number of residents in institutional settings continues to drop.
- Continued attention on early intervention is promoted.
- The number of students identified by schools as mentally retarded continued to drop, but with a slight increase in recent years.
- Employment possibilities are enriched by the implementation of practices such as supported employment.
- The notion of supports is validated and encouraged.
- New medical discoveries (e.g., genome research) offer exciting possibilities.

2

Definition and Terminology

OBJECTIVES

After reading this chapter, the student should be able to:

- Identify terms used to describe mental retardation
- Discuss the concept of disablism and how it relates to mental retardation
- Identify key points of the various definitions that have been developed
- Highlight the definitions of mental retardation developed by the American Association on Mental Retardation (AAMR) definition
- Highlight the various contemporary definitions promoted by specific professional organizations
- Discuss the issues surrounding the practical implementation of definitions
- List and discuss the factors that influence the prevalence of mental retardation

KEY TERMS

adaptive behavior

clinical judgment

developmental disability

developmental period

disablism

incidence

intellectual disability

mental retardation

prevalence

6-hour retarded children

standard deviation

subaverage general
intellectual functioning

Mental retardation is a complex condition worthy of close study. Essentially, mental retardation is an intellectual disability that affects the way individuals who have it adapt to and cope with the various environments in which they find themselves. This condition is manifest by difficulties in intellectual functioning and in the performance of everyday type of behaviors that would be expected of a person of similar age and from the same cultural background. Mental retardation is also multidimensional such that other factors like the capacity to function, the ability to function, and the opportunity to function must be considered when examining this condition (World Health Organization, 2001).

Mental retardation has been defined and will continue to be defined in various and differing ways, as illustrated in recent times by the proliferation of discussions related to this condition and the number of different definitions that exist. The importance and impact of getting definition right is illustrated in the following comment of Luckasson and Reeve (2001):

> Because the essence of a definition is that it separates something from another (named) thing, a major consequence of a definition is that can . . . make someone or something eligible or ineligible (as to serving on a jury), subjected to something or not subjected (as to involuntary commitment), exempted from something or not exempted (as from the death penalty), included or not included (as to protections against discrimination), entitled or not entitled (as to Social Security). (p. 49)

In addition to the various conceptualizations open to debate, mental retardation entails other meanings as well. On a very practical level, for instance: "For the individual and the family, mental retardation presents very practical concerns. For the community, state, and nation, it presents educational, social, economic, and political challenges" (Grossman & Tarjan, 1987, p. v).

The definition of mental retardation is explored in depth in this chapter, as we trace the evolution of how various individuals and organizations have perceived the condition. Ways of dealing with mental retardation on an individual basis are addressed throughout the book. Its challenge to society was underscored from a historical perspective in the previous chapter; current sociopolitical implications associated with a definition will be addressed in this chapter.

MENTAL RETARDATION IN CONTEXT

A complete online glossary is available on the Companion Website, which may be accessed at www.prenhall.com/ beirne-smith

Mental retardation is one type of developmental disability and generally refers to substantial limitations in present levels of functioning. These limitations are manifest in delayed intellectual growth; inappropriate or immature reactions to one's environment; and below-average performance in the academic, psychological, physical, linguistic, and social domains. Such limitations create challenges for individuals to cope with the demands they encounter each day, those that other people of comparable age and social or cultural background would be expected to deal with successfully on an ongoing basis. For example, in school settings these individuals display patterns of academic and social performance that are below their chronological peers' levels of mastery. Unlike other students who perform below grade level,

Stereotypes are all too often easy to make.

the principal reason that students with mental retardation do so relates to their problems in reasoning, dealing with abstract concepts, and problem solving. Their school-based difficulties are not primarily due to such factors as excessive absences from school or a specific learning disability—although such factors can contribute to their overall school performance.

Mental retardation encompasses a heterogeneous group of people with varying needs, presenting features, and life contexts. It is changeable, as some individuals may be asymptomatic at various times of their lives (before formal schooling and often later, as adults). Some professional orientations (AAMR, 2002) suggest that this condition is very much a function of the need for various levels of support. The severity of the condition ranges from mild difficulties in dealing with everyday activities to extreme limitations in basic areas of functioning that make the person dependent on others for basic skilled nursing care.

Mental Retardation as a Developmental Disability

As mentioned, mental retardation is an intellectual disability and also one type of developmental disability. In recent years, the concept of **developmental disability** has often been used to refer to individuals with mental retardation, particularly with adult populations. Although the term *developmental disability* covers a population of individuals other than those with mental retardation, its meaning clearly includes mental retardation. As defined in the Developmental Disabilities Assistance and Bill of Rights Act of 2000 (P.L. 106-402):

(A) IN GENERAL. — The term "developmental disability" means a severe, chronic disability of an individual that—

(i)   is attributable to a mental or physical impairment or combination of mental and physical impairments;

(ii) is manifested before the person attains age 22;

(iii) is likely to continue indefinitely;

(iv) results in substantial functional limitations in 3 or more of the following areas of major life activity:

(I) self-care, (II) receptive and expressive language, (III) learning, (IV) mobility, (V) self-direction, (VI) capacity for independent living, and (VII) economic self-sufficiency; and

(v)   reflects the individual's need for a combination and sequence of special, interdisciplinary, or generic services, individualized supports, or other forms of assistance that are of lifelong or of extended duration and are individually planned and coordinated. [§ 102(8)(A)(i–v)]

The federal definition accentuates functional limitations in major life activities, suggesting problems associated with a more involved population. Nevertheless, it also applies to persons with milder forms of retardation during some or all of their lives. The implication of chronicity and its potential inappropriateness with very young populations make it different from the most common definitions of mental retardation.

Alternative Conceptualizations

Alternative ways of thinking about mental retardation have emerged over the years. This section explores select perspectives that have had or are creating an impact on conceptualizing mental retardation.

One perspective, a phenomenological orientation, considers mental retardation to be solely a social invention (i.e., a reaction to people perceived as different), as some professionals have claimed (Blatt, 1987). Granted, identifiable biological manifestations exist in some individuals who have mental retardation, but we all have physical differences (e.g., freckles, musculature). Bogdan (1986) describes the phenomenological orientation:

> The generic term "disabled" and specific disability categories are ways of thinking about and categorizing others. Whether people are thought of as disabled and the criteria used to determine whether someone is disabled has [sic] to do with how the definers think about these things. (p. 347)

Mercer (1973a, 1973b), on the other hand, argues that neither a pathological nor a statistical approach to defining mental retardation is adequate for identifying cases of more mild retardation. As an alternative, she offers a social system perspective, which defines mental retardation as "an achieved social status in a social system":

> The status of mental retardate is associated with a role which persons occupying that status are expected to play. A person's career in acquiring the status of playing the role of mental retardate can be described in the same fashion as the career of a person who acquires any other status such as lawyer, bank president or teacher. (Mercer, 1973b)

Mercer's (1973a, 1973b) research findings suggest that individuals are labeled *mentally retarded* as a function of their performance in social situations. She advocates a more conservative definition of mental retardation, one that would make the measurement of adaptive behavior more practical. According to her view, multiple norm frameworks must be developed to adequately describe children from different sociocultural settings. That is, children must be described (and labeled, if necessary) in relation to their own social and cultural background, without prejudging that background as "deviant" or "deficient." Mercer also recommends that the identification and diagnosis of mental retardation be based on data that include the children's competencies as well as their deficits.

Think more about the power of language by visiting the Companion Website at www.prenhall .com/beirne-smith and selecting Chapter 2, Video Case Studies.

Gold (1980) developed a somewhat different sociological conceptualization of mental retardation. His perspective focuses on the ability or failure of society to provide adequate training and education as the measure of retardation rather than on the failure of the individual. Gold's ideas are reflected in the following statement: "The height of a retarded person's level of functioning is determined by the availability of training technology and the amount of resources society is willing to allocate and not by significant limitations in biological potential" (p. 148).

More recently, a clamor to deconstruct mental retardation has been proposed (Smith, 2002, 2003). Borrowing the argument from Szasz (1974) that the term *mental retardation* is "scientifically worthless and socially harmful" (*Note:* Szasz was referring to mental illness), Smith (2002) states that the "best definition of mental retardation may be no definition" (p. 64). Smith points to fundamental arguments made by Trent in his 1994 book *Inventing the Feeble Mind,* suggesting that mental retardation was constructed within the context of the residential institution for a number of reasons. Smith's position is captured in the following quote:

> Mental retardation and its various definitions are, in fact, manifestations of the typological thinking that inevitably creates a simplistic and misleading aggregation of people with very different needs and characteristics. . . . The time is overdue, however, for a fundamental questioning of the terms and practices associated with mental retardation. (Smith & Mitchell, 2001, p. 146)

Key Concepts to Keep in Mind

State Versus Trait. A distinction has been made between mental retardation as a state and as a trait. It has been stated by the American Association on Mental Retardation (AAMR) that "mental retardation is not a trait, although it is influenced by certain characteristics or capabilities of the individual. . . . Rather, mental retardation is a state in which functioning is impaired in certain specific ways. This distinction between trait and state is central to understanding" (AAMR, 1992, p. 10).

Individuals at the Margins. Individuals who have few needs for support or who are at the border of retardation create problems of identification and eligibility. Reschly (1988) has stated that as long as the system perceives mental retardation in terms of dichotomy—one either is or is not retarded—rather than a continuum, a problem will always persist in classifying individuals at the margins. This point is in great part because of (1) the way we conceptualize and measure intellectual abilities and (2) society's definition of acceptable behavior and toleration of behavior that is different.

TERMINOLOGY

Terminology in the field of mental retardation is almost always a topic that precipitates a lively discussion. The term *mental retardation,* used for more than 50 years (Luckasson & Reeve, 2001), is most often used in the United States. Worldwide, the term *intellectual disability* is the preferred designation. Whatever term is used, it needs to convey generally agreed-upon meaning and contribute to facilitating communication across a range of groups, including professionals, families, and individuals with this condition. This section will highlight the many different terms that have been, are being, and most likely will be used to name the condition of mental retardation.

Historical Terminology

As mentioned in chapter 1, people who are mentally retarded over time have been referred to as *dumb, stupid, immature, defective, deficient, subnormal, incompetent,* and *dull.* Historically, terms such as *idiot, imbecile, moron,* and *feebleminded* were used to label this population. Although the word *fool* referred to those who were mentally ill, and the word *idiot* was directed toward individuals who were significantly limited intellectually and socially, these terms were frequently used interchangeably (Hilliard & Kirman, 1965). Even today, the conditions of mental illness and mental retardation are regularly confused in the media and the popular press. For the sake of distinction, *mental illness,* broadly speaking, is a confused state of thinking involving distorted perceptions of people or one's environment. It may be accompanied by radical changes of mood. In this attempt to distinguish these two terms, it should be noted that an individual could have both conditions (i.e., what we refer today to as dually diagnosed).

The history of mental retardation is further complicated when we consider that retardation has been confused with physical deformity, cerebral palsy, dwarfism, epilepsy, and deafness. This confusion endures today to some extent because a combination of these conditions does occur at higher rates in this population.

One of the first steps in understanding a phenomenon is understanding the terms used to describe it, no matter how crude or limited they may be. In the past, *idiot* was used to refer to people of all levels of mental retardation, from mild to profound. It derives from the Greek *idiotes,* meaning "a layperson or unskilled worker." The word applied to untrained or ignorant people, and it was used in this sense until the 17th century (Penrose, 1966).

According to Kolstoe (1972), the *de praerogative regis* ("prerogative of the king" [of England]) issued between 1255 and 1290 defined an idiot as one who "hath no understanding from his nativity" (p. 2). About 200 years later, Sir Anthony Fitzherbert stated that an idiot was "such a person who cannot account or number, nor can tell who his father or mother are, nor how old he is, etc., so as it may appear he has not understanding of reason what shall be his profit or his loss" (Guttmacher & Weihofen, 1952). The key factor in identification as an idiot appears to be lack of understanding.

Idiocy was believed to be inborn and incurable. As mentioned in chapter 1, one of the first accounts of attempts to cure or at least ameliorate mental retardation was reported by Itard (1801/1962), who worked with a wild boy, Victor. A well-known physician of the time, Pinel, diagnosed Victor as an incurable idiot. Seguin, a student of Itard and following in his footsteps, also attempted to cure individuals with severe limitations; Penrose (1966) reports that "Esquirol referred to Seguin's mission as the removal of the mark of the beast from the forehead of the idiot" (pp. 4–5).

The concept of *idiot* was elusive and confusing, and it covered conditions that had little in common with each other; its primary use was to signify severe mental retardation. Although other terms such as *feebleminded, mental subnormality,* or *mental deficiency* were used to describe those with intellectual and social deficits, the confusion remained. Attempts to systematize the terminology and definitions of mental retardation have continued to present times, as evidenced in the debates raging today over the use of the term *intellectual disability.*

A different set of terms became popular in school settings. From the 1950s until the early 1980s, most students with mental retardation who were in school were labeled either *educable mentally retarded* (EMR) or *trainable mentally retarded* (TMR). EMR referred to students whose abilities were adequate to profit from an academically oriented curriculum; TMR referred to students whose programs emphasized the "training" of basic functional skills (e.g., daily living skills). Much of the classic literature on educating children and youth with mental retardation used these terms. However, the underlying thinking associated with these labels and the programmatic decisions based on them have changed dramatically in more recent times. As a result, their usage has declined to the point where it is rare to find situations where these terms are still used.

Current Terminology

Today, the most commonly used terms to refer to this condition are *mental retardation* and **intellectual disability.** As noted previously, the former term is primarily used in the United States. The latter term is commonly used in countries around the world (Patton, 2003). The International Association for the Scientific Study of Intellectual Disability (IASSID) uses this term in its name and that of its journal. Some professionals like the terms *intellectually challenged* or *mental disability.*

The term *intellectual disability* is receiving more support from professionals in the United States, as evidenced in the discussions to change the name of the American Association on Mental Retardation to the American Association on Intellectual Disability (Warren, 2003) and in its appearance in book titles/subtitles and journal articles (Simeonsson, Granlund, & Bjorck-Akesson, 2003). The use of the term *intellectual disability* has its critics as well (Garnett, 2003; Lower, 1999). Opposing arguments focus on the confusion, potential misinterpretation, and lack of inclusiveness that this term conveys.

Another interesting way to name this condition is to refer to it as being a type of learning disability, thus emphasizing what many professionals (see Baroff, 1999) argue is the core problem associated with the condition. In 1973, Dunn proposed the use of the term *general learning disabilities* (GLD) to refer to children and youth with mental retardation (i.e., school-age). He differentiated this term from *major specific learning disabilities* (MSLD)—a term that has endured until now to refer to individuals who demonstrate discrepancy between capacity and performance. Given the rise in popularity of the concept of learning disabilities that occurred in the 1970s, Dunn's GLD never caught on in professional circles. Interestingly, the term *learning disabilities* is used in the United Kingdom to refer to individuals with mental retardation. Simeonsson and colleagues (2003) remark that the term *learning disabilities* is preferable to *mental retardation* or *developmental disabilities,* and, as a result, they recommend that it be adopted.

In a similar way, Baroff (1999, 2003) recommends the use of the term *general learning disorder* (GLD) in place of *mental retardation.* In his proposed grouping of developmental disabilities, Baroff also suggests the use of the terms *specific academic learning disorder* (in place of *learning disabilities*) and *broad academic learning disorder* (in reference to slow learners).

The continual search for different terms yields diminishing returns. Any word can come to have a negative connotation, as reflected in the following true story. One school district, aware of the detrimental effects of labeling children "mentally retarded," began placing these children in an educational program designed to teach language, arithmetic, and reading very systematically, using an explicit teaching methodology. DISTAR (Direct Instructional Systems for Teaching Arithmetic and Reading), a series of commercial programs produced by Science Research Associates, was used. Before half the year was over, a group of concerned citizens asked that the program be abandoned because DISTAR was for "dumb" kids, and children not enrolled in DISTAR classes were making fun of the DISTAR children by yelling "DISTAR, DISTAR" at them at recess. It may be impossible to find acceptable terms and useful definitions without proper education and increased understanding of persons who are intellectually disabled.

DISABLISM AND MENTAL RETARDATION

Many groups in our society are not perceived favorably by the community at large. As Wolfensberger (1985) pointed out, "How a person is perceived affects how that person will be treated" (p. 128). If a certain group of people is perceived negatively, then its members will be treated less than favorably. Wolfensberger has identified groups of people who are devalued in our society, listing the major negative social roles into which these groups are typically cast. His analysis of this devaluation, although 20 years old, still is applicable today (see Table 2.1).

According to Wolfensberger, only mental disorder (i.e., mental illness) evokes more negative perceptions than mental retardation. It might be proper to mark the "Dread" column in Table 2.1 for mental retardation as well, because sufficient examples of this perception exist. For instance, consider the following scenario: parents shielding their children from a group of adults who are mentally retarded seated

TABLE 2.1
Socially Devalued Groups and the Common Historical Deviancy Roles into Which They Are Most Apt to Be Cast

People who are devalued due to:	Common Deviancy Roles								
	Pity	Charity	Menace	Sick	Sub-human	Ridicule	Dread	Childlike	Holy innocent
Mental disorder	X	X	X	X	X	X	X	X	X
Mental retardation	X	X	X	X	X	X		X	X
Old age	X	X		X	X	X		X	
Alcohol habituation	X	X	X	X		X			
Poverty	X	X	X		X		X		
Racial minority membership			X		X	X	X	X	
Epilepsy	X	X		X			X		
Drug addiction	X	X	X	X					
Criminal offenses			X	X	X		X		
Physical handicap	X	X				X			
Deafness/hearing impairment	X	X							
Blindness/visual impairment	X	X							
Illiteracy	X	X							
Political dissidence			X						

Source: From "An Overview of Social Role Valorization and Some Reflections on Elderly Mentally Retarded Persons," by W. Wolfensberger, 1985. In M. P. Janicki & H. M. Wisniewski (Eds.), *Aging and Developmental Disabilities: Issues and Approaches* (pp. 61–76), Baltimore: Paul H. Brookes. Copyright 1985 by Paul H. Brookes. Reprinted by permission.

near them on the bus out of concern that these adults are dangerous. Wolfensberger's analysis has three major implications: (1) persons who are considered retarded will be treated differently, likely badly; (2) this treatment reflects the way society conceptualizes deviancy roles; and (3) the perceptions and resultant treatment by others will greatly influence the behavior of people who are retarded.

It is precisely because many individuals with retardation are treated differently from the general population that the concept of disablism is relevant. **Disablism** (changed herein from the former term *handicapism*), similarly to racism, sexism, and ageism, results in mistaken beliefs, prejudices, and pejorative actions on the part of individuals or society in general. Bogdan and Biklen (1977), two professionals who brought this concept to the public consciousness, define it as a "set of assumptions and practices that promote the differential and unequal treatment of people because of apparent or assumed physical, mental, or behavioral differences" (p. 59). This concept applies to a range of people with disabilities, clearly including those who are mentally retarded.

Disablism is comprised of three key elements: stereotyping, prejudice, and discrimination. Many people view adults with retardation as childlike (stereotyping), which leads to the belief that they are incapable of making decisions for themselves (prejudice), which in turn results in others making decisions for them without their input or knowledge (discrimination). A practical example is the situation in which a person with mental retardation is not allowed to obtain a library card (discrimination) because it is believed (prejudice) that the person is incapable of being responsible for any books that are borrowed (stereotyping).

Disablism is manifest in various ways, most notably through language and medical portrayal. A particularly offensive example is the popular "moron" joke ("Why did the moron . . . ?"): As pointed out earlier, the term *moron* refers to an individual with limited intellectual capacity. These jokes are heard in everyday conversation and can be found in books of "tasteless jokes." Although people with mental retardation are not the only group to suffer from malicious jokes, they certainly are a prime target. Another language example involves the flippant use of the word *retarded* or *retard*. A recent piece in *USA Today* identified celebrities who had used this term to describe a person or situation in an unflattering way and provided quotes to support the point.

Disablism is also evident in media representations. For instance, the character Zero in the comic strip "Beetle Bailey" might be considered to have mental retardation, as he is always portrayed in uncomplimentary ways. A number of movies have included characters who have mental retardation in roles of differing levels of importance to the film. A list of some of the films with such characters is provided in Table 2.2. The table highlights films that use actors to portray characters with mental retardation, thus excluding the genre of documentary (e.g., *Best Boy/Best Man*). The table does not attempt to critique these films—we leave that up to the reader—so, it includes films with characters who contribute to the notion of disablism (e.g., *Charley, The Other Sister, I Am Sam*) as well as films that accurately portray a person with mental retardation (e.g., *What's Eating Gilbert Grape*).

Bogdan and Biklen also note that, far too often, newspaper reports associate criminal activity with disability, implying that the disability is somehow responsible for the crime. This perspective certainly has been evident in some media descriptions of people with mental retardation. It is important to be aware of instances of disablism and to strive to eliminate them. Far too often, blatant examples of disablism go unchallenged.

DEFINING MENTAL RETARDATION

Many definitions of mental retardation have been developed, all reflecting the different perspectives and perceptions of retardation at a given point in time. Blatt (1987) articulates this notion well:

> Because mental retardation is in the most fundamental and important ways a metaphor (people make of it what they want to, people interpret it in light of their own understandings and prejudices), the definition of "mental retardation" and the terms used to denote the condition represent a hodgepodge of (sometimes irreconcilable) values, words, and ideas. (p. 69)

Whether or not we agree with Blatt's statement, we must deal with the reality that definitions exist and are used to make decisions about persons with retardation.

Central to all of the earliest definitions of mental retardation is the notion of difficulties in social competence. Historically, this was the prime concern and therefore

TABLE 2.2

Motion Pictures with Characters Who Are Disabled or Gifted

Title	Disability of Key Character	Title	Disability of Key Character
At First Sight	VI	Miracle Worker, The	VI, HI
As Good as it Gets	E/BD; OHI	Moby Dick	PD
Awakenings	E/BD	Mr. Holland's Opus	HI
Bad Boy Buddy	E/BD	My Left Foot	PD
Beautiful Mind, A	GT; E/BD	Nell	ASD
Bedlam	MR	Of Mice and Men	MR
Being There	MR	One Flew over the	
Benny and Joon	E/BD	Cuckoo's Nest	E/BD
Best Boy	MR	Ordinary People	E/BD
Blackboard Jungle	AR	Other Side of the Mountain	PD
Born on the Fourth of July	PD	Other Sister, The	MR
Brother's Keeper	MR	Passion Fish	PD
Butterflies Are Free	VI	Patch of Blue, A	VI
Camille Claudel	E/BD	Philadelphia	OHI
Charley	MR	Piano, The	HI
Children of a Lesser God	HI	Places in the Heart	VI
Coming Home	PD	Powder	GT
Dancer in the Dark	VI	Radio	MR
Dominick and Eugene	MR	Rainman	ASD
Dr. Strangelove	PD	Regarding Henry	TBI
Dream Team	E/BD	Rudy	LD
Edward Scissorhands	PD	Scent of a Woman	VI
Elephant Man, The	PD	Searching for Bobby Fischer	GT
Fisher King	E/BD	See No Evil, Hear No Evil	VI
Forest Gump	MR	Shine	GT
Gaby: A True Story	PD	Sling Blade	MR
Good Will Hunting	GT	Sneakers	VI
Hand That Rocks the Cradle, The	MR	Stand and Deliver	AR
Heart Is a Lonely Hunter, The	HI	Steel Magnolias	OHI
Heart of the Dragon	MR	Sybil	E/BD
I Am Sam	MR	Terms of Endearment	OHI
I Never Promised You a		There's Something About Mary	MR
Rose Garden	E/BD	Tim	MR
If You Could See What I Hear	VI	Tin Man	HI
King of Hearts	E/BD	To Kill a Mockingbird	MR
King of the Jungle	MR	To Sir with Love	AR
La Strada	MR	Wait Until Dark	VI
Last Picture Show, The	MR	Whatever Happened to	
Little Man Tate	GT	Baby Jane	PD
Lorenzo's Oil	OHI	What's Eating Gilbert Grape	PD, MR
Man Without a Face, The	PD	Young Frankenstein	PD
MASH	VI, HI	Zelly and Me	E/BD

Key: AR, at risk; ASD, autism spectrum disorder; E/BD, emotional/behavior disorder/psychiatric issue; GT, gifted and talented; HI, hearing impairment; LD, learning disability; MR, mental retardation; OHI, other health impaired; PD, physical disability; TBI, traumatic brain injury; VI, visual impairment.

Source: From *Exceptional Individuals in Focus* (7th ed.), by J. M. Blackbourn, J. R. Patton, & A. Trainor, 2004, Upper Saddle River, NJ: Merrill/Prentice Hall. Copyright © 2004; reprinted by permission of Pearson Education, Inc., Upper Saddle River, NJ.

preeminent criterion. While in more recent times the importance of being able to deal adaptively with the demands of one's environment has remained important, this concept has been eclipsed by the relative importance given to intellectual functioning.

The major professional definitions of mental retardation published over the last 40 years have consistently used a framework that includes three criteria: deficits in intellectual functioning, difficulties in adaptive behavior, and manifestation during the developmental period. The specific interpretations, and weightings, of each of these criteria have changed, sometimes dramatically, over the years; however, all can be found in the major professional definitions. An explanation of each of these criteria will be provided later in this section.

This section has four major foci: (1) a brief examination of some early definitions, (2) a discussion of the series of definitions developed by the AAMR, (3) a look at other contemporary professional definitions, and (4) consideration of other definitions—some from a few years ago and some of more recent note—that are worthy of discussion.

Early Definitions

During the first half of the 20th century, two definitions of mental retardation—one developed by Tredgold and the other by Doll—were frequently cited. Tredgold (1937) defined *mental deficiency* as

> a state of incomplete mental development of such a kind and degree that the individual is incapable of adapting himself to the normal environment of his fellows in such a way to maintain existence independently of supervision, control, or external support. (p. 4)

Doll (1941) defined *mental deficiency* when he stated:

> We observe that six criteria by statement or implication have been generally considered essential to an adequate definition and concept. These are (1) social incompetence, (2) due to mental subnormality, (3) which has been developmentally arrested, (4) which obtains at maturity, (5) is of constitutional origin, and (6) is essentially incurable. (p. 215)

In 1969, Haywood and Stedman provided a definition that, not only referred to etiology, but also underscored the effects of mental retardation on learning and the resulting impact on social competence.

> In terms of its current usage, mental retardation is a global term encompassing over 200 etiological conditions with one common manifestation: impaired efficiency of learning, both in academic and social areas, which results in the inability to function adequately in society.

All of these definitions stress the concept of social competence. Arguably, Doll's definition is the most important of the early definitions, as it contains specific criteria (i.e., the first four criteria) that are precursors of elements that were used in subsequent definitions. The last two criteria in Doll's conceptualization of mental retardation spark discussion and disagreement to this day—particularly the notion of "incurability."

The AAMD/AAMR Definitions

In 1919, the American Association for the Study of the Feebleminded, which would later become the American Association on Mental Deficiency (AAMD) and is now known as the American Association on Mental Retardation (AAMR), appointed a Committee on Classification and Uniform Statistics. In 1921, this committee, in collaboration with the National Committee for Mental Hygiene, published the first edition of a manual defining the condition we now refer to as mental retardation. Subsequent revisions of the manual were printed in 1933, 1941, and 1957.

In 1959, a committee of professionals chaired by Rick Heber developed the fifth AAMD definition of mental retardation. That definition was reprinted with minor changes in 1961. The sixth revision was developed by a committee chaired by Herbert Grossman in 1973. Although the definition was similar to that developed by Heber's committee some years earlier, the interpretation was significantly more conservative. Fewer individuals could be identified as mentally retarded under the Grossman definition than under the Heber definition. It is important to mention that the 1973 AAMD definition was incorporated into the Education for All Children Act (EHA) of 1975 (P.L. 94-142) as the federal definition of mental retardation used in education.

Grossman's definition was reaffirmed, with minor revisions, in 1977, the next revision was published in 1983. The 1983 version, which, at the time, corresponded to definitions developed by the American Psychiatric Association (1980) and the World Health Organization (1978), described important considerations related to interpretation and clinical judgment used in classifying an individual as mentally retarded. This AAMD definition, like its predecessors, reflected a clinical perspective, relying on measurements and comparisons. Although the definition has been regularly discussed and often criticized within the field, it remained widely accepted and was used by the federal government. The ninth edition of the manual was published in 1992 (AAMR, 1992) and reflected a major paradigmatic shift, emphasizing a more functional definition of mental retardation and drawing attention to the importance of supports. Interestingly, this definition led to a splintering of professionals in the field of mental retardation, as a result of key conceptual, psychometric, and practical issues promulgated in the 1992 AAMR definition. In 2002, the AAMR (10th edition) issued the most recent definition, which maintained many of the philosophical ideas of the 1992 definition but did make conceptual and measurement changes to the adaptive skills areas associated with adaptive behavior functioning.

A review of the development of the AAMR definitions is worthwhile for a number of reasons. First, and perhaps foremost, up until the mid-1990s, the AAMR was considered the premier authority on definition. Examining the AAMR definitions also highlights the sociopolitical forces that were operative over the years, reflecting the evolution of the field and illustrating the changes in thinking about those identified as mentally retarded. Every AAMR definition since 1961 has used the term *mental retardation* and has included the three major components noted previously: subaverage general intellectual functioning, deficits in adaptive behavior, and manifestation during the developmental period. However, differences in interpretation of these three elements have occurred over the years. A detailed analysis of the more recent AAMR definitions follows and is summarized in Table 2.3.

TABLE 2.3

Comparison of Heber, Grossman, and Luckasson et al. AAMR Definitions of Mental Retardation

Term	Heber (1961)	Grossman (1973)	Grossman (1983)	Luckasson et al. (1992)	Luckasson et al. (2002)
General definition	Subaverage general Intellectual functioning, which originates during the developmental period and is associated with impairment in adaptive behavior.	Significantly subaverage general intellectual functioning existing concurrently with deficits in adaptive behavior and manifested during the developmental period.	Significantly subaverage general intellectual functioning resulting in or associated with concurrent impairments in adaptive behavior and manifested during the developmental period.	Substantial limitations in present functioning; characterized by significantly subaverage intellectual functioning, existing concurrently with related limitations in two or more of the following applicable adaptive skill areas: communication, self-care, home living, social skills, community use, self-direction, health and safety, functional academics, leisure, and work. Mental retardation manifests before age 18.	Mental retardation is a disability characterized by significant limitations both in intellectual functioning and in adaptive behavior as expressed in conceptual, social, and practical skills. This disability originates before age 18.
Subaverage intellectual functioning	Greater than one standard deviation below the mean.	Significantly subaverage: two or more standard deviations below the mean.	Significantly subaverage: defined as an IQ of 70 or below on standardized measures of intelligence; could be extended upward through IQ 75 or more, depending on the reliability of the intelligence test used.	Similar to Grossman (1983).	The criterion for diagnosis is approximately two standard deviations below the mean, considering the standard error of measurement for the specific assessment instruments used and the instrument's strengths and weaknesses.
Adaptive behavior	*Impairment in adaptive behavior:* Refers to the effectiveness of the individual to adapt to the natural and social demands of his environment. May be reflected in: 1. Maturation 2. Learning 3. Social adjustment	Defined as effectiveness or degree with which the individual meets the standards of personal independence and social responsibility expected of his age and cultural group. May be reflected in the following areas: *During infancy and early childhood:* 1. Sensory-motor skills development 2. Communication skills 3. Self-help skills 4. Socialization *During childhood and early adolescence:* 5. Application of basic academics in daily life activities 6. Application of appropriate reasoning and judgment in mastery of the environment 7. Social skills	Defined as significant limitations in an individual's effectiveness in meeting the standards of maturation, learning, personal independence, or social responsibility that are expected for his or her age level and cultural group.	Movement from conceptualizing adaptive behavior as a global entity to specification of 10 different adaptive skill areas—as presented in the definition.	Significant limitations in adaptive behavior are operationally defined as performance that is at least two standard deviations below the mean of either (a) one of the following three types of adaptive behavior: conceptual, social, practical; or (b) an overall score on a standardized measure of conceptual, social, and practical skills.

Term	Heber (1961)	Grossman (1973)	Grossman (1983)	Luckasson et al. (1992)	Luckasson et al. (2002)
		During late adolescence and adult life: 8. Vocational and social responsibilities and performances			
Developmental period	Birth to approximately 16 years.	Birth to 18 years.	Period of time between conception and the 18th birthday.	Conception to 18 years (Similar to Grossman, 1983)	Conception to 18 years (Similar to Grossman, 1983)
Assessment procedure	General intellectual functioning; may be assessed by one or more of the standardized tests developed for that purpose.	Same as Heber.	Same as Heber for intellectual functioning. Adaptive behavior assessed by clinical assessment and standardized scales.	Governed by a series of steps specifying requisite characteristics.	Limitations in intellectual functioning should be considered in light of three other dimensions in addition to adaptive behavior: participation, interactions, and social roles (health and context). Standardized instruments must be used. Significant limitations in adaptive behavior should be established through the use of standardized measures normed on the general population, including people with disabilities and people without disabilities. The use of valid assessment measures in addition to other sources of information is necessary. Clinical judgment continues to play an important role in the process.
Levels of severity	Borderline retardation IQ 68–84 Mild retardation IQ 52–67 Moderate retardation IQ 36–51 Severe retardation IQ 20–35 Profound retardation IQ < 20	_____ Mild retardation IQ 52–67 Moderate retardation IQ 36–51 Severe retardation IQ 20–35 Profound retardation IQ < 20	_____ Mild retardation IQ 50–55 to approx. 70 Moderate retardation IQ 35–40 to 50–55 Severe retardation IQ 20–25 to 35–40 Profound retardation IQ below 20 or 25 Cannot be determined	Traditional levels abondoned. System advocates use of intensities of needed support that are subclassified into four levels: • Intermittent • Limited • Extensive • Pervasive These levels are applied to the adaptive skill areas.	Use of a system based on intensities of needed support. (Similar to Luckasson et al., 1992)

FIGURE 2.1

The Normal Curve

Source: From "Methods of Expressing
Test Scores" (p. 8), 1955, *Test Service
Bulletin, 48.* Reprinted by permission.

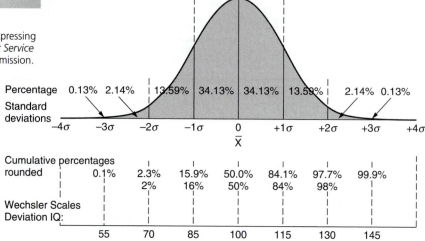

σ = standard deviation
X̄ = population mean—the average score
The Wechsler Intelligence Scales use a deviation IQ score with a mean of 100 and a
standard deviation of 15. In a normal distribution, a person who scores 1σ above
the mean receives a Wechsler score of 115. One who scores below 70 on a
Wechsler scale (>2σ below the mean) may be classified as mentally retarded if
impairments in adaptive behavior are also present.

The 1959 and 1961 Definitions. Committees of the American Association on
Mental Deficiency, chaired by Rick Heber, issued a definition in 1959 that was revised in 1961. The most notable difference between the two definitions was the introduction of the term *adaptive behavior* in the 1961 definition, replacing the 1959
terms *maturation, learning,* and *social adjustment.* The 1961 Heber definition stated:

> Mental retardation refers to subaverage general intellectual functioning which originates
> during the development period and is associated with impairment in adaptive behavior.

In this 1961 definition, **subaverage general intellectual functioning** refers
to performance of at least 1 standard deviation below the mean on a standardized intelligence test. The **standard deviation** is a statistic used to describe the
degree to which an individual's score varies from the average or mean score for
the population. With this criterion as a guide for diagnosis, it was possible to identify statistically almost 16% of the general population, and perhaps greater proportions of linguistically and culturally diverse groups, as mentally retarded.
Figure 2.1 illustrates the concepts of the normal curve, standard deviation, and population mean.

Adaptive behavior referred to the individual's adaptation to the demands of his
or her environment. Impaired adaptive behavior was considered in terms of standards and norms of appropriate behavior for the individual's chronological age
group. Moreover, as suggested, impaired adaptive behavior could be reflected in maturation, learning, or social adjustment.

- *Maturation:* The rate of sequential development of self-help and sensorimotor skills of infancy and early childhood during the preschool years (Heber, 1959, p. 3)
- *Learning ability:* The facility with which knowledge is acquired as a function of experience, particularly in school settings during the school years (p. 3)
- *Social adjustment:* The degree to which the individual is able to maintain himself or herself independently in the community and in gainful employment, as well as by the ability to meet and conform to other personal and social responsibilities and standards at the adult level as set by the community; reflected in large measure during the preschool and school-age years by the level and manner in which the child relates to parents, other adults, and age peers (p. 4)

Although deficiency in adaptive behavior was only loosely defined, use of this concept in the Heber definition represented a major departure from the earlier notions of Tredgold (1937) and Doll (1941) of incurability. The AAMR definition recognized that an individual might be deficient in one or more aspects of adaptive behavior at one time in life, but not at another. Favorable changes in social demands and environmental conditions, or in the individual's increased ability to meet natural and social demands, could mean that a person would no longer be called mentally retarded. The Heber (1959, 1961) definition established a very important point: Definition reflects an individual's current functioning, not an ultimate or permanent status.

In the 1961 AAMR manual, the **developmental period** was recognized as variable, but for purposes of definition it was judged to range from birth through age 16. This period represents the time during which primary growth and development occur.

Many professionals viewed the 1961 AAMR definition of mental retardation as an improvement over previous definitions, but it was not received without criticism. The concept of adaptive behavior caused considerable debate. Clausen (1972b) argued that the procedures for evaluating adaptive behavior were not adequate for diagnosis. This argument is still waged today, especially in response to the 1992 AAMR definition and its suggestion of limitations in adaptive skills areas. Clausen contended that diagnoses of mental retardation should be based solely on the data from psychometric evaluations. He revealed results of an earlier investigation showing that, in spite of the AAMR's inclusion of the concept of adaptive behavior in the definition, diagnoses of mental retardation were frequently made solely on the basis of intelligence test data (Clausen, 1967). This finding is reinforced today by the fact that intellectual functioning is still the primary factor used to describe and determine mental retardation.

Clausen's proposed psychometric definition was controversial and apparently unpopular, opposed on two basic grounds. First, such a definition could threaten the concept of mental retardation as an alterable or changeable condition. Intelligence test results are quite stable over time; hence, it was possible that important changes in observable behavior would not show on intelligence tests. The second criticism of the psychometric definition was that, on the basis of tests standardized on members of the majority culture, too many children from culturally diverse backgrounds had been misdiagnosed as mentally retarded.

It was generally recognized that the 1961 Heber definition was overinclusive (i.e., inclusion of the "borderline" category). As pointed out earlier, it was possible to identify statistically almost 16% of the general population as mentally retarded., using a ceiling of 85 IQ for this borderline category. In addition, as Greenspan and Switsky (2003) note, the problem was "exacerbated by the widespread ignoring by diagnosticians of the adaptive behavior criterion" (p. 6). Clausen (1972a) and others suggested that the definition be made more conservative by requiring that an individual IQ score be 2 or more standard deviations (instead of 1) below the mean on an intelligence test. Other professionals recommended that the loose connection between adaptive behavior and intelligence be strengthened. Both points have been consistently reflected in later revisions of the AAMR definition, albeit not necessarily solved in practice.

The 1973 AAMD Definition.   In 1973 the AAMD committee, now chaired by Grossman, was assigned to review the *Manual on Terminology and Classification in Mental Retardation.* The 1973 definition that emerged stated:

> Mental retardation refers to significantly subaverage general intellectual functioning existing concurrently with deficits in adaptive behavior, and manifested during the development period.

In this version, significantly subaverage intellectual functioning meant performance at least 2 standard deviations below the mean on an intelligence test (i.e., performance comparable to the lower 2.28% of the norm statistically). Adaptive behavior was defined in terms of the degree and efficiency with which the individual meets "the standards of personal independence and social responsibility expected of his age and cultural group" (Grossman, 1973, p. 11). Adaptive behavior was thus considered to be relative to the individual's age and sociocultural group. An expanded set of criteria was provided for the assessment of adaptive behavior. Deficits would manifest in the following ways:

- *During infancy and early childhood:* in sensorimotor skills development, communication skills, self-help skills, and socialization
- *During childhood and early adolescence:* in the application of basic academic skills in daily life activities, application of appropriate reasoning and judgment in mastery of the environment, and social skills
- *During late adolescence and adult life:* in vocational and social responsibilities and performances

The 1961 Heber definition included both subaverage intellectual functioning and deficits in adaptive behavior as necessary qualifying conditions for diagnosis. The relationship between adaptive behavior and intellectual functioning, however, was not clarified sufficiently. Children were consistently labeled mentally retarded on the basis of IQ alone. The two most important distinctions between the 1961 and the 1973 definitions were that (1) subaverage intelligence was defined as 2 standard deviations below the mean, underscored by the use of the word *significantly* in the definition, and (2) the relationship between adaptive behavior and intelligence was clarified and the importance of adaptive behavior was strengthened. Instead of simply requiring intellectual functioning and adaptive behavior to be associated, the committee stated that adaptive behavior deficits and subaverage intellectual functioning had to exist concurrently. In addition, the developmental period was extended to age 18, matching the age when many students finish schooling.

In spite of the extension of the developmental period, the 1973 revision became a much more conservative definition than those that preceded it. According to the 1961 AAMR definition, almost 16% of the general population could have been identified as mentally retarded from a purely psychometric perspective. According to the 1973 definition, less than 3% of the population could be considered mentally retarded from the same perspective. The 1973 revision of the definition resulted in a more than 85% reduction of the number of individuals who could be identified as mentally retarded. This comparison does not indicate the impact of the required connection between adaptive behavior and intelligence, but the two are moderately correlated at all levels of performance. Presumably, a number of individuals who might score 2 or more standard deviations below the mean on an intelligence test would not be referred for evaluation if they demonstrated appropriate adaptive skills.

During this time, two significant documents were published supporting a more conservative, cautious definition of people with mental retardation. The first was an article titled "Special Education for the Mildly Retarded—Is Much of It Justifiable?" by Lloyd Dunn (1968). Dunn, a respected authority in the field of mental retardation and former president of the Council for Exceptional Children, reported that many children from culturally different backgrounds were being incorrectly classified as mildly retarded and placed in special classes. The lack of adequate adaptive behavior scales, coupled with the convenient practice of identifying students as mentally retarded on the basis of IQ score alone, fostered the mislabeling of children who did not have mental retardation. Dunn (1968) stated:

> I have loyally supported and promoted special classes for the educable mentally retarded for most of the last 20 years, but with growing disaffection. In my view, much of our past and present practices are morally and educationally wrong. We have been living at the mercy of general educators who have referred our problem children to us. And we have been generally ill prepared and ineffective in educating these children. Let us stop being pressured into continuing and expanding a special education program that we know now to be undesirable for many of the children we are dedicated to serve.
>
> A better education than special class placement is needed for socioculturally deprived children with mild learning problems who have been labeled educable mentally retarded. Over the years, the status of these pupils who come from poverty, broken and inadequate homes, and low status ethnic groups has been a checkered one. (p. 5)

The Six-Hour Retarded Child, published by the President's Committee on Mental Retardation (PCMR, 1970), corroborated Dunn's charge that a significant number of culturally disadvantaged children, especially in urban areas, had been misclassified as mildly retarded and inappropriately placed in special education classes. These **6-hour retarded children** are classified as mentally retarded during the 6 hours they spend in an academic setting only, as they function within normal expectations outside school.

Although timely and raising real issues that needed review, the reports by Dunn and the PCMR were emotional, based on observation and a strong philosophical commitment rather than on rigorous empirical data. Nevertheless, strong face validity existed, and without question these two documents had a powerful impact on the field of mental retardation.

The 1977 AAMD Definition.   In 1977 the AAMD published its seventh manual on classification and terminology (Grossman, 1977). The wording of the 1977 definition is identical to that of the 1973 version, but the 1977 manual made a few modifications in its interpretation. To begin with, the definition of *significantly subaverage* remained 2 standard deviations below the mean, and the definition of *adaptive behavior* was essentially unchanged. The major change focused on the concept of **clinical judgment**—decision making that is based on the extensive experiences and expertise of an appropriately trained professional. The manual explains in detail the problems of measuring adaptive behavior, yet its importance is highlighted in the following sentence: "For a person to be diagnosed as being mentally retarded, impairments in intellectual functioning must co-exist with deficits in adaptive behavior" (Grossman, 1977, p. 12). The manual goes on to state:

> Individuals with [intelligence] scores slightly above these ceilings [2 standard deviations below the mean] may be diagnosed as mildly retarded during a period when they manifest serious impairments of adaptive behavior. In such cases, the burden is on the examiner to avoid misdiagnosis with its potential stigmatizing effects. (p. 12)

Later, the committee elaborated, stating: "A small minority of persons with IQ's up to 10 points above the guideline ceilings are so impaired in their adaptive behavior that they may be classified as having mild mental retardation" (pp. 19–20).

Although the 1977 definition was worded identically to the 1973 definition, the later manual allowed a diagnosis of mental retardation to be extended to individuals who, according to the previous definition, would not have been so classified. This point is often lost in discussion of the AAMR definitions. More importantly in the view of some professionals is that this manual clearly established the importance of clinical judgment as a necessary and viable component to the assessment process.

The 1983 AAMR Definition.   In 1983 the AAMR published its eighth manual on classification and terminology. The updated definition read:

> Mental retardation refers to significantly subaverage general intellectual functioning resulting in or associated with concurrent impairments in adaptive behavior and manifested during the developmental period.

Clinical judgment remained an important issue—so important that the appendix cited several short case studies followed by descriptions of the way decisions were reached from the information presented in the cases.

The tone of the manual emphasized that the content was carefully researched and contemplated before publication and that the decisions derived were logical, practical, and consistent with a need to explore a worldwide system of mental retardation. The authors collaborated with representatives of two other major classification systems so that the different systems would be as compatible as possible. The two other systems are the World Health Organization's (1978) system of *International Classification of Diseases, Clinical Modification* (9th ed.; ICD-9), and the American Psychiatric Association's (1980) *Diagnostic and Statistical Manual of Mental Disorders* (3rd ed.; DSM-III).

The AAMD manual defined *significantly subaverage* as an IQ of 70 or below on a standardized measure of intelligence. Yet this upper limit is intended as a guideline and could be extended to an IQ of 75 or more, provided behavior is impaired and clinically determined to be due to deficits in reasoning and judgment. In this definition, the strict use of standard deviations is discouraged, and the concept of the standard error of measurement inherent in all tests is emphasized:

> Clinicians using the system should be well aware that in determining whether a person is retarded and at what level of intellectual functioning the individual is operating, it is important to understand the concept of standard error of measurement and use it when making a clinical determination of retardation and level of functioning. (AAMR, 1983, p. 7)

No test is perfectly reliable, and some degree of random fluctuation in obtained scores is always expected. The standard error of measurement is an estimate of the degree to which the test scores would be expected to vary because of random error alone. For example, we know that the standard error of measurement on some tests of intelligence is 3 IQ points. If a child received a score of 72 on that test, the examiner should report that the student's true IQ would probably be within the range 69 to 75. The clinician would then decide whether other conditions, such as concurrent deficits in adaptive behavior or cultural difference, were present and associated with the level of performance on the IQ test. According to the 1983 AAMD manual (Grossman, 1983), an individual with an IQ of 75 or higher could be classified as mentally retarded if deficits in adaptive behavior were also present. On the other hand, an IQ of 70 to 67, or perhaps even lower, would not alone provide a sufficient basis for classifying a child from, for example, a minority culture as mentally retarded. The clinician would have to determine to what extent bias affected performance and whether deficits in adaptive behavior were present and associated with the attained level of performance.

You cannot measure something precisely unless you can define it precisely. Intelligence, achievement, and adaptive behavior are ready examples of rather imprecisely defined concepts, as Blatt (1987) emphasized. Therefore, it is naive to treat scores as precise when they are obtained by those measures. The standard error of measurement allows flexibility in interpretation, yet at the same time it provides reasonable structure.

The adaptive behavior component in the 1983 definition remained unchanged, but again, as discussed previously, the need for clinical judgment in borderline cases was emphasized. The measurement of adaptive behavior may involve observation, informal interview, or the use of a standardized scale. Adaptive behavior must be compared to norms for the individual's age and cultural group. The manual emphasized throughout that, because of the present state of affairs with adaptive behavior, clinical judgment must be used.

Although the conceptual basis of the developmental period did not change, the range did. The definition stressed that the developmental period begins at conception and extends through age 18. Thus, the incipient point of the developmental period was lowered and interestingly confronted the ongoing debate of when life begins.

Even though the 1983 manual was as up-to-date and definitive as possible and was supported by other professional organizations, the committee recognized that, as more data are collected and as new scientific knowledge and changing social issues arise, the definition of mental retardation will also inevitably change.

The 1992 AAMR Definition.   After 4 years of work, the Ad Hoc Committee on Terminology and Classification, chaired by Ruth Luckasson, published the ninth edition of the manual (Luckasson, et al., 1992). The new definition signaled many significant changes from its predecessors, as it is much more functional in nature. It stressed the interaction among three major dimensions: a person's capabilities, the environments in which the person functions, and the need for varying levels of support.

The wording of the 1992 definition differed from that of the 1983 version. Yet, the three major components (intellectual limitations, problems in adaptive areas, and age of onset) remained. The 1992 definition reads.

> Mental retardation refers to substantial limitations in present functioning. It is characterized by significantly subaverage intellectual functioning, existing concurrently with related limitations in two or more of the following applicable adaptive skill areas: communication, self-care, home living, social skills, community use, self-direction, health and safety, functional academics, leisure and work. Mental retardation manifests before age 18. (Luckasson et al., 1992, p. 1)

The following four assumptions were considered essential to the application of the definition:

1. Valid assessment considers cultural and linguistic diversity, as well as differences in communication and behavioral factors.
2. The existence of limitations in adaptive skills occurs within the context of community environments typical of the individual's age peers and is indexed to the person's individual needs for supports.
3. Specific adaptive limitations often coexist with strengths in other adaptive skills or other personal capabilities.
4. With appropriate supports over a sustained period, the life functioning of the person with mental retardation will generally improve. (Luckasson et al., 1992, p. 5)

Some key features of the 1983 definition remained (refer to Table 2.3) such as the age span of the developmental period. However, a number of substantive changes are evident in the 1992 definition. In addition to features already discussed, the other most notable changes include:

- The global notion of adaptive behavior was replaced by the identification of 10 adaptive skill areas.
- An individual would have to demonstrate relative limitations in two or more of the adaptive skills areas.
- The notion of maladaptive behavior was no longer operative.
- A three-step procedure for diagnosing, classifying, and identifying systems of support was recommended.
- A system for classifying individuals in terms of needed levels of support was introduced (discussed in the section of this chapter on classification) accompanied by the recommendation that reference to the former levels of severity (mild, moderate, severe, and profound) be discontinued.
- A profile of needed supports was presented that is based on four dimensions:
  - Intellectual functioning and adaptive skills
  - Psychological/emotional considerations

- Physical health/etiology considerations
- Environmental considerations
- An attempt was made to relate the definition to other functional definitions of disability (e.g., developmental disabilities).

The 1992 AAMR definition created much discussion within the professional and advocacy circles. Many people rejoiced in the attention given to levels of support needed for success that was a highlight of this definition. The 1992 definition, with some minor differences, was adopted by the American Psychiatric Association in 2000 with the publication of the most recent *Diagnostic and Statistical Manual of Mental Disorders, 4th Edition, Text Revision* (DSM-IV-TR).

Other parties, however, thought that the AAMR, influenced by philosophical themes, had strayed too far from the previous, generally accepted constructs of the 1983 definition. Members of Division 33 of the American Psychological Association (APA), were so enraged by elements of the new definition (e.g., the 10 adaptive skills areas) that this organization developed its own manual and definition in 1996. This action is notable because it meant that the AAMR definition was no longer the primary definitional source on mental retardation used across professions.

The 2002 AAMR Definition.   The AAMR Ad Hoc Committee on Terminology and Classification that was responsible for proposing the 2002 definition believed that this new AAMR definition builds upon the 1992 one. The 2002 AAMR definition states:

> Mental retardation is a disability characterized by significant limitations both in intellectual functioning and in adaptive behavior as expressed in conceptual, social, and practical adaptive skills. This disability originates before age 18.

Visit the Companion Website at www.prenhall .com/beirne-smith and select Chapter 2, Web Destinations to access AAMR's current definition, as well as many other websites that deal with definition and terminology issues.

The 2002 definition makes it very clear that five essential assumptions are understood when applying the definition:

- Limitations in present functioning must be considered within the context of community environments typical of the individual's age peers and culture.
- Valid assessment considers cultural and linguistic diversity as well as differences in communication, sensory, motor, and behavioral factors.
- Within an individual, limitations often coexist with strengths.
- An important purpose of describing limitations is to develop a profile of needed supports.
- With appropriate personalized supports over a sustained period, the life functioning of the person with mental retardation generally will improve.

In its efforts to refine the previous definition, the committee clearly acknowledged, discussed, and tried to address the substantial amount of criticism to the 1992 definition. The definition and the assumptions that go along with it contain obvious features from the 1992 definition (e.g., emphasis on levels of support) as well as new elements (e.g., a new taxonomy of adaptive skills areas). The theoretical model of mental retardation that is used throughout the manual is depicted in Figure 2.2.

FIGURE 2.2

Theoretical Model of Mental Retardation

Source: From *Mental Retardation: Definition, Classification, and Systems of Supports* (10th ed.) by Ruth Luckasson, Sharon Borthwick-Duffy, Wil H. E. Buntinx, David L. Coulter, Ellis M. (Pat) Craig, Alya Reeve, Robert L. Schalock, Martha E. Snell, Deborah M. Spitalnik, Scott Spreat, and Marc J. Tassé. Washington, DC: American Association on Mental Retardation, 2002. Reprinted with permission.

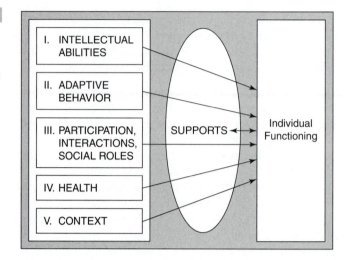

The model includes the major elements from the 1992 model, with some wording changes, along with the addition of a fifth dimension that involves participation, interactions, and social roles.

The 2002 AAMR definition of mental retardation uses the phrasing "significant limitations both in intellectual functioning and in adaptive behavior." The specific criteria for diagnosis is provided in Table 2.4. Specific examples of conceptual, social, and practical adaptive skills are presented in Table 2.5. The application of clinical judgment is still possible with this definition, as implied by the phrasing "approximately two standard deviations below the mean" (see Table 2.4). However, the criteria for establishing deficits in adaptive behavior are seemingly tightened in this definition with the specification of standard deviation cutoffs.

The new definition maintains the same age span for the developmental range that has applied since the 1983 AAMR definition: between conception and the 18th birthday. Interestingly, the 2002 AAMR definition introduced a little more flexibility in terms of classification, noting that different ways to classify an individual are possible—even the use of IQ range is allowed.

Contemporary Professional Definitions

Other definitional efforts, which are alternatives to the AAMR definition, have come into existence in more recent times. This has occurred because of periodic updating of various definitional sources (e.g., American Psychiatric Association, World Health Organization) or dissatisfaction with the 1992 AAMR definition and classification guidelines. Smith (1997) pointed out that various members within the AAMR differed greatly in their opinions of the revised definition. The most critical attacks on the 1992 AAMR definition were waged by Greenspan (1994, 1997), Jacobson and Mulick (1996), and MacMillan and his colleagues (Gresham, MacMillan, & Siperstein, 1995; MacMillan, Gresham, & Siperstein, 1993). Concerns, as highlighted previously, focused on the aspects of the definition related to the IQ cutoff level, the adaptive skills areas, and the levels of needed supports.

Definitional Component	Criteria
Significant limitation in both:	
Intellectual functioning	The criterion for diagnosis is approximately two standard deviations below the mean, considering the standard error of measurement for the specific assessment instruments used and the instrument's strengths and weaknesses. (p. 14)
Adaptive behavior	For the diagnosis of mental retardation, significant limitations in adaptive behavior should be established through the use of standardized measures normed on the general population, including people with disabilities and people without disabilities. On these standardized measures, significant limitations in adaptive behavior are operationally defined as performance that is at least two standard deviations below the mean of either (a) one of the following three types of adaptive behavior: conceptual, social, practical; or (b) an overall score on a standardized measure of conceptual, social, and practical skills. (p. 14)

TABLE 2.4
AAMR 2002 Definitional Criteria

Source: Luckasson et al. (2002).

Greenspan (1997) pointed out some important signs that indicated displeasure with the 1992 definition, including few state departments adopting the definition and the publication of a new manual on mental retardation by the American Psychological Association (Jacobson & Mulick, 1996). Greenspan went on to suggest that the publication of the 1992 definition had "served to undermine AAMR's credibility as the 'keeper of the MR definition' " (Greenspan, 1997, p. 181)—a distinction that AAMR was arguably able to claim heretofore.

Three alternative definitional perspectives developed by professional organizations are discussed next. The first is the 1996 definition published by the American Psychological Association (Jacobson & Mulick, 1996).

The 1996 American Psychological Association Definition. Spearheaded by Jacobson and Mulick, Division 33 of the American Psychological Association (APA) published its *Manual of Diagnosis and Professional Practice in Mental Retardation* in 1996. The rationale for developing the manual is reflected

TABLE 2.5

Examples of Conceptual, Social, and Practical Adaptive Skills

Conceptual
• Language (receptive and expressive)
• Reading and writing
• Money concepts
• Self-direction

Social
• Interpersonal
• Responsibility
• Self esteem
• Gullibility (likelihood of being tricked or manipulated)
• Naiveté
• Follows rules
• Obeys laws
• Avoids victimization

Practical
• Activities of daily living
  — Eating
  — Transfer/mobility
  — Toileting
  — Dressing
• Instrumental activities of daily living
  — Meal preparation
  — Housekeeping
  — Transportation
  — Taking medication
  — Money management
  — Telephone use
• Occupational skills
• Maintains safe environments

Source: Luckasson et al. (2002), p. 42.

in its preface: "a comprehensive statement of what MR is, what it means for the individual and society, and how to serve the needs of affected individuals is specifically called for at the present juncture" (p. xiv). APA's definition reads as follows:

> Mental retardation (MR) refers to (a) significant limitations in general intellectual functioning; (b) significant limitations in adaptive functioning, which exist concurrently; and (c) onset of intellectual and adaptive limitations before the age of 22 years. (p. 13)

After inspecting the APA's definition and manual, one realizes that it is essentially a restatement of the 1983 AAMR definitional constructs with some notable changes. The term *adaptive functioning* is used in place of *adaptive behavior,* and the upper limit of the age of onset has been extended from 18 to 22. Specific "criteria

The definition of mental retardation is a social and political one.

of significance" are provided for limitations in both intellectual functioning and adaptive functioning, as noted below:

Intellectual functioning: IQ or comparable normed score that is 2 or more standard deviations below the population mean for the measure
Adaptive functioning: a summary index score that is 2 or more standard deviations below the mean for the appropriate norming sample (p. 13)

Professionals with clinical and research interests who liked the 1983 AAMR definition of mental retardation found solace in the APA's definition. It avoids much of the psychometric dissonance created by the 1992 AAMR definition in both areas of intellectual functioning and adaptive behavior.

The 2000 DSM-IV-TR Definition. The most recent update to the *Diagnostic and Statistical Manual of Mental Disorders* was accomplished in 2000. This "text revision" was not a comprehensive revision of the manual; however, some changes were made to it. One area receiving attention was mental retardation.

The DSM-IV-TR definition of mental retardation is a derivative of the 1992 AAMR definition and contains the following wording:

The essential feature of Mental Retardation is significantly subaverage general intellectual functioning (Criterion A) that is accompanied by significant limitations in adaptive functioning in at least two of the following skill areas: communication, self-care, home living, social/interpersonal skills, use of community resources, self-direction, functional academic skills, work, leisure, health, and safety (Criterion B). The onset must occur before age 18 years (Criterion C) (p. 41).

According to this definition, *significantly subaverage intellectual functioning* is defined as an IQ "of about 70 or below (approximately 2 standard deviations below the

TABLE 2.6
Comparison of Adaptive Behavior/Adaptive Skill Areas Across Three Definitional Perspectives

AAMR (2002)	AAMR (1992)	DSM-IV-TR (2000)
3 areas	10 areas	11 areas
Conceptual:		
Language	Communications	Communication
Reading and writing	Functional academics	Functional academic skills
Money concepts		
Self-direction	Self-direction	Self-direction
Social:		
Interpersonal	Social skills	Social/interpersonal skills
Responsibility		
Self-esteem		
Gullibility		
Naiveté		
Follows rules		
Obeys laws		
Avoids victimization		
	Leisure	Leisure
Practical:		
Activities of daily living	Self-care	Self-care
• Eating		
• Transfer/mobility		
• Toileting		
• Dressing		
Instrumental activities of		
daily living	Home living	Home living
• Meal preparation		
• Housekeeping		
• Transportation		
• Taking medication		
• Money management		
• Telephone use		
	Health and safety	Health
	Community Use	Use of community resources
Occupational skills	Work	Work
Maintains safe environments		Safety

mean" (p. 41), and *adaptive functioning* is defined as "how effectively individuals cope with common life demands" (p. 42). Specific criteria for determining adaptive deficits for individual domains are not provided in the DSM-IV-TR manual. Table 2.6 shows the relationship of adaptive skills as stated in the 2002 DSM-IV-TR with the adaptive skills enumerated in the 1992 and 2002 AAMR definitions.

The 1993 ICD-10 Definition.   The *International Classification of Diseases* (10th ed.) is primarily a resource that is used worldwide in health care. Because the ICD-10 is so important internationally, recognition of how this resource defines mental retardation is warranted. Mental retardation is categorized under "Mental and Behavioral Disorders" and is defined as follows:

> A condition of arrested or incomplete development of the mind, which is especially characterized by impairment of skills manifested during the developmental period, skills which contribute to the overall level of intelligence, i.e., cognitive, language, motor, and social abilities. (ICD-10 p. 369)

Luckasson and colleagues (2002) note that the ICD-10 definition contains a number of problems; nevertheless, it is used by health care professionals. As a result, professionals who work in the health care fields need to know the definition and its inherent limitations.

Other Definitional Perspectives

Definitions of mental retardation have emerged from a number of other different sources. Three of these are discussed below—two of which were proposed some time ago and the last one recommended recently.

Behavioral Analysis Perspective.   Bijou (1966) took the position that mental retardation should be dealt with from a behavioral perspective. He suggests that:

> developmental retardation be treated as observable, objectively defined stimulus–response relationships without recourse to hypothetical mental concepts such as "defective intelligence" and hypothetical biological abnormalities such as "clinically inferred brain injury." From this point of view a retarded individual is one who has a limited repertory of behavior shaped by events that constitute his history. (p. 2)

The behavioral orientation provides one of the most logical bases for considering mental retardation a changeable condition. Without question, this orientation has had, and continues to have, an important impact on the development of educational and therapeutic interventions for individuals with mental retardation.

Educational Perspective.   Kidd (1977) argued the necessity of a definition of mental retardation that had a decided educational orientation. The definition he proposed stated:

> Mental retardation refers to subaverage general human cognitive functioning irrespective of etiology(ies), typically manifested during the developmental period, which is of such severity as to markedly limit one's ability to (a) learn and consequently to (b) make logical decisions, choices, and judgments, and (c) cope with one's self and one's environment. (p. 76)

Kidd's definition contained the major elements of other definitions; however, this defintion has a few twists. Kidd objected to the notion that subaverage intellectual functioning and adaptive behavior were separable. He also opined that the requirement that mental retardation must be manifest during the developmental period was problematic. In regard to this latter point, he asserted that, since brain damage manifested during the developmental period is often indistinguishable from brain damage manifested at a later time, it is logically indefensible to preclude the latter cases. This point has been raised in relation to death penalty cases with individuals who are suspected of having mental retardation. Robinson and Robinson (1976) remarked similarly:

> The specification that retardation be evident by age eighteen serves the conventional but perhaps dubious purpose of differentiating mental retardation from traumatic or deteriorative disorders originating in adulthood. (p. 31)

"Perceived Risk Status" Perspective.   The last definition reflects the most recent thinking of Stephen Greenspan. Interestingly, it is Greenspan's earlier conceptualizations of social competence to which the committee working on the 1992 AAMR definition referred when they began their discussions.

What is clear about Greenspan's thinking is that professionals' visions of what constitutes intelligent behavior need to expand beyond the singular focus on conceptual intelligence. Greenspan and his colleagues have arguably done the most work to promote the idea that social and everyday intelligence are as important as conceptual intelligence in understanding and defining mental retardation. It is important to recognize that Greenspan is proposing a conceptualization that includes different types of intelligent behavior (i.e., multiple intelligences). For years, Greenspan has promoted a tripartite model of intelligence that includes conceptual intelligence (IQ), practical intelligence, and social intelligence as the fundamental components. However, Greenspan's conceptualization differs substantially from the multiple intelligence model proposed by Gardner (2000). Fundamentally, Greenspan (1997) notes that mental retardation is clearly a cognitive disorder; however, he also points out that cognition can be used for a variety of purposes.

Greenspan (2003) has recently called for a major overhaul of the definition of mental retardation. His call for change is based in large part on two key factors: (1) the continued reign of IQ as "the foundation-stone for the definition and diagnosis of MR," and (2) the problems associated with the concepts of "adaptive behavior" and "adaptive skills." His main concern with the more recent term, *adaptive skills,* is that "it is an artificial, invented term that lacks a clear connection to what one might term the 'natural behavioral prototype' or phenotype for mental retardation" (p. 12–2). The definition that he proposes states:

> Mental retardation is a condition characterized by deficiencies in social, practical, and academic intelligence, typically attributable to known or presumed abnormalities in brain development, that cause an individual to be perceived, by knowledgeable professionals as well as laypeople in that individual's ecology, as needing long-term supports and services to enable him or her to function in society and to minimize the risks and dangers associated with failure in dealing with age-appropriate social, physical, and academic roles and challenges. Once a diagnosis of MR is made, individuals can be subclassified into broad disability severity categories (e.g., moderate, severe), based not on statistical units on standardized tests scores, but on intensity and pervasiveness of supports needed to maximize potential and minimize risk. (p. 12–2)

This definition does not specifically mention developmental period and there is no reference to the requirement that deficits must be found in both intellectual functioning and adaptive functioning.

SYSTEMS OF CLASSIFICATION

Systems for describing the various levels of mental retardation have been used for decades. The classification scheme that was used widely divided mental retardation into four levels based on IQ scores: mild, moderate, severe, and profound. Most of the major professional organizations, with the exception of AAMR, have retained the use of an IQ-based classification system. For example, the APA manual promoted a classification system that returns to four IQ ranges of severity: mild, moderate, severe, and profound. As noted in the manual, "Severity is determined by concurrent presence of IQ scores within four ranges and adaptive functioning consistent with each range" (Jacobson & Mulick, 1996, p. 14). Table 2.7 graphically depicts the classification systems used both historically and in recent times.

A constant clamor for changing the classification system has existed for some time. As highlighted earlier, the 1992 AAMR definition suggested a new classification system that abandoned the use of IQ levels. Rather, the ninth edition of the AAMR manual suggested the adoption of a system describing levels of support as a function of the different adaptive skill areas. This system of support intensities was maintained in the 2002 AAMR definition. The four intensity levels of possible needed supports were: *intermittent* ("as-needed basis"); *limited* (consistent over time, time-limited); *extensive* (regular involvement); and *pervasive* (constant, high intensity, provision across settings). The intent of this system is to explain a person's functional limitations in terms of the degree of support he or she needs to achieve personal growth and development.

OPERATIONALIZING DEFINITIONS

Previous sections of this chapter have focused mainly on conceptual issues of definition and classification; now we will look at how these systems are put into practice. The relationship between theory and practice in mental retardation is a tenuous one. This section approaches this topic from two perspectives: school and adult settings. In the school section, the discussion focuses on research that has examined state guidelines in the area of mental retardation and presents some ways that the definition of mental retardation has been operationalized in two specific states. In the adult section, select examples of operationalization issues are provided.

School Focus

State Guidelines.   Past studies of various aspects of state departments of education guidelines for defining, identifying, and classifying students with mental retardation (Frankenburg, 1984; Huberty, Koller, & Ten Brink, 1980; Patrick &

TABLE 2.7

Terminology and Levels of Severity of Retardation

Proponents	Generic Term	95	90	85	80	75	70	65	60	55	50	45	40	35	30	25	20	15	10	5	0
American Association for the Study of the Feebleminded	Feebleminded	Feebleminded						Moron				Imbecile					Idiot				
Tredgold & Soddy (Great Britain)	Mental deficiency							High grade; feeble-minded				Middle grade; imbecile					Low grade; idiot				
AAMR (Heber, 1961)	Mental retardation	Borderline mentally retarded						Mild			Moderate		Severe				Profound				
AAMR (Grossman, 1973)	Mental retardation							Mild			Moderate		Severe				Profound				
AAMR (Grossman, 1983)	Mental retardation							Mild			Moderate		Severe				Profound				
American Psychological Association (1996)	Mental retardation							Mild			Moderate			Severe			Profound				
American Psychiatric Association (2000) [DSM IV-TR]	Mental retardation							Mild			Moderate		Severe				Profound				

Note: Dashed rules indicate approximate cutoff points.

Reschly, 1982; Utley, Lowitzer, & Baumeister, 1987) have regularly found a great deal of interstate variability. Inconsistency is common in terminology, in the adoption of the federal definition of mental retardation (1983 AAMR definition: Grossman, 1983), and (when adopted) in the implementation of that definition as originally intended. A sense of this interstate variation can be gleaned from the findings of two studies of state guidelines in relation to definition, identification criteria, and classification systems that have been conducted.

The first study, conducted by Utley and colleagues in the latter 1980s, highlighted the reality that little commonality across states existed in terms of implementation. The second study, conducted in the late 1990s by Denning, Chamberlain, and Polloway (2000), was interested in determining the degree of impact the 1992 AAMR definition had on practice. These researchers found that once again little commonality existed across states. Furthermore, the 1992 AAMR definition was found to have had minimal impact on practice (i.e., changing state guidelines). Table 2.8 provides state-by-state and District of Columbia data.

Examples of Operationalization.   Two examples of how states have put into practice the conceptual elements of the definition of mental retardation are presented in this section. The first example, from Iowa, illustrates a methodology that incorporates the traditional elements (intellectual functioning, adaptive behavior, and developmental period) associated with definition and educational performance aspects. The second example, from Connecticut, provides a framework that utilizes a nontraditional conceptualization of mental retardation.

In 1996 and 1997, Iowa developed technical assistance guidelines for assisting with the identification of students with mental disabilities, the term used in this state. The major objective was to operationalize criteria that were based on the definition used in Iowa. The guidelines presented here are the result of a year-long collaborative effort of a study group composed of a variety of participants including parents, teachers, administrators, support personnel, and other professionals.

For a student to be classified as mentally disabled, the individual must meet all four criteria (Mauer, 1997, p. 192):

1. Intellectual functioning
   - Must include a variety of information sources, with the determination of mental disability the responsibility of the entire multidisciplinary team
   - Full scale IQ score of 75 or less
2. Adaptive behavior
   - Must include direct measures as well as indirect measures that evaluate the individual's performance in comparison to same-age peers from similar cultural backgrounds
   - Deficits identified in 2 or more adaptive skill areas
3. Developmental period
   - Age 21 and younger
   - Must show significant discrepancies that persist for more than 1 year
4. Educational performance
   - Must evaluate the individual's performance in the context of his or her current environment
   - Must identify deficits in all core academic areas (math, reading, language arts, science)
   - Defines significant deficit as individual scores at least 1 standard deviation below the mean of the national standardization sample
   - Must further validate standardized measures with in-school data that document differences between the individual's performance and the performance of same-age peers from the same cultural background
   - Must also include documentation of resistance to general education interventions in assessment of academic performance

In 2000, Connecticut's Department of Education published its *Guidelines for Identifying Children with Intellectual Disability/Mental Retardation* (State of Connecticut, 2000). The guidelines state: "Intellectual disability means significant deficits in conceptual, practical and social intelligence that adversely affect a student's educational performance and are manifested during the developmental period (birth to age 18)." A student must demonstrate deficits in all three components of intellectual competence. Specific eligibility criteria for each of the component intelligences are provided in the guidelines.

TABLE 2.8
Summary of State Guidelines

State	Term*	Definition†	IQ Cutoff	Require AB?	Age Ceiling	Classification System‡
Alabama	MR	GV	70	Yes	No	No
Alaska	MR	GA	2 SD	Yes	No	No
Arizona	MR	GA	2 SD	Yes	No	M/M/S/P
Arkansas	MR	GA	No	Yes	No	No
California	MR	GA	No	Yes	No	M/M/S/P
Colorado	SLIC	GA	2 SD	Yes	No	No
Connecticut	MR	GA	2 SD	Yes	No	No
Delaware	MD	GA	70	Yes	No	EMR/TMR/S
District of Columbia	MR	GA	70	Yes	No	M/M/S/P
Florida	MH	GV	2 SD	Yes	No	EMR/TMR/P
Georgia	ID	GV	70	Yes	No	M/M/S/P
Hawaii	MR	GA	2 SD	Yes	No	M/M/S
Idaho	MR	GA	70	Yes	No	No
Illinois	MI	GA	No	Yes	No	M/M/S/P
Indiana	MH	GA	2 SD	Yes	18	M/M/S
Iowa	MD	GV	75	Yes	21	No
Kansas	MR	LV	2 SD	Yes	No	MR/SMD
Kentucky	MD	O	2 SD	Yes	21	M/FMD
Louisiana	MD	GA	70	Yes	No	M/M/S/P
Maine	MR	GA	No	Yes	No	No
Maryland	MR	GV	No	Yes	No	No
Massachusetts	II	O	No	No	No	No
Michigan	MI	O	2 SD	Yes	No	EMR/TMR/S/P
Minnesota	MI	GA	70	Yes	No	M/M/S/P
Mississippi	ED	GA	2SD	Yes	No	EMR/TMR/S
Missouri	MR	GA	2SD	Yes	18	M/M/S/P

The Connecticut initiative is noteworthy because it was highly innovative. What makes the Connecticut situation so unique is that its definition of mental retardation is based on Greenspan's conceptualization of personal competence. Nevertheless, it comes with great challenges, such as getting diagnosticians, school psychologists, and other school-based personnel to accept a different way of doing things.

Adult Focus

Definitional issues in the adult sector are mostly concerned with qualifying for certain services such as Social Security and Medicaid. For instance, the Social Security Administration disability determination for mental retardation uses the following definition that looks a lot like definitions of mental retardation discussed earlier in the chapter, with some slight wording changes:

State	Term*	Definition†	IQ Cutoff	Require AB?	Age Ceiling	Classification System‡
Montana	CD	GA	No	Yes	18	No
Nebraska	MH	GA	2 SD	Yes	No	M/M/S/P
Nevada	MR	GA	No	Yes	21	M/M/S/P
New Hampshire	MR	GA	No	Yes	No	No
New Jersey	CI	LA	2 SD	Yes	No	M/S CI
New Mexico	ID	GA	No	Yes	No	No
New York	MR	GA	1.5 SD	Yes	No	No
North Carolina	MD	GA	70	Yes	No	EMR/TMR
North Dakota	MR	GV	70	Yes	18	EMR/TMR
Ohio	DH	GV	80	Yes	No	DH
Oklahoma	MR	GA	2 SD	Yes	18	No
Oregon	MR	GA	2 SD	Yes	No	No
Pennsylvania	MR	GA	80	Yes	No	No
Rhode Island	MR	GA	70	Yes	Yes	M/M/S/P
South Carolina	MD	GV	70	Yes	18	EMR/TMR
South Dakota	MR	GA	70	Yes	18	No
Tennessee	MR	LA	74	Yes	No	No
Texas	MR	GA	2 SD	Yes	No	No
Utah	ID	GA	No	Yes	No	No
Vermont	LI	GA	70	Yes	No	No
Virginia	MR	GA	No	Yes	No	EMR/TMR
Washington	MR	GA	2 SD	Yes	No	No
West Virginia	MI	LA	70-75	Yes	18	M/M/S/P
Wisconsin	CD	GV	70-75	Yes	No	M/M/S/P
Wyoming	MD	GA	No	Yes	No	No

*CD = cognitively delayed/cognitive disability, CI = cognitive impairment, DH = developmentally handicapped, ED = educational disability, ID = intellectual disability, II = intellectual impairment, LI = learning impairments, MD = mental disability, MNH = mentally handicapped, MI = mental impairment, MR = mental retardation, SLIC = significantly limited intellectual capacity.

†GA = Grossman adapted, GV = Grossman verbatim, LA = Luckasson adapted, LV = Luckasson verbatim, O = other.

‡EMR = educable mentally retarded, M/FMD = mild and functional metal disability, M/M = mild/moderate, M/SCD = mild and sever cognitive disability, P = profound, S = severe, SMD = severe multiple disabilities, TMR = trainable mentally retarded.

Source: Denning et al. (2000).

Significantly sub-average intellectual functioning with deficits in adaptive functioning initially manifested during the developmental period; i.e., the evidence demonstrates or supports onset of the impairment before age 22 (Reschly, Myers, & Hartel, 2002, p. 19)

For more about the application of definitions to death penalty cases, visit the Companion Website at www.prenhall.com/beirne -smith and select Chapter 2, Read and Respond.

In another context, the definition of mental retardation has become a very important topic in relation to the determination of mental retardation in death penalty cases in those states where the death penalty still exists—especially in those states where it exists and is being invoked.

The key point to be made about definitional issues in the adult sector is the recognition that whatever definition is written into the code of the state is what must be followed. However, sometimes definitions have not been incorporated into a specific part of a state's statutes. For example, the state of Texas exercises its right to execute individuals who have been convicted of capital crimes. Claims by individuals that they are mentally retarded must be addressed—but the state of Texas does not have a definition of mental retardation in its criminal code. Nevertheless, a definition does exist in the health and safety code and is sometimes referred to in criminal proceedings, although it does not have to be used. If, however, a definition exists in the criminal code, as is the case in most states, then that definition must be used for MR determinations.

Practical Realities

In many settings across the country, IQ has played and continues to play the dominant role in the decision-making process (Furlong & LeDrew, 1985; Greenspan, 2003; Polloway & Smith, 1987). Assessment of adaptive behavior is not being used in the ways that have been suggested.

For a number of plausible reasons, less importance is given to evaluation of adaptive behavior than to IQ. Zigler, Balla, and Hodapp's (1984) contention that the concept is "too elusive and ill-defined to be a criterion of mental retardation" (p. 218) is still relevant today. Zucker and Polloway (1987) offer another explanation:

> The concept of adaptive behavior has neither the psychometric history of IQ nor the stability across settings expected by diagnosticians for other scores. Although these concerns may actually represent strengths of adaptive behavior measures, their effect has been to prevent full utility of the measures. (p. 71)

Whatever the reason, adaptive behavior takes a backseat to intellectual functioning in the decision-making process. This reality undermines the value of determining typical behavioral regimens and may be a disservice to many individuals at the margin of eligibility.

What options does this situation leave us? We offer four different ideas. The first is to abandon the use of adaptive behavior as a criterion, as Zigler and colleagues (1984) suggest. They argue that mental retardation should be defined and assessed solely in terms of intellectual functioning. Greenspan's (2003) conceptualization of mental retardation fits this orientation, as his model stresses intelligence, albeit multiple intelligences. If, however, only conceptual intelligence is being considered, then this is too narrow a view of the terrain. Furthermore, it raises problems when we consider students whose linguistic, cultural, and economic backgrounds are significantly different from those of the majority population.

A second suggestion is that new, innovative assessment systems be developed. These could be based on multiple intelligence conceptualizations or incorporate behaviorally or functionally based measures.

The third view is grounded in the reality that adaptive behavior will continue to be a second-class citizen in the identification process. Instead of being a criterion, it

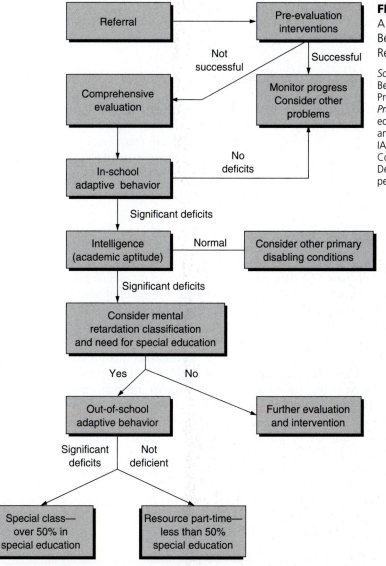

FIGURE 2.3

A Scheme of Use of Adaptive Behavior Information in Mental Retardation Classification

Source: From "Incorporating Adaptive Behavior Deficits into Instructional Programs," by D. J. Reschly, in *Best Practices in Mental Disabilities* (Vol.2), edited by J. R. Patton, E. A. Polloway, and L. R. Sargent, 1988, Des Moines, IA: Department of Education. Copyright 1988 by Des Moines, IA, Department of Education. Adapted by permission.

should play a supporting role in (1) justifying eligibility for individuals with IQs above 70, (2) questioning the certification of an individual with an IQ below 70 but with acceptable adaptive behavior skills, and (3) influencing placement and curricular decisions. This may not be the most desirable solution, but it may best reflect reality.

The fourth and last perspective is more stouthearted. It argues that we should continue to strive to develop a system in which in-school and out-of-school aspects of adaptive behavior play a key role. One conceptualization of such an idea promoted by Reschly (1988) and presented in Figure 2.3 promotes the integration of in-school and out-of-school measures of adaptive behavior as part of the evaluation process. The overriding goal is to identify students in need and provide services to them in the most appropriate manner.

INCIDENCE AND PREVALENCE

Prevention and treatment are two of the most pressing issues in the field of mental retardation. To determine causal factors and to deliver services and treatment efficiently, professionals have used estimates of the frequency of mental retardation: incidence and prevalence. Although the words *incidence* and *prevalence* are considered synonymous in some contexts, they have two distinctly different meanings.

Terminology Defined

Incidence refers to the number of new cases identified within a population over a specific period of time. The data for most estimates of incidence are obtained from cases that were clinically identified when individuals entered some form of intervention. Incidence figures are valuable for investigating the causes of a disability and developing prevention programs. For example, researchers have found that maternal age at a child's birth and the incidence of the chromosomal aberration that results in Down syndrome are related. That relationship was determined by comparing the incidence rates of Down syndrome births with populations of mothers from different age ranges. The incidence rate is higher for older mothers. Although researchers have not determined why chromosomal aberrations are more frequent among older mothers than younger ones, the relationship between maternal age and the incidence of Down syndrome leads to possibilities for prevention.

Prevalence refers to the total number of cases of some condition existing within a population at a particular place or at a particular time. Unlike incidence, prevalence is not concerned with the number of new cases. Therefore, it is not as useful in determining causal relationships. Prevalence statistics are, however, better than incidence statistics for determining need for services. Prevalence rates are frequently represented as percentages.

Prevalence may be conceptualized in two ways: identifiable and true (Grossman, 1983). *Identifiable prevalence* refers to the cases that have come in contact with some system. *True prevalence,* which is a larger figure, assumes that several people who may meet the definitional criteria of mental retardation exist unrecognized by our systems. True prevalence does not include those who once met criteria but no longer do so.

For several reasons, variations in estimates of the incidence and prevalence of mental retardation have been found across studies and populations. Among factors influencing the incidence and prevalence of mental retardation are differences in criteria and methodologies of the researchers and gender, age, community, race, and sociopolitical factors of the group under investigation. We look at each of these factors next.

Factors Associated with Prevalence Rates

A variety of factors can influence the prevalence rates of mental retardation. This section will explore four of them: definitional perspective, gender, community variables, and sociopolitical factors.

Definitional Perspective. The difficulty of defining retardation is reflected by the number of reviews on the prevalence of mental retardation that mention the imprecision in definition and general haziness of the concept. For example, in 1959, G. O. Johnson criticized one of the most widely quoted surveys that had been conducted (the Census of Referred Suspected Mental Retardation, conducted in Onondaga County, New York, in 1953). He did so because it used a broad definition of mental retardation and, therefore, possibly reported more cases than actually existed according to generally accepted definitions.

It is not unusual for prevalence figures to be estimated without a survey ever being conducted. Hypothetical prevalence statistics can be projected from formal definitions of mental retardation that rely entirely on psychometric data or depend substantially on such data (e.g., earlier AAMR definitions).

The impact that definition can have on prevalence figures is reflected by the intellectual functioning criterion used in the 1973/1977 AAMR definition contrasted with that of the 1983 AAMR definition. As noted earlier in the chapter, the cutoff score changed from 1 standard deviation below the mean to 2 standard deviations below the mean. The significance of definition is clearly obvious.

If IQ were the only criterion for defining mental retardation, approximately 2.3% of the population could be considered mentally retarded; in fact, the U.S. Office of Education reported in 1971–1972 that 2.3% of the school-age population was mentally retarded (0.8% moderate or severe, 1.5% mild). The PCMR estimated that approximately 3% of the population was mentally retarded; however, the validity of the 3% figure, which was cited widely in previous times, has been seriously challenged. As early as 1973, prevalence estimates of 1% were being favored (Mercer, 1973a). Most contemporary definitional perspectives of mental retardation suggest a prevalence figure below 1%.

In 1978, the National Institute of Handicapped Research funded a project to establish a means of providing national estimates of the incidence, prevalence, and other demographic characteristics of Americans with disabilities. The purpose of this effort was to provide an adequate statistical base for policy. Roistacher, Holstrom, Cantril, and Chase (1982) note that by 1978 more than 80 federal agencies (plus many more state and local agencies) were providing services to people with disabilities. Many of the agencies collected incidence, prevalence, and demographic data, but most agencies had different legislative mandates, resulting in different purposes for collecting data. Ultimately, the collected data lacked comparability across agencies. Roistacher and colleagues state that different definitions and data collection methodologies made aggregation of data impossible. Although definitional and methodological problems can be reduced, these researchers believe that developing an adequate statistical base for policy making would be beneficial. Furthermore, while knowing the numbers of people identified as mentally retarded is important, we are only beginning to learn about their demographic and clinical characteristics, attitudes and aspirations, service experiences, and adult outcomes. Collecting such information is important, but data at the national level reflecting a realistic picture of current events are needed if policy makers are to make informed decisions.

Gender.   In general, more males than females are identified as mentally retarded at all age levels. Three explanations attempt to account for these gender differences in prevalence. First, biological defects associated with the X chromosome have a greater probability of being manifested by males than by females. Second, it appears that different child-rearing practices and different social demands are associated with gender differences in prevalence. For example, aggressive behavior for males is typically reinforced during child rearing. An aggressive boy who is mentally retarded may not perceive the differences between appropriate and inappropriate situations for being aggressive. Individuals who exhibit behavior problems have greater chances of being identified as retarded than those who do not. Finally, society's demands for self-sufficiency traditionally have been higher for males than females (Robinson & Robinson, 1976); a lower degree of self-sufficiency is a marker for mental retardation, perhaps leading to males being disproportionately classified.

Community Variables.   Communities vary in their ability to absorb individuals with limited talents. For example, people are more apt to be identified as mentally retarded in urban communities than in rural ones (MacMillan, 1982). That variation has been subject to different interpretations. First, urban communities are generally perceived as more complex than rural communities. It is commonly believed that the social demands of urban communities are, therefore, more difficult to meet. In the past, individuals with borderline retardation from urban districts were more likely to be identified as mentally retarded, because urban districts tend to have better developed referral and diagnostic services. Some marginal cases may never be formally diagnosed in rural districts.

Socioeconomic conditions within communities are also related to differences in prevalence rates. Children who are born and reared in less enriched, lower socioeconomic groups are more likely to be labeled mentally retarded than children from suburban settings. Many attempts have been made to account for the much higher rates of mental retardation among children from lower socioeconomic groups and deprived environments. Interestingly, prevalence figures indicate that, as the severity of retardation increases, cultural and socioeconomic factors become less pronounced. In other words, just as many wealthy families as poor families have children with severe retardation.

Prevalence figures also vary according to a country's level of development. In less developed countries, the situation is paradoxical, as the AAMR's Committee on Terminology and Classification noted:

> In underdeveloped countries lacking mass immunization programs, proper nutrition, hygiene and sanitation, prenatal care for pregnant women, and other public health services, the incidence of mental retardation and other disorders is high. Under these conditions, whereas incidence may be high, prevalence may be comparatively lower because of excessive infant mortality. (Grossman, 1983, p. 75)

Another relevant fact is that such characteristics as literacy and cognitive ability, which are highly valued in more developed and literate societies, may not be so im-

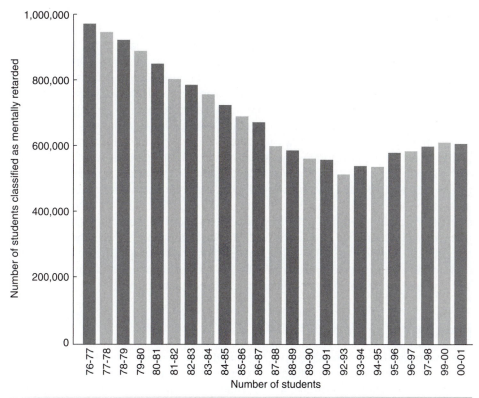

FIGURE 2.4
School-Identified Population, Ages 6–21 (1976–2001)

portant in settings that are largely subsistence oriented and have little if any interest or means to identify individuals who might have mental retardation.

Sociopolitical Factors. Evidence suggests that prevalence is influenced significantly by prevailing attitudes, policy, and practices. For instance, since the implementation of P.L. 94-142, the number of students classified as mentally retarded by school systems throughout the United States has dropped substantially. Polloway and Smith (1983) noticed this trend early on. Analyzing federal data for the period 1976–1981, they found that the number of students between the ages of 6 and 21 served under P.L. 94-142 and P.L. 89-313 dropped approximately 13%. An update of these changes through 2001 (see Figure 2.4) indicates that, in general, there has been a significant decrease in the student population. However, in recent years a slight increase has occurred. It is important to note that not all states and, for that matter, not all local education agencies have experienced the same exact trends. In the aggregate, however, fewer students are identified as mentally retarded since the federal mandate for special education was implemented in the mid-1970s.

The prevalence rates of students with mild forms of retardation have been most affected by a range of sociopolitical factors. This issue has become so acute that the viability of the concept of mild mental retardation has been questioned (MacMillan, Gresham, & Siperstein, 1996). MacMillan and colleagues argue that mild mental retardation "differs markedly from other cases of mental retardation" (p. 357) and recommend that a new term be used to describe this displaced group of students.

Why this dramatic change? In large part it is because of sociopolitical factors that influenced how we identify and serve students who are decidedly below the norm. One important reason for this change is a more conservative posture on identifying students as mentally retarded, especially if they are from culturally diverse backgrounds. Professionals in the field are noticeably wary, as they should be, of the misdiagnosis and misplacement of students who are linguistically and culturally diverse. Another reason is that a number of higher functioning students formerly identified as retarded are now receiving special education services elsewhere. Some students with mild cognitive limitations are now served under the category of learning disabilities—a label that is less stigmatizing than that of mentally retarded. Other factors are also playing a critical role in the changing numbers of students with mental retardation, such as the positive effects of early intervention efforts. Nevertheless, it is important to remember that much of what happens to people who are mentally retarded, including how many of them are so identified, is a function of prevailing social opinion and policy.

FINAL REFLECTIONS

The enactment of P.L. 94-142 and its expanded provisions as amended (1983, 1986, 1990, 1997, and 2004) gave official recognition to the importance of developing case registers of individuals with disabilities. That law required local education agencies to conduct and document efforts to identify all at-risk children residing within their jurisdiction (i.e., child find). After they have been identified as being at risk, the children must be evaluated to determine whether they are disabled and thus qualify for educational and related services. This task is enormous.

Most policy decisions result either directly or indirectly in allocations of resources to meet goals. Public policy makers include the president, members of federal and state legislatures, county commissioners, school administrators, professional organizations (e.g., Council for Exceptional Children), and special interest groups. Most persons who make or affect policies related to people who are mentally retarded are not professionals in the field. All of them, however, are involved in making decisions about the relative importance of different goals and deciding the appropriate expenditures of resources to meet each goal. Policy makers must identify the most beneficial set of goals and allocate the necessary resources. The prudence and the equity of policy decisions affecting those with mental retardation depend heavily on the decision makers' understanding of the demography of this group.

To understand the term *mental retardation,* we must begin by establishing a definition. Historically, a variety of attempts has been made to define concisely the condition implied by this term and its precursors. The AAMR definitions of Heber (1959, 1961) and Grossman (1973, 1977, 1983) have reflected the essential dual dimension of the concept of retardation. The more recent AAMR definitions (1992, 2002) represent a more functional perspective. Nevertheless, professionals continue to question and suggest alternatives (e.g., DSM-IV-TR, APA), and further evolution is inevitable.

Classification involves delineating specific subgroups of persons who are mentally retarded. This task has given rise to a variety of systems and specific terms. Historically, approaches have categorized persons according to level of severity (e.g., the former AAMR system). The current AAMR system now recommends that (a) classification be determined on the basis of levels of support across adaptive skill areas and (b) current systems based on IQ levels be abandoned. Yet, in practice, former systems of classification endure.

Prevalence figures in mental retardation have proven to be difficult to establish; significantly wide ranges have been reported in the literature. Although 3 % used to be cited by the government as an estimate of the prevalence of retardation, there is generally no support for this figure today. Most professionals suggest prevalence rates of less than 1%. Additional concerns in prevalence relate to variations based on gender, community environment, and sociopolitical factors.

To check your understanding of this chapter, go to the Companion Website at www.prenhall.com/beirne -smith and select Chapter 2. From there, you can access the Self-Test and Essay modules.

Summary

Mental Retardation in Context
- Mental retardation is a complex condition.
- The condition is characterized by substantial limitations in present levels of functioning.
- Mental retardation encompasses a heterogeneous group of people with varying needs.
- The definition of developmental disabilities overlaps significantly with the AAMR (1992) definition of mental retardation.
- Some professionals suggest that mental retardation be considered a social invention.

Terminology
- Various terms have been used formally to refer to mental retardation.
- Many nonprofessionals confuse the concepts of mental retardation and mental illness.

Disablism and Mental Retardation
- Many groups of people are not perceived favorably in today's society.
- *Disablism* is a term that refers to stereotyping, prejudice, and discrimination based on apparent or assumed physical, mental, or behavioral differences.
- Media portrayals of individuals with mental retardation provide both negative and positive examples.

Defining Mental Retardation
- Early definitions stressed the concept of social competence.
- The definitions developed by the AAMR have typically included three major components: subaverage mental functioning, deficits in adaptive behavior, and occurrence during the developmental period.
- The 1992 AAMR definition introduced a more functional perspective to explaining the condition.
- The 2002 AAMR definition reconceptualized the adaptive skill areas.

Contemporary Professional Definitions
- New definitions have emerged.
- The American Psychological Association developed a definition that was similar to earlier versions of the AAMR definition.
- The 2000 DSM-IV-TR definition contains derivatives from the 1992 AAMR definition.

Other Definitional Perspectives
- Alternative definitions (behavioral, educational) exist, and others will be developed.
- Greenspan recommends a definition that includes the concept of personal competence and multiple intelligences.

Systems of Classification
- Mental retardation can be classified in a number of ways, with the most common being etiological, intellectual, or behavioral.
- Traditional levels of mental retardation include mild, moderate, severe, and profound.
- The AAMR (1992) system advocated the abandonment of levels based on IQ and recommended that classification be determined on the basis of levels of needed support across adaptive areas.

Operationalizing Definitional Perspectives
- The relationship between what is discussed theoretically and what is put into practice can vary greatly.
- Research suggests that no one definition is used consistently in education throughout the United States.
- Two models developed by Connecticut and Iowa highlight the ways the definition has been interpreted.
- Definitional issues affect the adult sector.
- IQ continues to have more importance in determining whether a student qualifies as being mentally retarded.

Incidence and Prevalence
- The terms *incidence* (i.e., number of new cases) and *prevalence* (i.e., number of existing cases) refer to different types of statistical concepts.
- Prevalence figures have been difficult to determine, with a wide range reported in the literature.
- Most professionals believe prevalence rates to be less than 1%.
- Estimates of incidence and prevalence vary according to definitional perspectives, gender, community contexts, and sociopolitical factors.

3

Assessment of Individuals with Intellectual Disabilities

OBJECTIVES

After reading this chapter, the student should be able to:

- Discuss different types of theories of intelligence and intellectual development
- Identify and describe different instruments used in the practice of intelligence testing today
- Discuss different types of theories of adaptive functioning
- Identify and describe different instruments used in the practice of adaptive behavior assessment today

KEY TERMS

adaptive behavior

assessment

competence

deviation IQ

dissimulation

nature–nurture controversy

Wechsler scales

A complete on-line glossary is available on the Companion Website, which may be accessed at www.prenhall.com/beirne-smith

Assessment in general, and assessment of mental and special abilities in particular, covers a wide range of activities. Though assessment has been defined in different ways by different people, most agree that it is not so much an activity as a process, dynamic and ongoing, and one that changes with the needs of the individual. **Assessment** is the collection of information for educational, psychological, and vocational decision making.

The importance of testing and assessment is not lost on three of education's most prominent professional associations: the American Educational Research Association, the American Psychological Association, and the National Council on Measurement in Education (1999):

> Educational and psychological testing and assessment are among the most important contributions of behavioral science to our society. . . . The proper use of tests can result in wiser decisions about individuals and programs than would be the case without their use and also can provide a route to broader and more equitable access to education and employment. . . . Educational and psychological testing and assessment involve and significantly affect individuals, institutions, and society as a whole. (p. 1)

Educators are required to provide children with individual psychoeducational evaluations prior to placement in special education programs. Policies in most states prescribe that these evaluations include two critical assessment areas (for mental retardation): intelligence and adaptive behavior. Furthermore, educators must monitor the progress of students and assess the transition needs of students as they prepare to move from school to community living. Assessment plays an important role in the adult sector as well. Eligibility for services and identifying the support needs are two important areas. The legal proceedings for either juveniles or adults will often require the assessment of competence, capacity, and dissimulation. What follows is an in-depth look at the theories and assessment practices of intelligence and adaptive behavior and an introduction to other important assessments areas conducted with persons who have mental retardation.

ASSESSMENT OF INTELLIGENCE

The assessment of intelligence is a critical topic in the area of mental retardation. It is an essential activity for the purpose of making a diagnosis of mental retardation, as indicated in the previous chapter on definition. Moreover, as Luckasson and colleagues (2002) point out, "the assessment of intellectual functioning is a task that requires specialized professional training." This type of assessment has been and remains a highly charged topic (Bryant, 1997). This section of the chapter will explore the fundamental concepts associated with intelligence and the measurement of it, review key influences on how intelligence is assessed, introduce the major instruments developed for this purpose, and examine the most important issues associated with intelligence testing.

Conceptual Bases

The discussion of what intelligence is and how to measure it has been of great interest to psychologists and educators for many years. To this day, great variance can be found in regard to professional thought on these topics. This section provides a backdrop of the various definitions and major theories of intelligence that have emerged over the years.

Definitions of Intelligence.   Professionals from a wide range of backgrounds have attempted to define intelligence. The definitions that emerged over time reflected professional thinking during a particular era as well as certain sociopolitical factors that were operant. Some definitions grew out of the underlying theories of intelligence that were being proposed, as will be discussed in the next section. Table 3.1 highlights many of the noteworthy attempts to define intelligence; the table is an adaptation of a version created by Sattler (2001). Table 3.1 does not include some definitions noted by Sattler but does include the definition of intelligence provided in the 2002 AAMR manual (Luckasson et al., 2002) on definition, classification, and systems of support.

What is clear from examining the different definitions in the table is that no general agreement can be found. Anastasi and Urbina (1997) make three very important points in regard to defintion:

> . . . it should be noted that the unqualified term "intelligence" is used with a wide diversity of meanings, not only by the general public but also by members of different disciplines . . . and by psychologists who specialize in different areas or identify with different theoretical orientations. (p. 294)

> . . . tested intelligence should be regarded as a descriptive rather than an explanatory concept. (p. 295)

> . . . [a] major point to bear in mind is that intelligence is not a single, unitary ability, but a composite of several functions. (p. 296)

Theories of Intelligence.   Theories of intelligence are useful to the extent that they provide professionals with an organizing structure for understanding and evaluating how children learn. For teachers and other service providers in the community, the concept of intelligence is most useful when it helps to formulate instructional strategies.

Theories of intelligence can be evaluated from several points of view. For some people, particularly those who work in the field of education, intelligence can be an intricate and well-defined construct; for others, it may be little more than a generally held notion or idea, as noted by Anastasi and Urbina (1997) in the previous section. According to some theorists, it is the efficiency of the process that is important—for example, how much of a given task one can accomplish in a certain period of time. According to others, it may be the relationships among ideas that really matter. For still others, intellectual theories are best understood in the context of their origin (innate or acquired). While nearly all theories of intelligence contain some of these elements, Wechsler's (1958) definition of intelligence, as listed in Table 3.1, offers one of the most cogent explanations: "The aggregate or global capacity of the individual to act purposefully, to think rationally, and to deal effectively with his environment" (p. 7). A brief description of three very general types of theories of intelligence follows.

Traditional *psychometric theories* have their roots in differential psychology, the study of individual and group differences. Psychometric theorists assume that

TABLE 3.1

Some Definitions of Intelligence

Anastasi (1986)	"Intelligence is not an entity within the organism but a quality of behavior. Intelligent behavior is essentially adaptive, insofar as it represents effective ways of meeting the demands of a changing environment. Such behavior varies with the species and with the context in which the individual lives" (pp. 19–20).	Estes (1986)	"... intelligence ... is a multifaceted aspect of the processes that enable animate or inanimate systems to accomplish tasks that involve information processing, problem solving, and creativity" (p. 66).
Binet (in Terman, 1916)	"The tendency to take and maintain a definite direction; the capacity to make adaptations for the purpose of attaining a desired end; and the power of autocriticism" (p. 45).	Freeman (1955)	"... *adjustment or adaptation of the individual to his* [or her] *total environment,* or to limited aspects of it. ... The capacity to reorganize one's behavior patterns so as to act more effectively and more appropriately in novel situations. ... The *ability to learn.* ... The extent to which [a person] is educable. ... The *ability to carry on abstract thinking.* ... The effective use of concepts and symbols in dealing with ... a problem to be solved" (pp. 149, 150).
Binet & Simon (1916)	"... judgment otherwise called good sense, practical sense, initiative, the faculty of adapting one's self to circumstances. To judge well, to comprehend well, to reason well, these are the essential activities of intelligence" (pp. 42–43).		
		Gardner (1983)	"... a human intellectual competence must entail a set of skills of problem solving— enabling the individual *to resolve genuine problems or difficulties* that he or she encounters, and, when appropriate, to create an effective product—and must also entail the potential for *finding or creating problems*— thereby laying the groundwork for the acquisition of new knowledge" (pp. 60–61).
Carroll (1997b)	"... IQ represents the degree to which, and the rate at which, people are able to learn, and retain in long-term memory, the knowledge and skills that can be learned from the environment (that is, what is taught in the home and in school, as well as things learned from everyday experience)" (p. 44).		
Das (1973)	"... the ability to plan and structure one's behavior with an end in view" (p. 27).	Humphreys (1979)	"... the resultant of the processes of acquiring, storing in memory, retrieving, combining, comparing, and using in new contexts information and conceptual skills; it is an abstraction" (p. 115).
Detterman (1986)	"Intelligence can best be defined as a finite set of independent abilities operating as a complex system" (p. 57).		

Hunt (1985)	Intelligence is a collective term that refers to the possession of useful knowledge and special information-processing capabilities.		cial case of educing either relations or correlates" (p. 300).
Pellegrino (1986)	"Intelligence is implicitly determined by the interaction of organisms' cognitive machinery and their sociocultural environment. . . . [There is] the need to consider cultural values and context in any understanding of intelligence" (p. 113).	Sternberg (1986)	*". . . mental activity involved in purposive adaptation to, shaping of, and selection of real-world environments relevant to one's life"* (p. 33).
Sattler (2001)	"Intelligent behavior reflects the survival skills of the species, beyond those associated with basic physiological processes."	Stoddard (1943)	". . . the ability to undertake activities that are characterized by (1) difficulty, (2) complexity, (3) abstractness, (4) economy, (5) adaptiveness to a goal, (6) social value, and (7) the emergence of originals, and to maintain such activities under conditions that demand a concentration of energy and a resistance to emotional forces" (p. 4).
Snow (1986)	Intelligence is part of the internal environment that shows through at the interface between person and external environment as a function of cognitive task demands.	Wechsler (1958)	"The aggregate or global capacity of the individual to act purposefully, to think rationally, and to deal effectively with his [or her] environment" (p. 7).
Spearman (1923)	". . . everything intellectual can be reduced to some spe-		

Source: From *Assessment of Children: Cognitive Applications* (4th ed.) (p. 136) by J. M. Sattler, 2001, San Diego, CA: Jerome M. Sattler. Copyright 2001 by Jerome M. Sattler. Reprinted with permission.

underlying abilities account for most variations in intellectual functioning. The traditional psychometric theorists range from those who believe that a single trait accounts for all mental abilities (e.g., Spearman, 1927; Vernon, 1950) to multifactored theorists who believe that intelligence is best explained by a multitude of traits or factors (Guilford, 1967; Thorndike, 1927; Thurstone, 1938). Most, however, place these models at two ends of a continuum and believe that reality lies somewhere in between.

More recently, John Carroll (1993) proposed a three-stratum theory of cognitive abilities that allows for a general ability factor similar to Spearman's *g*, second-level factors referred to as broad ability factors (e.g., crystallized intelligence, fluid intelligence), and 50 or more primary (or narrow) abilities, many of which were previously identified by Thurstone. Carroll's three-stratum theory synthesizes the factor-analytic work of the last century and offers much promise for new developments in the years ahead.

Information-processing theories, perhaps better than any others, represent the second and most truly interdisciplinary approach to understanding intelligence. With contributions from anthropology, computer science, education, linguistics, and psychology, information-processing theorists focus on the methods by which a person processes information, taking it from sensory stimuli and transferring it to motoric output (Sternberg, 1985).

Among the many theories that emanate from an information-processing model, Sternberg's (1985, 1988) triarchic theory of human intelligence continues to receive some acclaim. The triarchic theory describes a complex and highly integrated system of mental operations that combines such influential elements as the internal world of the individual, the external world of the individual, and one's life experiences. Sternberg (1997) is careful to point out the underlying components and mechanisms in each of the three areas but cautions that while such operations may be found among people of all cultures, the values placed on specific problem-solving strategies and mechanisms may vary. For example, children of one culture may adapt more quickly to the environmental demands of a new community than other children, based on both past experiences and the social worth of the necessary skills. Consequently, what is deemed intelligent in one culture may not be viewed as intelligent in another. What further distinguishes Sternberg's theory from other contemporary theorists is an explanation of how information is processed within each of the three aforementioned areas. That is, he allows for the presence of higher order problem-solving skills, performance components that allow for the execution of those problem-solving skills, and knowledge acquisition components that allow one to attend, retrieve, and compare the necessary pieces of information.

Another major theory is Das, Naglieri, and Kirby's (1994) planning, attention, simultaneous, and successive (PASS) processes model. The PASS model of information processing is an extension and validation of Luria's (1980) early theory of human cognitive functioning. Luria first reported and others have since verified the presence of three functional units of information processing. The first functional unit allows a person to become aroused by and attend to environmental stimuli. The second functional unit is responsible for acquiring, holding, and then processing the information, of which there are two main approaches: processing multiple pieces of information all at once in an integrated manner (simultaneous) or processing information in a sequential, temporally organized (successive) manner. The third functional unit, known as the planning unit, provides the individual with the means to analyze cognitive activity, develop a problem-solving strategy, and then evaluate the efficacy of that solution. Das and colleagues (1994) have suggested that the PASS model offers psychologists and educators a number of options for responding to the special needs of children with disabilities.

The third major category of theories is the most broad and focuses on the ideas of *multiple intelligences.* Perhaps the best known is Gardner's (1993) theory of multiple intelligences. While reminiscent of the multifactored theories, Gardner's theory allows for multiple definitions of intelligence, including, among others, social and motoric intelligence. Although little in the professional literature validates Gardner's definitions, many educators have embraced it as a new and innovative perspective for considering intellectual functioning. From the viewpoint of people who work with persons with mental retardation, the assumption that all individuals are different and possess their own unique combination of strengths and weaknesses is very much in agreement with Gardner's premise that it is possible to be intelligent in specific yet nontraditional ways.

Another multiple intelligence perspective is provided by Greenspan (Greenspan & Driscoll, 1997; Greenspan, 2003). Greenspan has revised his model of personal competence over the years; however, at its core he has argued for a tripartite model of intelligence that includes conceptual, practical, and social intelligence. The notion of *intellectual competence* can be seen in the model of personal competence depicted in Figure 3.1. Greenspan's model separates "everyday competence" (i.e., a function of practical and social intelligence) from "academic competence" (i.e., comprised of conceptual intelligence and language—skills most relevant to school success). Greenspan notes that conceptual intelligence is "the element tapped by IQ measures (Greenspan & Driscoll, 1997, p. 134). The three types of intelligences promoted by Greenspan can be conceptualized in the following way:

- *Conceptual intelligence:* The ability to think about and understand problems found in formal learning settings
- *Practical intelligence:* Performance of everyday skills
- *Social intelligence:* An individual's social and interpersonal abilities

Nature Versus Nurture. If professionals view intelligence as fixed and predominantly inherited, then they may view their role as disseminators of information rather than cultivators of learning. This position assigns the responsibility of learning—and its opposite, nonlearning—primarily to the person receiving instruction. But if professionals (i.e., teachers) view intelligence as something that can be altered, they may see their jobs as instrumental in the learning process, thereby allowing them to view a person's learning as an indication of their own effectiveness (i.e., as teachers).

One's beliefs about intelligence and the ways in which individuals learn are very much related to the **nature–nurture controversy,** the question of whether intelligence is innate or acquired. Actually, few authorities claim either the extreme hereditarian or the extreme environmentalist position, believing instead that both factors work together in a sort of duet to influence one's abilities and patterns of responses (Plomin, 1994). The Swiss psychologist Jean Piaget (1952) referred to such a combination of biological and environmental factors as *epigenetic* in nature.

The bulk of this debate concerns the relative proportions of the two ingredients that combine to shape one's intelligence. Researchers generally agree that a person's upbringing affects cognitive development within the constraints of existing biological potential. But how rigid are those constraints? And how powerful are the environmental forces that influence them? Researchers are divided on these issues. Some— such as Bouchard, Lykken, McGue, Segal, and Tellegen (1990); Jensen (1998); and Pedersen, Plomin, Nesselroade, and McClearn (1992)—believe that the hereditary component can be quite strong, perhaps in excess of 70%. That is, 70% or more of the variation in intelligence is attributable to the person's genetic makeup. Others, such as Kamin (1974), believe that one's intelligence has nothing at all to do with genetics.

The actual estimate of heritability depends very much on which relationships are being investigated (e.g., monozygotic twins, dizygotic twins, biological siblings, adoptive

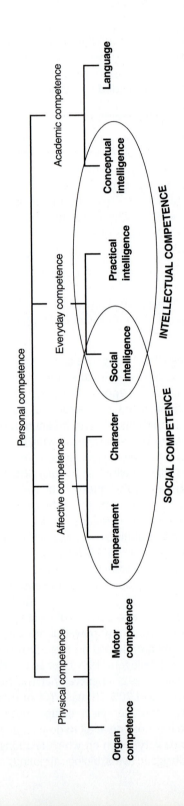

FIGURE 3.1

Greenspan's Model of Personal Competence

Source: From "The Role of Intelligence in a Broad Model of Personal Competence," by S. Greenspan & J. Driscoll, in D. P. Flanagan, J. O. Genshaft, & P. L. Harrison (Eds.), *Contemporary Intellectual Assessment: Theories, Tests, and Issues* (p. 133), 1997, New York: Guilford. Copyright © 1997 by Guilford Press. Reprinted by permission.

Teachers must help structure environments in ways that stimulate learning and intellectual growth.

siblings) and whether the siblings are raised together or apart and with or without their biological parents. It is not simply a matter of heritability alone, but how the inherited components interact with the environmental components (Mackintosh, 1998). Virtually everyone is familiar with intellectually gifted parents whose children never live up to their "expected" intellectual potential, just as most people are aware of families of very limited social, economic, and intellectual means who have raised children with extraordinary intellectual capabilities. Hence, there is no sure formula for creating the optimal blend between genetic makeup and environmental influence.

The best research to date seems to suggest that the heritability of intelligence is about 50%; however, as with all population estimates, that value is only applicable to the population at large and can vary markedly from individual to individual based on the person's circumstances (Plomin & Petrill, 1997). If heritability is estimated to be around 50%, then the remaining 50% is due to environmental influences—and one can safely say that one's intellectual potential is shaped to a large degree by non-hereditary factors that resonate through all parts of a person's life, into the school, home, and community. Educators and social service delivery personnel must therefore help structure environments in ways that stimulate intellectual growth. In addition, they must accept that changes are both constant and welcome additions where intellectual growth and development are concerned.

Intelligence Quotient. Many find the notion that one's intellectual capacity can be described with a single value unsettling. Although it is still possible to find tests that yield only one score and examiners who define a person's level of academic aptitude in terms of a single value, these tests and examiners are in the minority. The notion of a single IQ score is valid only if a single factor of general ability underlies all problem-solving operations. But since most people today do not believe in the notion of a lone ability factor, and no major intelligence test is based on a single, underlying dimension, the notion of IQ has indeed changed dramatically since its inception.

Though many of the terms once associated with intelligence and intelligence quotients are no longer accurate, they have remained in the American vocabulary and are worth knowing. The earliest and least sophisticated term for describing a person's level of intellectual functioning is *mental age*. Mental age is an estimate of one's intellectual level and is different from chronological age. A 5-year-old who successfully completes tasks typically performed only by children 7 years of age would be considered to have a mental age of 7 years. The concept of mental age and some loose applications of this concept are used regularly in the media and legal proceedings.

Louis Terman first introduced the term *intelligence quotient* (IQ) in 1916 as a better scoring index than mental age. While no longer used in practice, the ratio IQ is important in a historical sense and is calculated by dividing one's mental age by one's chronological age and multiplying by 100. The disadvantage of a mental age score as compared with a ratio IQ score, such as that proposed by Terman, is that it provides an index of a child's IQ test performance relative to others in a given age group—but this technique does not work for adults. Beginning in early adulthood, chronological age increases faster than mental age, making adults in general and older adults in particular appear less apt than they really are.

Today, deviation IQs are used in place of intelligence quotients for all age groups. Although many professionals still refer to these scores as "IQs," they are not IQs—at least not in the same way referred to 75 years ago when the concept was just originating. A **deviation IQ** is nothing more than a subtest raw score converted to a standard score for the examinee's own age group. The standard score for a particular child is derived by subtracting the mean raw score of all children in the respective age group from the raw score of the child, and then dividing that value by the raw score standard deviation for all children in that age group. The advantage of a deviation IQ is that a person's relative standing within a particular reference group can be compared with the scores of many others, including those of different ages and ability levels. This is the primary reason that most individually administered, norm-referenced intelligence tests used today include composite quotient scores that have a mean (M) of 100 and a standard deviation (SD) of 15. When subtests are components of an instrument, scaled scores are typically used that have a mean (M) of 10 and a standard deviation (SD) of 3.

Key Influences

Although the testing practices of today differ markedly from those of the time when they were first introduced, the premise has remained very much the same: to distinguish those who are successful at solving problems from those who are not. According to Ittenbach, Esters, and Wainer (1997), the act of assessment is actually a quest in search of an underlying truth. It is a means by which hypotheses are tested and verified using scientifically acceptable methods (Messick, 1988).

While the history of testing is virtually 4,000 years old, the history of modern testing is little more than a century old. Sir Francis Galton (1832–1920) is generally considered to be the founder of formal testing. However, it was actually one of his contemporaries, James McKeen Cattell (1860–1944), who is credited with coining the term *mental tests*. What made Galton and Cattell's influence on the mental testing movement so profound was not their shared interests in eugenics and individual differences so much as their particular blend of skills and abilities. Galton, part scientist and part philosopher, was trying to better understand the inheritance of mental abilities through physical traits, whereas Cattell was interested in differences in physiological functioning through performances on paper-and-pencil tests.

The critical link between the two investigators was mathematician Karl Pearson (1857–1936). According to Ittenbach and Lawhead (1997), "Galton had the ideas, but Karl Pearson had the mathematical acumen to sell it to the world" (p. 31). Cattell then applied the new mathematical operations to test scores of his experimental psychology students at the University of Pennsylvania. From there, the union of statistics and experimental psychology carried forward to all of American psychology.

As a construct, intelligence is a relatively well-accepted and time-honored notion of problem-solving ability. Yet, the definition of intelligence and the way in which it is measured are open to debate. Many have attempted to define intelligence, but few have set out to measure it with any degree of rigor. Those who have tried to measure intelligence have done so with the understanding that they were attempting to explain one of the most complex and elusive components of human functioning. Test developers have been careful to distinguish the construct of intelligence from its assessment (i.e., the manner in which information is obtained). Human service providers should be careful to do the same.

Alfred Binet.   The first effective test of intellectual ability was devised in the early 1900s by French psychologists Alfred Binet, Victor Henri, and Theodore Simon (Schultz & Schultz, 1996). Although Binet had a wide and varied career within the discipline of psychology, it is in the fields of intelligence and psychometrics that he has had "his most concentrated, enduring, and intellectually powerful influence" (Haywood & Paour, 1992, p. 1). In 1904, the French Ministry of Public Instruction appointed Binet to a commission to study the problems of educating children who were not likely to benefit from traditional classroom instruction and who would instead profit from slower paced educational programs—that is, children with learning problems.

As early as 1895, Binet had already argued in his writings that educational tests were far too narrow in scope and that new tests were needed to better understand the learning process. Thus, Binet and his colleague Theodore Simon devised an instrument to identify children who were considered lacking in mental ability. Their first test, the 30-item Measuring Scale of Intelligence, was published in 1905, then revised in 1908, and revised again in 1911 (as cited in Haywood & Paour, 1992). Their scale was different from others of the day in that it did not just tap sensory experiences but instead allowed for the evaluation of such mental abilities as comprehension, memory, and reasoning—intellectual skills deemed critical for scholastic success. In short, the Binet-Simon scale sampled higher level, complex processes that the authors believed to be essential elements of intelligence.

Binet and Simon went to great lengths to differentiate between the concepts of natural intelligence and acquired intelligence. They were interested in measuring one's capacity to learn rather than simply the amount of knowledge gained. Because reading and writing are learned skills, Binet and Simon's tests of intelligence were constructed to avoid measuring reading and writing. The initial version of their scale, for example, tested the child's ability to identify pictured objects, repeat a three-digit series, reproduce geometric figure drawings, define abstract words, and perform similar nonacademic tasks.

Among the many versions of the original Binet-Simon scale used in the United States in the early 20th century, it was actually Terman's Stanford Revision and Extension of the Binet-Simon Scale (Terman, 1916) that became the template for all subsequent revisions. Terman's version has since been revised in the country four times: in 1937 and 1960 with Maud Merrill; in 1986 by Robert Thorndike, Elizabeth Hagen, and Jerome Sattler (1986); and most recently by Gale Roid (2003). The 1937, 1960, and once again in the 2003 edition of the Stanford-Binet included such materials as toys and miniature objects (e.g., beads, balls, cars, dolls), which examinees were instructed to manipulate in various ways, and booklets and pictures (animals and household objects, etc.), about which they had to answer questions.

David Wechsler.   David Wechsler's (1896–1981) influence on assessment in the schools has been profound. Whereas the Stanford-Binet has served as the standard of intellectual assessment for a century now, the Wechsler scales have served as the workhorse. The **Wechsler scales** are a series of three individually administered intelligence tests, modeled after one another, in which a person's intellectual abilities are described using a verbal/motor framework (i.e., Wechsler, 1949, 1955, 1967, 1974, 1981, 1989, 1991a, 1997, 2003). The Wechsler scales have provided the preferred vehicle for the identification and classification of countless school-age children for nearly half a century. The adult scale is used frequently in community settings and legal proceedings as well.

Like Binet, Wechsler was trained as a clinician. Though he worked with adults rather than children, he too believed that intelligence was a unitary trait and that it was actually only one part of the broader construct of the human personality. Perhaps the most important feature of the Wechsler scales, and very likely the reason their use in the schools has far exceeded that of the Binet, is that the tests are remarkably similar across the preschool, elementary, and secondary age ranges. As opposed to earlier versions of the Binet in which children of different ages were tested using very different tasks, with the Wechsler scales, children of different ages are exposed to different items but to highly similar tasks, thereby adding an element of consistency to evaluations throughout a child's schooling. Sadly, America's educators will never come to know the instrument that Wechsler had intended to complete his battery of intelligence tests across the life span, the *Wechsler Intelligence Scale for the Elderly* (WISE), which was under development at the time of his death in 1981 (Kaufman, 1994).

When they first appeared, the Wechsler scales were distinguished by several other innovative features. For example, every Wechsler test is subdivided into smaller scales and subscales. The *Wechsler Intelligence Scale for Children 4th Edition* (2003), for example, consists of 15 subtests—10 core and 5 supplemental ones. Each subtest theoretically measures a different ability and is treated as a separate entity; combined, all subtests allow the examiner to assess global intellectual capacity. Wechsler (1939) believed that the Binet test of that era did not tap motoric performance, an important facet of intelligence, so he developed a performance scale that complemented the verbal scale in such a way that it offered problem-solving items that required judgment, reasoning, foresight, and planning, but little in the way of verbal ability.

Major Instruments

The Stanford-Binet and Wechsler scales have been and remain very popular with school personnel and are the most widely used instruments (Stinnett, Havey, & Oehler-Stinnett 1994). Despite their historical and clinical importance, however, they are facing increased competition from newer and arguably theoretically superior instruments. Some of these tests are readily available, inexpensive, and easy to administer and require little in the way of administrator training or time; however, they do not always meet state or local guidelines for use and very often do not provide all the information needed for an in-depth diagnostic evaluation.

The most commonly used instruments, including the Wechsler scales and the Stanford-Binet, 5th edition, along with key information about each instrument, are described in Table 3.2. The specific Wechsler scales and the Stanford-Binet 5 are discussed below in more detail due to the important role they play in educational and clinical practice.

TABLE 3.2

Measures of Intelligence (listed alphabetically)

Instrument	Publication Date	Age Range	Organization	Features
Comprehensive Test of Nonverbal Intelligence (CTONI) (Hammill, Pearson, & Wiederholt, 1997)	1997	6 yrs 0 mos to 90 yrs 11 mos	• Six subtests: • Pictorial Analogies • Pictorial Categories • Pictorial Sequences • Geometric Analogies • Geometric Categories • Geometric Sequences	• Includes measure of nonverbal problem solving and reasoning • Three quotients: • Nonverbal Intelligence Quotient • Pictorial Nonverbal Intelligence Quotient • Geometric Nonverbal Intelligence Quotient
Kaufman Assessment Battery for Children, 2nd ed., (KABC-II) (Kaufman & Kaufman, 2004)	2004	3 yrs to 18 yrs	• Major scales: • Simultaneous • Sequential • Planning • Learning • Knowledge • 18 subtests	• Dual theoretical foundation: • Luria neuropsychological model • Cattell-Horn-Carroll model • Global scores: • Mental Processing Index • Fluid-Crystallized Index • Nonverbal Index
Stanford Binet Intelligence Scale, 5th edition (SB5) (Roid, 2003)	2003	2 yrs 0 mos to 85+	• Verbal and nonverbal subtests for each of five factors: • Fluid Reasoning • Knowledge • Quantitative Reasoning • Visual-Spatial Processing • Working Memory	• Uses routing techniques • Includes extensive high-end items • Has improved low-end items
Test of Nonverbal Intelligence (TONI) (Brown, Sherbenou, & Johnsen, 1997)	1997	6 yrs 0 mos to 85 yrs 11 mos	• Two equivalent forms; 45 items arranged in order from easy to difficult	• Quick administration time
Wechsler Adult Intelligence Scale, 3rd edition (WAIS-III) (Wechsler, 1997)	1997	16 yrs 0 mos to 89 yrs 0 mos	• Subtests: **Verbal:** • Vocabulary • Information • Similarities • Comprehension • Digit Span • Arithmetic	• Scores: FSIQ, Index Scores, Subtest Scores

TABLE 3.2 **(continued)**
Measures of Intelligence (listed alphabetically)

Instrument	Publication Date	Age Range	Organization	Features
Wechsler Adult Intelligence Scale, 3rd edition (WAIS-III) (continued)			**Performance:** • Block Design • Object Assembly • Picture Completion • Picture Arrangement • Digit Symbol	
Wechsler Intelligence Scale for Children, 4th edition (WISC-IV) (Wechsler, 2003)	2003	6 yrs 0 mos to 16 yrs 11 mos	• Subtests: • Block Design • Similarities • Digit Span • Picture Concepts • Coding • Vocabulary • Letter-Number Sequencing • Matrix Reasoning • Comprehension • Symbol Search • Picture Completion • Cancellation • Information • Arithmetic • Word Reasoning	• Five composite scores: • Verbal Comprehension Index • Perceptual Reasoning Index • Working Memory Index • Processing Speed Index • Full Scale IQ
Wechsler Preschool and Primary Scale of Intelligence, 3rd edition (WPPSI-III) (Wechsler, 2002)	2002	2 yrs 6 mos to 7 yrs 3 mos	• Subtests: • Information • Word Reasoning • Comprehension • Similarities • Block Design • Matrix Reasoning • Picture Concepts • Picture Completion • Object Assembly • Symbol Search • Coding • Receptive Vocabulary • Picture Naming	• 5 composite scores: • Verbal IQ • Performance IQ • Processing Speed Quotient • General Language Composite • Full Scale IQ
Woodcock-Johnson Tests of Cognitive Ability (WJ III COG) (Woodcock, McGrew, & Mather, 2001)	2001	2 yrs to 90+	• Standard Battery: • Verbal comprehension • Visual-auditory learning • Spatial relations • Sound blending • Concept formation • Visual matching • Numbers reversed • Incomplete words • Auditory working memory • Visual-auditory learning-delayed • Extended Battery: • General information • Retrieval fluency • Picture recognition • Auditory attention • Analysis-synthesis • Decision speed • Memory for words • Rapid picture naming • Planning • Pair cancellation	• Overall score: General Intellectual Ability (GIA)—differentially weighted score as a function of age • Other scores: standard scores (M = 100, SD = 15); percentile ranks, age- and grade-equivalents scores; instructional ranges; discrepancy scores; Relative Proficiency Index (RPI) • Computer-scored only

Wechsler Preschool and Primary Scale of Intelligence, 3rd Edition. The Wechsler Preschool and Primary Scale of Intelligence, 3rd Edition (WPPSI-III; Wechsler, 2002) is a standardized, individually administered test of intelligence intended for use with children aged 2 years 6 months through 7 years 3 months. The WPPSI-III is third in a line of scales designed for young children (WPPSI, WPPSI-R). The purpose, as stated in the manual, is to assist with the diagnosis of exceptionalities of young children in educational and private practice settings.

A number of changes were made in this new version to keep pace with contemporary theories and practice, including the addition of six new subtests. The WPPSI-III has 15 separate subtests ($M = 10$, $SD = 3$), with different core subtests depending on the age of the child. The core test may be administered in 30 to 45 minutes (ages 2-6 to 3-11) or 45 to 60 minutes (ages 4-0 to 7-3). Five composite scores can be derived on the WPPSI-III: Verbal IQ; Performance (fluid) IQ; Processing Speed Quotient; General Language Composite; and Full Scale IQ.

Wechsler Intelligence Scale for Children, 4th Edition. The Wechsler Intelligence Scale for Children, 4th Edition (WISC-IV; Wechsler, 2003) is a standardized, individually administered test of intelligence intended for use with children and adolescents aged 6 years 0 months through 16 years 11 months. The WISC-IV is fourth in a series of time-honored and clinically tested instruments (WISC, WISC-R, WISC-III). The WISC-IV provides subtest and composite scores "that represent intellectual functioning in specific cognitive domains, as well as a composite score that represents general intellectual ability (i.e., Full Scale IQ)" (Wechsler, 2003, p. 1).

The purpose of the WISC-IV is to help with educational planning and placement, diagnosis of exceptionality, clinical and neuropsychological assessment, and educational and psychological research. The WISC-IV has 15 subtests—five are new to this edition—and all are identified as either core or supplemental. Three subtests from the previous edition (mazes, object assembly, and picture arrangement) were dropped. The subtests, their abbreviations, and a short description of each is provided in Table 3.3.

The three traditional global scales (verbal scale, performance scale, and full scale) have changed, reflecting current theory and practice. The new indexes ($M = 100$, $SD = 15$) are Verbal Comprehension Index (VCI), replacing Verbal IQ, and Perceptual Reasoning Index (PRI), replacing Performance IQ. In addition to these two indexes, two other composite scores can be derived from the results of subtests that were administered: Working Memory Index (WMI) and Processing Speed Index (PSI). The scores form each index, based on the core subtests only, are combined to create a child's total score (Full Scale IQ, or FSIQ). The 10 core subtests can be administered in 65 to 95 minutes.

Wechsler Adult Intelligence Scale, 3rd Edition. The Wechsler Adult Intelligence Scale, 3rd Edition (WAIS-III; Wechsler, 1997) is a standardized, individually administered test of intelligence intended for use with adults aged 16 years 0 months and older. The WAIS-III is a revision of the original Wechsler Adult Intelligence Scales (WAIS, WAIS-R). The purpose of the WAIS-III differs somewhat from that of the WPPSI-III and WISC-IV in that, like its forerunner the WAIS-R, it tends to be much more of a clinical rather than a school-based instrument.

TABLE 3.3

WISC-IV Subtests, Abbreviations, and Descriptions of Subtests

Subtest	Abbreviation	Description
Block design	BD	While viewing a constructed model or a picture in the Stimulus Book, the child uses red-and-white blocks to re-create the design within a specified time limit.
Similarities	SI	The child is presented two words that represent common objects or concepts and describes how they are similar.
Digit span	DS	For Digit Span Forward, the child repeats numbers in the same order as presented aloud by the examiner. For Digit Span Backward, the child repeats numbers in the reverse order of that presented aloud by the examiner.
Picture concepts	PCn	The child is presented with two or three rows of pictures and chooses one picture from each row to form a group with a common characteristic.
Coding	CD	The child copies symbols that are paired with simple geometric shapes or numbers. Using a key, the child draws each symbol in its corresponding shape or box within a specified time limit.
Vocabulary	VC	For Picture Items, the child names pictures that are displayed in the Stimulus Book. For Verbal Items, the child gives definitions for words that the examiner reads aloud.
Letter–number sequencing	LN	The child is read a sequence of numbers and letters and recalls the numbers in ascending order and the letters in alphabetical order.
Matrix reasoning	MR	The child looks at an incomplete matrix and selects the missing portion from five response options.
Comprehension	CO	The child answers questions based on his or her understanding of general principles and social situations.
Symbol search	SS	The child scans a search group and indicates whether the target symbol(s) matches any of the symbols in the search group within a specified time limit.
Picture completion	PCm	The child views a picture and then points to or names the important part missing within a specified time limit.
Cancellation	CA	The child scans both a random and a structured arrangement of pictures and marks target pictures within a specified time limit.
Information	IN	The child answers questions that address a broad range of general knowledge topics.
Arithmetic	AR	The child mentally solves a series of orally presented arithmetic problems within a specified time limit.
Word reasoning	WR	The child identifies the common concept being described in a series of clues.

The WAIS-III provides three composite IQ scores ($M = 100$, $SD = 15$): full-scale IQ, verbal IQ, and performance IQ. Fourteen subtests comprise the WAIS-III ($M = 10$, $SD = 3$), 11 of which are required; total administration time is approximately 90 minutes. As with the other two tests, bonus points are awarded for quick, correct responses.

Stanford-Binet, 5th Edition.   The Stanford-Binet, Fifth Edition (SB5) is an individually administered intelligence test that is appropriate for use with individuals from 2 to 85 years of age. This edition retains many features of previous editions and incorporates a host of new features as well.

The instrument is based on a hierarchical model of intelligence that includes a global *g* factor at one level and several broad factors at a second level. This second level in the SB5 is associated with a five-factor model of cognitive abilities: fluid reasoning, knowledge, quantitative processing, visual-spatial processing, and working memory.

The SB5 contains 10 subtests, 2 of which use a point-scale format of the 1986 edition and the remaining subtests of which use a functional-level format as used in previous editions of the Stanford Binet. Various combinations of the subtests provide different scales:

Full Scale IQ: All ten subtests
Abbreviated Battery IQ Scale: Two routing subtests (Object Series/Matrices and Vocabulary)
Nonverbal IQ Scale: Five nonverbal subtests associated with the five cognitive factors presented above.
Verbal IQ: Five verbal subtests associated with the five cognitive factors.

Some of the key changes in the SB5 from earlier editions include:

- Five factors of cognitive ability—four factors were used in the SB IV.
- Inclusion of five nonverbal subtests (Nonverbal IQ Scale).
- New item content—including items that measure very low functioning and very high giftedness.
- New artwork.
- Ability to compare verbal and nonverbal performance.
- Enhanced memory tasks.

The SB5 was normed on 4,800 individuals who closely matched the 2000 U.S. Census data. The manual reports very high reliabilities and comprehensive studies of concurrent and criterion validity. The key components of the SB5 are the examiner's manual, three easel-style item books, technical manual, test booklets, cards (child, layout), and a number of manipulatives.

"Culture-Free" Tests

Concern for children from bilingual and minority backgrounds has sparked the development of a number of "culture-free" measures in which there has been an effort to eliminate all cultural factors that might favor one group over another. One such test is the *Matrix Analogies Test* (Naglieri, 1985), an instrument that is purported to

For more information about the cultural considerations of assessment, and many other topics discussed in this chapter, visit the Companion Website at www.prenhall .com/beirne-smith and select Chapter 3, Web Destinations.

be a much purer measure of nonverbal reasoning ability than other tests. The examinee is shown a matrix of abstract designs with a missing element and is asked to select a design that best completes the picture.

Other tests such as the *Leiter International Performance Scale, Revised* (Leiter-R; Roid & Miller, 1997), the *Universal Nonverbal Intelligence Test* (UNIT; Bracken & McCallum, 1998), the *Test of Nonverbal Intelligence, Third Edition* (CTONI-3; Brown, Sherbenou, & Johnsen, 1997), the *Comprehensive Test of Nonverbal Intelligence* (Hammill, Pearson, & Wiederholt, 1997), and the nonverbal scales of many of the Wechsler tests (when administered in the respondent's native language) have also redefined the standards by which culture-fair intellectual assessment is now conducted.

Until the day when the process of evaluating intellectual abilities can be clearly separated from cultural influences at both obvious and subtle levels, there may never be a truly "culture-free" test. The most that can be hoped for in the meantime are tests that minimize the role of language and socially driven expectations and emphasize nonverbal skills and abilities, which many of these tests do quite well.

Issues Associated with Intelligence Testing

Considerable controversy surrounds the issue of intelligence testing at all levels of usage. Some critics of intelligence testing find fault with the tests, others with the examiners, and still others with the process. Critics further argue that test scores are subject to various forms of statistical and administrative error and that these scores can vary considerably from one time to another. These points are well taken. Following are brief discussions of some of the important and long-lasting disagreements that continue to plague the practice of intelligence testing.

Underlying Constructs and Test Content.

A major criticism of intelligence testing pertains to the perception by the public and some members of the profession that IQ tests inadequately cover the broad spectrum of abilities defined as intelligence. Much of this criticism stems from the lack of convergence between the theory and structure of existing tests and the current knowledge base of experimental evidence, particularly as it relates to children with special needs (Das et al., 1994). Authors and publishers of tests are quick to point out that the tests do not measure all components of one's cognitive development but rather a sample of abilities in several key areas. The key areas are most often representative of the author's beliefs about intelligence, given the current state of research in the area. Some tests are designed to cover areas that other tests fail to touch. For example, the WISC-IV has a strong fine-motor component, while the Binet does not. Furthermore, the Stanford-Binet V has subtests that contribute to a definable memory factor—the WISC-IV introduced a working memory index (WMI) for the first time in this edition. Though very different tasks are used in the respective tests, all fit into a broader framework for understanding the cognitive functioning of people with and without disabilities.

Test Selection and General Usage.

Examiners also vary with respect to their ability to select and use the best possible instrument for a given person. The basic problem is that, although the word *intelligence* is used to refer to the totality of a person's ability and potential, no finite samples of behavior can possibly demonstrate everything that is worth knowing about that person's capabilities. A major premise of most, if not all, major intelligence instruments is that a score on an IQ test is not synonymous with intelligence. Other nonintellective factors also play a crucial role in both test performance and daily living (Wechsler, 1991b).

One common purpose of today's tests, similar to those of Binet's time, is to predict likelihood for success in traditional academic settings. Although never perfect, the tests are indeed able to signal those for whom academic difficulties may be expected. Despite the defensible rationale for the original and continued development of these instruments, many people treat the tests themselves as if they were the offending party. One must wonder whether such frustration and anger are really directed toward the tests, toward what the tests predict (academic outcomes), or toward the process of implementing educational interventions. Rather than kill the messenger, why not do as Kaufman (1994) has recommended in regard to the WISC-III and *kill the prediction!* "The fact that most children who score very poorly on the WISC-III will also do poorly in school should not be accepted as a statement of destiny" (p. 7). Accurate and in-depth assessment followed by verifiable educational interventions can do much to change a child's likelihood for success in a given academic program.

Regulation of Access.   Another major criticism of IQ tests is that they regulate access to educational opportunities and relegate certain students from minority backgrounds to special education programs as a result of misidentification and therefore overidentification. The response is that school personnel use these tests to help understand why a student is encountering difficulty in traditional academic areas. Whether a child possesses special gifts or special limitations such as mental retardation, each child is entitled to an environment where full academic growth can be realized. IQ tests are not used to change the academic programs of students who are performing well in the classroom; rather, the tests are used by professionals only after the student, parents, teachers, or other service providers have reason to believe that the child or youth is not successful under normal classroom conditions. When used appropriately and within the context of a multidisciplinary team as mandated by the 2004 reauthorization of the Individuals with Disabilities Education Act (IDEA), IQ tests serve only to confirm the presence and nature of learning difficulties observed by others. Simply put, IQ tests are intended to reduce—not increase—the number of children qualifying for special education. When the opposite occurs, discovery should focus on the process being implemented.

Stability of IQ over Time.   The concept of intelligence was introduced at a time when the prevailing belief was that intelligence was hereditary and therefore a constant trait. Laypersons and professionals alike generally think of intelligence as a basic, enduring attribute of an individual. But if intelligence is a constant, why do IQ scores fluctuate? Anastasi and Urbina (1997) point out that, for people in general, test performance over the school years and into college is quite stable. However, "studies of individuals . . . may reveal large upward or downward shifts in test scores" (p. 326). When a child receives an IQ score of 95 at age 6, an IQ score of 89 at age 13, and an IQ score of 105 at age 16, does this mean that the child had average intelligence at first but lost intelligence between ages 6 and 13 and became brighter again by 16? Obviously not. The most likely explanation is that the student was influenced by emotional, motivational, or experiential factors.

Test Equivalence.   Different instruments contain different components (i.e., subtests and content) and often are built on slightly different constructs. As a result, different scores are possible. A related issue involves the issue of the norming sample. Different tests, and for that matter, different editions of the same test, will produce different results due to the fact that the sample on which the test was normed is different. Flynn (1998) found that scores likely will be lower when a new edition of a test is published. This phenomenon, commonly referred to as the "Flynn effect," is thought to be due to an increase in class IQ gains and the increased difficulty of the tests themselves. Kanaya, Scullin, and Ceci (2003) recently found that students in the borderline and "mild" range of mental retardation lost an average of 5.6 IQ points when retested on a renormed test.

Use of Strict Cutoff Scores.   Some definitional orientations such as the definition developed by the American Psychological Association use a strict cutoff score of 70 to determine subaverage intellectual functioning. Other definitional sources like AAMR and DSM-IV-TR are more flexible in this area. Table 3.4 includes the language of these three definitions in terms of cutoff scores. The definitions that are more flexible are based on the argument that *all* measures of intelligence have error and therefore an exact score is impossible to determine. Luckasson and colleagues (2002) state that "there can be little rationale for anything other than a relativistic standard for significantly subaverage intellectual functioning" (p. 58).

TABLE 3.4
General Subaverage Intellectual Functioning Criterion Across Three Definitional Perspectives

Definitional Perspective	Meaningful IQ Score Cutoff	Wording from Definitional Source
AAMR (2002)	"approximately" 70	"The criterion for diagnosis is *approximately* 2 standard deviations below the mean." (p. 14)
DSM-IV-TR (2000)	"about" 70	"Significantly subaverage intellectual functioning is defined as an IQ of *about* 70 or below (approximately 2 standard deviations below the mean)." (p. 41)
APA (1996)	"is" 70	"The criterion of significance *is* an IQ or comparable normed score that is 2 or more standard deviations below the population mean for the measure." (p. 13)

ASSESSMENT OF ADAPTIVE BEHAVIOR

The notion of examining what a person does in typical situations is often much more helpful than what a person can do or might do under the best of circumstances. Recently, increased attention has been directed toward the adaptive skills of persons with mental retardation. The acquisition of adaptive skills for most people is considered to be a continuous and naturally occurring set of events; for persons with mental retardation, however, the process is anything but continuous and very often plagued with difficulty.

Conceptual Bases

This section of the chapter will discuss the definitional perspectives of adaptive behavior, the evolution of the concept, and the relationship of adaptive behavior to intelligence.

Definitional Perspectives.   The term **adaptive behavior** represents a relatively new name for an old concept (Reschly, 1985). Prior to the Middle Ages, references to one's adaptive skills were informal, and care was provided based on behavioral deviance and physical deformity (Horn & Fuchs, 1987). In light of the long-standing recognition of the relationship between adaptive behavior and mental retardation,

Observig children's social and problem-solving skills is an important part of assessing adaptive behavior.

FIGURE 3.2

Clusters and Specific Adaptive
Behavior Areas

Source: From "Adaptive Behavior and
Mental Retardation," by
R. H. Bruininks, M. L. Thurlow, &
C. J. Gilman, 1987, *Journal of Special
Education, 21*(1), p. 74. Copyright
1987 by PRO-ED. Reprinted by
permission.

Self-help, personal appearance
  Feeding, eating, drinking
  Dressing
  Toileting
  Grooming, hygiene

Physical development
  Gross motor skills
  Fine motor skills

Communication
  Receptive language
  Expressive language

Personal, social skills
  Play skills
  Interaction skills
  Group participation
  Social amenities
  Sexual behavior
  Self-direction, responsibility
  Leisure activities
  Expression of emotions

Cognitive functioning
  Pre-academics (e.g., colors)
  Reading
  Writing
  Numeric functions
  Time
  Money
  Measurement

Health care, personal welfare
  Treatment of injuries, health problems
  Prevention of health problems
  Personal safety
  Child care practices

Consumer skills
  Money handling
  Purchasing
  Banking
  Budgeting

Domestic skills
  Household cleaning
  Property maintenance, repair
  Clothing care
  Kitchen skills
  Household safety

Community orientation
  Travel skills
  Utilization of community resources
  Telephone usage
  Community safety

Vocational skills
  Work habits and attitudes
  Job search skills
  Work performance
  Social vocational behavior
  Work safety

assessment of adaptive functioning is much more focused and quantifiable than ever before. Much progress has been made in the name of adaptive behavior in the 50-plus years since Doll's (1947) first *Social Maturity Scale* and the inclusion of the term *adaptive behavior* in the 1961 AAMR definition—but more work remains.

Although experts in the field appear to have reached some degree of agreement on the definition of adaptive behavior, and perhaps even on the skills that are believed to comprise it, the actual components of effective adaptive functioning remain much more puzzling. For example, in a content analysis of adaptive behavior measures, Bruininks, Thurlow, and Gilman (1987) found 10 different categories of behaviors composed of 45 different skills (see Figure 3.2). Complicating the measurement process are the realizations that adaptive behavior is a dynamic, ever-changing construct and that it is influenced by such factors as cultural norms, age-related expectations, and a combination of anticipated and idiosyncratic behaviors

(Horn & Fuchs, 1987). Whether one is interested in the construct of adaptive behavior or the operationally defined skills that undergird it, attention to tasks that are developmentally appropriate and contextually relevant are important considerations for people whose quests toward personal independence and social responsibility are not to be taken for granted.

Grossman (1983) defined adaptive behavior as the "degree with which individuals meet the standards of personal independence and social responsibility expected for age and cultural group" (p. 1). The American Association on Mental Retardation emphasized *definable skill areas* rather than the more abstract term of *adaptive behavior* in their 1992 definition. The most recent AAMR 2002 manual defines adaptive behavior as "the collection of conceptual, social, and practical skills that have been learned by people in order to function in their everyday lives." This definition of adaptive behavior has borrowed significantly from Greenspan's tripartite model of intelligence.

Though some people have criticized AAMR's earlier definitions of adaptive behavior as too elusive and ill defined (e.g., Zigler, Balla, & Hodapp, 1984), Kamphaus (1987) has defended the earlier definition as homogenizing, suggesting that it has provided the field with a focus and sense of direction that investigators in other areas have yet to obtain.

Whereas classification of mental retardation requires both an intellective (IQ) and nonintellective (adaptive) component, the formal emphasis on adaptive skills has encouraged a more balanced approach to diagnosis and service delivery where mental retardation is a concern. It is precisely because members of the profession have been willing to pursue a deeper understanding of adaptive behavior that service delivery to persons with mental retardation has vastly improved in recent years. The benefits of an agreed-on definition of adaptive behavior are only now leading to some consensus on its theoretical structure. Theories of adaptation are indeed longstanding but have, for the most part, remained outside the interest of most persons in the field of mental retardation—until recently. Following is a brief discussion of theories of adaptation from biological, psychological, and sociological points of view.

Evolution of the Concept.   Adaptation has historically been considered a biological phenomenon. The capacity of an organism to adjust to changes in the environment depends largely on two types of responses that (1) allow it to remain at equilibrium with itself (homeostasis) and (2) to function over a normal range of biologically acceptable environments (homeokinesis) (Prosser, 1986). While some such changes occur immediately (e.g., reaction to anxiety and fear, or fever in response to an infection), other changes may take days, weeks, months, or even years to occur (e.g., muscle development in response to maturation). Still others (e.g., a species' collective resistance to a disease or ability to survive in extreme conditions) may take many generations to evolve. Brandon (1990) has defined an organism's adaptedness in terms of biological properties and its capacity to survive in its own environment.

Individuals, alone or in groups, have their own beliefs, attitudes, and desires. Whereas biologists are interested in the adaptive mechanisms of biological systems, psychologists and educators are interested in the richness of the behaviors and their dependence on various environmental conditions (Staddon, 1983). In some areas of functioning, however, both biologists and psychologists have much to say about the responsiveness of people to certain environmental conditions—and responsivity to stress is one such example. According to Hobfall (1998), physiological psychologists have found a high degree of similarity among peoples' responses to single stressors but a high degree of variability among people's tendencies to respond to stressors in general. That is, people tend to have behavioral repertoires that they consider to be successful, specific, and adaptive when confronting stressful or unusual circumstances. For example, Piaget's (1952) early work in organization and adaptation of new information is a key component in our present-day understanding of cognitive development in children. For a child to interpret and adjust to the demands of the external world, new experiences must be understood and modified in the context of preexisting information. Although Piaget limited his work to children, the same principle can be extended across the life span to many different situations and areas of adjustment.

Many adaptive behaviors are less a function of the person than of the organization or social unit to which the person belongs. For example, Lumsden and Wilson (1985) reported that groups of people, like other animals, generate behavioral patterns that fit the social group to the environment. Even characteristics such as loyalty, morality, and altruism exist in groups of people and other animals because of their survival value to the group. A more obvious example of social adaptation may be found in social systems theory, a sociologically based theory often used to explain the structure and function of organized groups (Gordon, 1991). According to social systems theory, groups that survive over time are those whose development of organizational structures allows them to keep their place of importance in the broader social milieu. Status, roles, norms, and behaviors are as important for the social group as they are for the individuals within the group. Just as "children are born into a world of pre-existing, relatively stable social structures," so are social groups, dictating that they, too, must be "socialized to meet the expectations of the [broader] system" (Mercer, 1978, p. 71).

Adaptive behavior as a valued construct is now receiving the attention that other constructs in psychology and education have known for years. It may be years before the theoretical work of today pays dividends at the service delivery level. Necessarily, much of the research that has been conducted has emphasized the characteristics of the instruments instead of exclusively furthering the development of the construct itself. Among the research that is conceptually based is a growing consensus that adaptive behavior is a multidimensional construct rather than a unidimensional one, with as many as four to six stable factors (e.g., Thompson, McGrew & Bruininks, 1999; Widaman, Reise, & Clatfelter, 1994; Widaman, Stacy, & Borthwick-Duffy, 1993). There is also some evidence that the factor structures themselves may be hierarchical, with one or perhaps two broad factors (i.e., adaptive, maladaptive) having several underlying dimensions (Widaman & McGrew, 1996).

An example of a model that illustrates the hierarchical nature of adaptive behavior rather nicely is Greenspan's (Greenspan & Driscoll, 1997) model of personal competence (see Figure 3.1). According to Greenspan, "competent individuals can be defined both in terms of the qualities they bring to various goals and challenges, as well as by their relative degree of success in meeting those goals and challenges" (p. 131). In his model, and consistent with the published literature, are four broad domains of competence: physical competence, affective competence, everyday competence, and academic competence. Greenspan posits a number of lower-order factors that are contained in each of the aforementioned domains, factors that all have relevance for persons with mental retardation as well as for persons of all ability levels.

 To consider the educational implications of adaptive behavior assessment, go to the Companion Website at www.prenhall.com/ beirne-smith and select Chapter 3, Video Case Studies.

Adaptive behaviors, specifically, are the behavioral skills that are demonstrated in response to environmental demands (Widaman & McGrew, 1996). In 1992, AAMR shifted toward a more functional definition of mental retardation; references to the more vague term of adaptive behavior were replaced by 10 very specific adaptive skill areas: "communication, self-care, home living, social skills, community use, self-direction, health and safety, functional academic, leisure, and work" (AAMR, 1992, p. 1). The change to the more easily definable adaptive skills areas "is not intended as a refutation of the term adaptive behavior" (Luckasson et al., 1992, p. 38) but as a response to the limitations of the measurement process itself. It was believed that by emphasizing the 10 skill areas, the potential for agreement on identification and remediation of abilities is enhanced. As discussed earlier in the chapter, this did not occur; rather, a splintering of professionals took place. It is unlikely that the 2002 AAMR definition will correct the division that occurred in the mid-1990s.

Relationship to Intelligence.   Before intelligence tests were developed, mental retardation was characterized with respect to limitations in social and adaptive functioning (Nihira, 1999). Recent definitions of mental retardation continue to emphasize an individual's ability to function adequately within the individual's principal environment. According to Leland (1978), the ability to cope with the more social demands of one's environment is "the reversible aspect of mental retardation, and it reflects primarily those behaviors which are most likely to be modified through appropriate treatment or training methods" (p. 28).

Adaptive behavior played an increasingly important role in the diagnosis of mental retardation up through the early 1970s, but it wasn't until the 1973 AAMR definition that adaptive behavior joined intelligence as a prominent and complementary component in the diagnosis and classification of mental retardation (see Grossman, 1973). Although the two constructs share much in common and have been found to be moderately correlated (Harrison & Boney, 2002), they also stand apart in several substantive ways. First, examiners using measures of adaptive behavior attempt to obtain information about a person's usual actions, whereas intelligence tests are designed to obtain information about maximal performance. Second, adaptive behavior measures tap a number of different everyday living areas, whereas intelligence tests typically focus on higher order reasoning abilities. Third, intelligence tests are administered under very controlled conditions, while adaptive behavior information is typically obtained through semi-structured interviews with third-party respondents (people who know the person well).

Because of the importance of both adaptive behavior and intelligence, and the notion on the part of many that one may serve as a stand-in for the other, researchers have investigated the relationship between the two constructs. In a comprehensive review of 42 studies documenting the relationship between measures of intelligence and adaptive behavior, Harrison (1987) found a moderate relationship between the two constructs. Others, using more sophisticated statistical techniques, have also found that the two constructs represent separate but related entities (i.e., Ittenbach,

Spiegel, McGrew, & Bruininks, 1992; Keith, Fehrman, Harrison, & Pottebaum, 1987; McGrew, Bruininks, & Johnson, 1996).

Thus, research over the past 30 years seems to be confirming what clinicians have suspected for a long time: that adaptive behavior and intelligence represent distinct but related and complementary constructs. To many clinicians, unfortunately, the importance of the relationship between the two constructs seems to rest on the sometimes useful distinction of optimal (for intelligence) versus daily problem solving (for adaptive behavior). Schalock (1999) suggests that for service delivery to reach its full potential, practitioners and researchers should consider merging the two constructs within one overarching framework. He offers an overall model of competence with the areas of practical skills, conceptual skills, and social skills as the subdomains of interest. Although his model is similar in many ways to Greenspan's model of personal competence (Greenspan & Driscoll, 1997) described earlier, his premise of merging the two components reinforces Greenspan's point that what service providers are interested in and what the field still needs is a systematic means of formally bringing the two components together in a way that fully addresses the needs of persons with mental retardation. What psychologists want is a model that is conceptually sound and allows for psychometrically valid measurement.

A clear case of the classification and treatment dilemma occurs when children or youth are seen in one setting as mentally retarded (e.g., at school) but appear to function normally in another setting (e.g., with family and friends outside of school). Such is the problem of the well-known "6-hour retarded child" (President's Committee on Mental Retardation, 1970) described in chapter 2. In late adolescence and adulthood, people are looked upon as mentally retarded when they repeatedly prove incompetent in handling social and vocational responsibilities. Yet social and vocational problems need not grow directly out of ineptitude; it is very common to find adults who were identified as mentally retarded during their school years and who later function quite well in their postschool environments.

Key Influences

The concept of adaptive behavior has been shaped by a number of sociopolitical forces over the years. However, one person, and his colleagues, and one organization have had a dramatic impact on the notion of adaptive behavior.

Edgar Doll.   The Vineland Social Maturity Scale was developed in 1935 by Edgar A. Doll at the Vineland Training School in Vineland, New Jersey. The author's original purpose in constructing the scale was to provide a means of measuring social competence—or "social maturity"—to help in the diagnosis of mental deficiency. Recognizing the need for an "adaptive behavior" component in the classification of persons as mentally subnormal, Doll sought to devise a measure "distinguishing between mental retardation with social incompetence (feeblemindedness) and mental retardation without social incompetence (which is often confused with feeblemindedness)" (Doll, 1965, p. 2). He defined mental deficiency as the demonstration of intellectual inadequacy, social inadequacy, and arrested mental development.

American Association on Mental Retardation. From the early work of Edouard Seguin, the AAMR's first president, to the contributions of today's leaders, the American Association on Mental Retardation (AAMR) has served as the scientific leader in the field of mental retardation. As noted in chapter 1, Seguin's work on the physiology of mental retardation is well known. Less well known are the contributions of Goddard (1907), who challenged Seguin's early work, saying that while individuals who are mentally retarded were limited cognitively, they could still function quite well with adequate preparation and support. The problem, Goddard said, was with the instruction, not with the person; the pace of instruction needed to be slower and conducted with more patience.

Little more than a decade later, the organization's members felt a pressing need to define, diagnose, delineate, and otherwise specify the nature of the "defective delinquent," a term coined by Doll to represent individuals having trouble adapting to society. Meyers, Nihira, and Zetlin (1979) cite Doll's (1947) work as the formal beginning of adaptive behavior assessment. Believing that individual differences occurred in social competence just as in intelligence, Doll (1953) assumed that these differences represented a unitary trait, were developmental in nature, and were essential for an accurate diagnosis of mental retardation.

In 1965, the AAMR initiated a study of the broad dimensions of adaptive behavior. The study produced two adaptive behavior scales, one designed for children 3 to 12 years of age, and the other for adolescents and adults. The two scales were then combined into one; a second formal scale was then modified and standardized for use in the schools. They were revised in the early 1990s and now comprise the family of AAMR Adaptive Behavior Scales, one for residential and community settings and one for school settings.

Major Instruments

Contributions to the development of adaptive behavior assessment are not limited to the AAMR and Edgar Doll. However, the instrument that evolved from Doll's first scale and the instruments that emerged from the work of the AAMR are discussed in some depth below. Several other instruments that have helped influence the means by which adaptive behavior is measured and explained are also noteworthy. All of the major adaptive behavior instruments are listed and described in Table 3.5.

Vineland Adaptive Behavior Scales: Second Edition. The Vineland scales have been revised recently, and are now referred to as the Vineland-II (Sparrow, Cicchetti, & Balla, 2005). The new edition of the scale consists of three versions similar in name to the versions in the previous edition: interview edition, survey form; interview edition, expanded form; and teacher rating form. An additional form, titled "Survey Interview Parent/Caregiver Form" has been added to the instrument. The purpose of each of the forms is indicated in its title. The first two scales are administered to individuals who know the person being assessed, usually parents or caregivers. Teachers or other school-based personnel typically complete the teacher rating version—formerly the "Classroom Edition" in the previous edition of the

TABLE 3.5

Adaptive Behavior Measures

Instrument	Publication Date	Age Range	Adaptive Skill Domains/Subtests	Features

Vineland-II Adaptive Behavior Scales, 2nd edition (Sparrow, Cicchetti, & Balla, 2005)	2005	Birth to 90 yrs (Survey Interview, Parent/ Caregiver Rating, Expanded Interview forms)
		
		 3 yrs to 21 yrs 11 mos (Teacher Rating form)
			• Communication
			 • Daily Living
			 • Socialization
			 • Motor
			 • Maladaptive Behaviors
				• Four forms:
				   • Survey Interview
				   • Parent/Caregiver Rating
				   • Expanded Interview
				   • Teacher Rating
				 • Scoring Software

Adaptive Behavior Assessment System, 2nd edition (ABAS-II) (Harrison & Oakland, 2003)	2003	Birth to 89 yrs	• Communication
			 • Community Use
			 • Functional Academics
			 • Home/School Living
			 • Health and Safety
			 • Leisure
			 • Self-Care
			 • Self-Direction
			 • Social
			 • Work
				• Five forms:
				   • Parent (birth–5)
				   • Parent (5–21)
				   • Teacher/Day Care (2–5)
				   • Teacher (5–21)
				   • Adult (16–89)
				 • Scoring Software

AAMR Adaptive Behavior Scale-School, 2nd edition (ABS-S:2) (Lambert, Nihira, & Leland, 1993a)	1993	3 yrs to 21 yrs	**Part 1: Adaptive**
			 • Independent Functioning
			 • Physical Development
			 • Economic Activity
			 • Language Development
			 • Numbers and Time
			 • Prevocational/ Vocational Activity
			 • Self-Direction
			 • Responsibility
			 • Socialization
			
			 Part 2: Maladaptive
			 • Social Behavior
			 • Conformity
			 • Trustworthiness
			 • Stereotyped and Hyperactive Behavior
			 • Self-Abusive Behavior
			 • Social Engagement
			 • Disturbing Interpersonal Behavior
				• One form, two parts:
				   • Part 1: Adaptive Behavior Skills
				   • Part 2: Maladaptive Behaviors
				 • Factor scores:
				   • Personal Self-Sufficiency
				   • Personal-Social Responsibility
				   • Community Self-Sufficiency
				   • Social Adjustment
				   • Personal Adjustment

Instrument	Publication Date	Age Range	Adaptive Skill Domains/Subtests	Features
AAMR Adaptive Behavior Scale-Residential and Community, 2nd edition (ABS-RC: 2) (Nihira, Leland, & Lambert, 1993a)	1993	18 yrs to 60+	[see ABS-S:2]–plus Part 1: Adaptive • Domestic activity Part 2: Maladaptive • Sexual behavior	[see ABS-S:2]
Adaptive Behavior Evaluation Scale, Revised (McCarney, 1995)	1995	5 yrs to 18 yrs	• Communication Skills • Self-Care • Home Living • Social • Community Use • Self-Direction • Health & Safety • Functional Academics • Leisure • Work	• Two forms: • School Version Rating • Home Version Rating
Scales of Independent Behavior, Revised (SIB-R) (Bruininks, Woodcock, Weatherman, & Hill, 1996)	1996	Infancy to 80+	• Motor • Gross Motor Skills • Fine Motor Skills • Social Interaction and Communication • Social Interaction • Language Comprehension • Language Expression • Personal Living • Eating and Meal Preparation • Toileting • Dressing • Personal Self-Care • Domestic Skills • Community Living • Time and Punctuality • Money and Value • Work Skills • Home and Community Orientation	• Four cluster areas, 14 subscales • Three forms: • Full-Scale • Short • Early Development • Maladaptive behavior assessed by looking at areas of problem behavior • Short form of the scale is called *Inventory for Client and Agency Planning (ICAP)*—used in adult settings

Vineland. The new form for parents and caregivers is designed to obtain information on adaptive skills that must come from a home setting. These scales assess five domains of adaptive behavior: communication, daily living skills, socialization, motor skills, and maladaptive behavior (assessment of the last domain is optional).

Administration and scoring of the scales follow a structure in which items are organized developmentally according to domain. Raw scores are converted to Domain and Adaptive Behavior Composite standard scores ($M = 100$, $SD = 15$), percentile ranks, adaptive levels, age equivalents, and estimated adaptive level; Subdomain-scaled scores ($M = 10$, $SD = 3$) are also provided. An indication of problems in maladaptive behavior are indicated by maladaptive levels based on the optional Maladaptive Behavior Index.

Some of the other features of the Vineland-II include:

- New norms
- Expanded age range: Survey Interview, Expanded Interview, Parent/Caregiver Form—birth to age 90, Teacher Rating Form—ages 3 to 21-11
- Items have been updated to reflect more contemporary skill demands
- Item are organized by subdomain. A listing of the Vineland-II domains/index and subdomains is provided in Table 3.6
- Spanish versions of all forms are available

The Vineland continues to be a popular measure of social competency, and many now place it among the best measures of adaptive behavior.

AAMR Adaptive Behavior Scale—School, 2nd Edition. The AAMR Adaptive Behavior Scale—School, 2nd Edition (ABS-S:2) (Lambert, Nihira, & Leland, 1993a), is a norm-referenced, individually administered, comprehensive measure of adaptive and maladaptive behavior intended for use with school-age children. The instrument consists of two parts. Part 1 is divided into nine behavior domains impor-

TABLE 3.6
Organization of the Vineland-II

Domains and Index	Subdomains
Communication	• Reception • Expressive • Written
Daily Living Skills	• Personal • Domestic • Community
Socialization	• Interpersonal Relationships • Play and Leisure Time • Coping Skills
Motor Skills	• Fine • Gross
Maladaptive Behavior Index	• Internalizing • Externalizing • Other

tant for personal responsibility and independent living (independent functioning, physical development, economic activity, language development, numbers and time, prevocational/vocational activity, self-direction, responsibility, and socialization). Part 2 assesses social adaptation and maladaptive behavior and consists of seven domains (social behavior, conformity, trustworthiness, stereotyped and hyperactive behavior, self-abusive behavior, social engagement, and disturbing interpersonal behavior).

It should be noted that the ABS-S:2 and its companion scale, the ABS-RC:2 described below, are completely independent of one another and have their own unique features. However, both instruments offer a standardized interview format. The standardization sample appears to be relatively strong, with more than 1,000 children with and without disabilities from 31 states serving as the normative base. Percentiles, standard scores, and age equivalents are available to the examiner. Five factor scores are also available. Internal consistency estimates for all scores reportedly exceed .80 (Lambert, Nihira, & Leland, 1993b). Software designed to help with scoring and report writing is available from the publisher at an additional cost. Like the Vineland, the ABS is undergoing a revision and a new version will be available in the future.

AAMR Adaptive Behavior Scale—Residential and Community, 2nd Edition. The AAMR Adaptive Behavior Scale—Residential and Community, 2nd Edition (ABS-RC:2) (Nihira, Leland, & Lambert, 1993a), represents the AAMR's latest revision of a project begun in 1965 to study the broad dimensions of adaptive behavior. The ABS-RC:2 is a norm-referenced, individually administered, comprehensive measure of adaptive and maladaptive behavior intended for use with persons living in residential and community settings. The authors of the ABS-RC:2 report that the scale has a fourfold purpose: to determine strengths and weaknesses in a person's adaptive skills, to identify persons whose adaptive behavior is substantially and significantly different from those of same-age peers, to gauge the progress of persons receiving intervention services, and to serve as a valid measure of adaptive behavior in research studies (Nihira, Leland, & Lambert, 1993b).

The ABS-RC:2 consists of two principal sections: Personal Independence (Part 1) and Social Adaptation (Part 2). Information is obtained through a standardized interview format conducted by an examiner trained in psychodiagnostic methods. Item types vary; some take a Likert-type format with scores ranging from behavior not present (0) to behavior present in highest form (3), as, for example, when the examiner wishes to know how well a person is able to function when visiting a restaurant. For other items, the examiner may wish to know only whether a particular behavior is present. Examples of this type of behavior are taking food off others' plates, eating too fast or too slow, or swallowing food without chewing. In each of these cases, the response would be scored as either yes (1) or no (0).

Five types of profile scores are available through the ABS-RC:2: raw scores, percentiles, domain standard scores, factor quotients, and age equivalents. The ABS-RC:2 was standardized on 4,103 persons from 46 states and is reported in the manual to be representative of all persons with mental retardation nationwide using major demographic variables (Nihira, Leland, & Lambert, 1993b). Software is available from the publisher to help with scoring and report writing.

Best and Recommended Practices

Best practice in the assessment of adaptive behaviors requires several key consider-ations. Harrison and Boney (2002), while writing to a school psychologist audience, provide guidelines for effective practice:

- The examiner should incorporate adaptive behavior assessment into a com-prehensive data-based decision-making framework of providing services to children. Failure to link the assessment to the probable forms of interven-tion, at the outset, is to deny the very reason for which the assessment was conducted.
- The examiner should carefully select the scale(s) to be used based on the in-dividual child's needs for assessment and the specific information provided by the scales.
- The examiner should understand a scales limitation and take into account these limitations.
- The examiner should use multiple methods of adaptive behavior assessment, given the limitations of norm-referenced rating scales. This information from these sources should be integrated in a organized and logical manner. The use of both norm-referenced and non-norm-referenced measures (e.g., clinical in-terviews, observations, self-report techniques) is warranted, when possible.
- The examiner should obtain information from both parents and teachers when assessing the adaptive behavior of a child. It is important to obtain in-formation about adaptive skill functioning in both school and nonschool (e.g., home, work) settings. To use one at the exclusion of the other overlooks an important piece of information relative to everyday living skills.
- The examiner must always use a balanced consideration of adaptive behav-ior and intellectual assessment results when making decisions about a men-tal retardation classification.
- The examiner needs to recognize that adaptive behavior assessment has many important uses for students other than those with mental retardation. (pp. 1175–1176)

Issues Associated with the Measurement of Adaptive Behavior

Adaptive behavior has emerged as an important index in the identification of men-tal retardation and in programmatic aspects associated with intervention. However, its acceptance is not universal, and its measurement is still under some debate. Al-though most professionals and laypersons alike believe that there is a definite non-intellectual component to mental retardation, disagreement remains as to its role and function in the assessment-to-service sequence. An examination of the issues follows.

Realities of Existing Instrumentation.   First, measuring adaptive behavior seems to be much more difficult than simply defining it—and defining it certainly has not been easy. The adaptive behavior tests currently on the market all seem to measure different tasks in different ways. For example, some tests cover tasks considered to be important at home, others at school, and still others in residential facilities. Furthermore, some instruments assess social skills, others assess social intelligence, and still others assess social development. Some measures emphasize domestic skills, whereas others emphasize self-help skills. All represent very important but yet very different types of adaptive capabilities. It is no surprise, then, that researchers and clinicians alike are still struggling to find the true underlying dimensions of the construct known as adaptive behavior in commercially available instruments.

Role of Intelligence. A second major criticism pertains to the school-age population and the degree to which intellectual factors play a part in the determination of adaptive skills. Some researchers (e.g., Mercer, 1978) see intelligence as an unnecessary part of adaptive functioning, but others (e.g., Reschly, 1985) regard intellectual functioning as a crucial component of adaptive functioning. Problem-solving skills carry over from one environment to the next whether in school, home, play, or otherwise. As evidence continues to mount with respect to subtle but important distinctions between intelligence and adaptive behavior, it is imperative that new frameworks be developed that allow for the integration of both intelligence and adaptive behavior within one overarching framework. Greenspan's (Greenspan & Driscoll, 1997) model of personal competence (see Figure 3.1) offers such a framework by dividing personal competence into four key areas across which traditional measures of intelligence and adaptive behavior all play important roles.

Cultural Considerations. Another criticism of adaptive behavior scales pertains to their use in diverse cultures. Some contend that because they are used with intelligence tests, they are plagued by many of the limitations of intelligence tests from years past. Not so. That is not to say that adaptive behavior measures are perfect when it comes to culture fairness—they certainly are not. Whether one is actually interested in skills within a single culture or across many cultures, adaptive behavior is, by definition, culture bound. To know what is appropriate for a given age and reference group depends very much on the person's ability to decode and identify subtle and not-so-subtle cultural cues. The issue at hand, then, becomes one of validity and appropriateness rather than simply guilt by (historical) association. In short, what the field needs, according to Craig and Tassé (1999), are culturally competent assessment practices. That means good tests, with good norms, and good evaluators.

Interview Methodology. Although the practice of interviewing credible and knowledgeable informants is the typical way to obtain information about adaptive functioning on someone with whom the examiner is not familiar, this methodology is fraught with potential problems. Different people see different levels of competence in the same individual. Informants will sometimes guess when asked certain questions—this is particularly a problem with teachers when asked about out-of-school behaviors. Problems arise when the informant does not speak the language of the interviewer and a translator is used. Making sure that the original question is conveyed properly and understood clearly by the informant is problematic.

Role of Maladaptive Behavior.   Much confusion has existed in relation to these two constructs (McGrew & Bruininks, 1990). *Maladaptive behavior* refers to behaviors such as destruction of property, deviant sexual behavior, lying, stealing, physical aggression, and various psychotic behaviors. Whether the measure of maladaptive behavior should be part of the adaptive behavior regimen is at issue. According to Luckasson et al. (2002), "problem behavior that is 'maladaptive' is not a characteristic or dimension of adaptive behavior . . . although it often influences the acquisition and performance of adaptive behavior" (p. 75).

OTHER TYPES OF ASSESSMENT

Assessment of persons with mental retardation includes more than eligibility determination, which has been the thrust of most of this chapter. Three other areas are discussed in this section: educational assessment, community-related assessment, and assessment as it relates to legal proceedings.

Educational Applications

After a student is determined to qualify for services under IDEA via the category of mental retardation, the elements of how to provide an appropriate education are identified and ultimately implemented. Various mandates of IDEA require certain types of assessment. Three of these are addressed in the following discussion.

Progress Monitoring.   It is essential that how well a student is doing be evaluated on a regular basis for educational decision-making purposes. The use of frequent, data-based approaches to measure student learning must be part of a student's ongoing program. IDEA requires that measurable goals be written for those areas that interfere with a student's ability to access the general education curriculum. IDEA also requires that progress reports be given to the student's parents as frequently as for students who are not receiving special education services.

Transition Planning.   IDEA mandates that transition services be provided to students beginning at age 16. To effectively plan for a student's future, it is essential that a comprehensive transition needs assessment be undertaken. This process must be adjusted to the ability level of the student, but it should be based on the student's preferences and interests. One component of transition assessment should be the determination of occupational interests and aptitudes. This topic will be covered in detail in chapter 11.

High-Stakes Testing.   All students should participate in the district and state-level testing that is now part of the standards-based education movement, when appropriate. Many students with mental retardation will take part in the ongoing examinations that occur every year. Most of these students should qualify for some type of accommodation in the administration of the exam. Some of the students, particularly those with more significant disabilities, will be exempt from taking these exams. They, however, will have to take an alternative assessment.

Adult and Community Applications

Assessment in the adult sector can take many forms, from the informal assessments that are part of ongoing life skills instruction being provided in a living situation to more formal assessment used for qualifying for Social Security or for determining progress in various training programs.

One of the most intriguing instruments developed in recent years for use with adults is the *Supports Intensity Scale* (SIS). The intent of this scale is to identify needed supports for adults with mental retardation so that they can pursue a meaningful life. Specifically, the SIS measures what practical supports are required for a person to be proficient in 57 key life activities in seven core areas of competence (home living, community living, lifelong learning, employment, health and safety, social interaction, and protection and advocacy. The scale is not an adaptive behavior measure, although its core areas relate closely to adaptive behavior domains. The SIS differs in that it focuses on identifying "the extraordinary support that a person needs in order to participate in the activities of daily life" (Thompson et al., 2004, p. 11).

Legal Proceedings

Assessment plays a key role in a number of legal situations. For instance, it is not uncommon that an individual with mental retardation who encounters the legal system will be referred for psychological evaluation to determine his or her competence and/or capacity.

Capacity/Diminished Capacity.   *Capacity* refers to an individual's ability to knowingly commit a crime and is related to age (e.g., a child under the age of 8 is presumed by law in many states not to have the mental capacity to commit a crime). *Diminished capacity* refers to a person's "ability to establish either criminal intent or the motivation to engage in criminal behavior and to understand it as such" (LaDue & Dunne, 1997). A finding of diminished capacity requires the presence of a mental disorder.

Competence.   **Competence** refers to a person's competence to stand trial. It involves the person's ability to understand the charges brought against him/her, to understand the legal process, and to be able to assist his or her attorney in the defense. A competency evaluation might involve a number of different measures—one of which is likely to be an intelligence test. Keyes and Edwards (1996) recommend that a competence assessment for a person with mental retardation include the following: intellectual testing; perceptual-motor examination; achievement test (determination of literacy); adaptive behavior/skills; socioemotional scale; and an instrument specifically designed for the assessment of competence, such as the *Competence*

Read about several states' approaches to alternate assessment by visiting the Companion Website at www.prenhall.com/ beirne-smith and selecting Chapter 3, Read and Respond.

Assessment for Standing Trial for Defendants with Mental Retardation (CAST-MR; Everington & Luckasson, 1992). The CAST-MR includes separate sections on Basic Legal Concepts, Skills to Assist Defense, and Understanding Case Events.

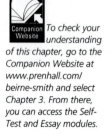

To check your understanding of this chapter, go to the Companion Website at www.prenhall.com/ beirne-smith and select Chapter 3. From there, you can access the Self-Test and Essay modules.

Dissimulation.   In some cases, especially death penalty cases where a claim of mental retardation is being made, assessment will focus on the determination of mental retardation. However, an argument made by the prosecution in some cases involves the issue of a person trying to feign mental retardation by intentionally trying to score low on various test and assessments that might be administered. Trying to give such a false appearance of mental retardation is known as **dissimulation** or malingering. Instruments such as the *Validity Indicator Profile* (Frederick, 2003) might be administered to detect whether a person' responses are valid.

FINAL REFLECTIONS

Assessment as it relates to individuals with intellectual disabilities takes many different forms. It is extremely important for professionals in this field, at the very least, to be familiar with the reasons for assessment and the various instruments and techniques that are used for the purposes discussed in this chapter. Moreover, it is important to realize that this chapter is only an overview, and that a more in-depth study of assessment is needed, the details of which are dictated by one's professional specialization.

Summary

Assessment of Intelligence
- Theories of intelligence may be evaluated along a number of dimensions, such as the source of one's knowledge, the amount of one's knowledge, or the pattern of one's mental processing ability.
- Most people believe that intelligence is epigenetic in nature, a combination of both biological and environmental factors.
- Deviation IQs are considered to be the best index of intellectual ability because they allow an examiner to compare a person's score with others of markedly different ages and ability levels.
- The first effective test of intellectual ability was the 30-item *Measuring Scale of Intelligence* designed by Alfred Binet and Theodore Simon in 1905. The most recent revision was published in 2003.
- The Wechsler scales are a series of three individually administered intelligence tests that are widely used in the field of mental retardation, with new editions of the preschool and school versions recently published.
- Criticisms of intelligence tests take several different forms: Some are directed at the tests themselves, others are directed at the examiners who conduct the evaluations, and still others are directed at the assessment process.

Assessment of Adaptive Behavior

- *Adaptive behavior* refers to a person's ability to meet age-appropriate and culture-appropriate standards of independence and personal responsibility.
- Adaptive behavior is considered to be a construct separate from but related to the construct of intelligence; moderate correlations between the two have been found.
- The first formal measure of adaptive behavior was Doll's (1935) *Vineland Social Maturity Scale,* developed at the Vineland Training School in Vineland, New Jersey.
- Several different measures of adaptive behavior have been developed over the years, ranging from simple behavioral checklists to in-depth diagnostic interviews.
- When measures of adaptive behavior are criticized, objections are usually directed at such things as the measurement process, the role of intelligence in adaptive functioning, and the culture-bound nature of adaptive behavior skills.

Other Types of Assessment

- Two key areas of assessment in school settings include the monitoring of progress that students are making and the identification of transition needs.
- An emerging focus of assessment in the adult sector is the determination of the levels of support that an individual needs across various settings.
- The assessment applications of individuals with mental retardation in legal proceedings may include issues such as the determination of competence.

Chapter

4

Individual Rights and Legal Issues

122

OBJECTIVES

After reading this chapter, the student should be able to:

- Understand fundamental concepts and legal bases for establishing the rights of persons who are mentally retarded
- Discuss the legal history for establishing educational, institutional, and community rights
- Understand the problems that occur when individuals with mental retardation are the victims of crime and are accused of crimes
- Identify future trends and issues pertinent to the lives of individuals who are mentally retarded

KEY TERMS

due process	habilitation	quasi-suspect class
equal protection	procedural due process	substantive due process

THE CONTEXT FOR SECURING INDIVIDUALS' RIGHTS

For the last several decades, the courts and Congress have played major roles in attempting to secure the rights of individuals with disabilities in the areas of education, employment, transportation, public accommodations, and communication. This assistance from the courts, state legislatures, and Congress was not always forthcoming. In the past, individuals with intellectual disabilities suffered discrimination, not only due to the views of society but also as a result of court decisions and legislation, which often reflected those societal views. For example, Yell, Rogers, and Rogers (1998) note that as early as 1893 a state court ruled that children with disabilities could be expelled from school (*Watson v. City of Cambridge,* 1893). Russo, Morse, and Glancy (1998) report that at one time, the majority of states required that certain individuals with disabilities be sterilized.

Brown v. Board of Education of Topeka, Kansas (1954) was an event that set the stage for increased educational opportunities and also served as a major legal turning point in the lives of people with disabilities (Yell, et al. 1998). Russo and colleagues (1998) refer to it as the "most significant ruling on education in the history of the United States" (p. 8). In this case, the Supreme Court ruled that the racial segregation concept of "separate but equal" was unconstitutional. Although this case was filed on behalf of African Americans, Turnbull and Turnbull (2000) made this observation:

> [If] *disabled* or *students with disabilities* is substituted for *Negro* and *nondisabled* is substituted for *white* wherever those words appear in *Brown,* we can understand why this case is important to the education of students with disabilities and how the Fourteenth Amendment became the constitutional basis for the rights of students with disabilities to be educated. (p. 10)

According to Newcomer and Zirkel (1999), litigation involving special education issues increased tremendously during the 1990s. Some court decisions were codified in the Individuals with Disabilities Education Act (IDEA) (Walther-Thomas & Brownell, 1998). In this chapter, recent litigation, legislation, major concepts, and future concerns are delineated.

Legal Bases for Establishing Rights

The three levels of government are federal, state, and local. Some powers are shared among these three levels, and other powers are primarily the domain of either federal, state, or local government. It is important to note that the U.S. Constitution and the laws passed by Congress are the supreme law of the land. Turnbull and Turnbull (2000) present a model of the three levels along with their corresponding governing documents (see Figure 4.1).

Companion Website

A complete online glossary is available on the Companion Website, which may be accessed at www.prenhall.com/beirne -smith

Federal Constitutional Arguments.   The Fourteenth Amendment to the U.S. Constitution contains two frequently invoked clauses: the **due process** clause ("nor shall any State deprive any person of life, liberty, or property, without due process of law") and the **equal protection** clause ("nor deny to any person within its jurisdiction the equal protection of the laws"). Many of the rights secured and services established for those with mental retardation have been achieved through litigation based on constitutional grounds, particularly on these two principles. Table 4.1 presents the constitutional

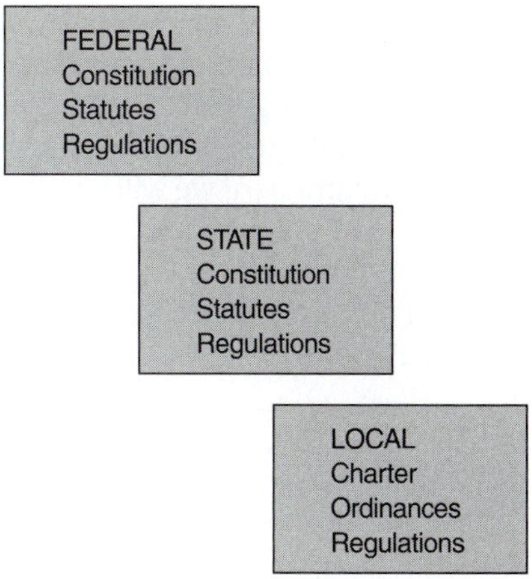

FEDERAL
Constitution
Statutes
Regulations

STATE
Constitution
Statutes
Regulations

LOCAL
Charter
Ordinances
Regulations

FIGURE 4.1

A Model of Public Law

Source: From *Free and Appropriate Public Education: The Law and Children with Disabilities,* by H. R. Turnbull, III, & A. P. Turnbull (6th ed., p. 4), 2000, Denver: Love. Copyright © 2000 by Love Publishing Co. Reprinted with permission.

TABLE 4.1

Constitutional Arguments Frequently Used in Litigation Involving Persons with Mental Retardation

Constitutional Argument	Constitutional Basis (Amendment)	Explanation	Example of Application
Equal protection	Fourteenth	No state shall deny to any person within its jurisdiction the equal protection of the laws	Right to education
Due process (substantive)	Fifth (federal) Fourteenth (state)	Protection from unreasonable action	Right to appropriate classification Right to treatment
Due process (procedural)	Fifth (federal) Fourteenth (state)	Guaranteed procedural fairness where the government would deprive one of property or liberty	Placement rights in the criminal justice system
Freedom from cruel and unusual punishment	Eighth	Protection from punishment that is found to be offensive to the ordinary person, that is unfair, or that is grossly excessive for the offense	Right to refuse treatment Right to treatment Rights in prison

arguments that have been used most frequently in cases involving persons with mental retardation. This table is only a brief guide to the constitutional issues; it is not a comprehensive list of all previous, present, or future bases for litigation.

Since the equal protection clause of the Fourteenth Amendment has been the backbone for many rights for persons with mental retardation, we will look at it more closely. There are three types of equal protection analysis (the application of equal protection to a specific claim): (1) "rational basis" or traditional analysis, (2) "intermediate" or "middle-tier scrutiny" standard, and (3) "strict scrutiny" analysis. Rothstein (1995) describes these different levels of scrutiny as follows:

> If the individual affected by the practice is a member of a "suspect class" such as a racial minority, or if the right at issue is a "fundamental right" such as a privacy, the practice will be strictly scrutinized (evaluated very carefully). Where the classification is not a specially protected class, or if the right is not an important one, the practice will usually be upheld if there is any rational basis for it. Individuals with disabilities have not been held to be members of a suspect class, but education has been recognized as deserving of "special constitutional treatment," and an intermediate test of heightened scrutiny has been applied. (p. 13)

When the courts apply the rational basis, or traditional analysis, they use a two-pronged test. First, they ask whether the purposes for different treatment sought by the state are legitimate. Second, they investigate whether a "rational" correspondence exists between the purposes of the state action and the classification.

The intermediate scrutiny standard is used when discriminatory practices are claimed against a group of people who share some of the characteristics of a "suspect class." A member of such a group is sometimes referred to as being a member of a **quasi-suspect class.** The U.S. Supreme Court decided in *Cleburne Living Center, Inc. v. City of Cleburne, Texas* (1984) not to grant suspect or quasi-suspect classification status to individuals who are mentally retarded. The Court stressed, however, that "irrational prejudice could not be the basis for unequal treatment" (Rothstein, 1995, p. 63).

The courts apply a strict scrutiny analysis where a practice affects a suspect classification or a fundamental interest. The state must demonstrate a compelling interest for the practice to be upheld.

Federal Statutes and Regulations.   Another mechanism for securing the rights of citizens who are mentally retarded that has had and will continue to have significance is federal legislation and its accompanying regulations. As more federal legislation is enacted, reference to it will occur more frequently. This is particularly noteworthy in light of the Supreme Court's reluctance to apply either the intermediate or strict scrutiny standards—standards that make it easier to win equal protection claims (Bateman, 1986).

To date, the United States has enacted a number of major pieces of legislation that have direct implications for persons with mental retardation. A list and accompanying description of some of the more important laws is provided in Table 4.2; select legislation will be discussed later in the chapter. Some of these federal laws have been reauthorized on many occasions. These legislative actions established mandates and provided a legal basis for arguing against unfair treatment.

TABLE 4.2
Major Federal Legislation Pertaining to Persons with Mental Retardation

Legislation	Year Enacted	Public Law No.	Features
Amendment to Vocational Rehabilitation Act	1973	93-112	* Prohibited discrimination against persons with "handicaps" (§ 504) * Provided a functional definition of "handicap"—mental or physical impairments that limit one or more of a person's major life activities * Included persons with conditions that would not be covered by later legislation (e.g., drug or alcohol addiction)
Education Amendments of the Elementary and Secondary Education Act 1965	1974	93-380	* Provided increased funding to assist states in meeting the right-to-education requirements * Required states to develop plans for implementing educational opportunities for all students with disabilities—including procedural safeguards
Developmental Disabilities Assistance and Bill of Rights Act	1974	94-103	* Broadened the term "developmental disabilities" * Provided grants to states and university-affiliated programs * Named the Individuals with Disabilities Education Act (IDEA) in 1990
Education for All Handicapped Children Act [Individuals with Disabilities Education Act (IDEA)]	1975	94-142	* Mandated a free, appropriate education for all students with "handicaps" in the least restrictive environment * Provided for nondiscriminatory testing, individualized education programs, procedural safeguards, and parent participation * Reauthorized most recently in 2004 as P.L. 108-446
Handicapped Children's Protection Act	1986	99-372	* Enacted in response to the Supreme Court's decision in *Smith v. Robinson* (1984) * Allowed courts to award reasonable attorney's fees to parents if the parents' complaint is successful
Americans with Disabilities Act	1990	101-336	* Landmark civil rights legislation—designed to eliminate discrimination * Provided civil rights protections to all persons with disabilities, including groups not previously addressed (e.g., HIV) * Incorporated a functional definition similar to the Vocational Rehabilitation Act of 1973—limitations in one or more major life activities * Stressed equal opportunity, independent living, and economic self-sufficiency * Addressed employment, public services (e.g., building, transportation), public accommodations (e.g., restaurants, museums), telecommunications

Source: Some information used in this table taken from Drew, Logan, & Hardman (1992).

State Constitutions, Statutes, and Regulations. All states have mandates regarding the education of their citizenry in their state constitutions (Underwood & Mead, 1995). The Fourteenth Amendment requires that states provide their citizens with equal protection. Therefore, state constitutions, statutes, and regulations can also provide a basis for legal action brought on behalf of individuals with disabilities.

Local Charters, Ordinances, and Regulations. Municipal, county, and other local provisions also play an important role in determining the rights of individuals who are mentally retarded. City charters, for instance, typically specify the establishment of various boards (e.g., school boards) and commissions. Ordinances like those that control zoning can be critical in terms of securing housing opportunities for this population. Regulations developed and issued by people in positions of authority, based on policy decisions of various legislative bodies, also affect citizens who are mentally retarded.

The Judicial System. The judicial system includes both a state and a federal court system—the latter composed of three levels. The federal judiciary is comprised of approximately 100 U.S. District Courts, which are the trial courts and represent the lowest level of authority. Cases from the U.S. District Courts are appealed to one of the 13 Circuit Courts of Appeals. The first 11 Circuit Courts of Appeals handle appeals from designated states and territories (see Table 4.3), another circuit handles cases from Washington, D.C., and still another circuit hears appeals from the entire nation on certain issues (Yell, 1998). Finally, at the highest level of authority is the U.S. Supreme Court.

State court systems are often organized on a similar three-tier system, but states may vary in the names they assign to each level (Rothstein, 1995). For example in some states the supreme court is the highest court, but in others, it is the lowest.

It is important to know the jurisdiction of a court. For example, the decisions of state courts in Alabama are not binding on state courts in Georgia. A decision by the

TABLE 4.3
Circuit Court of Appeals

Circuit	States and Territories in Each Circuit
1	Maine, Massachusetts, New Hampshire, Rhode Island, Puerto Rico
2	Connecticut, New York, Vermont
3	Delaware, New Jersey, Pennsylvania, Virgin Islands
4	Maryland, North Carolina, South Carolina, Virginia, West Virginia
5	Louisiana, Mississippi, Texas
6	Kentucky, Michigan, Ohio, Tennessee
7	Illinois, Indiana, Wisconsin
8	Arkansas, Iowa, Minnesota, Missouri, Nebraska, North Dakota, South Dakota
9	Alaska, Arizona, California, Guam, Hawaii, Idaho, Montana, Nevada, Northern Mariana Island, Oregon, Washington
10	Colorado, Kansas, New Mexico, Oklahoma, Utah, Wyoming
11	Alabama, Florida, Georgia

Source: From www.lawsononline.com.

11th Circuit Court of Appeals is binding in that circuit only, although the decision may be persuasive authority in another circuit (Yell, 1998). A decision by the U.S. Supreme Court is binding throughout the country.

Sources of Law

The sources of law that were discussed in the previous section and that contribute to the legal precedents that will be discussed in this chapter are documented in different ways. Table 4.4 lists the four sources of law, describes the legal resource that can be accessed, and provides an example of how the legal source is cited.

In addition, professionals working in the area of mental retardation should know how to obtain relevant information on legal issues. A variety of print and Web-based resources are available. Fiedler (2000) developed a useful list of resources for obtaining updated information on litigious and legisltive issues (see Figure 4.2).

LEGAL PRECEDENTS FOR INDIVIDUAL EDUCATIONAL RIGHTS

One of the more important areas related to individual rights involves education. Guaranteeing the educational rights of persons with mental retardation has not come easily. From wholesale exclusion to a present-day sense of empowerment and inclusion, many noteworthy legal battles were waged. This section discusses the following educational rights as they pertain to individuals with mental retardation: access to education (including eligibility); appropriate evaluation and classification; free appropriate public education (FAPE); least restrictive environment/appropriate placement; related services; extended school year; and disciplinary action (e.g., expulsion).

Access to Education

There is no federal constitutional right to an education. The U.S. Supreme Court reiterated this fact in *San Antonio Independent School District v. Rodriguez* (1973) when it stated that education is not a fundamental right guaranteed by the Constitution. The Supreme Court, however, earlier had discussed the importance of education in *Brown v. Board of Education* (1954):

> Today, education is perhaps the most important function of state and local governments. Both compulsory school attendance laws and great expenditures for education demonstrate our recognition of the importance of education to our democratic society. It is required in the performance of our most basic public responsibilities, even service in the armed forces. It is the very foundation of good citizenship. Today it is a principal instrument in awakening the child to cultural values, in preparing him or her for later professional training, and in helping the child to adjust normally to his or her environment. In these days, it is doubtful that any child may reasonably be expected to succeed in life if denied the opportunity of an education. Such an opportunity, where the state has undertaken to provide it, is a right which must be made available to all on equal terms.

Turnbull and Turnbull (2000) note that this case challenged the concept of "separateness in education" and that the "*Brown* plaintiffs and children with disabilities had undeniable similarities" (p. 11). Again, it is easy to see how the ruling in *Brown* provided legal arguments that could be used by attorneys for persons with disabilities.

TABLE 4.4
Sources of Law

Source of Law	Features	Legal Citations (Federal Level)
Constitutional Law	• U.S. Constitution is the supreme law of the land. • U.S. Constitution establishes basic parameters of the federal system of government. • All federal and state statutes, administrative regulations, and judicial decisions establishing case law are subject to provisions of the U.S. Constitution. • All state constitutions have public education mandates.	
Statutory Law	• Statutes are laws enacted by Congress and state legislatures. • Statutes tend to be broad and general in scope and language. • Federal statutes are organized by topic and published in *United States Code* (U.S.C.). Each title covers statutes on a specific topic (e.g., Title 20: education statutes).	• **20 U.S.C. Sec. 1400** = the location for IDEA is found in Title 20, Section 1400 of the U.S.C.
Regulatory Law	• Specific regulations that interpret statutes are developed by the executive branch of government. • Administrative regulations have the force of law. • Federal administrative regulations are published in the *Code of Federal Regulations* (C.F.R.). • The C.F.R. is organized by topics.	• **34 C.F.R Sec. 300.7(c)(6)** = the location of the definition of mental retardation used in IDEA is found in Title 34, Section 300 of the *Code of Federal Regulations*.

Case Law	• Case law is based on the result of litigation issued in published judicial decisions.
	• Decisions come from both federal and state court systems.
	• Federal courts are used when a dispute involves constitutional issues or federal statutes.
	• Published decisions are published in different sources:
	  • U.S. District Courts: *Federal Supplement*
	  • U.S. Courts of Appeals: *Federal Reporter* (a third edition is now available)
	  • U.S. Supreme Court—3 sources:
	    • *United States Court Reports* (abbreviated *U.S.*)
	    • *Supreme Court Reporter* (abbreviated *S. Ct.*) (published by West Publishing Company)
	    • *Supreme Court Reports, Lawyers' Edition* (abbreviated *L. Ed.*) (published by Bancroft-Whitney/Lawyers Cooperative)
		• **Stuart v. Nappi, 443 F. Supp. 1235 (D. Conn. 1978)** = decision from federal court in Connecticut that was decided in 1978; information is located in volume 443 of the *Federal Supplement* beginning on page 1235.
		• **Daniel R.R. v. State Board of Education, 874 F.2d 1036 (5th Cir. 1989)** = decision from the 5th Circuit Court of Appeals that was decided in 1989; information is located in volume 874 of the *Federal Reporter* (second series) beginning on page 1036.
		• **Board of Education of the Hendrick Hudson School District v. Rowley, 458 U.S. 176 (1982)** = decision from the Supreme Court that was decided in 1982; information is located in volume 458 of the *U.S. Court Reports* beginning on page 176.

Source: Information used in this table taken from C. Fiedler, *Making a Difference: Advocacy Competencies for Special Education Professionals,* 2000, pp. 67–69. Austin: PRO-ED.

FIGURE 4.2
Resources for Updated Information on Special Education Legal Issues

Print Resources
West's Education Law Reporter
Journal of Law and Education
Index to Legal Periodicals
Individuals with Disabilities Education Law Reporter
The Special Educator (published by LRP Publications)
Special Education Law Update (published by Data Research, Inc.)

Internet Websites
Axis Disability Rights Website
(http://www.island.net/-axis)
Contains articles related to advocacy, inclusion, and other special education issues.

Council for Disability Rights
(http://www.disabilityrights.org/)
Contains information on the Americans with Disabilities Act (ADA) and a parent's guide to special education.

Disability Resources on the Internet
(http://www.geocities.com/-drm/)
Contains information on Supplemental Security Income (SSI) and legislative updates.

Disability Rights Activist
(http://www.teleport.com/-abarhych/index.html)
Contains lots of information to foster advocacy on behalf of individuals with disabilities.

Internet Law Library
(http://law.house.gov/102.htm)

National Parent Network on Disabilities
(http://www.npnd.org/boutnpnd.htm)
Contains the Friday Fax, which addresses current disability issues, as well as the Monday Memos, which provides updated information. Links to IDEA legal issues and parent training and information centers.

Technical Assistance Alliance for Parent Programs
(http://www.taalliance.org)
Contains legislative updates.

EdLaw (http://www.access.digex.net/-edlawinc/)
Contains special education statutes and regulations, links to disability law on the Internet, and provides analysis on special education legal issues.

Thomas Legislative Information
(http://thomas.loc.gov/)
Maintained by the Library of Congress to provide access to a number of federal databases, including bills introduced in Congress, the Congressional Record, and U.S. Government Internet resources.

The Council for Exceptional Children
(http://cec.sped.org/home.htm)
Contains links to the ERIC Clearinghouse on Disabilities and Gifted Education, the National Clearinghouse for Professions in Special Education, and legislative information.

The National Center for Children and Youth with Disabilities (http://www.aed.org/nichy/)
Contains information on a variety of disability and law issues and information searches.

The Special Ed Advocate
(http://www.wrightslaw.com)
The Special Ed Advocate is a free online newsletter about special education legal issues, cases, tactics and strategy, effective educational methods, and Internet links.

Advocating for the Child
(http://www2.crosswinds.net/ washington-dc/-advocate/)
Contains a wealth of information on special education legal rights, responsibilities, and procedures.

Source: C. Fiedler, *Making a Difference: Advocacy Competencies for Special Education Professionals,* 2000, p. 70. Austin: PRO-ED. Reprinted by permission.

Keeping children with mental retardation out of school had been a long-standing practice in schools throughout the country, but in the early 1970s legal challenges to exclusionary policies were successful. This litigation paved the way for later federal legislation that would significantly alter the availability of educational services to students with disabilities.

Table 4.5 summarizes the most important historical court cases that either directly or indirectly led to establishing a right to education for children and youth with

TABLE 4.5
Summary of Early Right-to-Education Litigation

Litigants	Year	Highest Level of Judicial Review	Issues	Implications of Litigations	Arguments Used
Brown v. Board of Education of Topeka, Kansas	1954	U.S. Supreme Court	Segregation of students by race Impact of racial segregation on the child's motivation to learn	Segregation by race unanimously declared unconstitutional Established importance of education for advancement Established policy in favor of equal educational opportunity Generalized the purposes of education, not its fundamentality	Equal protection
Pennsylvania Association for Retarded Children (PARC) v. Commonwealth of Pennsylvania	1972	U.S. District Court (PA)	Class action suit—challenging the exclusion of children with mental retardation from free public education Access to education for all citizens with mental retardation Particular learning needs of this population	Consent agreement of both parties Established a right to education for children with mental retardation Established that all children with mental retardation could gain from education and training Demanded appropriate education Demanded preschool services if normal children received such Provided tuition grant assistance Provided due process mechanisms Required the identification of children not already identified Provided for education in the least restrictive setting	Equal protection Due process State statutes
Mills v. Board of Education of District of Columbia	1972	U.S. District Court (DC)	Class action suit—exclusion of all exceptionalities Access to education Use of waiting lists	Extended the logic of *PARC* to all disability groups regardless of the degree of the impairment Gained procedural safeguards Required timetable of implementation Acknowledged alternatives placement	Equal protection Due process District of Columbia Code

Case	Year	Court	Issue	Findings	Basis
San Antonio Independent School District v. Rodriguez	1973	U.S. Supreme Court	Claim that a discrimination exists due to being in a poorer school district Challenge to state-financing scheme Assertion that education is a fundamental right	Rejected wealth discrimination claim Left open the fundamentality of some identifiable quantum of education Reaffirmed the importance of education Indicated that denial of education could be used in terms of denial of freedom of speech and right to vote	Discrimination Equal protection
Lebanks v. Spears	1973	U.S. District Court	Challenged Louisiana's failure to provide education/training to a large number of children with mental retardation	Consent agreement Two features not found in *PARC* or *Mills*: (1) Education—oriented toward making every child self-sufficient or employable (2) Educational services to adults who were not given services as children Acknowledged additional factors for evaluation in addition to intelligence	Equal protection
Maryland Association for Retarded Children v. Maryland	1974	Circuit Court of Baltimore County	Class action suit on behalf of children with mental retardation and those with physical handicaps being denied free public education	Began to address "appropriateness" issue Required the state to provide the necessary funding	State statutes
In the Interest of H.G., A Child	1974	Supreme Court of North Dakota	Equal educational opportunity	Involved the highest level of judicial review prior to P.L. 94-142 (1975)	State statutes Equal protection

mental retardation. As the table shows, the arguments most frequently employed by plaintiffs in right-to-education cases include establishing the importance of education, using equal protection and due process claims, and addressing state and federal statutory provisions. For the most part, these plaintiffs have argued that if education is provided to the public in general, it should be available to all children regardless of level of ability or type of impairment.

Another critical factor established in two of the most important legal cases—*Pennsylvania Association for Retarded Children v. Commonwealth of Pennsylvania* (1972) and *Mills v. Board of Education of the District of Columbia* (1972)—is that all individuals with mental retardation can benefit from education or training. Without the prior establishment of this fact, opponents could have put up substantial opposition to providing educational services to many children and youth with significant disabilities and who had been excluded from schools. This issue of educability, while discussed professionally during this time (Kauffman & Krouse, 1981; Noonan, Brown, Mulligan, & Rettig, 1982), arose again later and was the focus of litigation in *Timothy W. v. Rochester School District* (1988). A brief analysis of these three cases is discussed next.

Pennsylvania Association for Retarded Children (PARC) v. Commonwealth of Pennsylvania.

Early in January 1971, the Pennsylvania Association for Retarded Children (PARC) and the parents of 13 children who were mentally retarded filed a class action suit in federal court on behalf of all Pennsylvania residents with mental retardation between the ages of 6 and 21 who were excluded from receiving educational services. At issue was the prevailing policy that denied these school-age children and youth access to public education. Expert testimony stressing the educational benefits that all children and youth with mental retardation could gain (i.e., attainment of self-sufficiency for many, and some level of self-care for others) weighed heavily in this case.

Although settled by means of court-approved consent agreement in October 1971, the *PARC* case had a profound impact on special education and children and youth with mental retardation. It established a precedent guaranteeing access to publicly supported education for all students who are mentally retarded. Through claims of violations of due process and equal protection rights, the plaintiffs were able to establish that certain Pennsylvania statutes were unconstitutional. Implications of this decision are listed in Table 4.5.

Mills v. Board of Education of the District of Columbia.

Not long after the consent agreement in *PARC* was reached, another civil suit was filed, this time in the District of Columbia. In *Mills v. Board of Education of the District of Columbia,* the parents and guardians of seven children charged that the board of education was denying their children a publicly supported education. All the plaintiffs in this case qualified as disabled. In August 1972, Judge Waddy ruled in favor of the plaintiffs, in effect declaring that a publicly supported education was the right of all children who were disabled, regardless of the type and severity of their condition. *Mills* actually extended many of the legal guarantees *PARC* had achieved for children who were mentally retarded to children with other disabling conditions. The defendants claimed that funds were insufficient to provide education to all such students. Judge Waddy's reply reflected the attitude of many concerning the exclusionary practices so long in effect:

The District of Columbia's interest in educating the excluded children clearly must outweigh its interest in preserving its financial resources. If sufficient funds are not available to finance all of the services and programs that are needed and desirable in the system, then the available funds must be expended equitably in such a manner that no child is entirely excluded from a publicly supported education consistent with his needs and ability to benefit therefrom. The inadequacies of the District of Columbia public school system, whether occasioned by insufficient funding or administrative inefficiency, certainly cannot be permitted to bear more heavily on the "exceptional" or handicapped child than on the normal child.

As noted in this decision, limited financial resources are not sufficient reason to exclude students from receiving an appropriate education. But financial resources are limited, and even with IDEA and its recent amendments in effect, financial issues will continue to demand attention.

After *PARC* and *Mills,* right-to-education suits were filed in many other states as well. Soon all students who were mentally retarded were to gain the right to the free, appropriate public education that had previously been denied them, as many of the provisions formulated in the *PARC* consent agreement were later incorporated into the Education for All Handicapped Children Act, now known as the Individuals with Disabilities Education Act (IDEA).

Timothy W. v. Rochester School District.   The assumption of a right to education has not gone unchallenged. In 1988, many years after the *PARC* and *Mills* cases were settled and after many years of the parents in this case trying to get special education services for their child, a federal district court in New Hampshire decided in the case of *Timothy W. v. Rochester School District* that, if it seemed that a student could not benefit from special education, the rights guaranteed under IDEA do not apply. This case involved a 13-year-old boy who was profoundly retarded and who had a host of other disabling conditions (respiratory problems, intracranial bleeding, hydrocephalus, seizures, hearing and vision difficulties). He was described as operating at a most basic level and as not having made any progress over a long period of time. In 1989, the First Circuit Court of Appeals reversed the lower court's interpretation of IDEA to allow exclusion from public education in some cases, reaffirming the basic principles underlying the intent of IDEA. The U.S. District Court had ruled that Timothy's potential for learning was "nonexistent." The First Circuit Court held that a student with significant disabilities like Timothy W. did not need to demonstrate an ability to "benefit" from special education services to be eligible for those services.

Underwood and Mead (1995) raised the question of what a court would do if a child is nonresponsive or unaware of his or her surroundings. The point that surfaces is whether a child with such features has any educational needs. This particular issue was not pertinent in the *Timothy W.* case; however, this issue might arise in the future.

Appropriate Evaluation and Classification

The use of intelligence measures as the primary determinant for identification and placement decisions has long been under scrutiny. The problems associated with intelligence testing have come under fire in a number of legal suits. *Hobson v. Hansen*

The inclusion of students with mental retardation was achieved on the basis of equal protection arguments.

(1967), *Larry P. v. Riles* (1972), *Diana v. State Board of Education* (1970), and *Parents in Action on Special Education (PASE) v. Hannon* (1980) have specifically considered the use of intelligence tests for this purpose.

Hobson v. Hansen. In *Hobson v. Hansen* (1967), the practice of denying to poor school-age children educational services equal to those of the more affluent was determined to be unconstitutional. The court found that students were being "tracked" into ability groups on the basis of instruments that seemed to be biased against African American students and those from lower socioeconomic groups. Schools in the District of Columbia were no longer permitted to use IQ measures to place children in tracks, and a close review of classification practices was ordered. This case is important to those interested in mental retardation because it addressed the consequences of being labeled mentally retarded.

Larry P. v. Riles. In *Larry P. v. Riles* (1972, 1974, 1979, 1984), the courts held that IQ tests could not be used as the primary determinant in placing African American students in classes for students classified as having educable mental retardation. Initially, intelligence tests could not be used to identify African American students as mentally retarded; in 1986 an expanded injunction was issued that banned the use of these instruments with African American students for any assessment purpose (Taylor, 1990). MacMillan and Balow (1991) note that, as a repercussion of *Larry P.,* the three largest school districts in California decided to ban the use of intelligence tests with all students, regardless of race, for special education purposes.

In 1988, however, a group of African American parents filed a complaint alleging that the 1986 order, which prevented their children from voluntarily taking IQ tests for purposes of placement in special education classes, violated their due process and equal protection rights. The court found that the plaintiffs' due process rights had been violated, ordering that the 1986 modification be vacated (*Larry P. v. Riles,* 1992).

Diana v. State Board of Education.   Just as *Larry P.* specifically concerned the problems of African American children who were being misclassified, other cases brought in California have focused on the problems of other ethnic groups in placement decisions. In *Diana v. State Board of Education* (1970), the injured party, representing Spanish-speaking children, argued that many such students had been placed in classes for students with mild retardation on the basis of individual intelligence tests that were considered culturally biased. The children involved in this lawsuit spoke primarily Spanish but were given intelligence tests in English. Although *Diana* was settled out of court, it resulted in clear changes in the methods and procedures used for identifying and placing students in special classes.

Parents in Action on Special Education (PASE) v. Hannon.   It would be misleading to suggest that the foregoing cases were the only lawsuits involving appropriate classification and placement, or that all litigation has been decided in the same way. In a class action suit filed in an Illinois federal district court—*Parents in Action on Special Education (PASE) v. Hannon* (1980)—the use of intelligence tests to place minority students in special classes designed for children with mild retardation again came into question. This time, however, the court ruled differently, declaring the tests nondiscriminatory and the practice valid when additional measures are also employed. The court closely examined specific intelligence tests for possible racial bias. So few items were found suspect that the court decided these measures should be considered culturally neutral. The court went on to underscore the importance of clinical judgment in the interpretation of IQ results and the decision-making process.

The diametrically opposed findings in *PASE* and *Larry P.* have added more confusion to an already controversial area. The misuse of IQ measures continues to undergo professional scrutiny, as concern for misdiagnosis and misplacement remains a top priority in the referral and placement process. As Taylor (1990) suggests, the issue of nondiscriminatory evaluation has not been put to rest. Interestingly, in 1994 the Ninth Circuit Court of Appeals, in *Crawford v. Honig* (1994), lifted the ban on using IQ tests for placing minority students in special education.

W.B. v. Matula.   In *W.B.v. Matula* (1995), another case relevant to the issue of identification and evaluation, a school district had failed to identify and provide an appropriate education to a student. W.B., the parent of the student, sued, and the Third Circuit Court of Appeals held that the plaintiff was not precluded from seeking monetary damages. Some attorneys who specialize in the area of special education law believe that this is a major ruling for those seeking damages (Bleemer, 1995).

Free Appropriate Public Education (FAPE)

Once an appropriate education was mandated by IDEA, it was inevitable that the term *appropriate education* would need to be defined. The issue is discussed routinely at individualized education program (IEP) meetings, but it was not formally addressed in the law until 1982. That year, the U.S. Supreme Court ruled in *Board of Education of the Hendrick Hudson Central School District v. Rowley*—the first case argued on the basis of P.L. 94-142 to reach this highest level of judicial review.

Board of Education of the Hendrick Hudson Central School District v. Rowley.   Although the plaintiff named in this particular litigation, Amy Rowley, was a student with a hearing impairment, the case has significant implications for students who are mentally retarded. This is because the Court specified criteria for a "free appropriate public education" in the majority opinion written by Justice William Rehnquist:

> According to the definitions contained in the Act, a "free appropriate public education" consists of educational instruction specially designed to meet the unique needs of the handicapped child, supported by such services as are necessary to permit the child "to benefit" from the instruction. Almost as a checklist for adequacy under the Act, the definition also requires that such instruction and services be provided at public expense and under public supervision, meet the State's educational standards, approximate the grade levels used in the State's regular education, and comport with the child's IEP. Thus, if personalized instruction is being provided with sufficient supportive services to permit the child to benefit from the instruction, and the other items on the definitional checklist are satisfied, the child is receiving a "free appropriate public education" as defined by the Act.

A number of important issues in interpreting IDEA arose in this case, and they have had and will continue to have bearing on litigation. First, the Court discussed the importance of a "basic floor of opportunity" for students—which means that all students should have reasonable opportunity for learning. The Court stressed that the act intends students to obtain special instruction and related services that are individually developed to provide educational benefit to students with disabilities. Unfortunately, the term *educational benefit* suffers from the same ambiguity that appropriate education does.

The issue that has received the most attention involves the "level of education" to be provided to students. What type of services should be provided, and to what extent must they be offered? In *Rowley*, the U.S. Supreme Court reversed the Second Circuit Court of Appeals' ruling that Amy Rowley was entitled to an interpreter. The Court's interpretation of congressional intent in enacting P.L. 94-142 suggested that programs do not have to develop students to their maximum potential. The Court noted that language addressing this particular issue was "noticeably absent" in the federal statute.

The *Rowley* decision initially sent shock waves through the field of special education, as many thought that students with disabilities would suffer if school systems took narrow interpretations of this case. Special education professionals feared that schools would have too easy a time demonstrating that students were getting "educational benefit" in programs that were not providing needed supportive services (DuBow & Greer, 1984). Blatt's (1987) concern was that schools would (1) have more freedom to decide what is acceptable for students with special needs, (2) no longer be motivated to provide optimal programs, and (3) meet a "far lesser" standard. This scenario, fortunately, has not materialized.

In the years subsequent to the *Rowley* decision, the courts began to expand their interpretation of "some educational benefit" to one of "meaningful benefit" (Osborne, 1996). Nevertheless, the Supreme Court in *Rowley* made it very clear that schools did not have to provide educational programs that would maximize the potential of students with disabilities.

FAPE and Private School Settings.   Federal regulations published in 1999 address the issue of children placed in private schools when the parents believe their children are not receiving a free appropriate public education (FAPE). If a hearing officer determines that the school district had not made FAPE available to the student and that the private school placement is appropriate, then the parents can be reimbursed. These regulations also state that the appropriateness of a placement does not depend on whether the placement meets state standards (C.F.R. §300.403[c]). There are several limitations on reimbursement. For example, to be eligible for reimbursement, the parents must have informed the IEP team that they were rejecting the placement of the school district and that they intended to place their child in a private school at the expense of the school district (C.F.R. §300.403[d][1][i]).

For a parent's perspective on the FAPE, go to the Companion Website at www.prenhall.com/beirne-smith and select Chapter 4, Video Case Studies.

Least Restrictive Environment/Appropriate Placement

Placing students who are mentally retarded in educational settings that are appropriate to their needs is becoming a major issue in the field. Debate goes on between those who want to maintain the guarantees of a continuum of service delivery options as specified in IDEA and those who advocate full inclusion in general education settings as the only option. IDEA mandates that a continuum of alternative settings be made available. The discussion about this issue will continue.

Turnbull and Turnbull (2000) assert that the 1997 amendments of IDEA strengthened the provisions of *least restrictive environment* (LRE). Although several cases have dealt with this issue—including *Roncker v. Walter* (1983)—three significant cases are discussed in this section.

Daniel R. R. v. State Board of Education.   In *Daniel R. R. v. State Board of Education* (1989), the Fifth Circuit Court of Appeals developed a two-faceted test to determine whether a placement is appropriate and consistent with the concept of LRE. The *Daniel* test requires attention to the following components, while considering other factors related to the student and school: First, can a student be educated satisfactorily in the general education classroom, with the use of supplementary aids and services? And second, if the student is placed in a more restrictive setting, is the student integrated to the maximum extent appropriate?

Sacramento City Unified School District v. Rachel H.   In *Sacramento City Unified School District v. Rachel H.* (1994), the court fashioned a four-prong test that considered: (1) the educational benefits to the student; (2) the nonacademic benefits;

(3) the effect of the student's presence on the general education teacher and students; and (4) the costs of having the student with a disability in the general education classroom (DeMitchell & Kerns, 1997).

Hartmann v. Loudoun County Board of Education.   In *Hartmann v. Loudoun County Board of Education* (1997), the Fourth Circuit Court of Appeals provided a three-part test for dealing with the least restrictive environment issue. The court ruled that including students in general education settings is not required, under the LRE mandate, when: (1) the student would not receive any educational benefit from placement in this setting; (2) any marginal benefit from placement in the general education setting would be outweighed by benefits that could only be provided in a separate special education setting; and (3) the student with disabilities is a disruptive force in the general education classroom. The last criterion raises some disturbing questions about who decides if a student is disruptive and how is this decision made.

General education consists of the general classroom, extracurricular activities, and nonacademic activities (20 U.S.C. §1414[d][1][A][iii]). A critical provision of the 1997 amendments is that the IEP must explain the extent that a student will not participate in these environments (20 U.S.C. §1414[d][1][A][iv]). Turnbull and Turnbull (2000) state that this provision, coupled with the stipulations of the amendments regarding discipline and financial considerations, codified the results of *Daniel R. R. v. State Board of Education* (1989) and *Sacramento City Unified School District v. Rachel H.* (1994).

Related Services

Under IDEA, students are entitled to related services, if needed, when those services allow a student to benefit from a free appropriate public education. It has not always been clear, however, whether certain services qualify as "related services," especially those services that are more medically oriented and that many students with more extensive needs may require. Two key cases that involved related services as the focal issue are discussed in this section.

Irving Independent School District v. Tatro.   In *Irving Independent School District v. Tatro* (1984), the U.S. Supreme Court ruled that a student with spina bifida was entitled to clean intermittent catheterization (CIC) services (a procedure that empties the bladder). The Court used a two-prong test to determine whether a service is a related service: (1) Is the requested service a supportive service necessary for the child to benefit from special education? Then, (2) is the requested service excluded as a medical service? If a service is a medical service, then it does not qualify as a related service. The Court decided that this supportive service (i.e., CIC) could be performed by a school nurse and therefore was not an excludable medical service. According to *Tatro,* only services that had to be performed by a physician were medical services that could be excluded as a related service.

Cedar Rapids Community School District v. Garret F.   Even with the ruling of the Supreme Court, lower courts differed in their interpretation of the second prong of the *Tatro* test. Some courts stated that a multifactor test considering such factors as cost could determine whether a service could be considered as an excludable medical service. In *Cedar Rapids Community School District v. Garret F.* (1999), the Supreme Court rejected this viewpoint, stating that there was no legal authority for use of a multifactor test to determine whether a service could be classified as a medical service and therefore be excluded as a related service. In the *Garret F.* case, Garret had been involved in a serious accident when he was 4 years old that resulted in a severe spinal cord injury. He used a wheelchair and was ventilator-dependent, requiring constant assistance. His ongoing needs included occasional pumping of an air bag attached to his tracheotomy tube, urinary bladder catheterization, and suctioning of his tracheotomy. He also required someone to be around him who knew emergency medical procedures (Boyle & Weishaar, 2001). His mother requested health care services (i.e., continuous one-on-one nursing services) to address his needs.

The Supreme Court agreed with the Circuit Court of Appeals, which stated that *Tatro* "established a bright-line test: the services of a physician (other than for diagnostic and evaluation purposes) are subject to the medical services exclusion, but services that can be provided in the school setting by a nurse or qualified layperson are not" (*Cedar Rapids Community School District v. Garret F.* 1997, p. 825). Although many would argue that the decision in *Tatro* was quite clear, the *Garret F.* decision reiterated the test unequivocally. At this point, there would appear to be little room for controversy on this issue. Nevertheless, the financial implications of this decision on schools is noteworthy, particularly where there are a significant number of medically fragile students.

Other Issues.   Other litigation further delineated what is considered to be a related service under IDEA. Transportation to and from a placement that has been designated as appropriate for providing special services is considered a related service, as found in two cases involving individuals with mental retardation: *Hurry v. Jones* (1984) and *Alamo Heights School District v. State Board of Education* (1986).

The issue of whether psychotherapy is a related service has major implications for schools, as such a ruling might require expensive services (e.g., out-of-state residential placement) that public schools do not provide. Various litigation produced differing outcomes. Several cases—including *T.G. v. Board of Education of Piscataway* (1983) and *Max M. v. Thompson* (1984)—have contested this issue and found psychotherapy to be a related service. Other litigation, *McKenzie v. Jefferson* (1983), found that the residential component of placement in a residential facility is medical in nature, not educational, and did not have to be paid for by a school district.

Extended School Year

A corollary to the FAPE issue is the provision of services beyond the normal 180-day school year. The first important case regarding the extended school year (ESY) was *Armstrong v. Kline* (1979). This case was originally filed in federal district court in Pennsylvania and later appealed to the Third Circuit Court of Appeals. The foremost issue in this litigation was that significant gaps (e.g., summer breaks) in the educational programs of certain students caused losses in skill development (regression) that required an unreasonable amount of time to make up (recoupment) and therefore entitled students to an extended school year. The decisions of both courts found the defendant's policy of limiting educational services to a maximum of 180 days inflexible, thus preventing students from receiving an appropriate education.

According to the 1997 amendments to IDEA, the school district must provide an extended school year if the IEP team determines that an extended school year is necessary to provide a child, regardless of the disability, with FAPE. The school district may not unilaterally limit the length, type, or amount of services.

Disciplinary Action

As mentioned earlier, the 1997 amendments codified the results of previous court cases. In regard to the issue of change of placement as a result of disciplinary action, IDEA incorporated the findings in cases such as *Honig v. Doe* (1988) and *J.B. v. Independent School District* (1995). Therefore, school districts may have already implemented many of the provisions of the amendments. The following list summarizes some of those amendments:

- There can never be a complete cessation of educational services (FAPE) for a student with a disability (C.F.R. 34 §300.121[a]).
- School personnel may unilaterally suspend students with disabilities for a total of 10 days or less (C.F.R. 34 §300.520).
- If a suspension or a change of placement is greater than 10 days, a manifestation hearing must be conducted to determine whether the misbehavior is a manifestation of the disability. If the misbehavior is not a manifestation of the disability, then the student can be disciplined the same as students without disabilities, but a complete cessation of FAPE cannot occur (C.F.R. §300.523).
- School personnel may unilaterally place a student who brings a weapon or illegal drugs to school in an interim alternative educational setting for 45 days (34 C.F.R. §300.520[a][2]).
- Even if a student is not currently receiving special education services, the student may be eligible for the procedural rights of IDEA if the school district had knowledge that the student had a disability (C.F.R. §300.527).

The issue of the continuation of educational services is controversial. This issue has been one of the central points of debate in the reauthorization of IDEA. Some proposals would allow school officials to terminate educational services to students with disabilities who bring weapons to school. In response to this proposed legislation that would terminate services, the Council for Exceptional Children and other organizations issued a policy statement that advocated for the continuation of educational services for extremely disruptive students. Because these groups recognize the importance of safety issues, the policy directive stated that this continuation of services could occur in alternative programs.

LEGISLATIVE MANDATES ESTABLISHING INDIVIDUAL EDUCATIONAL RIGHTS

Legislation has played a major role in guaranteeing the rights and addressing the needs of individuals with mental retardation. Some key pieces of legislation include the Developmental Disabilities Assistance and Bill of Rights Act of 1990 (P.L. 101-496) and the Carl D. Perkins Vocational and Applied Technology Education Act of 1990 (P.L. 101-392). However, three federal laws stand out and arguably have had the greatest impact on individuals with mental retardation: the Individuals with Disabilities Education Act (IDEA), Section 504 of the Vocational Rehabilitation Act, and the Americans with Disabilities Act (ADA). These three laws are discussed briefly below, along with one other piece of legislation—the No Child Left Behind Act (P.L. 107-110).

Individuals with Disabilities Education Act (IDEA)

This legislation was originally called the Education for All Handicapped Children Act (EHA), signed into law in 1975 as P.L. 94-142. It has been reauthorized five times—in 1983, 1986, 1990, 1997, and most recently in 2004 (as P.L. 108-446)—with each set of amendments having significant effects on the education of students with disabilities. The 1990 reauthorization (P.L. 105-47) changed the name to the Individuals with Disabilities Education Act (IDEA) and added two additional disabling conditions (autism and traumatic brain injury) to the list of 13 categories.

For more information about the legal implications of IDEA, and many other topics discussed in this chapter, visit the Companion Website at www.prenhall.com/ beirne-smith and select Chapter 4, Web Destinations.

The major provision of IDEA is that all students ages 3 through 21, who have disabilities and who need special education and/or related services, are entitled to a free appropriate public education (FAPE) in the least restrictive environment (LRE). Incentives exist for serving young children ages 0 to 2, and all states are providing such services. Key features of IDEA, along with a short description of what they mean, are listed in Table 4.6.

Section 504 of the Vocational Rehabilitation Act

In 1973, amendments to the Vocational Rehabilitation Act (P.L. 93-112) were enacted. Section 504 of this act is really a broad civil rights law that has become the "bill of rights for people with disabilities" by ensuring that individuals with disabilities could not be discriminated against, particularly in the areas of education and employment. The legislation specifically protects any individual who has a physical or mental impairment that limits one or more major life activities, who has a record of such an impairment, or who is regarded as having such an impairment. Major life activities include, but are not limited to, areas such as caring for oneself, performing manual tasks, walking, seeing, hearing, speaking, breathing, learning, and working. Clearly, this law applies to individuals with mental retardation, although in school settings IDEA applies more often for this population.

It should be noted that Section 504 applies only to programs, agencies, or organizations that receive federal financial assistance. However, given that most educational settings receive federal dollars in some fashion, the reach of this law is extensive.

TABLE 4.6
Key Features of the Individuals with Disabilities Education Improvement Act of 2004

Feature of IDEA	Brief Explanation
Free, appropriate public education	• Primary feature of IDEA: special education and related services to all who qualify.
Least restrictive environment	• Students with disabilities should be educated with their nondisabled peers to the greatest extent possible,
Nondiscriminatory assessment	• The nature of assessment should take into consideration best practices in assessment of students who come from culturally/ethnically/linguistically different backgrounds.
Due process provisions	• A variety of rights of students and their parents are protected by IDEA (e.g., notification, appeal, involvement).
Related services	• In addition to appropriate special education services, some students will need additional services such as physical therapy, counseling, transportation, nursing services.
State assessments	• All students with disabilities should participate in the evaluation process; most should be included in the district-wide and state-wide assessments that all students take; alternative assessments are used with students who are not able to participate in the typical assessments.
Transition	• A system that includes assessment and planning for the transition from school to postschool life should be in place for all students who are receiving special education services by age 16.

Source: C. Fiedler, *Making a Difference: Advocacy Competencies for Special Education Professionals,* 2000, p. 70. Austin: PRO-ED.

Americans with Disabilities Act (ADA)

Considered to be the most important piece of civil rights legislation to be enacted since the Civil Rights Act of 1964, ADA provides similar protections for and opportunities to individuals with disabilities. The law was enacted in 1990 (P.L. 101-336) and has provided protections for adults with disabilities in a wide range of settings, particularly in the workplace. The scope of the law extends to both public and private settings, and affects employment, public services, transportation, public accommodations (e.g., restaurants), and telecommunications. Rea and Davis-Dorsey (2004) note that, while ADA has some application in educational settings, IDEA and Section 504 tend to apply more frequently. Although some concern has arisen regarding how much of an impact this law has actually made on the lives of persons with disabilities, and some criticism has arisen from certain employers, the intent of the law is well founded and it continues to receive support from the public (Taylor, 1999).

No Child Left Behind Act

In January 2002, the No Child Left Behind Act of 2001 was signed into law. The overall purpose of this law is to ensure that all students are able to meet high state standards in education. This law requires, as does IDEA, that all students—including English language learners (ELLs) and those with disabilities—be assessed through state assessments. The law, operating under a 10-year implementation time line, states that all students will graduate from high school, be taught by highly qualified teachers, and be proficient in reading by the end of 3rd grade, and that all ELLs will be proficient in English. Some of the many requirements that schools must follow include the following:

- Annual testing of students against state standards
- Highly qualified paraprofessionals
- Support for students not meeting standards
- Accommodations to meet curricular and assessment needs of students with disabilities

Of particular significance to administrators and teachers working with students who have mental retardation is the emphasis on standards-based education and associated assessment. Schools can exempt only a set percentage of students from taking the high-stakes tests. As a result, the annual yearly progress (AYP) reports of a specific school and district can be influenced significantly by the inclusion of students with mental retardation in these tests. Johns (2004) has suggested that some schools have resorted to "pushing out" of school those students who might not fare well on the tests and thus affect a school's test score data.

As a result, the need for curricular adaptations to successfully implement NCLB becomes clearer as critical elements of NCLB are considered. Among the various aspects of this law is the need for standards-based curriculum and associated assessment. Today, most states have developed some form of standards-based education, and both NCLB and IDEA require that all students be provided opportunity in the state-mandated curricula and assessment.

LEGAL PRECEDENTS FOR INDIVIDUAL INSTITUTIONAL RIGHTS

This section introduces the legal maneuverings that have become the backdrop for many changes in institutional settings. Much of the section is devoted to a fundamental right that had been denied many of those confined to institutions for too long: the right to treatment. According to Hayden (1998), there were 71 court cases from 1971 to 1997 involving persons with mental retardation who were institutionalized. Hayden also notes that cases in later years alleged some of the same violations that were litigated in earlier years. Since 1997, other cases have arisen as well (e.g., the final decision in *Wyatt v. Stickney*). By 1998, 128 of the 346 state-operated institutions for individuals with mental retardation had closed.

Fundamental Issues

The terms *treatment* and *habilitation* are often used interchangeably, although some professionals do make a distinction. Both imply the delivery of some type of service, and they have been at the center of much discussion concerning those living in large, segregated residential facilities. Baer (1981) interprets the various courts' definitions of **habilitation** to mean "behavior change in the direction of those skills that cumulatively allow community living" (p. 91). Although this definition is very general, it does give a sense of purpose. Lakin and Bruininks (1985), analyzing the view of habilitation promoted in *Youngberg v. Romeo* (1982), remark that the U.S. Supreme Court defines *habilitation* as something that ensures "safety and freedom from undue restraint." The usefulness of this perspective is questionable.

Key Litigation

The right-to-treatment issue revolves around the notion that if individuals are placed, often involuntarily, in restrictive institutional settings, then constitutionally they are entitled to services. Many landmark cases have looked at this issue; a few are presented here. Most notable among them are *Wyatt v. Stickney* (1972), *New York Association for Retarded Children v. Rockefeller* (1973), *O'Connor v. Donaldson* (1974), *Halderman v. Pennhurst State School and Hospital* (1977), and *Youngberg v. Romeo* (1982). Because of their importance historically and implications today, each of these cases will be discussed below.

Wyatt v. Stickney. The legal impetus for reform was dramatized in 1972, in the litigation of the landmark case of *Wyatt v. Stickney.* This case had a direct impact on the adequacy of services in residential facilities for individuals with mental retardation. The plaintiffs in this class action suit built their case on the grounds that the residents of the Partlow State School (located in Tuscaloosa, Alabama) were being denied their right to treatment. Although this was a class action suit, it was originally filed by the legal guardian of Ricky Wyatt against the Alabama Department of Mental Hygiene in 1970. Specifically, in *Wyatt,* Ricky Wyatt (named plaintiff) represented all residents in the state of Alabama who were involuntarily confined in the state's hospitals.

The decision of Judge Johnson of the District Court for the Middle District of Alabama, North Division, declared that the constitutional rights of those residents were being violated under the Fourteenth Amendment. This state's failure to provide proper treatment in its residential facilities moved the court to draw up a precedent-setting 22-page appendix that defined minimum treatment standards for the state school to adopt. The order and the decree of the *Wyatt* decision were comprehensive in their coverage of residents' right to treatment and habilitation, records and review, physical environment, medication, and admissions policies. Minimum treatment standards as defined in *Wyatt* include the following:

1. Individuals who are borderline or mildly retarded shall not be placed in residential institutions.
2. Admission to a residential institution shall be granted following the determination that the client environment match is the least restrictive habilitative setting.
3. Institutions must attempt to move residents in the following manner:
   a. To a less structured living environment
   b. From larger to smaller facilities
   c. From larger to smaller living units
   d. From group to individual residence
   e. From segregated to integrated community living
   f. From dependent to independent living

To summarize the importance of *Wyatt,* consider what it achieved. First, the case focused exclusively on individuals with mental retardation residing in institutions. Second, the court issued a set of minimum standards and monitoring procedures for residential facilities that would serve as a model to other states. Third, the case recognized the constitutional rights of these residents.

The Fifth Circuit Court of Appeals later essentially upheld the earlier decision of the Alabama federal court, reemphasizing that residents have a constitutional right to treatment. Furthermore, this decision allowed the federal court to set standards and monitor their implementation.

In 1986, a consent agreement was approved in federal district court in Alabama, providing a settlement to this litigation, which had been initiated 14 years earlier. Over the course of time, the original *Wyatt* case had been reopened periodically to review the status of the implementation of what the court had ordered in Judge Johnson's original decision (*Wyatt v. Hardin,* 1975; *Wyatt v. Ireland,* 1979). The 1986 agreement was conciliatory; both plaintiffs and defendants made compromises. But as Marchetti (1987) describes it, "It appeared that all parties to the litigation and the federal court were seeking a justifiable reason for returning the mental health system back to the state's 'control,' while protecting the rights of the class members" (p. 249). Marchetti provides an excellent chronology of the *Wyatt* litigation, a concise description of the consent decree, and an interesting discussion of the implications of this action.

The *Wyatt* case was finally resolved in December 2003. Sundram (2004) summarized the meaning of this action:

> The case that is emblematic of an era in mental disability law, *Wyatt v. Stickney,* came to an end in federal court in Montgomery, Alabama, on December 5, 2003, when Judge Myron Thompson found that the state of Alabama had complied with the latest Settlement Agreement in this 33-year-old case, and dismissed the action. (p. 1)

New York Association for Retarded Children v. Rockefeller.
The case of *New York Association for Retarded Children v. Rockefeller* (1973) is commonly referred to as "the Willowbrook case," since the institution under scrutiny was the Willowbrook State School. Like *Wyatt,* the case originated after complaints were voiced concerning

reductions in staff. It focused on three major issues: overcrowding, understaffing, and the absence of community alternatives to institutionalization. Even though conditions did improve, the court's rulings were not as comprehensive and powerful as they had been in *Wyatt*. More significant, however, is the national attention it received. The Willowbrook case made more people aware of the deplorable conditions and lack of programming that existed in many such settings.

O'Connor v. Donaldson.

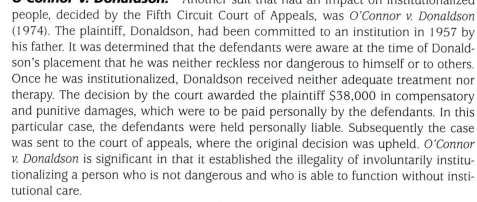

Another suit that had an impact on institutionalized people, decided by the Fifth Circuit Court of Appeals, was *O'Connor v. Donaldson* (1974). The plaintiff, Donaldson, had been committed to an institution in 1957 by his father. It was determined that the defendants were aware at the time of Donaldson's placement that he was neither reckless nor dangerous to himself or to others. Once he was institutionalized, Donaldson received neither adequate treatment nor therapy. The decision by the court awarded the plaintiff $38,000 in compensatory and punitive damages, which were to be paid personally by the defendants. In this particular case, the defendants were held personally liable. Subsequently the case was sent to the court of appeals, where the original decision was upheld. *O'Connor v. Donaldson* is significant in that it established the illegality of involuntarily institutionalizing a person who is not dangerous and who is able to function without institutional care.

Legal issues regarding guardianship continue to be discussed. To learn more, go to the Companion Website at www.prenhall.com/beirne-smith and select Chapter 4, Read and Respond.

Halderman v. Pennhurst State School and Hospital.

The first case concerning individuals with mental retardation who were residing in institutions to reach the U.S. Supreme Court was *Halderman v. Pennhurst* (1977). This case is fascinating because, in addition to the issues related to correcting unsatisfactory conditions at a large state-run facility (located in southeastern Pennsylvania), it ultimately sought to deinstitutionalize all residents, thereby closing down large, segregated facilities.

In the original action, begun in 1974, Terri Lee Halderman, a 20-year-old resident of Pennhurst, filed suit on behalf of herself and all present and future residents of the facility, alleging that subhuman conditions and the lack of habilitative programming at Pennhurst violated their statutory and constitutional rights.

In the first phase of the nonjury trial, begun in 1977, the court spent 32 days hearing testimony to establish the truth of Halderman's allegations. By the end of this exposition, any illusions of Pennhurst State School and Hospital as a facility for the "care and training" of persons with mental retardation were erased. The following excerpts from the opinion of presiding Judge Raymond Broderick suggest the quality of "care and training" afforded to residents there:

> Pennhurst is almost totally impersonal. Its residents have no privacy—they sleep in large, overcrowded wards, spend their waking hours together in large day rooms and eat in a large group setting. . . .
>
> All residents on Unit 7 go to bed between 8:00 and 8:30 P.M., are awakened and taken to the toilet at 12:00–12:30 A.M., and returned to sleep until 5:30 A.M. when they are awakened for the day, which begins with being toileted and then having to wait for a 7:00 A.M. breakfast. . . .

The physical environment at Pennhurst is hazardous to the residents, both physically and psychologically. There is often excrement and urine on ward floors, and the living areas do not meet minimal professional standards for cleanliness. Outbreaks of pinworms and infectious disease are common. . . .

Obnoxious odors and excessive noise permeate the atmosphere. Such conditions are not conducive to habilitation. Moreover, the noise level in the day rooms is often so high that many residents simply stop speaking. . . .

Residents' records commonly contain a notation that they would benefit from specific types of programming. However, such programming has, for the most part, been unavailable. The average resident receives only 1½ hours of programming per weekday and no programming on weekends. No one, except those in school, gets more than 3½ to 4 hours per day. If one factors out those programs which are not considered beneficial, the average drops to about 15 minutes per day. . . .

On the whole, the staff at Pennhurst appears to be dedicated and trying hard to cope with the inadequacies of the institution. Nearly every witness who testified concerning Pennhurst stated that it was grossly understaffed to adequately habilitate the residents.

The Broderick court held that confinement at Pennhurst clearly deprives residents of their right to nondiscriminatory habilitation, minimally adequate care, due process, equal protection, freedom from harm, and treatment by least restrictive means. Broderick ordered the eventual closing of Pennhurst and the establishment of suitable community settings to which residents could transfer. Moreover, he ordered that an individualized program plan (IPP) be developed for each remaining resident and that monitoring procedures be established for the duration of the facility's operation.

Pennhurst officials and their various codefendants appealed this decision in 1979 to the Third Circuit Court of Appeals. The appeals court affirmed the right of every individual with mental retardation to receive habilitative care in the least restrictive setting possible as well as his or her private right of action to enforce this right. Although the appeals court did not mandate Pennhurst's termination, it upheld 38 of the 41 paragraphs of Judge Broderick's order, along with his belief that persons with retardation would benefit most from community placement. The Third Circuit Court of Appeals based its judgment on statutory grounds—the 1974 Developmental Disabilities Assistance and Bill of Rights Act. The court stated that this legislation created substantive rights to habilitative services for individuals who were retarded.

In 1981, the U.S. Supreme Court reversed the appeals court decision. The High Court recognized the inadequate conditions at Pennhurst but did not believe that the congressional intent of the Developmental Disabilities Act created rights and required adequate treatment. McCarthy (1983) summarizes the Court's position: "The Supreme Court declared that the Act was not intended to create new substantive rights; it was designed to encourage, but not to mandate, better services for the developmentally disabled" (p. 519). McCarthy goes on to suggest that the Supreme Court position seems to be that it will strictly interpret funding legislation and will not demand that states provide services not explicitly stated in the laws.

In January 1984, out-of-court negotiations began between the parties involved in this case. By fall of that year, a settlement had been reached in which the state agreed to close Pennhurst, thus ending 10 years of litigation. Although this famous case did not achieve all the outcomes desired by the plaintiffs, *Pennhurst* will remain a byword in the movement to close institutions.

Youngberg v. Romeo.   In *Youngberg v. Romeo* (1982), the U.S. Supreme Court ruled that individuals with severe retardation who were involuntarily confined to any state facility had a constitutional right to habilitative services to ensure their safety and freedom from undue restraint—a decidedly restrictive view of habilitation. The Court reasoned that this right is based on the **substantive due process** provisions of the Fourteenth Amendment, which states that no state shall "deprive any person of life, liberty, or property without due process of law."

As Turnbull (1982) has indicated, the case affects professionals in significant ways. It spotlights the roles of professionals and professional differences of opinion by acknowledging that there are various models of treatment and a lack of consensus about which is best. The Court also recognized that professionals in the field of mental retardation are in much better positions than judges or juries to make decisions about treatment. Lakin and Bruininks (1985) note that the Supreme Court seems to have established a more limited role for federal courts in decisions of this type.

General education includes extracurricular and nonacademic activities, along with general classroom education.

LEGAL PRECEDENTS FOR INDIVIDUAL COMMUNITY RIGHTS

Adults with mental retardation living in community settings should be entitled to the same rights as other citizens. Gardner and Chapman (1985) developed a list of rights that persons living in community-based residential programs should enjoy (see Table 4.7). This list is not exhaustive, but it does give a sense of the rights we take for granted that have not always been available to people with mental retardation. To this list could be added other more controversial rights—such as the right to marry, the right to be parents, and the right to raise children. An overriding right for all is the right to associate with others. Several court cases have explored this topic.

Key Issues and Litigation

Much of the litigation directed at securing reasonable treatment in institutional settings (e.g., *Wyatt*) also suggested that efforts be undertaken to establish living conditions in community settings as close to normal and for as many individuals as possible. In line with this goal, advocates have championed the notion of community placement. The resultant community movement has taken hold, and many more individuals with mental retardation are pursuing their lives in more inclusive ways.

The right to live in community settings has not come without a struggle in many localities. This outcome has been most obvious in community opposition to

Right to services in the least restrictive environment
Right to normalized living conditions
Right to dignity and respect
Right to freedom from discomfort and deprivation
Right to appropriate clinical, medical, and therapeutic services
Right to vote
Right to religious worship
Right to private communication
Right to free association
Right to physical exercise
Right to seasonal, clean, neat clothing
Right to manage personal funds
Right to bed, dresser, and storage area
Right to privacy
Right to access to public media
Right to adequate nutrition
Freedom from unnecessary medication and mechanical, chemical, or physical restraints
Freedom from involuntary servitude
Right to equal protection and due process

TABLE 4.7
Rights of Persons in Community-Based Residential Programs

Source: From *Staff Development in Mental Retardation Services: A Practical Handbook* by J. F. Gardner & M. S. Chapman, 1985, Baltimore: Paul H. Brookes Publishing Co. Copyright © 1985 by Paul H. Brookes. Reprinted by permission.

the establishment of group homes. Henderson and Vitello (1988) state that three kinds of barriers can interfere with the community living movement: (1) local zoning ordinances, (2) state legislation that requires advance notification and in some cases permission from neighbors, and (3) restrictive covenants (e.g., people in a neighborhood are able to enforce a specific covenant to preserve the neighborhood's character). Of the three situations, the first has received the most attention.

Cleburne Living Center, Inc. v. City of Cleburne, Texas.   The case of *Cleburne Living Center, Inc. v. City of Cleburne, Texas* (1984) illustrates the problems that arise when a community opposes a group home. The principal obstacle in this case, as well as others like it, is the attempt to establish a group home in a "single-family residence" zone. In the past, group homes were commonly located in less desirable areas that were industrially or commercially zoned—areas for which permits were easier to obtain.

In this case, the Cleburne Living Center, Inc., was notified that a special-use permit would have to be approved before it could establish a group home for adults with mental retardation. The city council denied this permit on the basis that such a "hospital for the feebleminded" violated a local zoning ordinance. A suit was filed in federal district court claiming that the constitutional rights of these adults were being violated. The federal court upheld the city's decision to deny the request. On appeal, the Fifth Circuit Court of Appeals reversed the district court's ruling, citing that the ordinance was unconstitutional. This case was eventually appealed to the U.S. Supreme Court, which also found the zoning ordinance to be a violation of the plaintiff's equal protection rights.

Olmstead v. L.C.   A more recent case concerning community rights is *Olmstead v. L.C.* (1999). The Supreme Court decided that states should place individuals in community settings instead of institutions when the professionals deem that this setting is the most appropriate. The individual's wishes about where he or she lives must be considered, and the placement change must represent a reasonable accommodation for the states.

LEGAL ISSUES THAT SPAN A LIFETIME

Unfortunately, individuals with mental retardation are subject to the same ills and problems that affect the rest of society. The withholding of medical treatment, acts of sexual abuse, and domestic violence can impact the lives of the mentally retarded. They can also be the victims of crime or become criminal defendants. These problems have implications not only for the legal system but for educators as well.

Withholding Treatment

Individuals who are mentally retarded and who need organ transplants are often denied. Doctors and transplant center officials claim that they are not discriminating against individuals who are mentally retarded. They consider, however, how well the individuals will be able to take care of themselves and consequently their transplanted organs. They maintain that they are trying to give transplants to the individuals who will benefit the most. The result is that individuals with intellectual disabilities often do not receive organ transplants.

Hardie (2000) has chronicled the story of Julie, 27, a young woman with Down syndrome, who needed a heart-lung transplant. Hardie maintains that only one person with Down syndrome has ever received a heart-lung transplant, although there may be thousands of people with Down syndrome who need them. Perhaps Julie's mother said it best when she stated, "Doctors take an oath to doctor everybody. Don't [*sic*] that mean anything?" (p. H1)

Sexual Abuse

From childhood to adulthood, sexual abuse can be a concern for individuals with mental retardation. When one considers the characteristics that make individuals with disabilities—especially those who are mentally retarded—vulnerable, it is understandable that sexual offenders might select them as suitable targets. Indeed, according to Hume (1999), children with disabilities are abused (sexually and in other ways) at higher rates than children without disabilities. Generally, child sexual offenders look for children whom they consider to be susceptible to their advances. In explaining how victims are selected, one offender stated, "I would probably pick the one who appeared more needy, the child hanging back from others and feeling picked on." Another offender offered that he would "look for the kid who is easy to manipulate" (p. 8).

Reaching adulthood does not make those who are mentally retarded safe from sexual abuse. Sobsey (1997) reports that physical and sexual abuse rates are 4 to 10 times higher for adults with disabilities than for adults without disabilities. Sorensen (1997) relates that five women with mental retardation were raped by the owner of the home facility where they lived. Perhaps many of these crimes are not reported (Sobsey, 1997), and therefore it may not be possible to know the full extent of the problem.

Domestic Violence

If women without disabilities can become victims of domestic violence, then there is no reason to believe that women who are mentally retarded are somehow protected from this problem. Although literature focusing on women with mental retardation who are the victims of domestic violence is limited, Carlson (1997) explored the topic and contends that factors such as dependency, low self-esteem, and learned helplessness can increase the potential for domestic violence. Such women may not have contact with their families, which can help ensure continued exposure to violence.

Carlson (1997) relates the story of Nancy, a woman with mild retardation who lived independently in an apartment supervised by an agency that assisted individuals with developmental disabilities. Nancy finally admitted that she was being beaten by her boyfriend, William. Although Nancy wanted to end the relationship, she had been afraid to speak with the supervising agency about her problems. A representative from a domestic violence services organization and a caseworker from the supervising agency developed an intervention plan. They spoke with Nancy's landlord and with the police to inform them of the situation. They also obtained a restraining order against William, and the police agreed to notify and warn William not to harass Nancy. They taught Nancy several steps to take if William attempted to contact her.

Crime Victims

Sorensen (1997) contends that crimes are committed against individuals with disabilities at higher rates than individuals without disabilities. Moreover, Sobsey (1997) states that when these crimes are reported, law enforcement officials are hesitant to investigate and prosecute because they believe that the cases cannot be won. Sorensen asserts that even with the higher crime rates, prosecutors often have few caseloads that include individuals with disabilities. For instance, in the case of the five women who were raped (mentioned earlier), initially the local district attorney refused to prosecute.

Another tragic incident occurred when a man who was mentally retarded was poisoned and died after the owner of the home in which he lived collected and served him wild mushrooms (Sorensen, 1997). She served the mushrooms in an effort to save money on the grocery bill. The man had previously complained that he was not getting enough to eat. The woman was not charged with a crime. In other words, some prosecutors discriminate and do not provide individuals who are disabled with equal protection under the law.

When those who commit crimes against individuals with disabilities are prosecuted, they receive more lenient sentences as compared to sentences for crimes committed against individuals without disabilities (Petersilia, 1998). Sobsey (1997) found evidence of lighter sentences throughout the world. He relates the case of a mother in France who killed her autistic daughter; she received probation. Even in death, there may be no justice for individuals with disabilities.

Criminal Defendants

From the apprehension of the suspect to the execution of the convicted, the legal system is fraught with inequities for those who are mentally retarded (Petersilia, 1998). At each stage, individuals who are mentally retarded are at a decided disadvantage. However, it must be remembered that in any legal proceeding the individual is protected by **procedural due process,** the Fifth Amendment guarantee of the individual's right to a hearing, to be notified of a hearing, to be represented by counsel at a hearing, to be able to question and cross-examine witnesses, and to present witnesses.

At the apprehension stage, one police officer summed up the problem by stating that the mentally retarded are "the last to leave the scene, the first to get arrested, and the first to confess" (Petersilia, 1998, p. 5). It does not help that many police officers have not been trained to recognize and deal with individuals who are disabled. Laski and Keefe (1997) give an example of a man with autism who liked to walk back and forth in front of his home. Two police officers noticed him in front of his house and decided that he was a peeping Tom. In the confrontation that ensued, the officers threw him on the ground, which resulted in the man sustaining a physical injury.

At the interrogation stage, many factors can complicate matters for individuals who are mentally retarded. Some may wish to hide their disability (Edwards & Reynolds, 1997). They may not want police officers to know that they do not understand the questions, and consequently may avoid answering them (Keyes, 1997). In one study, Everington and Fulero (1999) found that individuals with mental retardation were less likely to understand their Miranda rights. They also concluded that individuals with mental retardation were "more likely to respond to leading questions and to coercion" (p. 218). Individuals who are mentally retarded may also confess to crimes that they did not commit, in an effort to please authority figures (Petersilia, 1998). Therefore, people with mental retardation may be wrongly convicted of a crime.

Death Penalty

Beyond the issue of those who are wrongly convicted, what should happen to individuals who are mentally retarded and guilty of a crime punishable by death? Keyes, Edwards, and Perske (1997) list some characteristics of individuals who are mentally retarded, including impulsiveness, lack of cause-and-effect reasoning, poor judgment, and, of course, lower intelligence. Keyes and his colleagues state that because of these characteristics, individuals who are mentally retarded lack the culpability necessary for imposition of the death penalty. They also calculated that 30 individuals with mental retardation were executed in the United States from 1976 to 1996.

In June of 2002, the U.S. Supreme Court ruled in *Atkins v. Virginia* that it was cruel and unusual punishment to subject individuals with mental retardation to the death penalty (see chapter 2, Table 2.9). This decision has had a profound effect on the cases of many individuals who are at the pretrial, trial, or postconviction stage. While not all states have a death penalty and other states use this form of punishment only rarely, there are states such as Texas, California, Florida, and Virginia that exercise the death penalty and have large numbers of individuals on death row. The issue of determining whether an individual has mental retardation is a complicated one. For a review of the key issues associated with persons who have mental retardation and the death penalty, see Everington, Olley, and Patton (in press.).

Implications

There may be common solutions to the aforementioned issues of the withholding of medical treatment, sexual abuse, domestic violence, and the problems inherent in the criminal justice system. These solutions may involve developing self-advocacy skills, advocacy by other organizations, and more training for doctors, educators, and law enforcement officials.

Students with disabilities should be taught how to advocate for themselves if they are being abused or accused of a crime. If they are accused of a crime, this self-advocacy may consist of merely teaching them to say, "I need to see a lawyer." As an example, one youth, Henry, who is mentally retarded, attended a special training program where he was taught this statement (Houchins, 1997). Henry witnessed two boys trying to burglarize a newspaper stand. A police officer drove up, and the offenders accused Henry of the crime. When the officer questioned Henry, he would only respond, "I need a lawyer." Henry also gave the officer a card that instructed him to call Henry's mother or the mental health retardation hotline. Subsequently Henry testified against the two boys, and they were convicted.

Self-advocacy skills may not be an option for everyone who is mentally retarded. If possible, these individuals should be taught how to access the services of organizations that can help protect them. However, individuals like Julie (the woman described earlier who needed an organ transplant) will need other parties to help save their lives. Parents, social workers, teachers, and other concerned individuals must be aware of organizations, both public and private, that can help. For example, the Association of Retarded Citizens (ARC) provides assistance to individuals accused of crimes. It also develops sentencing alternatives for convicted offenders with disabilities (Reynolds & Berkobien, 1997).

Possible solutions also hold implications for doctors, teachers, and law enforcement officials. Doctors may stereotype individuals with Down syndrome, viewing them as a monolithic group unable to care for themselves. Doctors may need more information about the services and support systems currently provided to individuals with disabilities. Teachers must specifically train students with disabilities to deal with issues of abuse and inform them of their rights in the criminal justice system. Many law enforcement officials also need additional training, and in fact some police departments have developed training programs (Fulton, 1997). The National Judicial College developed a curriculum to assist judges when they are dealing with individuals who are mentally retarded. Another organization that provides training is the Disability Rights Education and Defense Fund, Inc., founded in 1979 to protect and advance the civil rights of people with disabilities.

PERSISTING PROBLEMS

Two lingering problems are addressed in this section: noncompliance with IDEA, and improvement in the lives of people who were school-age prior to the passage of P.L. 94-142.

According to the National Council on Disability (NCD), there may be a problem with the enforcement of IDEA ("Back to School," 2000). Based on a review of Department of Education records from 1994 to 1998, the NCD concluded that "every state was out of compliance with IDEA requirements to some degree; in the sampling of states studied, noncompliance persisted over many years" (p. 1). The NCD also states that the Department of Education was not effectively using its enforcement authority to ensure compliance.

These are serious allegations. Current noncompliance with IDEA could have a detrimental effect on individuals with disabilities for many years into the future.

In contrast, members of the Council for Exceptional Children (CEC) counter that the report of the NCD did not accurately portray state compliance with IDEA, stating that some state noncompliance involved minor procedural violations ("Report Gives Unbalanced Impression," 2000). They agree, however, that efforts must be made to provide all students with their rights under IDEA.

Also troubling is the situation of those adults who grew up during a time in which FAPE was not provided (Kaye, 1997) and as a result may not be living their lives to their fullest potential. They may have deficiencies in such areas as functional academics, vocational training, and independent living. Kaye contends that more should be done to retrain these individuals.

The ramifications of a lack of FAPE in the past, coupled with possible state noncompliance with IDEA today, should be closely examined. These are both issues that could negatively impact those with disabilities. The NCD is urging Congress to ensure full implementation with IDEA. Congress, policy makers, educators, and parents should also question whether enough has been done to retrain individuals who were denied FAPE.

FINAL THOUGHTS

The fields of science and technology may hold much promise for individuals who are mentally retarded. Biotechnology may have an effect on the reduction of mental retardation in future years (Baker, 1997). Advances in gene therapy, genetic engineering, fetal surgery, human genome research, and biomedical research could have an impact on individuals with disabilities. Baker asserts that 21st century "medical technology may remove certain genetic markers or diminish any residual impact to the extent that only subtle physical or behavioral remnants will suggest that an individual needs support" (p. 378).

To check your understanding of this chapter, go to the Companion Website at www.prenhall.com/beirne-smith and select Chapter 4. From there, you can access the Self-Test and Essay modules.

Various types of technology are also beneficial. The uses of personal digital assistants (PDAs) and computers with individuals who are mentally retarded may be limited only by our imagination. Scientists have already developed wearable computers, and experts in the field are stating that man and machine will become one through this technology (Bookman, 2000a). Other scientists are attempting to combine living brain cells with electronics to create a bionic brain (Bookman, 2000b).

All of these areas may potentially involve the courts and legislation. Many legal and ethical questions may need to be answered. Will there be limitations—legal or ethical—on the uses of technology? How much input will individuals with disabilities and their advocates have in formulating policy? Who will decide the answers to these questions? Although these advancements hold much promise, there may also be room for abuse. Society will have the challenge of ensuring that technology will be used to help and not harm individuals with disabilities.

Summary

The Context for Securing Individuals' Rights

- *Brown v. Board of Education* (1954) was a significant ruling that provided legal precedents for individuals with disabilities.
- Certain legal terms such as *equal protection* and *due process* must be understood.
- Persons with mental retardation historically have been vulnerable to purposely unequal treatment.
- Mechanisms for securing rights are found at the federal, state, and local levels.

Legal Precedents for Individual Rights

- Individuals with disabilities are afforded certain rights regarding access to education, evaluation, classification, appropriate education, placement, related services, the extended school year, and expulsion.
- A noteworthy history of litigation exists that has tried to secure the right to treatment or habilitation for those confined to institutional settings.

Issues That Span a Lifetime

- Individuals who are mentally retarded may be denied certain medical services because of their disability.
- Issues relevant to crime, such as sexual abuse and domestic violence, can affect individuals who are mentally retarded.

Persisting Problems

- Congress and other officials must ensure compliance with IDEA.
- The training needs of individuals with disabilities who grew up prior to the provision of FAPE may need to be reevaluated.

Final Thoughts

- Technology may hold great promise as well as challenge for improving the lives of individuals with mental retardation.
- Many legal and ethical questions remain to be addressed.

5

Psychosocial Aspects of Intellectual Disability

OBJECTIVES

After reading this chapter, the student should be able to:

- Discuss the environmental correlates of intellectual disability
- Explain the relationship between poverty and intellectual disability
- Describe psychosocial interventions for people with intellectual disabilities
- Consider cultural implications for the treatment and understanding of people with intellectual disabilities

KEY TERMS

behavior genetics

compensatory interventions

cultural deprivation

cultural-familial mental retardation

ethnocentrism

feral children

nature–nurture controversy

psychosocial

6-hour retarded children

A complete on-line glossary is available on the Companion Website, which may be accessed at www.prenhall.com/beirne-smith

The eugenics movement is discussed in chapter 1.

T hroughout history, people have debated whether nature (a person's biological makeup) or nurture (learning that takes place within a person's environment) is responsible for shaping character. The **nature–nurture controversy,** ancient as it is, continues to be discussed in modern times. These days, however, few people attempt to defend an either-or philosophy. Most are willing to acknowledge that biology and environment both affect development, and that they interact and even influence each other. The discussion often seems academic; however, the nature–nurture debate has had a very real impact on persons with intellectual disabilities. The eugenics movement is probably the most dramatic and tragic example of this. However, the **psychosocial** position—the idea that environmental experience shapes behavior and attributes—has also had a huge influence on the identification and treatment of intellectual disabilities.

Despite the fact that a model of biology–environment interaction is widely accepted, people still argue over which is most important. The **behavior geneticists,** scientists who believe behavior is largely shaped by genetics, have attempted to argue through statistical analyses that the largest part of a person's intelligence, personality, interests, and behavior can be traced to biological disposition. The arguments can be quite compelling (cf. Rowe 1995). However, their analyses do not exclude environmental effects. In fact, their arguments indicate that environmental effects are strongest for persons whose experiences are out of the ordinary. As you'll see in this chapter, many of the psychosocial conditions that correlate with intellectual disability are just that.

This chapter explores some of the environmental correlates of intellectual disability. The relationship between poverty and mild mental retardation will be examined, as well as various types of interventions designed to compensate for environmental stressors related to poverty. Finally, we will turn our attention to the role of the environment in the success and happiness of people with intellectual disabilities, and the cultural factors that affect their treatment and understanding. Throughout the chapter, we will rely on classic research to illustrate not only what is known about psychosocial causes of intellectual disabilities, but also how this information was learned.

THE ROLE OF POVERTY

In 1959, the American Association on Mental Retardation (AAMR) for the first time acknowledged a subclassification called **cultural-familial mental retardation.** In current terminology, it is more common to hear of "intellectual disability that results from psychosocial disadvantage." The category is described as a form of mental retardation for which there is no discernable physiological cause. Instead, the disability is thought to be caused by certain environmental circumstances. The people who fall into this category tend to be labeled with mild or borderline mental retardation, and they tend to come from economically disadvantaged homes.

What is it about low socioeconomic status (SES) that lends itself to correlation with intellectual disability? Some have said that the higher rate of mental retardation in impoverished regions indicates a biological disposition that is inherited through the genes. Indeed, this was Goddard's opinion in his 1912 study of the "Kallikak" family, in which he stated:

We find on the good side of the family prominent people in all walks of life and nearly all of the 496 descendants owners of land or proprietors. On the bad side we find paupers, criminals, prostitutes, drunkards, and examples of all forms of social pest with which modern society is burdened.

From this we conclude that feeblemindedness is largely responsible for these social sores. Feeblemindedness is hereditary and transmitted as surely as any other character. We cannot successfully cope with these conditions until we recognize feeblemindedness and its hereditary nature, recognize it early, and take care of it.

In considering the question of care, segregation through colonization seems in the present state of our knowledge to be the ideal and perfectly satisfactory method. Sterilization may be accepted as a makeshift, as a help to solve this problem because the conditions have become so intolerable. (Goddard, 1912/1973, pp. 116–117)

Thankfully, the social response to intellectual disability is a bit more kind and gentle today. Although the possibility of genetic "pockets" of mental retardation cannot be discarded, we also understand that high rates of intellectual disability in a family or community does not necessarily mean that all of the cases are biologically based. In the case of impoverished homes, several circumstances may interact to prevent children from maximizing their intellectual potential. It is incredibly important to stress that this information should not be applied in a stereotypical fashion to all low-SES homes. In fact, the vast majority of people who live in poverty exhibit normal intelligence. However, *culturally deprived* homes—those that cannot provide the basic environmental stimulation necessary for optimal child development—are generally found to have low socioeconomic status. It is this **cultural deprivation** that is thought to result in intellectual disability.

In order to understand cultural deprivation, it is necessary to know what is important for intellectual development. Some characteristics of an optimally stimulating environment were offered by Ramey and Ramey (1996) and are compiled in Table 5.1.

Culturally deprived homes are often headed by single mothers who themselves have low IQ. Frequently, these mothers are quite young. They are often unemployed and/or rely on government assistance for survival. The households tend to be highly stressed, to have a bleak outlook on the future, self-imposed limits on dreams for the future, and an overall feeling of social oppression (Blatt, 1981). As depicted in Figure 5.1, the poverty creates stressors that impact the family, leading the next generation into poverty as well. Along the way, the conditions become prime for the onset of mental retardation. The logical question is: Can these problems be overcome? There is a body of research on **compensatory interventions,** or treatments designed to counteract the effects of poverty. We will discuss one such project next. Others will be discussed later in the chapter.

The Milwaukee Project

The role of cultural deprivation in the development of intellectual disability has long been discussed, but the most famous work in that area is most certainly the Milwaukee Project (Garber, 1988). The study began in the 1960s and was set in a Milwaukee housing project identified as having a higher than expected rate of mental retardation. The goal was to identify aspects of family or home environments that

TABLE 5.1

What Young Children Need in Their Everyday Lives to Promote Positive Cognitive Development and Good Attitudes Toward Learning

Encouragement of exploration: To be encouraged by adults to explore and to gather information about their environments.

Mentoring in basic skills: To be mentored (especially by trusted adults) in basic cognitive skills, such as labeling, sorting, sequencing, comparing, and noting means-ends relationships.

Celebration of developmental advances: To have their developmental accomplishments celebrated and reinforced by others, especially those with whom they spend a lot of time.

Guided rehearsal and extension of new skills: To have responsible others help them in rehearsing and then elaborating upon (extending) their newly acquired skills.

Protection from inappropriate disapproval, teasing, or punishment: To avoid negative experiences associated with adults' disapproval, teasing, or punishment for those behaviors that are normative and necessary in children's trial-and-error learning about their environments (e.g., mistakes in trying out a new skill, unintended consequences of curious exploration or information-seeking). *Note:* This does not mean that constructive criticism and negative consequences cannot be used for other child behaviors that children have the ability to understand are socially unacceptable.

Rich and responsive language environment: To have adults provide a predictable and comprehensible communication environment, in which language is used to convey information, provide social rewards, and encourage learning of new materials and skills. *Note:* Although language to the child is the most important early intervention, the language environment may be supplemented in valuable ways by the use of written materials or computer-based assistive technology devices.

Source: From "Early Intervention: Optimizing Development for Children with Disabilities and Risk Conditions," by C. T. Ramey & S. L. Ramey, in M. L. Wolraich (Ed.), *Disorders of Development and Learning: A Practical Guide to Assessment and Measurement* (2nd ed., p. 147), 1996, St. Louis: Mosby. Reprinted by permission.

may lead children who appeared to be normal at birth to develop mental retardation by the time they entered school.

The children identified for the study were determined to be "at risk" for mental retardation because they lived in this low-SES development and because their mothers were identified as having an IQ of 75 or below. Half of the families participated in an intervention while the other half received no intervention. At regular intervals, the children were administered a battery of tests, including tests of intelligence. The groups were then compared to determine whether the intervention (designed to introduce conditions common in households led by economically advantaged mothers who did not have an intellectual disability) led to decreased rates of mental retardation among the children.

Why do you think the researchers concentrated on children whose mothers had intellectual disabilities?

The intervention package consisted of two parts: family rehabilitation and child stimulation. In the family rehabilitation component, mothers were provided with paid instruction in job skills, followed by assistance in finding a job. The mothers (and some fathers) also were given instruction in daily life skills, such as counting money, paying bills, and so forth. Additionally, personal assistance and advocacy services were offered.

The child stimulation component provided routine medical care and screenings. The children were taken daily to a nursery care center, where the trained caretakers

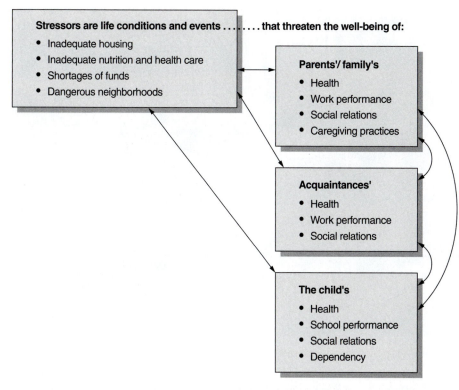

FIGURE 5.1

Environmental Stressors' Effects on Children Raised in Poverty

Source: From *Recent Theories of Human Development* (p. 215), by R. M. Thomas, 2001,. Thousand Oaks, CA: Sage. Copyright © 2001 by Sage Publications, Inc. Reprinted by permission of Sage Publications, Inc.

attempted to duplicate the types of interactions and experiences that previous research had identified as differentiating middle-class households from lower-class families. Sensory, motor, perceptual, cognitive, social, and language skills were targeted in different forms as the children developed.

Assessment information indicated that the children who received the intervention had IQs that averaged 30 points higher than those who did not. Additionally, they were significantly better at problem solving, exhibited more enthusiasm for learning tasks, and had significantly more advanced language skills. Follow-up assessments of IQ indicated that the differences continued through age 10, but the point range was smaller. Perhaps more startling, 60% of the control group children were classified as mentally retarded by the end of 4th grade, while none of the children who received the intervention package were so classified. It is important to note, though, that these positive outcomes did not necessarily lead to positive scholastic outcomes.

The Milwaukee Project generated a great deal of enthusiasm about the prospects of early intervention. However, the interventions were intensive. Some children were placed in foster homes. The infant stimulation and preschool programs were run for

Compensatory interventions target a variety of areas, including cognitive, motor, and social skills.

7 hours a day, 5 days a week. The personal assistance and advocacy services were provided by someone who established a personal relationship with the families. Interventions were individually tailored and were enhanced significantly by the strong personal relationships that study participants formed with the research teams.

Unfortunately, the enthusiasm generated by the Milwaukee Project would be marred by suspicion. Criticisms were made of the scientific rigor (or lack thereof) employed. Additionally, interested researchers had difficulty accessing the data for reanalysis. Still, the Milwaukee Project has remained influential. Generally speaking, the ideas it proposed are modeled by current early intervention programs, but the intensity is difficult for traditional social service organizations to match. (We will discuss other models of early intervention later in the chapter.)

The correlation between poverty and intellectual disability brings many challenges. One significant challenge relates to the unfortunate fact that many of the people living in poverty in the United States are members of minority groups. Combined with the environmental differences of poverty are the cultural differences of minority group membership. For that reason, a group of children may be at risk for being labeled with mental retardation upon entering school, although they may not exhibit characteristics as such in their home environments.

The 6-Hour Retarded Child

One of the most often cited concepts introduced by the President's Committee on Mental Retardation is the so-called "6-hour retarded child." The 1969 report defined **6-hour**

retarded children as "children and youth who were identified as being 'educably mentally retarded' only during their school hours and only during their school lives" (President's Committee on Mental Retardation, 1969). In other words, this group of children exhibited nothing to call attention to any cognitive limitations outside the school setting.

The report indicated that this was due to a reliance on IQ scores without regard to adaptive behavior indices. However, the question remained whether this group of students was truly fully functioning without intervention, or if they could, indeed, benefit from special services. What was known was that this group was disproportionately African American and poor.

See chapter 1 for information on the President's Committee on Mental Retardation.

In 1971, Garrison and Hammill published their landmark study, *Who Are the Retarded?* Briefly, the study described a subset of children with mental retardation rulings from Philadelphia-area schools, who had been placed in special classes. Garrison and Hammill applied a rigorous diagnostic assessment and determined that 25% of the children did not have mental retardation. The point of the study was that a single factor (IQ) should not be used to make placement and diagnostic decisions. However, there was a quiet suggestion that some of the children could be in those classrooms due to behavioral disorders or learning disabilities. (For a unique perspective on this issue, see Box 5.1.)

Garrison and Hammill did not provide demographic information about the children misplaced into special classrooms, but previous suspicion had been cast that minority children from impoverished neighborhoods were more likely to be labeled mentally retarded because of cultural differences. As can be seen in Table 5.2, African American children are still more likely than children from other racial groups to be labeled with mental retardation by the public schools.

Box 5.1 ✻ Reevaluating the Concept of Mental Retardation

The poem printed here was written by Marc Gold, a respected leader in the area of vocational training and a strong champion for the rights of people with mental retardation. The poem, read at the end of a speech that Gold gave in 1973, has been cited often since then and is used in the opening soundtrack of the film *Try Another Way*. Embedded in the poem is commentary about expectations, perceptions, testing, opportunities, and capabilities. The message of this poem is as relevant today as it was in 1973 and when its author reflected back on it (Gold, 1980).

An End to the Concept of Mental Retardation

Oh, What a Beautiful Mourning
If you could only know me for who I am
Instead of for who I am not,
There would be so much more to see

'Cause there's so much more that I've got.
So long as you see me as mentally retarded,
Which supposedly means something, I guess,
There is nothing that you or I could ever do
To make me a human success.
Someday you'll know that tests aren't built
To let me stand next to you.
By the way you test me, all they can do
Is make me look bad through and through.
And someday soon I'll get my chance,
When some of you finally adapt.
You'll be delighted to know that though I'm MR,
I'm not all handicapped.

Source: From "An End to the Concept of Mental Retardation: Oh, What a Beautiful Mourning," by M. W. Gold, in *Did I Say That? Articles and Commentary on the Try Another Way System* (pp. 143–144), 1980, Champaign, IL: Research Press. Reprinted with permission.

TABLE 5.2
Racial/Ethnic Composition (Percentage) of Students Ages 6–21 Served Under IDEA Part B During the 2002–03 School Year Mental Retardation Ruling

State	American Indian/ Alaskan	Asian/ Pacific Islander	Black	Hispanic	White	Total
Alabama	0.31	0.26	63.19	0.59	35.65	100.00
Alaska	37.51	5.73	5.73	3.94	47.07	100.00
Arizona	7.50	1.44	8.46	40.75	41.85	100.00
Arkansas	0.41	0.23	44.83	1.87	52.66	100.00
California	0.80	8.26	12.33	47.14	31.48	100.00
Colorado	1.14	1.91	12.62	32.31	52.02	100.00
Connecticut	0.40	1.47	27.82	21.35	48.97	100.00
Delaware	0.19	0.65	53.71	7.20	38.25	100.00
District Of Columbia	0.06	0.31	96.49	2.28	0.86	100.00
Florida	0.08	0.85	48.65	14.88	35.55	100.00
Georgia	0.11	0.73	62.51	3.30	33.35	100.00
Hawaii	0.14	83.81	2.00	3.16	10.90	100.00
Idaho	1.93	0.83	0.99	15.86	80.39	100.00
Illinois	0.07	1.58	42.46	12.31	43.57	100.00
Indiana	0.18	0.23	27.67	3.34	68.58	100.00
Iowa	0.67	0.83	7.62	3.78	87.09	100.00
Kansas	1.11	0.76	20.57	9.14	68.42	100.00
Kentucky	0.16	0.22	15.42	0.54	83.66	100.00
Louisiana	0.44	0.43	69.31	0.60	29.21	100.00
Maine	1.54	0.21	0.82	0.51	96.91	100.00
Maryland	0.44	1.72	60.82	2.80	34.22	100.00
Massachusetts	0.33	2.41	18.84	21.74	56.69	100.00
Michigan	0.77	0.95	36.00	2.99	59.29	100.00
Minnesota	3.44	3.71	11.71	3.84	77.30	100.00
Mississippi	0.08	0.36	75.00	0.44	24.13	100.00
Missouri	0.29	0.46	32.85	1.43	64.97	100.00
Montana	15.89	0.88	1.40	2.72	79.10	100.00
Nebraska	2.65	0.93	11.40	11.03	73.99	100.00
Nevada	2.52	5.51	20.41	25.18	46.38	100.00
New Hampshire	0.10	1.04	1.98	4.38	92.49	100.00
New Jersey	0.22	3.45	38.84	23.37	34.11	100.00

State	American Indian/ Alaskan	Asian/ Pacific Islander	Black	Hispanic	White	Total
New Mexico	12.65	0.70	3.86	56.67	26.11	100.00
New York	0.62	3.22	33.34	21.40	41.42	100.00
North Carolina	2.97	0.54	59.42	2.96	34.10	100.00
North Dakota	13.58	0.52	1.90	1.90	82.09	100.00
Ohio	0.14	0.26	32.07	1.87	65.65	100.00
Oklahoma	14.22	0.93	25.37	4.95	54.52	100.00
Oregon	2.46	2.58	5.70	10.37	78.89	100.00
Pennsylvania	0.21	0.47	21.66	5.93	71.73	100.00
Puerto Rico	0.01	0.01	0.18	99.78	0.02	100.00
Rhode Island	0.58	2.88	10.60	22.10	63.85	100.00
South Carolina	0.12	0.28	70.53	0.76	28.32	100.00
South Dakota	15.70	0.89	2.37	1.85	79.19	100.00
Tennessee	0.13	0.36	52.89	0.83	45.79	100.00
Texas	0.27	1.52	30.50	37.14	30.56	100.00
Utah	1.96	2.32	1.38	11.54	82.80	100.00
Vermont	0.96	0.72	1.44	0.48	96.41	100.00
Virginia	0.08	1.97	49.96	4.01	43.97	100.00
Washington	4.74	4.98	9.54	14.66	66.08	100.00
West Virginia	0.09	0.07	5.48	0.16	94.20	100.00
Wisconsin	1.84	2.35	21.04	5.11	69.66	100.00
Wyoming	1.82	0.66	1.16	9.57	86.80	100.00
American Samoa	0.00	100.00	0.00	0.00	0.00	100.00
Guam	0.00	95.56	2.22	2.22	0.00	100.00
Northern Marianas	0.00	98.15	0.00	0.00	1.85	100.00
Virgin Islands	0.00	0.00	79.26	19.68	1.06	100.00
Bureau of Indian Affairs	99.77	0.00	0.00	0.00	0.23	100.00
U.S. and Outlying Areas	1.14	1.83	34.47	12.50	50.06	100.00
50 states, District of Columbia, and Puerto Rico	1.07	1.80	34.48	12.51	50.15	100.00

Data based on the December 1, 2002 count, updated as of July 31, 2003.

Source: U.S. Department of Education. (2003). IDEA Part B Child Count (2002). In *Data Tables for OSEP State Reported Data.* Available from www.ideadata.org/tables26th/ar_aa15.htm

To think more about racial issues in special education, visit the Companion Website at www.prenhall.com/beirne-smith and select Chapter 5, Read and Respond.

Two theories exist about the 6-hour retarded children. First, it has been suggested that cultural differences made it difficult for the children to assimilate into the school culture, which was shaped by middle-class, White norms. However, when they returned to their home environments they were able meld into society. The other theory is that some of these children were identified by the schools because they struggled with the higher order cognitive tasks presented to them. They were able to function well in home communities that did not emphasize skills in math, reading, and language. As adults, they are able to choose career paths that do not require those skills. In essence, they are adapting to a very real cognitive limitation (Campbell & Fedeyko, 2001). Some are, in fact, able to "disappear" after school. Others, however, continue to struggle when they encounter situations outside the realm of their everyday lives (Richardson & Koller, 1996).

As with so many issues in social science, it appears that there is no definitive right or wrong answer to the question of the 6-hour retarded child. Generally, schools now require a more comprehensive evaluation for diagnosing mental retardation. However, what about those children who struggle in school, but are fine in other life arenas? What should happen to them? Clearly, many children have historically been placed in special classrooms due to cultural differences. Biases do exist in testing practices, as well. However, there are some basic philosophical questions at the root of this. How can schools effectively instruct children who are culturally different from the majority? Should adaptive behavior be assessed in reference to the home community, or the school community? How can these children best be prepared for life after school? The questions did not end with the 1970s. They still arise in public education today.

PSYCHOSOCIAL INTERVENTIONS

Largely in response to the literature on the relationship between cultural deprivation and intellectual disability, psychosocial researchers have attempted to formulate helpful interventions for prevention or to improve the lives of people who have mental retardation. Many positive outcomes have been accomplished, such as the development of infant and early childhood stimulation programs. However, while reading this chapter you will encounter a troubling trend among the psychosocial researchers and interventionists. Time and again, psychologists and educators promised more than they could deliver. Quite often, history would show that the interventions led to important outcomes—but these outcomes would be overlooked because the loftier goals that had been set in the beginning (e.g., to increase IQ or eradicate mental retardation) failed to be achieved.

The so-called "wild boy of Aveyron," one of the most notable examples of this trend, also happens to be one of the earliest reports of systematic special education. It involves the work of the imminent French physician Jean-Marc Gaspard Itard, who is considered one of the forefathers of special education.

The Wild Boy of Aveyron

As described in chapter 2, mental retardation by definition requires a person to have deficits in adaptive skills. These skills are learned largely through social modeling. IQ scores are also mitigated by social experience. Logically, then, people who are deprived of human contact would develop mental retardation. Isolated reports of persons growing up without significant human contact bear out this conclusion. These reports are generally based on the cases of **feral children**—children who grow up in social isolation, either through their own efforts or with the assistance of animals.

 To learn about other reports of feral children, as well as additional topics related to this chapter, visit the Companion Website at www.prenhall.com/ beirne-smith and select Chapter 5, Web Destinations.

This most famous feral child case was documented by Jean-Marc Gaspard Itard. In the 1790s, a legend emerged of a wild boy, approximately 12 years old, who lived in the woods of Lacaune in France, surviving by eating what was available in the forest and by stealing from local crops. After several sightings, he was captured and evaluated by leading educators of the time. It was thought that he was uneducable and congenitally retarded.

Itard was on the staff of an institution for the deaf, and was widely respected in his profession. He was greatly influenced by the Enlightenment philosophers, who believed that experience was the most important aspect of development. He decided to apply his methods to the instruction of the feral boy, whom he named Victor. His goal was to "awaken the boy's mind" (Malson, 1972).

In the beginning, Victor exhibited behaviors more similar to animals than to people. He did not wear clothing, nor did he seem to recognize or notice the sounds of the human voice. He could not open a door or use a chair to approach an out-of-reach object. He cared nothing for the activities of the other children. On the other hand, he possessed abilities most people did not. He could pick burning logs out of a fire without pain, could locate roots and berries by sniffing, and could bear intense cold. He did not speak, but possessed a single gutteral sound (Itard, 1801/1972).

In the first year, Itard listed five objectives for Victor's education: socialization, awakening of the senses, introduction to pleasurable activities, rudimentary speech functions, and recognition of symbolic representations. In his final report, following 6 years with Victor, Itard delineated three areas of instruction: sensory, intellectual, and emotional (Itard, 1801/1972).

The education of Victor was vigorous, methodical, and fruitful. Victor lived in Itard's home, under the care of a housekeeper. During his time with Itard and the housekeeper, Victor learned to adhere to basic rules of conduct (most of the time; there *was* an incident of tree climbing during a social engagement) and was able to perform household chores and personal grooming activities. A wider range of human senses became available to him (such as the differentiation between hot and cold, and the ability to appreciate comfort). He learned to recognize written letters and words, and to understand that they represented objects. He learned to communicate through pictures and signs. Additionally, and perhaps most importantly, he did establish relationships with Itard and the housekeeper. Although Itard described him as essentially selfish in his motivations, Victor would seek the approval of his teachers and tried to avoid upsetting them. He also exhibited signs of attachment of his caretakers, even showing affection at times.

Eventually, Victor came to see Itard's home as his own home. He ran away several times, but the last attempt was years into his training. When he made it back to the forest, he missed the comforts of home. He expressed symptoms of relief and joy when he saw the housekeeper again. By educating him in the ways of the world, Itard seemingly eradicated Victor's ability to survive on his own.

Interestingly enough, Itard's detractors considered his work with Victor a failure. Itard himself considered many parts of his work to be a failure. Victor was never able to develop advanced social skills. Additionally, he was never able to develop the ability to communicate through speech. This vexed Itard greatly. Speech, we now know, is a skill that has a critical period for development. If one does not learn to speak in the first 3 years of life, the full ability will not develop (although Gesell, 1941, reports adolescent onset of speech in another feral child called Kamala). However, it is impossible in modern times to look at Victor's progress and label his instruction a failure. This type of systematic instruction continues to be used in special education classrooms today.

Victor's story leaves open the question of whether his social isolation led to mental retardation. It is impossible to know—perhaps he was abandoned because of mental retardation. Philosophically, however, one must ponder this closely. If he truly had an intellectual disability before being abandoned, would he have been able to adapt so well to the wild? The story underscores the importance of the timing of intervention, especially in the area of speech.

Victor's story, like many children with language disorders, becomes even more complicated when considering the link between language and IQ. Just what would have happened if Victor had been educated at the age of 2 or 3? What if he had human contact throughout his life? Although we cannot answer those questions for Victor, there have been other studies that considered these ideas in general. We now turn our discussion to some of those.

Early Intervention Research

If there is one name that is most associated with early intervention research, it is most certainly Harold Skeels. Skeels began publishing the results of his longitudinal study in the 1930s. Working in an Iowa institution, Skeels placed 13 children under the age of 3 who were living in an orphanage into a ward of the institution with "brighter, older girls" (Skeels, 1942, p. 340). A group of children who remained at the orphanage were selected as the comparison group. Both groups of children were from underprivileged homes and were believed to have no organic cause for mental retardation. IQs at the beginning of the study ranged from 35 to 89 in the experimental group and from 50 to 103 in the group that remained at the orphanage.

The ward with the older girls was considered more stimulating because the girls lavished attention on the children. They assisted in the development of skills such as walking, talking, and playing. Additionally, they held, talked to, and played with the children. The nursery, where both groups lived prior to the study, was described as an average 1930s orphanage: "The outstanding feature was the lack of mental stimulation or experiences usually associated with the life of a young child in the ordinary home. Few contacts with adults were possible other than those involving physical care because of the large numbers of children and the limited staff" (p. 341).

The children who were moved to the more stimulating environment experienced gains in IQ that ranged from 7 to 58 points. Follow-up testing that occurred 2 to 4 years later indicated IQs remained higher overall, ranging from 2 to 61 points higher than at initial testing, although three children did lose ground between the end of the study and the follow-up period. However, several of the children moved out of the range of mental retardation.

The children who remained in the orphanage experienced the opposite outcomes. All but one of them lost IQ points during the experimental period (losses ranged from 8 to 45 points). At follow-up assessment, four had gained IQ points, while the rest lost points, ranging from 14 to 64. Five had dropped from average IQ into the ranges of mental retardation.

The message of this study was not only that children with environmentally imposed mental retardation could achieve normal IQ, but also that children with normal IQ could develop an intellectual disability, given a nonstimulating environment. Modern readers are probably also struck by the horror of institutional conditions that would enable the residents to provide better care for the children than the orphanage staff could provide.

Skeels and Skodak published a 30-year follow-up of these children in 1966. They did not readminister IQ tests, but did interview 24 of the original 25 participants. All 13 of the individuals who had received environmental enrichment were self-supporting and independent: "None of these members would now be identified as a former state ward, and a description of them as mentally handicapped at any time in their lives would be regarded as a hilarious joke by their present friends and associates" (Skeels & Skodak, 1966, p. 9).

Among the children who had remained at the orphanage, one person was described as an average citizen. This one person had received intensive intervention in nursery school after the study had been concluded. Median incomes for members of the experimental group were almost four times as much as median incomes for the orphanage group. In general, the authors felt their study documented the strength of the environment in shaping intelligence.

In the current climate, early intervention is generally conceived in two parts: infant/toddler programs and preschool programs such as Head Start. Efficacy studies present mixed results. An analysis of the available literature on the topic indicated that IQ gains tended to diminish after 3 years, with academic gains following suit within 5 to 6 years (Lazar, Darlington, Murray, Royce, & Snipper, 1982). This is in contrast with the results of the Milwaukee Project and another landmark study with similarly positive outcomes, called the Carolina Abecedarian Project (Ramey & Campbell, 1984). Campbell and Ramey (1994) speculated that this difference existed because of the length and intensity of those two projects. As mentioned in the discussion of the Milwaukee Project, the rigorous design of research projects is often difficult to duplicate in clinical practice.

The national Head Start program was born in a time of national optimism. It was a part of President Lyndon Johnson's War on Poverty and was engineered to provide compensatory services to children of poverty. However, in 1966 a report was published that indicated Head Start and similar programs provided no gains, or gains that were merely transitory (Coleman, 1966).

Scathing indictments followed the publication of the Coleman report. Because Project Head Start had so much public funding, the subject hit the popular press. One of the most compelling reviews was published in the *Wall Street Journal* (Freeman, 1968). However, the teachers and families of children enrolled in Head Start and other early childhood programs continued to provide positive feedback about their experiences.

Many of their claims were investigated and were upheld by the research. Preschool intervention was associated with improvements in motivation, basic health, parenting skills, and future placement in integrated settings (often avoiding institutionalization). These outcomes are good and worthwhile—but they were almost overshadowed by too-high expectations that early intervention would move large numbers of children into the normal ranges of intelligence and academic achievement (Scheerenberger, 1987).

 You can visit a preschool program by going to the Companion Website at www.prenhall.com/beirne -smith and selecting Chapter 5, Video Case Studies.

A thorough review of the research on early intervention leaves little doubt that children benefit from such services, even if they do not manage to meet the original goals (White, Bush, & Casto, 1986). The current research focuses more on the factors that increase the effectiveness of interventions (Heward, 2000). It appears that, like other methods of education, the most important factors are the intensity of the program and the degree of investment of the participants (Ramey & Ramey, 1992).

Once children enter the school years, the educational approach used can have a profound effect on their development. Other chapters of this book will discuss research and theory of educational approaches. However, one aspect of education is particularly pertinent to this chapter: the influence of segregation and labeling. These effects are important not only in the school years, but also in the adult years.

Segregation and Labeling Effects

In the 1960s and 1970s, leading researchers and teachers advocated for special classes for children with intellectual disabilities, so that they could receive intensive, individualized, functional instruction. However, there was a flip side to segregated classes. Research began to emerge that indicated special classes did not produce improved educational outcomes. Additionally, it was suspected that the children in those special classrooms were at best missing out on the important role of peer modeling. At worst, segregating them from the rest of the school simply because they were different violated their civil rights (Heward, 2000).

In the 1980s, the same arguments were made against institutionalization. As described in chapter 1, institutions were originally conceived to be training facilities. People with intellectual disabilities would receive training that would prepare them for life outside the facility. However, checking out of the institution was not a common practice. Institutions were now being accused of furthering their residents' disabilities (Trent, 1994).

The principle of *normalization,* as described by Nirje (1969) and Wolfensberger (1972), expounds upon the familiar adage, "Children learn what they live." Basically, these researchers believed that people with intellectual disabilities were being limited by the very devices that were supposed to liberate them. They suggested people with mental retardation would learn better by experiencing the environments for which they were being prepared. Research from the 1960s tended to support the idea that special classes did not equate to better outcomes (Hoelke, 1966; Kirk, 1964; Smith & Kennedy, 1967).

Dunn (1968) outlines several psychosocial reasons why segregated settings did not seem to help children with mild mental retardation. He leaned heavily on the idea that achieving the label *mental retardation* was "a destructive, self-fulfilling prophecy"

Preschool programs that include children with disabilities are becoming increasingly common

(p. 9). The impact comes not only from a diminished sense of self-efficacy, but also from lower expectations from significant others such as parents and teachers. Additionally, researchers were able to demonstrate that removing a child from the mainstream of education was demoralizing and worsened problems of adjustment (Meyerowitz, 1965).

Dunn's article generated quite a following and was largely responsible for a movement to abolish special classes altogether. However, in 1971 Donald MacMillan responded to Dunn's article, requesting a reexamination of the literature on special classes. According to MacMillan, many children were misplaced, but some children were deriving benefit from the special classes. He questioned the design of many of the studies cited by Dunn, indicating that it was possible that the children in regular classes did better because they had characteristics that both enabled them to perform better academically and to stay in a regular classroom in the first place. Additionally, most studies showed no academic difference, rather than academic impairment from special education. However, some studies indicated other advantages to special classrooms, including better postschool adjustment.

With regard to the social costs of segregation, MacMillan pointed to a study by Edgerton & Sabagh (1962) that stated the opposite of Dunn's assertions. These researchers found that for many people with mild mental retardation, being placed in a social structure with others with intellectual disabilities allowed them to achieve a greater feeling of high social status, since they were no longer perceived to be inferior.

In more recent years, the arguments for integrated educational and residential settings have taken on a different tone. Research can be cited to say that people with intellectual disabilities learn better in integrated settings, and other research indicates that specialized settings can help people learn. Many factors, including the skill of the teacher, intervene to influence whether learning occurs in any setting. Therefore, the question has now become one of civil rights.

The *inclusion* movement has its roots in the civil rights movement. Advocates of full inclusion believe all children should be allowed to participate in regular classrooms all the time. According to Taylor (1988), the continued existence of special classrooms and schools unnecessarily links the intensity of support to the restrictiveness of the setting, when intense supports could realistically be provided in integrated settings.

Advocates for a more moderate view on inclusion insist that it is unrealistic to believe that regular classrooms can, or should, effectively manage students with rare or unusually severe problems, especially if those problems will infringe upon the rights of the other children (Heward, 2000). In general, however, if a person can live and learn effectively in an integrated setting (possibly with additional supports), it is the person's right to be there (Turnbull, 1998). Perhaps Blatt (1987) put it best:

> Most people revere their freedom more than their very lives. Some insist that evidence is needed to justify deinstitutionalization. Did Lincoln require evidence to free the slaves? No. He needed only the belief that all people in this country who were neither dangerous to themselves or others deserved to be free. . . . The battle to evacuate institutions, or to integrate handicapped children in the public schools, is being fought on behalf of freedom for these people rather than improved clinical conditions and opportunities. The prepotent issue in this century will not be on the "right to treatment" but on each person's "inalienable right to freedom." (p. 357)

CULTURAL CONSIDERATIONS

Several authors have written of trends among certain groups with regard to levels of intelligence. These reports always bring about a firestorm of controversy. One of the loudest of those voices was Arthur Jensen, who reported in 1969 that African Americans tend to score lower on IQ tests than middle-class Whites because of unalterable hereditary factors. The psychosocial response was equally loud, and was led by sociologists such as Jane Mercer. According to Mercer (1973), children assigned a label of mental retardation and placed in a segregated setting because of the label had no choice but to live up to that label while at school.

The idea that children of minority races could be falsely labeled with mental retardation and that the labeling process itself was problematic for the children was the crux of the "6-hour retarded child" debate. But why did this happen? According to Edgerton (1981), majority group members are often victims of **ethnocentrism,** which is a worldview that is limited by one's own cultural experiences. This causes them to fail to recognize intelligence in different forms. Therefore, the researchers have often measured intelligence of people from other groups in culturally biased ways. The concept of adaptive behavior again becomes

What are the dominant values of American culture? What kinds of difficulties might a person with intellectual disabilities encounter in trying to uphold those values?

Box 5.2 　✻　 Excerpt from *The Cloak of Competence:* "Hank's Self-Perception"

Hank's view of himself is expressed repeatedly and clearly. He insists—and believes—that he is physically strong and has great endurance. His ability to lift heavy objects, to walk great distances, and to work long hours is an important source of his self-esteem. He likes to refer to himself as "a jack of all trades with a back like a mule." Most of all, he strives to avoid any suggestion that he is retarded. He knows that he was regarded as a mental retardate* at the time he was in Pacific, but it is doubtful that he has ever accepted this verdict. At any rate, he is diligent about hiding his past and denying that he is retarded. He has told no one that he was at Pacific, and he was horrified lest the research investigators somehow let slip something about his past. He is always eager to validate his competence by an assertion such as "I've lived long years alone here on the outs and I guess I've showed everyone I can take care of myself." He is equally prepared to explain the reason for his "problems": "My only handicap is a lack of schooling." He argues strongly that were it not for his neglected education he would be as "rich and famous" as anyone else. These explanations never vary. Hank has them well worked out.

Hank's vision of his future is equally clear. He wants to be "free," to have "a fresh start." He continually dreams and talks of becoming a gypsy, of being free to go and do what he pleases. He speaks of living alone on top of a high hill, saying, "The only roof I want over my head is the blue, blue sky." He realizes that he has made mistakes, particularly in falling so deeply in debt, and admits that it is wrong to "shoot for the moon." But he wants to be free of this debt, of his responsibilities, of long and hard work, of May [his wife], and of all supervision. He talks endlessly of getting "out from under the State," saying that the "State" has always been "over" him, telling him what to do. His practical procedures for achieving his needs include "getting hold of some money," "getting me a car," and then using this money and mobility to find a job as a male nurse at some distant sanitarium [institution] where "nobody knows about me."

*Note: Some of the language used in this excerpt is no longer considered acceptable, but was left in its original form for purposes of historical accuracy.

Source: From *The Cloak of Competence: Stigma in the Lives of the Mentally Retarded* (pp. 38–39), by R. B. Edgerton, 1967, Berkeley: University of California Press. Copyright © 1967 by the Regents of the University of California. Reprinted by permission.

vitally important to consider. Adaptive behavior is culturally relevant. To be considered adaptive, a person must understand what is necessary and valuable for life in his or her culture. When moving into a new culture, one must be able to adapt to the new values.

Edgerton's *The Cloak of Competence* (1967) sought to understand what was important for people with mental retardation to succeed living in the community. The study was a report of many interviews with people released from institutional care. Their experiences were quite varied—some marrying, some holding full-time jobs, some living with families; others ending up in jail, living in squalor, or being victimized in one way or another. Across the interviews, however, there was one recurring theme among all the different kinds of lifestyles: the need to appear normal. (See Box 5.2.)

Of course, some were better than others at blending in. Some thought they blended in, when really they did not. But all feared the consequences of their mental retardation label. In the preface to *Cloak,* Walter Goldschmidt theorizes that in order to be truly happy, a person needs a positive self-evaluation. How can you think well of yourself if you have a label that means you are less capable than most? The people Edgerton studied not only tried to hide their intellectual disability from others; most tried to hide it from themselves. When asked about their time in the hospital, many of them claimed they were there due to nervous breakdowns, seizures, or even alcoholism. These things, because they are treatable and because they are known to occur among "normal" people, were preferable to mental retardation.

The power and importance of *Cloak* lies in its attempt to share the humanity behind mental retardation. Some of the stories are happy; some are sad. Some are none too pretty. The experiences shared are quite diverse. But their successes and happiness were tied to the ability to pass for normal. Once again, adaptive skill shows itself to be of utmost importance. However, in this case, that skill is often very subtle; it is the ability to understand the fine nuances of human interaction, the unwritten rules of social behavior. This can be quite difficult for a person with cognitive limitations, but it can also mean the difference between acceptance and rejection.

To check your understanding of this chapter, go to the Companion Website at www.prenhall.com/ beirne-smith and select Chapter 5. From there, you can access the Self-Test and Essay modules.

Summary

The Role of Poverty

- Children of culturally deprived homes are at risk for the development of mental retardation.
- Proper nutrition, caring interaction, a responsive language environment, and stimulating surroundings are all required for optimal intellectual development.
- Compensatory interventions can provide benefits to children of culturally deprived homes.
- Some children of low-income, minority households may exhibit symptoms of mental retardation in school without noticeable difficulties in their home environments.

Psychosocial Interventions

- Special education methods were founded on the idea that destiny is not shaped entirely by genetics, and all people are capable of learning, growing, and changing.
- Although many important accomplishments can be made through psychosocial interventions, compensatory education cannot promise to eliminate all mental retardation and associated problems.
- The most effective compensatory intervention programs begin in infancy.
- In general, integrated settings are preferable for people with mental retardation to live and learn. There are many negative effects of segregation and labeling, which must be balanced against the ability of the integrated setting to provide meaningful support.

Cultural Considerations

- Cultural differences must be considered in the assessment of children from minority groups.
- A person's ability to adapt to cultural norms greatly affects his or her ability to function successfully in that society.
- Disability labels can have a self-fulfilling prophecy attached to them, due to decreased self-esteem and the lowered expectations of significant others.
- In Edgerton's classic study, *The Cloak of Competence,* people with mental retardation living in the community exhibited only one common theme: the desire to deny the presence of mental retardation.

Chapter

6

Biological Aspects and the Promises of Prevention

Edward A. Polloway, Ed.D.
Lynchburg College in Virginia

J. David Smith, Ed.D.
University of Virginia at Wise

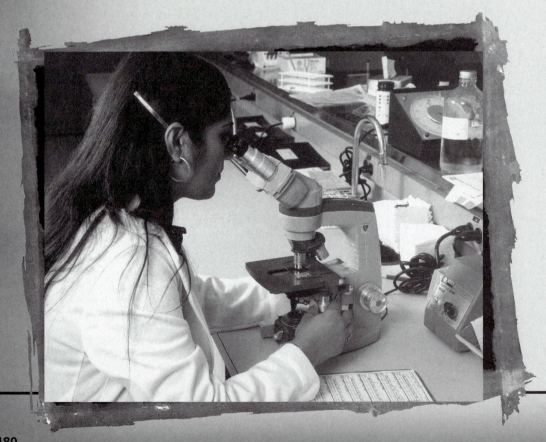

OBJECTIVES

After reading this chapter, the student should be able to:

- Provide an overview of causation
- Discuss the basic principles of genetics
- Identify and discuss the major biological causes of mental retardation
- Discuss various ways that mental retardation can be prevented
- Identify and discuss selected ethical issues facing the field

KEY TERMS

amniocentesis

autosomes

chromosomes

deletion

dominant inheritance

Down syndrome (DS)

fetal alcohol syndrome (FAS)

fragile X syndrome

genes

genetics

heterozygous

homozygous

Human Genome Project

hydrocephalus

hypoxia

innate

karyotypes

meiosis

microcephaly

monosomy

mosaicism

myelomeningocele

neurofibromatosis (NF)

nondisjunction

phenylketonuria (PKU)

polygenic inheritance

Prader-Willi syndrome (PWS)

recessive inheritance

Tay-Sachs disease

teratogens

translocation

trisomy

uniparental disomy

Williams syndrome

The authors acknowledge the significant assistance of Jessica Nayor, Betty Shelton, and Jeannine Vogel in the development of this chapter.

T he task of sorting out the many causes of mental retardation is formidable. From the beginnings of the study of retardation in the earliest part of recorded history to the more advanced efforts in the 21st century, the search for causation has been challenging. The goal of this chapter is to provide a foundation for understanding the complexities in the causes of mental retardation.

Causes of retardation and related developmental disabilities have traditionally been divided into two categories: biological (or physiological) and environmental (or psychosocial). Such a taxonomic grouping of causes might be thought to create a clear dichotomy of specific causes. However, most often, factors from both these domains are relevant in individual cases of these disabilities.

Although hundreds of specific factors have been identified as causative agents of mental retardation, the number of cases of retardation with unknown causes is still as large as those that are known and specifiable; that is, in approximately 50% of cases can a specific cause (i.e., a biological factor) be identified (Dykens, Hodapp, & Finucone, 2000). A key problem is that causes may be undetermined for the large category of people identified as having mild mental retardation.

A traditional perspective of causation is the two-group model that includes a group with organic (i.e., specific biological) causes and a second group presumed to be sociocultural, or historically cultural familial (Spinath, Harlaar, Ronald, & Plomin, 2004). The first group consists of known and specifiable biological causes often classified as pathological and/or clinical. Although such causes may result in retardation at all levels, most attention in the past was drawn to their etiology of more severe disabilities. Biological pathology can be identified in 60% to 75% of cases where the individual's IQ falls below 50 (McLaren & Bryson, 1987). But the traditional association of a single organic cause only with severe retardation is too simplistic; many individuals with high-incidence disabilities (i.e., mild retardation) may also be affected by physiological factors. The other traditional assumption—that mild retardation is the result of multiple, unspecifiable environmental events—has also given way to the fact that this is only a broad-brush distinction (Moser, 2000), and thus estimates suggest that 25% to 40% of all cases of mild retardation may have a specific identifiable cause (McLaren & Bryson, 1987) or that 10% to 50% of cases of mild retardation are related to genetic etiologies (Dykens et al., 2000). Furthermore, the assumption that sociocultural factors are all environmentally based has been challenged by contemporary studies of possible genetic influence (Spinath et al., 2004).

Clearly these data are influenced significantly by state prevalence rates (see U.S. Department of Education, 2002), in that states with high rates of identified retardation for ages 6 to 17 (e.g., Alabama: 2.39%, South Carolina: 2.23%) are likely to have a larger number of students with mild retardation and an associated lower percentage of identified biological causes than would a state with a lower prevalence (e.g., New Jersey: 0.35%, California: 0.48%). Despite these data, it is nevertheless important to recognize that many individuals with mild disabilities are also affected by genetic and other biological causes and that psychological and social influences are equally important in cases of severe disability. Finally, in the new millennium, there is increasing confidence that the cause of virtually all cases of mental retardation may become identifiable (Moser, 2000).

Given this confounding complexity, why should educators, psychologists, and other behavioral scientists spend time studying the causation of mental retardation? Kolstoe (1972), in his classic work, noted that familiarity with these causative factors facilitates multidisciplinary communication, is an essential element of professionalism, and is important in enabling professionals to make accurate information available to parents. Furthermore, in most situations etiological information from educators and child care professionals can contribute to a more accurate diagnosis. The role of teachers, for example, may include monitoring the effects of ongoing or progressive disorders that may hinder daily performance, preventing future occurrences through parent counseling, or facilitating immediate change (e.g., intervention in a case of child abuse).

Finally, research is beginning to identify educational and psychological intervention strategies that may be etiology-specific. Therefore, an understanding of causation may ultimately lead to alternative approaches to curriculum and instruction (e.g., Hodapp, 1997; Powell, Houghton, & Douglas, 1997). Hodapp (1997) suggests that the field of mental retardation has generated conflicting views of the relationship between etiology and behavior; on the one hand, the position is that specific genetic disorders have no specific effects on behavior, while an alternative is that genetic disorders are regularly and consistently associated with a distinctive behavioral pattern. He recommends a compromise between these two positions:

Hear a parent's perspective on the value of a diagnosis by visiting the Companion Website at www.prenhall .com/beirne-smith and select Chapter 4, Video Case Studies.

> A few different genetic disorders show an identical behavior among those affected, and this behavior differs from the behavior of individuals with other types of mental retardation. Thus, it is not as if all genetic disorders have identical effects on behavior nor that each genetic disorder has unique effects. Instead a few disorders show similar effects, which are, in turn, not shared by mixed etiological groups. (p. 70)

Dykens (2001) noted with some clear optimism that the value of etiological information would continue to grow, in part because:

> Behavioral researchers are playing a pivotal role in this ground swell of syndromic research. One long-term goal of this line of work is to examine links between genes, brain, and behavior. . . . Simply put, behavioral experts are needed to solve the behavioral half of these gene-behavior puzzles. In the short-term, behavioral . . . data can be put to immediate good use as guideposts for treatment and intervention, and such syndrome-specific recommendations have already been made for fragile X, Down, Prader-Willi, Williams, and other syndromes. (p. 1)

While a general awareness of causative factors is necessary for any professional in the field of mental retardation, the mechanisms of specific causes require multidisciplinary involvement. Input from various disciplines (e.g., biology, medicine, epidemiology, social work, psychology, psychiatry) and special education often is essential to determine whether a cause can be specified or is even relevant to treatment and/or education. That many causes of mental retardation cannot be currently identified also serves as a stimulus for continuing research.

Finally, while considering information on causation, it is important that the reader not lose sight of the fact that behind these data are people struggling with special challenges in their lives. As Blatt (1987) cautioned: "Treatises that deal with etiological conditions rarely recognize the human being [in] the superficially unattractive trappings of the condition" (p. 128). Readers must not overlook the fact that we are talking about real people who happen to have a given disability.

Our discussion of causes begins with attention to terminology and then focuses on genetics, other biological causes, and environmental influences. It concludes with attention to the prevention of mental retardation and related ethical issues.

TERMINOLOGY

As noted earlier, the task of understanding the causes of mental retardation and developmental disabilities is challenging, and translating specific terms for known causes into useful information can be particularly difficult. This section offers ways to understand some of the labels ascribed to selected causative factors.

The terminology used to identify various mental retardation syndromes currently comes from three sources: (1) conventional wisdom or practices related to a specific historical era, (2) names of persons who initially identified or described the condition, and (3) biomedical terms describing the cause or the resultant disabilities.

Several examples illustrate how historical names have been associated with mental retardation for syndromes. Perhaps best known is the archaic (and offensive)

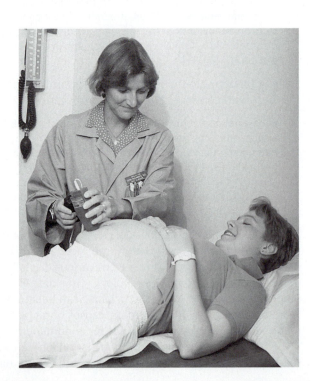

Ultrasound, or sonography, has led to our understanding of the prenatal environment.

term *mongolism,* which was coined by J. Langdon Down in 1866, two decades after Seguin's identification of the condition (Menolascino & Egger, 1978). For 100 years, this term, which was assigned simply because of Down's inaccurate observation that one frequent characteristic of the syndrome was facial similarity to Asians, prevailed in medical and psychological circles. Jordan (2000) summarized the context within which Down made his observations:

> "The inescapable observation that the expanding centers of manufacturing contained a population of overcrowded, chronically ill, malnourished Britons led to an alarming conclusion, namely, that the population was increasingly unhealthy and their retrogression in health and habits would be increased with each succeeding generation." Down noted that "the largest proportion of idiocy is to be found among the lower orders. . . . How can it be expected but that the mother . . . should propagate an enfeebled race?" In short, the British race appeared to be deteriorating at a rapid rate. In them, the appearance of features from other ethnic groups, in particular "the great Mongolian family," as Down phrased it, led him to see the *degeneracy* problem writ large on Britain's population. (p. 325)

Realization that Down syndrome is found in all racial groups (including persons from Mongolia) eventually aided in the much needed retreat from the racist term from the vocabulary of most professionals. Its use, however, unfortunately persists in some popular media.

A second, more direct way to identify a clinical syndrome is to attach to it the name of the researcher who contributed in a major way to its understanding. For instance, professionals now identify as *Down syndrome* the chromosomal condition disorder that J. Langdon Down originally described as mongolism. Other relatively well-known syndromes so named include Tay-Sachs disease, after the British and American physicians who described the characteristics of the condition in the late 1880s, and Lesch-Nyhan syndrome, named for two of the three researchers who first identified this disorder in 1964.

The third source of syndrome labels is biomedical terminology. Although some of these terms are frequently used by laypersons, their meanings are often obscure, in spite of their grounding in common forms. Thus, many of the labels convey primary features of the disorder, either causal or characteristic. Table 6.1 lists some of the more common terms used to identify clinical disorders. For each entry, the specific derivatives are noted, along with their common meaning and examples of their use.

Although labels are only an attempt to refer to complex phenomena, simply being familiar with the derivatives can be of assistance in understanding the nature of these disorders and the terms related to them. Several specific terms illustrate the system. For example, *toxoplasmosis* indicates a condition (*-osis*) of poisonous (*toxo-*) blood (*-plasm*). Although the clinical definition of toxoplasmosis is much more specific, the word, when analyzed, gives a fair suggestion of what the condition is about. Another example is *hydrocephalus.* The term refers to a disorder resulting from a blockage of cerebrospinal fluid, but breaking down the word into "water" (*hydro-*) and "head" or "brain" (*cephalo-*) provides a descriptive, if admittedly simplistic, picture of the condition. A third example is the disorder called **myelomeningocele.** As the term suggests, this condition is characterized by a

A complete online glossary is available on the Companion Website, which may be accessed at www.prenhall.com/ beirne-smith

TABLE 6.1
Biomedical Terminology

Stems and Affixes	Meaning	Example(s)
ab-, abs-	from, away	abnormal, abscess
amnio-	pertaining to embryonic sac	amniocentesis
anomalo-	irregular	chromosomal anomaly
auto-	self, same	autism, autosomes
-cele, -coele	sac, cavity	meningocele
-cephalo-	head, brain	hydrocephalus
-encephalo-	head, brain	encephalitis
endo-	inner, inside	endogenous
ex-, extra-	outside, away from	exogenous
fibro-	connective tissues	neurofibromatosis
galacto-	milk	galactosemia
glyco-, gluco-	sweet, sugar	glycogen, hyperglycemia
hydro-	water	hydrocephalus
hyper-	over, more than usual	hyperkinetic
hypo-	under, less than usual, lowered	hypothyroidism
-lepsy	seizure	epilepsy, narcolepsy
lipo-	fat	lipids
macro-, mega-	large	macrocephaly, acromegaly
meningo-	central nervous system membranes	meningitis
micro-	small	microcephaly
myelo-	marrow, spinal cord	myelomeningocele
neuro-	nerve	neurofibromatosis
-osis	condition of	toxoplasmosis
-plasia	cellular growth	skeletal dysplasia
-plasma	blood	toxoplasmosis
-plegia	paralysis	monoplegia, paraplegia
-semia	sign, symptom	galactosemia
-somy, -some, soma-	body	chromosome, trisomy
toxo-	poisonous	toxemia
-trophy	nutrition, nourishment	atrophy, dystrophy

Source: From Academy of Health Sciences, U.S. Army (1975).

saclike mass (*-cele*) on the spinal cord (*myelo-*) containing membrane tissue of the central nervous system (*-meningo-*).

GENETIC DISORDERS

Genetics is the study of heredity and its variations. As such, its scope is enormous and its complexities great. Advances in genetics over the past 60 years rival those in any area of science. The contributions of geneticists to understanding the causes of developmental disabilities are particularly noteworthy. In the last 20 years, this knowledge base has mushroomed due to research on gene mapping and DNA sequencing, most of it done under the auspices of the **Human Genome Project.**

For more information about the Human Genome Project, and many other topics discussed in this chapter, visit the Companion Website at www.prenhall.com/beirne-smith and select Chapter 6, Web Destinations.

An understanding of heredity begins with the study of genes. **Genes** are the basic biological units carrying inherited physical, mental, or personality traits. Approximately 30,000 genes are present in each human cell. Genes occupy specific positions on **chromosomes,** the threadlike or rodlike bodies that contain genetic information and material. As the Human Genome Project has progressed, the careful mapping and sequencing has reached a point where the full human genome will soon be completed.

Chromosomes vary widely in size and shape, but for human cells the normal pattern is consistent. Each cell contains 23 pairs of chromosomes. The embryo initially receives one member of each pair from each parent. There are two types of chromosomes: autosomes and sex chromosomes. **Autosomes** are matching pairs and constitute 44 of the 46 chromosomes within the usual human complement (i.e., 22 of the 23 pairs). Sex chromosomes make up the other pair. The letter X is used to represent the female sex chromosome and Y to represent the male sex chromosome. While the X chromosome contains a substantial amount of genetic information, the Y functions primarily as a determinant of male gender. At conception, an X chromosome is contributed by the mother, while either an X or a Y is contributed by the father. The XX combination creates a female, and the XY a male.

Ridley (2000), in his book on the human genome study and genetics, describes the genetic process in a unique way that facilitates further understanding. He notes:

> The human body contains approximately 100 trillion *cells.* . . . Inside each cell there is a black blob called a *nucleus.* Inside the nucleus are two complete sets of the human *genome* (except in egg cells and sperm cells, which have one copy each, and red blood cells, which have none). One set of the genome came from the mother and one from the father. In principle, each set includes the same 30,000 . . . *genes* on the same twenty-three *chromosomes.* In practice, there are often small and subtle differences between the paternal and maternal versions of each gene, differences that account for blue eyes or brown, for example. When we breed, we pass on one complete set, but only after swapping bits of the paternal and maternal chromosomes in a procedure known as *recombination.* Imagine that the *genome* is a book. There are twenty-three chapters, called *chromosomes.* Each chapter contains several thousand stories, called *genes.* . . . There are one billion words in the book, which makes it longer than 5,000 volumes the size of this one, or as long as 800 Bibles. If I read the *genome* out to you at the rate of one word per second for eight hours a day, it would take me a century. . . . This is a gigantic document, an immense book, a recipe of extravagant length, and it all fits inside the microscopic nucleus of a tiny cell that fits easily upon the head of a pin. (p. 7)

The precise and rather fragile roles of genes and chromosomes as building blocks of development are dramatically represented in mental retardation research. Table 6.2 provides an illustrative list of some relatively common genetic causes. The most prevalent general groups of biological causes of retardation are genetic transmission of traits (i.e., genetic disorders) and chromosomal abnormalities. But even in these seemingly clear-cut cases of genetic transmission, it is important to keep in mind that

TABLE 6.2
Most Prevalent Genetic
Conditions

Condition	Prevalence
Down syndrome	1.3 / 1,000
Klinefelter syndrome	0.8 / 1,000
Fragile X	0.6 / 1,000
Neurofibromatosis	0.33 / 1,000
Hypothyroidism congenital	0.25 / 1,000
Williams syndrome	0.1 / 1,000
Phenylketonuria	0.067 / 1,000
Prader-Willi syndrome	0.067 / 1,000

Source: From Moser (2000), pp. 225–250.

development is still shaped significantly by environmental influences. Ridley (2003) has pointed out that because research has revealed that there are only 30,000 genes in the human genome rather than the anticipated 100,000, environmental influences have taken on an even greater potency in human development. Further, it is essential to note that genes do not exist as the basis for causing disorders; rather, a specific disorder is most often the result when the gene is absent or does not perform its proper role (Ridley, 2000).

GENETIC TRANSMISSION

Many traits are transmitted from one generation to the next according to the makeup of a specific gene pair. Transmission can occur through autosomal dominant or recessive inheritance and through sex-linked inheritance. In **dominant inheritance,** an individual gene can assume "control" over, or mask, its partner and will operate whether the two elements of an individual gene pair are similar or dissimilar to each other. **Recessive inheritance** refers to genes that cannot control their partners. In a sense they "recede" when paired with a dissimilar mate and become influential only when matched with another recessive gene. Pairs of genes carrying the same trait are called **homozygous;** pairs carrying different traits are **heterozygous.** Homozygous pairs are necessary for recessive inheritance, whereas either homozygous or heterozygous pairs can lead to instances of dominant inheritance.

The dynamics of dominant and recessive inheritance are illustrated in Figure 6.1. Capital letters typically are used to indicate dominant traits; lowercase letters commonly denote recessive traits. In the typical case of dominant inheritance (Example A), only one parent would need to have the specific dominant trait in question, which is transmitted, theoretically, to two of their four children. In the common case of recessive inheritance (Example B), probability suggests that at each conception, chances are 1 in 4 that the child will be homozygous and will manifest the recessive trait (hh), 2 in 4 that he or she will be a heterozygous carrier for the succeeding generation (Hh, hH), and 1 in 4 that he or she will be homozygous for the dominant gene, therefore lacking the recessive gene altogether (HH).

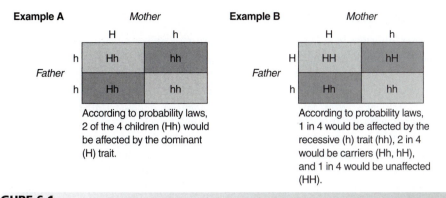

Example A

Mother

According to probability laws, 2 of the 4 children (Hh) would be affected by the dominant (H) trait.

Example B

Mother

According to probability laws, 1 in 4 would be affected by the recessive (h) trait (hh), 2 in 4 would be carriers (Hh, hH), and 1 in 4 would be unaffected (HH).

FIGURE 6.1
Dominant and Recessive Inheritance

Dominant Transmission

Dominant inheritance determines a variety of common traits, including brown eyes and prematurely white hair. Several rare physical disorders are carried as dominant traits. Frequently these disorders are structural; that is, they occur with visible, physical signs. General examples include Marfan's syndrome (which manifests itself through tall stature, loose joints of the limbs, and heart disorders) and achondroplasia (dwarfism). Relevant to our focus in this chapter, neurofibromatosis is an example of a dominant gene disorder that may involve mental retardation.

Neurofibromatosis (NF) is also known as *von Recklinghausen's disease,* named for the man who first described the disorder in 1882. The gene for NF has been identified as occupying a site on chromosome 17 (Rasmussen & Friedman, 1999). It affects about 1 in 3,000 newborns (Polloway & Rucker, 1997; Rasmussen & Friedman, 1999), with about 50% of the cases being inherited and the remainder caused by genetic mutations occurring spontaneously. It is identifiable by light brown patches (called café-au-lait) on the skin and/or by multiple, soft, fibrous swellings or tumors (neurofibromas) that grow on nerves or appear elsewhere on the body and can result in severe physical deformities (Clayman, 1989). It had been speculated that neurofibromatosis was the disorder that affected John Merrick (the "Elephant Man"), but this was later disproved. Surgical procedures for tumors may be recommended (i.e., when the growths cause complications or have a major effect on comfort or appearance), although the tumors may recur.

Neurofibromatosis varies greatly in how it is expressed (i.e., variable expressivity) from case to case. The café-au-lait patches are primarily a cosmetic concern, but the locations of the tumors will have an effect on mental development, which may be severe if they occur on the brain. Otherwise, the individual may function in the normal range of intelligence. The majority of children with NF, however, are likely to have academic problems, with an estimated 30% to 60% having learning disabilities (Nativio & Belz, 1990; Rasmussen & Friedman, 1999). A continuing concern is for the psychological consequences for individuals who see themselves as deformed and question whether they should have children.

Recessive Transmission

Recessive inheritance is commonly associated with blue eyes and a variety of other physical traits, but it also involves disorders capable of producing severe disabilities and serious health impairments. General health-related examples include sickle-cell anemia and cystic fibrosis, while examples of recessively transmitted mental retardation include phenylketonuria, Tay-Sachs, and galactosemia. Because transmission of recessive traits is a function of the union of two carriers (see Figure 6.1), controlling these disorders entails using genetic screening measures to identify unknowing carriers.

Recessive transmission is often related to those disorders that can be traced to dysfunction in the body's mechanisms for the processing of food—so-called *inborn errors of metabolism.* As Garrod observed in 1909 (cited in Ridley, 2000), perhaps that was what genes were: devices for making proteins. Garrod's classic observation was that "inborn errors of metabolism are due to a failure of a step in the metabolic sequence due to loss or malfunction of an enzyme" (p. 40). In particular, imbalances related to fats, carbohydrates, and amino acids have been well established as causative agents of retardation and related disabilities. However, their rarity is such that they result in a limited number of cases of mental retardation. Collectively they occur in approximately 1 in 4,000 births (Hall, 2000).

Metabolic disorders resulting from an increase in lipids, or fats, in the body's tissues are frequently progressive, degenerative diseases. The developmental profile is typically that of a normal progression until onset of the disorder, from which point the condition rapidly worsens. **Tay-Sachs disease,** for example, is inherited as an autosomal recessive trait. It is disproportionately prevalent among persons of Ashkenazic Jewish background (about 90% of Americans of Jewish descent are Ashkenazic and about 1 in 25 to 30 are carriers; Graziano, 2002), although recent findings have shown that it occurs more frequently among the general population than originally thought. Infants with Tay-Sachs disease appear normal at birth. The disease is typically manifested late in the child's first year, followed by a course of severe retardation, convulsions, blindness, paralysis, and death by the age of 4. There is no cure for Tay-Sachs disease, and it remains one of the most devastating causes of disabilities.

Diet control can also mediate the effects of genetic transmission of the amino acid disorder **phenylketonuria (PKU),** the most common of the genetic disorders and the most publicized success story in the preventive literature. PKU is caused by an autosomal recessive gene and, if left untreated, may be associated with aggressiveness, hyperactivity, and retardation. However, since it was first described by Ivar Asbjörn Folling in 1934, PKU has been virtually eliminated as a causative factor in severe retardation, despite its incidence of 1 in every 12,000 to 15,000 births. PKU has played a significant role in the field because it was the first inborn metabolic anomaly proven to cause retardation. Its discovery led to both increased research into etiology and a pronounced change in the aura of hopelessness that once surrounded mental retardation. Figure 6.2 illustrates the historical discovery process for PKU, and Box 6.1 provides an overview of Robert Guthrie's key work in this field.

As noted in Figure 6.2, the treatment regimen for PKU is related to restrictions in intake of phenylalanine, common in high-protein foods. Thus, the diet is predicated on the need for the substitution of other foods and synthetic proteins. With the elimination

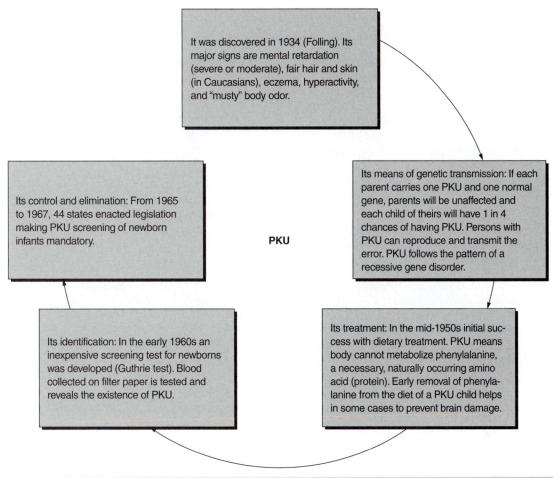

It was discovered in 1934 (Folling). Its major signs are mental retardation (severe or moderate), fair hair and skin (in Caucasians), eczema, hyperactivity, and "musty" body odor.

Its means of genetic transmission: If each parent carries one PKU and one normal gene, parents will be unaffected and each child of theirs will have 1 in 4 chances of having PKU. Persons with PKU can reproduce and transmit the error. PKU follows the pattern of a recessive gene disorder.

Its control and elimination: From 1965 to 1967, 44 states enacted legislation making PKU screening of newborn infants mandatory.

PKU

Its identification: In the early 1960s an inexpensive screening test for newborns was developed (Guthrie test). Blood collected on filter paper is tested and reveals the existence of PKU.

Its treatment: In the mid-1950s initial success with dietary treatment. PKU means body cannot metabolize phenylalanine, a necessary, naturally occurring amino acid (protein). Early removal of phenylalanine from the diet of a PKU child helps in some cases to prevent brain damage.

FIGURE 6.2
The History of Phenylketonuria (PKU)

Source: From President's Committee on Mental Retardation (1976), p. 25.

of phenylalanine from the diet, the deleterious effect is significantly reduced. Levitas (1998) summarized the nature of the legendary treatment for PKU as follows:

> Persons on this diet may not partake of the most common and widely enjoyed fast foods and barbecued staples in the American diet, making participation in family and community events difficult. . . . The diet can be heavy in carbohydrate snack substitutes, making it almost the opposite of what most people think of as a "diet"; new caregivers, and even casual contacts in the person's life, must be educated about the basis for the components of the diet, which must be strictly adhered to. The caregivers must be reminded to avoid all "diet foods" sweetened with Aspartame, which is a potent source of phenylalanine. The caregivers must learn to tolerate the liquid tyrosine supplement, which smells and tastes extremely "fishy." Fortunately, the liquid can be

Box 6.1 🌿 Robert Guthrie and the Discovery of PKU

Advances in the field of mental retardation and developmental disabilities have come in a variety of ways. Certainly key societal commitments have included support for research as well as for enabling legislation for educational programs and litigation to confirm basic human rights. However, behind most of these achievements often are individuals who have made a significant difference. As discussed in Koch's (1997) biography of Robert Guthrie, it is clear that he was one. Schroeder (1999) writes in his review of this book that it

> captures the science, the drama, the serendipity, and the chance events that resulted in the development over the last 50 years of screening tests for phenylketonuria (PKU) and of mass screening methods for metabolic errors in general as a major tool for the prevention of mental retardation. How did it happen that hundreds of millions of newborn infants around the world have been screened for a variety of metabolic dis-

orders largely due to the efforts of one man? That is a story worth tracing. One needs to observe Bob Guthrie's contributions as a scientist and as a human being. . . .

Three major contributions to newborn screening programs earn Bob Guthrie a place in the history of research in mental retardation: (a) he showed the blood specimens of three tiny spots on filter paper were safe and useful screening methods; (b) he developed the bacterial inhibition assay for phenylalanine in the blood spot, the first method of diagnosing PKU using blood; and (c) he advocated for mass screenings of newborns and children all over the world. This was a revolutionary concept, which required proselytizing in wide sectors of the medical and public health communities. His devising of inexpensive analytic methods was the key to their acceptance. That was the breakthrough from a public health standpoint.

flavored with fruit juices, vanilla, [and] honey and can be frozen into a "slushy" with flavorings. (p. 113)

The early results of diet treatment for PKU were most encouraging. Johnson, Koch, Peterson, and Friedman (1978) reported that a group of 148 treated PKU children did not significantly differ from the general population in the prevalence of congenital anomalies or major neurological defects. Intellectual development near or within the normal range thus was found to be achievable. Children treated very early—before they were a month old—had significantly higher IQs than those whose treatment began in the second month (Koch et al., 1988); continued adherence to the diet had positive results as well, while diet cessation in individuals continued to show a decrement in IQ (Levitas, 1998).

Two major problems remained, however. First, the diet prescribed for children with PKU can be unappealing and hard to follow, and it may be difficult to balance protein restrictions against the protein needs of developing children. For years, the special diet was generally discontinued by approximately school age, but this practice caused concern. For example, Matthews, Barabas, Cusack, and Ferrari (1986) reported decreases in social quotients for individuals for whom the diet was discontinued at age 5½ years. In children who maintained their diets to the age of 10, Fishler, Azen, Henderson, Friedman, and Koch (1987) found higher school achievement, intellectual level, language, and perceptual skills. Clarke, Gates, Hogan, Barrett, and MacDonald (1987) concluded:

The bulk of evidence appears to indicate that older children allowed access to unrestricted diets do experience some deterioration in intelligence, that this is associated with specific neuropsychological deficits that are not attributable simply to their intellectual [disability], and that this deficit is at least partly reversible by a return to dietary restriction. Although the data would support efforts to maintain older children with PKU on . . . restricted diets for as long as possible, the meager short-term clinical benefits, along with the well-known difficulty of re-introducing the therapeutic diet in older children . . . suggest that long-term return to dietary treatment is unlikely to succeed except in unusually highly motivated patients. (p. 260)

Research continues on the issue of treatment discontinuation in adolescents and adults with PKU; this research is likely to eventually yield definitive directions for future treatment (Griffiths, Smith, & Harvie, 1997). Levitas (1998) reviewed research in the area and gave a compelling case for a lifelong phenylalanine-free diet treatment for persons with PKU. Acceptance of this recommendation would have an obvious effect on a second issue (discussed next) that emerged with the study of PKU.

This second issue concerns women who were treated in childhood for PKU. As adults, their metabolic imbalances can harm their unborn children. In this instance, the problem is not a genetic one but rather an increased risk to the fetus during pregnancy due to the mother's elevated level of inappropriately processed phenylalanine. Consequences can include retardation, heart disease, and microcephaly (Schultz, 1983); therefore, women should reinstate their restricted diet during pregnancy. Evidence of this concern can be noted by consumers in common product warnings—for example on diet sodas or some low-fat foods (e.g., yogurt)—that these items contain phenylalanine. Unless pregnancy is avoided or dietary restrictions honored, Koch and colleagues (1988) indicate that the effects of maternal PKU could offset the preventive benefits of screening programs and dietary treatment interventions in infants.

Sex-Linked Inheritance

A third type of genetic transmission is through sex-linked (or X-linked) inheritance. This name derives from a variety of recessive traits carried on the X chromosome. Females have two X chromosomes, and a specific gene carrying a disorder can be dominated by its mate. But males (XY) will be affected by a single recessive gene carried on the X chromosome, because there is no second X chromosome whose genes could potentially dominate the pathology-producing recessive trait. Males have a Y chromosome, which does not carry genes that will counterbalance the X-linked gene. A female can be affected only if her father is affected and her mother is a carrier. Thus, the problem of sex-linked inheritance is particularly significant for males. Dykens and colleagues (2000) noted that more than 70 causes of disabilities can be traced to X-linked inheritance patterns.

In the general population, X-linked recessive traits of concern include color blindness, hemophilia, Duchenne-type muscular dystrophy, and a variety of other conditions that may be as much as 10 times more common in males than in females. The unique nature of sex-linked recessive inheritance is perhaps best illustrated by the presence of the disorder of hemophilia within the royal families of Europe. In a story often told, many of the ancestors and descendants of Queen Victoria of England, a carrier for hemophilia, either carried the disease or, in the case of some males, experienced the impact of this disorder. Most notably, Victoria's granddaughter, who married Nicholas II, the last czar of Russia, passed on hemophilia to their son, which ultimately became a contributor to the downfall of the Romanov dynasty (see Massie, 1967, for an ancestral outline reflecting the recurrence of hemophilia).

According to Dykens et al. (2000), there are greater than 70 different X-linked causes associated with mental retardation and developmental disabilities. Further, as much as 25% of mental retardation in males may be related to X-linked genes. While the more common pattern is X-linked recessive disorders, as discussed below relative to Lesch-Nyhan syndrome, there are also some conditions that are carried as dominant genes. The most common syndrome related to X-linkage that follows a unique pattern is fragile X syndrome.

In the field of mental retardation, a key example of sex-linked recessive inheritance is *Lesch-Nyhan syndrome.* The disorder, first identified in 1964 (Lesch & Nyhan, 1964), is inherited as an X-linked recessive and thus is much more common among males. According to Nyhan (1976), it is the second most common metabolic disorder (after PKU). The most striking manifestation of Lesch-Nyhan syndrome is an apparently uncontrollable urge to cause injury to oneself and, to a lesser extent, to others.

Typically, children with Lesch-Nyhan syndrome will begin displaying extreme self-injurious behavior (SIB) when acquiring teeth. They may bite ferociously and, in their frenzy, rip and tear tissue (Libby, Polloway, & Smith, 1983; Nyhan, Johnson, Kaufman, & Jones, 1980). Aside from SIB, they may hit, pinch, and bite others; use obscene language; spit; and engage in a variety of disruptive actions because of their inability to control their impulses (Hoefnagel, Andrew, Mireault, & Berndt, 1965). When unrestrained, they may scream as if terrified of the pain they might inflict on themselves; when restrained, they seem more calm.

Both biomedical and educational interventions have been attempted with children who have Lesch-Nyhan syndrome. Drug treatment to alter metabolism has proven efficacious on a short-term basis. Continued work on biochemical processes in the brain also offer great promise. Educational interventions with children with Lesch-Nyhan historically have included a variety of attempts at behavioral change, with varying levels of success (Anderson, Dancis, & Alpert, 1978).

Fragile X Syndrome

A disorder that was first noted in 1943 but began to receive significant attention after its formal discovery in 1979 is **fragile X syndrome.** After Down syndrome, this syndrome is the most common clinical type of retardation. It is also the most common hereditary cause of retardation (Lachiewicz, Harrison, Spiridigliozzi, Callanan, & Livermore, 1988). The actual mechanism for genetic transmission is quite complex. Its link to the X chromosome is in a fashion that varies from the recessive transmission pattern as previously discussed. General information about inheritance patterns for fragile X is as follows:

- One in 260 women are carriers.
- The most common form of transmission is from mother to son, which can be premutated (carrier) to mutated (affected), mutated (affected) to mutated (affected), or premutated (carrier) to premutated (carrier).
- A father can be premutated (unaffected and a carrier) and pass on the fragile X gene to his daughter.
- There is no male-to-male transmission.

Fragile X occurs in about 1 in 1,500 males and about 1 in 1,000 females in the general population (Clayman, 1989), although lower prevalence rates have been cited (Maes, Fryns, Ghesquiere, & Borghgraef, 2000). The source of the problem is the absence or severe deficiency of a specific protein (FMRP) that is deemed to be essential for the functioning of the brain (Bailey, Hatton, Tassone, Skinner, & Taylor, 2001). Research indicates that the protein level found in individuals was a key contribution to developmental outcomes (Bailey et al., 2001) and thus that children with higher levels of FMRP have higher levels of adaptive behavior (Hatton et al., 2003).

Diagnosis of fragile X can be made prenatally, although most often it is made clinically during early childhood after observation of developmental delays and/or the appearance of large ears (Buyse, 1990). Maes and colleagues (2000) provide a screening checklist for use with persons suspected of having the syndrome (see Table 6.3).

According to Barker (1990), common physical characteristics of fragile X include prominent jaws, macro-orchidism (large testes), long and thin faces, long and soft ears and hands, prominent foreheads, and enlarged heads. The syndrome has been associated in males with severe retardation, although reports of its occurrence in individuals with various levels of retardation (and also with normal intelligence) suggest the need for careful consideration of the contributions of environmental experience (Rogers & Simensen, 1987). Maes and colleagues (2000) report on the degree of retardation in a sample of persons with fragile X. For children, the statistics were 6.59%, profound; 29.9%, severe; 48.1%, moderate; and 15.6%, mild. For adults, the figures were 14%, profound; 71%, severe; and 21%, moderate. The nature of the sample, however, limits its generalizability to the overall population. Although males with fragile X are typically thought to be infertile, instances exist where this has not been the case.

Behavioral manifestations of fragile X may include attentional difficulties, repetitive speech, repetitive behaviors, and gaze avoidance, while speech and language patterns may include echolalia, preservative use of given utterances, and palilalia (i.e., repeating statements at increasing rates of speed and loudness) (Bellinger, Rucker, & Polloway, 1995; Belser & Sudhalter, 2001). Symons, Clark, Roberts, and Bailey (2001) researched the behavior of individuals with fragile X syndrome (FXS) in the classroom (as opposed to the more common laboratory research). They reported:

> Relatively low overall levels of severe behavior problems associated with gross motor stereotypes (e.g., hand flapping) or self-injury (e.g., hand biting) were observed. The finding that a broad measure of classroom quality, based on environmental and instructional variables, was significantly related to levels of classroom engagement

TABLE 6.3

Checklist for Fragile X Syndrome

1. Narrow and elongated face	15. Fearfulness
2. High forehead	16. Gaiety, cheerfulness
3. Prominent lower jaw	17. Hypersensitivity for changes
4. Large, protruding ears	18. Hand-biting
5. Macro-orchidism	19. Stereotypic hand movements
6. Hyperextensible finger joints	20. Flapping hands and arms
7. Hyperextensible joints (other)	21. Avoiding eye contact
8. Hyperactivity	22. Turning away the face
9. Sensory oversensitivity	23. Tactile defensiveness
10. Impulsivity	24. Rapid speed of language
11. Being chaotic	25. Being talkative
12. Shyness	26. Perseveration
13. Being too helpful	27. Echolalia
14. Approach-avoidance conflict	28. Imitation of own language

Source: From Maes et al. (2000).

suggests that how the teacher arranges and structures the classroom environment is critical for school success for students with FXS. . . . It appears that for this sample of students with FXS, classroom ecology was more important than biology for predicting levels of engagement. (p. 201)

This initial finding bears further attention as more naturalistic observations are considered in the future. Table 6.4 provides a summary of other characteristics.

A consistent relationship between fragile X and autism has been reported in the literature, with males with fragile X having a 5% to 46% prevalence of autism or autistic-like behaviors. Demark, Feldman, and Holden (2003) summarized research findings as follows:

- A definite subgroup of persons with fragile X appears to have behaviors commonly associated with autism (with some individuals meeting the diagnostic criteria for autism).
- Fragile X mutations may increase the risk of a child developing autistic-like tendencies.
- It is unclear what the precise relationship is between autism and fragile X.
- Fragile X mutations *may* increase the susceptibility for autism in conjunction with other genes associated with autism susceptibility.

Viewed from the reverse perspective, children with autism are found to have the fragile X pattern in about 15% of cases. While males with fragile X often exhibit autistic-type behaviors, they are usually less significant than the behaviors seen in persons who are clinically diagnosed as autistic. However, the similarity in behavior patterns does lead to difficulty in making a diagnosis of typical autistic-like behaviors versus clinical autism (Bellinger, Rucker, & Polloway, 1995; Cantu, Stone, Wing, Langee,

TABLE 6.4

Cognitive and Adaptive Strengths and Weaknesses in Persons with Fragile X

Strengths	Weaknesses
Verbal skills Repertoire of acquired knowledge	Auditory-verbal short-term memory Visual-perceptual short-term memory Sustaining attention, effort
Long-term memory for learned information Expressive and receptive vocabularies	Sequential processing Certain visual-spatial and perceptual organization tasks
Adaptive daily living skills, especially domestic and personal grooming tasks (males)	Shifting problem-solving strategies Integrating information (more readily measured in females) Adaptive socialization skills (females and males with autism)

Source: From *Genetics and Mental Retardation Syndromes* (p. 146), by E. M. Dykens, R. M. Hodapp, & B. M. Finucane, 2000, Baltimore: Paul H. Brookes. Copyright © 2000 by Paul H. Brookes Publishing Co. Used by permission.

& Williams, 1990). Finally it is important to note that individuals with fragile X who are also autistic tend to have lower adaptive skill levels and also more significant developmental and functional delays (Hatton et al., 2003), including in the areas of expressive and receptive language (Philofsky, Hepburn, Hayes, Hagerman, & Rogers, 2004).

 *To read about ongoing research on Fragile X, go to the Companion Website at www.prenhall.com/ beirne-smith and select Chapter 6, Read and Respond.*

Women who have the fragile X chromosome are frequently clinically viewed as carriers and may not be identified because of low expressivity (Barker, 1990); however, an estimated one third may also be partially affected and have learning disabilities (Rogers & Simensen, 1987). A pattern of varied strengths and weaknesses is particularly apparent in girls who have fragile X. Although not frequently mentally retarded, such girls are often learning disabled (Neely, 1991).

Polygenic Inheritance

The preceding discussion has focused on single-gene anomalies, reflecting the mechanism by which one gene controls one trait (or a given condition). Many traits, however, do not fit simple rules but are transmitted through **polygenic inheritance.** Polygenic (i.e., multiple genes) inheritance has particular importance for potential contributions to the etiology of the so-called psychosocial causes of retardation (see chapter 5). Unlike the one-gene/one-trait pattern of numerous disorders (e.g., PKU), in polygenic inheritance the interaction of multiple genes and networks influences individual intellectual functioning. Since the complexity of this phenomenon makes precise evaluation difficult in single cases, researchers depend on statistical data from population samples in seeking to understand polygenic inheritance. That is, "genetic predictions . . . have to be based on empirical data from population statistics. Simple genetic models just do not apply" (Scarr & Carter-Saltzman, 1982, p. 804).

CHROMOSOMAL DIFFERENCES

A second major source of biological causes of disabilities are chromosomal anomalies. Although these disorders are rare in the general population, their numbers are significant among cases of developmental disabilities in which cause can be specified.

The intensive research on chromosomes that began in the late 1950s and early 1960s has yielded a detailed portrait of both typical and atypical chromosomal patterns. These patterns are clarified through the use of **karyotypes.** The process of karyotyping includes taking a picture of the chromosomes in a human cell, enlarging it, cutting out the pictures of individual chromosomes, and then arranging the chromosomes by pairs from the largest (numbered as pair 1) to the smallest (pair 22), followed by the sex chromosomes (XX or XY).

Approximately 10% of pregnancies begin with some chromosomal imbalance, but most of these abort spontaneously during the first 3 months of pregnancy. A small number of these pregnancies proceed to full term, and the children born illustrate the potential effects of irregularities in the arrangement or alignment of autosomes or sex chromosomes. Chromosomal errors can be identified in approximately 1 in 200 live births.

While genetic disorders are classified as hereditary, chromosomal problems are often more accurately termed **innate,** since an abnormal chromosome arrangement is present at conception but is not the product of *hereditary* exchange. Disorders of this type usually result from abnormalities occurring during the stage of cell division called **meiosis.** During meiosis, individual reproductive cells divide and then pair up to form the genetic foundation of the embryo. The normal process includes 23 chromosomes from each parent, which are paired to form the new organism's complement of 46 chromosomes. Figure 6.3 illustrates the karyotypes for a male and a female with typical chromosomal patterns.

Several specific abnormalities that occur during the process of chromosomal arrangement and alignment result in either too much or too little chromosomal material being present. In **nondisjunction,** a given parental pair of chromosomes fails to split at conception, causing the formation of a group of three chromosomes (a **trisomy**) in lieu of the normal pair. A trisomy on chromosome 21 is the most common cause of Down syndrome; trisomies on 18 and 13 have also been noted in the literature. In **translocation,** a fragment of chromosomal material is located across from or exchanged with another chromosomal pair. For example, a translocation that results in Down syndrome occurs when a fragment broken off from chromosome pair 21 attaches to a chromosome from group 15. In **deletion,** a portion of the original genetic material is absent from a specific chromosome pair. Finally, **mosaicism** is an uneven pattern of dissimilar cells (such as of some cells with 46 and some with 47 chromosomes).

Before the 1950s, causes of the disorders now classified under chromosomal anomalies were unknown. Seminal research published by Lejeune and his colleagues (e.g., Lejeune, Gautier, & Turpin, 1959) and other geneticists then led to a much clearer understanding of the nature of chromosomal abnormalities. As mentioned earlier, aberrations in the number or arrangement of chromosomes are likely to damage the developing organism. Down syndrome and cri-du-chat syndrome are

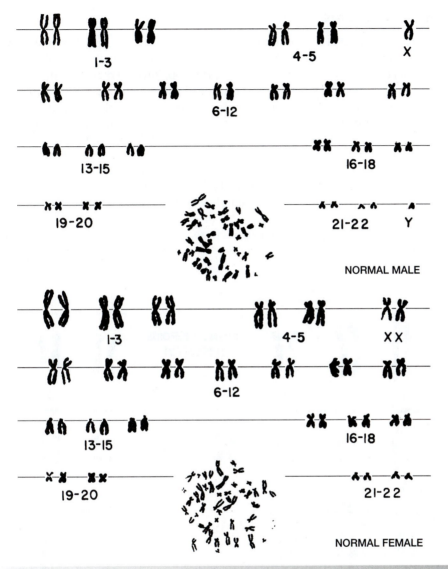

FIGURE 6.3
Typical Chromosomal Karyotypes

Source: From *Handbook of Mental Retardation Syndromes* (pp. 33–34), by C. H. Carter, 1975, Springfield, IL: Thomas. Reprinted by permission of Charles C Thomas Publisher, Ltd.

examples of autosomal disorders; Klinefelter and Turner syndromes come from sex chromosome abnormalities. As a broad generalization, disorders in autosomes are more often associated with mental retardation, whereas anomalies associated with sex chromosomes are more commonly associated with learning disabilities (Bender, Puck, Salbenblatt, & Robinson, 1986; Smith, Polloway, Patton, & Dowdy, 2004).

Down Syndrome

Down syndrome (DS) is the best known and most frequently researched biologically caused condition associated with mental retardation and developmental disabilities. In fact, Dykens and colleagues (2000, citing Hodapp) indicate that as many research articles have addressed Down syndrome as for all other genetic etiologies combined. For many laypersons, the concept of a person with mental retardation historically has often been synonymous with a Down syndrome individual. A reasonable estimate of the prevalence of the syndrome is about 1 in 700 to 1,000 births (Dykens et al., 2000), which amounts to roughly 5% to 6% of all persons identified as mentally retarded.

Study of DS has revealed three separate chromosomal causes. The first and most common, trisomy 21, is due to the failure of one pair of parental chromosomes to separate at conception, resulting in the child's having 47 chromosomes (see Figure 6.4). Trisomy 21 accounts for more than 92% of children born with Down syndrome (Dykens et al., 2000). This abnormality has historically been found more often in children born to older mothers, and researchers have suggested a variety of reasons.

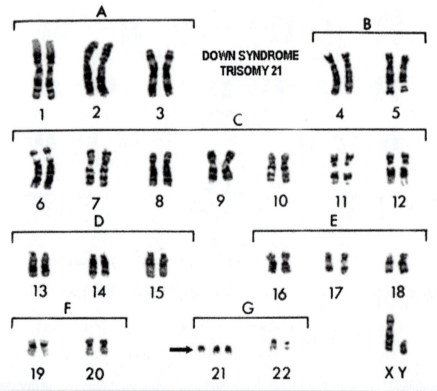

FIGURE 6.4
Karyotype of Trisomy 21

Source: From *Genetics and Mental Retardation Syndromes* (p. 39), by E. M. Dykens, R. M. Hodapp, & B. M. Finucane, 2000, Baltimore: Paul H. Brookes. Copyright © 2000 by Paul H. Brookes Publishing Co. Used by permission.

Specific factors that have been suspected of causing trisomy 21 include medication and drugs; exposure to radiation, chemicals, or hepatitis viruses; and the possible absence of a mechanism in the mother to abort the fetus spontaneously. Chapman, Scott, and Mason (2002, p. 54) hypothesized that "increased risk for Down syndrome among older, less-educated women may be due to deterioration of the ovum associated with the cumulative effects of chronic stress burden" (p. 54).

It is important to realize that, although risk is related to age and increases to approximately 1 in 30 births at 45 years old, age itself is a *correlate* and not the *cause*. With the increased public awareness of the correlation between age and risk of occurrence, many older parents undergo prenatal screening for Down syndrome and may then consider abortion. This fact, plus the reality that births to parents over age 40 are relatively rare, results in the large majority of births of children with Down syndrome actually being to younger parents.

A second form of Down syndrome is caused by a translocation transmitted hereditarily by carriers. Although this translocation is usually to chromosome pairs 13 or 15, the extra material comes from pair 21 and forms, in a sense, a partial trisomy. It is found on 3% to 5% of cases of DS (Dykens et al., 2000). Mosaicism, the uneven division that creates cells varying in chromosome numbers (some 47 and some 46), is a third and rarer form of the condition.

Down syndrome is frequently associated with a variety of medical challenges (see Table 6.5) and also a number of specific physical traits, with the latter including the following:

- Short stature
- Flat, broad face with small ears and nose
- Short, broad hands with incurving fingers

Medical Concern	Percentage Affected
Congenital heart defects	50
Hearing loss	66–89
Ophthalmic conditions (e.g., strabismus, refractive errors)	60
Gastrointestinal conditions	5
Endocrine conditions (e.g., hypothyroidism)	50–90
Dental conditions (e.g., crowding, periodontal disease)	60–100
Orthopedic anomalies (e.g., subclinical atlanoaxial subluxation)	15
Obesity	50–60
Skin conditions (e.g., eczema, dry skin)	50
Seizure disorders	6–13
Leukemia	0.6

TABLE 6.5
Medical Concerns in Persons with Down Syndrome

Source: From *Genetics and Mental Retardation Syndromes* (p. 63), by E. M. Dykens, R. M. Hodapp, & B. M. Finucane, 2000, Baltimore: Paul H. Brookes. Copyright © 2000 by Paul H. Brookes Publishing Co. Used by permission.

- Upward slanting of the eyes with folds of skin (epicanthic folds) at the inside corner of the eye
- Small mouth and short roof, which may cause the tongue to protrude and contribute to articulation problems
- Single crease across the palm
- Reduced muscle tone (hypotonia) and hyperflexibility of joints
- Incomplete or delayed sexual development

These traits vary greatly from one individual to another. Thus, no overgeneralizations should be made according to the defining characteristics that must or may be associated with Down syndrome. Many of the behavioral characteristics traditionally associated with DS have not been documented in research or require some further explication. For example, the stereotype of the child with Down syndrome who is cheerful, affectionate, rhythmic, and unusually dexterous has not been empirically established. Furthermore, while children with Down syndrome may exhibit more frequent and intense repetitive behaviors, Evans and Gray (2000) report that they did not differ from young children (matched on mental age) who were nondisabled in terms of the numbers of compulsive behaviors in which they engaged.

A very significant area of research on DS has been cognitive and intellectual functioning. Traditionally, the syndrome had been assumed to result most often in moderate retardation, with rare cases reaching a ceiling IQ of 70. Occasional anecdotal reports of ability and special talents, such as in the classic diary of Nigel Hunt (1967), were considered more interesting and unusual than typical.

The first comprehensive study that altered views on this issue was reported by Rynders, Spiker, and Horrobin (1978). Their review of 15 studies provided data on the intelligence test scores of children with Down syndrome that indicated a significant range in level of functioning and refuted the alleged ceiling IQ of 70.

Optimistic data on the abilities of children with Down syndrome then continued to accumulate with early intervention viewed as the key. Rynders and Horrobin (1990) provided further support in subsequent research supporting higher expectations for academic achievement in students with DS. They cautioned that IQs frequently diminish over time and, therefore, achievement levels should be stressed in assessing level of functioning and designing educational programs.

Individual case histories often support the positive views of the intellectual potentialities of persons with Down syndrome. For example, an illustration of the range of effects of the mosaic form of Down syndrome was offered by Turkington (1987), who described the life of a 35-year-old woman with Down syndrome who had completed an associate arts degree in early childhood education. The success of the 1990s television show *Life Goes On* was due in large part to the character portrayed by Chris Burke, a teenager with Down syndrome. The story in Box 6.2 provides another such case study.

Language development has also been researched extensively on persons with Down syndrome. One focus has been possible challenges in speech development due in part to the protruding tongue. However, expressive and receptive language also warrant careful attention, as Abbeduto and colleagues (2003) have noted:

Box 6.2 ⚘ Fighting Back

Arlington—Kathleen Schermer, a special education specialist at Yorktown High School, can recall vividly the day Sara Miller gently and kindly told off the slackers in her U.S. history class.

"One day, when the vast number of students weren't doing their homework, Sara turned around to the entire class and said, 'You know, I have Down syndrome and I am getting this work done and I know you can too,'" Schermer said. "The boys, if they could have slithered into the floor and evaporated, they would have."

Miller had lobbied long and hard to take the class, convincing administrators . . . she could handle the shift from her special education curriculum. In the end, she graduated from Arlington's Yorktown High in 2002 with a 3.2 GPA, two years on the swim team and a reputation for bringing positive energy to any situation.

Her teachers were so impressed they nominated her for a national award—and weren't too surprised when Miller . . . [was] one of three students with disabilities who won the 2003 "Yes I Can" award for self-advocacy by the Council for Exceptional Children. "The reason we chose Sara is because she . . . basically put her future in her hands and gained the confidence and support in her school," said Jess Forr, a program development specialist with the Council.

Today, Miller is participating in an extended education program at the Arlington Career Center where she is being trained to become an assistant in early childhood education. "I want to work with kids who have special needs. . . . I just like being there for them, being their companion and their friend. . . . I believe in determination. When I get something done, I'm happy with my life."

"She was our only child," said her mother. "We didn't have anything to compare her against, and we didn't consider there were things she shouldn't do."

She came to Yorktown High with a determination that she could do anything and a fear that other students would think she couldn't. She was the only student with Down syndrome at the school. "It scared me that they might think, 'she is so slow, she can't do that. . . . I wanted to slap them in the face [and say] 'No, I'm not like that. I'm very kind, very smart.'" As the years passed, she overcame her fears and grew to know many people at the school. She developed a few close friends in her special education classes but felt most comfortable with adults. . . .

High school "transformed me into a new person, more loose, comfortable," Miller said. "I felt safe there." Miller became an integral part of the swim team and Yorktown's Fellowship of Christian Athletes chapter, according to senior Jenny Varuska, 17.

She competed in races but also was one of the team's biggest motivators and made a point of congratulating members on their swims. "She gave us advice and told us we can trust God with anything and that's how she got through life," Varuska said. "A lot of people admired her. She had a lot to overcome but never showed a sign of being upset."

Source: "Fighting Back," by J. Kelly (2003), *Northern Virginia Journal.* Reprinted in the Lynchburg, VA, *News & Advance,* May 25, 2003, p. C-8. Used with permission.

The comprehension of syntax is more challenging than the comprehension of vocabulary for adolescents and young adults with Down syndrome. . . . These results suggest that language intervention for adolescents and young adults with Down syndrome must devote considerable attention to increasing the syntactic capabilities of affected individuals and that such interventions may need to be more intense than those targeting lexical skills. (p. 156)

Another area of emphasis has been considerations of plastic surgery. Such efforts, most notably in Israel and related to the work of Reuven Feuerstein and his colleagues, have demonstrated that the physical stigmata of Down syndrome can be reduced. May (1988) provides a good discussion of the rationales, benefits, and cautions of plastic surgery for people with Down syndrome. According to research reported by May and Turnbull (1992), the majority (88%) of plastic surgeons were familiar with the procedures, and 24% had performed it. Reasons given for the surgery included (in rank order): to normalize appearance, to improve speech and eating abilities, to improve breathing, and as a response to parental request.

An important area of research is life expectancy. In 1929, expectancy for individuals with Down syndrome was only 9 years; by 1990, that average had increased to more than 50 years (Eyman, Call, & White, 1991). As age increases, association of DS with Alzheimer's disease also increases. Individuals with Down syndrome apparently run a much greater risk of developing Alzheimer's disease (Stark, Menolascino, & Goldsbury, 1988; Zigman, Schupf, Lubin, & Silverman, 1987). The association is not unexpected, given the identified locus of two genes associated with Alzheimer's on chromosome pair 21. Epstein (1988) has pointed out that the loss of intellectual functioning associated with advanced age will be seen even more often in individuals with Down syndrome now that life expectancies have increased.

Several overriding points must be made clear. First, individuals with Down syndrome are primarily and foremost people who have needs, desires, and rights similar to those of other people. Thus, while a substantial amount of attention has focused on intellectual considerations, of at least comparable importance is research on socioemotional considerations such as developing friendships (Freeman & Kasari, 2002), emotional development (Kasari, Freeman, & Hughes, 2001), and family relationships (Cuskelly & Gunn, 2003). Second, the effects of intensive interventions with young children who have Down syndrome have been evaluated only since the late 1970s; thus, historical descriptions of DS are no longer accurate. For example, as reported in the popular press, Charles de Gaulle had a daughter with Down syndrome. At the time of her early death in 1948, he reflected the sentiments of parents of an earlier historical era when he comforted his wife by saying of their deceased daughter, "Come . . . now she is like everybody else." The perspective for this quote in the new millennium would rather much more clearly focus on the similarity and equality of people with Down syndrome in life rather than death.

Prader-Willi Syndrome

Another condition that has been linked to an autosomal abnormality is **Prader-Willi syndrome (PWS).** Most cases (i.e., approximately 70%) of Prader-Willi syndrome appear to be caused by deletion of a portion of the long arm of the paternal chromosome on pair 15. For a significant portion of the remaining 30%, the condition appears to be the result of maternal **uniparental disomy** of the 15th chromosome; that is, both chromosomes are contributed by the mother with none from the father (Holm et al., 1993; Scott et al., 1999).

Persons with PWS often have small features and stature and the condition has also been associated with mild retardation and learning disabilities. However, the most significant characteristics of PWS include insatiable appetite (and hence often obesity) and a pattern of obsessive-compulsive disorder (OCD) (Holsen & Thompson, 2004), often interacting with efforts to obtain food (Joseph, Egli, Koppekin, & Thompson, 2002). The biological mechanism underlying PWS brings about a preoccupation with eating that has prompted observers to suggest that, for a Prader-Willi child, "life is one endless meal." In fact, recent research points to the fact that individuals with Prader-Willi syndrome were more likely than a comparison group of individuals— including those both with retardation but not Prader-Willi and those without mental retardation—to indulge in eating food that was contaminated as well as to eat highly unusual combinations of edible and inedible foods (e.g., cake with grass) (Dykens, 2000; Dykens et al., 2000).

The characteristics associated with Prader-Willi syndrome generally become evident in two stages: an infantile hypotonic phase, and a childhood/adulthood obesity phase (Donaldson et al., 1994). Initially, a major paradox is the failure-to-thrive condition, given that failure to thrive subsequently turns into excessive eating and obesity as the child increases in age. In addition, babies with Prader-Willi generally experience hypotonia; thus, the term "floppy baby" has frequently been used to describe them during infancy. Between the ages of 1 and 3, the characteristics of the second phase of the syndrome begin to become apparent. This phase may include hyperphagia (i.e., an insatiable appetite) and constant preoccupation with food. Uncontrollable eating often leads to life-threatening obesity. Also noted during this phase are delayed psychomotor development, signs of cognitive impairment, and delayed and/or abnormal pubertal development (Scott et al., 1999, p. 4).

As persons with Prader-Willi syndrome develop, a pattern of significant behavioral difficulties often emerges, including temper tantrums, impulsivity, aggression, and stubbornness (Dimitropoulos, Feurer, Butler, & Thompson, 2001; Dykens, Cassidy, & King, 1999). In addition, some research indicates that individuals with Prader-Willi syndrome are more likely to engage in self-injurious behavior, with skin picking the most prevalent manifestation being reported (Dimitropoulos et al., 2001; Symons, Butler, Sanders, Feurer, & Thompson, 1999). Table 6.6 provides a summary of behavioral patterns.

Goldman (1988) noted that the association of Prader-Willi syndrome with obesity has led to the assumption that the expected life span for individuals with the disorder would be limited, at least in part because of the physical complications of being grossly overweight. In contrast, her research indicates that older individuals with the syndrome do exist but may be unidentified. Goldman describes two adult women for whom the desire to overeat continued with no evidence of their understanding the need to manage intake. They obtained food through their own devices: "Even when the environment is believed to be controlled, these persons evidently engage in some variety of successful covert foraging" (1988, p. 101).

Based on research by Dykens and Rosner (1999), individuals with PWS (as compared to those with nonspecified mental retardation) are more likely to enjoy eating, think about food, be upset with changes in routine, be impatient with delays, and have a low frustration tolerance, while they are less likely to have many friends and be energetic. Further, as Joseph and colleagues (2002) noted, the likelihood of OCD effectively distinguishes individuals with PWS from other persons with eating disorders.

TABLE 6.6

Person with PWS (4–46 Years Old) with Maladaptive Behaviors: Child Behavior Checklist

Maladaptive Behavior	Percentage
Overeats	98
Skin picks	97
Stubborn	95
Obsessions	94
Tantrums	88
Disobedient	78
Impulsive	76
Labile	76
Excessive sleep	75
Talks too much	74
Compulsions	71
Anxious, worried	70
Prefers being alone	67
Gets teased a lot	65
Peers don't like	60
Hoards	55
Steals (food, money for food)	54
Withdrawn	53
Unhappy, sad	51

Source: From *Genetics and Mental Retardation Syndromes* (p. 186), by E. M. Dykens, R. M. Hodapp, & B. M. Finucane, 2000, Baltimore: Paul H. Brookes. Copyright © 2000 by Paul H. Brookes Publishing Co. Used by permission.

Additional information on the mechanics of the disorder and the effectiveness of various treatment options continues to be available as research develops. Strategies that involve early intervention, exercise, monitoring of caloric intake, education about appropriate food choices, environmental controls, and specialized transition planning are indicated (Scott et al., 1997).

Williams Syndrome

Williams syndrome was poorly understood until its genetic base was identified in the 1990s. As such, the syndrome provides an apt example of the continued research on the genetic basis of specific syndromes and the efforts to derive treatment and educational implications from syndrome identification. The literature on Williams syndrome (e.g., Dykens et al., 2000; Dykens, Rosner, & Ly, 2001; Einfeld, Tonge, & Rees, 2001; Johnson, 2004; Mervis, Klein-Tasman, & Mastin, 2001) highlights the fact that it has an incidence of approximately 1 in 20,000 births. It is caused by the microdeletion of chromosome 7, with multiple genes involved (i.e., missing)—genes that impact *elastin,* a connective tissue. Common signs include being pixie-like and petite in physical appearance. Further characteristics include the following:

- Overly friendly
- Highly anxious
- An average IQ of 40 to 90, but with marked unevenness in patterns and a unique behavioral profile (according to Searcy et al., 2004, whose study of individuals with Williams syndrome reported 46% with IQs between 85 and 70, 45% between 69 and 66, and 9% between 54 and 40)
- Developmental delays in speech/language, motor and academic skills, but with unique patterns of development
- Well-developed vocabulary coincidental with difficulty in maintaining reciprocal conversation
- An ability to learn to read over time and with strength in phonics-based spelling
- Limited visuospatial development and poor visual-motor skills (e.g., handwriting problems)
- Limited mathematical and numerical knowledge
- Identified medical concerns including cardiac, digestive, and feeding difficulties

Sex Chromosomal Differences

Anomalies in the sex chromosomes have also been found to affect development adversely. Two such conditions are discussed next; their karyotypes are shown in Figure 6.5.

Klinefelter syndrome is a condition, initially described in 1942 by Dr. Harry Klinefelter, in which males receive an extra X chromosome so that they have an XXY configuration. The clinical pattern includes frequent social retardation, sterility and underdevelopment of the male sex organs, and the acquisition of female secondary sex characteristics. The syndrome may be associated with mild levels of intellectual retardation, although intellectual deficits increase with the number of X chromosomes (i.e., XXXY, XXXXY).* Because some children of the XXY pattern may not develop the formal syndrome, the term *Klinefelter syndrome* has now more often been replaced by describing individuals with the extra X chromosome as *XXY males* (Bock, 1997).

The incidence of XXY males is relatively high, with approximately 1 in 500 to 1,000 births. Although no specific cure exists, physical aspects of the condition can be alleviated through surgery and testosterone treatment. XXY males can have problems with auditory perception, receptive and expressive language, and a general deficit in processing linguistic information (Bender et al., 1983), as well as being prone to difficulties in the formation of positive social relationships, depression, and significant mood changes (Bock, 1997). Although often discussed in relation to mental retardation, XXY in males is more commonly associated with learning disabilities (consistent with the earlier note that sex chromosomal disorders are more often associated with learning disabilities).

---

*Webb (2000, pp. 11–12) concluded: "With the addition of sex chromosomes past three, mental retardation is almost always present, although these cases are few and far between. The range of mental retardation [may be in] the severe/profound range."

FIGURE 6.5
Sex Chromosomal Abnormalities

Source: From *Handbook of Mental Retardation Syndromes* (pp. 39, 45), by C. H. Carter, 1975, Springfield, IL: Thomas. Reprinted by permission of Charles C Thomas Publisher, Ltd.

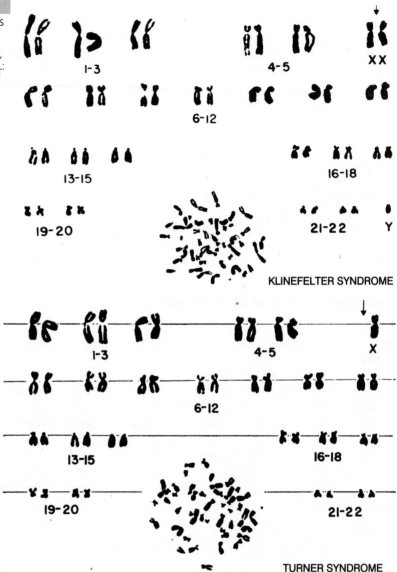

A sex chromosomal disorder in females, *Turner syndrome,* results from an absence of one of the X chromosomes (XO). It is the only syndrome with a true **monosomy** (i.e., one chromosome) and thus the only one in which individuals with the syndrome show fewer than 46 chromosomes. Its rarity—1 in 2,500 female births (Rovet, 1993)—is underscored by the fact that more than 95% of fetuses conceived with the XO pattern are spontaneously aborted.

Although Turner syndrome is not usually a cause of mental retardation, it is worthy of mention because it is often associated with learning disabilities. Some data indicate that the pattern of females with XO syndrome includes lower performance scale and full-scale IQ scores (but not lower verbal scores) and with somewhat lower educational and occupational attainments than their peers. Common problems are in spatial relations and hence mathematical abilities, memory, attention, and social competence (Downey et al., 1991; Rovet, 1993). Turner syndrome produces numerous deviations from normal development, with lack of secondary sex characteristics, sterility, and short stature as particularly common features.

CRANIAL MALFORMATIONS

Several conditions associated with retardation manifest themselves as cranial malformations. The most dramatic is anencephaly—literally, the absence of major portions of the brain. Although anencephaly, for obvious reasons, is not associated with any treatments, it has been the subject of exciting research. A major type of neural tube defect (i.e., a defect occurring in the brain or spinal cord), it has been associated with the 1998 federal requirements that food manufacturers of grain products must add the nutrient folic acid to their products because of its positive effects on the appropriate development of the fetal neural tube (see AAMR, 1996). This change in the dietary complement of folic acid has proved to have a significant reductive effect on this disorder as well as on *spina bifida* (i.e., a hole in the tube that surrounds the spinal cord that may or may not be related to mental retardation).

Two other cranial malformations are indirectly associated with mental retardation. Children who have **microcephaly** are characterized by a small, conical skull, a curved spine that typically leads to a stooping posture, and severe retardation. In rare cases, the condition can be transmitted genetically, probably as an autosomal recessive trait, but it is more commonly a secondary consequence of such conditions as congenital rubella or fetal alcohol syndrome (discussed later), or it may be the result of environmental exposure (e.g., radiation). Individuals affected by microcephaly have been characterized as imitative, good-natured, and lively. There is no known cure.

Hydrocephalus consists of at least six types of problems associated with interference in the flow of cerebrospinal fluid within the skull. The most common type of blockage results in progressive enlargement of the cranium and subsequent brain damage. Physical manifestations of this condition differ widely; however, an enlarged skull is not present in all cases. Hydrocephalus may result from polygenic inheritance or as a secondary effect of maternal infections or intoxications. The effects of this condition can be reduced in many infants by draining off the fluid, using shunts to decrease the cranial pressure. (*Shunts* are valves or tubes surgically inserted under the child's skin to pump the fluid away from the brain and maintain proper flow.) The results of shunt treatment have been very encouraging in preventing head enlargement, the symptom most often associated with an increase in the probability of retardation.

Milder cases of hydrocephalus may escape detection, with no ill effects noted. For example, some observers have hypothesized that Einstein may have had a mild, nonprogressive case of hydrocephalus (Beck, 1972).

OTHER CONGENITAL FACTORS

In addition to cranial malformations, other congenital factors include a variety of conditions that may be associated with harmful factors called **teratogens.** These can significantly affect prenatal (and, in some cases, postnatal) development. The first widespread public exposure to the awesome power of teratogenic agents came from the thalidomide tragedy in England in the 1960s. Intended as a relaxant during pregnancy, this drug caused severe physical deformities (e.g., missing and/or shortened limbs) in many fetuses. The discussion that follows focuses on some of the specific factors that have been identified as having teratogenic effects.

Maternal Disorders

The brain is especially susceptible to damage through maternal disease during the first 3 months of pregnancy. Infection of the mother by rubella (i.e., German measles) early in pregnancy has been found to result in fetal defects in up to 50% of these cases. This is particularly significant because rubella has historically been a disease of epidemic occurrence. Immunization procedures developed more than 30 years ago helped to limit its incidence, but trends in the 1990s indicate increases in the disease. In addition to retardation, *congenital rubella* can result in heart disease, blindness, and deafness. It has been one of the primary causes of severe multiple disabilities among children.

Congenital syphilis is another maternal disease that can damage the central nervous system and result in severe disabilities in developing fetuses. Perhaps the most alarming feature of this disorder has been its recent increasing prevalence after it had nearly been eradicated in the 20th century. This may be due in part to antibiotic-resistant strains of the disease. Research has also addressed the possible effects of maternal acquired immune deficiency syndrome (AIDS) as an agent of congenital disabilities.

One other significant cause of retardation that may function as an insult to the fetus is *blood-group incompatibility* between mother and unborn child. Most commonly, the condition occurs as a result of the Rh factor, a protein on the surface of some red blood cells. Rh-positive blood cells contain this protein; Rh-negative cells do not. When an Rh-positive male and an Rh-negative female conceive an Rh-positive child, neither mother nor fetus is adversely affected. At birth, however, the mother's immune system will react to the fetus's Rh-positive blood by forming antibodies to the Rh factor. These antibodies remain in the mother's system and will enter the bloodstream of the next Rh-positive baby conceived, attacking its central nervous system and possibly resulting in retardation, epilepsy, and cerebral palsy. Treatment of this immune response focuses on preventing the destructive antibodies from forming. One technique is to vaccinate the mother with Rh immunoglobulin serum midway through each suspected Rh-positive pregnancy and within 72 hours of its termination (whether by birth, miscarriage, or abortion). This serum destroys the Rh-positive cells that pass from the infant's to the mother's bloodstream, inhibiting the development of antibodies that would otherwise attack the next fetus carried. This procedure does not alter the mother's immune response mechanism but can remove the stimuli that trigger it.

Substance Exposure

A great deal of research has addressed the effects of drugs and industrial chemicals on fetuses. Particular attention has been given to nicotine, caffeine, lysergic acid diethylamide (LSD), and other related drugs. The results of exposure to these substances are clear, and we should assume that pregnant women should also avoid any other powerful chemical substance.

The first significant breakthrough of understanding in this domain was with alcohol consumption. Problems associated with alcohol have been generally acknowledged for years. For example, Haggard and Jellinek (1942) noted that "infants born to alcoholic mothers sometimes had a starved, shriveled and imperfect look" (p. 165). But despite this long-standing suspicion of teratogenic effects, only since the 1970s has the nature of **fetal alcohol syndrome (FAS)** been documented. Jones, Smith, Ulleland, and Streissguth (1973) coined the term *fetal alcohol syndrome* after studies of eight unrelated offspring born to chronically alcoholic mothers showed a recognizable pattern of major and minor malformations, growth deficiencies, and developmental disabilities.

The best estimates of FAS occurrence are between 1 and 3 cases per 1,000 births (Ackerman, 1998; Warren & Bast, 1988). Other studies have also reinforced this approximate rate of occurrence, placing the figure at 1 in 650 births (Webb, Hochberg, & Sher, 1988). At this rate, FAS is clearly among the leading known causes of mental retardation, along with Down syndrome (Abel & Sokol, 1986).

In FAS, the mother's heavy alcohol consumption has direct toxic effects on the fetus. Exact levels of consumption that cause FAS are not known, but those mothers who are alcoholic, who have several drinks per day, or who engage in binge drinking run a confirmed, significant risk of damaging their unborn children. Risk rates are particularly high during the first trimester of pregnancy. Research continues on the risks of light or moderate drinking. An important area of study has been *fetal alcohol effects* (FAE), a more subtle disorder associated with learning and attentional problems. Given the risk of FAE, a common recommendation is for total abstinence from alcohol drinking during pregnancy. Figure 6.6 provides the related government warning.

The characteristics of FAS can be separated into three primary features: central nervous system dysfunction (e.g., retardation), craniofacial malformations (e.g., cleft palate, microcephaly), and prenatal and postnatal growth development (e.g., low birth weight). A diagnosis of FAS is warranted when a child has a cluster of disorders within these three areas (Griesbach & Polloway, 1991).

Mann (2003) summarized the potentially educationally relevant concerns associated with FAS as including attentional deficits and distractibility, impulsivity, restlessness, inept social interactions, self-control problems, and memory, problem-solving, and organizational difficulties.

While fetal alcohol syndrome has frequently been associated with lower levels of functioning and hence mental retardation, also growing is evidence of difficulties associated with retention, abstract thinking, and mathematics. Kerns, Don, Mateer, and Streissguth (1997) report on a group of adolescents and young adults identified as having FAS and not being mentally retarded. They confirm the presence of learning-related challenges in this population. As they note: "Cognitive impairments of this nature and degree might account, in part, to the widespread

FIGURE 6.6
Government Warning: Alcohol
Consumption

Source: Warning label mandated by
Public Law 100-690, November 1989.

> (1) According to the Surgeon General, women should not drink alcoholic beverages during pregnancy because of the risk of birth defects.
> (2) Consumption of alcoholic beverages impairs your ability to drive a car or operate machinery and may cause health problems.

reports and observations of functional difficulties that individuals with FAS manifest in school, home, and community" (p. 691). Implications for educators are discussed further by Ackerman (1998), and for families and communities by Streissguth (1997).

Attention also has extended to other drugs, because of common reports of children exposed to drugs in utero. However, significant problems persist in determining the actual number, with estimates of 500,000 to 750,000 exposed children born each year (King, 2004). Although the research base is by no means clear, a number of possible characteristics have been noted for children who are at risk due to prenatal exposure to drugs. Such judgments must be made cautiously because the research base is confounded by, for example, lack of control for other factors; wide variance in substances, dosage, and purity; multiple drug exposures; and variant levels of prenatal care (King, 2004). Poulsen (cited in Vincent, Poulsen, Cole, Woodruff, & Griffith, 1991) indicated that problem areas could include the following:

- Exhibition of behavioral extremes
- Being easily overstimulated
- Low tolerance for changes
- Constant testing of limits set by adults
- Difficulty in reading social cues
- Difficulty in establishing and maintaining relationships with peers
- Language delays
- Sporadic mastery of skills
- Inconsistent problem-solving strategies
- Auditory processing and word retrieval difficulties
- Decreased capacity to initiate and organize play
- Decrease in focused attention and concentration

Considerations of substance exposure must always be set in a broader environmental context, as stressed by Brady, Posner, Long, and Rosati (cited in King, 2004):

> The long-term effects which will be found within the general population of drug-exposed children will not be explained by drug exposure alone. Before we can predict the developmental outcomes for these high-risk children we need further research into the additive and interactive effects of the multiple risk factors to which they are exposed, including in many cases the global effects of poverty, multigenerational substance abuse, and the impact of growing up in a drug-seeking environment. (p. 5)

PREMATURITY AND PERINATAL CONCERNS

The advances in technology for supporting premature and low-birth-weight children as well as for addressing prenatal concerns have dramatically changed the prognosis for these neonates over the last 30 years. For example, McNab and Blackman (1998) summarized research on mortality rates and indicate that from 1985 to 1995, the mortality rates in the United States for infants with birth weights of 500 to 749 grams (approximately 1 to 1.5 pounds) decreased 31%, while mortality for those 750 to 1,499 grams (1.5 to 3.5 pounds) decreased by 53%. They noted that consequently 47% of infants weighing 1 to 1.5 pounds survived the first year, while 80% of those between 750 and 999 grams did as well. For infants over 1,000 grams, the survival rate was more than 90%. Clearly, medical science significantly and positively affected the prognosis for these babies.

In addition to the complexity of causes of prematurity and low birth weight (see Figure 6.7), determining the effects of prematurity continues to be a difficult task. Full-term infants are born between 37 and 41 weeks, and normal birth weight is above 5.5 pounds (Widerstrom, Mowder, & Sandall, 1991). Extremely short pregnancies (less than 28 weeks) or very low birth weights (below 1,500 grams, or 3.5 pounds) frequently present problems. For less substantial deviations from the norm in term or weight, the results are not so clear. Data indicate that the relationship among prematurity, birth weight, and mental retardation is most significant for very low birth weight.

In addition to low IQ, prematurity has also been linked to increased occurrence of cerebral palsy, attentional deficits, and other neurological and medical complications. The technological efforts now available in neonatal intensive care units (NICUs) represent the most effective response to the challenges presented by these special infants by providing a medically responsive facility that coincidentally offers the neonate a psychologically supportive environment. Widerstrom and colleagues (1991, p. 114) cite the recommendations of Bennett (1986) for NICU practical guidelines:

- Recognize the unusual physiological stresses being endured by the premature infant.
- Modify the environment to decrease overstimulation (specifically screen out grossly bombarding and unnecessary sensory stimuli such as handling during periods of quiet sleep).
- Introduce diurnal rhythms to promote behavioral organization. Gradually facilitate reciprocal visual, auditory, tactile, vestibular-kinesthetic, and social feedback during alert periods.
- Immediately terminate or alter approaches that produce avoidance responses.
- Educate and assist parents in reading, anticipating, and appropriately responding to their own infant's cues and signals, thus fostering and reinforcing parents' feelings of competence.

Oxygen deprivation, referred to as **hypoxia** (low oxygen) or *anoxia* (no oxygen), can result from such birth difficulties as a knotted umbilical cord, extremely short or long labor, or breech birth. Anoxia has long been associated with pronounced deficiencies in the affected infant, including lower IQ scores (Graham, Ernhart, Thurston,

FIGURE 6.7
Low Birth Weight and Prematurity

Source: President's Committee on
Mental Retardation (1976), p. 31.

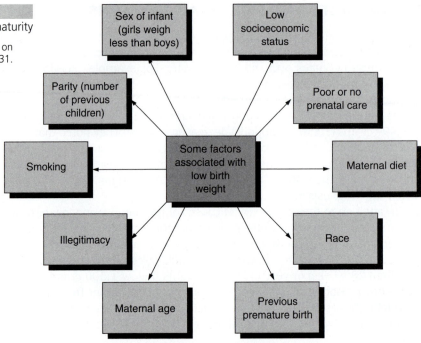

Prematurity: Gestation time of less than 37 weeks.
Low birth weight: Weight at birth equal to or less than 2,500 grams.

& Craft, 1962; McLaren & Bryson, 1987). The deficiencies it produces may vary greatly and are often unstable, so it is difficult to give an accurate prognosis for a child who experiences anoxia. Other problems at birth that can be traumatic include the delivery itself and the specific anesthetic procedures used.

McNab and Blackman (1998) provide an important summary of the challenges facing infants with birth complications and their families:

> Despite the ability of neonatologists to provide life-saving measures for very sick babies, allowing them to be discharged from the hospital, significant obstacles often face many of these infants and their families once they are home. Ongoing health problems in these children can hamper or delay the normal course of motor, cognitive, language, and social development. Community early intervention professionals such as educators, social workers, and physical, occupational and speech therapists can improve these children's long-term outcomes by being knowledgeable about these health problems and devising creative family-centered early intervention strategies. (p. 198)

POSTNATAL CONCERNS

A variety of postnatal traumatic events leading to disabilities can occur throughout early childhood. *Head injuries* account for the greater part of such cases. It has been estimated that 1 in 30 newborns will experience a serious brain injury by the end of the teen years (Allison, 1992). Some 89% of these injuries are caused by falls, bicycle and motor vehicle accidents, and sports-related activities. The highest risk years are actually between 15 and 25, with boys being twice as likely to be affected as girls, and with motor vehicle accidents being the most common cause of injury (Pipitone, 1992; Vernon-Levett, 1991). The relationship of auto accidents to brain injury has spurred the passage by all states of mandatory child restraint and seat belt laws.

Child abuse is a special concern, particularly because of its relationship to disabilities. Child abuse can result from and aggravate primary disabilities. Zantal-Weiner (1987) notes in her review that children with disabilities are less able to defend themselves from abuse, have greater difficulty determining appropriate and inappropriate contact and telling anyone of the abuse once it has occurred, are more dependent on those who abuse them, are less likely to report abuse, and are seen as less credible when they do report it. In addition to striking, other negative so-called disciplinary actions like violent shaking can potentially play a role in brain hemorrhage and retardation. Signs of a "shaken baby" include vomiting, seizures, blood pooling in the eyes, apnea (spells of interrupted breathing), irritability, sleeping difficulties, and drowsiness; outcomes may include hypertension, cerebral palsy, subcranial or subdural hemorrhages, coma, and death.

Lead poisoning, which may lead to encephalitis, is permanently and progressively damaging to the central nervous system because of lead's role as a neurotoxicant. It can cause seizures, cerebral palsy, and retardation. Other effects of lead poisoning include gastrointestinal disturbances (e.g., anorexia, vomiting) and central nervous system manifestations (e.g., convulsions, drowsiness, irritability). Although commercial paints no longer contain lead, poisoning is still a factor in residences where a child has access to old, peeling paint. Conscious urban renewal is reducing the scope of this problem through repainting with unleaded paints. In older homes, lead paint can also enter the body through inhalation of dust or fumes, such as during renovation work (Marino et al., 1990) or from the soil around the houses. The existence of high lead levels remains most serious in inner-city areas where abatement efforts have not been fully implemented. Elevated lead blood levels can also be caused by water from lead water pipes; by prolonged breathing of polluted air, as in towns with lead smelters and heavy traffic congestion; and by the young child's mouthing and eating objects containing lead (see Table 6.7). There may be no such thing as a safe level for heavy metals in the body (Stark et al., 1988); research continues on the potential effects on cognition in children who are exposed to low levels of lead contamination (Minder, Das-Smaal, & Orlebeke, 1998).

Nutritional deficiencies are also worth noting here, although these are obviously both prenatal and postnatal concerns. Developmental deficiencies can occur when either the mother or child has an inadequate diet. Malnutrition during gestation or the first 6 months of life hinders the development of brain cells and can lead to as much as a 40% deficit in their number. Resnick (1988) states that the first two trimesters may be most critical to the prevention of such lacks, although he also indicates that maternal nutrition before pregnancy may be even more important. Since later brain growth is in weight rather than in number of cells, the effects of early malnutrition have long been viewed as irreversible (see the classic research by Cravioto, DeLicardie, & Birch, 1966). However, it has also long been recognized that it is difficult to assess the true detrimental effect of poor nutrition because it tends to accompany other unfavorable

TABLE 6.7

Increased Risks for Lead
Poisoning

- Residence built before 1978
- Residence with chipped, cracked, or peeling paint
- Residence with lead pipes or lead-soldered copper pipes
- Residence near waste sites and lead industry
- Lead present in water above 500 ppm
- Leaded ceramics and leaded crystal, especially those imported from Mexico, Italy, and China
- Residence adjacent to major highways built before 1986
- Family members who work in industry using lead (battery plants, electronics, stained glass, and mining)
- Hobbies using lead (ammunition, molding, and fishing weights)
- Food from cans soldered with lead
- History of eating nonfood substances (e.g., paint chips, pencils, crayons, ashes, or dirt)
- History of poor nutrition, especially low iron, calcium, or Vitamin C
- Playing with old or imported lead toys and old keys
- Elevated lead level, above 10 micrograms per deciliter

Source: Adapted from Lynchburg College Lead Symposium (1997). Used with permission.

circumstances—inadequate housing, substandard living conditions, poor hygiene, and poor prenatal care, as well as diets high in calories but low in important nutrients.

PREVENTION

The purpose of this section is to survey the tools, techniques, and procedures that assist in the process of preventing retardation. Inspired by a 1970s government commitment to prevent the occurrence of 50% of all cases of retardation by the end of the 20th century (PCMR, 1976), researchers tackled virtually all causes of retardation. In every known case, a specific preventive measure was identified.

Graham and Scott (1988) developed a comprehensive model for conceptualizing prevention (Figure 6.8). They distinguished three levels of prevention: (1) primary, where risk conditions can be eliminated so that a condition never comes into existence; (2) secondary preventive efforts, which reduce or eliminate the effects of an existing risk factor; and (3) tertiary intervention, which assists a child who has a disability. Crocker (1992) and Polloway and Rucker (1997) have identified the specific activities associated with a comprehensive prevention program. These considerations are outlined in Table 6.8 and implicit in the discussions that follow.

Preconception

Preventive measures taken before conception can avert hereditary, innate, congenital, and other constitutional disorders. One basic tool is *genetic counseling,* an attempt to determine risks of occurrence or recurrence of specific genetic or chromosomal

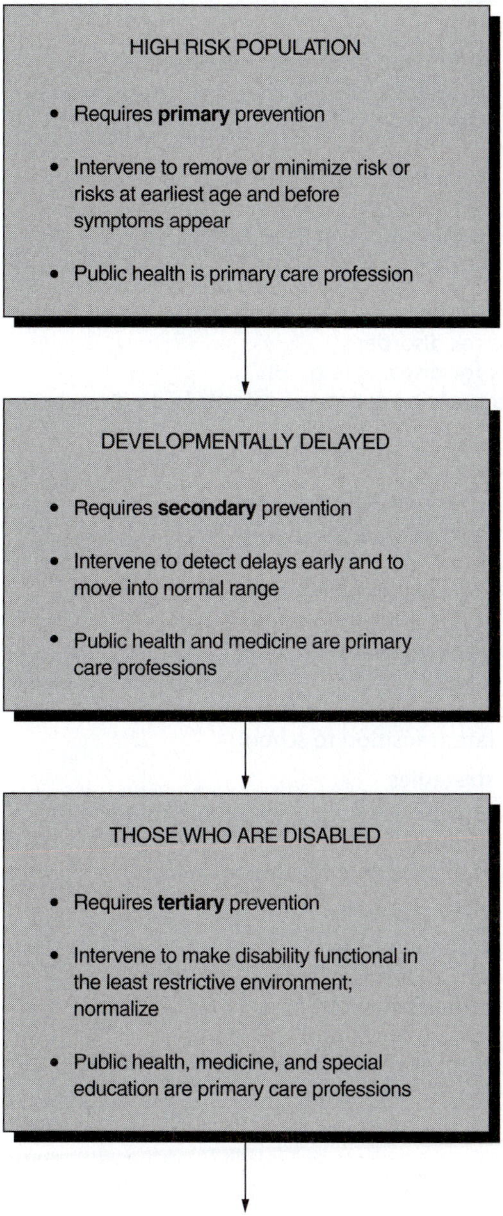

HIGH RISK POPULATION

- Requires **primary** prevention

- Intervene to remove or minimize risk or risks at earliest age and before symptoms appear

- Public health is primary care profession

DEVELOPMENTALLY DELAYED

- Requires **secondary** prevention

- Intervene to detect delays early and to move into normal range

- Public health and medicine are primary care professions

THOSE WHO ARE DISABLED

- Requires **tertiary** prevention

- Intervene to make disability functional in the least restrictive environment; normalize

- Public health, medicine, and special education are primary care professions

FIGURE 6.8
The Developmental Continuum of Risk

Source: From "The Impact of Definitions of Higher Risk on Services to Infants and Toddlers" (p. 25), by M. Graham & K. G. Scott, 1988, *Topics in Early Childhood Special Education, 8*(3). Adapted by permission.

disorders. The tools of the genetic counselor include the family history and personal screening. Study of the person's genetic and medical history is particularly concerned with evidence of spontaneous abortions or stillbirths, relatives' age at death and causes of death, and the existence of any interfamily marriages that might bear on the presence of specific genetic disorders. Screening is primarily for carriers of recessive trait disorders. Blood samples can be analyzed rather easily and inexpensively. Based on an

TABLE 6.8

Elements of a Comprehensive
Prevention Program

Prenatal strategies

Ensure family planning and timing of pregnancies
Provide genetic counseling
Test for genetic carriers
Provide adequate prenatal care and diagnostics
Reduce teenage pregnancy rates
Reduce births out of wedlock
Avoid alcohol and other teratogenic substances during
    pregnancy

Perinatal strategies

Screen newborns for disorders
Screen newborns for diseases (e.g., HIV)
Provide early intervention for at-risk infants (e.g., those born
    prematurely)

Preschool strategies

Enroll children in early intervention programs
Provide parental education and support
Avoid lead in environment
Avoid hazards associated with brain injury
Reduce occurrences of child abuse and neglect
Use safety restraints in vehicles
Immunize for diseases
Provide proper medical care and treatment
Plan for appropriate transition to school

School preventive strategies

Provide effective instruction and relevant curriculum
Involve parents in education
Provide a family life curriculum to future parents

Federal and state policy strategies

Commit to a reduction in poverty
Reduce the prevalence of homelessness
Provide public information about prevention
Support comprehensive prevention programs
Develop and provide universal health care programs

understanding of the mathematical probabilities associated, for example, with recessive, dominant, or sex-linked inheritance, prospective parents can make an informed decision about the risks of having a child who may have a developmental disability.

Other specific means of prevention are also available during the preconception period. Immunization for maternal rubella can prevent women from contracting this disease during pregnancy. Blood tests can identify the presence of venereal diseases. Adequate maternal nutrition can lay a sound metabolic foundation for later childbearing. Family planning in terms of size, appropriate spacing, and age of parents can also affect a variety of specific causal agents.

During Gestation

Two general approaches to prevention during pregnancy are prenatal care and analysis for possible genetic disorders. Numerous prenatal precautions can be taken to avert congenital problems. Adequate nutrition, fetal monitoring, and protection from disease are certainly the grounding of prenatal care. Avoidance of teratogenic substances resulting from both exposure (e.g., radiation) and personal consumption (e.g., alcohol and drugs) also relate specifically to this period.

Analysis of the fetus for the possible presence of genetic or chromosomal disorders is another key component of genetic counseling. Prenatal diagnosis is typically recommended when the mother is 35 or older, when the risk of the disorder is greater than the risk of the procedure, and/or when couples are known to be at risk (e.g., have had a previous child with the condition, are genetic carriers, or if there is an established risk due to familial patterns).

Prenatal screening may include the triple test (or triple screen), amniocentesis, chorionic villi sampling, fetoscopy, fetal biopsy, and ultrasound. The *triple screen* is a procedure that provides an analysis of three chemicals (i.e., maternal serum alpha-feto protein (AFP), unconjugated estriol, and human chorionic conadotropin) to provide an initial assessment of at-risk pregnancies (Dykens et al., 2000). As Apolloni (1998) noted, with the triple screen "each of these three analyses are derived from blood samples and considered in conjunction with related information (i.e., age and weight of the

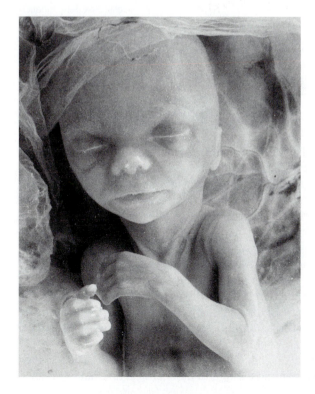

Prenatal precautions, including good nutrition, fetal monitoring, and protection from disease, can help avert congenital problems.

FIGURE 6.9

Amniocentesis

Source: From *Fetal Monitoring and Fetal Assessment in High-Risk Pregnancy* (p. 184), by S. M. Tucker, 1978, St. Louis: Mosby. Copyright © 1978 by C. V. Mosby. Reprinted by permission.

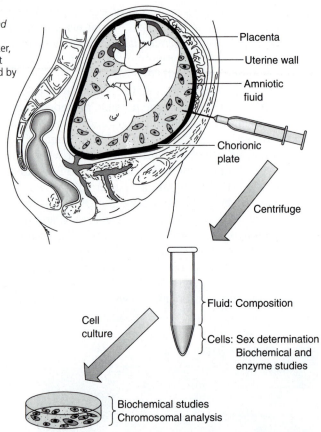

Placenta

Uterine wall

Amniotic fiuid

Chorionic plate

Centrifuge

Fluid: Composition

Cells: Sex determination
Biochemical and
enzyme studies

Cell culture

Biochemical studies
Chromosomal analysis

mother, ethnic group, gestational age of the fetus and the number of fetuses). . . . [It is] cheaper to perform, it is faster (results available in 1–3 days versus 2 weeks for amniocentesis), and there is no risk to the fetus. . . . It provides an initial direction for determining whether further diagnostics should be performed" (pp. 34–35).

Usually performed during the 14th to 16th week of pregnancy, **amniocentesis** involves drawing amniotic (embryonic sac) fluid for biochemical analysis of fetal cells (see Figure 6.9). In the majority of cases where amniocentesis is used, its primary purpose has been the detection of chromosomal errors such as Down syndrome. Generally, the technique is safe. However, potential parents should be informed of certain considerations, including the risk of about 0.5% or less of a miscarriage, the possibility of an unsuccessful culture of fetal cells, and the possibility of disorders remaining undiagnosed by the procedure. More recently, the procedure has been used earlier in gestation, but the risks are slightly increased.

Another technique for prenatal diagnosis is *chorionic villus sampling* (CVS), which can also provide information on chromosomal and biochemical anomalies. In CVS, chorionic tissue (the fluffy material that forms the placenta) is withdrawn. The test can be performed after approximately 9 weeks of gestation, with initial results (chromosomal analysis) available within 2 days and a full culture (for analysis) available within 2 weeks after sampling. The most significant advantage of the process is that it allows an earlier analysis of fetal status. It has been estimated that CVS is associated with a risk rate for miscarriage and other complications only slightly higher than that for amniocentesis (about 1% or less).

One other technique that has contributed to an understanding of the prenatal environment is *ultrasound,* or *sonography.* This technique can be used for possible determination of hydrocephalus, some central nervous system disorders, and limb anomalies. The technique is also used to determine the location for amniocentesis, to assist in delivery, and as a common adjunct to fetal therapy, which seeks to correct conditions existing in utero.

These analytical techniques have three purposes. Most encouraging, of course, is that negative tests assuage parental fears or anxieties. Second, the result can confirm suspicions of disorders and give the parents a chance to determine what to expect. They may also alert physicians to the need for careful monitoring prenatally, perinatally, and postnatally. Finally, the information can be used as a basis for decisions about termination of pregnancy. The use of these techniques, along with elective abortion, has significantly reduced the rates of a number of specific disorders—for example, in cases when DS is confirmed, studies range from 80% to 95% of those receiving these data consequently report a decision to terminate (Roberts, Strough, & Parrish, 2002)—although obviously it has also generated much controversy.

Roberts and colleagues (2002) researched the responses of mothers to the role of genetic counseling in the process of deciding whether to terminate pregnancy. They surveyed 69 women at risk for carrying a fetus with disability. A series of questions were asked including; would you terminate if a disorder were confirmed? (65% yes); were you encouraged to talk with a parent of a child with disability? (91.3% no); and was genetic counseling helpful? (91% yes for information on prenatal disorders, 13% yes for information on quality of life issues, and 17.4% yes in terms of being provided with positive and negative aspects of giving birth to a child with a disability).

Pueschel (1991) stressed that genetic counseling never results in value-free messages to parents. Professionals should not advocate a particular action but must transmit factual data and present alternatives. In the case of a genetic disorder, he notes that this could include terminating the pregnancy or allowing it to continue to term and, in the latter case, either caring for the child or seeking adoption.

Given the controversial nature of abortion at this time, it is worth noting the following key policy issues that continue to receive public scrutiny and debate:

- Funding for prenatal screening research
- Parental consent
- Trimester/length of term (when abortion can/cannot be considered)
- Federal funding for abortions
- Maternal health and safety

At Delivery

Prevention at delivery is based on anticipating possible problems. Pregnancies deserving of special attention include those involving very young or older mothers, inconsistent prenatal care, closely spaced pregnancies, drug exposure during pregnancy, and a history of previous children with genetic disorders.

Several specific measures are associated with the perinatal period. The most common is the *Apgar test* of vital signs (Apgar, 1953), an evaluation routinely given in U.S. hospitals at 1 and 5 minutes after the birth of a child. The physician rates each of the following factors on a scale of 0 to 2: heart rate, respiratory effort, muscle tone, skin color, and reflex response. An Apgar score of 8 to 10 suggests the newborn is healthy and responsive; scores of 5 to 7 and 0 to 4 indicate moderate and severe concerns for further attention, respectively. Initially, screening using such a scale can assist in preliminary decision making about children who may be at risk for specific disorders, and a more comprehensive assessment then follows. Intensive intervention can begin almost immediately for premature and other infants identified as having a particular difficulty.

Computer-assisted obstetric measures aid in the close monitoring of both mother and child. Another helpful measure for Rh incompatibility during the first 3 days after birth is injection of immunoglobulin serum, as described earlier (see the section titled "Maternal Disorders"). If a child is born to a mother who did not have the necessary series of injections in the course of a previous pregnancy, a complete transfusion of the newborn's blood can prevent the destruction of its blood cells by the mother's antibodies.

A third focus is on screening for specific genetic disorders (e.g., PKU). Federal guidelines call for screening for OPU, congenital hypothyroidism, and sickle-cell anemia. Related state guidelines range from 4 to 36 disorders (across states) for which screening is to occur. All states require subsequent notification of the health care provider, while fewer than half require direct notice to the parents.

Early Childhood

Several types of intervention are important during early childhood. Proper nutrition is critical throughout development, but particularly so during the first 6 months. Dietary restrictions for specific metabolic disorders should be maintained until no longer required. Avoidance of hazards in the child's environment can prevent head injury, and avoidance of exposure to substances such as lead and mercury are mandatory for proper development. Finally, key issues related to prevention during the early childhood period fall most appropriately within the psychosocial arena. For example, important considerations include maternal age and maternal education (e.g., Chapman et al., 2002); while maternal age may have complications for biological concerns, both age and educational level also have clear psychosocial implications (see chapter 5).

Perspective

The preceding discussion has highlighted a variety of preventive measures that target the various causes of retardation discussed earlier in this chapter. For biological causes, the advances of the last 40 years have been breathtaking. In terms of psychosocial causes, the successes that have been achieved are tempered by the obvious need for greater commitment. Whether society is willing to devote the necessary resources to breaking the poverty cycle and altering the effects of psychosocial causes, with the goal of reducing the prevalence of retardation, is still an unanswered question. Governmental commitment, especially at the federal level, is critical.

It is clear that, regardless of whether a child already has a disability, growing up in restricting conditions interferes with a child's opportunity to develop and mature as well as his or her more privileged peers. The negative consequences of an unstimulating environment must be diminished through the most promising intervention strategies. As Baroff (1974) wrote more than 30 years ago: "Equality of opportunity is a ghastly charade if individuals are so stunted by early experiences" that they do not take advantage of opportunities for treatment that are available (p. 116). By facilitating children's cognitive, academic, social, and emotional development, we increase the chances of having a future population of healthy, self-sufficient, mature adults. Intervention strategies with a preventive aim must work to identify children at risk and establish strategies designed to facilitate the development of each of them.

ETHICAL ISSUES

Remarkable developments in molecular biology and genetic engineering are reported daily in the popular press. Further advances in genetic science and medical technology will almost certainly change the course of the human experience. The eradication of what are now considered diseases, disorders, and defects may become possible before the end of the 21st century. As medicine advances, however, a critical question may be how diseases, disorders, and defects are defined. Is mental retardation, in this context, a disease, a defect, or a human difference? Is mental retardation a condition to be prevented in all circumstances, or is it part of the spectrum of human variation? Depending on the answer, what does this say about the status of people with this condition in a society that values human equality? What does it say about their fundamental value as people?

The danger that people with mental retardation will be further devalued as genetic interventions proliferate and become more accessible is illustrated by recent remarks by James Watson. Winner of the Nobel Prize and codiscoverer of DNA, Watson was also the first director of the Human Genome Project. In his capacity as leader of the effort to map and sequence the genetic makeup of human beings, Watson also advocated careful consideration of the ethical, legal, and social implications of the project. Yet, in an article titled "Looking Forward," Wastson questioned the value of the lives of people with severe disabilities. He spoke of the decisions faced by "prospective parents when they learn that their prospective child carries a gene that would block its opportunity for a meaningful life" (Watson, 1993, p. 314). In this article he speaks of parents who do not undergo genetic testing: "So we must also face up to the ethical and practical dilemma, facing these individuals who could have undergone genetic diagnosis, but who for one reason or another declined the opportunity and later gave birth to children who must face up to lives of hopeless inequality" (p. 315). Later Watson spoke to the German Congress of Molecular Medicine and condemned the eugenic philosophy that resulted in the atrocities of the Nazi era. Then, in a seeming contradiction, he advocated what might be termed "parental eugenics." He asserted that the "truly relevant question for most families is whether an obvious good will come from having a child with a major handicap." From this perspective, Watson said, "seeing the bright side of being handicapped is like praising the virtues of extreme poverty" (Lee, 1998, p. 16).

As it becomes possible to identify virtually all persons at risk for having a child affected by a genetic disorder (Moser, 2000), the excitement over prevention must be sobered by the ethical aspects of this capacity. It is therefore critical to consider carefully the actions that can be taken, versus those that should be taken, once a specific disability, or risk of a disability, has been identified.

The ethical implications of genetic engineering and its capacity for changing human nature has been discussed for a number of years, and it is coming into sharp focus now for the meaning of mental retardation. In 1969 Sinsheimer argued that the "new eugenics would permit in principle the conversion of all the unfit to the highest genetic level" (p. 13). He went on to assert that the "losers" in the uncontrolled genetic lottery included not only the children born each year with "gross evident defects" but also "the 50,000,000 Americans with an IQ of less than 90" (p. 13). Sinsheimer's shrill words strikingly portray how the ethical questions currently being raised concerning mental retardation may be prophetic of larger issues to come about the meaning of the human condition.

Our earlier discussion of amniocentesis focused on its use to detect specific genetic disorders, especially Down syndrome. Public encouragement to screen for the disorder led to an increase in the number of abortions of fetuses found to be affected. But, as Smith (1981) noted 25 years ago, "The ease with which the abortion of Down syndrome fetuses is accepted as the best alternative, even by people who otherwise oppose abortion, may be related to the conventional wisdom or popular misunderstanding of the level of mental retardation or other disabilities associated with this condition" (p. 9).

Another major ethical concern is the question of the right to life after birth of children who are disabled. Newspaper accounts of the cases of Baby Doe in Indiana; Baby Jane Doe in New York; Phillip Becker, a California teenager with Down syndrome; and Baby Gabriel in Canada sensitized the public to issues that for years had been quietly debated in professional circles. In most cases, the question is whether a child's disability should be a primary factor in the decision to provide maximum medical care. In addition to the important legal questions involved, philosophical issues are also significant in this arena.

An additional ethical issue is that of "do not resuscitate" orders (DNR) for persons with special needs. Given the complexity of the medical needs of some individuals, this area promises to be of great concern in the future. Smith's (1995) discussion of John Lovelace, an adult with mental retardation who was deinstitutionalized, provides a vivid discussion of this issue. Lovelace, at risk for a stroke due to a vascular abnormality in his brain, was deemed to be not a candidate for emergency treatment in the event of a health crisis. This decision was reached based on his retardation, absence of family, and his dependency on government-funded medical care. It was decided without his informed consent. (For further information on DNR orders and special education, see Sewall & Balkman, 2002.)

Box 6.3 ☙ Right to Treatment

The Board of Directors [CEC-MR (now DDD)] resolves that the fact that a person [has] mental retardation . . . is not a justifiable reason, in and of itself, for terminating the life of that person. Mental retardation alone is not a nullification of quality or worth in an individual's life and should not be used as a rationale for the termination of life through direct means nor the withholding of nourishment or life sustaining procedures.

The issue of pediatric euthanasia is complex and troubling to professionals. . . . A most basic question posed by this dilemma is that of who is to make the decision to deny treatment or nourishment to a child who has mental retardation. Most often involved in this decision are parents, physicians, and, in most cases which become public, the courts. Arguments have been made for and against the role of each of these parties in making such a decision.

Support for parents as decision makers derives from the concept that children are the property of their parents and that they have the final voice in any crucial matter concerning their offspring. Critics of this view believe that parents are often emotionally distraught and lack adequate information on which to base their decision when faced with such a dilemma. Their decision may be unduly influenced by fears concerning raising the child or of institutional placement.

Physicians often feel that they are in the best position to make an objective decision. It has been observed, however, that they often are motivated by their perception of what will prevent suffering in the family. It is argued that physicians should not be the decision makers because their duty is to preserve life, not to judge which lives deserve preservation.

Parents of newborns and physicians have rarely had the opportunity to experience living or working with individuals having mental retardation across the course of their lives. As special educators serving individuals with disabilities from infancy through adulthood, the Board . . . observes that mental retardation alone does not necessarily cause a life of pain, suffering or absence of life quality for the affected persons, and that it should not imply a justification for the termination of life. Research and experience . . . demonstrate that all people can learn, all can participate (at least partially) in the wide range of human experiences and most become productive citizens and are valued human beings by persons who truly know them.

Source: Adapted from "CEC-MR Position Statement on the Right of Children with Mental Retardation to Life Sustaining Medical Care and Treatment," by J. D. Smith, September 1988, *CEC-MR Report,* p. 2. Copyright © 1988 by the Council for Exceptional Children. Reprinted by permission.

Increasingly complex ethical issues require the scrutiny and advocacy of professional educators. As Smith (1989) noted, special educators may often be better informed than physicians concerning the possibilities and potentialities in the lives of children with disabilities. They are in a unique position to act as advocates (see Box 6.3).

FINAL THOUGHTS

Hundreds of specific etiological factors have been identified as causes of mental retardation and developmental disabilities. Nevertheless, in the vast majority of individual cases, a specific cause cannot be identified.

To understand etiology, we must first understand the principles of genetics, since a large percentage of biological causes stem from recessive, dominant, and sex-linked inheritance and from chromosomal abnormalities. Other causes include

To check your understanding of this chapter, go to the Companion Website at www.prenhall.com/ beirne-smith and select Chapter 6. From there, you can access the Self-Test and Essay modules.

prenatal infections and intoxications, brain injury, malnutrition, cranial malformations, disorders related to pregnancy, and environmental influence.

Prevention of retardation requires an intensive program that begins before conception and continues throughout the developmental period. Every specifiable cause of retardation has a preventive measure of one type or another.

Advances in medical technology have created ethical problems that society must face. Each person must accept the responsibility of becoming informed on these ethical issues and developing her or his own professional position.

Summary

Introduction
- The causes of mental retardation are many and varied.
- Professionals in the field of mental retardation need to have a general awareness of causes.
- Terminology used to describe various etiologies comes from three sources: conventional wisdom, names of specific people, and biomedical vocabulary.

Genetic and Chromosomal Considerations
- Genetics is the study of heredity with a focus on genes and chromosomes.
- Mental retardation can result from problems with genetic material on either autosomes or sex chromosomes.
- Genetic transmission can occur through autosomal dominant or recessive means or through X-linked patterns.
- Karyotypes are charts of chromosomes.
- The most recognizable condition associated with chromosomal anomalies is Down syndrome.

Other Etiological Considerations
- Cranial malformations involve conditions such as hydrocephaly.
- Many different toxic substances can significantly affect prenatal and postnatal development.
- Prematurity and other perinatal factors are related to developmental delays.
- Events such as head injuries and child abuse can also contribute to mental retardation.

Prevention
- Prevention requires an intensive program that begins before conception and continues throughout the developmental period.
- Every specifiable cause can be matched with one or more preventive measures.

Ethical Issues
- Advances in medical technology have created ethical problems that society must face.
- Special educators are uniquely qualified to act as advocates for children with disabilities when ethical issues arise.

7

Family Considerations

Audrey A. Trainor, Ph.D.
University of Wisconsin at Madison

OBJECTIVES

After reading this chapter, the student should be able to:

- Describe various conceptualizations of family models
- Explain relationships between key components of the family systems model
- Identify key characteristics of families
- Discuss the major forces influencing family functioning
- Discuss key issues faced by families throughout the life span

KEY TERMS

adaptability model

developmental model

family

family characteristics

family functioning

family interactions

family paradigms model

family support services

family systems theory

person-centered planning

wraparound services

Everyone is a member of a family, whether biological or social, organizational or spiritual, permanent or temporary—everyone has a family of one sort or another. Broadly speaking, a **family** is "two or more people who regard themselves as family and who perform some of the functions families typically perform. These people may or may not be related by blood or marriage and may or may not usually live together" (Turnbull, Turnbull, Shank, & Leal, 1995, pp. 24–25). Families may also include any person, organization, or institution that family members regard as having important influence in their lives (Knight, 2003). Goldenberg and Goldenberg (2000) state that these naturally occurring units have their own rules, roles, and methods of communication; they maintain their membership through good times and bad by such factors as affection, loyalty, and concern for one another. The family, then, represents the most basic and critical unit of a culture, the one with the strongest and most enduring influences.

AMERICAN FAMILIES

Several decades ago, the traditional family unit consisted of a mother, father, and two or more children; however, demographics in the United States have shifted and the makeup of the American family is now quite different. According to the U.S. Census Bureau (2003b), a "family household" is one in which the householder is related to at least one other member by marriage, birth, or adoption. Single parents now head nearly 17% of U.S. family households, to which 78% of the U.S. population belong (U.S. Census Bureau, 2003b). In 2000, the portion of family households in the United States headed by married couples decreased 3% from the 1990 census. Another shift is the number of families in which multigenerational members reside, accounting for 3.7% of all U.S. family households. These households are more likely to be found in urban areas where immigration rates are high, where the cost of affordable housing is high, and/or where high rates of very young women are bearing children without being married (U.S. Census Bureau, 2003b).

Although the demographics of families with a person who has an intellectual disability are not always different from the demographics of families in the general population, they are different in some important ways. Specifically, for example, in an analysis of household survey data conducted by the U.S. Census Bureau and focusing on people with mental retardation/developmental disabilities, Larson and colleagues (2000b) found that among those not living in large public residential facilities (institutions) in 1994 and 1995, 85% lived with relatives, as compared with 41% of people in the general population. Furthermore, only about 7% of adults with mental retardation were married and lived with their spouse, as compared with 47% of all adults in the general population. Interestingly, while the married rates were very different from one another, the formerly married rates (i.e., divorced, separated, widowed) were about the same for both groups.

Understanding the factors that influence the development of persons with mental retardation requires an understanding of the role of the family in the developmental process. Family involvement in the school community is generally considered desirable and an important factor in increasing the educational success of all students. In the 2000–2001 school year, 637,497 youth ages 3 to 21 received

Under IDEA, 2004	Parent/family members have the right/responsibility to . . .
§614(d)(1)(B)(i)	Be included as a member of the individualized educational program (IEP) team
§614(a)(1)(D)(i)(I)	Provide consent to formal special education evaluation/assessment plans
§615(b)(1)	Access any educational records of the child (once a child is receiving special education services)
§615(b)(6)(A)	Present a complaint about any matter relating to the identification, evaluation, or educational placement of the child
§615(g)(1)	Appeal decisions about complaints that result in hearings with the local education agency to the state education agency

TABLE 7.1

Selected Parental/Family Rights and Responsibilities Protected Under IDEA 2004*

*The rights and responsibilities contained in this table do not comprise an exhaustive list. Rather, this is a sample of those contained in IDEA.

services in special education in the category of mental retardation (U.S. Department of Education, 2002). For parents and family members of youth with disabilities, participation in the special education process is essential. In fact, the Individuals with Disabilities Education Improvement Act of 2004 (IDEA) mandates that teachers and administrators take a variety of measures to ensure that the rights of people with disabilities and their parents are protected. Table 7.1 provides a list of key mandates included in IDEA that protect the rights of parents. Keep in mind, however, that this list is not exhaustive.

Many of the protections included in IDEA present special challenges to both educators and families of children with exceptionalities. As families and schools interact with one another, beliefs and values about the roles of family members, as well as members with disabilities, the functions of families, and the purpose of education, each embedded in the special education experience, are constantly being mediated (Kalyanpur & Harry, 1999). Beliefs and values about family, parenting, disability, and education are shaped, in part, by our cultural identities, so the diversity of conceptualizations of these topics is boundless in a society as diverse as the United States. In fact, the diversity of the U.S. school-aged population is increasing, while the diversity of our teaching force has remained fairly homogeneous. While 84% of U.S. teachers are of European American descent (National Center for Educational Statistics, 2003), roughly 60% of U.S. schoolchildren were European American, 17% were African American, 17% were Latino, 4% were Asian American, and 1% were American Indian (National Center for Educational Statistics, n.d.). Birthrates that vary according to ethnicity and race, as well as current immigration trends, provide indications that student diversity will continue to increase (Artiles & Ortiz, 2002).

Of course, cultural identities and diversity are not limited to a person's race or ethnicity. Other elements of culture—including socioeconomic status, disability status, gender, sexual orientation, religious orientation, and language—also contribute to a person's cultural identity. By all accounts, the diversity of U.S. schoolchildren and their families is increasing by some of these factors as well. For example, 18% of the population in 2000 (a rate that doubled since 1980) reported speaking a language other than English at home (U.S. Census Bureau, 2003a). Additionally, the number of nontraditional families headed by gay or lesbian parents is increasing (Murphy, 1999; K. S. Peterson, 2004). Each family characteristic that helps define the identity of the family unit contributes to the emergence of unique preferences, strengths, and needs. Most importantly, cultural identities are dynamic and vary among group members. For example, generational differences among immigrant parents and their children can lead to important differences in values and beliefs held by members of the same group, and even the same family unit (Valenzuela, 1999). Educators must rise to the challenge of responding to the complex needs, strengths, and preferences of a diverse group of constituents. Understanding the social unit of the family, through a variety of disciplines of study, is one way to develop competency in this area.

UNDERSTANDING FAMILIES

The family represents the simplest yet oldest social unit of humankind. Whereas social scientists were once interested only in individuals, today they are interested in understanding people in general—large groups, small groups, and all groups in between. The family is one such example. The study of families and mental retardation has evolved from its roots in the examination of pathology and dysfunction, to its contemporary inquiry into the complexities of family processes (Stoneman, 1997). In light of the contributions of researchers from seemingly disparate disciplines, conceptualizations of families have been developed that provide a framework for understanding the makeup of the family in much greater detail. The models that have been proposed borrow heavily from other disciplines and differ markedly from the images of the American family promulgated in the 1950s. A brief discussion of three such models follows.

Family Paradigms Model

The **family paradigms model** of Reiss (1981) is based on a sociological framework focusing on the interactions of family members. This model classifies families into one of three different types based on their interpretation of and responses to events around them. *Environmentally sensitive families* comprise the first group and consist of people who see their life events as both knowable and orderly; all family members are expected to contribute to the sharing of ideas and efforts of orderly family functioning. *Interpersonally distant families* consist primarily of detached family members, loners, and those for whom independence is critically important. Consequently, members of these families put very little emphasis on interactions with others in the family. *Consensus-sensitive families* constitute the third group, those families whose need for conformance and family order is so strong as to isolate them from the rest of society. Dissension is not tolerated, especially when it comes from outside the family; family members quickly surrender their own ideas for what they believe to be the good of the family.

Adaptability Model

Beavers and Hampson (1993) offer an **adaptability model** that includes concepts typically used in the physical sciences. For example, families and family functioning may be placed on a grid in which one continuum ranges from severely dysfunctional to optimal, and the other continuum from centripetal to centrifugal (see Figure 7.1). Those at the healthy end of the spectrum are more likely to be open, adaptable, and goal-oriented, whereas the severely dysfunctional families are most likely to be rigid, have poor communication patterns, use ineffective coping strategies, and be inappropriately content with their existing family structure. Beavers and Hampson's connection with the physical sciences comes in the major tenet, *entropy,* or the degree to which families tend toward disorder. Centripetal forces are those that draw a family together, while centrifugal forces are those that push a family apart. The ability to balance out the attractive (centripetal) and repelling (centrifugal) forces is a major determinant of healthy family functioning. As Figure 7.1 illustrates, the healthy family is one in which choices are respected and members are allowed to move, within limits, into and out of the family unit as life events dictate.

A complete online glossary is available on the Companion Website, which may be accessed at www.prenhall.com/ beirne-smith

Developmental Model

The notion that families develop along predictable lines is not a new one. In fact, some say that the **developmental model** in family psychology actually represents an elaboration of traditional developmental psychology—that is, the development of the individual. Carter and McGoldrick (1999) have divided the family life cycle into six stages, beginning with single young adults who leave home to begin their lives in the community, and ending with families in later life. In between are the stages of newly joined families, families with young children, families with adolescents, and families who are transitioning their offspring into adulthood. Goldenberg and Goldenberg (2000) have identified a number of tasks families are expected to meet in their cycle of development. Separation from their families of origin, new relationships and behavioral patterns, and the resolution of dependency issues at each of the respective stages are examples of stage-related tasks that must be addressed for all families. For Carter and McGoldrick (1999), the family system is an intergenerational unit with three to five primary cohorts that move through life together (e.g., children, adults, older adults). Much of Carter and McGoldrick's model is based on simple common sense, with the addition of the notion that the actions of people of each generation profoundly affect the actions of the other generations, thereby creating and changing the actual course of development of the people in each succeeding generation.

Just as most major theories of human development have failed to account adequately for nonnormative patterns of development for persons with disabilities, so, too, have most theories of family development. The literature is replete with studies addressing stressful life events, transition issues, and quality-of-life issues at various stages of normative family development—yet the effect of persons with mental retardation on the family's growth and development is still far from certain. For example, whereas family care for a person with mental retardation terminated relatively early in life only a few decades ago, life expectancies are now

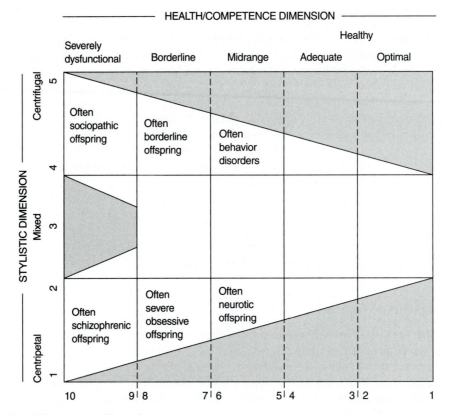

HEALTH/COMPETENCE DIMENSION

Health/Competence Dimensions

Severely dysfunctional. Poor boundaries, confused communication, lack of shared attentional focus, stereotyped family process, despair, cynicism, [and/or] denial of ambivalence.

Borderline. Shifting from chaotic to tyrannical control efforts, boundaries fluctuate from poor to rigid, distancing depression, [and/or] outbursts of rage.

Midrange. Relatively clear communication, constant effort at control, "loving means controlling," distancing, anger, anxiety or depression, [and/or] ambivalence handled by repression.

Adequate. Relatively clear boundaries, negotiating but with pain, ambivalence reluctantly recognized, some periods of warmth and sharing interspersed with control struggles.

Optimal. Capable negotiation, individual choice and ambivalence respected, warmth, intimacy, [and/or] humor.

FIGURE 7.1

Beavers and Hampson's Model of Family Functioning

Source: From "Measuring Family Competence," by W. R. Beavers & R. B. Hampson, in F. Walsh (Ed.), *Normal Family Processes* (2nd ed., p. 78), 1993, New York: Guilford. Copyright©1993 by Guilford Press. Adapted by permission.

Regardless of what model is used, early intervention is important.

commensurate with the population as a whole (Braddock, 1999; Eyman & Borthwick-Duffy, 1994), making planning for the later years a necessity for many. This added concern may well add stress to families in ways unforeseen just a few years ago.

FAMILY SYSTEMS

Each of the foregoing models informs our understanding of families in a very general way. However, a fourth conceptualization—**family systems theory**—has been particularly instructive in understanding family in the context of disability from a systems perspective. Families are highly diverse and dynamic entities. Family systems theory, applied to families with members who have disabilities, helps explain how various characteristics and interactions of families over time influence members' experiences both in special education and the larger society (Turnbull & Turnbull, 2001). Figure 7.2 provides an illustration of the family systems model.

In the remainder of this chapter, we will use the framework of family systems theory to explore the characteristics, interactions, functions, and life cycles of families with members who have mental retardation. We will examine how the inputs to the system (e.g., family characteristics) influence family interactions and family outputs, or functions. A key point to remember, however, is that this process is not linear. In other words, the components mentioned above are constantly occurring, influencing, and shaping one another. Also keep in mind that what follows is not a discussion of a storybook family, free from the stressors and problems of everyday living. Instead, the family is presented for what it is—a complex, dynamic, yet highly interdependent group of persons attempting to live, love, and work together.

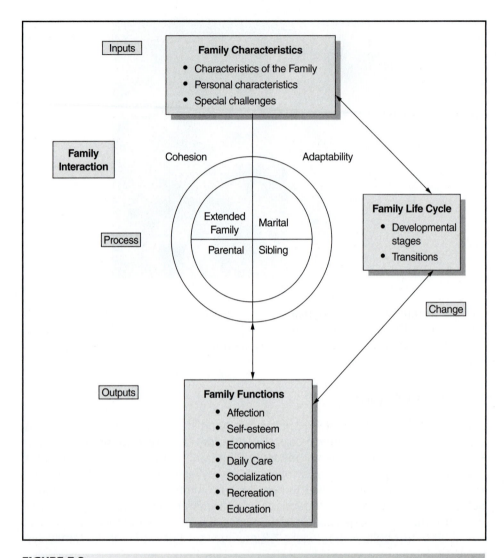

FIGURE 7.2

The Family Systems Model

Source: Adapted from *Families, Professionals, and Exceptionality: Collaborating for Empowerment* (4th ed.) by Turnbull and Turnbull © 2001, Reprinted by permission of Pearson Education, Inc., Upper Saddle River, NJ.

Family Characteristics

Families differ on a wide range of variables, contributing to our society's rich diversity. **Family characteristics** include size, structure (for example, who is head of the household, presence of stepparents, inclusion of multigenerational family members), cultural background (such as race/ethnicity, geographic origin, language use, religious practice and beliefs), and socioeconomic status (such as highest level of education completed by parents, occupation, income). These characteristics come together to comprise the unique identity of a family unit. In addition to family characteristics, the identities of families are made more complex by the characteristics of the individuals who belong to the family unit. The personality and health of each member, both physical and mental, influence the individual's contribution to the family unit. For example, how the head of the household copes with stress—including acknowledging and responding to disability—impacts the family unit and its ability to develop stress management strategies.

Family Interactions

According to family systems theory, the family's characteristics, the characteristics of each family member, their reactions to having a member with disabilities, and special challenges (e.g., living in poverty) all constitute attributes that the family unit brings to the context of the special education community (Turnbull & Turnbull, 2001). **Family interactions** impact family functions: Interpersonal relationships comprise the cornerstone of a family's existence. Inquiries into family relationships have generally included parent–parent, parent–child, and child–other relationships. Research interest in intergenerational relationships will likely increase as the family structure increasingly includes daily contact with grandparents and other relatives. All are embedded in larger social networks, and all have implications for persons with mental retardation. How does having a family member with mental retardation impact these interactions and relationships? How do these interactions influence the efficacy of the family to function? Two such relationships—parental and sibling—will be examined in some detail here.

Parental Relationships.   As was mentioned earlier in this discussion of family considerations, family characteristics vary greatly regardless of the presence of a child with a disability. Family structures, which contribute to the types of interactions among children and adult members, can include single parents, married or divorced parents, stepparents, guardians, adoptive parents, and extended family members who unofficially assume the role of parents. The roles and responsibilities, as well as the interactions among adults in the family, will ultimately impact the family's ability to function. Based on 1995 data, the most recent available, American divorce/separation rates range from 24% to 50% within the first 10 years of marriage, but these figures vary by employment status, age at time of marriage, and race/ethnicity, among other factors (Bramlett & Mosher, 2002). Although some studies have documented high rates of marital breakups among families of children with disabilities (e.g., Epstein, Cullinan, Quinn, & Cumblad, 1994; Hodapp & Krasner, 1995), and additional anecdotal evidence supports the notion that parenting a child with mental retardation acts as a stressor to parental relations, few conclusions on this topic can be drawn without more empirical evidence (Stoneman, 1997). Of course, quantifying or qualifying this stress is no simple task and past studies have been based on the presupposition that having a child with mental retardation would have deleterious effects on the family unit. While the perception that marital difficulties might be more commonplace in households where the needs of a child with mental retardation demand large amounts of time, money, and other resources seems plausible, parents may also come together to meet these needs, thus strengthening their emotional bond (Stoneman, 1997). Lastly, marital stress, which may or may not result in dissolution of the parental relationship, is difficult to quantify and compare.

Evidence exists to support the age-old axiom "two heads are better than one," when the efficacy of parents to address the needs of their children with mental retardation is explored. In a study of interactions between mothers and fathers (some married and some divorced) of children with severe intellectual and developmental disabilities, Simmerman, Blacher, and Baker (2001) found that fathers (both custodial and noncustodial) were highly involved in child-rearing activities and that their level of involvement impacted the stability of the relationship between parents. Further, these researchers found that the mothers' and fathers' satisfaction with the fathers' involvement ameliorated the perceived burdens of child rearing. When parents of children with mental retardation do perceive the disability experience to be stressful, parents are likely to experience it in different ways—mothers through caregiving, and fathers through more social, interactive means (Essex, Seltzer, & Krauss, 1999; Roach, Orsmond, & Barratt, 1999). Nevertheless, just as not all studies have reported increased incidences of stress in families of children with disabilities, not all studies have reported differences in levels of stress or coping ability between groups of parents (e.g., Beckman, 1991; Bolger, 1992). The key point here is to understand that adult relationships interact within the family system and impact the family's ability and approach to functioning. Furthermore, these interactions can vary according to the characteristics of the child or life span issues the family faces over time. According to Stoneman (1997), the more challenging characteristics of children with mental retardation, such as behavioral and emotional problems, as well as periods of life transitions (e.g., a child's completion of public schooling), have the potential to contribute to marital stress.

Not surprisingly, one of the greatest influences on the psychological health and well-being of a child is the psychological health and well-being of the parents. Said another way, the better the relationship between parents and the better integrated the family prior to the birth or adoption of a child with a disability, the better integrated the family is afterward. The adaptive capability of a family rests on two important factors: first, the general level of health and well-being prior to any adverse circumstances, and, second, the extent to which a family perceives the circumstances as adverse. Some families do not view disabilities as bad; they are simply viewed as individual differences. Hence, it adds little to their general level of stress. Furthermore, while there may indeed be increased levels of stress in many families of persons with mental retardation, increased levels of stress do not exist in all such families, and there is certainly no guarantee that the stress that is experienced leads to increased levels of maladjustment or psychopathology (Glidden & Johnson, 1999; Hannah & Midlarsky, 1999).

 For more information about sibling relationships, and many other topics discussed in this chapter, visit the Companion Website at www.prenhall .com/beirne-smith and select Chapter 7, Web Destinations.

Sibling Relationships.   The physical and emotional contact of siblings throughout life represents the most critical and enduring set of relationships life has to offer. Whereas parent–child relationships routinely span 40 to 60 years, sibling relationships may last 60 to 80 years. The challenges experienced by the brothers and sisters of persons with mental retardation are particularly complex. Although many researchers have focused on negative aspects of the sibling experience, others have found either no difference or positive experiences with respect to levels of adjustment (including pathology) between families with and without children with mental retardation (Glidden & Johnson, 1999; Hannah & Midlarsky, 1999).

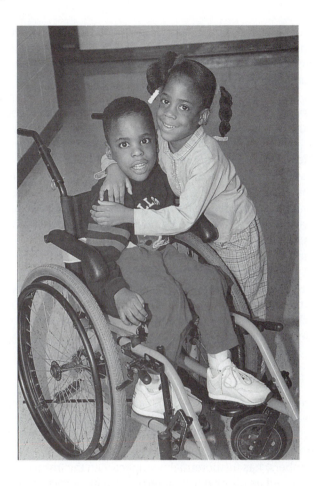

Nondisabled brothers and sisters often have special needs and concerns because of their sibling's disability.

Brothers and sisters without disabilities play many important roles in the lives of their siblings who have disabilities such as mental retardation. With a high degree of variability, siblings (whether chronologically older or younger than the child with a disability) may act as playmates, role models, antagonists, and/or defenders (NICHCY, 1988). Siblings may provide important entrée into peer groups (Geisthardt, Brotherson, & Cook, 2002). Siblings may act as caregivers, or they may engage in problematic behaviors. These behaviors may result from feeling jealous of the added attention a child with a disability commands from the parents, feeling guilty about being embarrassed or about refusing responsibilities associated with siblings with disabilities, or experiencing a number of other emotional reactions (Bauer & Shea, 2003). One important role often fulfilled by siblings is that of future caregiver. As parents age, they may designate their other children as guardians of their child with mental retardation, particularly if the disability impacts the child's self-care and independence in a limiting way.

Siblings without disabilities also benefit from having a brother or sister with a disability. Cuskelly and Gunn (2003) found that in the middle-class families who participated in their study, parents believed that their children without disabilities gained empathy when fulfilling the role of caregiver to their siblings with Down syndrome.

These researchers also found that brothers and sisters of children with Down syndrome did not have more responsibilities than their peers without siblings with disabilities. Providing support for the brothers and sisters of children with disabilities has been an ongoing project of the National Association of Sibling Programs (NASP). The organization, housed in Children's Hospital and Medical Center in Seattle, Washington, sponsors workshops for children, publishes a newsletter, and provides materials for teachers and counselors who work with siblings of children with disabilities (Meyer & Vadasy, 1996).

Other Family Relationships.   Relationships among family members are not limited to parental and sibling relationships. As the diversity of the family increases and many configurations of the family are formed, more information is needed regarding other relationships that have the potential to impact how families function. For example, the relationships between children, parents, and multigenerational, extended family members have not been studied in depth, yet these relationships may be central to culturally and linguistically diverse families, families with limited financial resources, as well as families in which children are born to adolescents and single parents. Also important is the notion that all relationships are dynamic. Interactions between brothers and sisters, as well as interactions between parents and children, naturally change over time. As people age and become more independent and competent, their needs and desires for family interactions vary.

Functioning

Family functioning essentially means how families take action to meet members' individual and collective needs (Turnbull & Turnbull, 2001). The ways in which families function span a variety of activities that impact members on a daily as well as long-term basis. For example, a loving and supportive family (functioning to meet the affective needs of its members) has the potential to impact both the immediate emotional health of a child, as well as his or her long-term feelings of security and happiness. Of course, how families define *loving* and *supportive* will vary. The complexity of family functioning is impacted both by family characteristics (e.g., cultural identities that shape how love and support are demonstrated) and the interactions among family members (e.g., the health and the strength of the parental relationship). Additionally, the dynamic and interrelated nature of the functions themselves contributes to this complexity. For example, functioning to meet the affective needs of family members may be influenced by other family functions, such as meeting the economic needs of the family. To illustrate, parents who are migrant workers might leave their children with extended relatives during seasons of work in order to earn money and provide food, shelter, and other material necessities for their children. During their absence, these parents may have difficulty expressing love and support on a daily basis because contact with their children will be limited. To assume, however, that children in this type of family do not feel loved and supported would be a mistake—because they may get their emotional needs met by other family members, or they may define *love* and *support* within the scope of their parents' actions, as well as a number of other possible scenarios. In order to support families who have children with disabilities, professionals must understand the complexities of family functioning and refrain from making assumptions and using stereotypes. Rather, educators must take time to get to know families and recognize the preferences, strengths, and needs of each one.

Families perform a variety of functions in addition to fulfilling emotional and economic needs—including daily living, educational, social, and recreational needs (Turnbull & Turnbull, 2001). Further, the efficacy with which these functions are completed varies not only from family to family, but can also vary during the life span of each family unit. For example, a highly functional family, adept at meeting the needs of its members, may experience dysfunction while dealing with the death of one of its members. Some of the functional demands on families with children with mental retardation are presented in Figure 7.3. Stress and coping theories, like the family systems theory, conceptualize families' abilities to function as dynamic, complex, and variable, depending on the family characteristics, interactions, life cycle, and environment or contextual variables (Stoneman, 1997). Active involvement in parental support groups has been associated with positive stress management functioning in families (Lustig, 2002); however, such involvement in parental support organizations and advocacy groups may be preferred by some parents (i.e., European American, middle-class) more than others (Turnbull & Turnbull, 2001). Table 7.2 provides a list of nationally organized parental/family support and advocacy organizations.

Hear a parent's perspective on family functioning and family stress by visiting the Companion Website at www.prenhall.com/ beirne-smith and selecting Chapter 7, Video Case Studies.

The family system, as well as each of its components, is an open system existing in the midst of environments and contexts that impact how the system works (Walsh, 2002). Important to note is that contextual variables such as poverty or economic boon, political power or disenfranchisement, peace or conflict of communities and societies form the backdrop for the family systems model. The exact points at which family characteristics, interactions, and functions converge with the environmental variables that make up their surroundings will designate the unique strengths, needs, and preferences of each family. Families can be resilient, vulnerable, neutral, or some

---

Financial
Home modifications to accommodate child's physical needs
Extra day-care or baby-sitting costs to meet child's special needs
Job accommodations to meet special needs of child

Physical
Extensive caregiving (i.e., inability to leave even older child or adult alone)
Sleep disruption because of child's physical or behavioral characteristics
Meeting child's therapeutic needs
Attending planning and team meetings

Medical
Refusals or limits to health insurance or medical care
Carry out daily medical treatments to meet child's physical needs
Time devoted to medical appointments

Social/emotional
Restricted time for leisure or social activities
Explanations to siblings and other family members about child's condition
Dealing with reactions from others
Acceptance of child's mental retardation
Scrutiny of private lives by a variety of professionals

FIGURE 7.3

Demands Faced by Families of Children with Mental Retardation

Source: From *A Family Centered Approach to People with Mental Retardation* (p. 15), by L. Leal, 1999, Washington, DC: American Association on Mental Retardation. Reprinted by permission.

TABLE 7.2

Parental/Family Support and Advocacy Groups

Organization	Web Site Address
American Association on Mental Retardation	http://www.aamr.org/
The Arc of the United States	http://www.thearc.org/
Development Disabilities Resource Center	http://www.ddrcco.com/
Exceptional Parent	http://www.eparent.com/
Family Village	http://www.familyvillage.wisc.edu/index.htmlx
Genetic Alliance	http://www.geneticalliance.org/
MUMS: National Parent to Parent Network	http://www.netnet.net/mums/
National Association for the Dually Diagnosed	http://www.thenadd.org/
National Down Syndrome Society	http://www.ndss.org/
Our-Kids	http://www.our-kids.org/
PACER Center: Parent Advocacy Coalition for Educational Rights	http://www.pacer.org/
Planned Lifetime Advocacy Network	http://www.plan.ca/

mixture of all three. Key to working with families who have members with mental retardation is the capacity to accept, acknowledge, and address each family as a unique entity. Ultimately, this means rejecting stereotypes that exist on the basis of mental retardation, race/ethnicity, socioeconomic status, gender, age, language, and a myriad of other variables, while listening to families as they articulate and act on their priorities.

FAMILY LIFE

Despite the complexities that create unique families with divergent experiences, having a family member with mental retardation increases the likelihood that families will encounter similar issues in relation to family and disability, particularly in the area of educational involvement. As early discussion in this chapter indicated, parents and family members of children with special needs have special roles in the educational experiences of their children (see Table 7.1). Related issues include interpreting disability; advocacy and collaboration with education, social service, and medical professionals; and planning for adult living. This list of issues is obviously not exhaustive; rather, it represents the kinds of issues that are being examined, explored, and discussed by family members and consumers, practitioners, and researchers.

Interpreting Disability

One characteristic salient to this discussion is individuals' responses to exceptionality. A variety of conceptualizations of parents' and family members' reactions to the addition of a member with disabilities exists. The revelation that a person has a disability can occur anytime in one's life. Often it occurs at or near birth, as is typical with mental retardation. One well-known framework, the five stages of acceptance

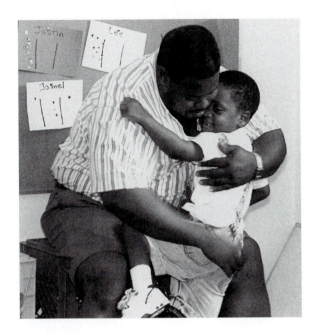

Families of children with mental retardation can vary greatly in their ability to cope with the extraordinary challenges that face them.

of a disability, corresponds with Kübler-Ross's (1969) stages-of-grieving model. Batshaw, Perret, and Trachtenberg (1992) have outlined five steps that they believe fairly represent the stages families of children with mental retardation go through in their acceptance of the disability, as follows:

- *Denial:* Parents and family members may resist the notion that their loved one is different from others. Refusal to accept the new information may be particularly acute when it pertains to a child who looks normal, is somewhat shy or reserved in temperament, and is an only or eldest child.
- *Depression:* Following an awareness that a disability exists and that the perceptions of qualified service providers (e.g., teachers, physicians, psychologists) have a basis in fact, family members often feel a sense of loss or even that the disability is greater than their resolve to overcome it. A general lack of interest in traditional social activities and normal daily activities is among the many indicators of a depressive episode.
- *Anger and guilt:* Once the depression subsides and the family realizes that the disability is not likely to overwhelm them, their energy level starts to rise, and they begin to respond to the new and unfamiliar situation. Along with the increase in energy and unfamiliar feelings comes a desire to fight back, to challenge the disability and challenge those they may consider to be responsible.
- *Bargaining:* When parents realize that they, too, have a role to play in the course of the disability, they often set out in search of mitigating factors that will allow them to regain some control in their fight to overcome the disability. In an era of medical miracles, it is not uncommon for families to begin doctor shopping, to search endlessly for someone or something that can diminish or even cure the child of the disability.

- *Acceptance:* Accepting the reality of a situation that is unwanted and unpleasant may be a difficult task. Once family members have accepted the permanence of the disability and found that its values and structures have remained relatively intact, they are free to continue their family functioning, growing and developing as a new family unit, living, loving, and learning to the fullest extent possible (see Box 7.1).

Although the stages presented here may offer a useful schema for service providers who routinely work with families of persons with mental retardation, the stages represent only one framework for better understanding family members' reactions to the presence of a disability in one of its members. Several caveats are in

---

Box 7.1   ☀   A Unique Parental Perspective

We who work with people with mental retardation are always inspired by parents who do things that make their child a significant part of the family. It is typical for proud parents to send out birth announcements of their new family member. Usually, these announcements are full of excitement and satisfaction. But how do you tell people that your newborn has mental retardation?

Sometimes interesting items come to our attention, and we do not know from where they came or who gave them to us; the following material falls into that category. It is a real birth announcement, but its authors are unknown. It demonstrates one of the most positive parental attitudes we have seen. We have omitted the child's name, date, and time of birth because it is not necessary; the important message is contained in the parents' words. This child, who has an intellectual disability, is lucky to be introduced into a family like this one.

We invite you to rejoice with us at the birth of our daughter

on

at

It is our belief as Latter-day Saints that we all lived a pre-earth life with our Heavenly Father. Certain valiant spirits were selected at that time for special missions during an earth life. One of these spirits has been chosen for our family. Our daughter is a child with Down Syndrome. We feel privileged to be entrusted with the care of this special child, who will return to her Heavenly Father at the end of her earth life and resume, for all eternity, her valiant status with her body and intellect completely restored.

order. First, little empirical work has been done to verify the actual presence or invariant nature of these stages. Second, not all families proceed through these stages in this sequence, if at all. Third, although many parents do experience a sense of loss with respect to the idealized child, this loss is not limited to children with disabilities. Virtually all parents must come to accept their children, their spouses, and themselves in light of who they are and not who they might have been. Many if not most parents experience a sense of joy and appreciation for the new realized child that they now have.

Other Perspectives.   To conclude that there is a single, normative response to the news that a child has a disability is naive. Not only does each family have its own unique way of responding to the news, but it is also quite common for a family's feelings and responses to the disability to vary throughout life. For some families, a mild disability is catastrophic; for others, a profound disability may be of little consequence. Family members from culturally and linguistically diverse backgrounds may experience and react to the birth of a child with disabilities quite differently from the stages described earlier. For example, some parents and family members may attribute disabilities to their religious origins, whereas others may be more fatalistic in their orientation and believe that the presence of a disability has provided them with motivation and strength to overcome adversity (Harry, 1992; Lue & Green, 2000; Skinner, Bailey, Correa, & Rodriguez, 1999). Yuan (2003) found that some parents use metaphors such as journeys, connections, or cycles to describe both the ups and downs of having a child with a disability. Because the concept of disability is culturally bound, diverse groups may define or describe disability with a high degree of variability. As a result, some parents and family members may not agree with medical or educational professionals' assessments that their children have disabilities. This difference of opinion should not be confused with the stage of denial described earlier; rather, to some parents, a disability may seem more like a difference in development, particularly if there is little physical evidence of the presence of a disability (García, Mendez-Pérez, & Ortiz, 2000).

Collaborating and Advocating

As indicated previously, families perform a variety of functions, including providing daily sustenance and emotional interactions, to meet the needs of their members. For families of persons with mental retardation, performing these functions may be necessary throughout the life of the person with mental retardation, affect virtually all life activity areas, and require advocacy for human and civil rights, as well as collaboration with professionals in the fields of education (the focus of this discussion), social services, and health care. The purpose of supportive services in each of these fields is to contribute to the quality of life of people with mental retardation, to increase their inclusion in the communities in which they and their families live and participate, and to promote autonomy among people with mental retardation. Values of normalcy, independence, and self-determination are heavily embedded in supportive services (Kalyanpur & Harry, 1999). Whether families embrace these underlying values with the same enthusiasm as they are espoused by support service systems must be determined on an individual family basis. This is important because the values of families will likely influence the extent and types of support they decide to access and utilize. In the area of education, advocacy and collaboration have been the subjects of extensive research and discussion (e.g., Bauer & Shea, 2003; Kalyanpur & Harry, 1999; Turnbull & Turnbull, 2001). This body of work documents the changing roles of family members in the lives of children with disabilities such as mental retardation, as they collaborate with service providers. Historically, family members, particularly mothers, have been faulted for the presence of a child's disability and were encouraged to transfer the care of their child with mental retardation to the trained professionals of a state institution rather than care for them at home. This is no longer true. Parents and other family members are accepting an increasing number of roles on behalf of their children with disabilities (e.g., teachers, political advocates, educational decision makers, and collaborators) (Turnbull & Turnbull, 2001).

Understanding what families want in a helping relationship implies understanding what they do not want. They do not want to be told what is best for their child, as much as they want options for care and action. Parents want to be seen as competent, capable, cooperative, and willing to pursue the right course of action once several paths have been identified. Families have known for years that professionals bring a special expertise to the disability at hand. Increasingly, professionals are coming to appreciate the special expertise that families bring to the therapeutic process. The term that we now use to describe family-centered involvement and decision making is *empowerment*. Without the family's help and input and, most important, the contribution of the family member in need of service, there would be no service delivery at all.

To read more about family caregiving issues, go to the Companion Website at www.prenhall.com/ beirne-smith and select Chapter 7, Read and Respond.

Accessing Educational Resources.   Special education legislation mandates that families' preferences, strengths, and needs impact decisions for educational placements. Parent participation in the special education process has been variable, ranging from parental satisfaction to passivity to antagonistic and litigious reactions. Parents and family members must have knowledge about disability and the education system to effectively participate. Preliminary research in the area of parents of children with mental retardation indicate that parents whose children have the more well-known types of mental retardation (e.g., Down syndrome) may have more resources to make informed decisions with regard to educational resources for their children (Fidler, Hodapp, & Dykens, 2002). Parents and family members do not always agree regarding which services are necessary to meet the needs of children with mental retardation, making collaboration challenging (Gaudet, Pulos, Crethar, & Burger, 2002). While contemporary issues in education may focus teachers' attention on standardized testing, parents may have other concerns. Parent-identified priorities for educational access and programming for children with mental retardation have included functional communication skills (Stephenson & Dowrick, 2000), issues of family and community belonging (Parette, Brotherson, & Huer, 2000), and issues related to inclusion and educational placements (Park & Turnbull, 2001).

One way to increase collaboration between family members and professionals is through the use of **person-centered planning** techniques (Bassett & Lehmann, 2002), in which the person with mental retardation and his or her family members actively participate with teachers and other professionals to address current educational needs and strengths, as well as develop plans for postsecondary life. In this model, the person with a disability is actively involved in mapping out his or her preferences, strengths, and needs, and connecting those to current and future plans for service provision. Preliminary studies of the use of such planning strategies with people with mental retardation and their families are favorable (Everson & Zhang, 2000). Parents have reported satisfaction both with the amount of input they were able to provide to professionals, and with the positive impact such involvement had on their children with severe mental retardation. Questions remain regarding the implementation of person-centered planning among people with disabilities and their families who are from linguistically and culturally diverse backgrounds, and the amount of time such planning takes to implement effectively.

Making the prescription for optimal service delivery so challenging is the realization that families of children with disabilities are not simply carbon copies of one another. While they may share much in common with other families, they have their own strengths and weaknesses, preferences and approaches, and, most important, attitudes about what is best for their loved one with mental retardation. Not surprisingly, the professionals with whom they work also have their own strengths and weaknesses, attitudes and preferences, and beliefs about what is right for the person in need of service. For the service delivery system to work as intended, the actions of both the service providers and the family members must be in concert with one another. Professionals and family members alike often need to be reminded of their unique but complementary roles in the service delivery relationship.

Building on the strengths of the family offers both parties a foundation for growth that might otherwise not be available. Leal (1999) identifies a number of possible sources of family strengths that professionals can use in their treatment plans. For example, professionals working with families with good, sound channels of communication can often use that communication to help facilitate treatment. This should include the use of sound cross-cultural communication strategies, so that professionals remain sensitive to the various backgrounds with which their families identify. Professionals striving to effectively collaborate with the families with whom they work must know a great deal about the individual family and its own approach to service delivery. See Figure 7.4 for a brief list of questions that service providers must ask themselves when providing such services. Families need the assistance of capable professionals. Professionals exist to help meet the needs of persons and families of persons with disabilities. Together, the two groups form an alliance that must be strong, resilient, and broadly based if the service delivery system is to work to the benefit of those for whom it is designed.

Accessing Supportive Care. **Family support services** can include respite care, family counseling, behavior training, and support groups for parents and siblings (Parish, Pomeranz-Essley, & Braddock, 2003). Family members assume the majority of caretaking responsibilities for their members with mental retardation. In fact, fewer than 15% of all people with mental retardation receive care in institutions or residential care facilities (Parish et al., 2003). Providing families with additional supports—such as respite care of the member with mental retardation

Do I respect the uniqueness of each family?
Do I value the expertise of family members?
Do I assume parents are competent or are capable of becoming competent?
Do I define and describe families in terms of their positive characteristics?
Do I consider how any one recommendation, support, service, or intervention might potentially affect all members of a family?
Have I identified immediate concerns and other unmet needs that might be consuming family members' time and energy?
Have I provided families with as much information as possible so they can make informed decisions?
Do I allow decision making to rest with the family, including the right to say no or refuse services?
Is my overall goal to build on family strengths?
Do I help families learn how to recognize their strengths and tap into information sources of support in order to reduce their need for formal support services?

for one afternoon a week, at which time family members can address their own personal, recreational, employment, or daily living needs—can be beneficial to the functioning of the family system. These options, however, may be scarce. Families may have to advocate diligently for supportive services, because funding for such services has typically been disproportionately provided to institutions and residential settings rather than to families who provide direct care to their members with mental retardation (Parish et al., 2003).

Accessing Financial Resources. Approximately 24% of all people with disabilities were employed in 2000 (Kaye, 2003). Employment rates for people with mental retardation vary according to the extent to which this disability impacts employment-related skills, the vocational and educational skills of the individual, and numerous other factors. For families and their members with mental retardation, obtaining additional financial resources may include sources other than competitive employment—such as Social Security and disability income supplements—once the member with mental retardation becomes an adult and exits the public school system. In addition to limitations of income from employment, the costliness of providing services for people with mental retardation often exceeds that of caring for members without disabilities. While some expenses may be covered by traditional health insurance or provided by the local education agencies (typically until age 22), other expenses such as vocational training, recreational support, and specialized daily living needs (e.g., motorized wheelchair or computer-assisted communication devices) can be more than an average family's budget may allow.

Accessing Care Coordination. A fourth but certainly not final area of needed supports is in the area of coordinated services. The ability to coordinate efforts effectively cannot be underestimated. The presence of duplicate, redundant, or competing services can be just as frustrating as the general lack of necessary services. Consequently, the notion of *wraparound services* has evolved. The term **wraparound services** describes an organized, integrated approach to service delivery that allows for a specially designed treatment plan at a specific point in time. Similar to individualized education programs (IEPs) used in the schools, wraparound services result from a meeting or meetings held by a service coordinator (or case manager), treatment team, and the family. According to Karp (1996), such services allow the "service coordinators to wrap the services around children and their families rather than forcing children into existing service programs" (p. 299). Wraparound services have the advantage of providing services in the natural environments in which families function.

Meeting the Demands of the Life Span

Chapter 11 also discusses the issues that come about as children with mental retardation become adults. Transitioning to postsecondary settings can be an incredibly hopeful and rewarding time for both the young adult with mental retardation and his or her family members. Simultaneously, transitions (postsecondary and beyond) can be tumultuous and difficult. One of the presuppositions in disability-related service delivery systems is that planning is worthwhile and can lead to success. This belief, while deeply embedded in the mainstream, European American, middle-class culture, is not universally valued by all members of our linguistically and culturally diverse nation (deFur & Williams, 2002). Some families, particularly those who are more fatalistic and collectivistic in their orientations, may believe that planning cannot change the path fate has defined for each of its members. As teachers and other service providers attempt to involve family members in transition planning, keeping abreast of the value system to which the family identifies is key to a productive relationship. Doing so does not mean that anyone should ignore the transition mandates outlined in chapter 11. Rather, the implication is that teachers should identify their own beliefs about transition and adults with mental retardation, explicitly discuss planning activities with consumers and families, provide a range of options for family participation, and listen to the family's preferences and observe its strengths and needs, thus following the cultural-responsive methods espoused in multicultural special education (Kalyanpur & Harry, 1999).

The importance of the values orientation of families is not minimized with the passage of time. Older adults with mental retardation represent a unique challenge for an increasing number of families today. Persons who were once strong, energetic, and responsible for family decisions frequently become less willing or less able to make the necessary decisions over time. When decisions of aging caregivers affect the life of an adult with mental retardation, another important transitional phase must be addressed—planning for the later years. Because of improvements in medicine, nutrition, education, and service delivery, persons with mental retardation, like those without mental retardation, are living longer than ever before. Not only is life expectancy for persons with mental retardation now similar to that of the general population, but in most cases that means outliving their parents (Braddock, 1999). Embedded in this new trend are new roles and expectations for virtually all family members—the parents, the siblings, and the adult offspring with mental retardation. As parents themselves age, their decisions regarding caretaker responsibilities for their children with mental retardation emerge

To check your understanding of this chapter, go to the Companion Website at www.prenhall.com/beirne-smith and select Chapter 7. From there, you can access the Self-Test and Essay modules.

as a driving force behind the decisions they make. For example, parents' perceptions of gender roles have the potential to impact decisions they make regarding selection of a brother or a sister to care for their sibling with mental retardation after the parents can no longer do so (Cuskelly & Gunn, 2003). In a study of 140 adult siblings of adults who resided in parental homes, Krauss, Seltzer, Gordon, and Friedman (1996) found that siblings maintained a connectedness with their brother or sister long after leaving home and that the siblings without mental retardation sustained "regular and personal contact, provided emotional support, and felt knowledgeable about the varied needs of their brother or sister with mental retardation" (p. 83). Approximately one third of the siblings surveyed intended to live with their sibling upon moving him or her out of the parental home. Birth order may also play a part in this decision-making process. In a study of siblings with Down syndrome, older siblings without disabilities did have more responsibility than their younger siblings without disabilities, but no more than older siblings in families in which no child had a disability (Cuskelly & Gunn, 2003).

The roles of parents and their children naturally change as both parties age. For parents of children with disabilities, adjusting their role as advocate and protector to one of supporter, thus promoting self-determination, may be quite challenging (K. Peterson, 2004). (For one family's experience, see Box 7.2, "A Rite of Passage.")

Box 7.2   ☸   A Rite of Passage

Following is a brief story about one family's attempt to provide their daughter, Lesley, with a reception that marked her entry into adulthood. This particular reception, considered by her family and friends to be an important developmental milestone, parallels that of many other young adults who do not have intellectual disabilities. Most important, perhaps, is the realization that this reception occurred at a time when movement toward community involvement and full community inclusion was only just beginning. Irrespective of her disability, Lesley was entitled to all of the benefits and trimmings that most young women long for as they enter adulthood. For Lesley's family, the process of planning and preparing for this big occasion was as important as the event itself. Following are the words of Lesley's mother as she reflects on that big day more than two decades ago:

On Lesley's 22nd birthday, we had a party for her at Eagle Creek State Park. The state park is not far from our home, is in the middle of a large nature preserve, and gives the appearance of being far from a large metropolitan area, which it is not. Though it was indeed a birthday party, it resembled a formal reception more than an actual birthday party. The reception was held on the grounds of the state park in a reception center, a large home formerly owned by the Eli Lilly foundation, the service arm of a large pharmaceutical company in Indianapolis, and donated to Eagle Creek park for such activities.

Prior to Lesley's 22nd birthday, we decided that every girl needed and deserves to have a formal reception of her own, one that requires a lot of planning and preparation. As a part of our preparation, we were sure to include all of the formalities that seem so dear to a young woman's heart—such as formal invitations, special napkins with her name and date of the reception on them, and a beautiful, many-layered cake. She needed to have the excitement of selecting the colors, planning the menu, planning the guest list, shopping for the cake, and so forth. It was to be a day for all to remember!

At the party itself we had a buffet, presents galore, and a guest book for people to sign as they entered the reception center. Similar to parties for other young adults without mental retardation, this guest list included immediate family members, friends, and other relatives. Parents of friends were not invited unless Lesley or the invited guest dearly wanted them. The guest list numbered about 40 people. Presents were listed according to guests so that thank-you notes could be written. In one guest's words, "Lesley had a beautiful gown on, the food was great, and the band made for a nice, festive atmosphere." Lesley is 46 now, and we have had several birthday parties for her since that summer afternoon over two decades ago. None, however, has matched the joy and splendor of her 22nd birthday.

Lesley no longer works at a sheltered workshop. She now works in the greenhouse of Dow Agro-Sciences. She is very dependable and has matured into a wonderful lady and very sociable person. Lesley has many happy and enthusiastic relationships at work and home. Most of her friendships away from work are with friends of the family and grew out of activities such as the Symphony Board, community opera, and People of Vision. Through these relationships and the interest others have taken in her, she has developed exceptionally well, verbally as well as socially. Dinner parties, bike rides, walks in the park, and lunch outings are some of the many opportunities that she is now able to take advantage of with her friends. Lesley also visits her sister, Clare, in Columbus, Ohio, at least once a year. They go shopping and do all the things sisters normally do.

At home, Lesley does almost all of the outside work, plus laundry and other errands for day-to-day life. Some of these errands include shopping for groceries at Kmart and Kroger while I wait outside. Her contributions to the home are particularly valuable now because of my arthritis. When Lesley is not working, we enjoy walking and hiking along the trails of Eagle Creek State Park. Because we live on a small farm west of Indianapolis, we have many animals. Lesley takes care of her ducks, cats, dogs, goose, and pony as well as many inside pets.

Throughout Lesley's life, I have stressed the importance of her making her own decisions. I couldn't help but notice an almost universal feeling with respect to this among the other mothers of Lesley's contemporaries. Whether it is raining or snowing, hot or cold, it is up to Lesley to dress appropriately—which she does very well. In addition, she takes full responsibility for her personal hygiene such as bathing, shampooing, brushing teeth, changing clothes, and so on—though I do help her change the linens on her bed. In other words, we have continued to treat her just as we would any of our other adult children.

This has not always been easy, however, as Lesley certainly understands that there are many privileges that she will never attain—and it hurts her. Our means of responding to her, her needs, and her hurts, when they arise, is simply to talk about them and remember that no one has a perfect life and that we will all have to be thankful for our blessings. We accept our disappointments and go on the best we can. Lesley has faith in God and in a life hereafter which, we believe, helps her immensely.

Interesting research has been conducted in the area of familial relationships in adulthood and mental retardation. For parents and their adult children without disabilities, adulthood has the potential to promote a close relationship in which adult children have insights into the actions and decisions their parents made as they were growing up. Likewise, older parents are able to relate to their adult children as peers. Participants in a longitudinal study of families with a child with mental retardation revealed close bonds among adult members as well (Essex, 2002). While mothers' close feelings with their adult children with mental retardation correlated with the level of education of the children and extent of functional skills, fathers' close feelings with their adult children were associated with marital satisfaction, among other variables.

Caring for a child with any type of disability can be demanding, no matter how able or stress-free the family may be. While support personnel do not want to interfere with the family's right to autonomy and self-determination, pragmatics dictate that as the family ages, different types of supports may indeed be needed. The supports may be directed in part at the disability, the age of the person with mental retardation, and/or the needs of the aging parents—whose own resources may be growing increasingly limited. In this case, it is not a matter of autonomy or self-determination, but rather of vigilance in advocacy to see that the older adult's needs are met in a timely and respectful manner (Thorin, Yovanoff, & Irvin, 1996).

Summary

Organization of the Family

- Whereas social scientists were once interested only in individuals, they are now concerned with understanding people in general, individually and collectively.
- Families function as a system; their characteristics, interactions, and functioning interact with environmental and contextual variables. The entire process is dynamic and variable throughout the life span.
- A family's patterns of responses are considered to be both a cause and a consequence of its development.

Family Issues

- Responding to disability is a highly individualized endeavor.
- The major determinant of the psychological health and well-being of a child with mental retardation is the psychological health and well-being of the parents.
- Foremost among the list of supports needed by families is a social support system that allows families to feel that they and their problems are valued by others.
- Collaboration among key members of the disability community can enhance family functioning. Such collaboration is determined, in part, by the congruency between the values and beliefs of the family and the support system to which it has access.
- The aging process of family members with and without mental retardation is a driving force behind decisions about the future.

T he best way to gain an understanding of individuals who have mild mental retardation is to spend time with those so labeled. We recognize, however, that many students enrolled in an introductory course in mental retardation may not have this opportunity. With this in mind, we designed this chapter to give the reader an understanding of the characteristics of this group.

MILD RETARDATION: DEFINITION AND OVERVIEW

By definition, individuals with mental retardation are distinguished from people who do not have retardation on the basis of intellectual functioning and adaptive skills. Significantly subaverage *intellectual functioning* traditionally has been described along a continuum of mild, moderate, severe, and profound, according to the degree to which a person's measured general intelligence deviates from the normal range. The term *adaptive behavior* historically has been used to convey the nature of one's personal independence and social responsibility.

In both of these domains, the amount or degree of deficit is of prime importance. According to the manual on definition offered by the American Association on Mental Retardation (AAMR, 2002), importance is given to the interaction of (1) the individual's capabilities, (2) the various personal and social environments that one encounters on a daily or regular basis, and (3) the individual's actual performance. Based on these interactions, persons with mental retardation will display

Although by definition, individuals who are retarded are different, they have the same needs as individuals who are not retarded.

Chapter

8

Characteristics of Persons with Mild Mental Retardation

OBJECTIVES

After reading this chapter, the student should be able to:

- Discuss the general descriptors and caveats that apply to this group
- Identify the demographic characteristics that describe this group
- Discuss those characteristics that affect performance in school and community: motivation, sociobehavioral, learning, speech and language, and physical and health characteristics
- Provide a description of educational placement, services received, and graduation rates

KEY TERMS

educable mental
   retardation (EMR)

grouping

learned helplessness

locus of control

mediation

selective attention

self-determination

sustained attention

trainable mental
   retardation (TMR)

T he best way to gain an understanding of individuals who have mild
mental retardation is to spend time with those so labeled. We recognize,
however, that many students enrolled in an introductory course in mental retardation may not have this opportunity. With this in mind, we designed this chapter to give the reader an understanding of the characteristics of
this group.

MILD RETARDATION: DEFINITION AND OVERVIEW

By definition, individuals with mental retardation are distinguished from people who
do not have retardation on the basis of intellectual functioning and adaptive skills.
Significantly subaverage *intellectual functioning* traditionally has been described
along a continuum of mild, moderate, severe, and profound, according to the degree
to which a person's measured general intelligence deviates from the normal range.
The term *adaptive behavior* historically has been used to convey the nature of one's
personal independence and social responsibility.

In both of these domains, the amount or degree of deficit is of prime importance. According to the manual on definition offered by the American Association
on Mental Retardation (AAMR, 2002), importance is given to the interaction of (1)
the individual's capabilities, (2) the various personal and social environments that
one encounters on a daily or regular basis, and (3) the individual's actual performance. Based on these interactions, persons with mental retardation will display

*Although by definition,
individuals who are retarded are
different, they have the same
needs as individuals who are not
retarded.*

different needs and require varying levels of assistance across adaptive skills areas; reciprocally, the need for assistance can influence the individual's level of functioning.

In this chapter, we examine the characteristics and needs of individuals who require little or no support systems in most adaptive skills areas. In the next chapter, we take a closer look at individuals who require more intensive levels of support.

The characteristic behaviors discussed in this section frequently are observed among people who have various levels of retardation at different stages of life. As previously mentioned, many factors influence individual functioning and behavior. Some of these variables are organic involvement, sensory or orthopedic impairments, problems relating to health, the nature of environmental demands, the family's concern and resources, the availability of medical and educational services, and the age at which the retardation was diagnosed and intervention was begun.

Individuals who are mildly retarded demonstrate intellectual functioning and adaptive behavior at the upper end of the retardation continuum. The 1992 AAMR definition assessed the intellectual functioning of individuals who are retarded as an IQ standard score of approximately 70 to 75 or below with concurrent deficits in adaptive skill areas. The most recent AAMR definition (2002) employs a standard deviation criterion (i.e., at least 2 standard deviations below the mean on an appropriate assessment instrument) for the intellectual and adaptive behavior components.

For more on the definition of mental retardation, see chapter 2.

According to the *Twenty-fourth Annual Report to Congress on the Implementation of the Individuals with Disabilities Education Act* (U.S. Department of Education, 2003), states and outlying areas reported serving 5,775,722 students ages 6 through 21 under IDEA during the 2000–2001 school year. This figure represents an increase of 28.4% since the 1991–1992 school year. Of these, 612,978—or 10.6% of all students ages 6 through 21 served under IDEA—were categorized as mentally retarded. States had the option of reporting children in the 3 through 9 age groups as developmentally delayed; 28 states took advantage of this option. An additional 28,935 students were served as developmentally delayed, some of whom are mentally retarded. Generally, 85% of the population of persons who are retarded are reported to be mildly mentally retarded (American Psychiatric Association, 2000). For more detailed data, see Table 8.1 and Table 8.2.

From the 1976–1977 school year, when the Department of Education began compiling statistics on students receiving special education services, until the 1990–1991 school year there was a distinct decline in the number of students identified as mentally retarded. Such variables as school districts' increasing reluctance to identify students from minority ethnic or culturally diverse backgrounds as mentally retarded, school districts' moving of higher functioning students who previously were labeled as mentally retarded to the less stigmatizing learning disabilities category, or the success of early identification and early intervention may account for this downward trend. Recently, the number of students identified as mentally retarded appears to have stabilized.

While the rate at which children with intellectual disabilities develop motor, social, and language skills may be noticeably slower than their peers, milder forms of retardation often are not suspected until the children enter school. Frequently, a combination of difficulty with academic subjects and behavioral problems generates

TABLE 8.1

Children Aged 6 to 21 Served Under IDEA Part B, School Year 2000–2001: All Disabilities, Specific Learning Disabilities, Speech or Language Impairments, Mental Retardation, Emotional Disturbance*

State	All Disabilities	Specific Learning Disabilities	Speech or Language Impairments	Mental Retardation	Emotional Disturbance
Alabama	92,274	42,093	15,972	20,224	4,854
Alaska	16,054	9,191	3,169	819	843
Arizona	87,298	51,059	15,209	7,215	5,312
Arkansas	52,862	22,490	9,569	11,773	488
California	587,636	344,595	125,095	35,549	22,188
Colorado	70,597	34,201	13,326	3,461	8,753
Connecticut	66,714	30,615	12,347	3,731	7,332
Delaware	15,108	9,049	1,650	2,039	675
District of Columbia	10,185	5,117	960	1,342	1,861
Florida	336,675	164,225	75,100	39,421	37,082
Georgia	154,732	48,665	32,726	30,204	24,100
Hawaii	22,032	10,722	2,326	2,692	3,371
Idaho	25,583	14,595	4,167	1,929	822
Illinois	267,576	134,494	56,079	27,712	30,699
Indiana	141,219	59,362	36,056	21,862	12,107
Iowa	66,881	33,809	4,223	16,494	9,905
Kansas	54,360	23,975	10,635	5,553	4,244
Kentucky	78,200	20,448	17,947	17,950	5,858
Louisiana	87,981	35,947	19,170	12,024	5,369
Maine	31,655	13,126	7,537	1,047	3,697
Maryland	102,074	44,316	23,893	6,698	9,116
Massachusetts	147,888	90,882	21,851	14,559	12,893
Michigan	201,519	94,511	39,912	24,121	19,147
Minnesota	98,432	38,802	16,370	10,097	17,592
Mississippi	55,337	27,318	16,230	5,800	683
Missouri	126,074	65,763	26,131	12,387	9,164
Montana	17,522	9,651	3,319	1,229	1,029
Nebraska	39,069	16,084	9,724	5,951	2,630
Nevada	34,484	21,703	5,728	1,757	1,822
New Hampshire	27,690	13,339	5,516	1,009	2,546
New Jersey	205,354	111,288	42,824	5,772	13,785
New Mexico	47,286	28,357	8,676	1,900	3,052
New York	386,842	204,158	59,337	15,801	42,925
North Carolina	155,706	66,965	27,622	28,844	10,267
North Dakota	12,405	5,620	3,390	1,232	1,035
Ohio	218,979	85,490	38,467	51,471	15,125
Oklahoma	79,184	44,631	14,294	8,475	4,171
Oregon	68,278	34,335	15,204	4,365	4,634
Pennsylvania	219,377	122,386	36,022	27,052	19,864
Puerto Rico	57,758	31,284	7,540	13,055	819

State	All Disabilities	Specific Learning Disabilities	Speech or Language Impairments	Mental Retardation	Emotional Disturbance
Rhode Island	28,113	15,683	5,052	1,206	2,540
South Carolina	94,147	43,037	21,165	16,954	6,002
South Dakota	14,539	7,405	3,222	1,441	778
Tennessee	115,164	54,371	24,922	14,493	3,590
Texas	455,200	258,386	71,091	24,904	35,323
Utah	48,136	27,973	8,836	3,183	3,471
Vermont	13,251	5,039	2,120	1,412	2,186
Virginia	153,215	74,858	23,381	14,190	12,947
Washington	107,091	50,756	15,934	6,591	4,908
West Virginia	44,888	18,986	10,992	9,229	2,124
Wisconsin	110,852	52,530	17,416	13,026	16,256
Wyoming	11,459	5,760	2,661	633	948
American Samoa	649	521	26	63	7
Guam	2,062	1,545	186	95	19
Northern Marianas	516	323	29	61	2
Palau	121	87	7	5	1
Virgin Islands	1,329	549	130	452	77
Bur. of Indian Affairs	8,110	4,747	1,325	424	625
U. S. and outlying areas	5,775,722	2,887,217	1,093,808	612,978	473,663
50 states, D. C., & P. R.	5,762,935	2,879,445	1,092,105	611,878	472,932

* Please see data notes for an explanation of individual state differences. Data based on the December 1, 2000, count; updated as of August 30, 2001.

Source: U.S. Department of Education, Office of Special Education Programs, Data Analysis System (DANS).

concern. Learning problems sometimes appear to be specific to one subject, such as reading, but more often these problems are recognized across subjects.

Children who do not have the verbal and communication skills of their age-mates may withdraw from interpersonal relationships or seek attention in inappropriate ways. Inappropriate social behavior can result from any number of factors. These children may misbehave from the frustrations of scholastic failure or because they cannot distinguish clearly between acceptable and unacceptable standards of behavior. Problem behavior also can be an attempt to gain acceptance from other children who might encourage deviant behavior.

Some individuals with mental retardation have significant psychiatric disorders as well, resulting in a dual diagnosis. Reber & Borcherding (1997) noted that a higher prevalence of these problems occurs among children who are mentally retarded than among those who are not retarded. We present a more detailed discussion of this topic later in the chapter.

TABLE 8.2

Children Aged 6 to 21 Served Under IDEA Part B, School Year 2000–2001: Autism, Deaf-Blindness, Traumatic Brain Injury, Developmental Delay[*]

State	Autism	Deaf-Blindness	Traumatic Brain Injury	Developmental Delay
Alabama	765	8	254	749
Alaska	195	5	70	10
Arizona	1,119	36	306	0
Arkansas	671	14	161	0
California	10,557	147	1,235	0
Colorado	453	69	246	0
Connecticut	1,225	55	87	0
Delaware	263	42	2	0
District of Columbia	103	10	25	13
Florida	3,626	50	415	0
Georgia	1,916	21	365	0
Hawaii	276	3	61	392
Idaho	291	15	147	1,384
Illinois	3,103	60	682	0
Indiana	2,621	31	482	0
Iowa	537	3	129	0
Kansas	619	10	183	652
Kentucky	864	14	189	4,224
Louisiana	1,145	12	301	2,156
Maine	444	4	108	0
Maryland	1,933	26	322	0
Massachusetts	575	48	302	0
Michigan	4,075	0	0	66
Minnesota	2,448	45	346	1,207
Mississippi	385	13	122	1,776
Missouri	1,589	49	336	26
Montana	163	18	61	0
Nebraska	337	10	191	126
Nevada	394	5	144	0
New Hampshire	342	5	61	353
New Jersey	2,925	29	61	0
New Mexico	225	18	218	668
New York	5,943	42	1,321	0
North Carolina	2,374	21	422	551
North Dakota	118	4	30	49
Ohio	2,217	17	471	0
Oklahoma	666	14	263	0
Oregon	2,516	33	307	0
Pennsylvania	3,304	41	1,456	0
Puerto Rico	473	30	25	0

State	Autism	Deaf-Blindness	Traumatic Brain Injury	Developmental Delay
Rhode Island	309	4	51	0
South Carolina	852	18	98	47
South Dakota	227	1	47	0
Tennessee	935	4	246	2,810
Texas	6,023	73	938	0
Utah	584	72	327	302
Vermont	160	6	75	570
Virginia	1,983	6	304	6,679
Washington	1,620	30	323	3,797
West Virginia	312	20	112	0
Wisconsin	1,823	7	321	76
Wyoming	94	0	80	0
American Samoa	1	0	1	0
Guam	16	1	2	24
Northern Marianas	2	0	0	25
Palau	1	0	0	0
Virgin Islands	6	0	1	33
Bur. Of Indian Affairs	6	1	11	170
U.S. and outlying areas	78,749	1,320	14,844	28,935
50 states, D.C., & P. R.	78,717	1,318	14,829	28,683

*Please see data notes for an explanation of individual state differences. Developmental delay is applicable only to children aged 3 through 9. Data based on the December 1, 2000, count; updated as of August 30, 2001.

Source: U.S. Department of Education, Office of Special Education Programs, Data Analysis System (DANS).

A number of terms have been used to describe individuals who have been iden-tified as mentally retarded and provided with special education and related services. Even though the use of traditional labels for levels of retardation (mild, moderate, se-vere, and profound) is discouraged in the most recent AAMR manual on definition, classification, and systems of supports, it is likely that these existing terms will con-tinue to be used. States, for the most part, have not been receptive to the AAMR sys-tems of support. Denning, Chamberlain, and Polloway (2000) reported that only four states adopted the AAMR system of supports approach for identifying and classify-ing students with mental retardation.

Educable mental retardation (EMR) and trainable mental retardation (TMR) are two terms that have a long history of use in school settings. Over time, these terms have fallen into disfavor with most professionals in the field; however, they are still used in some locations. The term *EMR* referred to students whose abilities were adequate for them to profit from an academically oriented curriculum; *TMR* referred to students

 *A complete online glossary is available on the Companion Website, which may be accessed at www.prenhall.com/ beirne-smith*

whose programs emphasized the training of basic functional skills (e.g., self-help skills). The underlying thinking associated with these terms and the programmatic decisions based on them have changed dramatically in recent years. As a result, their usage has declined drastically as well.

Although some data support the contention that individuals who are mildly retarded display more secondary problems than the population as a whole (Barlow & Durand, 1995; Borthwick-Duffy & Eyman, 1990), the vast majority of these individuals can lead satisfying and productive lives. Adults with mild mental retardation are capable of securing and maintaining employment and becoming economically self-sufficient. However, adult outcome data on the amount of unemployment and underemployment among adults who are retarded provide chilling realizations that much work still must be done. With increased knowledge about how individuals who are retarded learn, and with more effective methodology for improving their performance, we should be able to provide better programs, sensitive to both current and future needs.

DEMOGRAPHIC CHARACTERISTICS

Information about the characteristics and background of a given population enables us to understand, prepare for, and serve the needs of that group. For two reasons, the following discussion focuses primarily on the demographics of individuals with mild mental retardation. First, this segment of the population appears to have changed the most in the past few years. Second, individuals who need more intensive systems of support generally are not overrepresented in any given socioeconomic or racial group; they are distributed fairly evenly throughout the general population.

Gender

More boys than girls are labeled "mentally retarded." In Dunn's (1973) review of the literature on persons who are mildly retarded and his subsequent description of that population, he stated that students labeled as EMR were more likely to be male. This still holds true, if figures in studies characterizing individuals who are mildly retarded are indicative of the population as a whole (Epstein, Polloway, Patton, & Foley, 1989; Larson et al., 2000b; Polloway, Epstein, Patton, Cullinan, & Luebke, 1986; Wagner, Newman, & Shaver, 1989).

Reasons given for a preponderance of males include greater role expectations placed on males; aggressive behavior more often exhibited by males, leading to referral and subsequent labeling; and a higher probability of such biological factors as gender-linked influences affecting male children. A possibility also exists that gender bias in the diagnostic/classification process may disproportionately affect the number of males categorized as mentally retarded (U.S. Department of Education, 1996).

Ethnicity

Reviewers of demographic data historically have reported a disproportionate number of racial and ethnic minority children being labeled as mildly mentally retarded

(Doll, 1962; Dunn, 1973; Epstein et al., 1989; Manni, Winikur, & Keller, 1980; Polloway et al., 1986). During the 1960s, 1970s, and 1980s, the racial imbalance in the makeup of EMR classes became the focus of much litigation, which in part led to changes in the procedures for identifying and labeling children as mentally retarded. Perhaps our efforts at definitional changes and more stringent identification procedures have had some effect; overrepresentation of racial and ethnic minorities in programs for students who have intellectual disabilities is still evident, but the most recent figures for the mental retardation category are no longer statistically significant for race and ethnicity (see Table 8.3). According to the *Twenty-fourth Annual Report to Congress on the Implementation of the Individuals with Disabilities Education Act* (U.S. Department of Education, 2003), figures comparing 1986–1987 students (cohort 1) to 1999–2000 students (cohort 2) show that changes in the racial/ethnic distribution for all students with disabilities affected students in different disability categories in different ways. There was a decline in the proportion of students who were White for eight of the nine disabilities, including the mental retardation category. There was a small decline in the percentage of students who were Black for eight of the nine disabilities, but a small increase in the mental retardation category. Similarly, there was a small increase in the percentage of Hispanic students in the mental retardation category. The overrepresentation of African American and Hispanic students in programs for students with mental retardation may be attributed in part to relatively low income and the disabilities associated with poverty; such school-related factors as ambiguity and subjectivity in the assessment, referral, and placement processes; and variability in counting, analyzing, and reporting procedures. The increase in the percentage of Hispanic students in the mental retardation category also may be attributed to language differences between home and school. When all these variables are accounted for, however, a disproportionate representation of African American and Hispanic students still remains in programs for students with mental retardation.

Socioeconomic and Family Patterns

Information available on secondary school youth who have disabilities (U.S. Department of Education, 2003) indicates that these youth, when compared to the general population of youth, are more likely to:

- Live in blended rather than traditional two-parent families
- Have bilingual or bicultural backgrounds
- Come from families characterized by lower socioeconomic status
- Live in a family that has a significantly lower household income

The implication drawn from this information is that these factors may affect the educational performance, physical and health status, and adult outcomes of these youth. It is also important to recognize that these findings are related to all youth with disabilities—not just those with mental retardation.

Environmental deprivation as a variable in the etiology of mental retardation is recognized by the AAMR (2002) in its multifactorial approach to the causes of

TABLE 8.3

Changes in Racial/Ethnic Backgrounds and Language Use, by Cohort and Disability Category (Cohort 1 = 1986–1987; Cohort 2 = 1999–2000)

	Learning Disability	Speech/ Language Impairment	Mental Retardation	Emotional Disturbance	Hearing Impairment	Visual Impairment	Orthopedic Impairment	Other Health Impairment	Multiple Disabilities
Percentage who were:									
White									
Cohort 1	67.0 (3.1)	53.8 (4.4)	60.2 (3.5)	67.5 (3.7)	61.0 (3.5)	62.7 (4.9)	62.6 (4.4)	55.0 (4.8)	63.0 (6.3)
Cohort 2	62.5 (2.9)	66.5 (3.1)	55.2 (3.0)	61.5 (3.0)	60.8 (3.2)	60.9 (4.2)	64.3 (3.2)	74.9 (2.2)	65.3 (3.0)
Percentage point change	–4.5	+12.7*	–5.0	–6.0	–0.2	–1.8	–1.7	+19.9***	+2.3
Black									
Cohort 1	21.2 (2.7)	27.4 (3.9)	30.3 (3.3)	24.9 (3.4)	20.4 (2.9)	26.1 (4.4)	20.2 (3.7)	17.2 (3.7)	20.8 (5.3)
Cohort 2	18.4 (2.3)	16.8 (2.5)	32.6 (2.9)	24.2 (2.6)	17.7 (2.5)	19.5 (3.4)	14.9 (2.4)	15.0 (1.8)	18.3 (2.4)
Percentage point change	–2.8	–10.6*	+2.3	–0.7	–2.7	–6.6	–5.3	–2.2	–2.5
Hispanic									
Cohort 1	8.7 (1.9)	15.7 (3.2)	6.3 (1.7)	6.0 (1.9)	14.4 (2.5)	7.7 (2.7)	15.5 (3.3)	24.4 (4.2)	10.8 (4.0)
Cohort 2	15.4 (2.2)	14.3 (2.3)	9.5 (1.8)	10.5 (1.9)	16.1 (2.4)	15.4 (3.1)	16.6 (2.5)	7.2 (1.3)	12.0 (2.0)
Percentage point change	+6.7*	+1.4	+3.2	+4.5	+1.7	+7.7**	+1.1	–17.2***	+1.2
Percentage who do not use English at home:									
Cohort 1	13.0 (0.8)	7.6 (2.4)	5.9 (1.7)	1.5 (1.0)	18.0 (2.8)	5.6 (2.3)	7.6 (2.5)	10.3 (3.0)	33.5 (6.1)
Cohort 2	15.4 (2.2)	17.6 (2.6)	11.4 (2.0)	8.9 (1.8)	40.4 (3.3)	17.7 (3.3)	14.9 (2.5)	9.0 (1.5)	15.6 (2.3)
Percentage point change	+14.1***	+10.0**	+5.5*	+7.4***	+22.4***	+12.1*	+7.3	–1.3	–17.9**
Sample size: Cohort 1/2	383/630	219/471	323/607	288/575	626/612	339/489	300/627	229/1,226	281/739

Standard errors are in parentheses.

Statistically significant difference in a two-tailed test at the following levels: * $p<.05$, ** $p<.01$, *** $p<.001$.

Source: National Longitudinal Transition Study 2.

mental retardation (i.e., interactions among biomedical, social, behavioral, and educational risk factors). The description associated with identifying risk factors states that individuals who are retarded may experience family poverty, homelessness, inadequate parenting skills, parental substance abuse, or child abuse and neglect. Examples of interactions between or among risk factors might include "(a) maternal poverty and substance abuse, causing a lack of prenatal care and fetal alcohol syndrome, and (b) homelessness, causing lack of early intervention services" (AAMR, 2002, p. 135). In at least one study describing this population (Epstein et al., 1989), factors sometimes associated with low socioeconomic status—such as a preponderance of single-parent homes, children raised by people other than their natural parents, and family involvement with one or more community agencies for support services—have been substantiated as contributing elements.

The higher prevalence of milder forms of mental retardation among low-income families has been acknowledged for some time (Westling, 1986). As previously mentioned, this disproportionate representation appears to be almost entirely limited to those needing less intensive systems of supports. Socioeconomic conditions do not appear to affect the prevalence of those with more extensive and intensive needs (MacMillan & Reschly, 1998).

MOTIVATIONAL AND SOCIOBEHAVIORAL CHARACTERISTICS

Children with mental retardation have the same basic physiological, social, and emotional needs as their typically developing peers. Because of their experiences in dealing with environments in which they are less able to display appropriate adaptive skills, however, they often develop patterns of behavior that serve to distinguish them further from those who do not have retardation. For example, members of this group show a higher prevalence of emotional and behavioral problems (Barlow & Durand, 1995; Fraser & Rao, 1991; Lovell & Reiss, 1993). The motivational and behavioral characteristics presented in this section are generalizations supported by studies of groups of people with mental retardation. Because all individuals are unique and there is at least as much variability among those who are retarded as among persons who are not retarded, the following generalizations will not fit every individual.

Motivational Characteristics

Many early investigations came from research in the field of social learning theory and concentrated on distinctions between individuals who were mildly retarded and those who were not retarded. This discussion, however, has relevance for those with slightly more intensive needs as well.

Locus of Control. How one perceives the consequences of one's behavior is known as the individual's **locus of control.** Individuals who operate primarily from an *internal locus of control* see events—both positive and negative—as results of their own actions.

Those who see positive and negative events as controlled primarily by such outside forces as fate, chance, or the actions of other people have an *external locus of control*.

Young children tend to be externally oriented, perceiving many circumstances and events in their lives as being beyond their control. As children mature, however, they become more aware of the influence of their own actions. As a result, they gradually shift to a more internal locus of control, although this is not as true of students with mild disabilities. Students with mild retardation tend to remain more externally oriented than do their peers who are not disabled and thus demonstrate less adaptive capabilities as adolescents and adults (Wehmeyer, 1994). External control, therefore, is considered a more debilitating orientation, as it keeps individuals from accepting responsibility for their own successes and failures and from developing self-reliance and self-regulatory behaviors. Wehmeyer, Palmer, Agran, Mithaug, and Martin (2000) have stated that skill in **self-determination**—the ability to act instead of being acted upon—is critical for students to achieve positive adult outcomes. Zhang (2001) noted that self-determination facilitates community integration and helps individuals who are retarded to take charge of their lives. Self-determination allows individuals the opportunity to express preferences, make choices, take risks, assume responsibility, and exert control over their personal circumstances. (See Box 8.1.)

Learned helplessness is another term sometimes used to reflect the belief that failure will crown even the most extraordinary efforts (Stipek, 1993). Seligman (1975), who originated the concept of learned helplessness, noted that the phenomenon occurs when individuals perceive that events cannot be controlled by their actions. In school settings, for example, learners believe that regardless of the quality or quantity of their response, the outcome will be negative.

Expectancy of Failure.   *Expectancy* refers to the reinforcement that is anticipated as a result of a given behavior. Rotter (1954) postulated two types of expectancies. The first is the expectation of a particular type of reinforcement, such as a tangible reward or social approval. The second involves expectations generalized from the results of past experiences with particular types of problem-solving activities. In other words, new situations are approached with either the expectation of success or the expectation of failure, based on what the individual has experienced in the past.

Studies by Cromwell (1963), Cummins and Das (1980), and Schloss, Alper, and Jayne (1994) involving subjects with mental retardation found them to have a high expectancy of failure. Zigler (1973) and Balla and Zigler (1979) noted that an individual who has accumulated experiences of failure sets lower aspirations and goals in an effort to avoid additional disappointment. Heber (1964) pointed out that this fear of failure may become circular: The expectation of lack of success lowers the amount of effort put into the task; performance of the task is thus below what might be anticipated from the individual's capabilities; and the expected failure becomes reality.

Those working with individuals who demonstrate the debilitating attitude of expecting to fail must create situations that encourage and reward effort. It is important for these individuals to experience success and to recognize it when it occurs. However, it is equally important to teach them how to deal with failure and how to persevere.

Companion Website For more information about self-determination, and many other topics discussed in this chapter, visit the Companion Website at www.prenhall.com/beirne-smith and select Chapter 8, Web Destinations.

Box 8.1 🌿 Positive Supports

A Definition of Positive Supports

Positive supports are actions and beliefs that reflect respectful interpersonal relationships, choice, communication, inclusive communities, and self-determination to assist a person to become a more independent, contributing member of the community. They encompass a variety of strategies that are considered unconditionally for a person who may be exhibiting behaviors that challenge family members, educational staff, service providers, and/or the community. People also require positive supports during other times in their lives. A committed group of diverse people collaborate to identify, develop, and secure the needed supports, while acknowledging a person's individuality. Positive supports recognize people's rights to make informed choices, take risks, and contribute in the decision-making process.

Foundations of Positive Supports

- Community
- Being heard
- Individualized supports
- Ongoing support
- Enhanced quality of life

Core Elements of Positive Supports

- Active member of an inclusive community
- Person-centered planning
- Communication
- Choice
- Friendship
- Collaborative team
- Control resides with person
- Support during crises
- Teaching/building competencies

Positive Supports Questions to Ask

Is the support you provide to individuals with disabilities positive in its approach? Take a moment to answer the questions below to find out.

1. Does the person have the opportunity to make informed choices that impact his/her life (e.g., real life choices such as who, or what agency will provide support, hiring and firing staff, where to live/work, and what/how much to eat)?
2. Does the person have a way to communicate his/her needs and wants throughout the entire day?
3. Does the person have reciprocal relationships in his/her life? (While paid staff at times develop reciprocal relationships with a person, these paid relationships should not be the only ones a person has.)
4. Is the person an active member of the community, participating in events of his/her choice on an individual basis? (This does not include activities designed exclusively for individuals with disabilities.)
5. Is person-centered planning used to identify supports based upon the person's dreams, goals, strengths, and needs ensuring that the supports are unique to him/her?
6. Do supporters reevaluate what is needed when identified supports do not appear beneficial?
7. Do supporters listen to and acknowledge the concerns and requests that a person may have no matter how he/she makes that request (e.g., talking, use of behavior)?
8. Do supporters acknowledge that their own values, behavior, and needs may influence their interactions with and the behavior of others?
9. Do supporters respect the person's right to take risks after he/she has obtained relevant information and the support needed to evaluate the information?
10. Does the person advocate for him/herself to determine his/her own life?
11. Are identified supports flexible to meet the everchanging needs a person may have?
12. Do we recognize and accept the diversity of the people we work with and support?

Outer-Directedness.   Another result of attempts to avoid failure is a style of problem solving called *outer-directedness*. Instead of being self-reliant in problem solving, the outer-directed individual relies on situational or external cues for guidance (Bybee & Zigler, 1992).

While this type of behavior is certainly not limited to those with retardation, Zigler (1999) suggested that it prevails among this group because they have learned to distrust their own abilities, due to the frequency with which they have failed in the past. Efficient problem solving necessarily involves using both external cues and one's own cognitive resources. The use of external cues may be an appropriate adaptation to one's limitations (Bybee & Zigler, 1992). However, relying too heavily on external cues could result in a dependence on them, even for a task well within one's own capabilities (Balla & Zigler, 1979).

In the three motivational orientations discussed (locus of control, expectancy for failure, and outer-directedness), the detrimental effect of repeated failures is a recurring theme. Perhaps the most important implication for those working in the field is the necessity of providing children who are retarded with tasks at which they can succeed. This holds true for both social and academic settings. Allowing the child to be successful is an invaluable motivational tool. Yet all children, disabled and otherwise, need to learn to deal with failure as well. A sensitive teacher can shape classroom experiences in such a way that the child gains enough self-confidence through repeated successes to be able to rebound from the inevitable failure. Parents and teachers need to be sensitive to their own expectations for the child, so that they do not inadvertently reinforce the child's negative expectations. They must take care to avoid conveying the idea that they do not think the child is competent to handle tasks. Rather, parents and teachers should require all children to assume responsibilities that are within their grasp, make it clear exactly what is expected of them, and allow them opportunities to try.

Other ways to increase the chances of success are setting specific realistic goals, providing immediate feedback for specific behavior, and rewarding accomplishments. If the child has failed repeatedly at a certain task, the situation should be restructured to present a novel approach that makes success possible. Finally, although it is desirable to help children who are retarded become more inner-directed and self-reliant, their tendency to rely heavily on external cues should be used to advantage. Teachers and parents should provide appropriate behavior models for children.

Self-Regulatory Behaviors

Ultimately, we would like all individuals to exert control over their lives. For them to do so, it is essential that they develop self-regulation of many behaviors across different settings and maintain the behaviors over time. Field, Martin, Miller, Ward, and Wehmeyer (1998) define self-determination as "a combination of skills, knowledge, and beliefs [that enable individuals with disabilities] to engage in goal-directed, self-regulated, autonomous behavior" (p. 2). Despite the desirability of developing self-regulation in persons with mental retardation, Whitman (1990) warned that such individuals are likely to be delayed in acquiring this skill. This admonition is based on the fact that self-regulation is a linguistically guided process, and individuals who are retarded display linguistic limitations. Nevertheless, the goal of developing self-regulatory behaviors is warranted and attainable. Wehmeyer, Field, Doren, Jones, and Mason (2004) noted that recent research indicates that developing self-determination skills in students with disabilities results in more positive educational experiences and enhances adult outcomes. Similarly, Whitman (1990) offered the following strong rationale for promoting self-regulation in persons who are retarded:

> By exercising self-control, persons with retardation can increase the probability that they will act effectively without external direction, maintain what they have learned, and generalize learned responses to situations where training contingencies have not been applied. Moreover, by self-regulation of their behavior, they are more likely to be able to live in more normalized settings where close supervision is not possible. Finally, because independent action is valued by our society, individuals with retardation who become more autonomous are also more likely to be reacted to more positively by others, which in turn will increase their feeling of self-efficacy. (p. 348)

Wehmeyer and colleagues (2004) noted that there are several empirically validated models of self-determination that can serve as boilerplates for developing instructional materials to promote self-determination in students with disabilities.

Sociobehavioral Characteristics

Children and adolescents who have more severe mental retardation historically have been described as displaying more social and behavioral problems than their peers who are not disabled (Lovell & Reiss, 1993). According to Guralnick and Weinhouse (1984), in play settings, for example, young children who are severely developmentally delayed interact less frequently with their peers and engage more frequently in solitary or unoccupied activities. Similarly, in work settings, adults who are more severely retarded demonstrate difficulty in accepting criticism, resolving conflicts, following instructions, and engaging in conversation (Sherman, Sheldon, Harchik, Edwards, & Quinn, 1992). Studies focusing on students who are mildly retarded confirm similar problems in this population (Epstein, Cullinan, & Polloway, 1986; Polloway, Epstein, & Cullinan, 1985; Russell & Forness, 1985). Some of the specific problem areas include disruptiveness, attention deficits, low self-esteem (Polloway et al., 1985), overactivity (Polloway et al., 1986), distractibility and other attention-related problems (Epstein et al., 1989), and difficulty in interpersonal cognitive problem solving (Healey & Masterpasqua, 1992).

Individuals whose needs for support are minimal often have difficulty in establishing and maintaining interpersonal relationships (Heiman, 2000). They may, for example, have trouble developing close personal friends, as evidence has indicated that they are more often rejected than accepted by their peers (Polloway et al., 1986). This frequency of rejection is associated with the degree of inappropriateness of the behavior they display. Furthermore, inappropriate behavior and peer rejection may be apparent as early as preschool. Kopp, Baker, and Brown (1992), for example, found those preschoolers who were developmentally delayed demonstrated less positive affect and more disruptive and regressive behavior that interrupted play than did their peers who were not developmentally delayed. Findings from such studies have important implications for the social acceptance and subsequent formation of friendships of these students.

Read more about friendships and relationship issues by visiting the Companion Website at www.prenhall.com/beirne-smith and selecting Chapter 8, Read and Respond.

It is difficult to estimate the prevalence of mental health disorders in persons who are retarded due to problems in sampling and diagnosis. Generally, mental health disorders are more prevalent in individuals who are retarded than in the general population. Dosen and Day (2001), for example, estimated a prevalence of 7% to 26% in individuals in the general population and 9% to 74% in individuals who are retarded. This represents a two to three times higher rate among persons who are retarded. Lovell and Reiss (1993) found a higher incidence of behavioral and psychiatric disorders in individuals referred to as moderately retarded.

A wide range of behaviors may be evidenced in individuals who are retarded, including distractibility, hyperactivity, anxiety disorders, posttraumatic stress disorders, psychotic disorders, and personality disorders. Health-related problems as well as the effects of medication may affect attention and concentration, leading both to a slower, more limited acquisition of social skills and to an increase in inappropriate behaviors. The same types of mental health disorders are found in persons who have and do not have mental retardation, but the behavioral manifestations of psychiatric disorders will vary by individual. Some educators have hypothesized that the lower the intellectual level, the more pronounced the behavioral deviations. This suggests that individuals with greater need for supports would exhibit more behavioral problems than those with fewer need for supports. Additionally, there are numerous patterns of behavior that might result in a dual diagnosis. Table 8.4 provides some examples of psychiatric disorders that some individuals with mental retardation might display.

Because being able to meet more normal behavioral expectations is often a significant factor in the decision to include students with special needs in general education classrooms, social skill problems may contribute to more restrictive placements. Also, a great many variables influence the learning process. Better social, motivational, and behavioral adjustment is likely to relate to better academic functioning. Another major consideration is that successful adult adjustment requires competence in many social and behavioral areas. Curricular attention to this area would enable a more successful integration into community life.

Further implications extend into higher education, where professionals are trained to work with exceptional students. In the area of mental retardation, teachers need to prepare themselves for a diversity of social and behavioral problems and receive training in appropriate intervention and management techniques for dealing with them (Gumpel, 1994; Leffert & Siperstein, 1996). Training is also needed in ways to incorporate social skills into the curriculum and in methods and materials by which such skills may be taught.

LEARNING CHARACTERISTICS

We may think of learning as the process whereby practice or experience produces a change in behavior that is not due to maturation, growth, or aging. The definition implies (1) that the changed behavior is relatively permanent, as distinguished from responses to, for example, drugs or fatigue; and (2) that the learner is involved and participating, not just changing because of physical growth, maturation, or deterioration.

Major depression (in mental retardation requiring extensive support) Change in pattern of physical activity Change in sleep pattern Feeding problems Increase in challenging behaviors (aggression, self-injury, stereotypes) Loss of interest or pleasure in daily routines Persistent depressed or irritable mood Withdrawal from social interactions **Major depression (in mental retardation requiring intermittent to limited support)** Change in appetite and/or weight Diminished ability to concentrate Fatigue or loss of energy Feelings of worthlessness or guilt Insomnia or excessive sleeping Loss of interest in school and extracurricular activities Persistent feelings of sadness or despair Recurrent irritable or withdrawn behavior Recurrent thoughts of death or suicide **Mania** Decreased frustration tolerance and increased aggression Decreased need for sleep Elevated mood together with grandiose or paranoid thoughts Heightened sexual arousal (increased masturbatory or inappropriate sexual activity) Increased motor restlessness and agitation **Schizophrenia** Catatonic behavior Delusions Flat or inappropriate emotional expression Hallucinations Loosening of associations in speech **Obsessive-compulsive disorder** Repetitive purposeful behavior performed in response to obsessions Persistent thoughts that are senseless	**TABLE 8.4** Symptoms of Psychiatric Disorders in Children with Mental Retardation

Source: From "Dual Diagnosis: Mental Retardation and Psychiatric Disorders," by M. Reber & B. G. Borcherding, in M. L. Badshaw (Ed.), *Children with Disabilities* (4th ed., p. 408), 1997, Baltimore: Paul H. Brookes Publishing Co.; reprinted by permission.

Physical maturity, however, can result in behavioral changes. The development of such motor skills as walking appears not to be influenced by training or experience until the child has the necessary physical maturity. Delayed development is a characteristic of people who are retarded, and the degree of delay generally is related to the severity of the retardation and the presence of other inhibiting conditions. People who expect a person with disabilities to acquire skills at the same rate as persons who are not disabled may end up frustrated and may fail in their attempts to teach new skills. Instruction and practice will not supplant the maturation process, but studies of infant stimulation provide enough encouragement to justify instruction and practice to enhance development.

For more on intervention in infancy and early childhood, see chapter 10.

Learning is a hypothetical construct and, as such, cannot be measured directly. How much or how little learning has taken place can be inferred only from performance. If a student points to the object that the teacher has just named or spells a word correctly, then we assume that learning has taken place. If the student performs the task incorrectly or does not attempt the task at all, then we assume that learning has not occurred. Since learning can be measured only indirectly, we must be cautious in interpreting performance levels as direct indicators of learning. A great many factors influence whether and how an individual responds in any situation. Given appropriate supports and services, the majority of students who are mildly retarded can be educated effectively. Moreover, many of these students can be included successfully in general education settings for all or most of the school day.

Cognitive Development

Quantitative Versus Qualitative Perspectives.   Use of the concept of mental age (MA) to express the level of cognitive functioning of a given individual has given rise to differing orientations from which to view the cognitive development of persons who are retarded. For example, cognitive development may be viewed as quantitative and comparable among individuals of similar MA, regardless of chronological age. This perspective, the *developmental position,* assumes that cognitive development, at least for the youngster who is mildly retarded, is similar to that of a younger child who is not retarded. According to Kail (1992), Tomporowski and Tinsley (1994), and Zigler (1999), such children progress through the same developmental levels in the same sequence as do children who are not retarded, although at a slower rate and lower level of ultimate functioning. Proponents of this point of view believe that children who are retarded fail because they are presented with tasks beyond their current ability level. Educational programs based on a developmental model would, therefore, use traditional teaching strategies but be geared primarily to the individual's MA. The developmental view of cognitive growth can be thought of as a series of steps or stages in which new tasks are presented only when the child reaches the level of mental ability appropriate to that task.

Proponents of the *difference position,* however, view the cognitive development of persons who are retarded as being qualitatively different from that of those who are not retarded. Ellis and Dulaney (1991) contended that there are differences in the ways in which these individuals process information and that the main task of re-

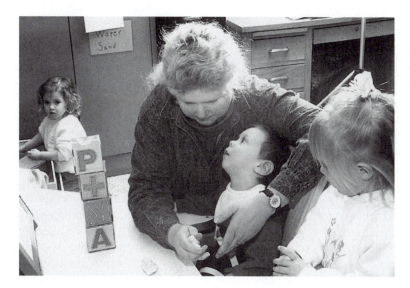

The degree of delayed development is generally related to the severity of the retardation and the presence of other inhibiting conditions.

search is to describe these areas of difference. The implications for teaching are that unique teaching methods and materials are needed to overcome or lessen the effects of the deficiency.

Research favoring one orientation over the other is plentiful. Firm conclusions, however, are difficult to reach because of the many variables that affect cognitive development (e.g., etiology of the retardation, motivational differences, problems associated with matching individuals based on MA). Regardless of one's position on this issue, the research in this area adds to our larger understanding of the learning process of individuals who are retarded.

Cognitive-Developmental Theory. Since much of the developmentally oriented research is based on Piaget's theory of carefully sequenced stages of development, we now briefly present this theory along with its application for learners who are retarded. We will describe some learning processes where distinctions between learners who are retarded and learners who are not retarded have been noted.

The original tenets of cognitive-developmental theory were formulated by Jean Piaget, based on observations of his own ("normal") children. He viewed mental development as a result of the continuous interaction with and adaptation to the environment, or the child's perception of it. According to Piaget (1969), each child progresses through stages of development in which various cognitive skills are acquired. The main stages of development, along with approximate age norms, are as follows:

1. Sensorimotor stage—birth to 2 years
2. Preoperational stage—2 to 7 years
3. Concrete operations—7 to 11 years
4. Formal, or abstract, operations—11 years and older

The sensorimotor stage is characterized by sensory experiences and motor activity. As young children become more aware of the surrounding environment, they begin to distinguish between themselves and other persons and objects. The second stage, preoperational, involves more than purely physical operations. Children begin to use symbols for the people and objects around them, assimilate customs, and acquire new experiences by imitating the actions of others. During the concrete operations stage, children develop further abilities to order and classify objects. Although their mental operations are more highly developed, children are usually limited to solving problems with which they have had direct or concrete experience. The ability to perform abstract thinking and reason by hypothesis is said to develop around the age of 11 or 12 and characterizes the formal operations, or abstract, stage.

Piagetian theory has been applied to children with mental retardation by Inhelder (1968) and Woodward (1963, 1979), who view these children as progressing through the same stages of cognitive development as their typically developing peers, with the major differences being in rate and highest level achieved. The age at which a child who is retarded will reach each stage will be later, and the more severe the retardation, the slower the progression through the stages. In addition, individuals who are mentally retarded may not achieve all stages of development. According to Inhelder, children who are mildly mentally retarded may reach the concrete operations level, but individuals who have been called moderately retarded will go no further than the preoperational stage. Those who are severely or profoundly retarded will remain at the sensorimotor level.

According to Piagetian theory, mental development progresses as a result of children's interactions with their surroundings. The educator's role, therefore, is that of a provider of materials and opportunities, appropriate to children's stage of development, with which they can interact. Teachers of students who are retarded need to be aware of the developmental sequences to determine a child's readiness for a particular task and to consider the rate and the expected optimal level of functioning when planning curricula for children with varying levels of retardation.

Processes Involved in Learning

Individuals who are mentally retarded, by definition, perform below average on tests of intelligence and are slow and inefficient learners. Whether one subscribes to the developmental or difference model of cognitive functioning, the practical issue of providing an optimal learning environment remains. Toward this end, a vast amount of research has been conducted in the area of learning and applied to individuals who are retarded. Most researchers have concentrated their efforts on one aspect of learning, such as attention or memory. In generalizing the findings to educational programming, however, we must emphasize that implications from various theories relating to separate aspects of learning should be used in combination to offer learners who are retarded the best opportunities for realizing their potential.

The major processes that are discussed in this section include attention variables, mediation strategies, and memory. The major features of these and other processes, along with the implications for instruction, are summarized in Table 8.5. The discussion that follows details some of the relevant research in these areas.

TABLE 8.5

Characteristics and Implications of Mental Retardation

Domain	Representative Problem Areas	Instructional Implications
Attention	Attention span (length of time on task) Focus (inhibition of distracting stimuli) Selective attention (discrimination of important stimulus characteristics)	Train students to be aware of importance of attention. Teach students how to actively monitor their attention (i.e., self-monitoring). Highlight salient cues.
Use of mediational strategies	Production of strategies to assist learning Organizing new learning	Teach specific strategies (rehearsal, labeling, chunking). Involve student in active learning process (practice, apply, review). Stress meaningful content.
Memory	Short-term memory (i.e., seconds over minutes)—common deficit area Long-term memory—usually more similar to persons who are nondisabled (once information has been learned)	Because strategy production is difficult, students need to be shown how to use strategies in order to proceed in an organized, well-planned manner. Stress meaningful content.
Generalization learning	Applying knowledge or skills to new tasks, problems, or situations Using previous experience to formulate rules that will help solve problems of a similar nature	Teach in multiple contexts. Reinforce generalization. Teach skills in relevant contexts. Remind students to apply what they have learned.
Motivational considerations	External locus of control (attributing events to others' influence) Outer-directedness (in learning style) Lack of encouragement to achieve and low expectation of others Failure set (personal expectation of failure)	Create environment focused on success experiences. Emphasize self-reliance. Promote self-management skills. Teach learning strategies for academic tasks. Focus on learning to learn. Encourage problem-solving strategies (versus only correct responses).
Cognitive development	Ability to engage in abstract thinking Symbolic thought, as exemplified by introspection and developing hypotheses	Provide concrete examples in instruction. Provide contextual learning experiences. Encourage interaction between students and the environment, being responsive to their needs so that they may learn about themselves as they relate to people and objects around them. *(Continued)*

TABLE 8.5
Continued

Domain	Representative Problem Areas	Instructional Implications
Language development	Delayed acquisition of vocabulary and language rules Possible interaction with cultural variance and language dialects Speech disorders (more common than in general population)	Create environment that facilitates development and encourages verbal communication. Provide appropriate language models. Provide opportunities for students to use language for a variety of purposes with different audiences. Differentiate cultural variance or language delay or difficulties. Encourage student speech and active participation.
Academic development	Delayed acquisition of reading, writing, and mathematical skills, decoding and comprehension of text Problem-solving difficulties in mathematics	Use learning strategies to promote effective studying. Promote literacy acquisition. Teach sight words with emphasis on functional applications (see Polloway, Miller, & Smith, 2003). Teach strategies for decoding unknown words and place skills in context of literacy development (Katims, 2001). Provide strategies to teach reading comprehension and math problem solving. Adapt curriculum to promote success.
Sociobehavioral considerations	Social adjustment Social perception and awareness Self-esteem Peer acceptance Suggestibility Classroom behavioral difficulties (e.g., disruptions, lack of involvement)	Promote social competence through direct instruction in social skills. Reinforce appropriate behaviors. Seek an understanding of reasons for inappropriate behavior. Involve peers as classroom role models. Program for social acceptance. Use peers in reinforcing interventions.

Source: From *Teaching Students with Special Needs in Inclusive Settings* (4th ed., p. 240), by T. E. C. Smith, E. A. Polloway, J. R. Patton, & C. A. Dowdy, 2004, Boston: Allyn & Bacon. Copyright © 2004 by Pearson Education. Reprinted by permission of the publisher.

Attention.   In any learning situation, **selective attention,** the ability to attend to the relevant aspects of the task at hand and discard the irrelevant aspects, and **sustained attention,** the ability to maintain one's concentration long enough to process and comprehend the information, are critical for successful learning. Attention has been described in a variety of ways but most teachers think of it in terms of selective and sustained attention. Teachers often refer to students who have problems in selective attention as being *distractible* and to students who have problems in sustained attention as having *short attention spans*. Krupski (1986, 1987) contended that the ability to attend or the quality of attention was the result of the interaction of three variables: (1) the child, (2) the setting, and (3) the task.

Typically, individuals who are retarded have difficulty with attention. Many researchers have attributed this difficulty to differences in information processing capacities; others have described it as problems in concentration or memory. Zeaman and House (1963) conducted much of the early research on attention, hypothesizing that individuals who are retarded differ from individuals who are not retarded in their selective attention. Their research found that individuals who are retarded required more trials to select the relevant dimension (color, shape, size) of a two-choice discrimination task. They concluded that individuals who are retarded require more time to learn to attend to the relevant dimensions of a task. In updating their theory, Zeaman and House (1979) noted a relationship between MA and the number of dimensions that a participant could attend to simultaneously. Learners who were retarded could not attend to as many dimensions simultaneously as could participants who were not retarded. This is particularly important if, as Brooks and McCauley (1984) maintained, such learners have less attention to allocate to "all domains of information processing" (p. 482). The research of Zeaman and House continues to generate investigations of selective attention in individuals who are retarded. The results of these studies have been mixed. Generally, however, researchers have found that these individuals are less able than individuals who are not retarded to perceive, select, and group relevant stimuli and discard irrelevant stimuli (Cha, 1992; Cha & Merrill, 1994; Eriksen & Yeh, 1985).

The results of studies of sustained attention have indicated that when required to make comparisons between the relevance of a task, individuals who are retarded exhibit a more rapid decline in vigilance than do individuals who are not retarded (Tomporowski & Simpson, 1990). Researchers have concluded that these differences are related to differences in information processing abilities (Tomporowski & Hager, 1992).

The instructional implications of this research include that teachers of individuals who are retarded should (1) present initial stimuli that vary in only a few dimensions, (2) direct the individual's attention to these critical dimensions, (3) initially remove extraneous stimuli that may distract the individual from attending, (4) increase the difficulty of the task over time, and (5) teach the student decision-making rules for discriminating relevant from irrelevant stimuli.

Grouping and Mediation Strategies.   After attending to a specific stimulus, an individual must organize and store it so that it can be recalled when needed. Spitz (1966) refers to this process as *input organization* and has conducted research to determine the functioning in this area of persons who are mentally retarded.

Spitz's (1966) research led him to theorize that the input step in the learning process was more difficult for subjects who were retarded than for other subjects, because of a deficiency in their ability to organize the input stimuli for storage and recall. This finding generated a great deal of research into strategies that teachers may use to enhance a student's ability to categorize incoming data. Two such methods are *grouping* and *mediation*.

Spitz (1973, 1979) sees **grouping,** or clustering material prior to its presentation, as more beneficial to the learner who is retarded than presenting material in random order. Restructuring the perceptual field for individuals who characteristically have difficulty at this stage of the learning process should facilitate memory and recall. Grouping is perhaps the simplest method of organizing information. Material may be grouped spatially, in different visual arrangements; temporally, with a pause or time lapse between items; perceptually, with certain items enclosed in a shape or configuration; or categorically, by content or commonality of items.

Stephens (1966) has further broken down the categories of grouping by content into physical similarity (e.g., items of the same color), function (e.g., articles of clothing), concepts (e.g., plants, animals), and sequential equivalence (e.g., subjects and objects as used in grammatical arrangements). Work by Stephens (1972) in presenting stimuli according to types of grouping indicates that the most basic type of grouping is that of physical similarity. As a child increases in MA, more advanced grouping strategies are used. This same progression was reported for subjects who were not retarded as well as for subjects who were mildly retarded.

A *mediator* is something that goes between or connects. In verbal learning, **mediation** refers to the process by which an individual connects a stimulus and a response. One approach to the study of verbal learning, *paired associate learning,* focuses on verbal mediation as a means of learning responses to stimulus words or elements. In this technique, the subject is generally presented with pairs of words. Then only the first word in each pair is repeated, and the subject tries to recall the second. Verbalizing the connection between the two stimulus words seems to enhance performance. In studies reviewed by Meyers and MacMillan (1976), researchers noted marked improvements in tasks of this type, even by subjects who were retarded, when the subjects were instructed in mediation strategies or provided with such mediators as sentences relating the stimulus to the response. The meaningfulness of the material and the use of stimulus words or objects familiar to the subject (Estes, 1970) also facilitated learning in paired associate tasks.

Several implications for teaching can be drawn from this research. First, materials presented to learners who are retarded should be familiar or have some relevance for them. Second, information should be grouped or organized into meaningful parts. Finally, such learners should be instructed in mediation strategies.

Memory.   Memory, the ability to retrieve information that has been stored, is one of the most heavily researched components of the learning process. As one would expect, individuals who are retarded tend to perform less well on tasks of memory than do their age- or grade-level peers. Moreover, the more severely retarded the individual, the greater the deficit in memory displayed.

Researchers have hypothesized that the root of memory problems in individuals who are retarded may be related to a lack of selective attention (Westling & Fox, 2000); inefficient or nonexistent rehearsal strategies (Brooks & McCauley, 1984); delay in developing learning sets (Merrill, 1990); or an inability to generalize learned skills to new settings, with different people, or in different ways (Stephens, 1972).

Polloway, Patton, and Serna, L. (2005) stated that an inability to generalize skills hampers the ability of individuals who are retarded to be more independent and reduces their need for external supports.

Early researchers of memory processes usually made a distinction between *short-term memory (STM)* and *long-term memory (LTM)*. Information recalled after a period of days or months or longer is usually referred to as being in LTM, whereas data stored from a few seconds to a few hours are in STM. Most early researchers contended that once learned, information is retained over the long term about as well by those who are retarded as by those who are not (Belmont, 1966; Ellis, 1963). In the area of STM, however, early researchers concluded that learners who are retarded appeared to have considerable difficulty (Borkowski, Peck, & Damberg, 1983; Ellis, 1963). Swanson and Cooney (1991) hypothesize that the memory function in learners with mild disabilities is developmentally delayed. Merrill (1990) found that learners with mental retardation required more time than their age-mates to reach levels of automaticity and fluency in memory processes and thus were less able to handle large chunks of cognitive information at one time.

Smith, Polloway, Patton, and Dowdy (2004) recommended stressing meaningful content and using specific strategy instruction to teach students to proceed in an organized, planned manner. Belmont and Butterfield (1971) and Brown, Campione, and Murphy (1974) reported success in efforts to improve STM performance among these learners, by direct teaching or by rehearsal or practice procedures, although the effects of the training appeared to be specific to the training task at hand and not readily transferable to other situations (Belmont & Butterfield, 1977).

The major rehearsal strategies noted by Mercer and Snell (1977) in their review of studies of STM were verbal rehearsal and image rehearsal. *Verbal rehearsal* relates to the concept of self-instruction and refers to labeling aspects of a task and verbalizing these labels aloud or silently while the task is being performed. In *image rehearsal,* a form of visualization, the individual is taught to associate aspects of a task with pictures of events that will help to recall them.

Drew, Hardman, and Hart (1996) and Dunn (1973) criticize the early research on memory problems in individuals with retardation as plagued with methodological problems that made interpretation difficult, and they note that currently, researchers of memory processes have moved toward an *information processing* model. Sternberg (1997) noted that information processing researchers investigate how individuals acquire, process, and use sensory stimuli.

Executive control and *metacognition* are components of an information processing model. These two terms apply to the process one consciously goes through to determine the need for a strategy, analyze a problem, anticipate outcomes of various actions, select a strategy to solve the problem, and monitor progress toward the solution (Raymond, 2000). Researchers have noted that learners who are retarded generally do not spontaneously employ executive control processes (Brown, 1974; Merrill, 1990; Sternberg & Spear, 1985), but that they can be taught to use them effectively (Borkowski et al., 1983; Sternberg, 1997). Other teaching techniques to facilitate recall include (1) organizing material into meaningful segments, (2) using reinforcement and incentives for remembering, (3) modeling use of appropriate strategies, (4) using spaced and repeated practice, (5) reminding and encouraging the learner to use rehearsal strategies, and (6) using reconstructive elaborations.

Observational Learning

Modeling, imitation, and *learning through observation* are the terms most often associated with *observational learning,* which refers to learning from demonstrations by others. Much of the research in this area has been done by Bandura (1986) and his associates. It substantiates the important role that observational learning plays in acquiring social behaviors, gender roles, language, and religious and political practices. In addition, modeling and imitation are involved in the development of new behaviors and the modification of existing ones, and they may result in the learning of inappropriate as well as appropriate responses.

Certain characteristics of individuals who have mental retardation give support to the use of this tool to teach new behaviors. The tendency of these learners to be outer-directed or look to others for cues or guidance in problem solving (Turnure & Zigler, 1964) and their suggestibility (Zigler, 1999) indicate that modeling can be effectively used for acquiring or changing behavior. Suggestions for using observational learning as a teaching tool include (1) being aware that any behavior may serve as a model, (2) using prompts or cues to direct students' attention, (3) calling attention to students who exhibit desirable behavior, (4) ignoring undesirable behavior so that others do not model it in an attempt to gain attention, and (5) rewarding imitation of appropriate behavior.

SPEECH AND LANGUAGE CHARACTERISTICS

Speech and language problems occur with greater frequency among individuals identified as mentally retarded than among those not so identified (Bernstein & Tiegerman, 1993; Warren & Abbeduto, 1992). This is not unexpected, since cognitive ability and language development are closely related. The speech problems most often seen are difficulties in articulation, voice, and stuttering (Hardman, Drew, & Egan, 1996). Common articulation errors include the substitution, omission, addition, or distortion of sounds, which make speech less intelligible. Language disorders that commonly accompany mental retardation include delayed language development and a restricted or limited active vocabulary (Spradlin, 1968). Language is so important to independent functioning that prospective parents, parents of high-risk children, and day care personnel should be trained in various means of encouraging language development.

As corroboration of the evidence that students who are mildly retarded display lower overall functioning than those classified similarly before the passage of P.L. 94–142 (the Education for All Handicapped Children Act of 1975), we see an increasing occurrence of secondary handicapping conditions (MacMillan, 1989; MacMillan & Borthwick, 1980). For example, Epstein and colleagues (1989) gathered information from the individualized education programs (IEPs) of 107 children identified as mildly retarded and receiving special education in northern Illinois. Speech and language problems were the most frequent secondary disability; well over half the students were eligible for and receiving speech and language therapy. Language deficits may be related to such factors as absence of or limited adequate speech and language models and less encouragement to use language. A disproportionate number of students who are mildly retarded are also members of cultural or ethnic minorities (U.S. Department of Education, 2003), which may also play a role in the language deficiencies found in this population.

Research on the language abilities of individuals who are retarded offers some interesting findings. Abbeduto and Nuccio (1991) studied the receptive language abilities of this group and found that students who were retarded focused on the formal, sequential aspects of spoken language rather than on its semantic, conceptual aspects. Individuals who were not retarded demonstrated the latter abilities. In a study on the use of repair behaviors (i.e., the speaker's effort to make an utterance understood when a listener indicates a problem in understanding), Scudder and Tremain (1992) found that students who were retarded displayed appropriate repair behaviors. However, as situations became more demanding, students who were retarded did not reuse effective strategies and became more frustrated.

Among those whose needs are more pronounced, speech and language disorders are even more common, because of not only their decreased intellectual development but also the increased possibility of concomitant disabling conditions. The motor dysfunction accompanying cerebral palsy, for example, can seriously impede the ability to produce intelligible speech. A higher prevalence of hearing impairment also exists in this population, and poor hearing affects articulation and may contribute to a further delay in the acquisition of language. Many students, especially those with Down syndrome, have frequent bouts of middle-ear infections during their childhood years (Pueschel, 1997). The conductive hearing loss these infections can cause also delays language and creates speech problems (Balkany, Downs, Jafek, & Krajicek, 1979).

One of the features typically found in the child with Down syndrome is a protruding tongue. Tongue reduction surgery, often in combination with facial surgery, has become increasingly common as a means of diminishing some of the more obvious characteristics (see Box 8.2). The usefulness of such surgery in improving speech, however, is dubious. Lemperle and Rada (1980) report more intelligible speech for a majority of 63 children with Down syndrome after undergoing surgery, although no formal speech evaluations were conducted. In other studies, Olbrisch (1982) and Lemperle (1985) sent questionnaires to families of children who had received tongue reduction surgery and reported that 88% and 68%, respectively, of the parents perceived speech improvement. Parsons, Iacone, and Rozner (1987) took formal speech assessment measures before surgery, 4 weeks after surgery, and again 6 months after surgery with 27 children with Down syndrome. The number of articulation errors did not differ significantly across time, although the parents were almost unanimous in perceiving speech improvement.

Box 8.2   ❖   Changing the Look of Mental Retardation

Plastic surgeons can straighten the slanted eyes, build up the cheekbones, and minimize the protruding tongue commonly found in children with Down syndrome. But should they? Plastic surgery remains the most controversial treatment offered Down syndrome children.

The 1½- to 2½-hour operation is fairly straightforward. Surgeons can build up the bridge of the nose, cheekbone, and chin with bone grafts or synthetics, change the slant of the eyes and cut fat from the lower eyelids. There are usually no facial scars because the work is done through the mouth or by cutting skin flaps behind the hairline. The tongue, which appears too large and protrudes from an unusually small mouth, is reduced by about one-fifth. Advocates of surgery believe that children with

Down syndrome are rejected partly because of their physical features, and that improving their appearance may result in greater social acceptance. Critics respond that there is little hard evidence that surgery has these effects. In fact, it has to be admitted that even the most gifted plastic surgeons can't make a child with Down syndrome look entirely normal. After surgery, the gait, neck, and body proportions are still unusual. Even the face remains clearly different. "I've yet to see a child after the operation," says Diane Crutcher of the National Down Syndrome Congress, "who doesn't look like a child with Down syndrome." Moreover, say some critics, the surgery is itself a kind of rejection, a message that the children are not acceptable as themselves. It is society's preoccupation with "good looks" that should

Before and after: Advocates of surgery say it reduces the stigma often associated with Down syndrome. Critics say it sends the message that the children are unacceptable in appearance as they are.

Photos courtesy of Dr. Kenneth Salyer, Dallas, Texas.

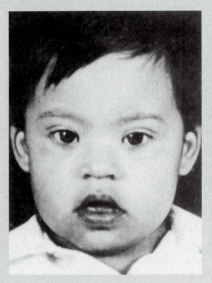
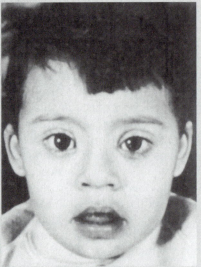

PHYSICAL HEALTH CHARACTERISTICS

In general, the physical health characteristics and needs of persons who are mildly retarded do not differ dramatically from those of other individuals. More pronounced physical and health concerns, however, tend to co-occur in individuals who are more severely retarded. The following discussion highlights selected conditions of retardation as well as general health considerations that have specific implications for individuals who are retarded.

change, these critics argue, not the faces of children with Down syndrome.

Even those who advocate the operation admit that not every child with Down syndrome is a good candidate for surgery, and both parents and child must go through an intensive screening process before their surgeon lifts a scalpel. "The surgery should be performed only in children whose quality of life can be improved by the procedures," cautions Garry S. Brody, clinical professor of plastic surgery at the University of Southern California. Surgery is immediately ruled out if the child is profoundly retarded or has life-threatening physical problems. In addition, parents must be realistic about what the surgery will and won't do. "If you think the child is going to roll out of the operating room with 20 more IQ points," says Crutcher, "you're going to be disappointed."

While controversial, plastic surgery remains an option for those willing to try every avenue. The American Society of Plastic and Reconstructive Surgeons operates a toll-free number (800/635-0635) for information on reconstructive and cosmetic surgery for Down syndrome, and offers a referral list of board-certified plastic surgeons qualified to perform the operation.

Source: From "Special Talents," by C. Turkington, 1987, *Psychology Today,* September, p. 45. Reprinted with permission from Psychology Today Magazine, copyright © 1987 (Sussex Publishers, Inc.).

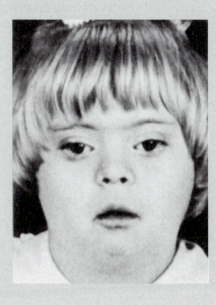 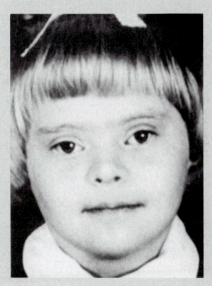

Motor and Sensory Development

We begin with motor development, which even in those who are mildly retarded may be delayed and markedly less accomplished than in the child who is not retarded. Motor deficits include problems of balance, locomotion, and manipulative dexterity (Bruininks, 1974). The growth rate may be slower, and these individuals may be shorter and lighter than children who are not retarded (Bruininks, 1974; Mosier, Grossman, & Dingman, 1965). Reschly, Robinson, Volmer, and Wilson (1988) demonstrated that, as the severity of retardation increases, so do problems in motor skills areas; this relationship is depicted in Table 8.6.

Sensory defects are also more common among individuals who are retarded, with visual and auditory problems frequently noted (Barlow, 1978). Color blindness appears to be more prevalent among individuals who are moderately retarded than among those who are more mildly retarded or who are not retarded (O'Connor, 1975). Early screening for sensory defects is essential, as specific correctional devices or types of intervention may be indicated. In fact, early identification of any health problems may be critical to the child's total development. Although the retardation itself may obscure problems or impede efforts to diagnose health problems, early intervention and treatment may lessen the effects of the disability and influence the rate and level of development the child may attain.

Selected Conditions

Down Syndrome.   A child who is retarded may be classified as a clinical type. To be regarded as a specific clinical type, an individual must show certain facial, body, and disorder characteristics relating to a particular syndrome associated with mental retardation. There are a number of these syndromes, but the one most frequently associated with mental retardation is Down syndrome.

Besides their distinct physical appearance, children with Down syndrome frequently have specific health-related problems. Many have structural defects of the heart that may threaten their survival, although surgical procedures can be successful in correcting the defect. Lung abnormalities are also frequent in children with

TABLE 8.6

Analysis of Motor Skills Across IQ Levels

IQ	N	$\bar{X}$*	s.d.	Total with Weaknesses[†] N	%
<50	39	2.10	1.07	29	74
50–54	33	2.18	1.10	23	70
55–59	35	2.46	1.07	17	49
60–64	52	2.48	0.96	25	48
65–69	59	2.53	0.95	24	41
70–74	121	3.08	0.91	26	21
75–79	155	2.95	0.88	40	26
80–84	118	2.97	0.85	30	25

* Mean scores were derived from a Likert rating scale that used the anchor points of 1 = Significant Weakness, 2 = Weakness, 4 = Strength, and 5 = Significant Strength.

[†]Total was formed by the sum of the Significant Weakness and Weakness ratings.

Source: From *Iowa Mental Disabilities Research Project: Final Report and Executive Summary,* by D. Reschly, G. Robinson, L. Volmer, & L. Wilson, 1988, Des Moines: State of Iowa, Department of Education. Copyright © 1988 by State of Iowa, Department of Education. Reprinted by permission.

Down syndrome, resulting in susceptibility to upper respiratory infections. The incidence of leukemia is higher than in the normal population. Other common health problems of children with Down syndrome are eye and ear infections, obesity, skin problems (primarily due to their characteristically rough and dry skin), problems of the teeth and gums, and hearing impairments (Pueschel, 1997).

Individuals who work with children with Down syndrome should be alert to signs of infection, particularly ear and upper respiratory infections, so that early medical treatment can prevent more serious problems. Physical education and exercise programs should also be provided, although the type and amount of activity required of a particular child should be planned with the guidance of medical personnel.

Cerebral Palsy. Not all children with cerebral palsy are mentally retarded (Pellegrino, 1997); however, a child who does have this condition presents a number of health-related problems. Cerebral palsy is a neuromuscular disability that may result from damage to the brain at birth or during the first 4 years of life. While the condition may include any number of intellectual, sensory, and behavioral disorders, the motor disability presents several potential problems. Because of fluctuating muscle tone, hypertonicity, or hypotonicity, children with cerebral palsy may exhibit atypical posture and movements that limit their participation in learning activities. Limbs that are not exercised may lose their usefulness altogether. Children with cerebral palsy, therefore, usually require professional assistance in handling and positioning. Some children may be in movement or exercise programs that need to be repeated at certain intervals during the day. According to Rainforth and York (1991), the goals of positioning assistance include stabilizing the body, maintaining proper body alignment, and increasing participation in learning activities. Professionals working with a child who wears a brace or cast should be alert to such signs of circulation problems as swelling, coldness, change of color, and evidence of infection, as well as other skin problems.

Individuals working with youngsters who are retarded and have cerebral palsy must be aware of a number of other problems that sometimes accompany the disorder. Speech difficulties complicated by lack of muscle control are common and often require speech therapy or other special educational measures. Visual and auditory problems are also seen more frequently in the child with cerebral palsy, and corrective measures to improve vision or hearing may be warranted. Difficulties with chewing and swallowing may present real hazards if the child is given foods such as hard candy, popcorn, or chewing gum. Teachers should consult the parents for specific instructions about eating and drinking. As with other disabilities, upper respiratory infections are common, and early symptoms should be reported, since the consequences of such infections may be severe.

Seizure Disorders. Seizures are a health problem often associated with cerebral palsy, but they are also characteristic of other conditions that may accompany mental retardation (Freeman, Vining, & Pillas, 1997). Because seizure disorders are significantly more common among individuals who are retarded than among individuals who are not, teachers working with these individuals should be trained to respond appropriately and be aware of the possible side effects of seizure control medication (Epstein et al., 1989).

Seizures vary from momentary disturbances, which may go unnoticed (absence, or petit mal), to episodes involving jerking of the muscles and loss of consciousness (tonic-clonic seizure, or grand mal). Some children experience an aura of sensation just before a seizure begins and may be able to give some indication that it is imminent. In some children, the likelihood of a seizure is increased by external factors, such as flickering lights or loud sounds, or the child's physical condition, such as being highly excited, ill, or fatigued. By being aware of these cues, teachers can be alert to circumstances that might precede or precipitate seizures.

Once a seizure occurs, it should not be interrupted. The major concern is to keep the child from injuring him- or herself. During a tonic-clonic (grand mal) seizure, the child should be eased to the floor, furniture and other objects pushed away, and, if possible, restrictive clothing loosened and the child turned on his or her side to aid breathing. Someone should remain with the child until the seizure ends and then allow the child to rest.

Substance Abuse.   Until recently, little was written on this topic as it pertains to individuals who are retarded, and the common perception was that this group was less likely to have problems than those without retardation (Ferrara, 1992). Although some studies support this perception (Christian & Poling, 1997; Delaney & Poling, 1990), reason for concern persists. Other sources suggest that problems associated with substance abuse, when it does occur, may arise more quickly and at lower levels of drug use for this group (Resource Center on Substance Abuse Prevention and Disabilities, 1992). This finding is extremely disturbing, given the fact that more individuals with retardation live in communities where this threat is widespread.

General Health Considerations

Nutrition.   Proper kinds and amounts of food are necessary for the general well-being of all children. Poor diet not only arrests biological development and diminishes resistance to disease and illness but is also a negative factor in social adjustment and academic learning (Cohen, 2000). Inadequate or unbalanced diets may be a result of insufficient food, poor supervision of meals and snacks, or lack of understanding of the importance of proper nutrition and how to provide it.

Illness and Disease.   As might be expected, children with retardation are more susceptible to disease and illness than their typically developing peers. Poor nutrition and lack of adequate health care (including immunizations) appear to be major factors in promoting problems among children from lower socioeconomic classes. Children who are mildly retarded often have additional disabling conditions or health problems that account for their relatively poor health. The frequency of heart and lung disorders among Down syndrome children is just one example.

Several specific problems are commonly noted among children who are retarded. Colds and upper respiratory infections are more frequent and often last longer than in other children. The seriousness of the symptoms can be compounded by the presence of other disorders such as cardiac conditions.

The incidence of dental problems is also relatively high among children who have mental retardation. Dental problems are often due to poor nutrition, failure to brush teeth properly or regularly, or absence of routine dental checkups.

Accidents and Injury.   Children who are developmentally delayed, as already indicated, can be poorly coordinated and awkward. Add to this the poor judgment and impaired reasoning that may come with subaverage intellectual ability, and a higher than average accident rate can be predicted. Conditions accompanying the retardation—limited vision, muscle weakness, motor disabilities, and seizures—may also contribute to increased injuries. This group can also suffer physical injury due to abuse (Zirpoli, 1986).

Physical Activity.   A certain amount of exercise and activity is necessary for the total well-being of any individual. For the child with mental retardation, a planned program of physical activity is essential for a number of reasons. Individuals who are mildly retarded may not differ appreciably in physical and motor skills from those who are not retarded, and sports and other physical activities may provide an opportunity for expression and achievements as well as an outlet for tension. Gains in physical strength and motor coordination as well as feelings of accomplishment often enhance social and personal adjustment.

While opportunities for physical education and recreation historically were neglected with respect to people who are mentally retarded (Chinn, Drew, & Logan, 1979), the current outlook is far more encouraging (Beasley, 1982; Halle, Silverman, & Regan, 1983). Provisions of the Individuals with Disabilities Education Act (IDEA) include not only physical education but also recreation and leisure education as related services that must be extended to all students. Community agencies and citizens' groups are becoming more actively involved in providing opportunities for recreation. The Special Olympics program remains a viable source of physical activity as well. Programs offered by colleges and universities designed to train professionals in techniques for working with students with disabilities in the area of physical education and recreation are increasing in number and scope.

EDUCATIONAL CHARACTERISTICS

In this section we examine various facets of the educational programs of students with mild retardation. Specifically, we focus on placement options, curricular and service issues, and performance characteristics.

Since the passage of P.L. 94-142, the Education for all Handicapped Children Act of 1975, Congress has required that all children with disabilities be served in the least restrictive environment (LRE). In accordance with the provisions of the Individuals with Disabilities Education Act (IDEA), recent data indicate that the general education classroom is LRE for the majority of students with disabilities. According to the U.S. Department of Education (2003), during the 1999–2000 school year, 95.5% of all students with disabilities were served in regular school buildings—and of those students, 47.3% were served in the general education class for 79% of the school day. This represents an 87.1% increase in the number of students with disabilities served in the general education class for 79% of the school day.

Companion Website *To learn about one student with mild intellectual disability, go to the Companion Website at www.prenhall.com/ beirne-smith and select Chapter 8, Video Case Studies.*

Although we have made progress in serving students with disabilities in more inclusive environments, the trend does not hold for all groups or categories of students. Elementary students are more likely than secondary students to be served in general education classrooms. Students with mental retardation are considerably less likely than students with learning disabilities and speech or language impairments to be served in the general education classrooms for the majority of the school day and—second only to students who are emotionally disturbed—are more likely to be served in separate public facilities.

Programmatic Realities

Preparing students to deal successfully with the demands of adulthood and to live as independently as possible should be the primary goals of any program. The particular demands of adulthood for which one needs to be prepared will vary somewhat depending on probable subsequent environments. Moreover, the nature of the program will also be influenced by the individual's level of schooling (i.e., elementary versus secondary). The emphasis of curriculum will change as a function of school level and needs of the individual. Figure 8.1 illustrates a two-dimensional (curricular approach and level of schooling) model for deciding the nature of instructional programs. Fundamentally, programs must develop a student's competence in the following areas: employment or further education, home and family, leisure pursuits, community involvement, physical and emotional health, personal responsibility, and interpersonal relationships (Cronin & Patton, 1993).

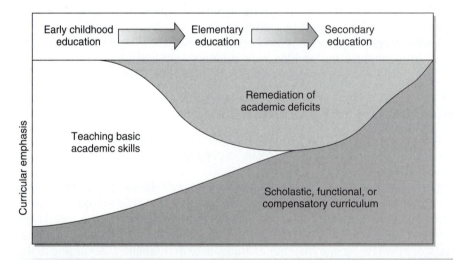

FIGURE 8.1

Curricular Emphasis Across Levels of Schooling

Source: Adapted from *Human Exceptionality: Society, School, and Family* (4th ed.), by M. L. Hardman, C. J. Drew, M. W. Egan, & B. Wolf, 1993, Boston: Allyn & Bacon. Copyright © 1993 by Allyn & Bacon. Adapted by permission.

Interestingly enough, however, while the literature favors a broad-based curriculum, studies of IEP goals for students who are mildly retarded indicate a strong emphasis on academic goals (Epstein et al., 1989; McBride & Forgnone, 1985). In light of the more recent descriptions of this population, it is not surprising that professionals in the field are calling for a more comprehensive approach to the education of students who are retarded, one that includes life skills preparation (Brolin, 1997; Cronin & Patton, 1993), social skills training (Gresham, 1982; Polloway et al., 1986), and vocational training (Brolin & Brolin, 1979; Edgar, 1987; Jaquish & Stella, 1986).

Related services are provided to students who have been identified as disabled to enable them to benefit fully from their educational program. It is likely that many individuals may have secondary impairments and will need additional related services. In the study by Epstein and colleagues (1989), the majority of the IEPs for students with mild retardation listed some type of secondary problem. Nearly 90% of the students had speech and language disorders; and sensory disorders (particularly visual impairment), convulsive disorders, and emotional and behavioral disorders were more common than in the general population. This study is consistent with other research (MacMillan, 1982; MacMillan & Borthwick, 1980) that characterizes many individuals who are mildly retarded as displaying multiple disabilities and therefore being in need of more related services and support personnel.

As inclusion becomes commonplace in our schools, we anticipate that more and more students with mild mental retardation will be provided services in general education settings. There is still a considerable amount of work that must be done to ensure that inclusion is successful. At a minimum, changes must be made in the personnel preparation programs of both general and special educators to provide these educators with the skills they need to ensure the success of *all* students who are educated in their classrooms.

Academic Achievement

Students who are retarded are likely to show deficits in all academic areas. The majority of students with mild retardation read at levels lower than expected for their MA, and of the various aspects of reading, comprehension appears to be the most difficult for them (Carter, 1975; Dunn, 1973). In mathematics, the majority of students can learn the basic computations; however, mathematical reasoning and appropriate application of concepts to problem-solving tasks are more difficult for this group. Functional arithmetic skills involving money, time, and measurement, because they are important for community living, are an integral part of the curriculum (Westling, 1986).

The school exit rate for students who are mentally retarded has remained fairly stable over the past 5 years. According to the U.S. Department of Education (1999), results of research studies on students with disabilities leaving school indicate that students who received vocational training during their secondary school years have achieved positive long-term results in terms of greater success at independent living, higher rates of employment, and greater community participation.

 *To check your understanding of this chapter, go to the Companion Website at www.prenhall.com/ beirne-smith and select Chapter 8, then choose the Self-Test module.*

Summary

Definition and Overview
- Not every person with mental retardation may display all the characteristics discussed in this chapter.
- This chapter focuses on individuals who require few or no supports systems in most adaptive skills areas.
- Those considered mentally retarded are part of a heterogeneous group.
- Individuals who have mild retardation have been referred to as *educable* or *trainable* in the past.

Demographic Characteristics
- More males than females are identified.
- Historically there have been a disproportionate number of racially different and ethnic minority children labeled as having mild mental retardation.
- Recent data support the description that many youth who with mental retardation live in blended families and come from families characterized by lower socioeconomic status.

Motivational and Sociobehavioral Characteristics
- Motivational characteristics include external locus of control, expectancy for failure, outer-directedness, and more limited self-regulatory behaviors.
- Social and behavioral problems are more likely among students who have mental retardation, with some students displaying psychiatric problems as well.

Learning Characteristics
- By definition, individuals with retardation have problems in cognitive areas; however, there is some difference of opinion whether cognitive development is qualitatively or quantitatively different from that of individuals who do not have retardation.
- Various processes associated with learning (attention, mediation strategies, memory) can be problematic for this group.

Speech and Language Characteristics
- Speech and language problems occur with great frequency among individuals who have retardation.
- Delayed language development frequently is a characteristic of individuals with retardation.

Physical Health Characteristics
- Motor development may be delayed in children with mental retardation.
- Sensory deficits are more common among persons with mental retardation.
- Individuals with Down syndrome have a number of physical features common to this condition.

- Cerebral palsy and seizure disorders occur more frequently in persons with mental retardation.
- The data on the extent of substance abuse in this group are equivocal at this time.

Educational Characteristics

- Students with mental retardation are being served more frequently in general education classrooms for greater portions of the school day.
- Studies of IEP goals indicate a predominance of academic goals.
- Many students with retardation qualify for related services.
- The school exit rate for students who have mental retardation has remained fairly stable over the past 5 years.

Characteristics of Persons with Severe Intellectual Disabilities

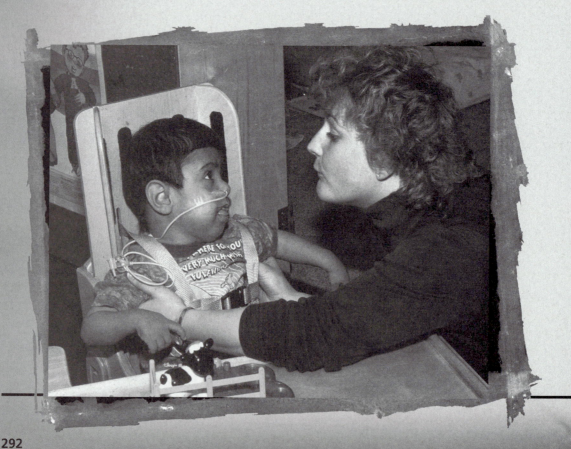

OBJECTIVES

After reading this chapter, the student should be able to:

- Explain basic demographic information about persons with severe intellectual disabilities
- Describe the physical and functional correlates of severe intellectual disabilities
- Identify and describe behavioral and emotional characteristics of persons with severe intellectual disabilities
- Discuss important educational concerns for persons with severe intellectual disability

KEY TERMS

behavior analysis

community-based instruction

community-referenced instruction

congenital conditions

full inclusion

functional assessment

functional curriculum

generalization

graduated guidance

outcomes-based assessment

task analysis

I n the previous chapter you were introduced to the group of people who comprise the majority of individuals with intellectual disability. But what about the rest? Who are they? What are they like? As the definition of mental retardation has changed throughout the years, so have social perceptions of persons with severe mental retardation. This chapter will consider some common characteristics of this population, including physical, functional, emotional, behavioral, communication, and educational considerations. Throughout the chapter, we will address some of the philosophical implications of education and treatment that have influenced the lives of persons with severe intellectual disabilities over the years.

SEVERE INTELLECTUAL DISABILITIES: DEFINITION AND OVERVIEW

Generally speaking, individuals who require more extensive supports than those described in the previous chapter are referred to as persons with severe intellectual disability. The "severe" label encompasses the groups specifically designated as having moderate, severe, and profound levels of mental retardation. This is quite a heterogeneous group with a wide array of abilities and limitations. TASH, the advocacy leader for persons with severe disabilities, offers the following description:

> [Severe mental retardation includes] individuals of all ages who require extensive ongoing support in more than one major life activity in order to participate in integrated community settings and to enjoy a quality of life that is available to citizens with fewer or no disabilities. Support may be required for life activities such as mobility, communication, self-care, and learning, and necessary for independent living, employment and self-sufficiency. (Lindley, 1990, p. 1)

People with severe intellectual disabilities often, but not always, have accompanying medical conditions that cause the mental retardation. Functionally, their abilities vary. Some are able to perform activities of daily living with a great deal of independence. Others require assistance in all areas, including eating, toileting, and changing position. In all, however, their disability is usually easily noticed and they require a great deal of support to attain their goals. Sometimes, it can even be difficult to determine what their goals are.

In this introductory section, we will discuss basic demographic information, as well as etiological and functional characteristics. Additionally, we will pause to consider how the bulk of the literature on education, supports, and interventions for people with mental retardation applies to this group.

Demographic Characteristics

Chapter 2 introduced the idea that the definitions of mental retardation are a reflection of the times in which they are drafted, that "people make of it what they want to, people interpret it in light of their own understandings and prejudices" (Blatt, 1987). People with more severe forms of intellectual disability have often suffered in the face of such perceptions. Miscalculation of their potential is documented throughout history. One need only look to such descriptions as provided by Goddard in 1920:

> Yet they are the persons who make for us our social problems. The emphasis here is on the word "incapable." This is the thing that we have heretofore ignored. We have known that these people *did not* compete successfully and that they *did not* manage their affairs with ordinary prudence, but we have not recognized that they were fundamentally *incapable* of so doing. (p. 5)

Unfortunately, the winds of change were slow to come. Nearly a half-century later, the same sentiment is reflected by another author: "The profoundly retarded individual is considered, on the basis of current knowledge and practices, incapable of profiting from any type of training or education" (Stevens, 1964, p. 4).

Why is the road to understanding the needs, capabilities, and *humanity* of these individuals so long? One reason may well be that it is difficult to understand that which we do not see. Besides the fact that individuals with severe forms of intellectual disability have known little community integration until recent times, our understanding is hampered by their status as a relatively rare segment of the population. As depicted in Figure 9.1, of the approximately 1% to 3% of the total U.S. population who have mental retardation, only about 15% experience the need for extensive supports. Specifically, about 10% are within the moderate range, with 3% in the severe range, and only about 2% in the profound range (American Psychiatric Association, 2000).

Severe forms of intellectual disability are generally recognized earlier in life than are the milder cases. More pronounced developmental delays and additional related medical conditions make this earlier diagnosis possible. Unlike the milder forms of intellectual disability, environmental deprivation is not usually an associated factor. Although certain associated prenatal factors, such as premature births, are more common in impoverished areas, the prevalence of the condition is relatively stable across all socioeconomic classes (APA, 2000).

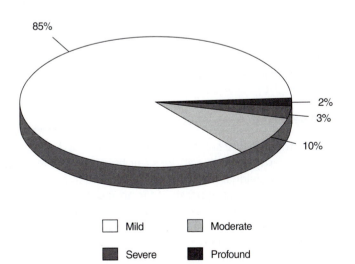

FIGURE 9.1

Breakdown of the Population with Mental Retardation

Source: Data taken from American Psychiatric Association (2000), pp. 43–44.

Physical Characteristics

For people with the most severe levels of intellectual disability, life is often complicated by the existence of concomitant conditions. Sometimes health and physical concerns are paramount, and the intensity of needed supports is much greater. The range of motor abilities for persons with severe intellectual disability ranges from very athletic to virtually immobile. Whereas some persons may be able to climb mountains, others may be unable to chew their food. Even the healthiest of individuals may have physical limitations that warrant extensive supports. For example, a person born without a right hand may require a prosthetic device, specially constructed tools and utensils, and extended time allowances for tasks requiring the use of two hands.

Biological conditions associated with mental retardation are discussed in chapter 6.

Medical conditions offer challenges for any person, regardless of talents or abilities. For people with severe intellectual disability, however, these challenges are often compounded by the inability to successfully communicate pain or discomfort. Additionally, they represent such a small segment of the population that their complex, specialized needs may not be especially well understood by health care providers.

A complete online glossary is available on the Companion Website, which may be accessed at www.prenhall.com/ beirne-smith

Health considerations for this group comprise both congenital conditions and acquired conditions. The term **congenital conditions** refers to those present from birth. Many of the disorders that result in mental retardation also cause physical and health problems, such as tumors, seizures, and organ failure. For such persons, medical concerns are usually chronic and sometimes intense.

Even those persons who do not have chronic congenital conditions may encounter significant difficulties when medical conditions are acquired. Illnesses that are fairly easily conquered in mainstream America may have more dire effects in persons with severe intellectual disability. Again, communication problems are often to blame. The inability to self-report feeling ill can result in benign illnesses progressing to more serious conditions before they are discovered. Even when the illness is known, other obstacles to overcome may include obtaining adequate nutrition, exercise, and hydration.

Oftentimes, the disorder that leads to intellectual disability also results in blindness, hearing impairment, deafness, or deaf-blindness. The impact of such disorders can be strong. Methods for teaching persons with sensory disorders must be integrated with methods for teaching people with intellectual disabilities in order to maximize each person's chances for successful living.

Functional Characteristics

It may seem logical to expect that as IQ decreases, the intensity of needed supports increases. This is often a valid assumption, but it does not hold true in every case. For example, it is possible for an individual who has an IQ below 50 to function with limited or intermittent supports, just as it is possible for an individual with an IQ above 55 to need extensive or pervasive supports. Though IQ is an integral part of the definition of mental retardation, it is generally not the most useful source of information about a person's needs and abilities.

While the range of skills and abilities possessed by individuals varies considerably, a few broad statements may be made about the functional characteristics of this group as a whole. People with severe levels of intellectual disability frequently have more than one disability, and they often have physical characteristics that draw attention. They learn new skills slowly and have difficulty applying knowledge gained in one context to another. They often have limited communication skills, and sometimes exhibit problem behaviors. It is important to note, though, that people with severe intellectual disabilities have a wonderful variety of personal attributes. Although progress may be slow, people with severe intellectual disabilities do learn—and they can form relationships based on love, fun, and common interests (Heward, 2002).

Having said all this, it is important to note that within this very small segment of the population there exists a great deal of heterogeneity. Much has been said in other chapters about the importance of adaptive behavior assessment. However, those assessments are based on information from very large groups of people, only a few of whom have severe intellectual disabilities. So, a person whose scores indicate profound mental retardation may be completely dependent on someone else for everything, including rolling over in bed, eating, and toileting. On the other hand, that person may be able to walk, talk, dress, and perform some household tasks. Therefore, the best way to understand the person's capabilities is to get to know the person.

See chapter 3 for a discussion of adaptive behavior assessment.

Philosophical Considerations

Most of the literature on mental retardation and special education was not written with this group in mind. When the earliest rumblings about instruction and training were made, the authors were really targeting people with mild to borderline levels of cognitive impairment. Likewise, the mid-20th century arguments about the right educational settings for students and the best residential arrangements for adults were by and large made for people with mild intellectual disabilities. It was really not until the late 20th century that anyone specifically turned attention to people with severe and profound mental retardation.

Should a child who cannot learn to read remain in a regular classroom? What if she cannot talk, or walk, or see, or hear? And if she needs help with toileting in the 7th grade? What if she eats through a gastronomy tube? After school, do we expect her to get a job? To live independently? How do her needs relate to the tenets of IDEA and No Child Left Behind? These are tough questions that get little attention outside the special interest groups that represent them.

Regardless of level of disability, the relationship between community access and skill development still exists. We simply cannot expect persons with severe intellectual disabilities to develop higher level skills unless they are involved with the community to which they are expected to conform. The more society is willing to invest in providing supports, the higher the likelihood that the individual will learn to function with less support. This is not to say that we can "cure" mental retardation. However, we can and should expect that the provision of meaningful supports will lead to improved outcomes over time (AAMR, 2002).

Later in this chapter we will return to the inclusion philosophy and its implications for persons with severe intellectual disabilities. For now, we will continue our examination of characteristics.

BEHAVIORAL AND EMOTIONAL CHARACTERISTICS

Over the years, much time and attention have been dedicated to assisting persons with intellectual disabilities to develop a repertoire of productive and socially adaptive behaviors. The ability to demonstrate appropriate behavior while inhibiting challenging behavior impacts many areas of a person's life (Hill & Bruininks, 1984; Larson, 1991; Reichle & Light, 1992). In addition to covering common behavioral issues, this section will describe the science of behavior analysis and the types of interventions commonly used to teach adaptive behaviors and reduce challenging behaviors. Additionally, we will address the issue of mental health in persons with severe intellectual disabilities.

Behavioral Issues

People with severe intellectual disabilities are likely to require assistance acquiring new skills, applying the skills they've already learned to new situations, and communicating their wants, needs, thoughts, and feelings (Heward, 2002). These skills are helpful in functioning successfully in the social world. For this reason, persons with severe intellectual disabilities are likely to concentrate a great deal of time on learning such adaptive skills (cf. Wehman & Kregel, 2004).

Compounding the problems associated with slower development of adaptive behaviors are the risks of developing challenging behaviors. People with severe intellectual disabilities sometimes develop difficult behaviors such as aggression and self-injury, as well as self-stimulatory behaviors like persistent rocking and hand flapping. However, the presence of severe intellectual disabilities should not be taken as the sole explanation for challenging behavior. Research has indicated that such behaviors are neither inevitable nor incorrigible in this population. Instead, they are strongly related to training and environmental circumstances (Luiselli & Cameron, 1998).

Although adaptive and challenging behaviors are generally thought to be separate constructs (Bruininks & McGrew, 1987), this is not to say they are unrelated. Challenging behaviors are often eliminated by teaching adaptive behaviors such as communication, choice making, and social skills (Horner & Carr, 1997; Reichle & Wacker, 1993; Van Houton & Axelrod, 1993). Additionally, both types of behavior have been shown to improve in enriched, accepting environments (Koegel, Koegel, & Dunlap, 1996).

Behavior Intervention

The idea that behavior and environment are related is nothing new. The work of psychologist B. F. Skinner (1953) first explained the relationship. Skinner termed the relationship *operant,* because the person voluntarily "operates" on the environment to get what he or she wants. The science of **behavior analysis**—the study of environmental events that change behavior—arose from Skinner's work. Behavior analysis is a logical tool for use with persons who have severe intellectual disabilities, because unlike other forms of psychological intervention, it does not require the person to report internal events such as thoughts and feelings that may be driving behavior. With behavior analysis, the psychologist is able to identify the events in the environment that are maintaining a behavior and manipulate them in order to encourage the development of new behaviors (Miller, 1997).

The usefulness of behavior analysis with persons who have severe forms of intellectual disability was further increased by the integration of functional assessment techniques. **Functional assessment** is a process of identifying the purpose, or function, of a given behavior in order to teach a more adaptive method of addressing that need. Although categorizations of behavioral function vary, the four functions presented by Iwata and colleagues (Iwata, Dorsey, Slifer, Bauman, & Richman, 1994; Iwata, Pace, et al., 1994) are commonly cited: social attention, escape from demand, access to tangible items such as food or toys, and self-stimulation or sensory reinforcement.

 For more information about functional assessment and many other topics discussed in this chapter, visit the Companion Website at www.prenhall/ beirne-smith and select Chapter 9, Web Destinations.

Functional assessment has become a widely accepted first step in developing behavior modification plans. The usefulness of the process is underscored by provisions of the Individuals with Disabilities Education Act (IDEA, 2004), which require that a functional assessment be conducted if a student with a disability is placed in an alternative educational setting for more than 10 days due to behavior. A functional assessment may involve direct observations of the student by a person trained in behavioral psychology, environmental manipulations in which the student's responses to various consequences are observed, or structured interviews with the student, his parents, or teachers (O'Neill, Horner, Albin, Storey, & Sprague, 1990).

Once a functional assessment has been completed, appropriate interventions may be developed. Many options are available for reducing challenging behaviors and increasing desired behaviors. Commonly, these interventions are based on the principles of *reinforcement*. That is, desired behaviors are reinforced, or followed by a pleasant consequence, while the desired consequence is withheld following challenging behaviors. For example, if a functional assessment indicates that Amy grabs people to get attention, attention would be withheld when she grabbed. In order to prevent her from developing new challenging behaviors, an appropriate method of gaining attention should be taught (Carr & Durand, 1985; Horner & Carr, 1997). For example, Amy could be given immediate attention for raising her hand, calling her teacher's name, or presenting a picture symbol.

Other forms of intervention are available that do not require direct training of the individual. Generally, such interventions involve making modifications to the person's environment (Horner & Carr, 1997). For example, if a functional assessment indicates that Bob only hits himself when he hears loud music, it makes sense to simply eliminate loud music from his environment. Similarly, behaviors identified as self-stimulatory may be addressed by giving the person access to alternative activities that provide the same sensory response (e.g., scheduling access to a trampoline for a person who jumps up and down). For people who engage in problem behaviors to access tangible items, providing noncontingent access to those items often eliminates the need for the person to engage in the behavior (Vollmer, Iwata, Zarcone, Smith, & Mazaleski, 1993).

A final note regarding problem behavior relates to the idea of life quality. People who live active, balanced lives have higher degrees of psychological and emotional health (Baroff, 1991). Simple adjustments regarding the exercise of personal choice or increased involvement with peers have often been shown to be successful

Quality of life will be discussed again in chapter 12.

"treatments" for problem behavior in this population (e.g., Horner, 1980; Koegel et al., 1996). When conducting behavioral assessments, it is important to consider such factors as personal choice making, involvement in reciprocal relationships, and active engagement in fun and meaningful activities.

Mental Health

Mental health is a dynamic construct. At times, most people experience emotional difficulties that result in transient problems. People with severe intellectual disabilities are no exception. Levitas and Gilson (2001) proposed a list of 16 stressors that commonly occur in the lives of persons with mental retardation and may result in a mental health crisis. Included in the list are occurrences such as the birth of siblings, being "surpassed" by siblings, starting and ending school, psychosocial and sexual maturation and the accompanying issues of sex and dating, and typical life and relationship transitions through the processes of aging, moving on, and death.

Additionally, in today's philosophical climate of encouraging productivity and independence, people with severe intellectual disabilities may feel pressure to "function at maximum performance and behavioral level at all times" (Levitas & Gilson, 2001). This can be an overwhelmingly stressful way of life. It is very important that educators, families, and caregivers are sensitive to this issue. It is often a reality that people with intellectual disabilities, perhaps because they are often reliant upon others for social cuing, are held to higher standards of behavior than the rest of the world.

The issue of dual diagnosis, as discussed in chapter 8, has implications for individuals with severe intellectual disabilities as well as those with milder forms of mental retardation. Mental illness is cited to occur at a higher rate in persons with mental retardation than in the general population (Borthwick-Duffy, 1994). Impulse control disorders, anxiety disorders, and mood disorders are cited as having a high rate of diagnosis in the severe to profound ranges (King, DeAntonio, McCracken, & Forness, 1994).

Diagnosing psychological disorders may be problematic in that the symptoms can be misinterpreted or altogether unnoticed for persons with severe or profound intellectual disabilities. For example, depressive symptoms are more likely to mimic acting out behavior (such as psychomotor agitation and irritable mood) than typical sadness (Charlot, 1998). Issues such as these have led to the questioning of the applicability of the DSM-IV definitions of psychiatric disorders to individuals with severe and profound mental retardation. Despite its limitations, the DSM-IV-TR—*Diagnostic and Statistical Manual of Mental Disorders, 4th Edition, Text Revision* (APA, 2000)—is the definitive diagnostic source for such disorders. The manual advises that information should be garnished from several sources in order to guard against misdiagnosis. Behavioral observations, interviews with the individual and his or her significant others, medical examinations, and psychometric evaluations are some examples of valuable sources of information for the diagnostic process.

COMMUNICATION CHARACTERISTICS

In our world, words are the building blocks of understanding. The ability to produce and interpret language is vital for successful living in society. For people with severe intellectual disabilities, communication skills are often jeopardized by difficulties with speech and language. This section will describe speech and language development, assessment and treatment of communication problems, and considerations for teaching communication skills.

Speech and Language Development

The development of speech and language is a complicated and fascinating process that is only partially understood. It appears the human brain is biologically predestined to code and decode language. The development of language has an impact on other cognitive processes such as memory and problem solving. Under normal circumstances, language learning and speech production are dynamic processes that begin at birth. Crying, reaching, and imitating are all precursors that indicate language readiness (Salkind, 1994).

For persons with severe intellectual disabilities, language development is usually delayed or interrupted. The rate of speech/language disorders among this group is estimated at 90% (National Institute of Neurological Disorders and Stroke, 1988). Although the problems are often grouped together, speech and language disorders are distinct phenomena that may occur together or separately. Speech problems occur when sounds are absent or distorted to the extent that the speaker cannot be easily understood. Language disorders may occur in two forms: receptive and expressive. Receptive problems are indicated when a person cannot understand, or decode, the rules of language. Expressive problems occur when the person cannot use the rules of language well enough to share his or her experiences (Paul-Brown & Diggs, 1993).

Investigations of the speech and language skills of persons with severe intellectual disabilities have indicated a wide array of skill levels, ranging from direct behaviors that reveal the person's wants and needs to gesturing to verbal fluency (Mar & Sall, 1999). Regardless of the mode of communication, people with more severe forms of intellectual disability are likely to take a practical approach to communication. That is, communication attempts are more likely to occur when the person wants to access an object or request assistance. More social functions, such as commenting on surroundings or asking about the well-being of others, are less frequently observed (McLean, Brady, McLean, & Behrens, 1999; McLean & Snyder-McLean, 1991).

Assessment and Interventions

Most people with severe intellectual disabilities will participate in a speech/language assessment at some point in life. Such assessments are usually part of the comprehensive evaluation procedures that are required for many types of services (Kubiszyn & Borich, 2002). Assessments may consist of teacher/family interviews, physical examinations, standardized tests, and/or direct observations by speech/language pathologists. Hearing evaluations are routinely administered, as well (Paul-Brown & Diggs, 1993).

Assessment results are used to design and implement interventions. For persons who use words to communicate but experience difficulties with producing specific sounds, a speech therapist may provide direct training through prompting and imitation exercises. Several computer programs have become available that may increase motivation or provide additional practice opportunities (Paul-Brown & Diggs, 1993). For many people with severe intellectual disabilities, however, the production of understandable speech is not possible. Interventions for those people must focus on assisting the person to communicate despite all obstacles (Kaiser, 1993a).

Among nonverbal communication methods, gesturing and manual signing are the most commonly used (Soto, Belfiore, Schlosser, & Haynes, 1993). Again, a wide array of skill levels are present among persons using manual language. Rudimentary forms of sign language include pointing and forming gestures that mimic the behavior desired (for example, pointing to a favored toy to indicate a desire to play with it; imitating the motion of bringing food to the mouth to indicate a desire to eat). People with more advanced communication skills may learn less obvious signs from organized sign languages, such as clapping the hands together to indicate "school" or crossing the arms at the wrists to indicate "work."

Still other persons with severe intellectual disabilities may benefit from some type of augmentative communication device. *Augmentative communication* may take many forms, including pointing to or presenting pictures of desired objects or activities. In a more sophisticated version, pictures are arranged on an electronic board and a synthesized voice is activated when the person touches the picture (Soto et al., 1993). Although all types of communication interventions can work, the rate of skill acquisition and the extent to which skills are maintained and generalized to new situations are dependent upon the instructional strategies used (Romski & Sevcik, 1993).

Augmentative communication is discussed more thoroughly in chapter 13.

Communication Training

The first step in ensuring that a person benefits from communication training is to choose the most appropriate mode or modes of intervention. Factors to consider include visual discrimination skills, motor skills, ability to keep up with a device, skills of the conversational partners, setting appropriateness, and preferences of the individual (Soto et al., 1993).

Once the communication mode has been selected, the teaching method must be considered. Research indicates that communication skills are learned more quickly and are retained for longer periods of time when *naturalistic* approaches are used (Kaiser, Yoder, & Keetz, 1992). In employing a naturalistic approach, teaching occurs during everyday activities at home, school, and in the community; the environment is arranged to encourage communication; the student's interests are incorporated as motivators to communicate; and natural consequences are provided (Halle, Alpert, & Anderson, 1984).

The importance of naturalistic instruction cannot be overemphasized. In order to maximize the student's potential for learning a new sign or picture, instructors begin by teaching words that represent favorite objects or activities. This will ensure that the reinforcement will be powerful and repeat trials will be welcome. Use of the new word should be incorporated into real-life situations, throughout the day, and across all settings. The favored items are placed in the environment so that they may be seen, but not accessed without communicating. All attempts to communicate are met with encouragement and corrective feedback (Kaiser, 1993b).

Perhaps the most important element of naturalistic language training is the use of natural consequences. In other words, when the student forms a sign or points to a picture, the item or activity requested should be immediately presented. Social praise is often paired with the object (Romski & Sevcik, 1993). While the addition of praise may be advantageous for some, teachers should be aware that the praise may be confusing for other learners. That is, the child may have difficulty learning whether the picture or sign represents the object or the teacher's attention (Bondy & Frost, 1994).

EDUCATIONAL CONCERNS

Little historical information is known about the education of persons with severe intellectual disabilities. Education of such persons simply was not a subject of great concern in centuries past. The contributions of 19th century reformists (e.g., Edouard Seguin, Samuel G. Howe) laid the groundwork for subsequent models of instruction for persons with mental retardation (Safford & Safford, 1996).

For a parent's perspective on educating a child with severe intellectual disabilities, go to the Companion Website at www.prenhall .com/beirne-smith and select Chapter 9, Video Case Studies.

Current literature analysis indicated three areas of concentration on this topic: curriculum choices, instructional strategies, and inclusion considerations. In this section, we will discuss each of those areas in turn. We end with a return to philosophy: What is the purpose of education for persons with severe intellectual disability, and how can we determine whether those goals have been met?

Functional Curriculum

People with severe intellectual disabilities usually have educational needs that are different from the majority of students in school. Ability to comprehend the three Rs is significantly limited. Instead, these children need to learn skills that will assist them in their everyday lives. For that reason, their education is best when based on a **functional curriculum**. A functional curriculum is one that teaches everyday life skills in order to maximize the student's potential for independence.

As described by Wehman and Kregel (2004), a functional curriculum might address such areas as money management, socialization, self-esteem, employment skills, travel and mobility training, community participation, home living skills, personal care, hygiene, and health and safety. Additionally, these skills must be taught in a meaningful way. People with severe intellectual disabilities often have difficulty with **generalization** (applying skills learned in one setting to other situations). Therefore, it is not good enough to talk about how to wash clothes; the student must have hands-on experience washing the clothes. Table 9.1 lists some examples of home skills curriculum with example activities.

Besides the obvious difficulties of designing an appropriate instructional environment for teaching such skills, perhaps the most difficult thing about a functional curriculum is the breadth of it. There are virtually no limits to the range of skills and

TABLE 9.1

Home Skills Curriculum with Example Activities

Curriculum Area	Key Activities
1. Planning and preparing meals	Planning a menu Preparing meals Using cooking equipment Storing food safely
2. Self-care, bathing, and hygiene	Showering or bathing Caring for hair Caring for nails Caring for teeth Toileting Washing hands and face
3. Cleaning and care of the home	Vacuuming Dusting and wiping surfaces Neatening and organizing
4. Cleaning and care of clothing	Washing and drying clothes Changing clothes as needed Folding and storing clothes
5. Telephone use	Calling for appointments or services Calling friends and acquaintances Calling in emergencies Answering calls from others
6. Leisure activities	Watching television Listening to music Performing hobbies Entertaining visitors
7. Safely procedures	Calling 911 in an emergency Evacuating during a fire Responding to smoke detectors Using a fire extinguisher Calling an ambulance or doctor if one becomes very sick Safely answering the door
8. Time management and scheduling activities	Adhering to a daily schedule Following a calendar Using alarm clocks
9. Negotiating with others and self-advocacy	Negotiating responsibilities with roommates Negotiating communal versus private property and areas within the home Negotiating with neighbors regarding issues such as noise, external lights, and so on Speaking up to ensure that important responsibilities are carried out by roommates or others Speaking up on one's behalf to ensure that needed supports are obtained

Source: From "Living at Home: Skills for Independence," by D. E. Steere & T. L. Burcoff, in P. Wehman & J. Kregel (Eds.), *Functional Curriculum for Elementary, Middle, and Secondary Age Students with Special Needs* (2nd ed., p. 297), 2004, Austin, TX: PRO-ED. Copyright © 2004 by PRO-ED, Inc. Reprinted by permission.

activities one could identify as necessary for independent life. Therefore, the selection of goals could be a cumbersome process. There are plenty of prepackaged assessment and development tools available to assist in the various steps of this process (cf. Forest & Pearpoint, 1992; Giangreco, Cloninger, & Iverson, 1998). In general, however, there is a simple, logical progression that begins with the question: What do the child and family want, and how do we help them get there? Orelove and Malatchi (1996) suggest the following sequence:

1. Determine the child's interests and dreams.
2. Determine the skills the child already possesses that will assist him or her in attaining those dreams.
3. Determine challenges the child will face in attaining those dreams.
4. Select the challenges to be addressed now and later.
5. Write goals and objectives that are measurable, associated with specific learning activities, age appropriate, and can be generalized to natural settings.

It is very important to realize that curriculum selection and development is an ongoing process. Once goals and objectives have been established, it is necessary to continually assess the child's progress and make changes as the child's needs change. Figure 9.2 depicts the process.

Instructional Strategies

Once goals, objectives, and teaching activities have been selected, it is important to think about the most appropriate method for teaching the desired skills. Usually skills are taught using behavioral principles, which begin with a **task analysis.** Task analysis is a process of breaking down a task into simple, ordered steps. The student is then taught to accomplish each step of the task using positive reinforcement. Reinforcement does not usually have to be elaborate; in most cases, simple praise is enough. In many cases, the feeling of accomplishment that follows the completion of the task is reinforcement enough. Sometimes, however, tangible reinforcement is needed. This, however, should always be faded away over time as the task is learned.

When following behavioral teaching strategies, instructional prompts are very important. The most effective teacher will give the least informative prompt necessary to cue the student. That is, one wouldn't want to provide hands-on assistance with shoe-tying if the child could accomplish the task with verbal instructions. Doing so could result in the child becoming dependent on others to initiate actions he already knows how to do. Kregel (2004) describes six different levels of prompting often used in educational settings:

1. *Ambiguous verbal prompts:* Teacher makes comments such as "Keep going" or "What's next?" that encourage a child to go on without specifying what needs to be done.
2. *Specific verbal prompts:* Teacher provides specific information that tells the student what to do next, such as "Pick up the plate."
3. *Modeling:* Teacher performs the correct action and then allows the student to attempt to perform the step.

FIGURE 9.2
Flowchart of the Instructional
Planning Process

Source: From *Educating Children with Multiple Disabilities: A Transdisciplinary Approach* (3rd ed., p. 380), by F. P. Orelove & D. Sobsey, 1996, Baltimore: Paul H. Brookes. Copyright © 1996 by Paul H. Brookes Publishing Co. Reprinted by permission.

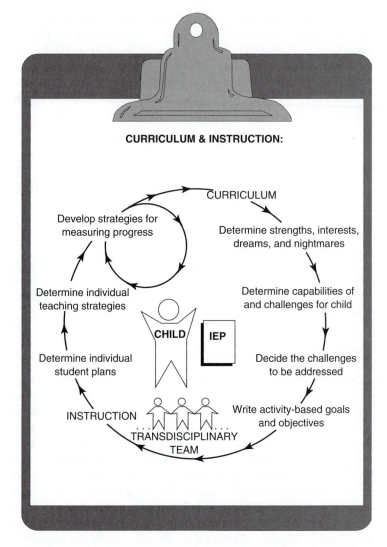

4. *Gestures:* Teacher uses methods of nonverbal communication, such as pointing to the place where an object belongs or gesturing to the student to turn an object over.

5. *Priming:* Teacher gives student just enough physical assistance to initiate performance of the step. When the student begins to move on his or her own, the teacher's assistance is removed.

6. *Physical assistance:* Teacher gives student hand-over-hand assistance to enable him or her to complete the task. This assistance is then faded from the hand, to the wrist, to the forearm, to the elbow, to the shoulder; the fading process is called **graduated guidance.**

Once skills are learned, the teacher's goal is to ensure that they are retained and generalized to appropriate situations. The process of fading tangible reinforcers has already been mentioned. This is absolutely necessary if the student is to generalize the skill to situations in which the reinforcer is not present. Tangible reinforcers should be replaced with more natural consequences, such as eating a freshly cooked meal or receiving compliments on nicely pressed garments.

Generalization is also encouraged by teaching the skills in a variety of settings and utilizing a variety of different instructors. Doing so reduces the possibility that the student is using an inappropriate cue. For example, a student who is learning to use a vending machine by visiting the same machine might be baffled by a machine that accepts money in a different way or delivers the product in a different place.

The same problem may arise when the student becomes accustomed to a single instructor. The teacher may have unconscious mannerisms that indicate whether the student is on the right track. The child may be relying on those mannerisms as a guide without the teacher's knowledge.

Read a teacher's perspective on working with this population by visiting the Companion Website at www.prenhall.com/beirne-smith and select Chapter 9, Read and Respond.

The need to encourage skill generalization is one of the main reasons special education has embraced the philosophies of **community-based instruction** and **community-referenced instruction.** Community-based instruction takes place in the community settings in which the behavior is expected to occur. Community-referenced instruction is related to actual incidents that naturally occur in the environment. It may take place in the classroom (Wehman & Kregel, 2004). A student who takes part in community-based instruction may actually go to the grocery store to shop during school hours. The student in the community-referenced instruction paradigm may learn to identify price tags in the classroom. Box 9.1 describes one program of community-based instruction.

Although most educators agree that a community-based curriculum would be best for teaching community-related skills, this requires the student to be removed from the school setting. Inclusion advocates say, however, that the time spent with other children in the school setting is as important as skills attained through a community-based curriculum. This is not the only controversy regarding people with severe intellectual disability and inclusion. In the next section, we will examine some of those factors.

Inclusion Considerations

The concept of educating children with severe intellectual disabilities in the public schools is really not very old. Even when the early right-to-education legislation was passed, it was obviously meant to apply only to children with mild mental retardation. Although school systems are now required to provide an education to all children, regardless of degree of disability, there still exists controversy over where this education must be provided.

The concept of **full inclusion**, a policy of all students being educated in inclusive environments 100% of the time, without regard to the severity of the disability, is receiving more attention in the professional literature. However, most parents, professionals, and advocacy groups still believe an array of options, including special classes, is preferable (Heward, 2002). It is not our goal here to influence the reader's opinion on that topic. Instead, we wish to describe ways in which this group can be successfully included, whether through full or partial inclusion. One thing is certain on this topic: Successful inclusion takes work (see Box 9.2).

Box 9.1 ⚜ Travel Training for Persons with Cognitive or Physical Disabilities

Traveling independently on public transportation is one occasion when a person with a cognitive impairment must perform with absolutely no assistance. Training a person with a cognitive impairment to use public transportation requires a comprehensive and individualized instructional program. Before a person with a cognitive disability can safely use public transportation, she or he must demonstrate 100% consistency in many functional skill areas, beyond simply learning the travel route to and from a destination.

Before travel training begins, a travel trainer determines a student's strengths and weaknesses, assesses how much support the student can expect from her or his parents or guardians, and reviews the travel route to determine the feasibility of traveling to a specific destination. Travel training begins only when the student is ready to learn the travel route and has support from parents or guardians. It's notable that a student with a cognitive disability does not necessarily have to know how to read a clock, make change, or understand survival signs to succeed in a travel training program, though these skills certainly are assets.

A comprehensive travel training program for people with a cognitive disability should consist of the following:

Phase 1: Detailed instruction in specific travel routes, fare costs, boarding and de-boarding sites, and the demonstration of pedestrian skills necessary for this travel route, as well as constant practice in life skills such as appropriate interaction with community workers and with strangers, use of public telephone, and appropriate behavior in public places.

Phase 2: Direct observation of the student by the travel trainer to verify that the student has learned all necessary travel skills taught in Phase 1.

Phase 3: Instruction in emergency procedures. Emergencies can include boarding the wrong transit vehicle, missing a stop, or losing one's fare or transfer pass.

Phase 4: Assessment of the student's interactive skills with strangers. Travel training programs may use plainclothes police officers or travel trainers whom the student has not met to approach the traveling student and try to extract personal information from him or her. Students pass this assessment procedure if they do not impart personal information to or leave with a stranger.

Phase 5: Indirect observation of the student. As the student walks to and from the transit stop and rides the transit vehicle independently, her or his performance is assessed at a distance by a travel trainer, who follows in a car. The student is aware that she or he is being observed.

Phase 6: Covert observation and assessment. The student is not aware that she or he is being observed.

Phase 7: Follow-up observations. Periodically, a student who successfully completes a travel training program should be covertly observed to verify that she or he is still practicing safe travel skills.

While different travel training programs may vary the order in which they teach travel skills, the teaching methods of travel training programs should be the same. The average length of a quality travel training program is 15 sessions, though training time will vary according to the complexity of the travel route and the nature of the student's disability.

Once a person with a cognitive impairment begins to travel independently along one travel route, typically, she or he learns other travel routes with relative ease. Sometimes intense instruction is required to travel to a new destination, especially if reaching the new destination requires new or more advanced pedestrian skills or different modes of transportation.

Source: Voorhees (1996), pp. 7–9.

Box 9.2 ☆ Making Inclusion Work

Successful school inclusion doesn't just happen. It takes sensitivity, preparation, creativity, and above all, work. The success will hinge on day-to-day interactions. The following is an excerpt from *Making School Inclusion Work: A Guide to Everyday Practices,* by Katie Blenk and Doris Landau Fine:

> An absolutely major issue in our school is that every child act positively toward his or her schoolmates. Even with our best efforts, there have been times that certain typical children have not acted appropriately to their schoolmates with special needs. This needs to be dealt with immediately and in a way that really sends the message home to the typical child.
>
> We had a child in our program who was very large for his age and could walk but not talk. To communicate with his peers he would yell sounds and pull on their clothes to get their attention. This was very disconcerting to two little girls who were into Barbie dolls, dresses and were a bit snobby to most of their friends in general. After this child with special needs decided he wanted them as friends, disaster struck. Comments like, "We don't like so-and-so," or "We don't like to play with him," could be heard.
>
> In our school this kind of behavior isn't tolerated under any circumstances, regardless of the children involved. In this particular case the staff was very concerned. We talked to the children and their parents, but I really felt it wasn't enough; these kids needed to understand more. Now kids will be kids, and little girls around six seem to catch that disease of being prissy and exclusionary to one another. And in all fairness no one really likes to be yelled at and pulled on.
>
> I waited until a day that the child with special needs wasn't in school and I gathered the class in my office. I told them that this child is trying to tell them things when he yells and pulls on them. And I made each child come up to me. I whispered a statement in their ear such as "I like your dress. It's really pretty," or "Congratulations, Stephanie, on your new baby brother." I had the child I whispered to go and say the whispered statement to whatever child I mentioned in the statement, but they couldn't use any words because they had to make believe they could not speak. One by one I saw these children go over, try to communicate with their friends, and not be able to. They experienced the complete frustration that so many non-verbal children go through. So, I said, now you know how your friend feels and why he pulls on you or yells sounds at you.
>
> The results of this exercise were astounding. Not only did the children stop the negative behavior towards their friend with special needs, but the two little girls actively started helping their friend and finding ways to communicate with him.
>
> This story raises a very important point. No matter how determined a team is to have a quality inclusive program, it doesn't just happen. Quality inclusion is an ongoing process of evaluation, change and facilitation; problems such as these will continuously crop up over the course of time and need to be dealt with effectively. The best way to teach is through hands-on activities, and the best way for these children to learn what they needed to learn was by experiencing it. You can tell the children how others feel, but to have them feel it can make significant changes quickly.

Source: From *Making School Inclusion Work: A Guide to Everyday Practices* (pp. 72–73), by K. Blenk & D. L. Fine, 1995, Cambridge, MA: Brookline Books. Copyright © 1995 by Brookline Books. Reprinted by permission.

One of the most important factors in the success of inclusion is the match between the child, the teacher, and the other students in the classroom. Blenk and Fine (1995) provide some guidelines for assessing the situation. First, it is important to make sure the child is given an adequate amount of time to adjust before judging the inclusion experience to be a failure. Additionally, a struggling child should be tried in another classroom for 3 to 6 months before giving up on inclusion altogether. Secondly, consider how this child's needs may conflict with the needs of the rest of the specific children in the class. For example, it might not be in anyone's best interest to place a child who is already severely shy and withdrawn into a classroom with children who are likely to criticize or ridicule him.

A third important aspect to consider is whether the classroom (including the classroom teacher) is flexible enough to embrace the different needs of this child. In a perfect world, all classrooms would be. In reality, however, many are not. Teachers must be able to try different approaches and sometimes have different rules for children with severe disabilities. Additionally, they may be asked to provide assistance in ways that are very different from what other children require. When this happens, teachers should be given adequate training and information before being presented with the situation.

Wherever a child may be physically placed, inclusion has not truly occurred unless the child is accepted by peers. Successful inclusion policies attempt to increase involvement on both ends. There are many documented cases of young elementary-aged children embracing the included child without much interference from adults. However, it is often necessary to do some preplanning. Table 9.2 provides some suggestions for encouraging typically developing children to engage children with disabilities.

If inclusion experiences are to generalize to other life areas, however, it is important for the included child to learn how to attract friends. There are some packaged curricula available for this (cf. Kapp-Simon & Simon, 1991). Behavioral instruction can also be effective. However, little attention has thus far been paid to this very important area of development.

Although we want inclusion to be a pleasant experience for all, there are also some tough lessons that can be learned when bad things happen. We really don't live in a world where everyone is nice and accepting of everyone else. Sometimes the benefit of an inclusive environment is that the child will learn to handle people who aren't so nice (Schultz & Carpenter, 1995).

TABLE 9.2

Suggestions for Recruiting Peers to Assist Students with Disabilities

1. Informally ask students if they would like to interact with a given student, and provide opportunities to do so.
2. Ask the teacher who might benefit academically, socially, and emotionally from working with a student having severe [disabilities].
3. Ask the school counselor, especially at the secondary level, to identify students who may benefit from such interactions.
4. Assign students to the same cooperative learning groups for a few weeks to help establish relationships.
5. Have students with severe sensory and intellectual impairments join extracurricular activities and clubs.
6. Ask the student council or other school leaders if they are interested in getting to know or supporting some students.

Source: From "The Important Role of Peers in the Inclusion Process," by J. E. Downing & J. Eichinger, in *Including Students with Severe and Multiple Disabilities in Typical Classrooms* (pp. 129–145), 2002, Baltimore: Paul H. Brookes. Copyright © 2002 by Paul H. Brookes Publishing Co. Reprinted by permission.

Studies of skill acquisition of persons with severe intellectual disabilities who have increased interactions with the community verify this expectation. Kennedy and Itkonen (1994) indicate social gains under such conditions. Several authors, including Snell (2000) and Wilcox and Bellamy (1982) have noted, for example, that students with more severe intellectual disabilities who participate in a community-based curriculum find and retain jobs at a greater rate than do those who participate in self-contained educational programs.

On the topic of increased interactions between persons who have disabilities and those who do not, questions about the impact on society at large naturally arise. Research has indicated that authority figures and nondisabled peers develop helpful, accepting, positive attitudes toward persons with severe intellectual disabilities after inclusive experiences (Strully & Strully, 1989). Block and Rizzo (1995) discuss the development of facilitative attitudes of nondisabled peers and authority figures after inclusive experiences. Over time, reports of positive outcomes for both the person with and the nondisabled peers have become more frequent (c.f. Gaylord, Abery, & Schoeller, 1997). So, it would seem that community involvement with persons who have severe intellectual disabilities can be a positive experience for all.

Educational Outcomes

John Dewey (1966) told us that good schools should work to develop good citizens. With this philosophy in mind, leaders in the field of special education took on the responsibility of ensuring that students with severe intellectual disabilities left school with the skills required to live successfully in society. In order to measure success, educators would have to define specific outcomes of interest. Although conceptualizations differ, most proposed outcomes could fall into one of three categories: independence, productivity, and community integration.

Independence is a broad construct that encompasses many aspects, most notably self-reliance and self-determination. Self-reliance refers to a person's ability to take care of himself or herself. Skills that reflect self-reliance range from feeding oneself to living in a home alone. Educational programs offer many opportunities to encourage self-reliance. As described earlier, self-determination refers to a person's ability to set and navigate his or her own life course. Skills that educators may help to develop include making choices, communicating preferences, setting achievable goals, and self-advocating (Wehmeyer, 1993).

In our society, independence is largely tied to productivity, which is generally defined as holding a job and being economically self-sustaining. Therefore, the most desirable outcome for all individuals, including those with severe intellectual disabilities, is competitive employment. In order for this to occur, education and training must focus on vocational instruction and on-the-job skill development. Research generated during the past 20 years demonstrates that competitive employment is a viable outcome for persons with severe intellectual disability (Moon, Inge, Wehman, Brooke, & Barcus, 1990). Rusch, Enchelmaier, and Kohler (1994) identified the following as outcome components for successful school-to-work transition: development of individual transition plans; demonstration of improved work opportunities; job placement in competitive, integrated settings; and documentation of progress in employment-related skills.

Most proposed educational outcomes will be in the categories of independence, productivity, or community integration.

Without social integration, the value of living a productive and independent life is questionable. Common activities that the majority of the population can take for granted are sometimes difficult for a person with severe intellectual disabilities to access. Barriers to accessing such community resources may include lack of knowledge of such resources (Schleien, Ray, & Green, 1996), deficits in social skills (Gaylord-Ross & Chadsey-Rusch, 1991), and social self-consciousness (Zetlin & Turner, 1985). Elective participation in religious activities is an example of a commonly overlooked element of true community membership. Riordan and Vasa (1991) indicated that clergy were aware of few persons with disabilities in their congregations, so provisions for their education and participation in rites of passage have been infrequent. Peer groups are important sources of social support for all people—and persons with severe intellectual disabilities are no different. We all share the need for human interaction. Although we are still learning how, educational settings provide a wonderful opportunity for teaching the person to overcome such barriers, and for teaching nondisabled peers to prevent many of those barriers from being constructed.

In the current educational climate, the term *educational outcomes* is often associated with **outcomes-based assessment,** the practice of judging the value of an educational program by the progress each child makes. With the initiation of the No Child Left Behind Act, this policy has been linked to school funding. For obvious reasons, there have been problems making children with severe intellectual disabilities fit into the overall assessment schema of a given school district. There has been discussion about whether their outcomes fit with school-wide, district-wide, and state-wide outcome goals. However, the law does not require all children to participate in the same assessment or to be held to the same standards. Children with severe mental retardation are likely to be assessed with alternate standards and procedures, such as portfolios of work completed during the year. Although these alternate assessments have been described as cumbersome and difficult to standardize because of the individualized curriculum, with creativity and ingenuity it is hoped that they will help ensure a practical education for all.

Although the areas of emphasis under NCLB are reading, mathematics, and science, student outcomes within those areas can still be functional. Table 9.3 includes examples of functional academics for students included in the general curriculum. This way of thinking about education can lead to the development of useful outcome goals (McLaughlin & Warren, 1994).

Employment is one of the most important educational outcomes. This issue is discussed thoroughly in chapters 11 and 12.

TABLE 9.3

Traditional Academic Content Areas and Examples of Functional Activities

Academic Content Area	Examples of Functional Activities
Reading	Read a newspaper article Read a recipe Read the signs on restroom doors Read instructions for video game Read a job application Read a course schedule of classes for college
Math	Add sales tax to purchase order Use calculator to add grocery item totals Compare prices at a local video store Calculate income tax return Compute square footage for a carpentry task
Science	Calculate boiling point for candy recipe Use medication chart Plant and harvest vegetable garden Identify weather to select appropriate clothing
Social studies	Register to vote Identify cultural holidays and customs Identify headlines in newspapers Determine bus route in the community
Health	Brush teeth and practice proper oral hygiene Plan balanced meals Identify and purchase items for class first aid kit Identify health services in the community Label sexual feelings and attitudes
Expressive writing	Write a thank-you note Dictate a personal story Write a biography for college entrance application

Source: From "Functional Academics," by P. S. Wolfe & R. M. Kubina, in P. Wehman & J. Kregel (Eds.), *Functional Curriculum for Elementary, Middle, and Secondary Age Students with Special Needs* (2nd ed., p. 118), 2004, Austin, TX: PRO-ED. Copyright © 2004 by PRO-ED, Inc. Used by permission.

Companion Website *To check your understanding of this chapter, go to the Companion Website at www.prenhall.com/ beirne-smith and select Chapter 9. From there, you can access the Self-Test and Essay modules.*

Summary

Definition and Overview

- People with moderate, severe, and profound levels of intellectual disability are generally grouped together in the category called "severe."
- Of the 1% to 3% of the population estimated to have mental retardation, only 15% have greater than mild disabilities.
- Severe intellectual disability is usually biologically based, and people with severe intellectual disabilities often experience multiple disabilities.
- Functional abilities of this group vary significantly and are related to experience and training. It is important that people with severe intellectual disabilities have inclusive experiences.

Behavioral and Emotional Characteristics

- The development of adaptive and challenging behaviors is influenced by training and environmental factors.
- The tools of behavioral psychology have been successful in teaching a wide array of adaptive behaviors and decreasing challenging behaviors.
- People with severe intellectual disabilities experience many life stressors that may have a negative effect on emotional health.
- Mental illness is suspected to occur at greater rates among persons with mental retardation than in the general population, but diagnosis is complicated by a lack of formalized assessment measures, barriers in communication, and atypical demonstration of symptoms.

Communication Characteristics

- Most persons with severe intellectual disabilities have some form of speech/language disorder.
- Gesturing and manual signing are the most commonly used methods of nonverbal communication among persons with severe intellectual disabilities.
- Naturalistic teaching methods have been shown to be the most effective approach for teaching communication skills.

Educational Concerns

- People with severe intellectual disabilities should be educated with a functional curriculum that prepares them for future life in the community.
- Instructional strategies should be tailored to the student and geared toward generalization.
- Successful inclusion experiences are dependent upon the match between the child, the teacher, and the other students in the classroom.
- Positive inclusion experiences can benefit nondisabled peers as well as students with severe intellectual disabilities.

10

Infancy and Early Childhood

with
Sylvia L. Dietrich, Ph.D.
University of Alabama

OBJECTIVES

After reading this chapter, the student should be able to:

- State the rationale for early childhood special education
- Discuss the legislation and implementation affecting early childhood special education programs
- Describe assessment procedures used with infants, toddlers, and young children who have disabilities
- Discuss considerations in programming for young children

KEY TERMS

at risk

criterion-referenced testing

curriculum

curriculum-based assessment

developmental delay

early childhood special education

early intervention

family assessment

individualized education program (IEP)

individualized family service plan (IFSP)

judgment-based assessment

norm-referenced test

play-based assessment

transition

RATIONALE FOR EARLY CHILDHOOD SPECIAL EDUCATION

Educational programs for infants and children with disabilities were virtually nonexistent 25 years ago—but today's society is recognizing the importance of the early childhood years and the need for early identification and intervention for infants, toddlers, and preschoolers who have special needs. Several factors have contributed to this recognition and support, including research support for early education, evolving social policies on early education, expanding legislation for young children and their families, and an increasing number of early intervention programs for young children with special needs (Lerner, Lowenthal, & Egan, 2003).

 A complete online glossary is available on the Companion Website, which may be accessed at www.prenhall.com/beirne-smith

Early childhood special education is a system of services for special needs children from birth through 5 years of age. *Special needs children* are children who have been diagnosed with a disability, developmental delay, or who are considered at risk for school and learning failure.

Among the first to draw attention to the importance of the early years were Marie Montessori, Friedrich Froebel, and G. Stanley Hall. Other researchers have added their support. For example, Bloom (1964) found that children develop 50% of their total intellectual capacity by age 4 and 80% by age 8. White (1975) concluded that the period between 8 months and 3 years is of utmost importance in the development of intellectual and social skills. In addition, Hayden and Pious (1979), McDaniel (1977), Smith and Strain (1984), and Weissman and Littman (1996) have argued that for children with physical, social, emotional, or mental disabilities, educational programming should begin shortly after birth.

The rationale for early childhood special education has been built on research that clearly demonstrates the correlation and importance of the early experiences of children to their later growth and development. Bricker and colleagues (Bricker & Cripe, 1992; Bricker, Pretti-Frontczak, & McComas, 1998; Bricker & Veltman, 1990) define the theoretical underpinnings of early intervention programs:

1. Children with developmental disabilities require more and/or different early experience than children without disabilities.
2. Formal programs with trained personnel are necessary to provide the required early experience to compensate for developmental difficulties.
3. Developmental progress is enhanced in children with disabilities who participate in early intervention programs. (Bricker & Cripe, 1992, p. 9)

Bailey and Wolery (1993) provide a knowledgeable argument for early childhood education. According to these authors, high-quality early intervention can successfully detect problems when they are distinct and remedial, change the behavior of children in different areas of development, prevent the secondary consequences of primary disability, reduce the cost of serving these children at a later age, and provide assistance and training to families in need. Similarly, in a review of early childhood programs for disadvantaged and high-risk children, Barnett (1995) concludes that high-quality early education programs positively affect children's intelligence quotient, school achievement, grade retention, placement in special education, and social competence. Guralnick (1998) concurs that comprehensive early childhood education reduces the decline in intellectual development that occurs without appropriate intervention.

Additionally, in a review of early intervention findings from the Abecedarian Project, Project CARE, and the Infant Health and Development Program, Ramey and Ramey (1992) found that the benefits of daily early educational intervention in the first 5 years of a child's life can improve a child's intellectual performance and academic achievement at least until early adolescence. Daily intervention activities considered essential to such outcomes are for the child (1) to be encouraged to explore the environment; (2) to be guided toward basic thinking skills, such as sorting and sequencing; (3) to celebrate and reinforce accomplishments; (4) to practice the skills learned and to expand on these skills; (5) to avoid negative consequences during the trial-and-error process of learning; and (6) to provide a full verbal and written language experience for the child.

Families of children who are developmentally delayed or at risk for developing a disability form the other side of the rationale for early childhood special education (Baird, 1997; Raver, 1999; Thorp, 1997; Turnbull & Turnbull, 2000a, 2000b). These families involved in the early intervention system are also recipients of services as they learn how to parent a special needs child.

SERVING YOUNG CHILDREN WITH DISABILITIES

Federal legislation has played a critical role in the provision of services to young children with disabilities and their families. Two laws that have strengthened this role are P.L. 99-457 and P.L. 102-119. Both laws are now incorporated into IDEA and were written to provide comprehensive services to young children with disabilities and their families. P.L. 99-457 (the Education of the Handicapped Act Amendments of 1986) has several important features including (1) the extension of rights and protection of the Individuals with Disabilities Education Act (IDEA) to preschoolers ages 3 to 5, with disabilities; (2) stipulation of national policy for early intervention by establishing incentives and assistance to states for the extension of existing special education services to infants, toddlers, and preschoolers; (3) financial assistance offered to states to develop and implement a statewide, comprehensive, coordinated, multidisciplinary, interagency program of early intervention services for infants and toddlers with disabilities, birth through age 3, and their families; (4) recognition of the importance of the family on the child's overall growth and development; (5) development and implementation of a variety of models beyond the traditional education models usually employed with young children and their families (Lerner et al., 2003). P.L. 102-119 (the IDEA Amendments of 1991) reorganized how infants, toddlers, and preschoolers with disabilities receive services under IDEA and added to the law such critical features as early intervention services, personnel preparation, and the concept of serving children in "natural environments."

The preschool population is categorized into two age groups by both P.L. 99-457 and P.L. 102-119, with different provisions for each group. Part B covers preschoolers (ages 3 through 5), extending the provisions of IDEA to preschool children with disabilities. Part C covers infants and toddlers (birth through age 2), addresses the needs of very young children with disabilities, and focuses on the child's developmental and medical needs as well as the importance of the family (Lerner et al., 2003).

Services to children who are retarded are well-designed and systematically implemented.

IDEA Part B: Preschool Children with Disabilities

Part B of IDEA (P.L. 105-17) mandates that all states provide a free appropriate public education to all eligible children with disabilities, ages 3 through 5. Part B further extends full rights and protection to these children by mandating services for them and permitting the noncategorical reporting of children ages 3 through 9. Schools may elect to identify children either with a noncategorical term, such as *developmental delay,* or by the category of disability.

To see a sample IEP, go to the Companion Website at www.prenhall.com/ beirne-smith and select Chapter 10.

For preschool children ages 3 through 5, service providers can decide if they would like to develop an individualized family service plan (IFSP) or an **individualized education program (IEP)**. The majority of agencies utilize IEPs to outline programs and services that will be delivered to young children with special needs. See Table 10.1 for a list of required IEP components.

According to the *Twenty-fourth Annual Report to Congress on the Implementation of the Individuals with Disabilities Education Act* (U.S. Department of Education, 2002), during the 2000–2001 school year states reported serving 599,678 children ages 3 through 5 with disabilities under IDEA (see Figure 10.1). This number represents a 37.6% increase in young children served from the year 1992–1993. The increase may be attributable in part to expanded Child Find activities and to states' success in transitioning children from Part C to Part B (U.S. Department of Education, 2002).

Chapter 10.

TABLE 10.1

Components of the Individualized Education Program (IEP)

Subpart C—Services

Individualized Education Programs §300.347 Content of IEP.

(a) **General.** The IEP for each child with a disability must include—

(1) A statement of the child's present levels of educational performance, including—

   (i) How the child's disability affects the child's involvement and progress in the general curriculum (i.e., the same curriculum as for nondisabled children); or

   (ii) For preschool children, as appropriate, how the disability affects the child's participation in appropriate activities;

(2) A statement of measurable annual goals, including benchmarks or short-term objectives, related to—

   (i) Meeting the child's needs that result from the child's disability to enable the child to be involved in and progress in the general curriculum (i.e., the same curriculum as for nondisabled children), or for preschool children, as appropriate, to participate in appropriate activities; and

   (ii) Meeting each of the child's other educational needs that result from the child's disability;

(3) A statement of the special education and related services and supplementary aids and services to be provided to the child, or on behalf of the child, and a statement of the program modifications or supports for school personnel that will be provided for the child—

   (i) To advance appropriately toward attaining the annual goals;

   (ii) To be involved and progress in the general curriculum in accordance with paragraph (a)(1) of this section and to participate in extracurricular and other nonacademic activities; and

   (iii) To be educated and participate with other children with disabilities and nondisabled children in the activities described in this section;

(4) An explanation of the extent, if any, to which the child will not participate with nondisabled children in the regular class and in the activities described in paragraph (a)(3) of this section;

(5)

   (i) A statement of any individual modifications in the administration of State or district-wide assessments of student achievement that are needed in order for the child to participate in the assessment; and

   (ii) If the IEP team determines that the child will not participate in a particular State or district-wide assessment of student achievement (or part of an assessment), a statement of—

     (A) Why that assessment is not appropriate for the child; and

     (B) How the child will be assessed;

(6) The projected date for the beginning of the services and modifications described in paragraph (a)(3) of this section, and the anticipated frequency, location, and duration of those services and modifications; and

(7) A statement of—

   (i) How the child's progress toward the annual goals described in paragraph (a)(2) of this section will be measured; and

   (ii) How the child's parents will be regularly informed (through such means as periodic report cards), at least as often as parents are informed of their nondisabled children's progress, of—

     (A) Their child's progress toward the annual goals; and

     (B) The extent to which that progress is sufficient to enable the child to achieve the goals by the end of the year.

Source: IDEA Part B, Subpart C—Services: Individualized Education Programs. Available online at IDEA Law and Resources, on the Web site of the Council for Exceptional Children (http://www.cec.sped.org/law_res/doc/law/regulations/searchregs/300subpartC/Csec300.347.php).

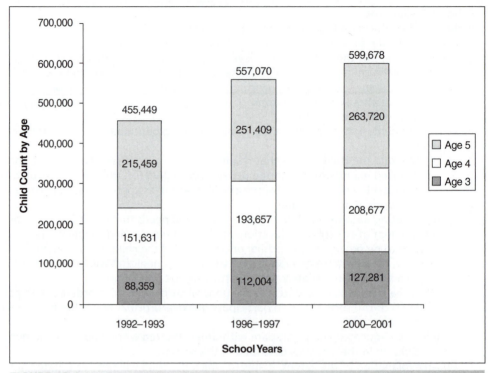

FIGURE 10.1

Preschoolers Receiving Services Under IDEA, School Years 1992–1993, 1996–1997, and 2000–2001

Source: U.S. Department of Education, Office of Special Education Programs, Data Analysis System (DANS).

IDEA Part C: Early Intervention Program for Infants and Toddlers with Disabilities

According to the *Twenty-fourth Annual Report to Congress on the Implementation of the Individuals with Disabilities Act* (U.S. Department of Education, 2002), the number of infants and toddlers served under Part C of IDEA grew 40%, from 165,351 on December 1, 1994, to 230,853 on December 1, 2000 (see Figure 10.2). According to anecdotal reports from states, the increase in the number of children served can be attributed to improved Child Find efforts, more efficient data collection procedures, and staff training (U.S. Department of Education, 2002).

Part C of IDEA addresses the provision of services for infants and toddlers with disabilities. Whereas Part B mandates services for children aged 3 through 5, Part C authorizes financial assistance to the states through grants to address the needs of infants and toddlers with disabilities and their families. Features of Part C are described below.

Eligibility.   To be eligible for the infant/toddler program, children must be experiencing **developmental delays** as measured by appropriate diagnostic instruments and procedures in at least one of five areas: (1) cognitive development, (2) physical

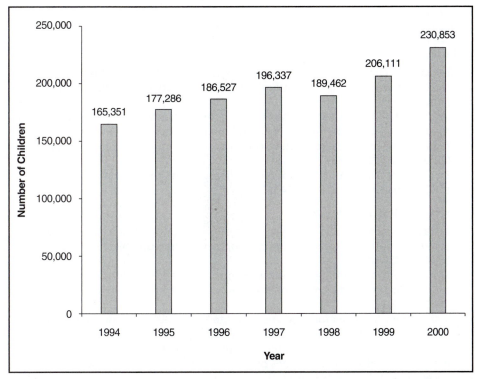

FIGURE 10.2
Infants and Toddlers Served Under IDEA Part C, 1994–2000

Source: U.S. Department of Education, Office of Special Education Programs, Data Analysis System (DANS).

development, including vision and hearing, (3) communication/language and speech development, (4) social or emotional development, or (5) adaptive development. Also included are children whose diagnosed physical or mental condition has a high probability of resulting in developmental delays. Each state must define the term *developmental delay* for identifying infants and toddlers for service.

Individualized Family Service Plan (IFSP). An **individualized family service plan (IFSP)** is required for infants and toddlers and their families receiving services under part C. The IFSP underscores the significant role of families in the lives of infants and toddlers with disabilities. Each IFSP must include (1) present levels of functioning, (2) a statement of family strengths and needs, (3) expected outcomes, (4) specific services provided, (5) projected dates of initiation and duration of services, (6) name of the service coordinator, and (7) steps taken to support the transition to the preschool program. Notably, under Part C, family members other than the child with a disability may be receiving services. The primary recipient of the services may be a parent, through parent training and counseling. Finally, under Part C, the IFSP must be reviewed, at the least, in 6-month intervals. See Table 10.2 for further information on IFSPs.

For more information about topics covered in this chapter, including sample IEPs and IFSPs, visit the Companion Website at www.prenhall.com/beirne-smith and select Chapter 10, Web Destinations.

TABLE 10.2

Components of the Individualized Family Service Plan (IFSP): Part C of IDEA

The IFSP must:

1. Be based on a multidisciplinary assessment of the unique strengths and needs of the infant or toddler and identify the appropriate services to meet those needs [20 U.S.C. § 1436 (a) (1)]
2. Include a family-directed assessment of the resources, priorities, and concerns of the family and identify the supports and services necessary to enhance the family's capacity to meet the developmental needs of the infant or toddler [20 U.S.C. § 1436 (a) (2)]
3. Be developed in writing by a multidisciplinary team that includes the infant or toddler's parents [20 U.S.C. § 1436(a) (3)]

Further, the IFSP must include:

1. A statement of the child's present levels of physical, cognitive, communication, social or emotional, and adaptive development, based on objective criteria [20 U.S.C. § 1436 (d) (1)]
2. A statement of the family's resources, priorities, and concerns relative to enhancing the development of the family's infant or toddler [20 U.S.C. § 1436 (d) (2)]
3. A statement of the major outcomes expected to be achieved for the infant or toddler and the family, and the criteria, procedures, and time lines used to determine the extent to which progress toward achieving the outcomes is being made and whether modifications or revisions of the outcomes or services are necessary [20 U.S.C. § 1436 (d) (3)]
4. A statement of the specific early intervention services necessary to meet the unique needs of the infant or toddler and the family, including the frequency, intensity, and method of delivering services [20 U.S.C. § 1436 (d) (4)]
5. A statement of the natural environments in which early intervention services shall be provided appropriately, including justification of the extent, if any, to which services will not be provided in the natural environment [20 U.S.C. § 1436 (d) (5)]
6. The projected dates for initiation of services and anticipated duration of services [20 U.S.C. § 1436 (d) (6)]
7. Identification of the service coordinator who will be responsible for implementating the plan and coordinating with other agencies and persons [20 U.S.C. § 1436 (d) (7)]
8. The steps to be taken to support the toddler's transition to preschool or other appropriate services [20 U.S.C. § 1436 (d) (8)]

Source: U.S. Department of Education (2004).

Service Coordinator. The service coordinator is responsible for the implementation of the IFSP and gives guidance to the family. The service coordinator organizes and manages the efforts of the various agencies and oversees transition of the infant or toddler to a new placement.

Interagency Coordination.   The governor of each state must designate a lead agency and an Interagency Coordinating Council to implement Part C. The lead agency is responsible for entering into formal interagency agreements to provide comprehensive services to infants and toddlers with disabilities and their families. The law requires coordination of services at local, state, and federal levels.

Multidisciplinary Services.   There must be a comprehensive multidisciplinary evaluation for the infant/toddler and family. Other services may include family training and counseling, home visits, special instruction, speech/language pathology and audiology, occupational and physical therapy, psychological services, diagnostic and evaluative medical services, early identification screening and assessment services, health services necessary to enable the infant or toddler to benefit from other early intervention services, social work services, vision services, assistive technology devices and assistive technology services, and transportation and related costs (U.S. Department of Education, 2002).

Implications of the 2004 Reauthorization of IDEA upon Young Children and Their Families

The 2004 reauthorization of IDEA will impact the way services are delivered to young children and their families and fall into two broad categories: IEP/IFSP concerns and service delivery options.

IEP/IFSP Considerations.   IDEA (2004) deletes benchmarks and short-term objectives for children with disabilities, except for those children who take alternate assessments aligned to alternate achievement standards. For young children with disabilities who will be entering Preschool Special Education from a Part C early intervention program, IDEA requires the IEP team to consider the individualized family service plan currently in place for the child. Theoretically, this should enable the multidisciplinary team to get a broader and deeper understanding of the young child with disabilities and develop a more appropriate intervention plan for the child based on individual strengths and needs.

Service Delivery Options.   As discussed, IDEA 1997 placed preschool services for young children under Part B and maintained services for infants and families under Part C. IDEA (2004) provides states with the option of developing a birth through age 6 program. If chosen, a new state program must be developed and implemented jointly by the Part C lead agency and the state education agency. If a state elects to apply for this program, parents of children eligible for preschool services under section 619, who were previously receiving services under Part C, may choose to continue early intervention services under Part C until their children enter, or are eligible under state law to enter kindergarten. The state policy must ensure that these Part C services for preschoolers with disabilities include an educational component that promotes school readiness and incorporates preliteracy, language, and numeracy skills. Parents retain the right to transition their eligible preschool child to Part B preschool at any time before the child enters kindergarten.

Identifying Children Who Are At Risk

Under Part C of IDEA, individual states have the freedom to include children who are at risk for developmental delays if services are not provided. States may choose to service children who are at risk, but they are not required by law to do so.

One of the major dilemmas in implementing at-risk early intervention programs lies in the definition. As defined by Heward (2000), **at risk** "refers to children who, although not currently identified as having a disability, are considered to have a greater-than-usual chance of developing a disability. The term is often applied to infants or children who, because of conditions surrounding their births or home environments, may be expected to experience developmental delays at a later time" (p. 4). Common examples of risk factors include the socioeconomic status of the family, the intellectual abilities of the parents (especially the mother), and the number of children in the family.

Zervigon-Hakes (1995) concluded that three types of children are at risk. The categories are as follows:

1. *Established risk:* Children in this category have known genetic and biomedical conditions that affect their lives. Chromosomal disorders and sensory loss are examples of established risk factors.
2. *Biological risk:* These children have developmental histories that suggest the presence of a biological problem, but the problem is not apparent. Low birth weight and premature birth are examples of biological risk factors.
3. *Economic and social risk:* Children who fit this group have no known medical or biological problem, but they do experience life situations that can give rise to problems. Persistent poverty, inadequate health care, and substance or child abuse are examples of economic and social risk factors.

Head Start

To learn more about Head Start, go to the Companion Website at www.prenhall.com/ beirne-smith and select Chapter 10, Read and Respond.

Head Start, now more than 40 years old, is the largest program providing comprehensive educational, health, and social services to young children and their families with low socioeconomic status (Buscemi, Bennett, Thomas, & Deluca, 1996). Head Start was one of the initiatives of President Lyndon Johnson's War on Poverty within the Economic Opportunity Act of 1965. The purpose of Head Start was to break the cycle of poverty by providing education and social opportunities for children from low-income families. Head Start delivers services not only to children who may be at risk but also to young children with disabilities. In 1972, legislation required Head Start to provide services to a minimum of 10% of children with disabilities. The Head Start Bureau reported in 2000 that children with disabilities represented 13% of Head Start enrollment.

ASSESSMENT IN EARLY CHILDHOOD SPECIAL EDUCATION

Assessment is the process of collecting information about a child for the purpose of making critical decisions regarding the child. The three major purposes of assessment are identification and diagnosis, program planning, and program evaluation.

Assessment information is obtained through a variety of methods including testing, interviewing, observing children, and working with families. Part C of IDEA stipulates that families, to the extent they choose, should be involved in the assessment process. Families have valuable information and knowledge regarding their young children who are being evaluated that will facilitate in the overall assessment process.

Guidelines for the assessment of young children and their families are derived from an ecological framework. Several ecological factors—including culture, background, life experiences, and the child's overall development—contribute to the child's overall functioning and therefore should be considered during the assessment process (Meisels, 1996).

Recommended practices for assessment of young children, as proposed by the Division for Early Childhood (DEC) of the Council for Exceptional Children, stipulate that assessment must be useful, acceptable, authentic, collaborative, convergent, equitable, sensitive, and congruent (Bagnato & Neisworth, 2000; DEC Task Force, 2000). These eight qualities operationalize the concept of developmentally appropriate practice (DAP) and parents as partners in assessment for early intervention. The recommended practice guidelines in the area of assessment are as follow:

- Families and professionals collaborate in planning and implementing assessment.
- Assessment is individualized and appropriate for the child and family.
- Assessment provides useful information for intervention.
- Professionals share information in respectful and useful ways.
- Professionals meet legal and procedural requirements and meet recommended practice guidelines.

Defining the Population

Young children with disabilities and young children who are at risk for academic failure are eligible to receive special services. Furthermore, aside from categories of disabilities stipulated under IDEA, young children who receive a label of *developmental delay* can also receive special services.

Disability Categories.   Young children with an identified disability may be eligible for special services. These categories of disabilities are incorporated in Part B of IDEA and include autism, deaf-blindness, hearing impairment/deafness, mental retardation, multiple disabilities, orthopedic impairments, other health impairments, serious emotional disturbance, specific learning disability, speech or language impairments, traumatic brain injury, and visual impairments/blindness.

Developmental Delay.   Children generally are considered developmentally delayed if they show a delay in one or more of the major developmental domains—which include language and communication, gross and fine motor development, cognition, and socioemotional development. Criteria used to identify children as developmentally delayed vary from state to state, but are found by determining the percent of delay or by looking at the amount of standard deviation from the norm that the child performed on standardized tests. Typically minimal criteria include a 40% or greater delay in one area or 25% or greater delay in two developmental domains, or 2 standard deviations below the mean in one area of development or 1.5 standard deviations below the mean in two developmental areas (Benner, 2003).

At each state's discretion, under Part C of IDEA, young children who are at risk for developmental delays may receive assessment and intervention services. Children who have a high probability of experiencing developmental delays include those who could be considered at established risk, biological risk, and or environmental risk.

Stages in the Assessment Process

There are six stages in the assessment process in early childhood special education including (1) Child Find/case finding, (2) developmental screening, (3) diagnosis, (4) individualized planning of programs and interventions, (5) performance monitoring, and (6) program evaluation (Cook, Tessier, & Klein, 2000). Each of the six stages is described below.

Stage 1: Child Find/Case Finding.   Child Find is the initial step in the assessment process and the purpose is to locate young children who might need intervention programs and services. The goal of Child Find is to encourage individuals and agencies to take a comprehensive look at the young children whom they encounter in order to refer for screening those preschoolers who may need early intervention. Locating children in the community who have disabilities or who are at risk for having disabilities is a challenging task. Some parents may be unaware that their child is not developing normally. Other parents do not know that services are available for their child. In some cases, because of denial of a problem or cultural tradition, parents are reluctant to admit that their child has a disability.

Stage 2: Developmental Screening.   Developmental screening is a relatively quick way to survey a group of children and identify those who may need further evaluation because of a potential problem. The results of the developmental screening should not be used for diagnosis, placement decisions, or providing labels of disabilities.

Stage 3: Diagnosis.   The purpose of diagnosis is to answer questions about the problem and types of interventions that will help this child. To answer such questions, in-depth testing, informed clinical judgment, and information gathered by an interdisciplinary team—including the families—are necessary components.

Observation, interview, case history, informal tests, and standardized tests may be used to obtain information for diagnosis. The Division for Early Childhood Task Force (2000) recommends that trained professionals choose only norm-referenced tests that are reliable, valid, and normed with children who are similar to those being tested. This diagnostic information becomes the basis for determining eligibility for special education and services and should include information about the severity of the problem as well as the child's strengths and needs.

Stage 4: Individualized Planning of Programs and Interventions. If the diagnosis indicates a need for early intervention, then the next stage of the assessment process occurs—assessment for individualized planning of programs and interventions. Assessment for program planning uses observation of the child, interviews with families and caregivers, and information from other professionals who have worked with the child and criterion-referenced instruments. In the planning process, the close relationship between assessment and intervention should be highlighted. The assessment results are most useful when they can be immediately implemented to plan goals and objectives for the child (Bagnato & Neisworth, 2000).

The assessment should answer these questions: What are the areas of the child's strengths and weaknesses? What instructional goals should be set for this child? The areas considered in the planning process for preschoolers are as follows:

- Language and communication abilities
- Fine and gross motor development
- Cognitive abilities
- Self-help adaptive skills
- Socioemotional growth

Frequently, performance in one developmental domain influences development in the other domains. Therefore, it is recommended that a developmentally inclusive assessment of competence be completed to assist with planning. Following are some guidelines for assessment for planning programs and interventions (DEC Task Force, 2000):

- Assess at regular intervals. Understand and revise the goals and objectives with family participation for each child.
- Obtain multiple checks on the child's abilities.
- Report the child's strengths and set priorities for intervention.
- Make sure that assessment is appropriate for each child and the family.
- Assess the child in a variety of natural settings, including the home. Families often report that their child can do tasks at home that the child could not successfully perform during the testing situation in a clinical setting.
- Share the information from the evaluation with the team members and the family.
- Both families and team members collaborate in implementing assessment results and in planning interventions.

Stage 5: Performance Monitoring. Once the child is in an intervention program, progress should be monitored frequently. Monitoring progress requires multiple checks through observations, developmental checklists, and rating scales. Activities for performance monitoring include the following (DEC Task Force, 2000):

- Collect data on a regular basis about the areas of concern.
- Analyze the data to determine the mastery of targeted skills.
- Note progress the preschooler has made in accomplishing the stated goals and objectives on the IEP or IFSP.

- Judge the effectiveness of the intervention. Should instruction be modified? Note whether the child can generalize the learned skills to other settings when needed.
- Use this information to make decisions about further intervention and services.
- Make changes that are needed in the intervention plan.

Stage 6: Program Evaluation.   An important purpose of assessment is to evaluate the intervention program itself. Program evaluation is an objective, systematic procedure for determining the progress of the children and the effectiveness of the total intervention program (Bricker, 1996). Program evaluation should be multidimensional, taking into account both child-centered goals and family objectives. The program evaluation should include both formative evaluation, done during the operation of the program, and summative evaluation, done at the completion of the program to implement needed changes (Lerner et al., 2003).

Types of Assessment Instruments

The multiple measures and methods used to obtain information about young children include formal assessments such as norm-referenced, and criterion-referenced tests. In addition, other informal, alternative means of assessment are also available.

Formal Assessment Instruments.   One category of formal assessment consists of **norm-referenced tests,** which compare a child's performance to a norm group of children who have many attributes similar to the child being tested. For example, a norm-referenced test would evaluate a child's motor skills and then compare the results to children of similar age who do not have a disability. **Curriculum-based assessment,** on the other hand, measures a child's mastery of a specific set of tasks or skills. Such **criterion-referenced testing** is useful for program planning since results are easily linked to curriculum objectives.

Informal Assessment Methods.   Informal assessments also play a critical role in the program development for young children with disabilities. These alternative measures stress observation of children in their natural, everyday environments and are referred to as *ecologically based evaluation* since the child is viewed as interactive with the environment (Cavallaro, Haney, & Cabello, 1993). A combination of multiple measures and observations of the child in natural settings is necessary for a holistic and complete evaluation. Informal assessment methods include observation, checklists and rating scales, assessment of multiple intelligences, assessment of emotional intelligence, play-based assessment, dynamic assessment, performance and authentic assessment, judgment-based assessment, and family assessment.

Observation is a powerful technique for obtaining information about young children and is performed simply by observing them in their natural environments. Observational methods can include anecdotal records, running records, specimen descriptions, event sampling, checklists, and rating scales.

Play-based assessment offers a useful, natural method for evaluating young children who have disabilities or who are at risk. Since play follows a regular developmental sequence during childhood, the child's play activities can provide a measure of maturity and competence making play-based assessment suitable for any functioning child between the ages of 6 months and 6 years (Linder, 1990). Play-based assessment provides the format to obtain information on the child's developmental skills as well as patterns of interaction with others.

Dynamic assessment is an ecological approach that evaluates the child's ability to learn in a teaching situation rather than measuring what the youngster already knows in a testing situation (Lerner, 2000). Through teaching the child, the teacher determines how the child learns, what seems to be interfering with the child's ability to profit from instruction, and how the child responds to intervention. During dynamic assessment, the teacher provides appropriate support to enable the child to master tasks that were previously too difficult, through a process called *scaffolding.*

Performance and authentic assessment reflect a child's learning in various situations. In *performance assessment* the child may be asked to perform a task that is contrived—for example, brushing hair at different times from usual. Performance assessment requires multiple observations of the same task before conclusions are made about the child's abilities. *Authentic assessment* is similar to performance assessment, but the skill is preformed in a real-life situation when needed.

Judgment-based assessment uses clinical judgments from multiple sources to collect information about children and to supplement the data obtained from norm-referenced and criterion-referenced instruments (Losardo & Notari-Sylverson, 2001). It is often difficult to obtain information about the capabilities of children with severe disabilities because of their response limitation on formal and informal tests. In judgment-based assessment, input from families, teachers, and professionals assists in making clinical judgments about the strengths, needs, and abilities of the child. Such information is used to plan appropriate interventions.

Family assessment emphasizes the importance of family involvement as equal partners on the interdisciplinary team; the family members are valid and unique sources of information in assessing and making clinical judgments about their child's performances in a variety of function areas. A recommended practice in early childhood special education, therefore, is to include the family, to the extent desired, in decision making about assessments and interventions for their child (DEC Task Force, 2000). When the family members are included in the assessment process, it not only ensures their input but also assists them in identifying their priorities, goals, and objectives for their child. Useful information that can be gathered as a part of family assessment can be categorized as follows (McLean, Bailey, & Wolery, 1996):

- Child needs and characteristics likely to affect family functioning (e.g., temperament, responsiveness, consolabilty, regularity, motivation, and persistence)
- Parent–child interactions
- Family concerns (e.g., medical and dental care, respite, finances, orientation about child development)
- Critical stressful events or crisis times
- Family strengths, including personal resources
- Social and emotional support within the family, and an outside support system

Issues in Early Childhood Assessment

The assessment of young children with disabilities is a key component in the delivery of quality services. Quality assessment cannot be performed without the cooperation of the family and highly trained examiners. The key to forming a successful partnership is to involve the family at the initial stages of the assessment process. At these beginning stages, professionals and families should meet to share information and concerns regarding the assessment procedures. Informed participants are able to design an individual assessment that conforms to the needs of the child and the family. All questions regarding the choice of the assessment materials, procedures, and personnel should be fully explained. The assessment should be multidimensional and information should be gathered on multiple occasions (DEC Task Force, 2000).

Few components are as important to successful assessment, evaluation, and intervention as the training of early childhood service providers. Although recommendations for best practice vary from school to school and district to district, adequate preparation of professionals should be a constant. To increase the quality of services provided, examiners should have formal education in such areas as child development, assessment of mental and special abilities, and educational interventions—in addition to formal, supervised, field-based training experiences. Examiners may be required to modify test instructions and physically guide a child through the explanation process in order for the child to comprehend the requirements of the task. As this process demands a great deal of flexibility and understanding on the part of the examiner, he or she must be thoroughly familiar with the test materials and must have an organized plan or sequence of activities to facilitate comfortable interactions with the child (Bondurant-Utz & Luciano, 1994).

Equally important is the psychometric integrity of the respective instruments. Although the reliability and validity of preschool instruments have been criticized in recent years, their vulnerability appears to be diminishing as users have been demanding and test publishers have begun providing instruments with the same level of sophistication as those used with school-age populations (Fewell, 2000; McConnell, 2000). Standardized instruments with large, nationally representative normative samples, theoretically valid content areas, published validity information, and user qualification criteria are all hallmarks of a good instrument. Assessment instruments that are commonly used with young children with disabilities are highlighted in Table 10.3.

Each child is unique, regardless of disability or classifying conditions. Factors such as age, place of residence, socioeconomic status, genetic factors, environmental factors, personality, and cultural heritage shape the developmental and educational status of the child and must be considered within the unique components of the child's development. Researchers have found that while some developmental patterns signal the possibility of difficulties later on, others do not—making early identification of certain disabilities extremely difficult. Logically, then, the occurrence of a disability such as mental retardation only serves to complicate a procedure that is already delicate and fragile. Early childhood service providers must asses these abilities using methods and instruments that fairly yet appropriately identify the disability and its related areas. Understanding how children grow and develop relative to their own unique conditions and abilities is essential to designing sound intervention strategies (Drew, Hardman, & Logan, 1996).

TABLE 10.3

Types of Assessments Used with Young Children

Instrument	Areas Tested	Norm-Referenced (N) or Criterion-Referenced (C)	Age Range	Types of Scores
Assessment, Evaluation, and Programming System Measurement for Three to Six Years (Paul H. Brookes)	Cognitive Adaptive Social/emotional Fine motor Gross motor	C	3–6 years	Domain percent scores

Battelle Developmental Inventory
 	
(Riverside Publishing Company)
	Adaptive
	Social/emotional
	Communication
	Motor
	Cognition
		N	Birth–6 yrs	Standard scores
				  (Mean=100; SD=15)
				Developmental
				  percentiles
				Age equivalents

Brigance Inventory of Early Development—R (Curriculum Associates)	Preambulatory motor Gross motor Fine motor Self-help Speech and language General knowledge Readiness Basic reading Manuscript writing Basic math	C	Birth–7 yrs	Estimated developmental age scores
Carolina Curriculum for Preschoolers with Special Needs (Paul H. Brookes)	Cognition Communication Social Adaptive Fine motor Gross motor	C	2–5 years	Estimated developmental age scores
Developmental Assessment of Young Children (PRO-ED)	Cognitive Communication Social/emotional Physical Adaptive behavior	N	Birth–5 yrs 11 months	Standard scores (Mean = 100; SD = 15)
Developmental Assessment for Individuals with Severe Disabilities—2 (PRO-ED)	Social/emotional Language Sensory motor Activities of daily living Basic academics	C	Birth–6 yrs	Developmental age equivalents
Devereux Early Childhood Assessment (The Psychological Corporation)	Social Emotional	N	2–5 years	Standard scores (Mean = 50; SD = 10)
Hawaii Early Learning Profile for Special Preschoolers (Vort Corporation)	Self-help Motor Communication Social Learning Cognitive	C	3–6 years	Estimated developmental age scores *Continued*

TABLE 10.3
Continued

Instrument	Areas Tested	Norm-Referenced (N) or Criterion-Referenced (C)	Age Range	Types of Scores
Learning Accomplishment Profile—Diagnostic (Kaplan, Inc.)	Physical Self-help Social Academic Communication	N	30–60 months	Z scores Age equivalent scores
Mullen Scales of Early Learning (American Guidance Service)	Gross motor Fine motor Expressive language Receptive language Visual perception	N	Birth–5 years 7 months	Standard scores (Mean = 0; SD = 1)
Peabody Developmental Motor Scales (Riverside Publishing)	Gross motor Fine motor	N	Birth–5 years	Standard scores (Mean = 100; SD = 15)
Portage Guide to Early Education—R (Cooperative Educational Service Agency)	Infant stimulation Socialization Language Self-help Cognitive Motor	C	3–6 years	Estimated developmental age scores
Preschool and Kindergarten Behavior Scales (PRO-ED)	Social skills Problem behaviors	N	3–6 years	Standard scores (Mean = 100; SD = 15)
Preschool Language Scale—3 (PLS-3) (The Psychological Corporation)	Receptive language Expressive language	N	Birth–7 years	Standard scores (Mean = 100; SD = 15)
Social Competence and Behavior Evaluation—Preschool Edition (Western Psychological Services)	Social competence Affective expression Adjustment	N	2 years 6 months–5 years	Standard scores (Mean = 50; SD = 10)
Social Skills Rating System (American Guidance Service)	Social skills Problem behavior Academic competence (K–6th grade only)	N	3–5 years	Standard scores (Mean = 100; SD = 15)
Test of Early Language Development—3 (TELD-3) (PRO-ED)	Receptive language Expressive language	N	2 years–7 years 11 months	Standard scores (Mean = 100; SD = 15)
Vineland Social Emotional Early Childhood Scale (American Guidance Service)	Social Emotional	N	Birth–5 years 11 months	Standard scores (Mean = 100; SD = 15)

Variables also exist in terms of time of day of alertness with each child, in particular with infants. Results can be affected if the child is not rested, fed, comfortable, and attentive. This means that only a few hours per day may be available for optimal testing. The child's stage of development will also impact the test results. During particular developmental stages, children are strongly attached to the primary caregiver, which means that the primary caregiver must be present with the child for assessments to occur.

Children who are delayed in development may not comprehend the testing process and may need repeated prompts and encouragement as well as repeated explanations. The extra time required then impacts the physical and mental endurance of the child to attend to the task at hand, which at times, requires extra sessions to complete the assessment.

DESIGNING PROGRAMS FOR YOUNG CHILDREN

When designing and implementing programming for young children with disabilities, several factors must be taken into consideration—including legal issues, service delivery models, curricular models and issues, and transition. These and other components will be discussed in the following sections.

Legal Issues

The placement of young children with special needs is affected by IDEA 1997, P.L. 99-457, and P.L. 102-119. Services vary according to age of the child.

Services for Infants and Toddlers. Under Part C of IDEA, which is permissive legislation, states can apply for federal grants to establish a state-wide coordinated system of **early intervention** services to eligible infants and toddlers, with disabilities or who are at risk, and their families. An individualized family service plan (IFSP) is required for each eligible infant or toddler and the family. Infants and toddlers are eligible for services if they are identified as developmentally delayed, as determined by each state.

Early intervention services must include a multidisciplinary assessment, service coordination, and a written IFSP developed by a multidisciplinary team including the parents. Services should be designed to meet the developmental needs of the child and concerns of the family, covering areas such as special education, vision, assistive technology, social work, audiology, early identification, family support, health, medical (for evaluation purposes only), psychological services, occupational and physical therapy, transportation, speech and language therapy, and transition. Necessary services are outlined in the IFSP. A statement of the natural settings where early intervention services are delivered must be included. Natural settings include the home, child care centers, play groups, or any other settings for typical infants and children.

Services for Preschoolers. Under IDEA 1997 (P.L. 105-17), all states must provide a free appropriate public education (FAPE), including special education and related services for 3- through 5-year-old children with disabilities. Necessary services are stipulated in either an IFSP or IEP for all eligible children. Although services for 3- to 5-year-old eligible children are not considered to be as family-focused as services for infants and toddlers, parents or guardians play an important role in the education of their children, as contributing members of the interdisciplinary team that is conducting the assessment and stipulating the programming and services for the child.

Service Delivery Models

The educational needs of young children with disabilities differ from those of their school-age counterparts. To meet the diverse needs of younger children, greater flexibility and variety in service delivery options are needed. Primarily, four settings are used to provide services to young children with disabilities: (1) hospital-based settings, (2) home-based settings, (3) center-based settings, and (4) a combination of home- and center-based settings. Each of these options has certain benefits and disadvantages, as summarized in Table 10.4.

Hospital-Based Services.   Due to the emphasis on early detection among the medical and educational communities, newborns who are at high risk may be placed in neonatal intensive care units for specialized care. These units provide specialists in neonatology to care for the child and to provide education, guidance, and support for the parents. Referrals are made based on the individual children and their families (DEC Task Force, 1993).

Home-Based Services.   Home-based settings are used to provide services to children in their own home. The interventionist comes to the child's home and works individually with the child and the family. Most importantly, the interventionist works with the parents (or caregivers) to implement the activities and trains the parents to work with the child. Home-based services are considered more normalized because the natural environment for the child is the home. Visits by the early interventionist are scheduled weekly or biweekly as needed. Progress of the child is monitored by the family members and the interventionist.

This early intervention and training actively involve and educate the family so that they can participate at a higher level in planning later in the child's life, when the learning environment shifts away from the home. From a monetary viewpoint, home-based services are less expensive, as facilities do not need to be provided for education and transportation costs are incurred only by the interventionist. Home-based settings offer a realistic option in rural areas where it is impractical for children to travel long distances to early childhood centers.

A possible disadvantage of the home setting is that it may place undue stress on parents as they become the child's primary teacher. This role of parent as teacher may interfere with the role of parent as nurturer of the child. Specialists and related service providers may not be available to come to the home, so that services available to the family may not be as comprehensive as at an early childhood center. Also, parents may not have any contact with or support from other parents, as they would in a center-based program.

TABLE 10.4
Advantages and Disadvantages of Service Delivery Models

Model	Advantages	Disadvantages
Home-based	Rapport with family is more easily established.	Parents are responsible for implementing much of the intervention.
	Family routines are less likely to be disrupted.	Teachers spend potential planning and instructional time traveling from site to site.
	Children are more at ease, less frightened in familiar surroundings.	No opportunity exists for peer interaction and socialization.
	Materials can be designed to meet the needs of the natural setting.	
	Building and maintenance costs are unnecessary.	
Center-based	All primary and support services are housed in one location.	Cost of providing facilities and range of services is high.
	Teachers have more time for planning and instruction.	Center may need to provide transportation and bus aides, which increases cost.
	Situation promotes peer interaction and socialization.	Families may move and time may be lost in reorganizing bus routes or locating the family.
Combination	Greater flexibility in delivering services is possible.	Same as with home- and center-based models.
	Same as with home- and center-based models.	
Consultation	More efficient use of staff time.	Parents are responsible for implementation of the intervention.
		Imposes on parents to transport children.
		Limited amount of service can be provided to child or family.

Center-Based Services.   Services in center-based programs take place in a single location outside the home. Professionals consider center-based programs most appropriate for preschool-age children who require services from a team of specialists, who need peer models or peer interaction, and whose parents are not always available to participate in their education. Some programs accommodate only children with disabilities while others include children both with and without disabilities. Usually, the children attend the center for 3 to 5 hours per day, 4 to 5 days per week. Effective center-based programs have curricula that are unbiased and nondiscriminatory and are housed in buildings that are physically accessible to the children and their parents.

The advantages of center-based programs include the availability of a wide variety of specialists, increased opportunity for contact with children who are developing normally, and a support group for parents. Disadvantages of such programs include the expense of transportation, the cost and maintenance of the facility, and reduced individual contact for the family with an interventionist.

Combination Programs. Combined home- and center-based programs have the advantages of both settings. The combined program has flexibility and can be individualized to meet each child's needs. The child can receive the full range of services in the center and also benefit from the naturalistic environment of the home (Cook et al., 2000).

Curricular Models

A **curriculum** is defined as a set of experiences designed to accomplish specific developmental or learning objectives (Hanson & Lynch, 1995). In developing curriculum, three tasks need to be addressed: (1) establishing the *content,* or what is taught, (2) finding appropriate skills for each child, and (3) identifying methods for teaching the content and skills (Wolery & Fleming, 1993). The curriculum for early intervention programs should provide for a child's holistic development through integrated learning experiences, be based on a sound theory of learning, contain specific guidelines for implementation, and include comprehensive plans for evaluation (Bricker, 1998).

The philosophy underlying the curriculum for young children who are at risk or who have disabilities involves the following components (Cook et al., 2000; Driscoll & Nagel, 2002):

- *The content:* The content of the curriculum must have meaningful goals for the child, and the curriculum content should be culturally relevant. The content of the curriculum should foster the development of the child with special needs and encourage self-directed learning and positive relationships.
- *The child's stage of development:* The curriculum design and the activities selected should be appropriate for the child's stages of development.
- *Intervention strategies:* The philosophy underlining the curriculum should lead to the selection of methods that are effective in teaching children with special needs.
- *Social relationships:* The curriculum should provide activities that nourish social relationships. The context for teaching skills should involve social interactions of the child with significant adults, such as caregivers and teachers, as well as with other children.

Young children with special needs are increasingly receiving services in integrated or inclusive settings. (The case study "Maggie and Ida" presents one child's story.) The following are guidelines and offer useful considerations in developing a curriculum for inclusive settings (Richey & Wheeler, 2000):

- Young children, both those with and without disabilities, should share a common curriculum.
- Adaptations should be made so that the curriculum is appropriate for children with diverse learning styles and competencies. Instructional techniques should include both child- and teacher-directed activities.
- Experiences should stem from child initiations, as well as teacher-initiated activities.
- Play experiences should foster active engagement and interaction of all the children.
- An ecological approach should involve professionals and families in coordinating the curriculum to meet the needs of every child participant. Involving families helps to ensure the ecological validity of the curriculum.

Maggie and Ida

Maggie Erickson, a preschool student, and Ida Singer, an 87-year-old elder who volunteers in the Intergenerational Inclusive Preschool Program, have become important parts of each other's lives. Just how important can be seen in the following excerpts from conversations with Cathy Erickson, who is Maggie's mother, and with Ida.

Maggie's mother says: My daughter, Maggie, attends the JCC preschool for two days each week. Ida comes in every morning that Maggie is at school to help her. During the evenings, Maggie and I talk about everyone at the JCC preschool and Maggie always speaks of Ida with fondness. Like any child, Maggie is sometimes slow about getting ready to go to school. When that happens, I remind her, "You will get to see Ida today!" and before I know it, she is out the door. Last year, Maggie had to have a cast put on her leg and she needed to stay home from school. She was thrilled when Ida made a special trip to visit her at our home.

Elders such as Ida provide love and acceptance to the children with disabilities and their classmates, and the children provide the same to the elders. Elders also contribute a wealth of life experience to the children and to the classroom curriculum. Too often, families who have children with disabilities tend to become isolated. It is nice to know that there is another adult in Maggie's life who can provide her with support and acceptance.

"Grandma" Ida says: I have always had a very wonderful feeling about grandparents. I never knew my own grandparents, but I've always thought they are very special—you can learn from them. I'm a different kind of grandma for the preschool children. Their grandmas are all young—busy and socializing. I'm the spoiling grandma.

When Maggie first came to the preschool, she used to play mostly by herself, with the dolls. At first she really needed me there. I tried not to hover over her or "smother" her with attention. I'm sure it is easy to do that, but I thought if I gave her too much attention, she couldn't grow. So I try to take a backseat. I keep an eye on what Maggie is doing, in case she needs my help, but also interact with all of the kids.

Now Maggie is mixing well with the children. She is benefiting on her own because she is doing a lot on her own. She likes everybody.

I never realized that 3-year-olds were so smart. You can carry on a conversation with a child and learn a lot from them. For instance, even though I have a disability— I walk with a cane—the children learn to handle it. They realize that I can't pick them up readily. They learn that people have limitations. Like with my glasses. They would ask, "Why do you have to wear glasses, Ida?" They said, "Take them off!" I took them off and asked, "So how do I look?" "You still look like a grandma!" It keeps me young—keeps me younger—knowing that the children accept me for who I am.

I think it is important to get the different generations together. I think it is beneficial to the kids to have an overall picture of what people are—of what older people are, of what younger people are, of the different ways there are to live. If kids see an older person who can help themselves, it leaves an impression.

Working with the children makes a difference in how I feel about myself. I feel capable. It gives me a challenge, something to look forward to. If the children respond to something I do or say, then I feel good. I have a good feeling when I leave the classroom.

Source: From "Maggie and Ida," by L. A. Heyne, 1996, *Impact, 9*(4), p. 11. Copyright © 1996 by Institute on Community Integration, University of Minnesota, Minneapolis. Reprinted by permission.

We now turn our attention to some specific curriculum models. Keep in mind, however, that to date, no single curricular approach has been demonstrated to be superior to the others with all children. In practice, most early intervention programs combine approaches. When all is considered, professionals agree that the curriculum should be based on the individual needs of the child and the family.

Cognitive-Developmental Curriculum.   This model is based largely on the work of the Swiss psychologist Jean Piaget. Piaget considered the child an active agent in the learning process of trial-and-error experiments. According to Piaget, skills develop hierarchically and children pass through developmental stages in a highly predictable fashion. The following major ideas are emphasized in the cognitive curriculum (Driscoll & Nagel, 2001; Kostelnik, Soderman, & Whiren, 1999):

- Activities should allow children to develop their own thinking.
- Activities should be appropriate for the child's stage of development.
- A child's concepts and learning develop through direct day-to-day experiences.
- Encouragement and reinforcement foster cognitive learning.

Behavioral Curriculum.   The basis of the behavioral curriculum is the theory that a child's learning can be enhanced by changing and managing the events in the child's environment. From the behavioral view, the environment must be carefully structured, manipulated, and managed to foster effective learning. The specific objective of the behavioral model is to teach the child functional, age-appropriate, and useful skills. Skills are taught in the behavioral curriculum according to the child's or infant's needs in the present or projected future environment. The model defines skills precisely in behavioral terms and states criteria for performance clearly and

Supporters of behavioral curriculum maintain that the structure can be relaxed and skills integrated as learning progresses.

quantitatively. Supporters of this approach maintain that children who lack essential skills require a highly structured approach to learning and that the structure can be relaxed and skills integrated as learning progresses. Wolery, Bailey, and Sugai (1988) report that experimental evidence indicates that the behavioral curricula help children with disabilities, but the method remains controversial. Fewell and Kelly (1983) point out that opponents of the behavioral approach argue that the use of such an approach inhibits the cognitive and emotional development of young children with disabilities by prohibiting interaction with the environment.

Ecological-Functional Curriculum: The ecological-functional curriculum is based on the idea that young children must live and learn in many different environments—such as the home, school, or neighborhood—and that each of these environments has interactive effects on the child and the family.

The ecological-functional curriculum recognizes diversities in family cultures, languages, values, and ethnic backgrounds, thereby promoting individual family priorities. The selected curricular activities should be functional and meaningful for the child in the current setting as well as in a future setting.

The DAP Curriculum. Developmentally appropriate practice (DAP) contains guidelines for early childhood education programs as recommended by the National Association for the Education of Young Children (NAEYC) (Bredekamp & Copple, 1997). The DAP curriculum is an integrated, holistic approach to the education of young children. It is strongly influenced by the Piagetian constructivist theory. Developmentally appropriate programs assist children to grow socially, emotionally, cognitively, and physically and reflect children's learning activities. The DAP curriculum strongly recommends that children with disabilities be fully included in natural environments with typically developing children, with required services and supports provided to meet the needs in these settings (Bredekamp & Copple, 1997).

DEC Recommended Practices.   The Division for Early Childhood (DEC), a division of the Council for Exceptional Children, has incorporated many practices of DAP in the development of its recent curriculum guidelines (DEC Task Force, 2000). Several earlier criticisms of DAP have been addressed in this document, which demonstrates that the DAP philosophy of early childhood education has gradually blended with the early childhood special education philosophy (Carta, 1994; DEC Task Force, 2000; Umansky & Hooper, 1998).

The recommendations of both DAP and DEC are to identify relevant practices for all children and to understand when modifications of teaching methods are required for specific children (DEC Task Force, 2000). As more young children are included in natural settings, the fields of both early childhood and early childhood special education must continue to work together to address the needs of all children.

Three curricular models that have integrated the DAP guidelines and DEC recommended practices are activity-based intervention, learning centers, and a naturalistic perspective. Activity-based intervention is child-directed and uses routines as the structure to provide direct instruction and child initiated activities.

IMPLEMENTING PROGRAMS FOR YOUNG CHILDREN

Programs for infants and preschoolers differ from programs for school-age children in the amount of time spent in school and in the goals and objectives for learning. Yet teachers of young children face similar challenges in arranging the classroom and scheduling the school day. Workable classroom arrangements and effective scheduling are crucial to the success of infant and preschool programs.

Classroom Accommodations and Adaptations

Organizing the physical space in the classroom is the first step in facilitating learning. Designing the optimal classroom requires careful planning. Among the factors teachers must consider are the following:

1.   *The space available:* State education agencies usually dictate the minimum allowable space for infant and preschool classrooms. But the shape of the room and the presence of such fixed features as windows, sinks, and toilets sometimes inhibit optimal classroom arrangements. Polloway and Patton (1997) suggest that teachers begin planning room arrangement by drawing a rough sketch of the room, then adding in such basic equipment as tables, desks, and chairs. In designing classroom space, materials should be placed to facilitate student learning and involvement. Teachers should be mindful of their schedule and create a traffic flowchart to and from activities in the classroom with discernible boundaries that separate areas of instruction.

2.   *The physical needs of the students:* The physical needs of preschool children who have disabilities often differ from those of their typically developing peers.

Teachers need to take the equipment needs of young children with disabilities into consideration, allowing adequate room for movement with wheelchairs, walkers, and other equipment needs.

3. *Group arrangements:* Infant and preschool programs use a variety of group arrangements during the school day. Individual work areas should be located together in a quiet area. Group work areas should be away from the individual work area and should be flexible and fluid to allow for configuration and reconfiguration of small-, medium-, and large-group activities. The various areas should be plainly labeled to facilitate flow within the classroom, enable students to identify their assigned area, and promote student involvement.

4. *The purpose of instruction:* Lesson objectives frequently suggest the location and type of space needed. Activities that involve direct teacher instruction (e.g., language learning) require a more structured, quieter setting than activities that involve only teacher supervision (e.g., free play). Peer interactions may involve individual, parallel, or cooperative activities. Thus, the design of the classroom also must consider how the students will interact socially. A classroom that encourages social development will include appropriate locations for solitary, parallel, and cooperative activities. In an inclusive classroom, each child as well as the group must be considered in determining how and where instruction will be delivered.

5. *Material accessibility:* Searching for materials stored in out-of-the-way places can waste valuable teaching time, and materials that are not readily available are less likely to be used. Also, because fostering independence is an important goal of early childhood special education programs, teachers should avoid making materials difficult for children to locate and secure on their own. Lund and Bos (1981) suggest placing instructional areas close to material storage places, keeping frequently used materials close together to facilitate accessibility, and labeling or color-coding storage areas.

6. *Personal territory:* Like their school-age counterparts, children in preschool arrive with a variety of personal possessions. A safe and accessible space is needed in the classroom to store outerwear, storybooks, toys, and so on. Gray (1975) points out that personal space in the classroom contributes to the child's sense of belonging. Lund and Bos (1981) suggest using cubbies or lockers for children's personal belongings and picture cues to assist students in identifying their personal space.

In considering these six points, the teacher is viewing the individual child from various perspectives that will enable the teacher to determine not only what is best for the child but also to what extent the child can be included in a general education classroom for meaningful participation with children who are not disabled. One way to help teachers arrive at the proper balance for children with special needs is to use the preschool checklist presented in Figure 10.3 (Drinkwater & Demchak, 1995). The checklist covers the areas of scheduling and instructional arrangements, socialization and communication, alternative communication, and appearance of the child to aid teachers not only in including children with special needs in a general education classroom but also in creating goals to enable the inclusion to be successful. Benefits that Drinkwater and Demchak attribute to including students with special needs in the general education classroom are "(a) enhanced skill generalization, (b) increased self-initiations in social situations, (c) equivalent development gains to nondisabled peers, (d) preparation for

Teacher: _____   Student: _____

Date: _____

SCHEDULING AND INSTRUCTIONAL ARRANGEMENTS

yes   no   1. Is the child positioned so that he or she can see and participate in the activity?

yes   no   2. Is the child positioned so that other children and teachers may easily interact with her or him (e.g., without an adult between the child and other children, not isolated from other children)?

yes   no   3. Is the child involved in the same activities as other children?

yes   no   4. Does the child engage in activities at the same time as other children?

yes   no   5. Is the child actively involved in activities (e.g., plays a role in group activities, asks/answers questions)?

yes   no   6. Is the child given assistance only as necessary?

yes   no   7. Does the child use the same or similar types of materials during activities as other children?

yes   no   8. Are the least intrusive, natural prompts and contingencies used, if needed, to help the child to participate in the activity?

yes   no   9. Are the materials appropriate for the chronological age of the child?

yes   no   10. Does the child participate in activities that are appropriate for his or her chronological age?

SOCIALIZATION AND COMMUNICATION

yes   no   1. Does the child have a way to communicate (e.g., signs, gestures, pictures, speech) with other children?

yes   no   2. Do the other children know how to communicate with the child (e.g., use gestures, understand simple signs, respond to pictures)?

yes   no   3. Does the child socialize with other children (e.g., playing at free time, using playground equipment)?

yes   no   4. Is the socialization/interaction with other children facilitated (e.g., children are prompted and reinforced for initiations and interactions)?

yes   no   5. Do teachers interact in the same way with the child as with other children (e.g., praise, hugs)?

yes   no   6. Is the child given opportunities to demonstrate competence (e.g., line leader, passing out snacks, helper of the day)?

ALTERNATIVE COMMUNICATION (If this section is not applicable to the child, please skip to the next section.)

yes   no   1. If the child uses an alternative communication system (e.g., signing, picture cards), do other children know how to use it?

yes   no   2. Do teachers know how to use the alternative communication system?

yes   no   3. Is the alternative communication system always available to the child?

APPEARANCE OF THE CHILD

yes   no   1. Does the child have accessories that are similar to those of other children (e.g., small backpack, hair clips)?

yes   no   2. Is the child's dress age appropriate?

yes   no   3. Is clothing for activities appropriate (e.g., paint shirts; napkins, not bibs)?

yes   no   4. Are personal belongings (e.g., change of clothing, diapers) carried discreetly?

yes   no   5. If the child has special equipment, is it kept clean?

yes   no   6. Is the child's hair combed and kept neat?

yes   no   7. Are the child's hands clean and dry?

yes   no   8. Is the child's clothing changed as necessary to maintain a neat appearance?

FIGURE 10.3

Preschool Checklist: Integration of Children with Disabilities

---

SUMMARY OF THE PRESCHOOL CHECKLIST

Scheduling and Instructional Arrangements: _____/10

Socialization and Communication: _____/6

   Alternative Communication: _____/3 (if applicable)

Appearance of the Child: _____/8

Total Score: _____/24 (or 27 if Alternative Communication is applicable)

GOAL AREAS

Please feel free to use this section to set goals for yourself and your assistant(s) on ways that you can more fully include the targeted student in preschool activities and routines.
Goal areas to lead to fuller inclusion:

_____

_____

FIGURE 10.3

Continued

Source: From "The Preschool Checklist; Integration of Children with Severe Disabilities," by S. Drinkwater & M. Demchak, 1995, *Teaching Exceptional Children, 28*(1), pp. 4–8. Copyright © 1995 by the Council for Exceptional Children. Reprinted by permission.

dealing with the real world, (e) increased communication skills with peers and family members, and (f) increased number of nondisabled friends" (1995, p. 7).

Transition

Early childhood special education services are divided into two components: early intervention services for infants and toddlers from birth to age 2, and preschool services for children 3 to 5 years of age. **Transition** is the process of moving or changing a child from one service component or delivery system to another (Hanson, 1999). Ideally, the transition should be a smooth passage or an evolution rather than a sudden and unsettling relocation. An expansion of the concept of transition includes changes that occur within a specific program. Such changes occur when a child moves to a new class, starts with a new teacher, begins service with another service provider, or changes schedules and routines (Bailey & Wolery, 1993).

Young children who have been in B–3 programs must make the transition to a preschool program when they reach age 3. The next significant transition for young children who have special needs occurs at about age 6, as the child moves into either an integrated kindergarten environment or a special education program in the elementary school. Families and children must adjust to new locations, new teachers and staff, and changes in program format, curriculum, and emphasis. The level of parental involvement, intensity of parental contact, or availability of services for parents changes in each location and at the various age levels of the child.

Meet a child preparing to transition out of birth–3 services by visiting the Companion Website at www.prenhall.com/ beirne-smith and selecting Chapter 10, Video Case Studies.

FAMILY INVOLVEMENT

IDEA stipulates that families participate on the IFSP and IEP committees as collaborators. The law also requires that family needs and resources be assessed and the parents be counseled about their child's needs and assisted in acquiring services for the child. Family members have the opportunity for active participation in the writing of the IFSP and IEP and in the child's instruction. The law does not explicitly define *family,* but the definition used in this chapter refers to "two or more people who regard themselves as a family and who perform some of the functions that families typically perform. These people may or may not be related by blood or marriage and may or may not usually live together" (Turnbull, Turnbull, Shank, & Leal, 1995, pp. 24–25).

When professionals gain information about the family in an individual and personal way, then the professional is in harmony with the family's strengths, weaknesses, desires, expectations, priorities, and needs. Turnbull and Turnbull (2000b) note that, historically, families and parents have been viewed as fulfilling eight major roles: (1) the source of the child's disability, (2) organization members, (3) service developers, (4) recipients of professionals' decisions, (5) teachers, (6) political advocates, (7) educational decision makers, and (8) collaborators.

Heward (2000) outlines seven roles that parents of children with special needs fulfill:

1.   *Teaching:* Many children learn skills in an incidental fashion, but children with special needs must be directly instructed to learn many tasks. Since families are in day-to-day contact with these children, the family becomes the first teacher in early childhood. Some families must further learn to use special equipment and devices in order for their children to function in society.

2.   *Counseling:* In addition to the normal counseling role that parents deal with in addressing emotions, feelings, and attitudes, the parents of the child with special needs must also deal with greater intensity in these areas due to the disability. The disability itself must be addressed with the child, siblings, and greater society. The parents must guide the child through the day-to-day life with a disability.

3.   *Managing behavior:* Again, this is in addition to the normal role of parenting in training children toward the behavioral expectations of society. Many times parents first must be taught how to handle behavior so that they in turn can teach the child and then society at large.

4.   *Parenting siblings without disabilities:* No two children without disabilities are identical, but the difference is magnified when a disability is present. Parents must learn to parent both their children with and without disabilities so that all their children reach their full potential. In the course of their parenting, parents also must teach siblings without a disability about the disability itself and how this disability impacts the sibling with the disability, the family, and the siblings without the disability.

5.   *Maintaining the parent-to-parent relationship:* Having children decreases the time that parents have for themselves as a couple, but when a child with a disability is born, the time shrinks even further. To find time for themselves as a couple, the parent must leave the child with a disability in a competent care situation. This

requires additional stress for the parent in an already stressful situation, as the care-taker must be educated in the role of the parent. In addition to time is the factor of money. Many disabilities require additional funds to care for the child who is dis-abled, which decreases the funds available for parent time as a couple.

6. *Educating significant others:* Just as parents must educate caretakers of their child with a disability, the parent also must educate those in the family and the com-munity who come in contact with their child. Children with disabilities require con-sistency in their lives, and this happens only when the family and the community can be educated and respond in a single-minded fashion toward the child with a disability.

7. *Relating to the school and community:* The parents' role is that of advocate for their child. No one knows the child as intimately as the parent. The school and com-munity, therefore, should seek to include the parents in an active collaborative role for the benefit of the child with a disability and for the benefit of the school and com-munity. When all who work with the child are acting in a manner that is consistent, then the child with a disability benefits.

Summary

Companion
Website To check your understanding of this chapter, go to the Companion Website at www.prenhall.com/ beirne-smith and select Chapter 10. From there, you can access the Self-Test and Essay modules.

Rationale for Early Childhood Special Education
- Research supports the importance of early childhood special education in growth and development of infants, toddlers, and young children with dis-abilities or who are at risk.
- The focus of early childhood special education is on early intervention and programming.

Serving Young Children with Disabilities
- Recently passed laws recognize the need for special education early inter-vention services for infants, toddlers, and young children—with disabilities or at risk for disabilities—and their families.
- IDEA Part B extends the rights and privileges of IDEA to preschoolers and their families.
- IDEA Part C establishes new priorities for meeting the needs of infants and toddlers with disabilities and their families.

Assessment in Early Childhood Special Education
- Assessment includes three major purposes: (1) identification and diagnosis, (2) program planning, and (3) program evaluation.
- Assessment is a multistage process including (1) Child Find/case finding, (2) de-velopmental screening, (3) diagnosis, (4) individualized planning of programs and interventions, (5) performance monitoring, and (6) program evaluation.

Designing and Implementing Programs for Young Children
- Educators responsible for planning and implementing appropriate early in-tervention services must identify current resources, coordinate existing

programs, and develop innovative service delivery models with the informed consent of the family.

- Professionals must make classroom accommodations and adaptations based on space available, physical needs of the students, group arrangements needed, purpose of instruction, material accessibility, and personal territory.
- As children with special needs and their families move through the various service options in special education, planned transition services are necessary.

Family Involvement

- As stipulated by IDEA, families participate on the IFSP and IEP committees as collaborators.
- Parents of children with special needs fulfill the following roles for their children: (1) teaching, (2) counseling, (3) managing behavior, (4) parenting siblings without disabilities, (5) maintaining the parent-to-parent relationship, (6) educating significant others, and (7) relating to the school and community.

Chapter

11

School Years

350

OBJECTIVES

After reading this chapter, the student should be able to:

- Discuss the key fundamental provisions of the Individuals with Disabilities Education Act (IDEA)
- Explain the educational environment options available under IDEA for students who have intellectual disabilities
- Describe educational assessment and program planning procedures used with students who have intellectual disabilities
- Discuss key elements of educational programming for elementary-age learners with mental retardation, with special attention to curricular and instructional issues
- Discuss key elements of educational programming for secondary-age learners with mental retardation, with special attention to curricular and instructional issues

KEY TERMS

annual goals	IEP team	parity
behavioral objectives	inclusion	reciprocity
benchmarks	individualized education program (IEP)	Regular Education Initiative (REI)
collaborative consultation	job coach	related services
collaborative teaming	mainstreaming	short-term objectives
curriculum	natural supports	transition services

T hus far, we have dealt with the causes, characteristics, and assessment of individuals with mental retardation. This chapter, using the information presented previously, focuses on the critical task of developing and implementing educational programs that give all individuals with intellectual disabilities, regardless of their limitations, the opportunity to participate as much as possible in the activities of their daily environment.

We look at a number of key aspects in the process of educational programming for elementary- and secondary-age learners, beginning with an overview of the fundamental components of the Individuals with Disabilities Education Act (IDEA). Next, we review the educational environment options and consider the appropriateness of these placement alternatives. In the subsequent section, we examine the basic elements of program planning, with an emphasis on the individualized education program (IEP). Then we address programming for elementary-age learners by identifying various curricular orientations used in schools, discussing the curricular needs of students with mental retardation, and highlighting key instructional features. Finally, we look at educational programming for secondary-age learners, discussing educational placements for secondary students with mental retardation, curricular emphases at the secondary level, transition planning, and vocational preparation.

IDEA: AN OVERVIEW

The purpose of this section is to identify the major elements of IDEA that have a direct effect on the educational programming of students with mental retardation. Thirty years have passed since the initial passage of the Education for All Handicapped Children Act of 1975 (EHA, P.L. 94–142). In spite of various efforts to restrict its interpretation, its influence on the delivery of services to students with mental retardation has been profound—bolstered by significant amendments over the years that have strengthened and expanded various provisions of the law.

On December 3, 2004, President Bush signed into law the most recent reauthorization of IDEA (P. L. 108-446). IDEA (2004) enhances certain existing provisions of the law and adds significant new aspects to the legislation. Most provisions of P.L. 108-446 go into effect on July 1, 2005.

One significant and controversial addition to IDEA (2004) is the definition of and requirement for "highly qualified" special education teachers, as follows:

Sec. 602(10). "Highly Qualified."

1. Requirements for all special education teachers:
   a. All special education teachers come under NCLB definition (Sec. 9101); *plus* special education teachers must:
   b. Have state special education certification *or* have passed state licensing exam *and* have license to teach special education;
   c. Have not had certification or licensure waived on emergency, temporary, or provisional basis; *and*
   d. Have at least a bachelor's degree.

2. Requirements for special education teachers teaching students under alternate achievement standards (used for teachers teaching core academic subjects *only* to children assessed against alternate standards as established under NCLB regulations):
   a. Must *either* meet NCLB highly qualified requirements (Sec. 9101) for any teacher new or not new to the profession; *or*
   b. Meet NCLB requirements for elementary teachers or middle school teachers with subject knowledge appropriate to the level of instruction being provided.
3. Requirements for special education teachers teaching multiple subjects (applicable to those teaching two or more core academic subjects *only* to children with disabilities):
   a. Must *either* meet NCLB highly qualified requirements for any teacher new or not new to the profession; *or*
   b. If not a new teacher, must demonstrate competence in all subjects taught under NCLB, which may include "high objective uniform state standard of evaluation" (HOUSSE) covering multiple subjects; *or*
   c. If a new teacher who is highly qualified in math, language arts, or science, must demonstrate competence in other core subjects taught, as under NCLB, which may include a HOUSSE, *not later than 2 years after being hired.*
4. This definition does not create a right of action by a single student or class of students for failure of the teacher to be highly qualified.
5. Teachers deemed highly qualified under this provision are considered highly qualified for the purposes of NCLB.

According to Mandlawitz (2006) the controversy surrounding the marriage of the NCLB highly qualified definition of "any public elementary or secondary school teacher" arose because "NCLB requires that new teachers teaching multiple core subjects, as defined in NCLB and now in the IDEA, have an academic major or advanced degree, or pass a competency exam in each subject area taught. Teachers not new to the profession under NCLB may demonstrate competency based on a 'high objective uniform State standard of evaluation' (HOUSSE), which may involve multiple measures of teacher competency established by the individual state" (p. 3). Mandlawitz notes that this may prove particularly difficult for middle or high school special education resource teachers who are required to provide services to students for a full range of academic subjects. Thus, IDEA allows special education teachers to meet either the NCLB or HOUSSE option—or for teachers deemed highly qualified in math, language arts, or science, to establish competence not later than 2 years after being hired in any other core academic area taught.

Key Components of IDEA

Other key provisions form the essential components of IDEA (2004), as described below.

Free Appropriate Public Education.   A *free appropriate public education* (FAPE) means that school districts must provide special education and related services

To think more about educational accommodation requirements set forth in IDEA, go to the Companion Website at www.prenhall.com/beirne-smith and select Chapter 11, Read and Respond.

FIGURE 11.1
Related Services Specified in IDEA

Source: IDEA (1993),
§300.24(b)(1–15).

Audiology
Counseling services
Early identification and assessment of disabilities in children
Medical services
Occupational therapy
Orientation and mobility services
Parent counseling and training
Physical therapy
Psychological services
Recreation
Rehabilitation counseling
School health services
Social work services
Speech-language pathology services
Transportation

necessary for students with special learning needs. These services are available to all students, regardless of severity of disability, and are provided at no cost to the family. If school programs cannot meet a student's specific needs, other agencies must provide necessary services at public expense.

The schools also must furnish any number of related services when deemed necessary to ensure an appropriate education. Many students with mental retardation will qualify for one or more related services. A listing of related services is provided in Figure 11.1.

Appropriate Evaluation.   IDEA requires that a "full and individual initial evaluation" be conducted prior to a student with mental retardation receiving special education and related services for the first time. The parents, SEA or other state agency, or LEA may request an initial evaluation. The law also requires the following safeguards: parents' informed consent, implementation of nondiscriminatory evaluation practices, evaluation by a team, use of more than one procedure, testing in the language and form most likely to yield accurate performance information, and reevaluations conducted when necessary.

Furthermore, *all* children with disabilities must participate in *all* state-wide and district-wide assessments, with IEP designated accommodations and alternate assessments. Allowances for alternate assessments are included in IDEA, but such assessments must be aligned with the state's academic content, achievement, or alternate standards.

Individualized Education Program.   An **individualized education program (IEP)** is a written document summarizing a student's learning program, and it is required for every student who qualifies as having a disability. The major purposes of an IEP are to establish learning goals for an individual child, to determine services the school district must provide to meet those learning goals, and to enhance communication among parents and other professionals about a student's program. Both the stated goals and the services to be delivered should depend on an analysis of a

Companion Website *A complete online glossary is available on the Companion Website, which may be accessed at www.prenhall.com/ beirne-smith*

student's present levels of performance. The required elements of the IEP are discussed in more depth later in the chapter.

The 1997 IDEA amendments emphasize that attention must be given to "how a child's disability affects the child's involvement and progress in the general curriculum." Although consideration of a student's involvement in general education has been part of IDEA over the years, the most recent amendments now require a statement explaining the extent, if any, to which the student will not participate with students who are not disabled. Statements related to the student's participation, or lack of participation, in state- and district-wide assessments must also be included in the IEP. The 1997 amendments also increased the role of the general education teacher in the development of the IEP.

The 2004 amendments retained the commitment to provide **transition services** to students. A statement of needed transition services is required beginning at age 16. Such services are defined within the law as follows:

> The term "transition services" means a coordinated set of activities for a child with a disability that—
>
> (A) is designed to be within a results-oriented process, that is focused on improving the academic and functional achievement of the child with a disability to facilitate the child's movement from school to postschool activities, including postsecondary education, vocational education, integrated employment (including supported employment), continuing and adult education, adult services, independent living, or community participation;
>
> (B) is based on the individual child's needs, taking into account the child's strengths, preferences, and interests; and
>
> (C) includes instruction, related services, community experiences, the development of employment and other postschool adult living objectives, and when appropriate, acquisition of daily living skills and functional vocational evaluation. (IDEA, §602[34])

Two provisions from the 1997 reauthorization of IDEA were continued in the 2004 amendments. First, by age 16, and updated annually thereafter, a statement of transition service needs must be in place. Second, "beginning at least one year before the child reaches the age of majority under State law," a statement that the student has been informed of his or her rights that will transfer to the student on the age of reaching majority must be completed.

Least Restrictive Environment.   Schools must educate children with mental retardation—to as great an extent as possible—in general education settings with their peers who are not disabled. The *least restrictive environment* principle provides an opportunity for students with mental retardation to attend school in the most inclusive setting possible, which, most often, is defined as the general education (i.e., regular class) setting.

Parent and Student Participation in Decision Making.   Parents have always been encouraged, at least legally, to participate in the special education process. Parental consent must accompany every decision affecting a child or youth who is disabled. Specifically, parents must consent to the evaluation of a student's educational abilities and needs, the determination of necessary services, and the actual placement of a child in any type of special program. In addition, parents have the right to obtain an *independent educational evaluation* (IEE) of their child. Lastly, parents have had the right to challenge or appeal any decision related to any aspect of the special education process.

The 2004 amendments make it clear that parents are primary members of the IEP team. The amendments also strengthen efforts to increase student involvement in the decision-making processes of their education, especially as this relates to transition planning.

Procedural Safeguards.   A number of safeguards were included to protect the rights of both parents and their children. Parents are guaranteed the following rights: to obtain all educational records, to secure an IEE, to request a due process hearing, to appeal decisions, and to initiate civil action when appealing a final hearing decision. The 2004 reauthorization of IDEA retained the disciplinary provisions of the 1997 law but clarified the language related to manifestation determination, suspensions and conduct that is not a manifestation of a disability, and provision of educational and interim alternative services. The 2004 reauthorization also added provisions for a "resolution session" prior to a due process hearing, imposed status limitations for presenting complaints or making court appeals, and added procedures to determine surrogate parents for a child who is homeless or a ward of the state.

EDUCATIONAL ENVIRONMENT OPTIONS

The trend today toward providing beneficial, humanistic services to persons who are mentally retarded has led to changes in the structure of American schools, with a clear emphasis on providing appropriate education within inclusive settings whenever possible (Smith, Polloway, Patton, & Dowdy, 2004). The intent of this section is to provide a historical context for the evolution of services for children and youth with mental retardation and to discuss the various educational environments in which students with mental retardation are taught in schools today.

Evolution of Service Delivery

The free public school system in the New World was established in 1642 (Spring, 1986). Before that time, education was mostly limited to church-sponsored programs for which the provision of equal education for all children was not a concern. During the early part of the 19th century, states enacted laws that required communities to offer educational opportunities but did not make attendance mandatory. These efforts at mass education emphasized the importance of curricular content and not the needs of individual children. For the most part, children with mental and physical disabilities were excluded from school.

When students with mental retardation were provided an education, it was typically done in segregated settings—often in separate schools. The "two-box" arrangement (Reynolds, 1989) (i.e., students with disabilities served in special education settings and students without disabilities served in general education settings) exists to this day. However, the incipient elements of a more inclusive system were woven into the Education for All Handicapped Children Act of 1975 (EHA, P.L. 94-142), with its stipulation that education should be provided in the least restrictive environment. Nevertheless, the original act established, and all subsequent amendments/reauthorizations have maintained, the need for a continuum of educational alternatives.

As Reynolds (1989) has noted and Polloway, Smith, Patton, and Smith (1996) have documented, the history of special education is one of progressive inclusion. Over time, we have moved from exclusion to inclusion in school settings of students with disabilities. This trend, which includes phases when terms such as *integration* and *mainstreaming* were commonplace, has led to the current era of inclusive education. The conviction is to educate all students who are disabled, including those who are mentally retarded, in general education settings whenever possible.

The goal of the movement toward more inclusive education for students with mental retardation is to provide them with educational opportunities that will maximize their potential, give them access to the general education curriculum, and ultimately allow them to acquire the knowledge and skills to function fully in society. Interestingly, wholehearted agreement on how best to accomplish this goal is the subject of ongoing debate in the field of special education. Some special educators support full integration and the dissolution of the current special education system that maintains other placement options. Others maintain that a full range of placement alternatives is necessary to meet the special needs of students with disabilities.

From our perspective, professionals responsible for determining the initial educational environment for any student who is mentally retarded should look first at the most inclusive setting. However, whichever setting is chosen, it should be considered with the option to make appropriate changes as the needs of the individual student dictate. Furthermore, the movement of students who are mentally retarded from more segregated to more inclusive settings should drive educational programming. At the very least, this means that students who are included in general education settings must be provided the appropriate supports and services to ensure their success in the inclusive setting.

Setting Options

As mentioned previously, a continuum of options exists for providing an appropriate education to a student who is mentally retarded. The various educational environments that are used by the U.S. Department of Education (DOE) are regular class, resource room, separate class, public separate facility, private separate facility, public residential facility, private residential facility, and home/hospital environment. Although some states use different terminology to describe placement options, here we will use the DOE designations for organizational purposes.

The information on where students with mental retardation are served in schools can be found in the annual reports to Congress that the U.S. Department of Education publishes each year. The *Twenty-fourth Annual Report to Congress on the Implementation of the Individuals with Disabilities Education Act* (2004) reflects a significant increase in the number of students with disabilities currently being served in general education settings.

Regular Class (General Education)

When placement decisions are made judiciously and reviewed routinely, the goal of providing the most beneficial services to students who are mentally retarded with minimal segregation from their peers is attainable. Many students who are mentally retarded can reach this goal in the general education classroom with only minor adaptations in instructional procedures or the learning environment.

Instructing students who are mentally retarded in the general education classroom requires teachers who are highly skilled and sensitive to these learners' needs. Successful inclusion is most likely to be achieved when five critical dimensions are in evidence (see Figure 11.2).

According to Keogh (1990), special education and general education teachers must be able to maintain a reasonable balance between the special needs of students who are disabled and other students in the classroom. In addition to creating settings characterized by the attributes noted in Figure 11.2, general education teachers need to be skilled at judging the capacity of their students to learn and adjust instruction accordingly. They must also be able to predict and intervene, when problems arise among peers, and know how to handle the insecurities of students with mental retardation who cannot compete with their peers in all areas.

Instructional Supports.   In certain instances general education teachers are able to teach pupils who are mentally retarded in their classrooms with the help of some special education materials. The material may be a high-interest, low-vocabulary reading series, a programmed reader, a job-related mathematics book, or any material or hardware that allows the teacher to individualize instruction. This level of special education support requires a highly skilled general education teacher who is willing and able to accommodate, modify, and adapt instruction to meet the needs of learners who are mentally retarded.

Personnel Supports.   In this arrangement, the special education teacher collaborates with the general education teacher in a variety of ways. For instance, the special education teacher may be involved in demonstrating materials or equipment,

FIGURE 11.2
Critical Dimensions of Inclusive Classrooms

Source: From *Teaching Students with Special Needs in Inclusive Settings* (3rd ed.), by T. E. C. Smith, E. A. Polloway, J. R. Patton, & C. Dowdy, 2001, Boston: Allyn & Bacon. Adapted by permission.

- Sense of community and social acceptance
- Appreciation of student diversity
- Attention to curricular needs
- Effective management and instruction
  - Successful classroom management
  - Effective instructional techniques
  - Appropriate accommodative practices
  - Instructional flexibility
- Personnel support and collaboration

assessing the child's needs, developing teaching strategies, or providing instructional assistance as a co-teacher in the general education classroom. This level of support also requires that the general education teacher be willing to accommodate, modify, and adapt instruction to meet the needs of learners who are mentally retarded.

The success of either of these two arrangements depends on a reasonable student–teacher ratio. When classrooms are overcrowded, teachers become frustrated; frustrated teachers are less likely to attempt to accommodate the special needs of students who are disabled.

Itinerant Services. Some school districts use itinerant services as a way of providing needed supports to the general education teacher. Itinerant teachers travel from school to school and provide consultative and instructional services as needed. These teachers visit each of their assigned schools periodically, usually working in individualized or small-group instruction with students who have special needs that hamper their scholastic progress. Since these services are limited (visits are typically weekly or biweekly), responsibility for these students' education rests largely with the general education teacher.

The use of *paraeducators* (i.e., educational assistants, teacher's aides) has increased significantly as a way to provide support to students with mental retardation—especially those with more extensive needs—in general education settings. Paraeducators can fulfill many different roles in supporting students in general education settings.

Resource Room Services. The purpose of the resource room is to provide educational support to students who are mentally retarded and their teachers. The main difference from the previous educational arrangement is that the support provided occurs outside the general education classroom. In this arrangement, students with intellectual disabilities remain in the general education classroom for the majority of the school day and receive supplemental instruction on a regularly scheduled basis in the resource room.

The role of the resource teacher is to instruct students and to consult or collaborate with the general education teacher, other service providers, and parents or guardians (see Figure 11.3). In a finely tuned resource program, there is consistency between what occurs in the resource room and what occurs in the general education classroom. Goals and objectives are similar, and methods of teaching and procedures for evaluating students and programs are coordinated and compatible. Such a program requires general and special education teachers who are attuned to the needs of the students and are highly skilled in both instructional methodologies and collaboration.

Separate Class

Special class programs provide a self-contained instructional environment for students who are unable to profit fully from education in the general education classroom. Classes of this kind usually serve no more than 10 to 15 students and often have an aide to assist the teacher. The aide's duties may vary from preparing materials to instructing small groups under teacher supervision.

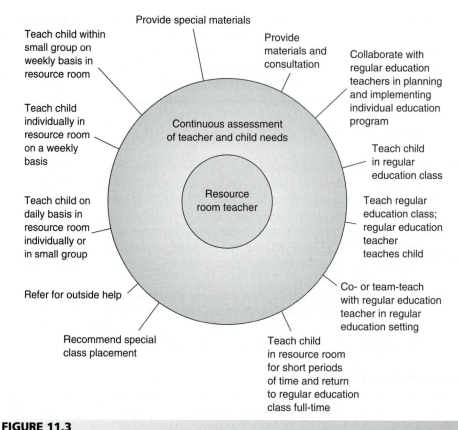

FIGURE 11.3
Service Alternatives for the Resource Room Teacher

Self-contained special classes are designed for children who cannot keep up with the pace of instruction in a general education classroom or for whom the nature of the curricular content is not appropriate. Generally, the special education class consists of a group of children identified as mentally retarded and in need of specialized intervention in terms of curriculum and instruction. Students typically receive all their academic instruction in the self-contained class; however, in some cases, they may divide their academic day between self-contained class instruction in some subjects and general education class instruction in others. Although special class students usually participate in general physical education, art, and music classes, they are largely segregated from the larger school environment.

Segregation in self-contained special classes is a significant concern, as such placement can be debilitating in its potential to stigmatize the student or discourage the development of social relationships with peers. Every effort must be made to determine the types and intensities of supports needed for the student to succeed in more inclusive environments. However, this need must be balanced by the assurance that the curricular needs of students are being met appropriately. The placement of students in self-contained settings can be justified only after a thorough examination of student needs.

Separate Facilities

Historically, school districts placed the majority of their students who had mental retardation in special schools. Under this arrangement, students were bused to a day school whose sole purpose was to serve students with disabilities. In separate schools, it is possible to control for all the variables in the learning environment—scheduling, physical facilities, instructional climate, and so forth. Arguments favoring this arrangement suggest that such settings provide maximum benefit to certain students who have not faired well in their neighborhood schools.

The disadvantage of special schools is the absence of contact with peers who are not disabled. Thus, the educational experience presents an unrealistic picture of the world and eliminates the benefits that students with intellectual disabilities gain through modeling and socialization with their typically developing peers. Such gains can be substantial, and as a result, few public school districts continue to have separate facilities for students whose academic and behavioral needs are not severe.

Separate Residential Facilities

In cases in which a student with mental retardation has educational and social disabilities so pronounced as to warrant round-the-clock attention, the student might attend a special residential school. Facilities of this kind have very low pupil–staff ratios, which benefit the students by allowing intensive instruction and support. Such facilities, however, deny pupils who are mentally retarded the opportunity to interact with peers who are not disabled.

It is important to note that a very small number of students have needs so severe that they require the highly specialized treatment offered in residential facilities. Many of these individuals have behavioral disorders or physical conditions that demand close attention. The environment of a residential school may, then, for some individuals, be the least restrictive environment in which they can function effectively. Even then, according to IDEA, constant monitoring is essential, so movement back to other more inclusive educational placements can be considered.

Home/Hospital Environments

Homebound instruction and hospital tutelage represent the last two educational environments available for school-age children and youth with mental retardation. These options are usually considered more temporary settings for those students who are unable to participate in other settings, often due to illness or injury.

Homebound instruction is similar to hospital instruction in that it is provided for students who are temporarily unable to attend school. Itinerant or general education teachers usually furnish the instruction. Since it is costly, segregates the child from peers, and provides limited time for instruction, homebound instruction should be considered a last resort.

Hospital instruction is usually temporary and limited to students who are recovering from an illness or accident. For students confined to a hospital or convalescent home for serious, chronic afflictions, however, hospital instruction is a continuing process. Itinerant or general education teachers often teach such students, although some children's hospitals have fully developed educational programs. Such programs usually employ a multidisciplinary approach to the treatment of the individual's illness or injury and often include certified special education teachers who work with other team members in designing and implementing the educational component of the treatment plan.

Focus on Inclusion

Researchers and educators have long questioned the efficacy of separate, special class placement for students with disabilities. In recent years, the entire system of delivering services to students with disabilities has come under fire. In the mid-1980s, the Office of Special Education and Rehabilitation Services of the U.S. Department of Education advanced a proposal called the **Regular Education Initiative (REI)** (Will, 1984). In this proposal, Will recommended fundamental changes in the ways in which we educate students with disabilities, including those categorized as mentally retarded. The REI proposed a merger of special and general education services that would result in providing educational services to students with disabilities within the framework of the general education system.

As a result of the REI, professionals in special education began to make distinctions between the traditional special education practice of mainstreaming and the newer reform-based practice of inclusion. Generally, the term **mainstreaming** refers to the practice of placing students who are disabled in the general education classroom (physical integration) to the extent appropriate to their needs. Some mainstreamed students would spend their entire school day in the general education classroom, but most utilized the resource room option. The special educator assumed primary responsibility for the education of students who were mainstreamed. The term **inclusion,** on the other hand, implies more than simple physical integration. It is predicated on the idea that students with disabilities are welcomed and embraced as participating and contributing members of the general education classroom. The general educator assumes primary responsibility for the education of students who are included.

Strong proponents of inclusion have viewed mainstreaming as an irresolute attempt to integrate students who are disabled in general education settings. In addition, some advocates of inclusion recommend the elimination of the full continuum of services for students who are disabled. Moreover, they argue that current special education practices—particularly identification, categorization, and separation of services—have proven ineffective in meeting the needs of large numbers of students with disabilities. One of the most powerful arguments against the placement of students in special education settings outside the general education classroom is that the instructional methodologies used by special educators (i.e., what happens in special education) are not that "special" and more like those of general educators (Lilly,

Students who are retarded profit from being in an education environment that is as normal a setting as possible.

1986). Perhaps the most compelling argument for inclusion is that placement in a special education class is no more effective than placement in a general education class (Glass, 1983; Skrtic, 1991). However, those concerned about the demise of the availability of a continuum of services also have challenged the research questioning the effectiveness of special education. They point out that this research is less than substantial and methodologically flawed (Hallahan, Keller, McKinney, Lloyd, & Bryan, 1988; Kauffman, 1987; Schumaker, & Deshler, 1988).

Staunch opponents of providing education to students with mental retardation in inclusive settings argue that diluting or eliminating hard-won services for students who had been poorly served in or excluded from general education programs without analysis of what will happen is dangerous (Keogh, 1988). Furthermore, many parents, students, and general and special education teachers are, for the most part, satisfied with the continuum of services (Guterman, 1995; Semmel, Abernathy, Butera, & Lesat, 1991). Inclusion opponents also have noted that the potential of the general education system to serve students with disabilities is untested. Inclusion opponents have pointed out that the necessary resources and supports and services required to serve these students appropriately in general education settings currently are not available (Baker & Zigmond, 1995; McKinney & Hocutt, 1988).

Research on inclusion has determined that in order for inclusion to be successful, certain instructional conditions must be present, including the following:

- Teachers must be philosophically committed to meeting the needs of all students in the general education classroom.
- Teachers must have time to plan and think about the needs of diverse learners.

- Teaching practices that meet the needs of all students must be incorporated into the instructional program.
- General education teachers must collaborate with special education teachers to assess, teach, and monitor student progress.
- Short-term, intensive instruction from a special education teacher needs to be available for some students with disabilities.

Efforts are under way to expand the role of and provide support for the general education teacher in educating students with special needs. Such innovations as teacher assistance teams (Chalfant & Pysh, 1989) and mainstream assistance teams (Fuchs, Fuchs, & Bahr, 1990) are designed to restructure referral procedures to include a prereferral component intended to limit the number of students referred to and subsequently placed in special education programs. Such approaches as collaborative consultation (Idol, Nevin, & Paolucci-Whitcomb, 1999), collaborative problem solving (Knackendofel, Robinson, Deshler, & Schumaker, 1992), peer collaboration (Pugach & Johnson, 1989), and peer coaching (Showers, 1985) are designed to deliver support to general education teachers in accommodating the needs of students with disabilities in their classrooms. Collaboration is a common element in each of these innovative approaches.

View an inclusive classroom by visiting the Companion Website at www.prenhall .com/beirne-smith and selecting Chapter 11, Video Case Studies.

We believe that inclusive settings are desirable and should always be considered for placement of students with mental retardation. However, we would quickly add that such consideration should be guided by the critical dimensions of successful inclusive settings that were highlighted in this section. We also think that it is important to be cognizant of the fact that a select group of students with mental retardation, particularly those whose needs are pervasive and not easily addressed by conventional interventions, will benefit from having available to them a range of educational options.

Final Thoughts on Placement

The characteristics of the individual, the philosophy and mission of the school, the parents, and the community influence the individual's assignment to an educational program. Child-related variables include the nature of the disability, motivation, academic skills, and behavioral characteristics. School variables include the nature of the general education class program, the availability of appropriate special education facilities, and the competence of educators. Parental and community factors include parental support, home environment, and community services.

Although these factors influence placement decisions, the strongest determinant in keeping with the prevailing trend toward inclusion should be the attempt to educate students who are disabled in as normal a setting as is feasible. The student should be integrated as much as possible within the school, the home, and the local community. In essence, programs that segregate students with disabilities from the normal environment are the least desirable placement alternative.

ASSESSMENT AND PROGRAM PLANNING

This section explores the important topics of assessment and the development of individualized education programs. Recall that the topic of assessment, particularly as it relates to eligibility determination, was covered in chapter 3. This chapter focuses on the use of assessment to generate information useful for program planning purposes.

Assessment for Programming

Comprehensive, accurate assessment is critical to the delivery of appropriate educational services to students with mental retardation. As one of the mandated components in the assessment process, educational assessment has three general purposes:

- To provide data that are usable by the interdisciplinary team in determining eligibility for special education services
- To determine the student's present level of performance and future instructional needs
- To evaluate the outcomes of educational programs

For students with intellectual disabilities, educational assessment has two additional purposes:

- To identify the supports needed to further the learner's independence, productivity, and community integration
- To evaluate the effects of the supports (AAMR, 1992)

The first step in conducting a comprehensive educational assessment is to evaluate referral information and the accompanying documents (e.g., school records, work samples) to determine the areas for further assessment. Each technique that is selected should be multifaceted and tailored to the needs of the individual student. Furthermore, observations should be conducted across settings and over time. Once the initial test battery has been selected and administered, the resulting data should be analyzed to determine areas in need of further testing. The process of testing and analyzing data should continue until the tester is satisfied that all necessary information has been collected.

A comprehensive educational assessment should have several outcomes. First, it should give an overall picture of the student's present level of performance. Second, it should pinpoint the specific strengths and weaknesses in the student's behavioral repertoire. Third, it should clarify the logical next steps in the student's development—often the next steps on the assessment scale. Instead of coming up with a single score or label, the assessment process should yield many individual items of information and point to many different areas where instruction would be beneficial in moving the student toward more independent functioning.

As mentioned in chapter 10, norm- and criterion-referenced assessments provide the assessor with different kinds of information. In *norm-referenced* assessment, a student's performance is compared to the performance of age- or grade-level peers. Norm-referenced measures provide a global picture of the student's level of functioning. Standardized achievement or intelligence tests are likely to be norm-referenced. Such measures are useful in obtaining information for placement decisions but are more limited in providing the type of information needed for program planning.

Criterion-referenced or *curriculum-referenced* assessments measure a student's mastery of specific, observable behavior and are more useful for program planning purposes. In criterion-referenced assessment, the student's performance is measured against a preset criterion (e.g., 80%) or the student's previous performance on a task, skill, or concept. Curriculum-referenced assessment is one type of criterion-referenced assessment. In curriculum-referenced assessment, the student is tested on what was taught. Both criterion- and curriculum-referenced assessments are useful in determining instructional objectives. Curriculum-referenced assessment, however, is more easily incorporated in daily lessons and thus provides the teacher with a clearer picture of the student's ongoing progress.

Hundreds of behavioral criterion-referenced assessment tools are available. They either include a range of skill areas or focus on one or two discrete areas (e.g., sight-word vocabulary, mathematical facts, or dressing behavior). Several disciplines (e.g., speech/language and physical therapy) have highly specialized but useful tools. Tools vary in their usefulness and objectivity, and prospective users must examine them carefully.

When selecting an assessment tool, the professional must take care to match its complexity and difficulty level with the student's level of performance. Special care, for instance, must be taken when selecting an assessment instrument for use with individuals whose cognitive functioning falls at the lower end of the scale. Testers must take care to select instruments that give credit to individuals who are lower functioning for rudimentary behaviors and that are sensitive to slight improvements in skill levels. For this reason, many teachers choose to develop their own assessment tools. Teacher-developed assessment tools often reflect what is being taught in the classroom and thus are useful in guiding the teacher in planning instruction and measuring student progress.

Whatever assessment tool is selected, teachers must ensure that the data collected are usable for the purposes of formulating goals and objectives for the IEP, planning instruction, or evaluating student learning. Finally, teachers must be aware that "testing conducted for the purposes of making a diagnosis and developing or evaluating educational programs measures an individual student's functioning level or ability at a given point in time, not the actual potential of that student" (AAMR, 1992, p. 113). In other words, assessment should be an ongoing process that is part of an ongoing educational program.

The IEP Team

The 2004 amendments of the IDEA stress the importance of the **IEP team**. This team essentially is charged with the task of developing a comprehensive and appropriate educational program for a student with a disability. As specified in the law [§ 614 (d) (1) (B)], the team should be composed of the following members:

- The parents of the student
- At least one general education teacher of the student (if the student is participating in general education)
- At least one special education teacher of the student
- A representative of the school system (public agency) who is (a) qualified to provide, or supervise the provision of, specially designed instruction to meet the unique needs of students; (b) knowledgeable about the general education

curriculum; and (c) knowledgeable about the availability of resources of the school system

- An individual who can interpret the instructional implications of the evaluation results
- Other individuals, at the discretion of the parent or the school system
- The student, if appropriate

To meet the challenges and responsibilities of formulating the IEP and making a placement decision, IEP team members rely heavily on assessment data. Usable assessment data, therefore, are critical to the effective functioning of this team. The rationale behind the use of an IEP team is that students who are mentally retarded (as well as students with any disability) have a variety of needs that can best be met through input from individuals with a broad range of training, experience, skills, insights, and perspectives.

Each has an important contribution to make to the team effort. Typically, the size of the team increases proportionally to the degree or intensity of the student's needs. For instance, for some students who are mentally retarded and have extensive needs, the IEP team is likely to include a speech/language pathologist, a physical therapist, and an occupational therapist, to name a few. The team must make a coordinated effort to decide about such critical areas as instructional objectives, educational placement, instructional strategies, and evaluation. To maximize effects and avoid duplication of efforts, the team should meet regularly to plan and review programs and should carefully delineate each person's responsibilities.

Developing the IEP

An individualized education program (IEP), as described earlier, is a written plan of action that specifies an individual's progress toward specific educational goals and objectives. The purpose of the IEP is to organize and integrate the total educational program to maximize instructional benefits for the learner. As previously emphasized, usable assessment data are necessary to fulfill this purpose. The IEP provides a measure of accountability for teachers and schools. The intent of IDEA is that teachers use the IEP as a functional guide to confer with other service providers and parents about the educational program, to develop instructional plans, and to record student progress.

Historically, IEP committees have used levels of intellectual functioning to make placement decisions and to design educational programs for students who were mentally retarded. Students with more severe retardation, for example, often were placed in more restrictive, less inclusive settings and provided instruction in such basic areas as self-care, communication, and socialization: The supports-based definition of mental retardation (Luckasson et al., 2002) recommends that the responsibilities of the IEP committee for students who are mentally retarded move beyond merely "matching" the student with a particular setting or set curriculum to an IEP committee that does the following:

- Collects and analyzes a broader set of assessment information (adaptive skills and limitations; physical, medical, and psychological characteristics and needs; and environmental strengths and limitations)
- Translates these assessment data into a profile of needed supports to compensate for, improve, or overcome the student's current performance in specific areas of weakness
- Develops plans (i.e., IFSPs [individualized family service plans] IEPs, ITPs [individual transition plans]) to address how the educational services and other needed supports will be delivered to the individual, involving agencies beyond the school when appropriate
- Designs programs that include the student, to the greatest extent possible, in educational, social, and leisure activities with peers who do not have disabilities and supplies the educational supports to enable successful inclusion and prevent segregated programs
- Evaluates the individual's progress under these plans and makes improvements on at least an annual basis considering assessment data, diagnosis, actual services and supports delivered, location of placement, the individual's progress, and the family's and student's degree of satisfaction (AAMR, 1992, p. 116)

Companion Website For more information about topics covered in this chapter, including sample IEPs and instructional strategies, visit the Companion Website at www.prenhall.com/ beirne-smith and select Chapter 11, Web Destinations.

General Components.   IDEA specifies the components but not the form of the IEP, so formats vary widely by locality. The 2004 amendments to the IDEA state that every IEP must have the following general components:

- *Statement of the student's present levels of educational performance.* This should include how the disability affects progress of the student in the general education curriculum and participation in appropriate activities.
- *Statement of measurable annual goals.* Derived from assessment data, **annual goals** are statements of what a student can reasonably be expected to achieve in the course of one school year.
- *Statement of benchmarks or short-term objectives.* Benchmarks, or short-term objectives, which previously were required for all students with an IEP, are now required only for children who take alternative assessments aligned to alternate achievement standards—that is, only for children who are severely cognitively disabled. **Benchmarks** or **short-term objectives** are behaviorally stated objectives based on annual goals that provide a clear direction for instruction and ongoing evaluation of student progress. Examples of behaviorally stated objectives are provided later in this chapter.
- *Statement of the special education and related services and supplemental aids and services and a statement of the program modifications or supports for school personnel that will be provided.* Each IEP must contain a statement of the type of special education services provided (e.g., resource) and who is responsible for providing those services. **Related services** refer to additional services (see Figure 11.1) needed to ensure that the program meets all of the student's educational needs. Related services may be delivered directly to the student, or they may take the form of family services (e.g., parent training). The law also requires that all modifications and requisite supports for the student be doc-

umented. This requirement helps with advancement toward attaining the stated goals and continued progress in the general education curriculum as well as in extracurricular and other nonacademic activities.

- *Explanation of the extent, if any, to which the student will not participate with nondisabled students in the regular class.* The extent of participation varies according to the individual's unique needs and is determined by the expected benefits on a case-by-case basis. Some students may benefit from full inclusion in the general education program, while the needs of others may prohibit participation in the general education program at the time in question.
- *Statement of any individual modifications in the administration of state- or district-wide assessments of student achievement.* The 1997 amendments make it clear that students with mental retardation are expected to participate in high-stakes testing. If, however, participation, with or without accommodations, is not appropriate for a student, an explanation must be provided, and an alternative plan for assessing the student must be offered.
- *Projected date for the beginning of the services and modifications and the anticipated frequency, location, and duration of those services and modifications.* Each IEP must contain an indication of the date on which special education services will begin and their anticipated duration. Identification of the educational environment(s) in which services are to be delivered is also required.
- *Statement of how the student's progress will be measured and how the student's parents will be regularly informed.* This statement provides more evidence of the increased attention to accountability promulgated in the 1997 amendments.

Transition Service Needs. The IEP must include a statement, "beginning not later than the first IEP in effect when the child is 16 and updated annually, of appropriate measurable postsecondary goals based on age-appropriate transition assessments related to training, education, employment, and where appropriate, independent skills" [§ 614 (d) (1) (A)]. This statement also must cover transition services, including courses needed to assist in reaching the goals.

Age of Majority. Beginning at least 1 year before the student reaches the age of majority, which varies from state-to-state, each IEP must contain a statement of information regarding rights transferred on reaching the age of majority.

IEP Goals and Objectives/Benchmarks

Determining goals and objectives/benchmarks is an important aspect of developing the IEP. IEP team members and teachers who write IEP goals and objectives must attend carefully to the results of assessment data. Teachers can draw on a number of sources to determine appropriate educational goals and objectives, remembering that a goal is relevant only to the degree to which it is functional for each individual and reasonably attainable during the school year. Goals and short-term objectives/benchmarks can be drawn from curriculum guides, assessment instruments that provide meaningful information on pertinent behaviors, state standards, or careful observation of a learner's needs in everyday settings.

As mentioned previously, *goals* refer to the broader, long-term outcomes. Examples of *functional* areas addressed by long-term goals are improving self-care skills, such as clothing selection; developing the skills associated with a specific occupation; or learning to make a weekly home budget. Examples of *academic* areas addressed by long-term goals are increasing mathematics skills in counting money, increasing sight vocabulary skills, or improving handwriting skills. Instructional or behavioral objectives/benchmarks are derived from long-term goals and refer to logically arranged sequences of specific, short-term steps toward meeting the annual goal. These objectives/benchmarks are important not only for planning purposes but also for monitoring the progress of a student.

Behavioral objectives are statements that specify an observable behavior, the conditions under which it will occur, and the acceptable standard for accuracy against which to measure performance. Listed below are hypothetical examples of behavioral objectives that are appropriate for teaching functional skills to elementary-age students with severe mental retardation:

- Given five coins of different denominations, Pedro will arrange the coins in order from most valuable to least valuable at least four of five times.
- Given a toothbrush, toothpaste, and a cup of water, Mikala will brush her teeth, moving the brush along all surfaces and using a circular brushing pattern for at least 2 minutes.
- When prompted, Curtis will maintain eye contact with the teacher for at least 2 seconds within 5 seconds of the cue.

Teachers of students with severe intellectual disabilities too often concentrate instruction on discrete skill areas and fail to teach the student to generalize the use of the skill to other settings, with other people, or to similar tasks. Generalization is discussed in greater detail later in this chapter. For now, at the planning stage, it is important for teachers to remember that when they write a behavioral objective for teaching a skill in isolation, they also must write a corresponding objective for teaching generalization of the skill.

For the last behavioral objective in our list above, for example, the teacher might write an objective that requires the student to use the skill with various people. For example:

- When prompted, Curtis will maintain eye contact with the teacher, the aide, or a peer for at least 2 seconds within 5 seconds of the cue.

Methods, Materials, and Activities

Most IEP formats used in school districts today include space for the teacher to specify methods, materials, and activities that will be used to meet the annual goals and objectives/benchmarks. Specifying methods, materials, and activities at the planning stage assists teachers in thinking through how they will instruct the student in the classroom.

Methods.   Instructional methods involve actively structuring the learning environment to promote learning of targeted objectives. Specifically, the teacher is concerned with choosing instructional methods that facilitate effective, efficient learning. These variables and corresponding instructional strategies and techniques are discussed later in this chapter.

Materials.   Teachers should choose instructional materials that help promote active learning of targeted skills. Materials can run the gamut—including textbooks and other print materials (e.g., handouts, workbooks), multimedia and software, audio- and videotapes, models/realia, games and toys, and a range of assistive devices. Teachers should use materials that add interest to the lesson, are age-appropriate, closely match the student's ability level, and lead directly to skill acquisition. Materials geared for general education classrooms should be used, with or without adaptation, whenever possible.

Many checklists and scales are available to assist teachers in evaluating materials for use in their classrooms (see Figure 11.4 for an example of a materials evaluation checklist). Many teachers develop their own instructional materials, which are usually less expensive than commercially produced materials and often motivate their students more because they can be personalized.

Activities.   Teachers also plan individual and small- and large-group activities that help in the acquisition of target behaviors. Activities can involve performing motor behaviors, talking, gesturing, writing, classifying, counting, role-playing (participating in simulations), and so on. Activities should be varied to add interest to the curriculum and should provide many opportunities for learners to actively respond. When appropriate, they should take place in real-life settings (e.g., a store or laundry), so that the transition from the simulated to the real-life environment is easier.

Monitoring Progress

According to IDEA, the learners' progress toward targeted annual goals must be measured regularly and conveyed to parents periodically. Highly effective teachers measure learner progress on a daily basis and use the results of the evaluation to make teaching decisions. These teachers test what is taught and use the results of the evaluation to determine what to teach next. Progress (or lack of progress) signals the teacher when to move on to more complex objectives, when to repeat instruction, or when to change instructional objectives, methods, materials, and activities. Data on student performance, used to guide educators in the decision-making process, may be obtained in many different ways. Often, the simplest procedures (e.g., recording the number of correct and incorrect oral responses) provide the teacher with the most accurate indication of learner progress.

EDUCATIONAL MATERIALS EVALUATION CHECKLIST

Title: _____ Subject/Skill Area: _____
Publisher: _____ Brief Description: _____
Address: _____

Yes/No INSTRUCTIONAL SCOPE AND SEQUENCE

___ 1. Are the scope and sequence of the material clearly specified?
___ 2. Are behavioral objectives or learner outcomes specified?
___ 3. Are student prerequisite skills specified in a hierarchical order?
___ 4. Are skills, concepts, and facts ordered in a logical manner from simple to complex?
___ 5. Does the instructional sequence proceed in small steps appropriate for difficult-to-reach students?

Comment: _____

CONTENT

___ 6. Do the concepts and skills included adequately represent the content area?
___ 7. Is the content consistent with the stated objectives?
___ 8. Is the information presented in the material accurate?
___ 9. Is the information presented in the material current?
___ 10. Are various points of view concerning treatment of minorities, persons with handicapping conditions, ideologies, social values, sex roles, socioeconomic status, and so forth, objectively presented?
___ 11. Are the content and topic of the material relevant to the needs of difficult-to-teach students as well as to other students in the general classroom?
___ 12. Is the content appropriate to the
       a. chronological age of the targeted student(s)?
       b. mental age of the targeted student(s)?

Comment: _____

INITIAL ASSESSMENT/PLACEMENT

___ 13. Does the material specify and provide a method for determining initial placement into the material?
___ 14. Does the initial placement tool contain enough items to accurately assess and place the learner into the material?

Comment: _____

ONGOING ASSESSMENT/EVALUATIONS

___ 15. Does the material specify and provide a method for determining ongoing progress in the material?
___ 16. Are there sufficient evaluation items to accurately measure student progress?
___ 17. Are procedures and/or materials for ongoing record-keeping provided that are useful to the student and teacher?
___ 18. Is student progress monitoring possible by self-recording or charting?

Comment: _____

INSTRUCTION

___ 19. Are instructional procedures for each lesson clearly specified?
___ 20. Does the material provide for a maximum amount of direct teacher instruction on the skills/concepts presented?
___ 21. Does the direct teacher instruction provide for active student involvement and response?
___ 22. Are the direct instructional lessons adaptable to small-group/individual instruction?
___ 23. Are a variety of cuing and prompting techniques used to elicit correct student responses?
___ 24. When using verbal instruction, does the instruction proceed in a clear, logical manner?
___ 25. Does the material provide for teacher modeling and demonstration when appropriate to the skills and concepts being taught?
___ 26. Does the material specify correction and feedback procedures for use during instruction?

Comment: _____

PRACTICE

___ 27. Does the material contain appropriate practice activities that contribute to mastery of the skills/concepts?
___ 28. Are the practice activities directly related to the desired outcome skills/behaviors?

Comment: _____

REVIEW/MAINTENANCE

___ 29. Are practice and review of content material provided?
___ 30. Are review and maintenance activities systematically and appropriately spaced?
___ 31. Are adequate review and maintenance activities provided for the difficult-to-teach student?

Comment: _____

MOTIVATION/INTEREST

___ 32. Are reinforcement procedures built in or suggested for use in the material?

___ 33. Are procedures specified for providing feedback to the student on his or her progress?

___ 34. Has the material been designed to motivate and appeal to students?

Comment: _____

ADAPTABILITY TO INDIVIDUAL DIFFERENCES

___ 35. Has the material been adequately field-tested with students with learning difficulties?

___ 36. Can the pace be adapted to variations in student rate of mastery?

___ 37. Can the method of response be adapted to the individual needs of the student?

___ 38. Can the method of instruction be adapted to the individual needs of the student?

___ 39. Can the student advance to subsequent tasks after demonstrating proficiency?

___ 40. Can the student be placed in the material at the learner's own level?

___ 41. Does the material offer alternative teaching strategies for students who are failing to master an objective?

Comment: _____

GENERAL USE CHARACTERISTICS OF THE MATERIAL

___ 42. Is a teacher's manual or set of teacher guidelines for use provided?

___ 43. Are teacher instructions clear, complete, and precise?

___ 44. Are teacher skills needed for appropriate use of the material with students specified?

___ 45. Is the amount of teacher preparation time for initial and daily use of the material specified?

___ 46. Is the estimated amount of daily or weekly time required of the student for effective use of the material specified?

___ 47. Are instructional grouping strategies provided for appropriate use of the material?

___ 48. Are the types of student responses needed for effective use of the material clearly specified for both instruction and practice situations?

___ 49. Is there a simple procedure for verifying correct responses and detecting errors in response?

___ 50. Are correction procedures specified when a student makes an error?

___ 51. Are other materials/media required for effective use of this material?

PHYSICAL CHARACTERISTICS AND COSTS

___ 52. Is the initial cost per student reasonable?

___ 53. Is the replacement cost per student reasonable?

___ 54. Are there extra costs involved in effective use of the material (e.g., duplication, extra materials, equipment, etc.)?

___ 55. Is the material consumable?

___ 56. Is the material durable?

___ 57. Is the material warranted?

___ 58. Is the material safe?

___ 59. Can the materials be easily stored and organized for classroom use?

___ 60. Is the format of the material clear, attractive, and in a type size and style appropriate for targeted students?

___ 61. Are the directions and illustrations for use by the student clear?

___ 62. Are the auditory components of the material clear and adequate?

Comment: _____

EVALUATION SUMMARY

APPROPRIATE USE(S) WITH TARGETED STUDENT(S)   Comment _____

___ Initial Assessment

___ Monitoring Progress/Mastery

___ Instructions

___ Practice

___ Reteach

___ Motivation

___ Not Appropriate

FIGURE 11.4

Educational Materials Evaluation Checklist

Source: From *Teaching the Mildly Handicapped in the Regular Classroom* (2nd ed., pp. 125–127), by J. Q. Affleck, S. Lowenbraum, & A. Archer, 1980, Upper Saddle River, NJ: Merrill/Prentice Hall. Copyright © 1980 by Merrill/Prentice Hall. Adapted by permission.

Final Thoughts on IEPs

Developing, writing, and monitoring IEPs is quite time-consuming, and some teachers report that the burden of the paperwork outweighs the usefulness of the document (Deno & Mirkin, 1980; Morgan & Rhode, 1983; Smith, 1990; Sugai, 1985). Computerized systems have proven useful as a time-saving device for developing and managing IEPs. Computers enable team members and teachers to collect and store student data efficiently, analyze the data rapidly, and produce multiple, legible copies of reports for educational planning (Nolley & Nolley, 1984; Smith & Wells, 1983). Some special educators have expressed concern that computer-generated IEPs foster a "cookbook" mentality and do not reflect a truly individualized program; Jenkins (1987), however, found that computer-generated IEPs were of higher quality than handwritten IEPs.

PROGRAMMING FOR ELEMENTARY-AGE LEARNERS

Educational programming for elementary-age learners with intellectual disabilities involves a number of interrelated and mutually influencing components. Educational programs must be designed, implemented, and evaluated systematically so that educators' decisions will have an optimal effect on the development of each learner. Such programming requires that educators consider variables related to the student, the teacher, and the environment.

The programming process we describe next can work for all educational programs regardless of the learner's age, placement, or level of support needed. Based on the assessment process described earlier in the chapter, the first step is to determine the learner's current level of educational performance, followed by the identification of instructional needs. This particular sequence should result in the development of a comprehensive IEP. The next crucial step is the arrangement of the teaching/learning environment to facilitate the acquisition and maintenance of knowledge and skills deemed appropriate.

Providing effective instruction to any group of students is daunting, due to the complexity of this process when done correctly. Polloway, Patton, and Serna (2001) have developed a model that depicts the many dimensions of effective practice (see Figure 11.5). Without question, many of the instructional variables noted in the model are largely under the direct control of the teacher. However, many teachers are creating learning situations that strengthen the student's engagement in the learning process (e.g., student-directed learning).

Characteristics Revisited

Students who are mentally retarded often have characteristics that teachers must address to make learning profitable for the student. This topic was covered in great detail in chapters 8 and 9, however, three particular characteristics are extremely important to the instruction and are worth revisiting here.

The first characteristic is the tendency to have an *external locus of control;* that is, individuals who are mentally retarded may think they have little control over the

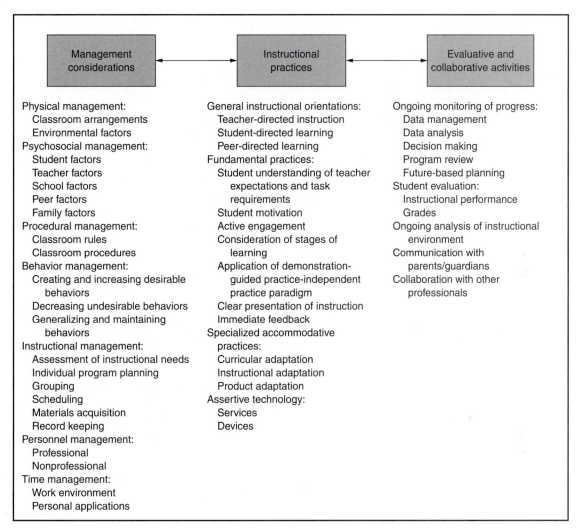

FIGURE 11.5

Dimensions of Effective Practice

Source: From *Strategies for Teaching Learners with Special Needs* (7th ed.), by E. A. Polloway, J. R. Patton, & L. Serna, 2001, Upper Saddle River, NJ: Merrill/Prentice Hall. Copyright © 2001; reprinted by permission of Pearson Education, Inc., Upper Saddle River, NJ.

environment or the consequences of their actions. The teacher can use several strategies to help students become more internally oriented. First, students must acquire skills that are adaptive and functional, so that they actually achieve a measure of control over their environment. Second, instruction should teach the students to associate their actions with their consequences and then to anticipate probable consequences so that they can choose appropriate behaviors. An effective strategy for teaching this type of skill is role-playing, which allows the student to repeatedly practice, in a nonthreatening situation, choosing and using suitable adaptive behaviors. Another strategy involves the use of a social learning contract that spells out, in writing or in pictures, the environmental factors linking various situation-specific behaviors and their possible positive, negative, and neutral results.

A second characteristic that teachers must address is the high *expectancy for failure* shown by many learners who are mentally retarded. This negative orientation is readily understandable, as many students with mental retardation have histories—sometimes extensive ones—of failing to learn new skills. Not only may these individuals anticipate failure when trying to learn new tasks, but they may even refuse to attempt new tasks. Teachers can counteract this commonly seen feature in several ways. First, they should look closely at the results of their assessments and set reasonable, achievable goals and objectives based on the student's demonstrated level of performance/functioning across skill areas. Second, they should structure the instructional program for success by breaking down objectives into small learning steps (via task analysis) and using a rich schedule of positive reinforcements. Third, they can reward effort and improvement along with reaching the objective. Fourth, they can teach students to use overt (i.e., spoken aloud) or covert (i.e., progressive whispers, inner talking, or thoughts) self-talk to monitor or reinforce their own behavior. These and similar strategies can help make students more willing to try new tasks and may lead to positive comments—"I can do it"—that indicate they feel they are likely to succeed, not fail. These types of techniques enhance the development of self-directed learning opportunities.

A third characteristic of learners who are mentally retarded is *outer-directedness,* or a tendency to rely regularly on external cues or instructions for behavior. We all use external cues; however, many individuals with mental retardation may depend on them. For example, a student who needs help with work may wait for the teacher to notice the problem and give advice and instructions. Teachers can reward more self-directed behaviors such as actively asking the teacher for help or independently identifying several possible solutions to the problem and then trying each one until the solution is reached. In every case, teachers must look beyond general characteristics to plan programs based on each individual's characteristics.

Goals for the Student

The educator's primary goal in teaching is creating educational situations in which the student acquires knowledge, concepts, and skills that have been targeted. Meeting this goal involves making wise decisions about placement, assessment, the student, curriculum, instruction, and evaluation. Ultimately, the instructional environment must be arranged properly and effective practices instituted. Doing so ensures that the student with intellectual disabilities (1) acquires a wide variety of academic, social, and functional skills, (2) learns when and where to use them, (3) generalizes learned skills to other new settings and situations, and (4) maintains the skills over time. The educator must keep these four objectives in mind. In this way, the tasks of teacher and learner will be complementary.

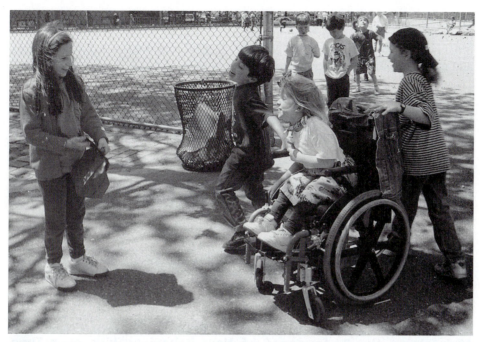

Although children with disabilities have special instructional needs, they are, above all, children.

Acquiring a Variety of Adaptive Behaviors.   Children and youth who are mentally retarded must function successfully in school, home, job, and community settings. To do so, they must acquire knowledge and develop skills in many areas, including many life-related skills (e.g., self-care), mobility, communication, social interactions, academics, health and safety, leisure, and vocational pursuits. While the teacher must target useful learning objectives in each of these areas, the degree to which each area is taught and the instructional procedures selected will vary, of course, according to the individual needs of the student.

Learning When and Where to Use the Skills.   Students who are mentally retarded must learn to observe and respond to environmental cues that signal that a particular behavior is warranted and appropriate in that setting. In other words, along with being able to perform a skill to a certain level of mastery, students must recognize the proper conditions for its performance. For example, when is it appropriate to approach, shake hands with, and introduce oneself to another person? At a party when a new person arrives, on the street to a complete stranger, or in a work setting while in the midst of completing a task? Or when is it appropriate to add numbers? When making a withdrawal from a checking account, when estimating the total cost of groceries to be purchased, or when determining the number of hours worked? Or when should one reach and grasp an object? When handed a soft toy, when given a bowl of hot cereal, or when within reach of another person's hair or eyeglasses? Discrimination tasks like these require learners with mental retardation to observe each setting, to determine relevant cues, and then quickly and reliably to decide which behavior from their repertoire is appropriate. The teacher must structure educational programs so that students learn to attend to relevant cues, make adaptive responses, and receive positive reinforcement for their efforts.

Generalizing Adaptive Behaviors to Other Appropriate Settings.
Generalizing behaviors is a corollary of learning skills. The person who is mentally retarded must be able to identify similar tasks for which a behavior is appropriate and respond correctly in those instances. For example, determining the amount of money owed when eating in different fast-food restaurants, repotting several types of plants and flowers, and filling out job applications for different clerical jobs all require the generalization of learned skills to new settings.

Another important element is the student's ability to generalize responses from the training situation to the real-life environment in which the behavior should occur. Whenever possible, skills developed in a classroom setting should also be trained in an authentic environment (i.e., community-based instruction). Teachers should not assume that teaching a student to count change in a classroom store, for example, will result in the student's being able to count change at a fast-food restaurant or a grocery store.

Maintaining the Performance of New Behaviors/Skills over Time.
Many crucial behaviors and skills must continue in the person's repertoire past formal training into future environments and situations that occur throughout life. Here again, the quality of the instructional program (i.e., the extent that effective practices are incorporated) can either facilitate or hinder the generalization, maintenance, and adaptation of new behaviors.

A key to successful educational outcomes for many students with mental retardation is the selection of *functional behaviors* as goals to be addressed by the IEP. A functional skill or behavior is one that is useful to students and that gives them some control over their environment in terms of obtaining positive and consistent results. A student will probably not maintain a nonfunctional behavior over time.

When selecting functional skills, teachers must ask whether the skill is likely to be useful in the student's present or projected future environments. Is it age-appropriate? Is the student likely to retain the skills over time? If the answer is no, then teachers should reconsider the nature of the individualized program that has been developed and identify more useful behaviors.

Regardless of the student's level of functioning, the educator should ask the following questions when selecting each target goal to be addressed in an individual's educational program:

- What skill clusters or activities does the person need to function in a variety of settings in the same way as do his or her same-age peers (e.g., in home, school, leisure, community, work)?
- What skill clusters of activities will the person need to learn in the near future to function like peers in these targeted environments (e.g., home, school, leisure, community, work)?

- What skill clusters or activities, either present or needed by the student, are highly preferred by the student?
- Which of these skill clusters are critical, essential, or of high priority to this student (or family) in terms of adult areas of functioning?
- Which of these skill clusters, if any, are critical to the student's health and safety?
- Which activities will promote increased independence and interdependence in inclusive community settings?
- Which activities will contribute to the student's happiness, acceptance by others, and personal life satisfaction?
- Which activities either cannot be taught or can only be taught with great difficulty (performed very infrequently, require great travel, necessitate simulation to teach)?
- Which activities (1) are or will be age-inappropriate, (2) are highly time-limited (not valuable beyond the student's near future), or (3) have questionable future value? (AAMR, 1992, pp. 130–131)

Educators' Collaborative Efforts

The emerging nature of instructional practice in schools today is highlighted by increased collaboration among school-based personnel. Nowhere is this more evident than when students with disabilities are placed in inclusive settings. Recalling the critical dimensions of successful inclusion depicted in Figure 11.2, one of the essential dimensions is "personnel support and collaboration."

Collaboration is referred to by a variety of terms (e.g., *peer collaboration, collaborative problem solving, consultation*). Each of these approaches differs in how the collaborative process is implemented. There are, however, some commonalities among the approaches.

First, all approaches view collaboration as a process rather than as a service delivery model. Knackendofel and colleagues (1992), for example, define **collaborative teaming** as "an ongoing process whereby educators with different areas of expertise voluntarily work together to create solutions to problems that are impeding students' success, as well as to carefully monitor and refine these solutions" (p. 1). The definition of collaboration formulated by Idol and colleagues (1999) suggests that **collaborative consultation** is an interactive process that enables people with diverse expertise to generate creative solutions to mutually defined problems.

A second commonality is that all collaborative approaches are built on the principles of parity and reciprocity. Parity and reciprocity refer to the mutuality of the process. **Parity** means that all members are accorded equal status; no single individual is viewed as the expert, and all contributions are judged solely on their merit as a feasible solution to the problem. **Reciprocity,** as defined by West, Idol, and Cannon (1989), means "allowing all parties to have equal access to information and the opportunity to participate in problem identification, discussion, decision making and all final outcomes" (p. 1).

The most common collaborative approaches used in schools today include collaboration-consultation, peer support systems, teacher assistance teams, and co-teaching. Figure 11.6 provides more detailed information on each of these approaches.

Approach	Nature of contact with student	Description
Collaboration-consultation	Indirect	General education teacher requests the services of the special education teacher (i.e., consultant) to help generate ideas for addressing an ongoing situation. The approach is interactive.
Peer support systems	Indirect	Two general education teachers work together to identify effective solutions to classroom situations. The approach emphasizes the balance of the relationship.
Teacher assistance teams	Indirect	Teams provide support to general education teachers. Made up of core members plus the teacher seeking assistance, it emphasizes analyzing the problem situation and developing potential solutions.
Co-teaching	Direct	General and specific education teachers work together in providing direct service to students. Employing joint planning and teaching, the approach emphasizes the joint responsibilities of instruction.

FIGURE 11.6
Types of Collaborative Efforts

Source: From *Cooperative Teaching: Rebuilding the Schoolhouse for All Students* (p. 74), by J. Bauwens & J. J. Hourcade, 1995, Austin, TX: PRO-ED. Used by permission.

Curricular Considerations

So far in this chapter, we have discussed the fundamental provisions of IDEA, the educational environment options available, and procedures that should guarantee access to an appropriate education for all elementary-age learners with intellectual disabilities. Access alone, however, does not guarantee success. It is time now to turn our attention to curriculum. Decisions about what and how to teach are critical to the success of students who are mentally retarded. This point has been emphasized throughout the chapter.

Elementary-age learners with mental retardation have diverse learning needs, as heterogeneity certainly exists within this group. This diversity results from variations due to level of intellectual functioning, certain individual characteristics, age, present and projected future life situations, previous educational experiences, family factors, cultural and socioeconomic background, and a host of community variables (e.g., rural versus urban). To accommodate the diverse learning needs of these students, educators must first address what is taught in school. A primary concern in programming for students who are mentally retarded is the curriculum.

Curriculum has been defined in various ways. Hoover and Patton (1997) define **curriculum** as planned learning experiences that have intended educational outcomes. Armstrong (1990) defines it as a "master plan for selecting content and organizing learning experiences for the purpose of changing and developing learners' behavior and insights" (p. 4).

School-age learners who are mentally retarded have a wide range of skill levels and instructional needs. Therefore, curricula designed for this group of students must be individualized, functional, and comprehensive. Such curricula are built around the assessed needs of the student and based on a life span perspective, not just focusing on the typical school ages of 5 to 18 years. Comprehensive curricula cover a wide range of content areas and levels of difficulty. Polloway and colleagues (2001) describe a comprehensive curriculum as one that does the following:

- Responds to the needs of the individual student at the current time
- Accommodates the concurrent needs for maximum interaction with nondisabled peers, provides access to the general education curriculum, and gives attention to crucial curricular needs that are absent from the general education curriculum
- Develops from a realistic appraisal of potential adult outcomes of individual students
- Remains sensitive to graduation goals and specific diploma track requirements (p. 165)

Figure 11.7 describes decision-making variables that should be considered when designing a comprehensive curriculum for learners who have mental retardation.

Curricular Orientations

Polloway and colleagues (2001) have adapted a model of program orientations originally proposed by Bigge, Stump, Spagna, and Silberman (1999) that identifies four general curricular orientations: general education curriculum without supports/accommodations, general education curriculum with supports/accommodations, special education curriculum with a focus on academic and social skill development or remediation, special education curriculum with a focus on adult outcomes.

General Education Curriculum Without Supports/Accommodations.
This orientation places students with mental retardation in general education classrooms, exposing them to the same exact curriculum as their classmates. The key feature here is that these students do not receive any assistance. This orientation will be the curricular option of choice when students exit special education.

A concern related to this approach includes the ability of students with mental retardation to deal successfully with the academic content presented. Another concern relates the functionality of the content to which students are exposed. In other words, are the student's long-term curricular needs being met?

General Education Curriculum with Supports/Accommodations. This orientation places students in general education classrooms but employs a variety of supports and other mechanisms to assist students as well as the general education teacher.

FIGURE 11.7
Decision-Making Variables

Source: From "Comprehensive
Curriculum for Students with Mild
Handicaps" by E. A. Polloway,
J. R. Patton, M. H. Epstein, &
T. E. C. Smith, 1989, *Focus on
Exceptional Children, 21*(8), p. 8.
Copyright © 1989 by Love Publishing.
Reprinted by permission.

1. Student variables
   - Cognitive-intellectual level
   - Academic skills preparedness
   - Academic achievement
   - Grade placement
   - Motivation and responsibility
   - Social interactions with peers and adults
   - Behavioral self-control

2. Parent variables
   - Short- and long-term parental expectations
   - Degree of support provided (e.g., financial, emotional, academic)
   - Parental values vis-à-vis education
   - Cultural influence (e.g., language, life values)

3. Regular class variables
   - Teacher and peer acceptance of diversity (classroom climate)
   - Administrative support for integration
   - Availability of curricular variance
   - Accommodative capacity of the classroom
   - Flexibility of daily class schedules and units earned toward graduation
   - Options for vocational programs

4. Special education variables
   - Size of caseload
   - Availability of paraprofessionals or tutors
   - Access to curricular materials (for specific curriculum models)
   - Focus of teacher's training
   - Consultative and materials support available
   - Related services available to students

Tutorial assistance provides additional instruction to the student on content covered in class. The advantages of tutorial instruction are that students, parents, and teachers tend to view this approach as less stigmatizing than remedial instruction; students may be motivated by instruction that corresponds to instruction in the general education classroom; and it allows the student to be maintained in the general education classroom. The disadvantage of this approach is that it is a short-term response that usually does not address the long-term needs of the student. That is, it may assist the student in succeeding in the class for which tutoring is provided, but it will not necessarily teach the student skills needed to succeed in subsequent classes.

A *learning strategies approach* focuses on teaching the student *how* to learn rather than *what* to learn. Such approaches emphasize the learner's role as an active participant in the learning process. The advantage of a learning strategies approach is that it clearly provides a student-focused system for dealing with the subject matter being presented in the general education classroom. It also emphasizes generalization of skills and concepts. Disadvantages are that many students who are mentally retarded lack the entry-level skills necessary to succeed with this approach, and it may be difficult to motivate students to learn a strategy that has long-term rather than short-term benefits.

Cooperative teaching is based on collaboration between the general education teacher and the special education teacher and is designed to provide the support needed to maintain students with disabilities in the general education classroom. The advantages of cooperative teaching are that it draws on the combined expertise and knowledge base of the general education and special education teachers, and it provides a way to promote content learning and integration. The main disadvantage of cooperative teaching is that it requires a set of collaborative skills that few teachers have refined in their personal preparation programs.

Special Education Curriculum with a Focus on Academic and Social Skill Development and Remediation. This orientation has as a basic tenet the notion that some type of specialized instruction is implemented. Most of the time, as dictated by the directives of the 2004 amendments of IDEA, the nature of what is taught is based on the goal of furthering the student's progress in the general education curriculum.

A *basic skills remedial approach* is most often used in elementary special education programs. In this approach, the student's skill deficits are identified and remedial instruction to address areas of academic need is provided. The advantage of the basic skills approach is that it directly addresses the identified needs of the student. Some disadvantages of this approach do exist. When a heavy emphasis on academic deficits is operative, teachers are apt to overlook the student's areas of strength. This approach may fail to program for generalization of skills learned. An overemphasis of this type of orientation may be inappropriate for secondary students who, at this point in their schooling, need instruction in a plethora of other adult outcome areas.

A *social skills remedial model* is characterized by its concentration on developing social competence in students with mental retardation. The advantage of this approach is that social competence is necessary to the student's success in general education settings and ultimately in most adult settings. Another important aspect of this orientation is that many students who have not developed appropriate social skills or who have developed inappropriate ones need direct instruction of social skills. The disadvantage of this approach is that few social skills curricula have demonstrated meaningful, observable change in students' behavior or generalization to other settings.

Special Education Curriculum with a Focus on Adult Outcomes. *Adult outcomes curricula* emphasize the acquisition of knowledge and development of skills that are directly related to the demands of adulthood and adult adjustment. Different taxonomies exist that provide schematas for organizing the various domains of adulthood in which some degree of competence will be needed. For instance, in one taxonomy, "life domains" might include community involvement, education, vocation, home and family, and recreation, while "support domains" would include personal development and emotional and physical health. One advantage of this approach is that adolescents often have positive perceptions about curricula that they find more relevant to their lives and therefore may be motivated by such an approach. A potential disadvantage of this approach is that, without systematic attention to adult outcomes, the curriculum may provide limited long- or short-term benefits.

Instructional Considerations

The goal of instructional programming for elementary-age students who are mentally retarded is to create a learning environment in which all learners reach their highest possible level of potential in a reasonable amount of time. Designing an instructional program that is both effective and efficient requires teachers to act as responsible, reflective decision makers and to exploit the knowledge that has been gained about practices that constitute effective teaching.

Over the past three decades, researchers in education have investigated the relationship between teaching and learning in an effort to identify instructional factors that influence academic outcomes for students who are disabled, including those who are mentally retarded. (Figure 11.5, introduced earlier in the chapter, organizes these important findings on effective practice.) Initially, this research focused on factors that were intrinsic to the learner. More recently, these studies have looked at a host of instruction-related variables that can have a profound effect on learning. A series of systematic studies now provides us with a knowledge base from which we can describe effective instruction for students with disabilities.

The results of this research confirm what we have long suspected: that teaching and learning are complex processes that involve both unique contributions from and interactions among the teacher, the learner, and the environment. Some variables that affect learning (e.g., learner aptitude) are influenced by but are not under the direct control of the teacher. However, the teacher can manipulate other variables to make learning a more efficient and successful experience for learners with intellectual disabilities.

Christenson, Ysseldyke, and Thurlow (1989) identify 10 instructional factors that affect student achievement. These factors provide a useful set of ideas that teachers and administrators should consider in their efforts to provide appropriate educational programming to students with mental retardation. Summarized, these factors are:

1. *The degree to which classroom management is effective and efficient.* Effective classroom teachers are proactive in their management of time, class routines, and student behavior. They anticipate and plan for potential problems in the classroom. They make students aware of goals and expectations. They establish class rules and routines, routinely monitor student behavior and progress, and are fair and consistent in their application of rewards and punishment. Effective teachers protect instructional time. They secure administrative support to minimize interruptions in their classrooms and arrange the class schedule and activities to limit time lost during transition and instruction.

2. *The degree to which there is a sense of "positiveness" in the school environment.* Student achievement is higher in classrooms in which teachers foster positive attitudes toward learning. Effective teachers demonstrate their belief that all students can learn by setting high but realistic goals for student performance, actively monitoring and rewarding student progress, and stating explicitly that they expect all students to succeed.

3. *The degree to which there is an appropriate instructional match.* Effective teachers adapt instruction to meet the particular needs of each student. They use assessment data to determine each student's current level of performance, interests, motivation, use of strategies, processing skills, and persistence for learning and match these to the student's stage of learning and task difficulty. They also assess the appropriateness of environmental conditions in the classroom to determine if the time allocated for instruction is sufficient to ensure learning.

4. *The degree to which teaching goals and teacher expectations for student performance and success are stated clearly and understood by the student.* Skilled teachers communicate goals effectively and frequently. They inform students of the quantity and quality of work needed for acceptable performance on a task. They preset criteria for mastery and provide students with task-specific feedback and correction. They provide equal opportunity for all students to respond and to participate in learning activities, and they reinforce or correct responses in a manner that facilitates student improvement on the task.

5. *The degree to which lessons are presented clearly and follow specific instructional procedures.* Effective teachers demonstrate concern for the quality of instruction in their classrooms. They encourage active student participation by using a demonstration-prompt-practice sequence and actively monitor student responses. They tie old knowledge to new learning by beginning each lesson with a review of previously learned material, and they include an overview of the lesson in their introduction. They use step-by-step presentation of instructional material to make explicit what skill is to be learned, why the skill is important, when the skill is useful, and how to apply it. They check student understanding of task demands frequently. They use positive reinforcement, spaced and repeated practice, and varied activities to gain and maintain student attention and to promote generalization.

6. *The degree to which instructional support is provided for the individual student.* Effective teachers use diagnosis, prescription, monitoring, interactive teaching, and record keeping to adjust instruction to meet the particular needs of individual students. They provide varied types and degrees of practice based on the student's ability or level of functioning. They adjust the amount of time devoted to learning certain tasks, skills, or concepts. They instruct the student in *how* to learn, in addition to *what* to learn.

7. *The degree to which sufficient time is allocated to academics and instructional time is used efficiently.* Effective teachers recognize that time is a valuable teaching resource over which they exercise considerable control. These teachers work to increase student achievement by increasing the amount of time students are actively engaged in learning or by decreasing the amount of time students need to learn. They allocate sufficient time to instruction, use effective instructional procedures, and ensure that students are successfully engaged in academically relevant tasks.

8. *The degree to which the student's opportunity to learn is high.* Effective teachers provide frequent opportunities for students to respond. They interact frequently with students. They provide prompts or cues that lead the student to a correct response. They carefully sequence instruction to maintain high rates of accuracy. They use such teaching procedures as choral response, peer tutoring, and cooperative learning to increase students' opportunities to respond. Finally, they ensure that all students have an equal opportunity to participate.

9. *The degree to which the teacher actively monitors student progress and understanding.* Effective teachers use frequent and active monitoring of student progress. In addition to asking for a response to questions, they ask the students to demonstrate and describe how they perform the task. They scan the classroom frequently to monitor students' attention to task.

10. *The degree to which student performance is evaluated appropriately and frequently.* Effective teachers use frequent evaluation and ensure that the evaluation is congruent with what is taught. These teachers use data from their evaluations to make teaching decisions about the needs of individual students and what to teach next.

PROGRAMMING FOR SECONDARY-AGE LEARNERS

From Edouard Seguin in the 1850s, to Richard Hungerford in the 1940s, to the present professional focus on transition to adulthood—practitioners in the field of mental retardation have recognized the need to prepare each student to be a contributing member of society. Seguin firmly stated that occupational preparation should have a place in educational programs. A century later, Hungerford outlined a comprehensive program of vocational education. His program, entitled "Occupational Education," was designed to build vocational and social competence skills. The program included occupational education, vocational training, and vocational placements (Hungerford, DeProspo, & Rosenzweig, 1948).

Professionals in special education, general education, and vocational education need to move forward in the development of stronger career preparation programs that prepare such individuals to be gainfully employed and to fit naturally into their communities. Today, many practitioners are seeking to provide more realistic vocational training for students who are mentally retarded, to integrate them into general vocational education training programs, and to assist them in making a successful transition from school to work.

In this section of the chapter, we focus on a number of issues pertinent to the transition and vocational education of secondary-age individuals with mental retardation. Key issues include the nature of the settings in which students with mental retardation are placed at the secondary level; curricular emphases at the secondary level; transition planning and services; and vocational preparation.

Educational Settings and Curricular Considerations

Students with mental retardation who are at the secondary level are likely to be found in a number of educational settings. Although more students with mental retardation are remaining in general secondary education classrooms at a national level, during the 1999–2000 school year, 51% of these students (in all 50 states, the District of Columbia, and Puerto Rico) spent more than 60% of their instructional time outside of general education (U.S. Department of Education, 2002). According to this same report, only 12% of these secondary-age students spent less than 21% of their instructional day outside of general education. The implication of these figures is that many students with mental retardation at the secondary

Setting	Percentage of Total
Outside regular class	
<21%	12.19
21–60%	31.50
>60%	50.61
Separate public facility	3.68
Separate private facility	0.83
Residential (public) facility	0.39
Residential (private) facility	0.30
Home/hospital setting	0.50

TABLE 11.1
Students with Mental Retardation, Aged 12 to 17, Served in Different Educational Environments Under IDEA, School Year 1999–2000

Source: U.S. Department of Education (2002).

level will spend an appreciable amount of their day in some type of special education or other setting. The exact figures for the various educational options are provided in Table 11.1.

The curricular challenge for students with mental retardation at the secondary level is to balance the IDEA requirement to provide access to the general education curriculum while addressing the functional needs of students. As Patton and Trainor (2002) noted, it is quite possible to align functional topics with state content and performance standards. The challenge is to provide an engaging program that relates to standards and prepares students for the lives they will have after school is completed.

Transition Planning and Services

Prior to the enactment of IDEA, local educational agency personnel had begun to recognize the need to prepare students who were mentally retarded more comprehensively for life after high school. The literature had documented this need (Rusch & Phelps, 1987), and according to Will (1984), planning for the postschool adjustment of students with disabilities had already been targeted nationally as a top priority. Comprehensive transition planning—which involves assessing needs, developing individual plans, carrying out the plans, and involving key personnel from the receiving environments—is necessary to best prepare individuals for the subsequent settings in which they will find themselves (Patton & Dunn, 1998). Transition planning and services are needed to help students with disabilities reach their fullest potential as adults. Halpern (1994), in a position paper approved by the Division on Career Development and Transition (DCDT) of the Council for Exceptional Children, refers to transition as

> a change in status from behaving primarily as a student to assuming emergent adult roles in the community. These roles include employment, participating in post-secondary education, maintaining a home, becoming appropriately involved in the community, and experiencing satisfactory personal and social relationships. The process of enhancing transition involves the participation and coordination of school programs, adult agency services, and natural supports within the community. The foundations for transition should be laid during the elementary and middle school

years, guided by the broad concept of career development. Transition planning should begin no later than age 14, and students should be encouraged, to the full extent of their capabilities, to assume a minimum amount of responsibility for such planning. (p. 117)

A number of critical points are evident in this definitional perspective. First, individuals must be prepared for a number of different adult roles—of which employment is only one. Second, cooperation and communication are essential for this process to work. Third, transition efforts (instruction and planning) need to begin at an early age. The instructional aspect of this point, discussed in the previous chapter and addressed thoroughly by Clark, Carlson, Fisher, Cook, and D'Alonzo (1991), suggests that the precursors of transition planning and services should start at the elementary level. Furthermore, the comprehensive planning piece must begin many years before the student exits the school system. Fourth, a major effort needs to be made to empower students to become key players in their own transition planning process.

The transition planning process is, at its core, a shared responsibility of the school, the home, the student, and adult service providers. The process, if implemented appropriately, should lead to (1) the acquisition of important knowledge and skills and (2) the linkage to essential supports and services in the community—all of which contribute to assisting the individual to deal with the challenges and the demands of everyday life. Ultimately, if this outcome is achieved the individual is likely to experience some sense of personal fulfillment in his or her life.

The goal of transitional planning is to ensure that a plan for postschool life includes the teaching of requisite skills (including vocational skills) and establishing a support network before the student exits school. This process depends on the development of a comprehensive set of transition goals.

The prospect of adjustment by adolescents who are mentally retarded to the world of work and community living depends greatly on how well various transition

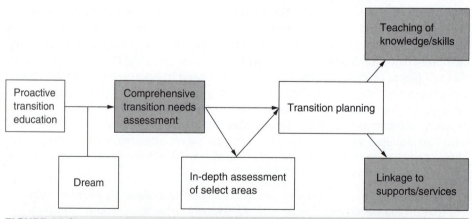

FIGURE 11.8

Transition Planning Process

Source: From *Transition from School to Young Adulthood: Basic Concepts and Recommended Practices,* by J. R. Patton & C. Dunn, 1998, Austin, TX: PRO-ED. Copyright © 1998 by PRO-ED, Inc. Reprinted by permission.

activities occur. The cooperative efforts of local education personnel, vocational rehabilitation counselors, postsecondary education staff, other adult service providers and various community agencies that assist such young adults are vital.

The transition planning process involves a progression of activities (see Figure 11.8). The process begins with an explicit system of transition education, provides a time for students to "dream" about their future, includes a mechanism for assessing a student's transition strengths and needs, and leads to the development of transition goals (instructional and linkage). Sometimes, a need for more in-depth information is needed that necessitates conducting further assessment, as noted in Figure 11.8.

Assessing Transition Needs. A variety of techniques yields information that can be useful for transition planning. Certain instruments, however, have been developed specifically for assessing transition-related areas. A list and brief description of some of the more popular instruments are provided in Table 11.2. For a more in-depth discussion of transition, see Clark (1998), Sax and Thoma (2002), and Sitlington and Clark (2006).

TABLE 11.2
Transition Assessment Instruments

Instrument	Features

Enderle-Severson Transition Rating Scales	• Two versions:
	  • One version designed for mild (ESTR-J-Revised, 2003)
	  • One version designed for severe (ESTR-III, 2003)
	• Subtests: employment; recreation and leisure; home living; community participation; and postsecondary education
	• Completed by classroom teacher and/or parent or primary caregiver

Transition Behavior Rating Scale, Second Edition	• Two versions:
	  • School version (TBS-2-SV)
	  • Self-report version (TBS-2-SRV)
	• Screening measure of behavioral characteristics
	• Subscales: work-related behaviors; interpersonal relations; and social/community expectations

Transition Planning Inventory, Updated Version	• Three versions
	  • Student version
	  • Home version
	  • School version
	• Identifies transition strengths and needs
	• Domains: employment, further education; leisure; daily living; health; community participation; self-determination; communication; and interpersonal relationships

Given that the transition process should be predicated on the student's preferences, interests, and needs, it is worthwhile soliciting information about various transition domains from the student. For this reason, many transition instruments request information from the student as well as from school-based personnel and the family. Information gathered through the implementation of a comprehensive transition needs assessment results in the acquisition of data on which school-based planning can be based.

Developing Transition Goals.   As mentioned previously in this chapter, the IEP must include transition information for the student no later than age 16. This is extremely important so that sufficient time can be allocated to coordinate a program of studies for the remainder of the high school years so that the student can move successfully from school to community living. It is equally important to consider all adult domains and not just the employment/education area. The commonly cited transition domains that should be considered during the assessment and planning process include communication, community involvement, daily living, employment, financial/income management, health (physical and emotional), independent living, leisure/recreation, personal/interpersonal relationships, postsecondary education, self-determination, transportation/mobility, and vocational training. A sample of goals written for a secondary student with mild mental retardation is provided in Figure 11.9.

The importance of empowering individuals with the necessary knowledge, attitude, and skills to make decisions about their current and future lives is being recognized by transition professionals across the country. Along with empowering students, families also must be intricately involved in the process (Wehmeyer, Morningstar, & Husted, 1999). A few notable curricular materials have been published in recent years that have been designed specifically to enable students to be the primary decision maker in their lives (see Field & Hoffman, 1996) and to become actively involved in the transition process (Halpern, Herr, Doren, & Wolf, 2001; Martin & Huber Marshall, 1996).

The idea that a variety of postschool options for individuals with mental retardation is possible should also be maintained. More programs for students with mental retardation have been established at the college level. Grigal, Neubert, and Moon (2005) have focused on how to assist students who have significant disabilities transition to programs at the college level.

Vocational Preparation

In this section, we discuss topics concerned with key elements of vocational preparation programs, including the identification of job opportunities for students who are mentally retarded. In the remainder of the chapter we explore traditional and emerging vocational training options, vocational assessment, vocational placement and follow-up, and select programming issues.

Key Features of Vocational Preparation Programs.   Regardless of the model one follows for developing a systematic view of how ultimately to prepare students who are mentally retarded for the world of work, the model chosen must contain several crucial elements. Among those elements are adequate program objectives, provision of counseling services, and a distinct stage for developing specific general job and

Employment	**PLEP:** Jimmy currently holds paid and work-study positions. He needs to expand his knowledge of available career options and requirements, and explore career interests. **Instructional goal:** Jimmy will identify two career options and skill requirements of each. **Linkage goal:** Jimmy will meet with a vocational counselor to complete an occupational interest assessment.
Postsecondary education/ training	**PLEP:** Jimmy is enthusiastic about attending a job-training program. His math, reading, and written language skills are not at grade level. He has little knowledge about furthering his employability skills. **Instructional goal:** Jimmy will follow written directions and complete program applications with 85% accuracy on the first draft. **Linkage goal:** Jimmy will meet with a job coach and explore what type of job training program would best meet his needs.
Daily living	**PLEP:** Jimmy is not able to utilize public transportation with consistent success. He also has difficulty using banking facilities. He does not have the skills to maintain an independent household. **Instructional goal:** Jimmy will demonstrate his ability to read and comprehend 10 key sight words related to transportation and banking. **Linkage goal:** Jimmy will be introduced to a caseworker for the state to find out more about group home availability in his community or area.
Leisure	**PLEP:** Jimmy is able to perform certain indoor and outdoor recreational activities. He needs to be involved in these activities in the larger community setting. **Instructional goal:** Jimmy will identify and attend three community events. **Linkage goal:** Jimmy will attend school club orientation night and select one extracurricular activity to join.
Community participation	**PLEP:** Jimmy has volunteered in a community program. He remains unaware of community resources available to him. **Instructional goal:** Jimmy will use a modified telephone book of community resources to determine contacts for a minimum of three services he may need. **Linkage goal:** None at this time
Health	**PLEP:** Jimmy has a positive self-image. He needs more information on arranging medical care and reproductive issues. **Instructional goal:** Jimmy will assess the seriousness of five hypothetical medical situations and identify two appropriate responses to each situation. **Linkage goal:** None at this time
Self-determination	**PLEP:** Jimmy displays confidence that he knows himself. Self-advocacy continues to be an area of need. **Instructional goal:** Jimmy will utilize a strategy to aid in decision-making process. **Linkage goal:** Jimmy will attend a support group for adults with disabilities to address issues of self-advocacy.
Communication	**PLEP:** Although Jimmy can read, he needs additional instruction in life skills reading. Jimmy has difficulty using written forms of communication. **Instructional goal:** Jimmy will learn and use a minimum of six key phrases, such as "I'll return at . . .", commonly used in written notes. **Linkage goal:** Jimmy will enroll in life skills reading course.
Interpersonal relationships	**PLEP:** Jimmy enjoys spending time in work-related environments and socializing with coworkers. Generalizing appropriate social behavior from one setting to another is an area of need. **Instructional goal:** Jimmy will demonstrate appropriate responses to stressful work-related situations in role-playing activities. **Linkage goal:** Jimmy will attend school club orientation night and select one extracurricular activity to join.

FIGURE 11.9

Present Levels of Performance (PLEP) and Selected Goals[*]

[*]Based on existing assessment data, other goals might be needed.

Source: From *Case Studies in Transition,* by A. Trainor, J. Patton, & G. Clark, 2005, Austin, TX: PRO-ED. Copyright © 2005 by PRO-ED. Reprinted by permission.

vocational skills. These elements are not the only ones that can cause a vocational preparation program to succeed or fail, but if one or any combination of them is missing, then the program will be less than optimal. Without clear program objectives, vocational preparation efforts will lack direction. Without counseling services, program participants will not always make the best choices when confronted with career decisions. Lastly, unless students learn a host of general job skills along with some specific entry-level vocational skills, many participants will leave the program without skills that they can put to use.

Developing Program Objectives.   Analyses of comprehensive vocational preparation programs reveal that program objectives are delineated clearly. While not all programs will have the same objectives, because of differences in students' characteristics, jobs available in the community, and so on, certain objectives should be almost universal.

The objective that should lead off any preparation program is the development of a continuing career profile of the student's skills and interests. Because students enter a program with different skill and interest levels, the program coordinator must assess these skills and interests to determine the appropriate beginning training level for each student. For example, if a student is interested in auto mechanics and has already been working in this area, she would probably be placed ahead of others just beginning an auto mechanics training program. As the student moves through the program, the instructor should gather and record additional information that reflects the trainee's changing or developing skills and interests. This information can then be used to motivate the student, as well as to convince employers that she is a desirable job candidate.

A second program objective should be to engage each student in actual or direct paid job experiences and activities. This objective is important because, as the Arc of the United States has stated, many programs that attempt to train persons who are mentally retarded for different kinds of work have been too academically oriented. As discussed earlier in this chapter, although academic skills are important, they should not be emphasized to the neglect of life skills (Polloway, Patton, & Serna, 2005). This oversight can be corrected by allowing the student on-the-job training opportunities, with support services and in any reasonably safe environment, whether it is a typical school or factory.

A third, related objective for all career development/vocational preparation programs is the development of entry-level vocational skills for every student. For this, students work on actual job sites both to learn how to adjust to the demands of the job and fellow workers and to begin building a repertoire of the requisite skills for employment in the particular area of work. For instance, the best way for aspiring cement masons to learn the latest mortaring techniques is to apprentice with a skilled craftsman under whose direction they can handle genuine masonry tools and do the actual cementing. Experiences of this kind are particularly beneficial for students who are mentally retarded.

The fourth important objective of all programs is to provide job placement and follow-up services for students who have completed or will complete the preparation program. Since many of the persons we are concerned with are likely to qualify for services from vocational rehabilitation or other employment-oriented agencies, personnel from those agencies can often provide placement and follow-up services. In other instances, schools may have their own vocational placement facilities. What is important here is to make placement and follow-up one of the goals of vocational preparation programs.

Providing Counseling Services. Counseling is another essential ingredient in a vocational preparation program. Rehabilitation counseling is a related service that students with disabilities are entitled to receive under IDEA. A rehabilitation counseling professional should be knowledgeable about career development, employment preparation, and methods to help the student achieve independence and integration in the community.

Developing Vocational Skills. The culminating phase in the vocational training process involves the development of some specific vocational skills. We explore this topic more extensively a little later in the chapter, but we give here an overall view of what should take place at this time. First, job availability in the community should be studied, and present and projected jobs should be analyzed to determine what skills are necessary to perform these jobs. Next, all students should have a thorough vocational evaluation completed to determine aptitudes and abilities. Once this is done, students should be trained on the basis of their present skill level, their interests, and projected job availability. Following training, students should be placed on permanent job sites. Worker and employer should receive follow-up services that identify potential problem areas and provide interventions to ameliorate or minimize the consequences of these problems. Finally, professionals should evaluate the program for how well it has prepared the student for employment and for how well community employment needs have been met.

Identifying Job Opportunities. The success of any vocational preparation program depends to a great extent on the accurate identification of available and appropriate jobs in the community. To meet the goal of job placement, personnel involved in preparing individuals who are mentally retarded for employment (e.g., vocational adjustment coordinators) should conduct surveys of available community employment options on a regular basis. Information from this survey should then be used to conduct job analyses. A job analysis is the process of systematically analyzing the demands of working environments (Sitlington & Clark, 2006). Survey data should also be used to assess student skills and to develop goals and objectives for the vocational preparation program. Omitting this critical step may result in preparing students for jobs that are scarce or in mismatching students with jobs that are inappropriate for their skills or interests.

Vocational Training Options

Various school-based options are available for providing vocational training to students with disabilities. Figure 11.10 highlights the newer options that are most commonly

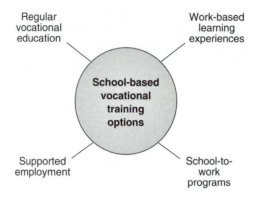

FIGURE 11.10
Contemporary Vocational Training Options

found in schools today (also see Sitlington et al., 2005). In addition, traditional work-study programs are still used in some schools.

Traditional Work-Study Program.   The high school work-study program has been a frequently used model for teaching vocational and occupational skills to students who have few needs for support. Traditionally, the high school work-study program usually runs over a 3-year period, encompassing grades 10 to 12. In the first year, lessons emphasize areas such as transportation, budgeting, peer relationships, personal hygiene, and measurement. Units are usually part of the academic portion of the program, which covers half of the school day. The student spends approximately half the day in the formal classroom setting and half in more practical instruction. In this part of the program, job analysis and job explorations, as well as specific assessment of the student's vocational skills and interests, begin.

During the second year of the program, students refine their skills by learning how to complete a job application and how to behave in a job interview. At this time, they develop some rudimentary skills in a number of areas, such as clerical work, food service, carpentry, or automobile repair.

During the third year of the program, students begin to concentrate on work skill refinement in one or two specific areas, spending part of the day on an actual job and the remaining time in school. As this year draws to a close, students spend more time on the job and less in school.

Because of requirements and constraints resulting from legislation passed over the last 20 to 25 years, work-study programs are not present in public schools to the extent that they were in the 1960s (Halpern, 1992). Elements of these programs, however, are found in various other vocational training models and transition programs.

Vocational Education.   Vocational education is an established discipline characterized by coursework found at the secondary level designed to prepare students for gainful employment as skilled or semiskilled workers. Professionals who are certified in the area of vocational education teach the courses.

Vocational education is composed of seven occupational areas: agriculture, business and office, health occupations, marketing, family and consumer sciences (i.e., home economics), trade and industry, and technology and technical education (i.e., industrial arts). Vocational education programs can be found either on the campuses of high schools or in separate vocational technical centers.

The typical problems associated with providing appropriate educational services to students with special needs in inclusive settings—highlighted earlier in the chapter—apply to regular vocational education as well. For students with mental retardation to succeed in these settings, such programs will need to be capable of making certain curricular modifications. Furthermore, sufficient supports must be available to the vocational education staff.

Vocational education presents some major challenges (e.g., academic requirements) to students with mental retardation. However, as Sitlington and colleagues (2006) note, it possesses some very positive features for many students with mental retardation.

Work-Based Learning Experiences. A number of community-based opportunities may be available to students with mental retardation. These include cooperative education, student internship programs, youth apprenticeship programs, school-based enterprises, and job shadowing activities. In general, these programs allow students to gain valuable real-world job knowledge and/or experience.

School-to-Work Programs. In 1994, Congress passed the School-to-Work Opportunities Act. This legislation was intended to prepare all students for work and further education. Students with mental retardation can be included in these school-to-work (STW) transition programs. The major thrust of the legislation was to provide a variety of school - and work-based learning opportunities, along with a coordinated set of connecting activities (e.g., partnerships) through the high school. Benz and Lindstrom (1997) offer a detailed description of the STW program.

Supported Employment/Workplace Supports. Supported employment is paid employment for those with disabilities who need some degree of support on the job. Most professionals consider a supported employment model much more preferable to the long-standing sheltered employment model as a way to employ individuals with mental retardation (Wright, King, & National Conference of State Legislatures Task Force on Developmental Disabilities, 1991). As Wehman and colleagues (1998) stress, supported employment is based on a set of values (see Figure 11.11) that have been generally accepted by those within the field of mental retardation. McLaughlin and Wehman (1996) describe four types of supported employment programs:

- *Individual placement model:* A **job coach** or employment specialist provides on-the-job training to the individual. The job coach provides services and gradually decreases the time spent with an employee. At any point, however, the job coach can continue to provide services to the employee as needed. The job coach tries to make a successful match between the employee and the job.
- *Mobile work crew model:* Individuals with disabilities work in groups that travel from one work site to another. The supervisor is usually an employee of a

supported employment agency. The work crew performs jobs such as custodial work on contracts negotiated by the supported employment agency with the business. One advantage, according to McLaughlin and Wehman (1996), is that individuals can have different job experiences by changing work crews.

- *Enclave model:* Employees with disabilities work in an integrated setting at a business or industry. They are allowed to compete for all job opportunities. Their supervisors are human service workers who remain on-site permanently.
- *Entrepreneurial model:* Workers with and without disabilities work at a not-for-profit job site. Their supervisors are human service workers who serve permanently in those positions.

A key player in the supported employment model is the employment specialist or job coach. According to Winking, DeStefano, and Rusch (1988), the job coach helps make the match between the employee and the job and learns the job that will be taught to the individual with the disability. Winking and colleagues add that in a survey of program coordinators at supported employment agencies, program coordinators stated that the competencies needed by job coaches are flexibility, good oral and written communication skills, the ability to cope and manage stress, confidence, and

FIGURE 11.11

Supported Employment Values

Source: From "Barriers to Competitive Employment for Persons with Disabilities," by P. Wehman, V. Brooke, M. West, P. Targett, H. Green, K. Inge, & J. Kregel, in P. Wehman (Ed.), *Developing Transition Plans,* 1998. Austin, TX: PRO-ED. Copyright © 1998 by PRO-ED. Reprinted by permission.

Commensurate wages and benefits—People with disabilities should earn wages and benefits equal to that of coworkers performing the same or similar jobs.

Community—People need to be connected to the formal and informal networks of a community for acceptance, growth, and development.

Everyone can work—Everyone, regardless of the level or the type of disability, has the capability and right to a job.

Focus on abilities—People with disabilities should be viewed in terms of their abilities, strengths, and interests rather than their disabilities.

Ongoing supports—Customers of supported employment services will receive assistance in assembling the supports necessary to achieve their ambitions as long as they need supports.

Real jobs—Employment occurs within the local labor market in regular community businesses.

Right to the opportunity—Regardless of their disability, everyone has the right to an opportunity to work in the employment of his or her choice.

Self-determination—People have the right to make decisions for themselves.

Systems change—Traditional systems must be changed to ensure customer control, which is vital to the integrity of supported employment.

the ability to take the initiative. Some of the duties of the job coach are to write task analyses, provide social skills training, maintain regular contact with parents, and provide job safety instruction. Winking and colleagues report that the work of a job coach can be quite varied, perhaps performing manual labor one moment, for example, and then attending an important meeting with a company representative the next.

Even though the job coach/employment specialist has traditionally played an important support role within the supported employment model, attention is being given to a broader notion of work supports, of which a job coach is only one. The importance of extending services through the use of **natural supports** has been underscored in recent times. A taxonomy of work supports that are available to persons with mental retardation in the workplace has been developed by Wehman, Bricout, and Kregel (2000). Four major categories comprise this taxonomy: agency-mediated supports, business-mediated supports, government-mediated supports, and family- and community-mediated supports (see Figure 11.12).

Individuals with mental retardation who are trained through a supported employment model may fare better in competitive employment than those who have worked only in a sheltered setting (Goldberg, McLean, LaVigne, Fratolilli, & Sullivan, 1990; Wehman et al., 1989). The benefits of supported employment for the em-

---

Agency-mediated supports

Job coach assistance

- Specialized training
- Compensatory strategies

Compensatory strategies (e.g., memory aids)
Assistive technology
Counseling
Substance abuse services
Medical services
Specialized transportation
Vocational rehabilitation counselor

Business-mediated supports

Job restructuring
Workplace accommodations

- Environmental modifications
- Assistive technology
- Task modification
- Schedule modification

Coworker mentoring

- Job task training and support
- Social support

Job creation
Employee assistance programs
Employment consultant (hired by business)

Government-mediated supports

Social Security work incentives

- Plan for achieving self-support
- Impairment-related work experience

Tax credits

- Work opportunity tax credit
- Disabled access credit
- Tax deduction to remove transportation and architectural barriers: Medicaid waiver

Family- and community-mediated supports

Personal care attendant
Peer mentors
Family members as job developers
Friends and neighbors
Social support networks

FIGURE 11.12
Taxonomy of Work Supports

Source: From "Supported Employment in 2000: Changing the Locus of Control from Agency to Consumer" (p. 130), by P. Wehman, J. Bricout, & J. Kregel, in M. L. Wehmeyer & J. R. Patton (Eds.), *Mental Retardation in the 21st Century,* 2000, Austin, TX: PRO-ED. Reprinted by permission.

ployee with mental retardation may include competitive wages and desirable fringe benefits, long-term retention, and career ladder opportunities (Wehman et al., 2000). Benefits also exist for society in general, as more individuals with mental retardation become productive employees and contributing members of the community.

The supported employment option is faced with significant challenges today, as Wehman and his associates have noted (Wehman et al., 2000; Wehman & Kregel, 1995): "Many supported employment programs still yield employment outcomes that have fallen short of initial expectations. Lack of earnings and fringe benefits, integration in the workplace, employer attitudes, job retention, and job satisfaction remain issues of concern in supported employment program evaluation" (Wehman et al., 2000, p. 117). Nevertheless, supported employment remains an attractive option and one that is needed for some individuals with disabilities (Sitlington et al., 2000).

Vocational Assessment

Various methods can be used in vocational assessment, including personality tests, self-report devices, and rating devices (Sitlington et al., 2005). The most commonly used, and perhaps the most useful, are written tests, observation of work samples, vocational assessment, and interviews.

We can group written assessment devices into at least two categories: aptitude tests and interest inventories. *Aptitude tests* measure the abilities and traits of an individual in a certain area. For example, an aptitude test that measures word-processing abilities should indicate whether a person can word-process or learn how to word-process. Educators most often use results of these tests to predict an individual's chances for success in a stated field. An example of an aptitude test is the *OASIS-3 Aptitude Survey* (Parker, 2001a).

Interest inventories assess the student's feelings and preferences about types of occupations rather than measure potential proficiency. The *Harrington-O'Shea Career Decision-Making (CDM) System,* revised edition (Harrington & O'Shea, 1992), and the *OASIS-3 Interest Survey* (Parker, 2001b) are two such devices. The CDM-revised has two levels. Level 1 is written at a 4th grade reading level and is designed for those with lower reading skills, including students in special education. Level 2 is designed for high school and college students. Both levels address abilities, job values, school subject preferences, and interests. The *OASIS-3 Interest Schedule* measures 12 interest factors related to occupations listed in the *Guide to Occupational Exploration* (GOE). The GOE allows individuals to research occupations within the 12 interest areas by providing job descriptions. It is particularly helpful to persons who have a more limited knowledge of careers. The specific factors are artistic, scientific, nature, protective, mechanical, industrial, business detail, selling, accommodating, humanitarian, leading/influencing, and physical performing.

Another way to assess work skills is through a work sample or job simulation. This procedure evaluates each individual's rate of production and general job-related behaviors. One example of a job simulation device is the *Jewish Employment and Vocational Service Work Samples* (JEVS) package. Brolin (1982, 1986) has described these work samples as being composed of 28 tasks that measure worker skills in 14 general industrial categories. During the evaluation, which covers a 2-week period, the person being evaluated is required to perform work-related tasks that vary from simple (lettering signs) to complex (disassembling and rebuilding equipment).

Another procedure recommended for determining an individual's transition needs is curriculum-based vocational assessment. This type of assessment derives from an evaluation of a student's performance within the vocational curriculum (Ianacone & Leconte, 1986). The data collected can be used to guide efforts to improve curriculum and to assist program personnel in decision making (Porter & Stodden, 1986).

Interviewing can also be used as an effective method to obtain as much information as possible. A fundamental tenet of this approach is that the interviewee must understand the purpose of the interview. Some of the information obtained should include the interviewee's likes, interests, and future goals. The interviewer should attempt to verify the interviewee's statements through the use of follow-up and parent interviews, or rating scales, with special attention given to any discrepancies in the data from the various sources.

Although these instruments and procedures do yield valuable information about students' vocational capabilities, they frequently have been criticized for several reasons. First, the reading level for many of the paper-and-pencil tests is too high for many students who are mentally retarded (reading levels for these instruments are usually at or around a 6th grade level). Second, few, if any, items relate directly to women. Third, socioeconomic differences are ignored (the preponderance of items reflects a middle-class orientation). Finally, racial and cultural diversity concerns are not taken into account. Work sample evaluations are criticized because they are expensive and time-consuming, often requiring extensive travel to and from the work site. The question of accuracy of the interview method is a problem as well. The information may be biased or limited in value as a result of misinformation or insufficient information. This is why the interviewer must attempt to verify statements made during the interview.

Vocational Placement and Follow-Up.   Once a student has acquired some vocational skills, either the school or some other agency or organization, such as vocational rehabilitation, seeks to place the student on a permanent job site. Smith and Payne (1980), Sitlington and Clark (2006), and Wehman (1990) suggest a number of procedures to aid the placement specialist. The following list summarizes these procedures:

- Make as many personal contacts with local employers as possible.
- Use local clubs to advertise your program, as well as to secure information concerning placement sites.
- Become more selective in the use of job sites as the program grows.
- Consider employers an integral part of the program. Use them at different levels of the program—for example, the prevocational as well as the vocational level.
- Obtain information from such resources as state job service centers, the state division of vocational rehabilitation, and the local Chamber of Commerce and job-training partnership program.
- Program personnel should review the budget to ensure that job placement concerns are receiving the most favorable level of funding.

In the better designed employment models, individuals receive follow-up services as needed, on a continuous basis (McLaughlin & Wehman, 1996). Information gained during the follow-up period can be used to assess program effectiveness. The relationship between follow-up and evaluation makes it possible for future as well as present program participants to benefit.

Companion Website *To check your understanding of this chapter, go to the Companion Website at www.prenhall.com/ beirne-smith and select Chapter 11. From there, you can access the Self-Test and Essay modules.*

Summary

IDEA: An Overview
- IDEA has stressed, since its onset, that all students with disabilities are entitled to a free appropriate public education in the least restrictive environment.
- The most recent amendments to the law, which occurred in 2004 continued the fundamental provisions of the law.
- A major theme that evolved out of the recent amendments was the relationship of a student's program to the general education curriculum.

Educational Environment Options
- School-identified students with mental retardation are served in a variety of settings.
- The most common placement is in a special education setting outside the general education classroom.
- Relatively few students are in general education classrooms for the greater part of their instructional day.
- The number of students served in separate facilities remains low; however, this practice does still occur.
- The use of various placement options varies greatly from state to state.

Assessment and Program Planning
- Obtaining useful assessment information for the purpose of program planning is critically important.
- Comprehensive assessment is essential to the development and ultimate implementation of appropriate special education programs.
- Recent amendments to IDEA clearly specify the membership of the IEP team.
- Required components have changed as a result of the recent amendments.

Programming for Elementary-Age Learners
- Key elements of effective instruction should be characteristic of interventions.
- Educational programs for students with mental retardation involve a number of interrelated and mutually influencing factors.
- Curricular considerations in planning educational programs for students with mental retardation are very important.
- Ten instructional variables should be considered in designing effective programs.

Programming for Secondary-Age Learners

- Secondary students with mental retardation are likely to be found in a number of educational settings.
- Transition planning for the postschool needs of students with disabilities has been targeted as a top national priority.
- A variety of assessment techniques yield information that can be useful for transition planning.
- Vocational preparation for secondary students with intellectual disabilities involves vocational assessment, vocational training, vocational placement and follow-up, and educational programming issues.

Chapter
12

Adult Years

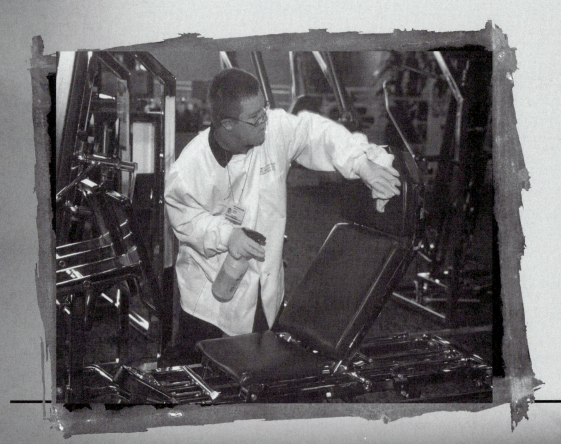

OBJECTIVES

After reading this chapter, the student should be able to:

- Describe various types of residential arrangements available to people with intellectual disabilities

- Identify important considerations in the employability of people with intellectual disabilities

- Explain the ways in which interpersonal relationships and community involvement can be affected by intellectual disabilities

- Discuss how the graying of America is affecting people with intellectual disabilities and their caregivers

- Address the concept of quality of life and related topics

KEY TERMS

community residential setting (CRS)

day habilitation programs

foster home

group home

home and community-based services (HCBS)

intermediate care facilities for persons with mental retardation (ICF/MRs)

public residential facility (PRF)

sheltered workshop

supported employment

supported living setting

I n this chapter, we discuss issues of adulthood. Adulthood is a wonderful time, constantly changing and characterized by an infinite number of issues. Our focus is, therefore, broad. We will attend to practical issues, such as living, working, and participating in the community. Additionally, we will discuss some of the hottest topics in intellectual disabilities today—namely, quality of life, interpersonal relations, and issues of aging. We begin with the most basic question: Where do adults with mental retardation live?

RESIDENTIAL AND COMMUNITY LIVING

Dramatic changes have occurred in the lives of adults with intellectual disabilities during the last several years. Yet, few have been as striking as the exodus of people from large public residential facilities to smaller community-based homes. *How* a person lives usually begins with *where* a person lives. For some people with mental retardation, that may mean an active life that includes interacting with neighbors, catching a bus to work, and planning for a party; for others, it may mean spending hours alone in a room, not knowing where to go or whom to visit.

The shift in placement patterns from residential to community settings has been both profound and far-reaching. What began in the late 1960s as a modest but humanely justifiable initiative has, 40 years later, transformed into a national and increasingly international movement toward improved services for people with developmental disabilities (see Mansell & Ericsson, 1996).

Today, the vast majority (85%) of people with mental retardation reside in traditional homes outside the service delivery system (Larson et al., 2000a). This is certainly the most desirable arrangement. However, it is sometimes necessary for persons with intellectual disabilities and their families to seek residential placement. Reasons for out-of-home placement vary, but most modern studies indicate the reasons are more related to family factors than to the characteristics of the person with mental retardation. Family factors may include caregiver stress, impact on siblings, difficulty obtaining effective community-based services, and concern for the child's future (who will provide care when the current caregiver is no longer able?) (Bromley & Blacher, 1991; Hanneman & Blacher, 1998; Llewellyn, Dunn, Fante, Turnbull, & Grace, 1999; Mirfin-Veitch, Bray, & Ross, 2003). The decision is often a protracted one; a long heart-wrenching process that has more to do with daily stress than with critical events (Bromley & Blacher, 1989, 1991; Kobe, Rojahn, & Schroeder, 1991).

In the remainder of this section, we will describe various types of living arrangements available to adults with intellectual disabilities. We begin with the most restrictive type of setting, institutional life—and end with the least restrictive type, independent living. The categories used are those defined by Amado, Lakin, and Menke (1990).

Institutions

Today's institutions—large congregate living settings for people with mental retardation and/or other types of developmental disabilities—can be subdivided into three types. The first type, termed **public residential facilities (PRFs),** are state-supported, fully staffed facilities equipped to provide services to 16 or more live-in residents at

A complete online glossary is available on the Companion Website, which may be accessed at www.prenhall.com/ beirne-smith

a time. There are two categories of these state-operated institutions: (1) those that provide services to persons with mental retardation and developmental disabilities exclusively, and (2) those that offer services to persons with mental illness primarily but who also have mental retardation. In addition to the state-supported facilities, a second type of institution is the fully staffed, privately (or local government) operated residential facility that provides services to 16 or more people with mental retardation and developmental disabilities. The third type of institution is nursing homes—large group facilities offering medical, nursing, and personal care to persons with and without mental retardation. Usually, nursing home care is provided to elderly persons or to people with medically fragile conditions.

The types of services offered by PRFs vary from institution to institution. It is common for large congregate care settings to offer a wide range of services irrespective of the residential population. For example, boarding schools, colleges and universities, professional and military schools, and even large summer camps must offer an assortment of programs to meet the needs of their residents. The larger the program, the wider the range of services that must be offered. However, large, congregate care settings for people with disabilities must, out of necessity, offer a vast array of services in fairly large concentrations. Therefore, most PRFs offer a variety of educational, social, recreational, medical, and health-related services. The range and depth of services is made even more challenging by the broad age range of residents, typically including everyone from birth through 90 or more years of age.

If services provided by institutions reflect the residents' needs, then it can safely be said that the PRFs of today are markedly different from the PRFs of 50 years ago. In the 1950s, the average institution had more than 1,500 residents, with some facilities housing as many as several thousand people at any one time. The decline in daily residency since the late 1960s has been both substantial and consistent (see Figure 12.1). For

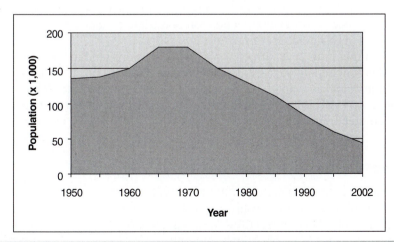

FIGURE 12.1

Average Daily Population of Persons with Mental Retardation and Related Conditions Living in MR/DD Large Public Residential Facilities, 1950–2002

Source: Data taken from Prouty, Smith, & Lakin (2003), p. 8.

example, the average daily total population of residents in large PRFs was 44,066 in 2002, down from an all-time high of 228,500 in 1967. This 81% drop in residency is best quantified by the following population-based ratios. While there were 116 people per 100,000 in the general population living in PRFs in 1967, there were only 15 per 100,000 in 2002. Currently, six states (Alaska, New Hampshire, New Mexico, Vermont, Rhode Island, West Virginia) and the District of Columbia have no remaining MR/DD PRFs. And, between 1996 and 2002, a total of 45 large public residential facilities closed, a closure rate of 6.5 facilities per year (Prouty, Smith, & Lakin, 2003).

Not only have the facilities changed, but the characteristics of persons served in PRFs have changed as well. In 2002, only 4.5% of all PRF residents were 21 years of age or younger, compared to 49% in 1965. More than half of today's residents are between the ages of 40 and 62. A modest increase has been noted in the proportion of the population in PRFs who are over age 62 (3.7% in 1977 versus 9.2% in 2002).

Today's institutional residents are also more likely to have severe forms of mental retardation or to have significant functional impairments or concurrent sensory, neurological, or psychiatric conditions (Lakin, Larson, Prouty, & Coucouvanis, 2003). Table 12.1 denotes specific characteristics of persons residing in PRFs.

One might imagine from the prior data that all movement for individuals as well as residential agencies is one-directional—that the deinstitutionalization of America has led to a mass exodus from institutions into the community. Although these trends are correct and supported by the data, there remain people who must either move into a PRF for the first time or transition back into a PRF from a community residential setting. New admissions are down to a fraction of what they were 30 years ago (approximately 2,149 persons in 2002), but they do indeed still occur and tend to be youth and young adults more so than persons from any other age group. Furthermore, these new admissions tend to be less cognitively impaired than the general PRF population. The profile of persons requiring readmission to PRFs tends to mirror that of the new admissions. Interestingly, that means a higher percentage of persons with mild or no mental retardation and slightly older rather than younger residents (Lakin et al., 2003).

The fact that both new admissions and readmissions tend to have higher levels of cognitive functioning suggests two important phenomena. First, cognitive and adaptive functioning are not the only factors responsible for PRF placement; and second, many of the community initiatives for persons with more extreme support needs seem to be working.

The University of Minnesota's Institute on Community Integration publishes an annual report on the progress of the deinstitutionalization movement, titled Residential Services for Persons with Developmental Disabilities: Status and Trends.

Community Service Systems

A **community residential setting (CRS)** is typically much smaller in size and scope than a large public residential facility and, more important, is located in a traditional residential neighborhood. While CRSs by definition have 15 or fewer residents, many if not most are actually family homes and only resemble some of the smaller congregate care facilities on paper. Often, the distinctions are subtle and made based on the guidelines of the respective funding agencies. Just as no two PRFs are exactly alike, no two CRSs are exactly alike, either.

TABLE 12.1

Characteristics of Residents of Large State MR/DD Facilities, 1977–2002

Characteristic		June 30 of the Year					
		1977 (*N = 151,112*)	*1987* (*N = 94,695*)	*1996* (*N = 68,320*)	*1998* (*N = 51,485*)	*2000* (*N = 47,329*)	*2002* (*N = 44,066*)
Age	0–21 years	35.8%	12.7%	5.0%	4.8%	4.5%	4.5%
	22–39 years	41.3	54.1	44.6	38.1	34.4	30.9
	40–62 years	19.2	27.3	42.7	48.9	52.7	55.4
	63+ years	3.7	6.0	7.7	8.2	8.4	9.2
Level of intellectual disability	Mild/no ID	10.4	7.2	7.4	7.6	10.2	10.4
	Moderate	16.4	9.8	8.9	9.5	9.8	9.9
	Severe	27.6	20.0	17.8	18.3	17.7	16.7
	Profound	45.6	63.0	65.9	64.6	62.3	63.0
Additional conditions	Cerebral palsy	19.3	20.5	22.6	23.5	21.9	19.4
	Behavior disorder	25.4	40.7	45.7	44.4	47.4	52.4
	Psychiatric disorder	NC	NC	31.0	34.3	42.0	45.7
Functional limitations	Needs assistance or supervision walking	23.3	29.5	35.7	38.9	35.4	37.0
	Cannot communicate basic desires verbally	43.5	54.8	59.4	59.6	59.4	58.1
	Needs assistance or supervision in toileting	34.1	46.6	57.0	59.5	55.9	56.1
	Needs assistance or supervision in eating	21.4	37.8	50.9	56.4	48.4	51.4
	Needs assistance or supervision in dressing self	55.8	60.5	66.1	69.9	65.3	62.6

NC = Statistic not collected in that year.

Source: From "Characteristics and Movement of Residents of Large State Facilities," by K. C. Lakin, S. A. Larson, R. W. Prouty, & K. Coucouvanis, in R. W. Prouty, G. Smith, & K. C. Lakin (Eds.), *Residential Services for Persons with Developmental Disabilities: Status and Trends Through 2002* (pp. 31–46), 2003, Minneapolis: University of Minnesota, Institute on Community Integration, Research and Training Center on Community Living. Used with permission.

The orientation of these settings is usually a function of the characteristics and needs of their residents. Community residential settings vary in size, location, number of residents, staffing patterns, and degree of handicapping conditions of residents. The level of mental retardation does not determine the most appropriate residential setting. The match between an individual's needs and those of the setting defines the quality of the living arrangement. Areas in which community settings may differ include residents' role in facility policy, degree of residents' privacy, staff philosophy of community involvement, residents' responsibilities within the facility, and decor and furnishings.

At one end of the spectrum of community residential settings are **intermediate care facilities for persons with mental retardation (ICF/MRs).** These facilities serve as a residential hybrid between the large PRFs and the small family-type homes. While there are large ICF/MRs with room for 16 or more persons (namely, PRFs), the ICF/MRs in this case meet the definition of community residential settings in that they are likely to have 15 or fewer persons and reside in traditional residential neighborhoods. They are generally staffed by a number of paid educational, medical, and social service personnel who also provide services similar to those offered in the larger institutional settings. For some persons with mental retardation leaving the institutional setting, an ICF/MR is a first stop along the community residential setting continuum.

At the other end of the community setting continuum are **supported living settings,** such as supervised apartments. In an increasing number of cases, these dwellings are owned or leased by the resident who lives in the dwelling; that is, the resident holds the mortgage or lease. Although a paid professional staff member may have responsibility for some or all of the formal operations of the setting, the assistance provided is one of support rather than overarching responsibility (e.g., payment of rent, connection of utilities, contact with maintenance personnel). The support provided depends on the adjustment and adaptive capabilities of the people in these settings.

Between these two ends of the continuum of CRSs lie foster homes and group homes. **Foster homes** are traditional family homes that are licensed by the state to provide care for persons who, for whatever reason, cannot live in their own family home. Some foster homes accept people with or without mental retardation, whereas others are licensed specifically for the care of people with developmental disabilities. Either way, foster care is one way a person with mental retardation may experience traditional family life.

The **group home** is the most common community living arrangement available to adults with mental retardation and developmental disabilities. In these homes, a group of persons with mental retardation or other developmental disabilities lives within a residential neighborhood and receives support and supervision from live-in counselors. Some homes are transitional; others serve as long-term residences. Many evoke images of comfortable family settings with decorations and personal belongings of the residents to encourage a sense of ownership and responsibility among household members.

Presented in the preceding section was a fairly detailed account of the extent to which PRFs have decreased in size over the past three decades. Commensurate with the rather astounding decrease in the number of people living in PRFs has been an equally large increase in the number of people living in CRSs. In 2002, 81% of people receiving residential services resided in a CRS. Between 1982 and 2002, the number of people living in foster care increased 146%. Likewise, the number of people living in homes that they own or lease has seen a surge in more recent years. Between 1993 and 2002, this number increased 156%, to an estimated 86,694 persons (Prouty et al., 2003).

Box 12.1 ⚜ Independent Living

Timmy and Carol Savage presently live in an apartment, on their own and as independent as any couple could possibly be. Tim spent 37 years of his life in the state's institution for those who are mentally retarded, after which he lived in a group home. Tim now works full-time sanding picture frames for ACME Industries, while Carol performs routine maid services for the Best Western Inn. According to Tim, and, incidentally, confirmed by the landlord, "We pay on time, every time. We don't get behind."

Tom Houston, housing developer for the disabled with Mental Retardation Services, explains it has been a long process of educating landlords and neighbors alike that those who are mentally retarded are more similar to than different from those pegged as normal: "Many landlords have very legitimate concerns about disabled individuals, because if a tenant is impeded in his performance of his duties as a tenant, it could result in a loss to the landlord."

The Savages have access to a citizens advocacy program that matches a volunteer from the community with a "special friend," a process by which the program hopes to develop lasting friendships. The layperson acts as an advocate for the human and legal rights of the person with retardation. It is simply one more way that differences can be diminished; volunteers grow in their understanding of the disabled.

Houston feels compelled to assure a prospective landlord that when a tenant who is disabled has inadequacies, a professional or a layperson such as a citizen advocate will compensate. Some people like the Savages need little supervision. They have demonstrated a consistency of behavior that assures a landlord of their ability to handle most of their duties as tenants with little guidance from others.

When a client is deemed ready for independent living, Houston helps him work out an agreement for monthly rent payments, including utilities, which are not to exceed one quarter of the individual's gross income.

Once an apartment is found to suit everyone's purposes, a 1-year lease is signed. The client is guaranteed that his rent subsidy will be renewed annually for the next 5 years.

"Some landlords are very responsive," says Houston. They call him up when they have a vacancy because they like the program and go out of their way to help the tenant. For the landlord, "It's just a cut-and-dried agreement, strictly business. He wants to know, 'Am I going to get my checks on time? Is my lease going to be violated?'"

Houston says over and over again that these tenants are turning out to be reliable. They like structure and adhere rather consistently to a routine once good habits are taught them. But Houston is quick to point out that "it's not a humanitarian thing. It's a good business deal. I wouldn't be on the phone to you," he tells a landlord, "if I didn't feel it was good business."

Family and Independent Living

As stated earlier, the majority of adults with intellectual disabilities live in regular homes outside the realm of any residential service system. Some are dependent on family for support, but others live independently or marry and have children (see Box 12.1).

Research on family living is limited. Most of it focuses on caregiver stress, service needs, and similar problems. The reason for this is quite practical—social science research is usually undertaken to solve some sort of problem. Generally speaking, though, most people with intellectual disabilities living with family are doing well and report no unmet needs (cf. Larson, Lakin, & Huang, 2003).

Nevertheless, some families do experience obstacles that require assistance. In the past, those obstacles presented more of a risk for out-of-home placement than is currently necessary. This change is in large part due to the **home and community-based**

To learn more about Medicaid services, and a variety of topics covered in this chapter, visit the Companion Website at www.prenhall.com/ beirne-smith and select Chapter 12, Web Destinations.

services (HCBS) Medicaid waiver program. With HCBS, families can access services that previously could be obtained only by admission to an ICF/MR program. Examples include caregiver respite, personal care, nursing, behavior intervention, and home-making assistance.

The HCBS program is growing rapidly. In 2002, there were almost 9 times as many HCBS recipients as there were PRF residents. Not only does this program enable more people to avoid institutional placement, but it also saves public money. ICF/MR placement costs almost $100,000 per person per year; HCBS averages less than $40,000 (Prouty et al., 2003). Why? HCBS services are tailored to the person; people receive only the services they need and want. ICF/MRs must provide a large array of services to all residents and pay for those services from a common pool. The cost is the same for a person who needs only one or two services as it is for a person who needs 10 or more types of service.

As we will discuss later in the chapter, sometimes people with intellectual disabilities live on their own, marry, or even have children. As you can imagine, however, they usually do not have high-paying jobs. For many, the goal of home ownership and/or complete independence has been out of reach for financial reasons. HCBS has helped. But there are other endeavors that have also been very helpful in this area. One of the most important is the National Home of Your Own Alliance (HOYO). HOYO provides technical assistance to people with disabilities who wish to buy a home. Assistance ranges from explaining the process, to helping find financial assistance with closing and renovation costs, to educating buyers about the responsibilities of home ownership.

EMPLOYMENT AND OCCUPATION

The routines, rhythms, and responsibilities of work are all part of adult life, and are no less significant for the person with mental retardation than for the person without mental retardation. Changes in legislation, social policy, and public attitudes have allowed more people to share in the benefits of productive employment than ever before. Whereas people with disabilities were once thought to possess little potential for gainful employment, even individuals with the most pervasive support needs are now

Career goals are appropriate for all students.

considered by employers to be quite capable of performing complex vocational tasks (Chamberlain, 1988; Tilson, Luecking, & Donovan, 1994; Wehman & Kregel, 1985).

The ultimate goal of habilitation is placement in a regular, competitive job—yet some adults with intellectual disabilities cannot meet this goal. Today a number of employment options are available. Economic conditions, extent and adequacy of training, flexibility of employment sites, and individual characteristics all interact to determine which option is most appropriate for a specific person at a given time. In this section, we will explore a variety of vocational options and their application to people with intellectual disabilities.

Education and Training

Continuing education, whether formal or informal, is receiving growing emphasis as a means of achieving professional advancement, recreational outlets, and personal enrichment for persons with and without intellectual disabilities. Institutions of higher learning (e.g., junior colleges, colleges, universities) have begun offering credit and noncredit courses to the general public to promote and further stimulate interest in continued educational development. Continued lifelong learning is essential for people to reach maximum levels of independence and to adapt to an ever-changing world. Consequently, lifelong learning is a logical endeavor for adults with intellectual disabilities.

Instruction may occur in a number of different settings. Often, it takes place at the employment site or training center. The place of residence can also provide non-traditional educational opportunities; for example, educational programs are often part of the weekly schedules of many if not most group homes. Another setting sometimes used for continuing education for adults with intellectual disabilities is the community college. Some colleges and universities have established programs for adults with mental retardation, while others meet the needs of this group by providing counseling, remedial coursework, and other supplemental services.

Adult education programs specifically for students with intellectual disabilities have also been established. Many of them follow programs developed at the Metro College for Living in Denver, Colorado, and the Night College in Austin, Texas. In addition to their educational curriculum, these colleges often furnish meaningful leisure-time activity. Programs such as the College for Living and the Night College have broadened the opportunities for these adults to expand their behavioral repertoires and to participate in activities that foster dignity, responsibility, and contributions to others. They are a source of pride for the participants and also provide firsthand experiences for persons interested in pursuing careers in the human services field. Because they use regular college campuses and community resources, they also help educate those without mental retardation about the skills and abilities of those who have mental retardation.

A more traditional approach to education and training is the **sheltered workshop** program. Sheltered workshops consist of programs that provide daytime activities for persons who require continuous supervision. These workshops provide both long- and short-term placements, stress self-sufficiency over employability, and serve persons with intermittent to pervasive support needs. Most workshops provide

Well-designed employment models ensure that individuals receive follow-up services on a continuing basis to assess program effectiveness.

basic rehabilitation services, including screening, evaluation, training, placement, and follow-up services. Sheltered workshops have been criticized for their segregated nature and have received less funding and support as the community-based movement has increased (Murphy, Rogan, Handley, Kincaid, & Royce-Davis, 2002).

Like sheltered workshops, **day habilitation programs** are designed to meet the needs of adults who do not yet have the skills for the workplace. Whereas sheltered workshops focus on vocational skills, day habilitation programs are designed to continue to develop a broader set of skills such as homemaking and self-care. They may also provide training in vocational skills and, in some cases, employment services.

Supported Employment

In the realm of intellectual disability, few would question the statement that the de-institutionalization movement is the most important development of the past quarter-century. Supported employment must certainly come in second. **Supported employment** is a process of enabling people with disabilities to work in the competitive workplace by providing them with the supports they need to be successful. Some supports are transitory, such as job training and determining appropriate accommodations. Other supports may be more permanent, such as the use of technology.

Nationally, more than 140,000 people participate in supported employment (Wehman, Revell, & Kregel, 1998). This number includes people with all types of disabilities, not just mental retardation. The program is popular because it provides a meaningful service to people with disabilities and a valued product for employers. Through Vocational Rehabilitation Services (VRS), for instance, employers are often given financial incentives to hire a supported employment enrollee. After a period of time, the financial incentives are removed. By that time, it is hoped that the person is functioning as well as any other person in that job.

TABLE 12.2
Supported Employment Values

Value	Value Clarification
Presumption of employment	Everyone, regardless of the level or the type of disability, has the capability to do a job and the right to have a job.
Competitive employment	Employment occurs within the local labor market in regular community businesses.
Self-determination and control	When people with disabilities choose and regulate their own employment supports and services, career satisfaction will result.
Commensurate wages and benefits	People with disabilities should earn wages and benefits equal to that of coworkers performing the same or similar jobs.
Focus on capacity and capabilities	People with disabilities should be viewed in terms of their abilities, strengths, and interests rather than their disabilities.
Importance of relationships	Community relationships both at and away from work lead to mutual respect and acceptance.
Power of supports	People with disabilities need to determine their personal goals and receive assistance in assembling the supports for achieving their ambitions.
Systems change	Traditional systems must be changed to ensure customer control, which is vital to the integrity of supported employment.
Importance of community	People need to be connected to the formal and informal networks of a community for acceptance, growth, and development.

Source: From "Competitive Employment: Has It Become the 'First Choice' Yet?" by P. Wehman, W. G. Revell, & V. Brooke, 2003, *Journal of Disability Policy Studies, 14,* 165. Copyright © 2003 by PRO-ED, Inc. Adapted with permission.

Supported employment is designed to provide only the amount of support needed, for only the amount of time needed for the person to work independently in a competitive market for a competitive wage. It is based on a set of values, as described in Table 12.2. The values are consistent with the values of self-determination, community integration, and consumer choice (Wehman, Revell, & Brooke, 2003).

Self-determination will be discussed later in the chapter.

Competitive Employment

The category of competitive employment represents employment on the open market, usually alongside persons without disabilities. More adults with mental retardation are obtaining placements in independent, competitive settings than ever before. Although supported employment is often a first step toward competitive employment, adults seeking this form of employment are as likely to obtain jobs through family, friends, or their own efforts as through organized vocational programs.

Forces still act against job attainment. Sources of economic support often will be reduced when a person obtains even a minimum wage job. For example, Rabasca

To read about a non-traditional employment venture, go to the Companion Website at www.prenhall.com/beirne-smith and select Chapter 12, Read and Respond.

(1999) has reported that "as many as 70% of persons with severe cognitive and physical disabilities are unemployed even though three out of four say they would like to work" (p. 29). Factors such as loss of cash payments, loss of health insurance/benefits, and lack of guidance about relevant educational employment opportunities are all cited as potential impediments to full employment integration.

It is easy to ask why people would resist paid employment in favor of social support. For some, it is a valid question. It is important to remember, however, that most people with intellectual disabilities are likely to hold unskilled labor positions. These jobs tend to pay minimum wage or a little higher. Most people have difficulty living on minimum wage; and people with disabilities often have additional expenses.

Thankfully, some progress has been made in reducing the financial penalties to people who find work but still need social support. However, there is still plenty of room for improvement.

INTERPERSONAL RELATIONSHIPS

Social relationships constitute the heart and soul of community integration (Kennedy, Horner, & Newton, 1989). Few will argue the importance of family, friends, and significant others to one's overall well-being. Sadly, however, a major finding within social integration research is that persons with intellectual disabilities tend to be accepted less often and rejected more often than persons without intellectual disabilities, leading to less satisfaction with personal relations (Taylor, Asher, & Williams, 1987). In this section, we will explore the very important construct of interpersonal relationships, and their place in the lives of adults with mental retardation.

Friendship

The recognition that meaningful personal relationships should be included as a desired outcome arose when physical inclusion practices resulted in continued feelings of rejection and isolation. Unfortunately, while many adults with intellectual disabilities report a substantial number of friends, Kennedy and colleagues (1989) found a limited number of "companions who remained a part of a participant's social sphere for more than a few months" (p. 195).

Knox and Hickson (2001) conducted a small study on the meaning of close friendship to people with intellectual disabilities. In this study, the participants were asked to identify their close friends and then describe what made that person a friend. A number of themes emerged that were quite consistent with common conceptions of friendship. Among those were that friends have common interests and enjoy each other's company, that they spend time together, and that they have a long-standing relationship that is expected to continue.

In a comprehensive review of the literature on social networks, Abery and Fahnestock (1994) found peers with disabilities, family members, and primary care providers to constitute the core of the social support system, much more so than for persons without intellectual disabilities. Knox and Hickson (2001), likewise, found that all of the people identified as "true friends" were other people with mental retardation. This is troubling for people who support a model of inclusion, as it is difficult to tell if the absence of friends without disabilities is due to the person's choice or to lack of social responsiveness in the mainstream.

Offsetting these difficulties is the finding that adults with intellectual disabilities tend to make greater use of their rather limited social support networks than do adults without intellectual disabilities (Rosen & Burchard, 1990). The many benefits to others of investing in social relationships with persons who have mental retardation—such as an increased tolerance of others, a reduced fear of persons with disabilities, and added friendships—cannot be overlooked (Peck, Donaldson, & Pezzoli, 1990).

The challenge, it appears, is in helping the world see the value of friendship with a person who has an intellectual disability. The literature on this topic is sparse, but a few theories do exist. One such theory is that people with mental retardation are often, if incorrectly, viewed as recipients, but not contributors, to the relationship. Another factor is a tendency toward a rather shy and reticent temperament, particularly in integrated settings (Abery, Thurlow, Bruininks, & Johnson, 1990). Finally, the lives of people with intellectual disabilities are often sheltered so much that they have decreased opportunities to get to know others, or to learn how to behave in a way that attracts friends.

So what is to be done? Sometimes nothing besides getting out of the way. Oftentimes, well-meaning "helpers" actually block friendships from forming, either by discouraging the person from following their interests or by overprotection. This is a problem when people so focused on inclusion forget that the person may value some friendships with others who have disabilities (Abery, 1997).

Having said that, though, there are certain distinct advantages to adults with intellectual disabilities forming friendships with typical peers. Though presence of mental retardation per se does not indicate social skill deficits, peers and confidants who can model effective social behaviors in community settings certainly enhance those skills. Peers without mental retardation offer opportunities for social involvement not always available to peers with mental retardation. For example, in a study involving 245 children, adolescents, and young adults from nine states, Brinker (1985) found that students without disabilities extended more social bids to students with mental retardation than did peers who have mental retardation. Equally important, students without mental retardation responded to more social bids from students who have mental retardation than did peers with mental retardation.

Sometimes people with intellectual disabilities will need more structured help in making friends. Possibilities include teaching the person with intellectual disability where and how to find others with common interests, and educating nondisabled peers about the person behind the disability (Schoeller, 1997). In truth, what works for one will not work for all. However, it may be desirable to increase involvement in valued community roles, such as volunteerism. This balances the idea that the person needs to be taken care of with the thought that the person has something to offer (Harlan-Simmons, Holtz, Todd, & Mooney, 2001).

Additionally, joining community organizations such as churches, sports leagues, and fitness clubs will increase exposure to others in the community. However, the person really should join clubs or groups that have an interesting purpose. If he joins a group simply to be included, it is likely he will find he has nothing in common with the members. Common interests are one of the first steps toward a friendship (Abery, 2003).

Dating, Marriage, and Sexuality

The need for physical and emotional intimacy is an important part of life for all people, and mental retardation does not change this. As discussed in chapter 1, however, fear and ignorance have led to a culture in which those needs are expected to be suppressed by people with intellectual disabilities. Although progress has been made, laws are still on the books in some states forbidding people with mental retardation to marry (Levesque, 1996).

Despite the existence of these laws, people with mental retardation do experience romantic love and observe the cultural rituals of dating and marriage. There is a tendency among the larger population to minimize the importance of these relationships, but in truth they are integral to a person's quality of life.

Sexual development and sexual activity may comprise the most controversial issues pertaining to adults with intellectual disabilities. Although the sexual development of persons with mental retardation is, for the most part, no different from that of persons without mental retardation, many misconceptions remain. Parents, peers, and professionals continue to hold on to a number of misconceptions ranging from a lack of interest in sex on the part of the person with intellectual disability to a fear that they will reproduce "their kind."

For many, the movement toward less restrictive living arrangements brings with it a number of opportunities not previously encountered in more restrictive settings. Many professionals argue that dating, marriage, and sexual activity are a normal part of daily living and should not be prohibited. Others disagree, citing a number of unfortunate and even life-threatening consequences of sexual activity as possible outcomes—for example, exploitation, unwanted pregnancy, sexual and physical abuse, and sexually transmitted diseases (Schwier & Hingsburger, 2000).

A number of factors make the right to socially appropriate romantic and sexual expression a bit more difficult. These include the heightened supervision and supports in comparison with individuals without intellectual disabilities; lack of accurate information typically provided by service providers about sexual development and functioning; and fewer socialization opportunities in which to try out new behaviors, roles, and expectations. Something as simple as negotiating the boundaries between risk and opportunity for growth remains a paramount issue for adults with intellectual disabilities (Schwier & Hingsburger, 2000).

As the service system has become more sensitive to human needs, a demand for practical sex education has been announced in the literature. However, carrying out that education can be uncomfortable. As such, sex education has often centered around body part identification and personal hygiene. This has led to inadequate knowledge and increased frustrations (McCabe & Cummins, 1996).

Increased independence and current patterns of social interaction now evidenced in the community necessitate, in practical terms, that the issue of sexuality no longer be ignored (Sundram & Stavis, 1994). Despite the finding that people with intellectual disabilities have less understanding of sexuality, there are also findings that they are at increased risk of pregnancy and sexually transmitted diseases (McCabe & Cummins, 1996).

AGING WITH MENTAL RETARDATION

Trends and Demographics

Few trends characterize America more than the graying of its population. People with intellectual disabilities are graying right along with the rest of the world. In the year 2000, there were approximately 641,000 people with developmental disabilities over the age of 60. By 2030, this number is estimated to double (Heller, Janicki, Hammel, & Factor, 2002). Helping to drive these numbers is the increased life expectancy of people with intellectual disabilities. As recently as the 1930s, life expectancy was 19 years. In 1993, it was 66 years (Janicki, Dalton, Henderson, & Davidson, 1999).

As people with intellectual disabilities age, so do their families and other primary caretakers. In the not so distant past, parents of children with disabilities usually outlived their child. This is no longer true, and families are having to plan ahead.

Happily, the world is learning more about healthy aging. It is now widely accepted that physical fitness, good nutrition, and an optimistic outlook all converge to make the aging process itself less debilitating. Additionally, science has contributed a great deal in terms of medicines and technology that extend the healthy life. These findings have been extended to the lives of people with intellectual disabilities as well. Still, the conditions associated with mental retardation often become complicated in later life. The most striking example of this is the relationship between Down syndrome and Alzheimer's dementia. Other conditions are also related to age-related changes, such as a loss of gross motor functioning in persons with cerebral palsy (Janicki, 2001).

For more information on these conditions, see chapters 6 and 8.

Aging with Dignity

Though it is heartening that people with intellectual disabilities are living longer, it sometimes takes a lot of forethought to ensure they do so with dignity. Not only is there the risk of the person outliving his or her caretakers, but there is also the large issue of financing a long life. Additionally, living longer is an advantage only if that life can be enjoyed.

Aging caregivers have been noted to experience a great deal of worry about their adult family member with intellectual disability. Not only must they worry about practical matters, such as where the person will live and who will care for him or her in the event of the caregiver's death, they must also worry about how happy the person will be in the new arrangement.

Additionally, aging caregivers often experience their own health-related problems. This complicates matters in obvious ways, especially for caregivers of persons with severe mental retardation and/or additional physical disabilities. When the caregiver's health suffers, his or her ability to provide physical assistance or to provide continuous supervision may decrease. Additionally, anxiety and stress may increase.

Equally important, when the caregiver's role begins to change, so does the context of the relationship. Sometimes the change is negative, as when the adult with intellectual disability does not understand why the caregiver is less involved or is introducing new people into their lives. Quite often, however, it is noted that the adult with intellectual disability rises to the occasion by providing care to the caregiver and forming a more interdependent relationship (Janicki, 2001).

To assist families in planning for their loved one's future, the Arc of the United States and the Rehabilitation Research and Training Center on Aging with Developmental Disabilities at the University of Illinois, Chicago, have developed *A Family Handbook on Future Planning* (Davis, 2003). The handbook covers a variety of practical issues, such as guardianship, trust funds, wills, and government benefits. It provides information about how to access services and negotiate through the bureaucratic maze so often associated with social service systems.

The handbook can be accessed through the Arc's Web site (www .thearc.org).

In the midst of this coping with change, one must not forget to live! American communities historically have not been friendly to the challenges of aging, but this is changing. The Americans with Disabilities Act has done much to improve access to public buildings and transportation systems. Additionally, as the aging community has grown, this group is increasingly being seen as a target market. Communities now proudly announce themselves as a great place to retire. With all of this publicity and attention come services, homes, and activities of interest to the group.

Chapter 13 will discuss the rapidly expanding technology applications for people with mental retardation.

Technology is also enhancing the lives of older Americans. Examples include telehealth equipment that allows patients to interface with their health care providers from home; electronic "panic buttons" that allow people to call for help from anywhere in their homes; and global positioning systems (GPS) that can help caregivers monitor the whereabouts of people with dementia, who are prone to wandering into unsafe areas.

COMMUNITY INVOLVEMENT

Community Acceptance

Few things are more important to the success of the community adjustment process than the goodwill, acceptance, and support of the public. Known simply as *community acceptance,* the public's knowledge and attitudes are key components in the psychological health and well-being of the environment in which persons with intellectual disabilities live. Zoning laws, program proposals, and mandates of elected officials are essential and formal means of acceptance. Less formal but equally important are the subtle, day-to-day gestures of acceptance and support put forth by one's neighbors each day.

Although the public in general and communities in particular support the idea of community acceptance, there are substantial barriers yet to overcome. It is now coming to light that the public's understanding of intellectual disability is deeply rooted in the structure of society. The roles and status people with intellectual disabilities are allowed to achieve are tied firmly to the extent to which people in the community believe the new members are different from themselves (e.g., appearances, behaviors, values) (Calvez, 1993; Quinn, Sherman, Sheldon, Quinn, & Harchik, 1992). Simply stated, the more "normal" people appear, the more rights, privileges, and autonomy they are afforded in day-to-day living. Cnaan, Adler, and Ramot (1986) offer a New Jersey Department of Health study in which 50% of all planned community residential settings in that state were not opened due to community resistance. Specific fears have ranged from a decrease in property values to concerns for the health and well-being of neighborhood children (Lubin, Schwartz, Zigmond, & Janicki, 1982; Ryan & Coyne, 1985).

Fortunately, fears and reactions such as those just mentioned can generally be changed or averted altogether. People with mental retardation are often thought to be unable to live independently and in need of close and constant supervision. These low expectations and the fears associated with them often dissipate when individuals get to know persons with mental retardation and recognize their abilities and potential. Seltzer (1984) found that efforts to educate the public about mental retardation and group homes correlated positively with community opposition and that "opposition is less likely when the community becomes aware either after the residence begins operations or more than six months before it opens" (p. 7). The implication of these findings is that it might be better to adopt a low-profile entry strategy rather than a high-profile one when establishing a community residential setting.

To facilitate acceptance of persons with intellectual disabilities and their community residential facilities, professionals must address the need for public education. Efforts must be made to inform the public about the nature, causes, and implications of mental retardation and even how to respond to people with intellectual disabilities. These educational efforts must provide opportunities for interaction that are both positive and progressive. The deinstitutionalization project of New York State serves as a model of comprehensive community education and involvement. Public media reports providing information on the needs and nature of mental retardation, task forces comprising community members who locate appropriate group home sites, and speakers' bureaus to address community concerns form the basis of this campaign to obtain community support. Not surprisingly, evidence in the literature suggests that positive outcomes are likely when planned and cooperative opportunities are created.

Recreation and Leisure

Like all people, adults with intellectual disabilities need recreational and leisure activities to balance the rigors of daily living. Unfortunately, far too many individuals with mental retardation remain outside the mainstream of community life in these areas. According to the *National Consumer Survey* (Temple University Developmental Disabilities Center, 1990), 1 of every 3 persons with mental retardation in the United States has an expressed need for recreational/leisure integration but is unable to acquire it.

Schleien, Meyer, Heyne, and Brandt (1995) provide an extensive review of the literature related to leisure skills and leisure education for persons with intellectual disabilities and conclude that the benefits of a high-quality leisure program are many. For example, skills learned during play extend across the curriculum (e.g., language, problem solving); increases in socially appropriate free time activities decrease the likelihood of socially inappropriate free time behaviors; and a well-developed repertoire of free time activities increases the quality of the relationships with family and friends.

Advocates have begun demanding that community recreational opportunities available to persons without mental retardation be extended to persons with mental retardation. The demands have been heard. Programs ranging from special skill-building programs to competitive international competition are now under way. While most human service providers are aware of the Special Olympics, less well known but potentially more important for encouraging community acceptance is the Special Olympics' Unified Sports program in which athletes with and without disabilities participate in equal numbers on the same teams in local, regional, national, and international competitions. The growth of the Unified Sports program remains unparalleled among organized athletic programs for persons with disabilities.

Park and recreation clubs, drama groups, day camps, craft guilds, jogging clubs, cooking groups, and other special organizations for combined involvement of persons with and without intellectual disabilities are being formed with increasing frequency. The continued development of special equipment such as modified bowling balls and walkers for ice skating has broadened opportunities for participation in sports in ways not imagined even a few years ago (e.g., Schleien, Ray, & Green, 1996).

If programs are so plentiful and efforts so numerous, why do 1 in 3 persons report an unmet need for recreational/leisure services? According to Ittenbach, Abery, Larson, Spiegel, and Prouty (1994), adults with mental retardation face three major barriers to recreational/leisure integration. First is the issue of lack of a friend or companion with whom to share the activity. No matter how enjoyable an activity is, it is more fun when it can be shared with someone else. Second is the general lack of guidelines for planning and implementing integrated programs available to recreational specialists. New guidelines have been developed in recent years, but more are needed. Third is a lack of skills necessary to take advantage of such programs. A willingness to try and pursue new activities is in part dependent on success in other, related, areas.

Services and Supports

All adults require services for community living. Whether working, shopping, banking, or pursuing recreational pastimes, very few people are able to live successfully without the services and supports of others in the community. Some adults, like those with intellectual disabilities, require more support services than others—services that are specific, costly, and critical to the community living status of a particular person.

Several studies have been conducted to determine the service needs of persons with intellectual disabilities living in the community. In their review of research on supports required by residents of foster homes, group homes, and institutions, Ittenbach, Larson, Spiegel, Abery, and Prouty (1993) found medical services, social and recreational services, case management services, and income assistance to be the major support services needed for daily living (see Table 12.3).

Not surprisingly, communities vary tremendously in the availability of services rendered. Complicating the situation further are the unique needs of the person, the family, and the community—all of which must be considered when attempting to match a person to a given environment and an environment to a person in need of supports.

Supports are resources and strategies that promote a person's well-being and functioning (AAMR, 2002). This is a broad definition that includes, but is not limited to, services. Supports may be provided by people, organizations, technology, or very low-tech devices such as picture recipe cards. It must be remembered that a support becomes a *hindrance* the moment it is no longer necessary. Supports should enhance each person's sense of confidence, self-esteem, and independence (Abery & Fahnestock, 1994).

TABLE 12.3

Support Services Needed and Used by Persons with Mental Retardation

Types of Support	Supports Needed[*]	Supports Used In Small Communities[†]	Public Institutions[‡]
Financial			
Health insurance	46		
Income assistance	55		
Payment or provision of medical equipment/supplies	37		
Payment or provision of medication	52		
Medical			
Dentist	66	95	96
Medical specialists		49	
Nurse	12	38	
Nutritional/dietitian		19	
Occupational therapist	32	15	16
Physical therapist	33	20	19
Physician	67	99	100
Psychologist		32	
Professional counselor	24	10	15
Speech/communication	40	33	17
Other			
Advocacy	34		5
Social/recreational	55		35
Social worker/case manager	60	62	
Transportation	50	62	16

Note: All values reported here are percentages. Small community facilities housed 1 to 6 persons with mental retardation. National Consumer Survey results include responses identified by 30% or more of the respondents. The absence of a value in any category means that the use of this type of support was not evaluated in the study.

[*] N = 13,075 (Temple University Developmental Disabilities Center, 1990)

[†] N = 336 (Hill, Lakin, Bruininks, Amado, Anderson, & Copher, 1989)

[‡] N = 997 (Hill, Lakin, Sigford, Hauber, & Bruininks, 1982)

One of the hallmarks of a supports approach is the notion that the supports are individualized and selected by the person who uses them. They should be tailored to help the person meet his or her personal goals. Therefore, they should be easily accessed and useful in all the domains of life. Figure 12.2 illustrates the processes of supports assessment and planning.

Coordinating the various supports needed in different environments can be an exceptionally difficult task. Input should be sought not only from professionals involved in such areas as education, psychology, and medicine, but also from family

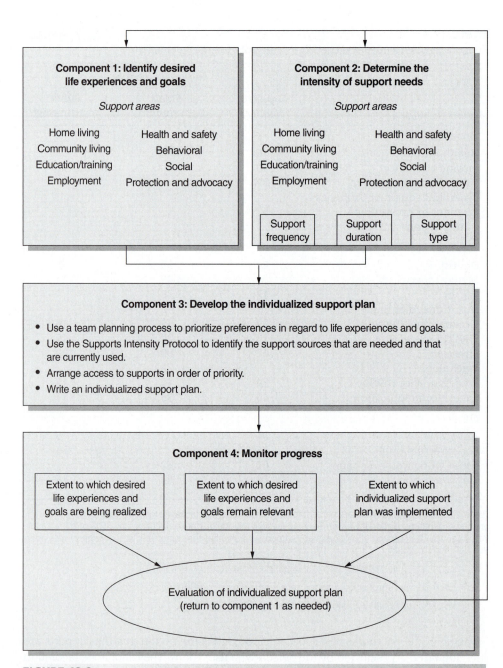

FIGURE 12.2
Four-Component Support Needs Assessment and Planning Process

Source: From "Integrating Supports in Assessment and Planning," by J. R. Thompson, C. Hughes, R. L. Schalock, W. Silverman, M. J. Tassé, B. Bryant, et al., 2002, *Mental Retardation, 40,* p. 391. Used with permission.

members and the person with intellectual disability. The involvement of family members is valuable not only for their ideas but because they can assist others in understanding the many ways their loved one expresses any preferences, needs, and opinions. Every person can justifiably expect to be treated with respect and dignity; this includes participation in his or her own life planning.

Sometimes the greatest support is information about other resources or about legislation that protects and promotes the welfare of persons with disabilities. The U.S. Department of Education's Office of Special Education and Rehabilitative Services funds parent information centers in each state to address parent concerns. Similarly, within the Department of Health and Human Services, the Administration on Developmental Disabilities and the Administration on Children and Families maintain family preservation/family support initiatives.

The movement toward greater community involvement and independent living arrangements has also furthered the cause of technological support development. By mandating equal access to community facilities, public transportation, and job opportunities, the Americans with Disabilities Act (ADA) forced human ingenuity (Bleyer, 1992) and includes everything from architectural accommodations to job task reconceptualization (Johnson & Lewis, 1994).

One of the biggest obstacles people with intellectual disabilities encounter relates to financial dependence. Adults with mental retardation to not have the same income and financial independence as adults without mental retardation. As financial dependence increases, lack of access to other community-based programs increases. Lack of discretionary income affects more than just the ability to purchase desired goods and services; it makes a person less likely to participate in certain social, recreational, and vocational activities, missing out on many of the benefits of community living.

As a way to provide regular income and health service coverage to persons with intellectual disabilities, a number of federally funded programs are available. Following is a brief discussion of four programs (also see Figure 12.3).

Social Security Disability Insurance Program.   The Social Security Disability Insurance (SSDI) program offers monthly cash benefits to persons and the dependents of persons 65 years of age and younger who were previously insured but who have left the workforce because of a disability. Eligibility is based on two factors: (1) the presence of a disability according to Social Security Administration guidelines, and (2) insured status through prior employment. Although childhood benefits typically cease at 18 years of age, dependents who are disabled continue to qualify for SSDI benefits as long as the disability continues. Most adult dependents with disabilities receiving such services have a developmental disability such as mental retardation, autism, or cerebral palsy; cash benefits continue under this category as long as the person is a dependent.

Supplemental Social Security Income Program.   The Supplemental Social Security Income (SSI) program offers monthly cash benefits to persons and dependents of persons who are aged or disabled and whose income falls below a certain level. The SSI program is a federally funded program supplemented by state funds to meet the basic living needs of its recipients. All but seven states provide funds to supplement federal

FIGURE 12.3
Matrix of Entitlement Programs

Source: From *How to Provide for Their Future* (p. 26), by the Association of Retarded Citizens of the United States. Copyright © 1984 by the Association of Retarded Citizens of the United States. Reprinted by permission.

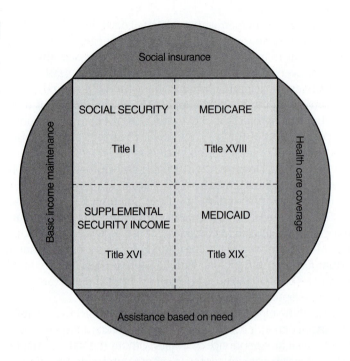

Matrix representing relationships among Social Security (SSDI, ADC), Medicare, Supplemental Security Income (SSI), and Medicaid for persons with disabilities. The criteria for eligibility based on disability are uniform for all programs in all states. The economic criteria differ. Social Security and Medicare are federally administered according to uniform rules in all states. SSI basic entitlements are federally administered according to uniform rules; most states provide state supplementation under state-specific criteria. Medicaid is a federally assisted, state-administered program. In most states, SSI-eligible persons are also eligible for Medicaid. In addition, some persons who meet the disability criteria may meet the economic criteria (means tests) for Medicaid even if ineligible for SSI. Children with disabilities may be eligible for SSI, Medicaid, or both.

benefits. The benefits are designed to reach those not previously employed and, thus, not covered by the SSDI program. As a group, SSI recipients are younger than SSDI recipients because of no requirement for prior insurance coverage and work history.

Medicare.   Medicare is a federally funded program that provides health insurance coverage (e.g., hospice, hospital, home health care) to persons with and without disabilities over the age of 65 and to persons who have left the workforce due to a disability prior to age 65. Disability criteria are identical to those in the previous two categories; eligibility requirements are closely aligned with SSDI requirements. Dependents of SSDI recipients are not covered until age 20.

Medicaid.   Medicaid is a jointly operated federal and state health care program for people who cannot afford private insurance or medical services. Originally commissioned to serve the acute health care needs of persons with low incomes, "it has now become the nation's primary program for financing long-term care services to elderly and disabled individuals" (U.S. Department of Health and Human Services, 1990, p. 102). Adults with mental retardation typically qualify for Medicaid. Though states are required to operate within federal guidelines, services vary widely from state to state. Disability criteria for the federal portion of the program are the same as for the other three previously mentioned programs; however, state eligibility criteria may vary. Under Medicaid, the federal government reimburses states for a portion of the costs incurred.

Risks and Vulnerabilities

A final thought on community life relates to risks and vulnerabilities. The reasons people with intellectual disabilities are at increased risk for victimization are easy to imagine. Stories of physical, emotional, and sexual abuse are heartbreaking. Exploitation is also a common story.

For many reasons, people with intellectual disabilities often learn to trust others before themselves. The unmet friendship needs discussed earlier in this chapter also leave them vulnerable to manipulation by anyone who gives that wanted attention and acceptance. Hope (1997) describes a sad tale of a boy who joined a gang for just those kinds of reasons.

Abuse is, of course, the biggest vulnerability of all. It is well documented that intellectual disability increases the risk for all types of abuse (Conway, 1994; Furey, 1994; Sobsey & Doe, 1991; Williams, 1993). Unfortunately, people with mental retardation often don't recognize that they are being abused, or they don't have the ability to predict when abuse is inevitable (Murphy, Coleman, & Abel, 1983). Additionally, research indicates difficulties identifying an appropriate solution when abuse is recognized (Khemka & Hickson, 2000).

Of course, teaching people to recognize their own victimization and to respond to that recognition appropriately is absolutely necessary. However, for people who have not attained that skill yet, it is important for others to be watchful for signs of victimization. Signs may include drastic changes in behavior, shying away from touch, withdrawal, skill regression, substance abuse, sleep and appetite change, and new fears. Recapitulating the abusive act also occurs (Davis, 2000).

The best way to help prevent abuse is to be a friend and advocate. People who have stable, trusting relationships are less likely to be victimized. They are also more likely to confide the nature of their interactions with others to the people they know care.

Another type of risk is that associated with substance use and abuse. Service providers express growing concern that as people with intellectual disabilities move into more normative and less protective settings, the risk of substance use and abuse increases.

The available data on drugs of abuse by persons with mental retardation are scant. However, Christian and Poling (1997) have reviewed the published literature and conclude that people with mental retardation are experimenting with drugs of abuse, but in seemingly smaller proportions than those without mental retardation. They further suggest that while people with mental retardation seem to be at no greater risk of addictive behaviors by virtue of their disability, those who are currently taking other prescription medications for related disorders are at greater risk for more serious complications due to the use and abuse of the controlled substances. Other consequences are also noteworthy: decreased levels of independence, increased difficulties with cognition and social adjustment, and delayed acquisition of important new social and problem-solving skills (Watson, Franklin, Ingram, & Ellenberg, 1998).

QUALITY OF LIFE

Although the deinstitutionalization movement grew from the idea that institutional living prevented persons from living fulfilling lives, early studies of the effects of moving out of an institution were largely confined to behavioral outcomes (cf. Kim, Larson, & Lakin, 2001; Larson & Lakin, 1989). As other gains were realized, the term *quality of life* began to be explored (e.g., Schalock, Keith, Hoffman, & Karan, 1990). Many endeavors to precisely define and delineate the term have been undertaken, and far too many aspects have been proposed to cover here. However, the general idea has emerged that life quality is related to the degree to which a person feels in control of his or her life, and is happy with the way life is going. In this section, we will discuss several concepts related to this idea, including self-determination, person-centered planning, advocacy, and personal satisfaction.

Self-Determination

Why do so many people without mental retardation try so desperately to distinguish themselves from others when persons with retardation try so hard to be like everyone else? This phenomenon has two interpretations. In 1967, Edgerton used the phrase "cloak of competence" to describe the lives of 53 persons recently released from institutions who, he believed, attempted to cloak themselves in an air of normalcy. He was referring to their efforts to assume roles, behaviors, and life stories that essentially denied to themselves and others the reality of the label and their previous years in an institution. In contrast to this is the more recent trend toward self-affirmation and self-determination in which adults with disabilities acknowledge their limitations but fail to let them stand in the way of optimal daily living.

Self-determination is defined as a person's right to navigate his or her own life path—to make their own choices about how they wish to live. At its core lies a person's ability to make informed decisions. Philosophically, the construct is a lofty one that relates to existential ideas about life. In practice, though, it translates to decisions about where and with whom to live, vocational choices, leisure time, and supports needed or wanted. Unfortunately, Wehmeyer and Metzler (1995) found that people with intellectual disabilities were likely to make choices about food, clothing, and leisure time, but less likely to make choices about where they live. In sum, we are still in the infancy of the self-determination movement.

Person-Centered Planning

Although the concept of quality of life represents a laudable leap in philosophy, one seemingly valid complaint has been lodged again and again: There is no such thing. That is, there is no universal construct because each person judges his or her own quality of life based on different criteria. Whereas one person may value independence above all else, another person may value relationships with significant others (Hatton, 1998).

The strategies of person-centered planning arose parallel to the interest in quality of life and self-determination. Designed to increase the volume of people's own voices and keep "helpers" on track in their helping, proponents of person-centered planning adhere to the notion that outcomes are diverse and individualized. In other words, the person should be enabled to express his or her own goals, and outcome assessment should be based on the movement made toward attaining those goals. (See Box 12.2.)

Person-centered planning begins by asking the person what he or she wants life to be like. People who care about the individual are invited to join the process; their role is especially important when planning with a person who has severe mental retardation. They are sometimes called upon to speak for the person or to translate the person's attempts to communicate. Other persons involved in the planning process include service providers and educators who are able to identify resources for attaining goals. For each goal that is set, a diagram for the future is made. Diagrams include

---

Box 12.2 ☀️ Self-Determination and Choice

How do the concepts of self-determination and choice relate to everyday life? The Research and Training Center on Community Living at the University of Minnesota offers the following suggestions to people evaluating residential service providers:

1. How much control do residents have over choosing their own room and house mates?
2. In what way are residents involved in hiring and evaluating staff?
3. Can residents choose not to do tasks they don't want to do?
4. How does this agency assure people have privacy when they want or need it?
5. To what degree are residents involved in planning their menu and weekly food shopping?
6. Can residents eat meals at times or places other than the standard?
7. Do all residents have free access to healthy, nutritious food?
8. How are the people who live here encouraged to exercise their full range of rights (e.g., using the telephone, voting, etc.)?
9. To what extent can residents decorate their rooms to their own liking?
10. To what degree do residents have control over how shared living areas are decorated?
11. Describe how residents are supported in handling their personal money.
12. What rules do those who live here need to follow and how were they developed?
13. Is there a schedule for daily activities (e.g., bed times) and weekly activities (e.g., shopping) at the homes where you provide support?
14. Describe how staff support residents in making informed choices and decisions.
15. How do staff support residents to make group decisions?
16. How do staff ensure residents are aware of their rights and comfortable reporting violations?

Source: From *Questions to Ask Providers When Making Decisions About Residential Supports for Family Members with Disabilities,* by the Research and Training Center on Community Integration, University of Minnesota, 1999, Minneapolis: University of Minnesota, Institute on Community Integration. Reprinted by permission.

the steps necessary for getting from where the person is to where the person wants to be, as well as the supports and resources to be accessed along the way. Outcomes are clear, individualized, and easily measured (Forest & Pearpoint, 1992).

Advocacy

Advocacy is the formal representation of one's interests in an effort to bring about changes in the broader social order. For persons with mental retardation, that means the elimination of barriers to full community living and inclusion. The true spirit of advocacy, however, extends well beyond simple legal rights, to include the more basic rights of autonomy, independence, and self-determination. Furthermore, it also includes such things as the freedom to live and move in the least restrictive environment, have gainful and productive employment, and marry and have a family (Schalock & Kiernan, 1990, p. 163). Over the past several decades, the advocacy movement has become a very popular and potent consumer force.

Despite the fact that most adults with intellectual disabilities find mere survival sufficiently complex, many communities are still raising legal and social obstacles to the notion of full community living. Consequently, persons with intellectual disabilities continue to be represented by many local, state, and national advocacy organizations. The President's Committee for People with Intellectual Disabilities, the Council for Exceptional Children, TASH (formerly known as The Association for Persons with Severe Handicaps), and the ARC of the United States (formerly known as the Association for Retarded Citizens) are examples of such organizations. Additionally, legislation such as the Vocational Rehabilitation Act, the Developmental Disabilities and Bill of Rights Act, and the Americans with Disabilities Act have helped tremendously. But it is only through the patience and persistence of persons with intellectual disabilities, their parents, professionals, and friends of persons with mental retardation that community initiatives and recent legislation have grown from simple ideas into participatory reality.

Many adults with intellectual disabilities are quite capable of expressing their opinions about issues that are important to them, but their concerns are sometimes very different from those of their care providers and often must be elicited using focused or nontraditional means (Foxx, Faw, Taylor, Davis, & Fulia, 1993; Lohrmann-O'Rourke & Browder, 1998). Advocates can help make the wishes and preferences of persons with mental retardation known to others. At a less formal level, advocates can help by evaluating the availability and appropriateness of services at the local or community level and then serving as catalysts for change. Advocates can help people with intellectual disabilities get jobs, stay in school, negotiate public transportation, and move about one's environment in a humane, respectful way. Advocates can also help by providing companionship to individuals who often have few friends. The role of advocates as models of acceptance cannot be underestimated and cannot be replaced by paid service delivery personnel.

Several types of advocacy now exist (see Table 12.4). Among the different types of advocacy is self-advocacy, a relatively new and highly effective movement that is increasing in popularity nationwide. One excellent example of an or-

Learn more about self-advocacy by visiting the Companion Website at www.prenhall.com/ beirne-smith and selecting Chapter 12, Video Case Studies.

TABLE 12.4
Types of Advocacy

Type	Advocate	Purpose
Systems (corporate) advocacy	An independent collective of citizens	Represent the rights and interests of groups of people with similar needs Pursue human service system quality and progressive change
Legal advocacy	Attorneys-at-law	Represent individuals or groups of individuals in the litigation or legal negotiation process
Self-advocacy	Individuals whose rights are at risk of being violated or diminished	Represent one's own rights and interests; speak on one's own behalf
Citizen advocacy	A mature, competent, volunteer citizen	Represent, as if they were his or her own, the rights and interests of another citizen

ganized effort of self-advocacy is People First, a movement in which individuals with disabilities have organized themselves at the local, state, and national levels to identify common needs and lobbying power. Systems advocacy is another type of advocacy in which a group of individuals with and without disabilities forms to better serve the needs of persons with disabilities. ARC is one such example. Though a relatively new social movement, advocacy has been heralded as a major force that can and will ensure success for persons with intellectual disabilities in the coming years.

Personal Satisfaction

The concept of personal satisfaction is a much broader construct than the outcomes discussed thus far. This is because personal satisfaction is a function of all of the other outcomes, plus other factors that may or may not be known. It is a reflection of the person's general sense of happiness.

Assessment of a person's happiness or satisfaction can be difficult. Multiple measures are often necessary, providing an opportunity for the person to share experiences at their own level and on a wide array of topics (Dudley, Calhoun, Ahlgrim-Delzell, & Conroy, 1998).

At its most basic level, personal satisfaction is the level of contentment and fulfillment felt by a person with respect to his or her person–environment match. While some see personal satisfaction as synonymous with overall quality of life, others see the two constructs as somewhat different (e.g., Edgerton, 1990; Heal, Borthwick-Duffy, & Saunders, 1996; Stark & Goldsbury, 1990). A major point of

To check your understanding of this chapter, go to the Companion Website at www.prenhall.com/ beirne-smith and select Chapter 12. From there, you can access the Self-Test and Essay modules.

difference in the positions is the amount of control people have over the parts of their lives that bring them satisfaction. Without getting caught up in the philosophical nature of the debate, adults with intellectual disabilities are indeed entitled to a life that is both satisfying and of the highest quality possible. Whether or not one's life in the community meets these criteria is up to the individual. More difficult, perhaps, is their proficiency in keeping society's mores and standards from inappropriately affecting their own sense of self-worth and self-determination.

Most adults with intellectual disabilities want very much to be part of a system that is often hesitant to welcome them. Whether it is more accurate to see these adults as resisting exposure for who they are or as simply not considering themselves to have a disability, it is safe to say that the label of mental retardation is not a comfortable one. The development of a positive sense of self is a life-long endeavor for adults without mental retardation; why should it be any different for adults with mental retardation? The answer is quite simple: For adults with mental retardation, the stakes are higher and the cards are often stacked against them.

Summary

Residential and Community Living

- Deinstitutionalization has been one of the most profound changes in the lives of people with intellectual disabilities over the past quarter-century.
- Most people with intellectual disabilities live in traditional homes, outside the service delivery system.
- Residents of institutions today tend to be older, have more functional limitations, and have more severe behavioral issues than in the past.
- Many types of community residential services exist, and offer varying degrees of support.

Employment and Occupation

- Service providers are becoming more adept at supporting people in the workplace.
- Adult education programs are offered in a variety of contexts, ranging from sheltered workshops to university courses.
- Supported employment is a valuable first step toward competitive employment.
- Barriers to competitive employment include low wages and potential loss of economic assistance.

Interpersonal Relationships

- Most people regard relationships as the most important aspect of their lives.
- People with intellectual disabilities often report their friendships are limited to family and paid caregivers.
- Even today, people with intellectual disabilities are often denied the right to love, marry, and express their sexuality.

- As the community-based movement progresses, more opportunities for intimate relationships will be presented.

Aging with Mental Retardation
- Like the rest of America, people with intellectual disabilities are living longer and healthier lives than ever before.
- Aging is sometimes complicated by other conditions associated with mental retardation, such as Down syndrome or cerebral palsy.
- As adults with mental retardation age, so do their caretakers. Many families are faced with the challenge of planning for life after the caretaker is no longer able to help.
- People with intellectual disabilities are deriving benefit from social change that is embracing an aging population.

Community Involvement
- Social acceptance can be enhanced by proper preparation and exposure to people with mental retardation.
- People with intellectual disabilities report difficulties accessing desirable recreation and leisure activities.
- Supports and services should be individually tailored, selected, and desired by the individual.
- Increased independence does present increased risks. People with mental retardation are at risk for maltreatment.

Quality of Life
- Self-determination refers to an individual's right to make choices and plans for his or her own life.
- Person-centered planning is a process for determining how someone can achieve his or her own goals.
- Several types of advocacy exist, including advocacy organizations, legal advocates, citizen advocates, and self-advocates.
- The ultimate goal of life is personal satisfaction—the degree to which one is content with his or her life circumstances.

Chapter

13

Assistive Technology Applications

OBJECTIVES

After reading this chapter, the student should be able to:

- Discuss the concept of assistive technology and its relevance in the special education classroom
- List and discuss the various definitions of assistive technology
- Identify the current trends and issues surrounding assistive technology
- Discuss the benefits of assistive technology
- List and discuss the policies and legislation of assistive technology
- List competencies that teachers need to implement assistive technology
- Explain assistive technology modifications that can be implemented in the classroom
- Discuss strategies for overcoming barriers to assistive technology
- Compare and contrast issues surrounding assistive technology at the preschool, school-age, and postschool levels

KEY TERMS

aided systems

Americans with Disabilities Act (ADA)

assistive technology

Assistive Technology Act of 2004

assistive technology services

augmentative communication

communication boards

conversation aids

keyguards

speech input and recognition

Technology-Related Assistance for Individuals with Disabilities Act

touch screens

unaided systems

virtual reality

tudents who have disabilities need a variety of adaptations to experience
success in school as well as in other facets of their lives. Over the years,
various assistive technologies have been developed to empower individuals with retardation to cope with everyday chores or procedures that seem
simple or natural for individuals without mental retardation (Bryant & Bryant,
1998a). Bryant and Bryant (2003) noted that technology is a way to foster independence for individuals with disabilities: "AT devices serve as a vehicle to help
individuals with disabilities do what they want to do, when they want to do it"
(p. 2). According to the Association for Retarded Citizens (ARC, 1997), technology can assist individuals who are retarded in overcoming barriers to independence and inclusion. Assistive technology (AT) compensates for the functional
limitations of the user and serves as a liberating agent for the individual. Hasselbring (1998) stated that assistive technology allows persons with disabilities to

TABLE 13.1
Current Trends and Issues Shaping the Use of Technology in Education

Types of Issues Having Impact on Technology in Education	Topics Under Each Issue	Current Issues Having Impact on Technology in Education	Implications for Technology in Education
Societal	Economic trends	Higher education costs	Distance learning emphasis to make education more cost-effective
	Political trends	Politicians call for lower-cost, more effective education	More reliance on DL and other technologies to increase consistency of quality, stretch scarce resources
	Social trends	Recognition of need for technology literacy	Computers becoming a required student purchase
		Increased communications results in less privacy	Possible suspicion of technology-delivered education
		Growing popular distrust of technology	Possible suspicion of technology-delivered education
Cultural/equity	Economic/ethnic	Lower-income schools equals less access to computers	Low-income students must have equal access to technology
		More minority students in lower-income schools	Minority students must have equal access to technology
	Multicultural	"Computer culture" is pervasive in society	Students must use computers regardless of cultural bias
	Gender	Technology remains a male-dominated area	Females' use of computers in education must increase
	Special needs	Special devices and methods can allow special-needs students equal access to technology but are expensive to obtain and implement	Disabled students must receive equal access to technology regardless of high costs to educational system

Types of Issues Having Impact on Technology in Education	Topics Under Each Issue	Current Issues Having Impact on Technology in Education	Implications for Technology in Education
Educational	Directed vs. constructivist views	Directed uses of technology (drill, tutorial) are proven effective but often considered passé	Demonstrated effective technology uses may be discarded
		Constructivist uses are emphasized but little evidence exists on their effectiveness	More research needed on newer technology uses
	Single-subject vs. interdisciplinary	Past emphasis on teaching subjects in isolation	Continued emphasis on use of single-skill software
		Current trend toward integrated curriculum or merging several subjects into one activity	Increasing use of multimedia and other technologies that support more complex, interdisciplinary activities
Technical	Rapid change	Technology changes too quickly for teachers to keep up	The latest technologies are in limited use in education
		Educators cannot afford most current technology	Schools usually have out-of-date equipment, materials
	Complexity	Teacher training is not keeping up with technology developments	Majority of teachers have insufficient training in technology materials and uses
		Schools lack the infrastructure to keep up with new technologies	Schools cannot take advantage of newest, most powerful technological developments

Source: From *Integrating Educational Technology into Teaching,* by M. D. Roblyer & J. E. Edwards, 2000, Upper Saddle River, NJ: Merrill/Prentice Hall. Reprinted by permission.

become an integral part of school and the community. Similarly, Grabe and Grabe (2000) noted that technology that permits collaboration can foster interactions between students with disabilities and their peers who are not disabled. On a different note, Belson (2003) stated that AT can bridge the gap for students with disabilities who do not have the same academic or instructional needs as their peers who are not disabled. Male (2003) concurred that AT can empower students with disabilities and make them more effective, efficient learners. Lesar (1998) noted that assistive technologies have the potential to reduce or prevent individuals from experiencing socioemotional and intellectual disabilities. For these reasons, educators have begun to explore technologies that have the potential to serve as solutions in helping students meet the demands of the classroom, the environmental demands of the workplace, and even the demands that can be found in the comfort of one's home (see Table 13.1).

Any technology application must match the individual's needs with the potential benefits.

DEFINITION OF ASSISTIVE TECHNOLOGY

Although **assistive technology** has been defined broadly, it can be thought of as any device that has the ability to enhance the performance of persons with disabilities (Lewis, 1998). Congress did not want to limit the range of tools and equipment that might be made available to individuals with disabilities by committing to a specific definition. As a result, Congress developed a general definition to be reflected in the Individuals with Disabilities Education Act of 2004 (IDEA). The IDEA defines assistive technology as the following: "Assistive technology device means any item, equipment, or product used to increase, maintain, or improve the functional capabilities of a child with a disability. The term does not include surgically implanted medical devices or removal of such a device" (Sec. 602 (1) B).

A complete online glossary is available on the Companion Website, which may be accessed at www.prenhall.com/ beirne-smith

The **Technology-Related Assistance for Individuals with Disabilities Act** of 1998 (Tech Act, reauthorized in October 2004) defines an assistive technology device as "any item, piece of equipment or product system, whether acquired commercially modified, or customized that is used to increase, maintain, or improve functional capabilities of individuals with disabilities" (p. 102, Stat. 1046). The Association for Retarded Citizens' (ARC, 1997) position on the use of assistive technology appears in Table 13.2.

Examples of commonly used AT devices that illustrate the formal definitions include positioning equipment, mobility devices, computer applications, adaptive toys and games, adaptive environments, electronic interfaces, homemade battery-powered toys, medical equipment, prostheses, and alternative and augmentative communication aids (Parette, Brotherson, Hourcade, & Bradley, 1996).

TABLE 13.2

Association for Retarded Citizens' Position on Assistive Technology

---

People with mental retardation have the ability to use assistive technology and should be given the opportunity.

Assistive technology devices designed to meet individual needs must be available throughout the life spans of children and adults with mental retardation and must be maintained and in working order, to be useful to support inclusion in the community.

Information on technology should be available to people with mental retardation, their families, friends, and support providers.

The principles of universal design* must incorporate the unique needs of people with mental retardation.

Technological innovators, designers, and manufacturers must be educated to the needs and preferences of individuals with mental retardation to ensure the production of useful products.

Individuals knowledgeable about people with mental retardation and current technology must be involved in assessing the needs of the person to ensure the selection of appropriate technology.

Effective use of assistive technology requires that (1) training must be provided to such groups as consumers, families, employers, educators, and other professionals, and (2) effectiveness must be evaluated on an ongoing basis.

Decisions regarding assistive technology must include consumer preferences based on experience with the device and service.

Universal design refers to designs that make all assistive technology products accessible to all people. Adherence to principles of universal design ensure that devices accommodate for individual preference and abilities; are easy to understand and are used regardless of the user's experience, language, or cognitive skills; and minimize adverse consequences of accidental or unintended actions.

Source: From *Assistive Technology Position Statement,* by the Association for Retarded Citizens, 1997, Arlington, TX: Arc of the United States. Available at the Web site of the Arc of the United States (http://www.thearc.org/posits/astec.html). Used with permission.

Lewis (1998) reported two purposes of assistive technology. First, technology can augment an individual's strengths by counterbalancing the effects of a disability. Second, it can provide alternative methods for performing a task so that disabilities can be compensated for or bypassed entirely. For example, an individual with difficulties in reading who possesses good listening skills can listen to books on tape rather than reading the print versions. Persons with poor computational skills but good fine-motor skills can use a handheld calculator. Those with poor spelling ability but a measure of computer literacy can write with a word processor that offers assistance in spelling. Similarly, persons with poor vision or poor motor skills can write using voice-to-text technology.

According to Blackhurst (1997), the assistive technology used for individuals with disabilities can range from such high-tech solutions as a speaking keyboard to low-tech solutions like a pencil grip. Included is the idea of a no-tech solution that involves the teaching or training of a device. The following list illustrates the continuum of technologies as described by Blackhurst:

- *High-tech* solutions involve the use of sophisticated devices, such as computers and interactive multimedia systems.
- *Medium-tech* solutions use less complicated electronic or mechanical devices, such as videocassette players and wheelchairs.
- *Low-tech* solutions are less sophisticated, such as adapted spoon handles, Velcro fasteners, or raised desks that can accommodate a wheelchair.
- *No-tech* solutions require no devices or equipment. These might involve the use of systematic teaching procedures or the services of related services personnel such as physical or occupational therapists. (1997, p. 42)

The expense of a device is often the determinant of where it will fall on the low-tech to high-tech continuum. Parette and Murdick (1998) noted that often, the more expensive the device, the more high-tech the design. Usually, the expense is a result of the device having greater sophistication and better use in varying situations, and requiring more training for the teacher and the student to use effectively (Lewis, 1993). Low-tech devices generally are inexpensive and often require little training for their use. In general, less emphasis should be placed on the categorization of the devices as being low- or high-tech and more emphasis should be placed on the suitability of the device for the individual student. Given that students with disabilities possess individual interests, strengths, and weaknesses, we may conclude that an AT device appropriate for one person may be inappropriate for another. Similarly, a device that may assist an individual in one setting may be inappropriate in a different setting (Bryant, Erin, Lock, Allan, & Resta, 1998). Once an individual's needs have been targeted and appropriate technology has been applied, then the technology has the potential to provide a variety of needs for the individual who is retarded.

To determine the type of technology or supports that a particular student may need, it is a good practice to begin with no-tech or low-tech solutions and work up to more sophisticated levels of the continuum. However, it is critical to address the issues of individual needs and differences. Applying technology involves matching the individual's demonstrated needs with the potential benefits possible through the use of the technology (Parette & Murdick, 1998). Bryant and Bryant (2003) refer to a *setting-person-feature match* and urge decision makers to consider whether the technology is reasonable, relevant to setting demands, and effective. These authors provide a list of questions that decision makers should consider when selecting assistive technology devices (see Table 13.3).

BENEFITS OF ASSISTIVE TECHNOLOGY

Assistive technology provides a variety of benefits for individuals who are disabled (e.g., see Table 13.4). Technology assists individuals who are retarded in overcoming barriers to independence by compensating for their daily limitations. Further, AT can decrease dependence on others by allowing individuals to become or remain integrated into their chosen communities (Bieniewski, 1999; Bryant & Bryant, 2003;

TABLE 13.3
Adaptation Considerations

1. **Purpose of the adaptation**

   What is the intended purpose of the adaptation?
   Is there a specific target group for whom the device is an adaptation?
   For what tasks is the adaptation intended to be used (e.g., reading, communication)?

2. **Requirements to use the adaptation**

   What abilities must the user/student possess in order to use the adaptation successfully?

3. **Environmental accessibility**

   Is the adaptation transferable across environments?
   Can the adaptation be transported easily?
   What are the requirements to use the adaptation in various environments (e.g., electrical, furniture)?

4. **Technical components**

   Does the adaptation involve electrical hardware and software?
   Is there voice input or speech capabilities?
   Does the user/student need to access a keyboard to use the adaptation?
   Is the adaptation compatible with other technological components?

5. **Ease of use**

   How easy is the adaptation to learn to use?
   Are there technological components that might take time to learn (e.g., programming)?
   Does use of the adaptation promote the individual's independence?

6. **Training requirements**

   How much training is required by the user, family, teacher/caregiver?
   What kind of follow-up training might be necessary?
   Is technical support readily available to troubleshoot when technology problems arise?

7. **Maintenance requirements**

   How durable is the adaptation?
   How reliable is the adaptation?
   What regular maintenance is necessary to ensure continued use of the adaptation?
   Who will do the maintenance?
   How long will maintenance take to correct problems?
   What "loaner" options are available?

Source: Bryant & Bryant (2003), p. 38.

TABLE 13.4

Academic Advantages of Assertive Technology as Reported by the U.S. Congress in 1988

Drill and practice to master basic skills
Development of writing skills
Problem solving
Understanding abstract mathematics and science concepts
Simulation in science, mathematics, and social studies
Manipulation of data
Acquisition of computer skills for general purposes and for business and vocational training
Access and communication for traditionally unserved population of students
Access and communication for teachers and students in remote locations
Individualized learning
Cooperative learning
Management of learning activities and record keeping

Source: From *Power On! New Tools for Teaching and Learning,* U.S. Congress, Office of Technology Assessment, 1988, Washington, DC: U.S. Government Printing Office.

"Study Points," 1999). Specifically, individuals may communicate with others, engage in social activities and recreation, and increase their daily living skills with the assistance of technology (ARC, 1997). In addition, assistive technology allows students to make more progress in speech and language therapy, occupational therapy, physical therapy, mobility, orientation, and other related service programs.

Technologies can be beneficial in assisting individuals daily in learning and working (Belson, 2003; Male 2003). Assistive technology allows students with mental retardation to receive educational services in the same school and classroom as students who do not have individual education programs. Technology provides students with additional access to instruction and other school activities and allows them to learn from classroom activities at a faster rate. Researchers at the North Central Regional Educational Laboratory (Valdez, McNabb, Foertsch, Anderson, Hawkes, & Raack, 2000) concluded that "technology offers opportunities for learner-control, increased motivation, connections to the real world, and data-driven assessments tied to content standards that, when implemented systemically, enhances student achievement as measured in a variety of ways, including, but not exclusively limited to, standardized achievement tests" (p. 1). These researchers also concluded that technology plays an important role in K–12 education, but noted that it will not solve all educational problems. Technology makes learning more enjoyable, interactive, and customizable. According to Valdez and colleagues, these attributes of technology can increase students' interest in learning and improve their attitudes toward the subject matter.

In 1993, the National Council on Disability conducted a 19-month survey that summarized the benefits of AT devices and services. The following are some of its findings:

- Almost three quarters of school-age children with disabilities were able to remain in a general education classroom and 45% were able to reduce school-related services.
- Sixty-two percent of working-age persons were able to reduce dependence on family members, 58% were able to reduce dependence on paid assistance, and 37% were able to increase earnings.
- Eighty percent of elderly persons studied were able to reduce dependence on others, half were able to reduce dependence on paid persons, and half were able to avoid entering a nursing home.
- Almost one third of assistive technology users indicated that their family saved money, averaging around $1,110 per month, with assistive technology. At the same time, one quarter of the users indicated that they experienced additional equipment-related expenses that averaged around $287 per month.
- Of the 42 users of assistive technology who reported having paid jobs, 92% reported that the assistive technology enabled them to work faster or better, 83% indicated that they earned more money, 81% reported working more hours, 67% reported that the equipment had enabled them to obtain employment, and 15% indicated that the equipment enabled them to keep their jobs.
- When asked to estimate the impact of equipment on their quality of life, assistive technology users reported that without the equipment, their quality of life on a scale of 1 to 10 was about 3; as a result of the equipment, it jumped to approximately 8.4 points. (pp. 1–2)

See much more about the benefits of assistive technology by visiting the Companion Website at www.prenhall.com/beirne-smith and selecting Chapter 13, Video Case Studies.

Because benefits for using assistive technology are evident, individuals with intellectual disabilities should be introduced to possible assistive technologies at an early age and educators and other service providers should be trained in selecting, implementing, and evaluating assistive technology for the individuals they serve.

POLICIES AND LEGALITIES SURROUNDING ASSISTIVE TECHNOLOGY

Individuals with Disabilities Education Act

The Individuals with Disabilities Education Act (IDEA) guarantees the right of all children with disabilities to a free and appropriate public education in the least restrictive environment. As a part of IEP/IFSP planning, parents, teachers, and administrators are required to consider technologies that may help a child meet the IEP/IFSP goals and objectives. With the passage of the 2004 amendments to the IDEA (P.L. 108-446), all teachers are expected to have knowledge and skill in various areas of special education. With this in mind, special and general education teachers should consider the appropriateness of assistive technology as a tool or an intervention for all students who have IEPs. Teachers who possess little knowledge about assistive technology may have difficulty fulfilling this requirement without special training or assistance. Special educators currently working in the field may need to gain new competencies in the area of assistive technology. The 1997 IDEA amendments also suggested that general educators should receive professional development to help them better to teach individuals with disabilities in their classrooms.

Lahm and Nickels (1999) noted that special educators must have an understanding of the legislation and regulations related to technology used in special education as well as develop a personal philosophy on the use of technology to guide them in the implementation of technology devices. Also, teachers need to know the terminology related to assistive technology to communicate accurately with others about its purpose. Furthermore, the IDEA specifies guidelines in assisting parents, professionals, and students in the selection, use, and acquisition of technologies. As defined in Section 602 of P.L. 108-446, *assistive technology service* includes the following:

- The evaluation of the needs of a child with a disability, including a functional evaluation of the child in the child's customary environment
- Purchasing, leasing, or otherwise providing for the acquisition of assistive technology devices by a child with a disability
- Selecting, designing, fitting, customizing, adapting, applying, maintaining, repairing, or replacing assistive technology devices
- Coordinating and using other therapies, interventions, or services with assistive technology devices, such as those associated with existing education and rehabilitation plans and programs
- Training or technical assistance for a child with a disability or the family of such a child
- Training or technical assistance for professionals (including individuals providing education or rehabilitation services), employers, or other individuals who provide services to employ, or are otherwise substantially involved in the major life functions of a child with a disability

Individualized Education Program (IEP).   The 2004 reauthorization of the IDEA requires IEP teams to consider assistive technology as a critical factor when developing a student's individualized education program (IEP). (As described in chapter 11, an IEP team may include the teacher, speech therapist, occupational therapist, physical therapist, and any other person who works with the student.) The 2004 IDEA requires schools to provide assistive technologies for a student with a disability if services and equipment are necessary to ensure a free appropriate public education (§300.308).

One of the new requirements in the IEP section of the federal law is that for each student eligible for special education services, the IEP team must "consider whether the child needs assistive technology devices and services" (§ 614[d] [3] [B] [v]). A student's IEP should reflect necessary assistive technologies that have the potential to provide the child with an appropriate education. If assistive technology is represented in the IEP, then team members must take measures to provide technologies as stated in it. Discussions about assistive technology should be documented on the IEP and/or in the meeting notes. Team decisions made and their rationale must be included in the IEP as well as determinations regarding assistive technology evaluations. If assistive technology and/or services are needed, then those also must be reflected in the IEP. When assistive technology is used to enable a student an appropriate education, the assistive technology must be provided at the school's expense.

Individualized Family Service Plan (IFSP).   The cooperation and participation of parents and siblings of an infant or toddler with a disability can enhance the use and practicality of assistive technology. Families of younger children with disabilities participate in the development of an individualized family service plan (IFSP). The family's participation is reflected in the IFSP that is usually prepared when a child is first diagnosed with a disability. During these early years, emphasis is placed on providing services to the child and the child's entire family. The focus on family distinguishes early intervention programs from programs that are developed for school-age children.

The IFSP is developed by a multidisciplinary team and contains statements about the family's resources and concerns with the intent to enhance the development of the special needs of the infant or toddler (Dunst, Trivette, & Deal, 1988). Consequently, family routines, values, and resources also must be considered when planning for technologies (Brinker, Seifer, & Sameroff, 1994). During the development of the IFSP, parents often target specific goals for their child (Butler, 1988; Parette et al., 1996). As parents come to see how assistive technology can improve their child's productivity, they increasingly request technologies and early intervention services to be documented and provided through the child's IFSP. Indubitably, children in this category can benefit from technology as early as it can be provided.

Assistive technologies affect the entire family. Thus, the entire family should play an active role in all processes regarding assistive technologies (Dunst et al., 1988). Considering that family cultures differ greatly from those of the school system, when determining the use of technology the IFSP team should address issues of independence, acceptance, and changes in the family routines ("Technology in School," 2000). Consequently, assistive technology devices are of little value to young children or their families without appropriate follow-up services. Problems can occur when families are not provided support services or training in methods of integrating the assistive device in the child's natural environment (Lesar, 1998). Support services ensure that the child and his or her family can adequately and readily use technologies on a regular basis. **Assistive technology services** may include such supports as purchasing and leasing devices and equipment; customizing and adapting devices; repairing devices; training the child and parents in the use of devices; and coordinating interventions, therapies, and services with assistive technology devices (RESNA Technical Assistance Project, 2000).

Assistive Technology Act of 2004

The Technology-Related Assistance for Individuals with Disabilities Act of 1998 (the Tech Act), which was due to sunset in 2004, was reauthorized as the **Assistive Technology Act of 2004** (AT Act). The AT Act is a reauthorization of one of the most influential and beneficial laws supporting the development of programs that ensure access to appropriate assistive technology devices and services for individuals and their families (Bryant & Bryant, 1998a). The AT Act directly addresses the need for increased access to technology by individuals with disabilities and their families. The law provides flexibility to states in responding to the technology needs of their citizens with disabilities and builds on the accomplishments achieved by states over the past decade through assistive programs funded under the act.

The purpose of the 2004 AT Act is to provide financial assistance to states to engage in activities that assist them in maintaining and strengthening a permanent comprehensive state-wide program of technology-related assistance. In addition, the act identifies federal policy that facilitates payment for technology devices and technology services, to identify those federal policies that prevent such payment and to eliminate inappropriate barriers to such payments. Specifically, the AT Act mandates accommodations and accessibility for individuals with disabilities to promote full participation and integration into society.

The 2004 AT Act is intended to target individuals with disabilities of all ages and their family members, guardians, advocates, and authorized representatives. Also targeted are individuals who work for public or private entities that have contact with individuals with disabilities, educators and related services personnel, technology experts, health and allied health professionals, employers, and other appropriate individuals and entities.

Specifically, the reauthorized Assistive Technology Act of 2004 waives the sunset provision, so that the AT Act now will be regularly reauthorized and will do the following:

To access the original language of legislation related to assistive technology, and to locate a variety of resources related to topics covered in this chapter, visit the Companion Website at www.prenhall.com/ beirne-smith and select Chapter 13, Web Destinations.

- Strengthen existing successful state assistive technology programs
- Authorize additional resources so each state will receive additional monies for protection and advocacy services
- Refocus training and technical assistance
- Emphasize the provision of assistive technology devices and services to ensure that technology will be available where individuals need it—in schools, on the job, and in the community
- Require programs to provide device demonstration, equipment loan, device reutilization/recycling, and financing systems, including low-interest loan programs
- Focus training and technical assistance to improve service planning for individuals with disabilities and to ensure that service providers have information on assistive technology
- Require states to focus on two populations: students with disabilities receiving transition services and adults with disabilities maintaining or transitioning to community living (thus aligning the AT Act with such recent federal priorities as the Individuals with Disabilities Education Act and the Americans with Disabilities integration mandate in the *Olmstead* decision; see chapter 4)
- Authorize projects of national significance to increase public awareness and encourage research and development
- Improve technical assistance, data collection, and the public Internet site

Americans with Disabilities Act

The **Americans with Disabilities Act (ADA)** of 1990 (P.L. 101-336) is a civil rights bill intended to eliminate discrimination against individuals with disabilities (Lewis, 1993). The ADA similarly requires the delivery of auxiliary aids and services as needed to assure equal access to programs and services offered by the school. Equal access includes the provision of auxiliary aids and services that are needed for effective communication with individuals who have disabilities. Although the ADA does not focus directly on technology, the law places requirements on public schools to provide access to the same services for individuals with and without special needs. In addition, technologies may be used to meet the law's requirements. As one requirement of the ADA, schools must be careful not to create barriers for any children.

TEACHER TRAINING

Perhaps one of the most difficult issues schools will face in meeting the assistive technology needs of their students is developing sufficient staff expertise. The 2004 amendments to the IDEA mandated that any state receiving a State Program Improvement Grant is required to use no less than 90% of the grant for professional development. Professional development for general educators, special educators, and related service personnel should include training in selecting, implementing, and modifying assistive technologies. The 1998 Tech Act added that general and special educators must receive more professional development and training so that they can deliver appropriate instruction (also see Yell & Shriner, 1997). Figure 13.1 illustrates the types of technology knowledge that teachers should possess, and Box 13.1 summarizes standards for educators.

Bryant and colleagues (1998) reported three competencies that educators must possess to implement assistive technologies adequately. First, educators must have access to necessary AT hardware and software. Second, educators should be comfortable with the use of the assistive technologies. Finally, educators should have access to adequate resources and training that assist with the implementation of assistive technologies. More specifically, Bausch and Hasselbring (2004) noted that AT service providers must be able to:

- Assess/evaluate students who have been referred for AT
- Match students to the most appropriate devices
- Consult with school faculty and/or individual teachers
- Train students, teachers, and families on using specific devices
- Collaborate with IEP team members
- Provide professional development training to school staff
- Purchase equipment
- Collaborate with other staff to include students with disabilities into the general education classroom
- Adapt and modify the curriculum
- Follow up and evaluate AT implementation (p. 101)

Roblyer and Erlanger (1998) summarized guidelines that make teacher training programs more effective. These guidelines call for emphasizing hands-on integration; training over time; modeling, mentoring, and coaching; and post-training access:

- *Hands-on integration emphasis:* Hands-on activities are necessary for teacher training. Skills needed to integrate technology cannot be effectively learned in a classroom watching demonstrations or listening to an instructor. Teachers in training must have an opportunity to navigate through a program and

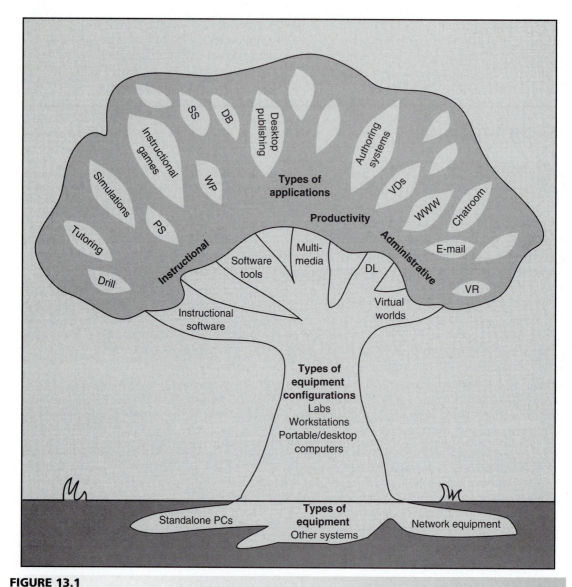

FIGURE 13.1
The Educational Technology Tree of Knowledge

Source: From *Integrating Educational Technology into Teaching,* by M. D. Roblyer & J. E. Edwards, 2000, Upper Saddle River, NJ: Merrill/Prentice Hall. Reprinted by permission.

complete a set of steps of creating new products. However, the focus should be on how to use the technology in the classroom.

- *Training over time:* Professionals are discovering that traditional models of staff development—particularly those "one-shot" programs for the entire staff—are ineffective for teaching computer skills. Training in technology

Box 13.1 ✿ NETS for Teachers

Educational Technology Standards and Performance Indicators for All Teachers

Building on the NETS for Students, the ISTE NETS for Teachers (NETS • T), which focus on preservice teacher education, define the fundamental concepts, knowledge, skills, and attitudes for applying technology in educational settings. All candidates seeking certification or endorsements in teacher preparation should meet these educational technology standards. It is the responsibility of faculty across the university and at cooperating schools to provide opportunities for teacher candidates to meet these standards.

The six standards areas with performance indicators listed below are designed to be general enough to be customized to fit state, university, or district guidelines and yet specific enough to define the scope of the topic. Performance indicators for each standard provide specific outcomes to be measured when developing a set of assessment tools. The standards and the performance indicators also provide guidelines for teachers currently in the classroom.

1. Technology Operations and Concepts

Teachers demonstrate a sound understanding of technology operations and concepts. Teachers:

- Demonstrate introductory knowledge, skills, and understanding of concepts related to technology (as described in the ISTE National Education Technology Standards for Students)
- Demonstrate continual growth in technology knowledge and skills to stay abreast of current and emerging technologies

2. Planning and Designing Learning Environments and Experiences

Teachers plan and design effective learning environments and experiences supported by technology. Teachers:

- Design developmentally appropriate learning opportunities that apply technology-enhanced instructional strategies to support the diverse needs of learners
- Apply current research on teaching and learning with technology when planning learning environments and experiences
- Identify and locate technology resources and evaluate them for accuracy and suitability
- Plan for the management of technology resources within the context of learning activities
- Plan strategies to manage student learning in a technology-enhanced environment

3. Teaching, Learning, and the Curriculum

Teachers implement curriculum plans that include methods and strategies for applying technology to maximize student learning. Teachers:

- Facilitate technology-enhanced experiences that address content standards and student technology standards
- Use technology to support learner-centered strategies that address the diverse needs of students
- Apply technology to develop students' higher order skills and creativity
- Manage student learning activities in a technology-enhanced environment

4. Assessment and Evaluation

Teachers apply technology to facilitate a variety of effective assessment and evaluation strategies. Teachers:

- Apply technology in assessing student learning of subject matter using a variety of assessment techniques
- Use technology resources to collect and analyze data, interpret results, and communicate findings to improve instructional practice and maximize student learning

(Continued)

• Apply multiple methods of evaluation to determine students' appropriate use of technology resources for learning, communication, and productivity

5. Productivity and Professional Practice

Teachers use technology to enhance their productivity and professional practice. Teachers:

• Use technology resources to engage in on-going professional development and life-long learning
• Continually evaluate and reflect on professional practice to make informed decisions regarding the use of technology in support of student learning
• Apply technology to increase productivity
• Use technology to communicate and collaborate with peers, parents, and the larger community in order to nurture student learning

6. Social, Ethical, Legal, and Human Issues

Teachers understand the social, ethical, legal, and human issues surrounding the use of technology in PK–12 schools and apply those principles in practice. Teachers:

• Model and teach legal and ethical practice related to technology use
• Apply technology resources to enable and empower learners with diverse backgrounds, characteristics, and abilities
• Identify and use technology resources that affirm diversity
• Promote safe and healthy use of technology resources
• Facilitate equitable access to technology resources for all students

Source: International Society for Technology in Education (2003).

should be ongoing. Teachers need time to reflect, plan, and experiment on their successes and failures with computer technology. Teachers will need time to ask questions, get feedback, and explore new ideas. Successful staff development provides adequate examples and gives teachers opportunities to use technologies.

• *Modeling, mentoring, and coaching:* Instructors who model the use of technology in their own teaching have been acknowledged as the most effective teacher trainers. Research has indicated that one-to-one mentoring and coaching programs are effective for novice teachers. Most teachers seem to learn computer skills through colleague interaction, collaboration, and information sharing.
• *Post-training access:* Teachers need to have adequate access to technology for training to be successful. In addition, teachers need access to technology after training to practice what they have learned.

BARRIERS TO ASSISTIVE TECHNOLOGY

Although assistive technology adaptations are used to circumvent disability-related barriers, it is common to encounter barriers and complications when implementing such technologies. A national survey (Wehmeyer, 1998) indicated that in many cases, individuals who are retarded and their families are unaware of the possible benefits that they could receive from assistive technology. Wehmeyer further reported that if they are aware of such benefits, they are not informed about the devices available, how to fund them, or where to obtain adequate assessment and training. Wehmeyer's conclusions were supported by the National Council on Disability's (2000) report, *Federal Policy Barriers to Assistive Technology,* which noted that the two biggest barriers for consumers of assistive technology were lack of knowledge about appropriate assistive technology and lack of funding to purchase assistive technology. Consumers consistently reported to the NCD that they did not have information on the availability of assistive technology, where to find assistive technology, where to get evaluations, or what were their rights. Further, consumers reported great uncertainty about how to fund their need for assistive technology. Consumers stated that they could not afford the cost, insurance companies refused their claims, and no public funding was available.

See chapter 8 for specific information about the disproportionate representation of minority and low-income individuals in programs for individuals who have intellectual disabilities.

As noted in chapter 8, a disproportionate number of individuals who are served in programs for persons with retardation come from minority populations, low-income backgrounds, and/or single-parent or blended families. Another barrier to the use of assistive technology by individuals with retardation is related to the "digital divide" that separates those who have access to computer-based information and those who do not. The National Telecommunications and Information Administration (NTIA, 1999) characterized Whites, Asians/Pacific Islanders, individuals with higher incomes, and individuals who are more highly educated or who come from dual-parent households as "information rich," and individuals with lower incomes and education levels or from certain minority populations as "information poor." Similarly, the U.S. Census Bureau (1998) reported that African Americans or Hispanics are less likely to have Internet access from any location than Whites or Asian/Pacific Islanders have access from home. This is important because household access is the traditional way in which Internet access is defined (NTIA, 2000).

Teacher expertise represents another significant barrier to the use of assistive technology by individuals who are retarded. Interestingly, novice teachers report being no more competent or prepared than experienced teachers (NCD, 2000). Bryant and colleagues (1998) reported three barriers that prevent novice teachers from using technologies or cause teachers to abandon technologies altogether. The first barrier includes limited access to technology. Some individuals with mental retardation lack the information necessary to acquire assistive technology. More unfortunately, teachers may lack knowledge to ensure that their students with physical or other disabilities receive necessary or appropriate technologies. Colleges of education at universities often have limited equipment funding and sometimes are at the bottom of the university equipment funding priority list. This results in untrained or poorly trained teachers. Further, as Bausch and Hasselbring (2004) pointed out, the great number of AT devices available makes service providers' choices difficult. These dilemmas can prevent or limit the appropriate education that individuals with retardation are entitled to receive.

Educators commonly receive minimal technology training in their preservice training. The second barrier would include limited professional development opportunities. A challenge of integrating assistive technology in the classroom is the lack of faculty training and technical support within many colleges of education. Educators need time and training to explore new and progressive AT devices and to implement those in their classrooms. As stated earlier in this chapter, the 2004 IDEA amendments mandated professional development for all educators who teach students with disabilities. Therefore, training is essential for educators to be competent in integrating assistive technology. Specifically, Bausch and Hasselbring (2004) noted that AT service providers must be trained in (1) selecting appropriate AT devices from the ever increasing number of available AT devices, (2) the operation and implementation of AT devices across all learning environments in which the student must function, and (3) providing the necessary support once an AT device is adopted.

A third barrier is the lack of incentives. This dilemma can be perceived within classrooms and at the university or college level. Bausch and Hasselbring (2004) reported that recent data indicate that college and university special education programs are not providing adequate training in assistive technology and that when such training does occur, it is often provided by departments outside special education that do not emphasize the unique educational needs of students with disabilities. These authors recommended that special education programs in higher education must acknowledge the importance of providing their students with the skills and knowledge of AT and begin to infuse AT content into their curriculum. The result is that preservice teachers enter the workforce unprepared in AT and school districts are forced to provide in-service training or individuals must seek outside sources of training. Unfortunately, educators at all levels often have little incentive to make a major investment of their time in attempting to integrate assistive technology into their teaching.

Any encountered barriers to assistive technology can leave individuals with mental retardation, their families, and professionals feeling frustrated that they have not acquired success in implementing technologies. Clinton (1995) reported frustrations that may accompany the use of assistive technology. It is common for parents who provide support to have unrealistic expectations that technology will cure disabilities. Some special education teachers and students are frustrated when technology requires initial training. For this reason, it can be easier when technologies offer plug-and-play solutions when possible, so students can direct their efforts to learning. Although recent advances have been made in assistive technologies, disabilities for which present technology offers no solutions still exist. However, there is hope that advancements in the future will lesson these frustrations.

To read more about barriers to assistive technology, go to the Companion Website at www.prenhall .com/beirne-smith and select Chapter 13, Read and Respond.

MODIFICATIONS

Bryant and Bryant (1998b) reported that instructional modifications include changes to teaching procedures, curricula, management, materials and technology, and the physical environment to facilitate learning. According to the AT Act of 2004, assistive technology may require simple, low-tech modifications or universal designs that are appropriate for use by individuals with a wide range of functional capabilities. Off-the-shelf technologies can become adaptive when they are used to enhance the learning of a student who is retarded (Lewis, 1998). For example, an audiotape becomes assistive when it is used to compensate for an individual's memory or note-taking problems. In addition, low-tech modifications such as

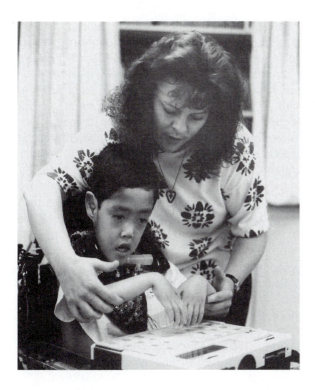

Modifications to standard computer keyboards might need to be considered for students with limited hand and finger mobility.

sticky notes, flags, and highlighters can enhance a student's organizational skills. Such modifications require minimal time and training to be implemented in the classroom.

Simple and uncomplicated modifications are sometimes all that are needed to allow a student to use a computer software program (Olson & Platt, 2000). Standard computer keyboards pose a number of problems for some students with mental retardation (Kincaid, 1999). Various modifications may need to be considered so that students with limited hand and finger mobility can access computer technology. Before a student can use computer technology for a given task, an appropriate method for inputting information must be available.

Word processing has the capability of helping individuals improve their writing skills (MacArthur, 1996). Students who are retarded often possess limited conceptualization of editing and revising; thus, such students limit their revisions to minor errors that fail to strengthen a written document as a whole. Therefore, using a word processor may not only teach students with intellectual disabilities to edit their writing better, but also can help these students to make frequent revisions without labored rewriting. MacArthur, Graham, and Schwartz (1991) reported that word processing not only reduces resistance to revising as a whole but also eliminates errors due to transcription. They further noted that word processing has the potential to facilitate other revision operations such as moving content and deleting material.

Today, word processors are accompanied with additional tools that can guide students with mental retardation as they learn to write. For example, most word processors are programmed with spell-checkers that can prompt students as they transcribe. Spell-checkers typically perform two functions: they identify misspelled words, and they suggest correct spellings (MacArthur, 1996). However, spell-checking by use of a word processor may not promote greater spelling skills, especially for weak spellers. As MacArthur stated, spell-checkers sometimes fail to teach spelling skills, since they simply compensate for poor spelling. Also, unless students are instructed in the proper use of spell-checkers, the content of the product may suffer. As any teacher knows, students sometimes view spell-checkers as obliterating the need to proofread the finished product.

Other computer-based learning tools can facilitate instruction that is individualized to the needs of students who are retarded. For instance, *widgets* are computer-based tools that go beyond the controlled, sequenced software programs that teachers traditionally use for drill and practice. According to Miller, Brown, and Robinson (2002), widgets are "small computer programs that are created using an authorized software program and can be stored on CDs or accessed via the Internet" (p. 24). Teachers can create their own widgets or use widgets created by other teachers. Widgets can be used by teachers to model, demonstrate, or elaborate on instructional tasks, skills, or concepts with an individual student or with a group of students who have similar instructional needs. Widgets allow teachers to decide when to move to a more challenging or less challenging problem or to a new learning objective. Thus, teachers are able to make sound instructional decisions based on how students are performing on the tasks, skills, or concepts being taught.

Handheld computers or personal digital assistants (PDAs) are finding a home in classrooms that serve students with disabilities. The portability and versatility of PDAs make them a useful instructional and communication tool for teachers and students. Bauer and Ulrich (2002) reported on the potential uses of PDAs in an inclusive classroom of 6th graders. Uses by students and teachers included the following:

- To self-monitor behavior
- To self-record grades and monitor student progress
- To beam lecture notes and the content of overheads directly from the teacher, rather than relying on a scribe or note-taker
- To beam long-term assignments
- To read books—young adult novels by recognized authors available for download free via the Internet
- As reminders for medication, to initiate a new task, or to move to another part of a test or assessment
- As a parent–teacher communication tool
- As a graphing calculator
- To facilitate student collaboration and peer support (p. 20)

Over the past decade, technology has not only advanced but also become increasingly powerful. Some emerging technologies should be given merit based on their capability to enhance the learning of individuals who are retarded. For example, virtual reality is one emergent technology that has notable potential for individuals with intellectual disabilities. **Virtual reality** involves the use of 3-D graphics combined with direct manipulation and provides for the illusion of immersion into a virtual world (Olson & Platt, 2000). When applying virtual reality, the individual interacts with a computer-simulated environment in detail. One of the most unique characteristics of virtual reality is its potential for contextualized instruction (Bottge & Hasselbring, 1993). Virtual reality simulates real-life experiences and can be used to construct conceptualized learning environments that promote generalization of skills (Lewis, 1998) or target the assessment and rehabilitation of functional skills and cognitive processes (Rizzo et al., 2001). Indeed, the concept of virtual reality portrays a promising future for individuals who are retarded. The future of virtual reality has the potential to level the playing field by providing unique modifications and accommodations for persons with intellectual disabilities.

Now, we explore the ways AT modifications impact various stages of the life span.

Early Childhood

Young children learn from playing. Because play often involves social interaction, children have the opportunity to interact with and learn from others. Through this interaction, children develop their cognitive skills, learn new concepts, and enhance their motor and perceptual capabilities. However, some children who are retarded lack the ability to interact socially due to their physical disabilities. Technology can make it possible for these young children to interact at an early age, so that they can have opportunities similar to those of children without disabilities. The key to success is to introduce the technology to children and their families as early as possible.

Computers can help young children with mental retardation to develop language. The goal of any language development program is to provide young children with the tools for independent communication. Some children will learn to speak, some will learn sign language, and others will need the assistance of augmentative communication. **Augmentative communication** refers to a set of approaches used to improve the communication skills of persons who do not speak or whose speech is not intelligible (Lewis, 1993; Olson & Platt, 2000). There are two basic types of augmentative communication: aided and unaided systems (Snell, 1993). **Aided systems** require the use of a picture or word board, a notebook, or a computerized aid. **Unaided systems** require the individual to use only hand or body motions to communicate (e.g., sign language). Augmentative communication options can range from high- to low-tech devices including such aids as symbol systems, manual communication boards, electronic communication devices, speech synthesizers, and communication enhancement software. Communication boards, a low-tech alternative to augmentative communication, assist young children in language expression. **Communication boards** are usually made of cardboard or another material and are used to display choices for children who cannot speak (Ysseldyke & Algozzine, 1990). For example, the young child can communicate by selecting from the options presented on the board. Table 13.5 briefly describes other assistive technologies for young children.

As mentioned earlier in this chapter, children benefit from receiving assistive technology at an early age. Under the 2004 IDEA regulations, AT services for young children include a number of specific supports. Initially, a child must have an evaluation of his or her unique technology needs, including a functional evaluation in the child's customary environment. Furthermore, professionals should consider

TABLE 13.5
Technologies for Young Children

> **Bump-and-go toys:** Examples are police cars and fire engines with flashing lights and sirens and a train with smoke, sound effects, and flashing lights.
>
> **Stuffed animals that move:** Examples are a dinosaur that walks on its hind legs, moving its head and front legs as its eye light up, and a pig that walks, wags its tail, says "oink" and wrinkles its nose.
>
> **Toys for dramatic play:** Include a toy sewing machine, blender, and mixer.
>
> **Musical toys:** Examples are a switch-operated drum, a musical top, and adapted versions of the Fisher-Price record player, music box radio, and music box TV.
>
> **Busy boxes activated by lightly touching built-in switches:** With the 5-Function Activity Center, the child touches an orange plate to turn on a light, a blue plate to play a radio, and a yellow plate to feel vibration. Pulling the string activates a music box, and moving the roller produces a buzzing sound.
>
> **Radios and tape recorders:** Include an adapted AM/FM radio with earphones.

Source: From *Special Education Technology: Classroom Applications* (1st ed.), by R. B. Lewis. Copyright © 1993. Reprinted with permission of Wadsworth, a division of Thomson Learning (http://www.thomsonrights.com).

purchasing, leasing, or providing for the appropriate AT device. Acquisition encompasses selecting, designing, customizing, fitting, adapting, applying, maintaining, repairing, or replacing assistive technology devices. During this time it may be critical to coordinate therapies, interventions, or services associated with the child's IEP or IFSP. Finally, service delivery systems are responsible for providing training and technical assistance to the child, the family, and the professionals who provide services to them (Assistive Technology Act, 2004). Agencies that serve young children recognize the need for assistive technology and labor to meet challenges in a fashion that provides appropriate technology, trains professionals and families in the use of assistive technology, and demonstrates unique ways for families to access assistive technology (Lesar, 1998). As documented by professionals, it is critical for families to take an active part in implementing assistive technology (Brinker et al., 1994; Parette et al., 1996).

School Age

The task of providing school-age students with a free appropriate public education (FAPE) is made more challenging with the 2004 reauthorization of the IDEA. As mentioned earlier, IEP teams are charged with the task of considering necessary assistive technologies for students with disabilities. In some instances, general education teachers are required to attend and participate in IEP meetings. As schools grow increasingly inclusive, general educators' involvement in IEP development should grow accordingly. Similarly, special educators should remain current on the progression of assistive technologies. Also, as schools grow more inclusive, students who are retarded may be challenged to participate in learning experiences that develop receptive and expressive literacy.

All too often technology is viewed as a stand-alone classroom element. Teachers may consider the computer as a place where students go to receive positive reinforcement when they have completed all their class work, or where students work on drill-and-practice activities. Technology can be an even greater vehicle for instruction, curricular access, and accommodation if that technology is incorporated into the curriculum and not viewed as an adjunct to teaching and learning activities (Rocklage & Lake, 1998). Technology should be viewed as a tool, much like a pencil or pad of paper. Also, students should be encouraged to use these technology tools across all learning and discovery activities within and outside the classroom.

Many classroom tasks involve expressing literacy in writing, and computer software that assists the writing process can be useful in inclusive settings (Bryant & Bryant, 1998a; Lewis, 1998). Students with disabilities may struggle when trying to perform tasks that require them to communicate knowledge. For this reason, it can be helpful for school-age children to use technologies that level the playing field. Computers are increasingly being used to overcome visual, hearing, and physical disabilities. For students with extremely limited physical mobility, there are computers that can be operated just by moving the eyes. Computers are powerful teaching tools for all students.

Because students usually respond to instructional software programs by typing on the computer keyboard, they sometimes may need assistance. Various modifications can assist students as they engage in such a task. Some students may benefit from the use of brightly colored stickers to illuminate keys that are frequently used with a software program. Keyguards can reduce the possibility of students hitting the wrong keys as they attempt to enter information. **Keyguards** are devices that fit over the regular computer keyboard and have holes cut out for an individual to access the keys on the keyboard with a stick, stylus, or finger (Olson & Platt, 2000). Another option that assists students who are retarded in using computer technology is the touch-sensitive screen (Merbler, Hadadian, & Ulman, 1999). **Touch screens** overlay the computer's monitor with a touch-sensitive grid that is aligned with characters or graphics on the screen. A touch-sensitive screen allows students to use a stylus or finger to deliver input into the computer, simply by pointing at the computer screen. Once students are provided modifications to assist them in entering information into a computer, they can begin to learn skills that enhance their writing capabilities.

Recent advances in computer technology entail speech input and recognition (Merbler et al., 1999). **Speech input and recognition** programs are based on special software that permits students to input their ideas into the computer using their voices. Such systems can be beneficial for students who have limited hand and finger mobility, although this method of inputting will not be appropriate for students who have speech impairments. Merbler and colleagues (1999) report that consistency of speech (e.g., pronunciation of words) is needed for these systems to work effectively.

Computers and word processing software enable students to put ideas in writing without the barriers imposed by paper and pencil. Providing students with a word processor can be useful but should be accompanied with other training as well. MacArthur and colleagues (1991) stated that students who are retarded will not edit and revise papers unless they receive specific instructions in the editing process. Therefore, simply providing a student with a word processor may not be enough for students who are retarded. Indeed, teaching the editing process is critical for these students.

Teachers can teach the editing capabilities of the word processor during the writing process. Computer editing can reduce or eliminate problems such as multiple erasures, torn papers, illegible handwriting due to poor fine-motor skills, and the need to constantly rewrite text that needs only minor modifications. Moreover, spell-checkers can improve the written expression products of students who are retarded. Although grammar-checkers are becoming more efficient, these programs have not been found to be helpful for many students with writing problems (MacArthur, 1996).

A common reason for abandoning assistive technologies is due to the individual's, the family's, or the service provider's inability to maintain or adapt a device to meet the needs of the individual (Lesar, 1998). This dilemma can be bypassed or prevented entirely in the classroom if teachers are given necessary supports. Merbler and colleagues (1999) noted some recommendations that can help teachers maximize assistive technology and student potential in their classroom:

- Use open-ended devices that permit customizing for the user and/or task.
- Find the lowest technology solution that can provide a level of performance or function rather than a complex, high-technology device or system. Simply changing a student's angle of view of a computer monitor (e.g., placing the monitor at eye level as opposed to hairline level or above) could reduce strain and improve performance.
- Collaborate with other teachers. There are too many technologies developing too quickly for one teacher to monitor advancement in technology independently. Sharing expertise can help.
- Collaborate with parents to ensure that assistive technology devices that go home are properly used and maintained. Parents can also be an excellent source of evaluative information on how effectively a device or piece of software is working.
- Don't believe that you have to master a device or software application completely before you begin using it. Many times an application can be used successfully early in the learning curve, and learning by doing can promote eventual mastery.
- Assistive devices should match the age, gender, and preferences of the user to promote acceptance and use.
- The arrangement and separation of controls should be predictable and natural. Feedback to the user must be meaningful.
- Be sure that your school or school system has a comprehensive policy covering assistive technology, including the protection of student and teacher privacy, the repair and maintenance of equipment, and the home use of the school purchased equipment. Be sure also that the policy states who is the assistive technology resource for IEP teams.

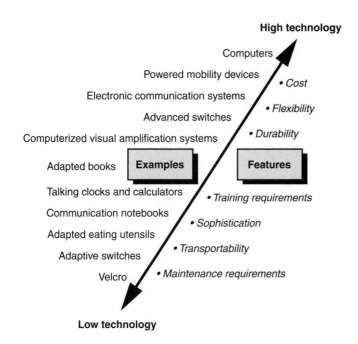

High technology

Computers

Powered mobility devices
• *Cost*

Electronic communication systems
• *Flexibility*

Advanced switches

Computerized visual amplification systems
• *Durability*

Adapted books **Examples**   **Features**

Talking clocks and calculators
• *Training requirements*

Communication notebooks
• *Sophistication*

Adapted eating utensils
• *Transportability*

Adaptive switches

Velcro   • *Maintenance requirements*

Low technology

FIGURE 13.2
Attributes and Examples in the Continuum of Low- and High-Tech Assistive Technology Devices

Source: From "Assistive Technology and IEPs for Young Children with Disabilities," by H. P. Parette and N. L. Murdick, 1998, *Early Childhood Education Journal, 25*(3), 193–197. Reprinted by permission.

- Simply purchasing assistive technology equipment will not ensure its use. Funds also must be allocated to ensure that teachers and other potential assistive technology service providers receive training in the use of the equipment.
- Do not be afraid to experiment. Assistive technology is a very young field, and everybody is learning.*

Figure 13.2 illustrates the continuum of low-tech to high-tech devices.

Although assistive technologies are necessary for some children, some parents are unaware of how to request technologies. California Assistive Technology System (1999) recommends the following steps for parents to request technology for their child:

> A written request should be made to the school asking for the assistive technology that the student needs or stating the student's need if you don't know exactly what is needed. Once your request is made, the local education agency has 15 days to give you a proposed assessment plan. Parents have 15 days to consent to the proposed assessments. Once the local education agency receives the parent's consent, it has 50 days to complete the assessment and develop the IEP. (p. 1)

---

*From "Using Assistive Technology in the Inclusive Classroom," by J. B. Merbler, A. Hadadian, & J. Ulman, 1999, *Preventing School Failure, 43*(3), pp. 113–118. Reprinted with permission of the Helen Dwight Reid Educational Foundation. Published by Heldref Publications, 1319 Eighteenth St., NW, Washington, DC 20036-1802. Copyright © 1999.

Postschool Years

The adult years of individuals with mental retardation can be fulfilled with meaningful occupations, socialization, communication, and recreation. In fact, the development of technological devices has contributed greatly to the integration of the individuals who are retarded (Morris & Blatt, 1986). However, some persons cannot experience successful adulthood without the assistance of technology. For the adult population, assistive technology should target means and methods for allowing them to experience a comfortable, possibly independent, and productive life.

Technology training for adults who are retarded should be emphasized during transition programming. More specifically the technology training should focus on an individual's support needs in the community, at home, and with employment (Hallahan & Kauffman, 1997). Generally, students who are retarded need technological supports as they prepare for their adult roles as workers, consumers, and participants in a community (Lewis, 1993). They may need technical assistance in managing money, preparing meals, grooming, maintaining a clean house, and keeping one's clothing clean. For example, adults who are retarded may use switches for chores such as brushing their teeth or making tea. In addition, those on the vocational track may need supported technology to help them accomplish their jobs with a degree of success.

The use of computer technology has considerable promise for adults with mental retardation. Today, these individuals are accommodated for cognitive impairments that are impediments to independence and self-determination. Those who might not be able to balance a checkbook due to a lack of prerequisite skills can use a computer to overcome that barrier. However, few software programs are designed for adults with intellectual disabilities (Wehmeyer, 1998). Present software programs are often too difficult, and when they are not, they are usually age-inappropriate. Even when software may be obtainable, existing operating systems create a barrier for individuals with retardation.

 *To check your understanding of this chapter, go to the Companion Website at www.prenhall.com/ beirne-smith and select Chapter 13. From there, you can access the Self-test and Essay modules.*

One key to an adult's ability to live in a community successfully is the ability to socialize and recreate. Conversation aids can be designed to enable adults who are retarded to engage in social activities (Snell, 1993). **Conversation aids** are books or tablets organized by topic according to home and community environments used by individuals who are retarded to enhance their ability to communicate and/or socialize. The adult can select photos, pictures, or illustrations for places, people, or objects. The photos are placed into the tablet and attached to the student. With the proper training, the student can learn to use the conversation aid to converse with family or peers.

Table 13.6 presents the contact information for a variety of organizations that can provide further information on selecting and using appropriate assistive technology for persons with mental retardation.

TABLE 13.6
Useful Resources and Web Sites

The Arc of the United States 1010 Wayne Avenue, Suite 650 Silver Spring, MD 20910 301-565-3842 www.thearc.org	CSUN: Center on Disabilities California State University, Northridge 18111 Nordhoff Street Northridge, CA 91330-8340 818-677-2578 www.csun.edu/cod/center.html

Inclusive Technologies
Temper Complex
37 Miriam Drive
Matawan, NJ 07747
732-441-0831
www.inclusive.com
	The Association for the Severely
	  Handicapped
	29 West Susquehanna Avenue,
	  Suite 210
	Baltimore, MD 21204
	410-828-8274
	www.tash.org

RESNA 1700 North Moore Street, Suite 1540 Arlington, VA 22209-1903 703-524-6686 www.resna.org	
	ABLEDATA 8630 Fenton Street, Suite 930 Silver Spring, MD 20910 800-227-0216 www.abledata.com
National Rehabilitation Hospital Assistive Technology Research Center 102 Irving Street, NW Washington, DC 20010-2949 202-877-1000 www.nrhatrc.org	Trace Research and Development Center 2107 Engineering Centers Building 1550 Engineering Drive Madison, WI 53706 608-262-6966 www.trace.wisc.edu
Closing the Gap P.O. Box 68, 526 Main Street Henderson, MN 56044 507-248-3294 www.closingthegap.com	
	United Cerebral Palsy 1660 L Street, NW, Suite 700 Washington, DC 20036 202-776-0406 www.ucp.org
Council for Exceptional Children 1110 North Glebe Road, Suite 300 Arlington, VA 22201 703-620-3660 www.cec.sped.org	AT Network 1029 J Street, Suite 120 Sacramento, CA 95814 800-390-2699 www.atnet.org
National Easter Seal Society 230 West Monroe Street, Suite 1800 Chicago, IL 60606 312-726-6200 www.easterseals.com	

▄▄▄▄▄ ■ **Summary** ▄▄▄▄▄▄▄▄▄▄▄▄▄▄▄▄▄▄▄▄▄▄

Definition of Assistive Technology

- The IDEA defines assistive technology as "any item, piece of equipment, or product system, whether acquired commercially off the shelf, modified, or customized, that is used to increase, maintain, or improve the functional capabilities of a child with a disability."
- Assistive technology can range from high-tech sophisticated devices to no-tech solutions that require no devices or equipment.

Benefits of Assistive Technology

- Assistive technology assists individuals with retardation in overcoming barriers toward independence by compensation for their daily limitations.
- Technologies can decrease dependence on others by allowing individuals to become or remain integrated into their chosen communities.
- Assistive technology allows persons with retardation to receive similar educational services as students without disabilities.

Policies and Legalities Surrounding Assistive Technology

- In accordance with the IDEA, special and general education teachers should consider the appropriateness of assistive technology as a tool or an intervention for all students who have individual education programs.
- The Assistive Technology Act of 2004 provides flexibility to states in addressing the need for increased access to technology by individuals with disabilities and their families.
- The ADA requires the delivery of auxiliary aids and services as needed to assure equal access to programs and services.

Teacher Training

- Teachers must have access to necessary hardware and software, should be comfortable with the use of technology.
- Teachers should have adequate training to implement assistive technologies effectively.

Modifications

- Technologies for young children should provide opportunities for interaction and play at an early age.
- IEP teams are charged with the task of considering necessary assistive technologies for school-age children who have mental retardation.
- Keyguards, touch-sensitive screens, and speech input and recognition systems provide assistance for individuals with intellectual disabilities as they use computers.
- Technology training for adults with retardation should be emphasized during transition programming.
- Technologies for adults should address the individual's support needs in the community, at home, and with employment.

KEY TERMS

formal supports   informal supports

Those of us interested in mental retardation are very much concerned about where we have been, where we are today, and where we will be in the future. Much is happening in the field of mental retardation, as evidenced in the educational, legal, and medical arenas. To predict what will happen in the future, however, without the gift of clairvoyance is difficult, and the best we can do is base our hunches on the trends and changes that the field is presently experiencing.

It seems evident that everyday life will continue to become more demanding and technologically sophisticated for everyone. Some indicators of this trend are provided below:

- The nature of work will be different. Many jobs will be more technically demanding, many more jobs will be automated, and individuals outside the United States will perform a significant number of basic jobs. Moreover, most of the available jobs will be in the service industry.
- Society will experience a significant aging effect. The number of older individuals is going to increase.
- Health care will become more sophisticated and more expensive. Questions remain as to how to ensure that all citizens have access to coverage.
- Economic conditions in the United States (e.g., the federal budget deficit) will remain problematic, constraining spending in many areas—especially in the areas of programs and services.
- Educational systems will keep changing. The No Child Left Behind initiative is here to stay. More students with mental retardation will be served in inclusive settings. Technology will continue to be used in innovative ways to deliver instruction and enhance learning.

Changes in the social, economic, and technological dimensions as well as in our lifestyles will have a profound impact on persons who are mentally retarded. In an informational society, it will be important to use developing technology to the advantage of those with retardation, on the one hand, and to prepare them to use various technologies, which will be very much part of everyday life, on the other. More than two decades ago, McHale (1980) suggested that some individuals will be able to take advantage of future changes, and some will not, so that there will be "haves" and "have-nots" in the informational society. Without assistance—that is, planning and preparation—most persons with mental retardation will fall into the have-not category unless care is taken to consider requisite home, community, and workplace skills needed for success in tomorrow's environments. The paradox is that new developments, by and large, will be beneficial to those with intellectual challenges. Consider, for example, the use of PDAs in the workplace to assist a person in the performance of a job-related task. But those with mental retardation are also at risk of being left behind as new types and levels of competence are created (e.g., wireless networks in public and private facilities).

One of the outcomes of a technologically more advanced society is that certain demands of everyday life are made easier—such as the use of pocket-size cellular telephones or new types of thermometers. But the limitation for many adults who are mentally retarded is that they do not know how to use these devices and—perhaps a more fundamental issue—they are unable to acquire them. This situation certainly holds true in regard to the use of computer technology as well.

THE DEMANDS OF ADULTHOOD

A case was made in chapter 11 for adequately preparing individuals with mental retardation for the major demands of adulthood. As indicated, these demands require competence in the following areas: employment/education, home and family, leisure pursuits, community involvement, physical/emotional health, and personal responsibility and relationships (Cronin, Patton, & Wood, 2005). Ensuring that students acquire competence in dealing with the challenges of adulthood will require innovative practices and will occur only if serious attention is directed to issues concerning curriculum, instructional technique, and transition planning.

Curricula must be based on what students will need in order to function in their likely subsequent environments. Comprehensive curricula must also be:

- Responsive to the needs of an individual student at the current time
- Reflective of the need to balance maximum integration with nondisabled peers against critical curricular needs
- Derived from a realistic appraisal of potential adult outcomes of individual students
- Aligned with state content and performance standards
- Sensitive to graduation goals and specific diploma track requirements

To be responsive to the areas of adulthood identified here, curriculum development efforts must consider how best to prepare students for a variety of life situations, including current and future workplace scenarios.

Employers themselves have identified important general job skills that are needed in today's workplace. These include some skill areas that can be troublesome to students with mental retardation and, unfortunately, that are not consistently taught as part of their programs. If they are needed, then they will have to be taught, and resources are available for doing this (Wehman & Kregel, 2005).

To teach the skills needed for success in the workforce and in life, learning is enhanced when it occurs in community-based settings. This recommendation must be balanced against the need to have students in inclusive settings as much as possible and providing students access to the general education curriculum. Establishing an equilibrium between these competing factors is possible but requires innovative options.

Transition planning for students who are mentally retarded must be based on a realistic evaluation of their needs, including all the major life domains (Clark & Patton, 2005). Transition plans should consider students' current and future environments as well as the nature of the support systems that students will have available to them when they leave school. Pursuant to requirements mandated in the Individuals with Disabilities Education Act (IDEA), transition planning must be based on a student's needs, interests, and preferences. As we know, legislating something does not guarantee that it actually will have benefit for those it is intended to help.

SYSTEMS OF SUPPORT

Within a rapidly changing service delivery system has come a heightened awareness of and need for stronger and better support systems for persons with mental retardation, with particular attention given to the development of natural support systems. While professionals and laypersons alike continue to disagree as to the best method of serving persons in community settings, few will argue that the face of residential services has changed markedly over the past several decades and will surely continue to do so for the foreseeable future (Lakin, Bruininks, & Larson, 1992).

While the issue of supports is certainly not a new one, the reframing of the American Association on Mental Retardation (AAMR) definition and classification system in 1992, and revalidated in 2003, using supports as a major component in defining mental retardation certainly is. While not all professionals embraced this new way of conceptualizing the way we think about mental retardation, the idea of levels of support need has grown in popularity, as exemplified in new ways to identify support need (Thompson et al., 2004).

Regardless of which paradigm one adopts, the realities of designing, providing, and accessing systems of support for persons with mental retardation remain both difficult and challenging. A subtle but necessary component of any paradigm is the issue of formal versus informal supports. Cooley (1989) distinguished between formal and informal support services in this way: **Formal supports** are generally organized programs consisting of professionals trained to provide necessary and specific services for persons with disabilities (e.g., assistive technology, formal education, income assistance, medical services). **Informal supports,** on the other hand, are those services generally provided through intrapersonal or interpersonal means by either the person with the disability or the person's family, friends, or neighbors. While the skills of such persons may indeed be special (e.g., companionship, general problem solving, home modifications, transportation), they are generally not considered to be those of a trained professional.

Both types of supports are essential for daily living. Bradley and Knoll (1995) believe that while the 1970s were a time of rapid deinstitutionalization, they were also a time of increased specialization for service providers. With the 1980s came a new emphasis on individualization and meeting the needs of the whole person, not just the demands of the disability. That is, service providers no longer thought solely in terms of matching people to society but also of helping society meet the needs of people with mental retardation. This particular approach has been an ambitious one, requiring input from many different people and from many different perspectives.

Where formal, organized programs were once the primary means of social service delivery in the field of mental retardation, individualized programs are now being used to complement or replace altogether the more formal programs of the 1970s and 1980s. For many persons, including those whose support needs are extensive to pervasive, informal supports may provide the most basic and enduring supports of all.

Viewing a person with mental retardation as someone for whom skills and abilities are unique, just as their barriers and supports are unique, does much to free the person from the stigma of eternal clienthood (Bradley & Knoll, 1995). Beneath the new model of supports provided by AAMR is the assumption that skills and abilities change over time. So, too, should one's supports.

AN AGENDA FOR FUTURE RESEARCH

Science, more often than not, deals with the unexpected, the unexplainable, and the unknown. Consequently, predictions of the future can often be as interesting as they are inaccurate. In an age when technological breakthroughs are apt to be as wonderful as they are astounding, it gives one reason to be optimistic. Yet, one must remain cautious, and predictions must be tempered with the realization that breakthroughs, however remarkable, may never come soon enough for those who need them the most.

As long as there is mental retardation, there will continue to be a need for ongoing research about and for those with mental retardation. Such areas as etiology, development, education, and community living have potential significance. Beneath these areas of significance, however, lie equally important strata of developments waiting to be uncovered, theoretical and conceptual tenets that guide future investigations. Research, both basic and applied, should continue to be supported and encouraged by all members of the service delivery system. Persons and families of persons who rely on this research must demand the highest quality research possible. No longer should the decisions to proceed with major policy issues and practice strategies be made in the absence of sound and verifiable research. The costs to the persons with mental retardation, families of persons with mental retardation, and society are far too high.

SOME FINAL THOUGHTS

We hope that the future will be characterized by improved conditions for those with intellectual challenges. There is good reason to believe that influences such as advocacy groups, interest groups, and—most important—social attitudes will continue to drive the quantity and quality of programs and services for those who are mentally retarded.

Blatt has given us much to think about in his many writings. In his last major publication, *The Conquest of Mental Retardation* (1987), he provided some thoughts that can help guide us as we prepare for the future:

We will conquer mental retardation not only by better science, but by a better way of life. . . . Increasingly specialized knowledge about mental retardation will, in itself, do relatively little to ameliorate the problems faced by mentally retarded people. . . . In order to understand and respond to the voices of mentally retarded people, we must understand ourselves, our society, our institutions (in the broader sense), our values and our traditions. (p. 11)

We can influence the future in many ways by what we do or, at the very least, try to do today. We can no longer remain passive observers, but must become active participants in solutions to the problems and needs of persons who are mentally retarded. Our attention should focus not only on individuals with mental retardation but also on the public—because the key to the future rests there. Without realistic understanding of and positive sentiment toward those who are mentally retarded, which must be nurtured by what happens today and reflected in financial support for our efforts, the outlook for this group is not favorable. Our highest priorities should be the inclusion of people who are mentally retarded in the worlds of all people, active participation on behalf of all advocates, and the continued search for new knowledge.

adaptability model Family model connected to the physical sciences and addresses the degree to which families tend toward disorder.

adaptive behavior "Degree and efficiency with which the individual meets the standards of personal independence and social responsibility expected of his age and cultural group" (Grossman, 1983, p. 1; see chapter 2).

aided systems Augmentative communication systems that require the use of a picture or word board, a notebook, or a computerized aid.

Americans with Disabilities Act (ADA) Civil rights bill intended to eliminate discrimination against individuals with disabilities.

amniocentesis Analysis of amniotic fluid during the second trimester of pregnancy to allow for biochemical analysis of fetal cells; can indicate presence of genetic and chromosomal disorders and indicate sex of fetus.

annual goals Statements of what the student with disabilities can reasonably be expected to achieve in the course of one calendar year.

assessment Collecting information through observation, testing, and task analysis to determine strengths and weaknesses for the purpose of making decisions.

assistive technology Devices used to enhance the performance of persons with disabilities.

Assistive Technology Act of 2004 Formerly the Tech Act of 1998, the law that supports the development of programs that ensure access to appropriate assistive technology devices and services for individuals with disabilities and their families.

assistive technology services Services that may include such supports as purchasing and leasing devices and equipment; customizing and adapting devices; repairing devices; training the child and parents in use of devices; and coordinating interventions, therapies, and services with assistive technology devices.

at risk Term describing a child who is in danger of substantial developmental delay because of medical, biological, or environmental factors if early intervention services are not provided.

augmentative communication Methods used to improve the communication skills of persons who do not speak or whose speech is not intelligible.

autosomes Twenty-two matched pairs of chromosomes (44 of the normally present 46).

behavior analysis The study of environmental events that change behavior.

behavior genetics The science that studies the relationship between heredity and human attributes.

behavioral objectives Statements that specify an observable behavior, the conditions under which it will occur, and the acceptable standard for accuracy against which to measure performance.

benchmarks *See* short-term objectives.

chromosomes Threadlike bodies containing genes (hereditary factors) occupying specific loci.

clinical judgment Judgment used in clinical situations derived from data-based expertise and experience.

collaborative consultation Process through which people with diverse expertise determine solutions to mutually defined problems.

collaborative teaming Process through which educators with different areas of expertise voluntarily work together to create, monitor, and refine solutions to problems that impede students' success.

communication board Devices that employ icons or pictures to assist persons with communication.

community-based instruction Teaching a skill to a student in the actual environment as opposed to teaching the skill in a classroom with the expectation of transference, generalization, and application of knowledge when skill use is required.

community-referenced instruction Educational programs that are directly related to actual incidents that occur naturally in the environment.

community residential setting A small living arrangement (15 or fewer residents) located in a traditional neighborhood. These are often family or foster homes.

compensatory interventions Treatments designed to counteract the effects of poverty.

competence *See* intellectual competence.

congenital conditions Conditions present from birth.

conversation aids Books or tablets organized by topic according to home or community environments used by individuals with mental retardation to enhance their ability to communicate and/or socialize.

cultural deprivation The state of being without the basic environmental stimulation necessary for optimal child development.

cultural-familial mental retardation A form of mental retardation for which there is no discernable physiological cause, and is thought to be caused by certain environmental circumstances.

curriculum The sequence and content of what is taught in school.

curriculum-based assessment A criterion-referenced type of test, with test items drawn directly from the instructor's teaching materials; considered to be a highly effective measure of student performance.

day habilitation programs Adult educational programs that are designed for those who do not yet have the skills for the workplace. They generally concentrate on a broad set of skills such as homemaking and self care in addition to vocational skills and employment services.

deletion In genetics, a process where a portion of original genetic material is absent from a specific chromosomal pair.

developmental delay Refers to delay in one of five areas: (1) cognitive development; (2) physical development, including vision and hearing; (3) communication, language, and speech development; (4) social or emotional development; and (5) adaptive development.

developmental disability A severe, chronic disability that occurs during the development period and results in substantial limitations in certain major life functions.

developmental model The notion that families develop along predictable lines.

developmental period Typically refers to the period from conception to age 18; age span varies across different sources.

deviation IQ In contrast to ratio IQ, assumes IQ is normally distributed with 100 as average and a standard deviation that is the same for every age level.

disablism (formerly *handicapism*) Practices and beliefs that promote differential treatment of individuals because of apparent or assumed physical, mental, or behavioral differences.

dissimulation Refers to a person trying to feign mental retardation by intentionally trying to score low on various tests and assessments that might be administered. Dissimulation might be an argument made by prosecutors against persons in death penalty cases.

dominant inheritance Inheritance in which an individual gene has control or can mask the other gene in the pair.

Down syndrome (DS) Best-known and most frequently researched biologically caused condition associated with mental retardation. Down syndrome is found in roughly 5% to 6% of all persons identified as mentally retarded, and found more often in children born to older mothers.

due process A constitutional guarantee that prohibits any state from depriving any person of life, liberty, or property, without due process of law.

early childhood special education A system of services for children from birth to 5 years of age who are disabled, developmentally delayed, or at risk of developmental delay, and their families.

early intervention System of services usually provided free of charge for children who are disabled, developmentally delayed, or at risk of developmental delay and their families.

educable mental retardation (EMR) Term used to refer to students whose abilities are adequate to become self-sufficient and learn academic skills through the upper elementary grades. The individual's score on an individual test of intelligence is approximately 55 to 70.

equal protection The principle of the Fourteenth Amendment, which allows the same rights and benefits to all citizens according to government practice unless there is a compelling reason to withhold these rights.

ethnocentrism A world view limited by one's own cultural experiences.

eugenics movement The science movement that manipulates breeding to improve the quality of the human race.

family A group of individuals consisting of immediate and distant relatives who are related through birth, adoption, or marriage; a group of people who love and care for each other.

family assessment Recognizes family members as valid and unique sources of information in assessing and making clinical judgments about a child's performance in a variety of function areas.

family characteristics Refers to the size, structure, cultural background, and socioeconomic status of the family.

family functioning Refers to how families take action to meet members' individual and collective needs.

family interactions Attributes that the family unit brings to the context of special education—the family's characteristics, the characteristics of each family member, their reaction to having a family member or members with disabilities, and special challenges (e.g., living in poverty).

family paradigms model Classifies families into one of three different types—environmentally sensitive, interpersonally distant, consensus-sensitive—based on their interpretations of and responses to events around them.

family support services Services beyond basic residential and vocational/habilitative services that people with mental retardation require for normal community living.

family systems theory Explains how various characteristics and interactions of families over time influence family members' experiences both in special education and larger society.

feral children Children who grow up in social isolation, either through their own efforts or with the assistance of animals.

fetal alcohol syndrome (FAS) Term used to refer to offspring born to chronically alcoholic mothers who show a pattern of major and minor malformations, growth deficiencies, and developmental disabilities.

formal supports Assistance provided to an individual by someone outside the person's social network; includes vocational training and service coordination.

foster home Traditional family homes that are licensed by the state to provide care for a person who, for whatever reason, cannot live in their own family home.

fragile X syndrome The most common hereditary cause of mental retardation. The source is the absence or severe deficiency of a specific protein (FMRP) deemed essential to the functioning of the brain.

full inclusion A policy of all students being educated in inclusive environments 100% of the time, without regard to the severity of the disability.

functional assessment Examination of the content in which a behavior occurs and the purpose that the behavior serves.

functional curriculum A curriculum that teaches everyday life

skills in order to maximize the student's potential for independence.

generalization Applying skills learned in one setting to other situations.

genes The basic biological units carrying inherited physical, mental, or personality traits.

genetics The study of heredity and variation.

graduated guidance A process of reducing prompt levels by giving hand-over-hand assistance, then fading from the hand to the wrist, to the forearm, to the elbow, and then to the shoulder.

group home A community living arrangement in which persons with intellectual or other developmental disabilities live within a residential neighborhood and receive support and supervision from live-in counselors.

grouping Clustering material based on sameness prior to presentation.

habilitation The acquisition and use of skills to allow for successful functioning in independent living and employment.

heterozygous Having to do with pairs of genes carrying different traits.

home and community-based Services (HCBS) A Medicaid waiver program through which families can access services which previously could only be obtained by admission to an ICF/MR program.

homme sauvage Human savage.

homozygous Having to do with pairs of genes carrying the same trait.

Human Genome Project A concerted, multinational effort to identify the location and function of all parts of the genetic code of humans.

humanism A philosophy that emerged in the Renaissance era that stressed people's worth as human beings and the freedom to develop.

hydrocephalus A disorder resulting from blockage of cerebrospinal fluid in the cranial cavity that causes an enlarged head and undue pressure on the brain.

hypoxia Low oxygen, which can result from such birth difficulties as knotted umbilical cord, extremely short or long labor, or breech birth.

IEP team The team charged with developing a comprehensive and appropriate educational program for a student with a disability.

incidence The number of new cases of a condition identified within a population over a specific period of time.

inclusion Placing students who are disabled, regardless of the type or degree of disability, in general education classrooms. The general education teacher assumes primary responsibility for students who are included.

inclusive environments The placement of people with special learning needs in settings with typical peers who have no special learning needs.

individualized education program (IEP) Individually written plan of yearly instruction by a committee required by the Individuals with Disabilities Education Act (IDEA) for every child or youth who is disabled.

individualized family service plan (IFSP) A document prepared as part of the voluntary component of P.L. 99-457, developed by a multi disciplinary team with the assistance of the child's parents or guardians, and detailing the year's plan for the child with disabilities, aged birth to 2, and the child's family.

informal supports Assistance provided to an individual by others who are a natural part of the individual's personal/social world.

innate Inherent; use of abnormal chromosome arrangements present from conception but most often not the product of hereditary exchange.

intellectual disability   A term commonly used to refer to the condition of mental retardation.

intermediate care facility for persons with mental retardation (ICF/MRs)   Residential settings that are licensed by the Centers for Medicaid and Medicare Services to provide education and training in addition to room and board.

job coach   A person who provides on-the-job training to individuals with disabilities.

judgment-based assessment   An appraisal according to a scale or checklist usually developed by a classroom teacher to measure abilities not typically identified by standardized instruments.

karyotypes   Graphic chromosomal pictures in descending order based on size.

keyguards   Devices that fit over the regular computer keyboard and have holes for a person to access the keys of the keyboard with a stick, stylus, or finger.

learned helplessness   A pattern of submissiveness that develops in individuals when they believe that their actions are of no consequence and that outcomes are beyond their control.

locus of control   The hypothetical construct that people attempt to reach a goal within their own power (internal locus of control) or through events controlled by others (external locus of control).

mainstreaming   The practice of placing students who are disabled in the general education classroom to the extent appropriate to their needs, although the special education teacher assumes primary responsibility for students who are mainstreamed.

mediation   (1) A memory strategy in which an individual connects a verbal label and information to be learned; (2) the process parents and school systems may use to agree upon identification, placement, and evaluation of a student with special needs.

meiosis   The division and pairing of gametes to form the genetic foundation for an embryo.

mental retardation   "Significantly subaverage general intellectual functioning resulting in or associated with concurrent impairments in adaptive behavior and manifested during the developmental period" (Grossman, 1983, p. 11; see chapter 2).

mental test   An obsolete name for an intelligence test.

metabolic disturbance   *See* phenylketonuria.

microcephaly   Characterized by a small, conical skull, a curved spine that typically leads to a stooping posture, and severe retardation.

monosomy   One chromosome.

mosaicism   (1) Uneven division of cells in mitosis, resulting in unequal or extra chromosomes; (2) a form of Down syndrome in which not all cells have unusual chromosome composition.

myelomeningocele   A condition characterized by a saclike mass on the spinal cord containing membrane tissue of the central nervous system and cerebrospinal fluid but no spinal nerves on the spinal cord.

natural supports   The resources accessed by persons with disabilities that promote independence, productivity, and community integration. Natural supports are selected from resources preexisting in the person's environment and are provided without the aid of technology or services agencies.

nature–nurture controversy   The debate as to whether intelligence is innate or acquired.

neurofibromatosis (NF)   Identifiable by light brown patches on the skin (café-au-lait) and/or by multiple, soft fibrous swellings or tumors (neurofibromas) that grow on nerves or appear elsewhere on the body, and can result in severe physical deformities. The gene for NF has been identified as occupying a site on chromosome 17. Also known as von Recklinghausen's disease.

nondisjunction   The failure of one pair of chromosomes to split correctly at meiosis, resulting in a trisomy; produces such conditions as Down syndrome (trisomy 21).

normalization   The process of providing for and, to the maximum extent possible, treating an individual with special needs in the mainstream of society as if the individual had no special needs.

norm-referenced test   A test that has been given to a large number of subjects and for which standard procedures for administration, scoring, and interpretation are published; standard procedures must be followed for results to be valid.

outcomes-based assessment   The practice of judging the value of an educational program by the progress each child makes.

parity   Equal status of all members involved in the collaborative consultation process; no single individual is viewed as the expert, and all contributions are judged solely on their merit as a feasible solution to the problem.

pedigree studies   Examination and research on a particular topic through generations.

person-centered planning   Involving the person who is intellectually disabled and other significant people in that person's life in the planning process.

phenylketonuria (PKU)   An inherited metabolic disease resulting from the absence of an enzyme for digestion that causes a toxic buildup of substances in the blood and urine; if undiagnosed at birth, it causes mental retardation.

play-based assessment Provides the format to obtain information about a child's development skills as well as patterns of interactions with others.

polygenic inheritance Inheritance in which more than one gene pair affects the appearance of a particular trait.

Prader-Willi syndrome (PWS) Condition linked to an autosomanal abnormality. Persons with PWS often have small features and stature. The condition also has been linked with mild retardation and learning disabilities.

prevalence The total number of cases of a disorder existing within a population at a particular place or at a particular time.

procedural due process Guaranteed by the Fifth Amendment, the right to fairness in regard to property or liberty. In P.L. 108-446, it refers to the individual's right to a hearing, to be notified of a hearing, to be represented by counsel at a hearing, to be able to question and cross-examine witnesses, and to present witnesses.

psychosocial The relationship between environmental experiences and cognitive, behavioral, and affective attributes.

public residential facility State-supported facilities designed to accommodate 16 or more live-in residents at any one time.

quasi-suspect class A group for whom there will be an intermediate or heightened analysis of alleged equal protection statutory violations.

recessive inheritance Inherited traits that do not express themselves

when paired with dominant genes and are influential only when matched with another identical recessive gene.

reciprocity Providing equal access to information and the opportunity to participate in problem identification, discussion, decision making, and outcomes to all persons involved in the collaborative process.

Regular Education Initiative (REI) A proposal in which Will (1986) recommended fundamental changes in the way in which we educate students with disabilities, including those categorized as mentally retarded.

related services Supportive services (e.g., special transportation, speech or language therapy, occupational or physical therapy) needed to ensure that the special education program meets all of the student's educational needs.

right to education Correct, free, and appropriate public school education for all children regardless of ability, age, race, religion, or gender.

selective attention The ability to attend to the relevant aspects of the task at hand and to discard the irrelevant aspects.

self-determination The ability to act instead of being acted upon.

sheltered workshop Programs that provide daytime vocational-related activities for persons who require continuous supervision.

short-term objectives Behaviorally stated objectives based on annual goals that provide a clear direction for instruction and ongoing evaluation of the progress of students with disabilities.

6-hour retarded children Term describing children who are considered mentally retarded at school but appear to function normally with family and peers outside of school.

sociopolitical forces Societal and civic strength.

speech input and recognition A software program that permits students to input their ideas into the computer using their voices.

standard deviation The unit used to measure the amount by which a particular score varies from the mean with respect to all the scores in a norm sample.

sterilization The process of rendering an individual unable to produce offspring.

substantive due process A constitutional guarantee that provides for protection against unreasonable governmental action.

subaverage general intellectual functioning Significant difficulties in general mental capability usually quantified using performance on an intelligence test approximately two standard deviations below the mean.

supported employment The placement of individuals with special needs into competitive employment positions with a job coach who does on-the-job training and supervision to facilitate employment and enhance job retention.

supported living setting A relatively independent living arrangement in which staff members provide the least intervention necessary for the person to live successfully.

sustained attention The ability to maintain concentration long enough to process and comprehend information.

task analysis A process of breaking a task down into simple, ordered steps for teaching purposes.

Tay-Sachs disease An inherited autosomal recessive trait typically manifested late in a child's first year, followed by a course of severe retardation, convulsions, blindness, paralysis, and death by age 4.

Technology-Related Assistance for Individuals with Disabilities Act The Tech Act of 1998, reauthorized as the Assistive Technology Act of 2004; supports the development of programs that ensure access to appropriate assistive technology devices and services for individuals with disabilities and their families.

teratogens Substances that can negatively affect prenatal development and result in a severely deformed fetus.

touch screens Devices that overlay the computer's monitor with a touch-sensitive grid that is aligned with characters or graphics on the screen, allowing the student to deliver input by touching the screen with a stylus or finger.

trainable mental retardation (TMR) An educational term for individuals functioning in the lower range of mental retardation who will not benefit from general education training but who require training in basic functional skills (e.g., self-help skills). Their score on an individual test of intelligence is usually 35 to 55.

transition (1) A carefully planned educational process bridging the gap between school and employment; (2) the passage or change from one stage or level to the next (e.g., 3rd to 4th grade, preoperational stage to concrete operations).

transition services Those services, such as vocational rehabilitation or postsecondary vocational training, provided to individuals with disabilities and leading to employment.

translocation Exchange of a fragment of chromosomal material within the same chromosome or to another chromosome; can result in Down syndrome.

trisomy Formation of a group of three chromosomes in lieu of a normal pair.

unaided systems Augmentative communication systems that use only hand and body motions to communicate.

uniparental disomy Both chromosomes are contributed by the mother with none from the father.

virtual reality The use of 3-D graphics combined with direct manipulation to provide the illusion of immersion into a virtual world.

Wechsler scales The Wechsler Intelligence Scales used for identification and classification of countless preschool children, school-age children, adolescents, and adults for nearly half a century.

Williams syndrome Caused by the microdeletion of chromosome 7, with multiple genes involved. Common signs include being pixie-like and petite in physical appearance.

wraparound services A name given to an organized, integrated approach to service delivery that allows for a specially designed treatment plan at a specific point in time.

References

Abbeduto, L., Murphy, M. M., Cawthon, S. W., Richmond, E. K., Weissman, M. D., Karadottir, S., & O'Brien, A. (2003). Receptive language skills of adolescents and young adults with Down or fragile X syndrome. *American Journal on Mental Retardation, 108,* 149–160.

Abbeduto, L., & Nuccio, J. B. (1991). Relation between receptive language and cognitive maturity in persons with mental retardation. *American Journal on Mental Retardation, 96,* 143–149.

Abel, E. L., & Sokol, R. J. (1986). Fetal alcohol is now a leading cause of mental retardation. *Lancet, 2*(8517), 1222.

Abery, B. H. (1997). What is social inclusion all about? *Impact, 10*(3), 2–3, 26.

Abery, B. H. (2003). Social inclusion through recreation: What's the connection? *Impact, 16*(2), 2–3, 32.

Abery, B. H., & Fahnestock, M. (1994). Enhancing the social inclusion of persons with developmental disabilities. In M. F. Hayden & B. H. Abery (Eds.), *Challenges for a service system in transition: Ensuring quality community experiences for persons with developmental disabilities* (pp. 83–119). Baltimore: Brookes.

Abery, B. H., Thurlow, M. L., Bruininks, R. H., & Johnson, D. R. (1990). *The social support networks of transition-age young adults with mental retardation.* Paper presented at the annual meeting of the American Association on Mental Retardation, Atlanta.

Abeson, A., & Davis, S. (2000). The parent movement in intellectual disabilities. In M. L. Wehmeyer & J. R. Patton (Eds.), *Mental retardation in the 21st century* (pp. 19–34). Austin, TX: PRO-ED.

Abroms, K. K., & Bennett, J. W. (1980). Current genetic and demographic findings in Down's syndrome: How are they represented in college textbooks on exceptionality? *Mental Retardation, 18,* 101–107.

Academy of Health Sciences, U.S. Army. (1975). *Introduction to Military Medicine and Surgery* (Study Guide 6). Fort Sam Houston, TX: Author.

Ackerman, M. E. (1998). *Fetal alcohol syndrome: Implications for educators.* (ERIC Document Reproduction Service No. ED426560)

Affleck, J. Q., Lowenbraum, S., & Archer, A. (1980). *Teaching the mildly handicapped in the regular classroom* (2nd ed., pp. 125–127). Upper Saddle River, NJ: Merrill/Prentice Hall.

Alamo Heights Independent School District v. State Board of Education, 790 F.2d 1153 (1986).

Allison, M. (1992). The effects of neurologic injury on the maturing brain. *Headlines, 3*(5), 2–10.

Amado, A. N., Lakin, K. C., & Menke, J. M. (1990). *1990 chartbook on services for people with developmental disabilities.* Minneapolis: University of Minnesota, Center for Residential and Community Services.

American Association on Mental Retardation (AAMR). (2002). *Intellectual Disabilities: Definitions, classification, and systems of support* (10th ed.). Washington, DC: Author.

American Association on Mental Retardation (AAMR). (1983). *Mental retardation: Definition, classification, and systems of support* (8th ed.). Washington, DC: Author.

American Association on Mental Retardation (AAMR). (1992). *Mental retardation: Definition, classification, and systems of support* (9th ed.). Washington, DC: Author.

American Association on Mental Retardation (AAMR). (1996, Summer). Folic acid additive to grain ordered by FDA. *AAMR News and Notes, 10,* 8.

American Educational Research Association, American Psychological Association, National Council on Measurement in Education. (1999). *Standards for educational and psychological testing.* Washington, DC: American Educational Research Association.

American Psychiatric Association. (1980). *Diagnostic and statistical manual of mental disorders* (3rd ed.). Washington, DC: Author.

American Psychiatric Association (APA). (2000). *Diagnostic and statistical manual of mental disorders* (4th ed., text revision). Washington, DC: Author.

Anastasi, A., & Urbina, S. (1997). *Psychological testing* (7th ed.). Upper Saddle River, NJ: Merrill/Prentice Hall.

Anderson, L., Dancis, J., & Alpert, M. (1978). Behavioral contingencies and self-mutilation in Lesch-Nyhan disease. *Journal of Consulting and Clinical Psychology, 46,* 529–536.

Apgar, V. (1953). A proposal for a new method of evaluation of the newborn infant. *Current Researches in Anesthesia, and Analgesia, 32,* 260–264.

Apolloni, K. (1998). The triple test. *Advance for Speech-Language Pathologists and Audiologists, 10,* 34–35.

Armstrong, D. G. (1990). *Developing and documenting the curriculum.* Boston: Allyn & Bacon.

Armstrong v. Kline, 476 F. Supp. 583 (1979).

Artiles, A. J., & Ortiz, A. A. (Eds.). (2002). *English language learners with special education needs.* McHenry, IL; Center for Applied Linguistics.

Assistive Technology Act. (2004). Washington, DC: U.S. Government Printing Office.

Association for Retarded Citizens (ARC). (1997). *Assistive technology position statement.* Arlington, TX: Arc of the United States. Retrieved December 8, 1999, from the Arc of the United States Web site (http://www.thearc.org/posits/astec.html).

Atkins v. Commonwealth of Virginia, 536 U.S. 304 (2004).

Back to school on civil rights: Advancing the federal commitment to leave no child behind. (2000, January/February). *LDA Newsbriefs, 35,* 1, 24.

Baer, D. (1981). The nature of intervention research. In R. Schiefelbusch & D. Bricker (Eds.), *Early language: Acquisition and intervention* (pp. 559–573). Baltimore: University Park Press.

Bagnato, S.J., & Neiwsorth, J.T. (2000). Assessment is adjusted to each child's development. *Birth—5 Newsletter, 1*(2), 1.

Bailey, D. B., Hatton, D. D., Tassone, F., Skinner, M., & Taylor, A. K. (2001). Variability in FMRP and early development in males with fragile X syndrome. *American Journal on Mental Retardation, 106,* 16–27.

Bailey, D.B., & Wolery, M. (1993). *Teaching infants and preschoolers with handicaps.* Upper Saddle River, NJ: Merrill/Prentice Hall.

Baird, S. (1997). Seeking a comfortable fit between family-centered philosophy and infant-parent interaction in early intervention: Time for a paradigm shift? *Topics in Early Childhood Special Education, 1,* 139–163.

Baker, J. M., & Zigmond, N. (1995). The meaning and practice of inclusion for students with learning disabilities: Themes and implications from the five cases. *Journal of Special Education, 29*(2), 163–180.

Baker, P. C. (1997). Presidential address 1997: Benchmarks for the next millennium. *Mental Retardation, 35,* 373–380.

Balkany, T. J., Downs, M. P., Jafek, B. W., & Krajicek, H. J. (1979). Hearing loss in Down's syndrome: A treatable handicap more common than generally recognized. *Clinical Pediatrics, 18,* 116–118.

Balla, D. A., & Zigler, E. (1979). Personality development in retarded persons. In N. R. Ellis (Ed.), *Handbook of mental deficiency: Psychological theory and research* (2nd ed., pp. 154–168). Hillsdale, NJ: Erlbaum.

Bandura, A. (1986). *Social foundations of thought and action: A social cognitive theory.* Upper Saddle River, NJ: Merrill/Prentice Hall.

Barker, M. (1990, April). *Clinical overview of the fragile X syndrome.* Paper presented at the 68th annual meeting of the Council for Exceptional Children, Toronto, Canada.

Barlow, C. F. (1978). *Mental retardation and related disorders.* Philadelphia: Davis.

Barlow, D. H., & Durand, V. M. (1995). *Abnormal psychology: An integrated approach.* Pacific Grove, CA: Brooks/Cole.

Barnett, W. S. (1995, Winter). Long-term effects of early childhood programs on cognitive and school outcomes. *The Future of Children: Long-Term Outcomes of Early Childhood Programs, 5*(3). Available at the Future of Children Web site (http://www.futureofchildren.org/).

Baroff, G. S. (1974). *Mental retardation: Nature, cause and management.* New York: Wiley.

Baroff, G. S. (1991). *Developmental disabilities: Psychosocial aspects.* Austin, TX: PRO-ED.

Baroff, G. S. (1999). General learning disorder: A new designation for mental retardation. *Mental Retardation, 37*(1), 68–70.

Baroff, G. S. (2003). Mental retardation: Some issues of concern. In H. N. Switzky & S. Greenspan (Eds.), *What is mental retardation: Ideas for an evolving disability* (pp. 64–74). Washington, DC: American Association on Mental Retardation.

Bassett, D. S., & Lehmann, J. (2002). *Student-focused conferencing and planning.* Austin, TX: PRO-ED.

Bateman, B. (1986). Equal protection for the handicapped. *Special Education Today,* p. 14.

Batshaw, M. L., Perret, Y., & Trachtenberg, S. W. (1992). Caring and coping; The family of a child with disabilities. In M. L. Batshaw & Y. Perret (Eds.), *Children with disabilities: A medical primer* (3rd ed., pp. 563–578). Baltimore: Brookes.

Bauer, A. M., & Shea, T. M. (2003). *Parents and schools; Creating a successful partnership for students with special needs.* Upper Saddle River, NJ: Merrill/Prentice Hall.

Bauer, A. M. Ulrich, M. E. (2002). I've got a Palm in my pocket: Using handheld computers in an inclusive classroom. *Teaching Exceptional Children, 35*(2), 18–22.

Bausch, M. E., & Hasselbring, T. S. (2004). Assistive technology: Are the necessary skills and knowledge being developed at preservice and inservice levels? *Teacher Education and Special Education, 27*(2), 97–104.

Bauwens, J., & Hourcade, J. J. (1995). *Cooperative teaching: 'Rebuilding the schoolhouse for all students* (p. 74). Austin, TX: PRO-ED.

Beasley, C. R. (1982). Effects of jogging program on cardiovascular fitness and work performance of mentally retarded adults. *American Journal of Mental Deficiency, 86,* 609–613.

Beavers, W. R., & Hampson, R. B. (1993). Measuring family competence. In F. Walsh (Ed.), *Normal family processes* (2nd ed., pp. 73–103). New York; Guilford.

Beck, J. (1972). Spina bifida and hydrocephalus. In V. Apgar & J. Beck (Eds.), *Is my baby alright? A guide to birth defects* (pp. 288–298, 400–414). New York: Simon & Schuster.

Beckman, P. J. (1991). Comparison of mothers' and fathers' perceptions of the effect of young children with and without disabilities. *American Journal on Mental Retardation, 95*(5), 585–595.

Bellinger, D. M., Rucker, H., & Polloway, E. A. (1995). Fragile X syndrome in males: Diagnostic, behavioral, and educational implications. (ERIC Document Reproduction Service No. ED406787).

Belmont, J. M. (1966). Long-term memory in mental retardation. *International Review of Research in Mental Retardation, 1,* 219–255.

Belmont, J. M., & Butterfield, E. C. (1971). Learning strategies as determinants of memory deficiencies. *Cognitive Psychology, 2,* 411–420.

Belmont, J. M., & Butterfield, E. C. (1977). The instructional approach to developmental cognitive research. In R. V. Kail & J. W. Hasen (Eds.), *Perspectives on the development of memory and cognition* (pp. 437–481). Hillsdale, NJ: Erlbaum.

Belser, R. C., & Sudhalter, V. (2001). Conversational characteristics of children with fragile X syndrome: Repetitive speech. *American Journal on Mental Retardation, 106,* 28–38.

Belson, S. I. (2003). *Technology for exceptional learners.* Boston: Houghton Mifflin.

Bender, B. G., Fry, E., Pennington, B., Puck, M., Salbenblatt, J., & Robinson, S. (1983). Speech and language development in 41 children with sex chromosome anomalies. *Pediatrics, 71,* 262–266.

Bender, B. G., Puck, M. H., Salbenblatt, J. A., & Robinson, A. (1986). Cognitive development of children with sex chromosome abnormalities. In S. D. Smith (Ed.), *Genetics and learning disabilities* (pp. 175–201). San Diego: College-Hill Press.

Benner, S. M. (2003). *Assessment of young children with special needs: A context-based approach.* New York: Thompson.

Bennett, W. J. (1986). *What works: Research about teaching and learning.* Washington, DC: U.S. Government Printing Office.

Benz, M. R., & Lindstrom, L. E. (1997). *Building school-to-work programs: Strategies for youth with special needs.* Austin, TX: PRO-ED.

Bernstein, D. K., & Tiegerman, E. (1993). *Language and communication disorders in children.* Upper Saddle River, NJ: Merrill/Prentice Hall.

Bieniewski, M. (1999). *Assistive technology.* Available online at the Tripod Web site (http://members.tripod.com/mwb626/scripts/techb.html).

Bigge, J. L., & Stump, C. S. (1999). *Curriculum, assessment, and instruction for students with disabilities.* Belmont, CA: Wadsworth.

Bigge, J. L., Stump, C. S., Spagna, M. E., & Silberman, R. K. (1999). *Curriculum, assessment, and instruction for students with disabilities.* Belmont, CA: Wadsworth.

Bijou, S. W. (1966). A functional analysis of retarded development. *International Review of Research in Mental Retardation, 1,* 1–19.

Binet, A., & Simon, T. (1905). Methodes nouvelles pour le diagnostic du niveau intellectuel des anormaux. *Année Psychologique, 11,* 191–244.

Blackbourn, J. M., Patton, J. R., & Trainor, A. (2004). *Exceptional individuals in focus* (7th ed.). Upper Saddle River, NJ: Merrill/Prentice Hall.

Blackhurst, A. E. (1997). Perspectives on technology in special education. *Teaching Exceptional Children, 29*(5), 41–48.

Blatt, B. (1981). A concept of educability and the correlates of mental illness, mental retardation, and cultural deprivation. In B. Blatt (Ed.), *In and out of mental retardation* (pp. 41–56). Baltimore: University Park Press.

Blatt, B. (1987). *The conquest of mental retardation.* Austin, TX: PRO-ED.

Bleemer, R. (1995). Court allows special education damages trial. *New Jersey Law Journal, 142*(9), 6.

Blenk, K., & Fine, D. L. (1995). *Making school inclusion work: A guide to everyday practices.* Cambridge, MA: Brookline Books.

Bleyer, K. (1992). The Americans with Disabilities Act: Enforcement mechanisms. *Mental and Physical Disabilities Law Reporter, 16*(3), 347–350.

Block, M. E., & Rizzo, T. L. (1995). Attitudes and attributes of physical educators associated with teaching individuals with severe and profound disabilities. *Journal of the Association for Persons with Severe Handicaps, 20*(1) 80–87.

Bloom, B. S. (1964). *Stability and change in human characteristics.* New York: Wiley.

Board of Education of the Hendrick Hudson Central School District v. Rowley, 458 U.S. 176 (1982).

Bock R. (1997). Understanding Klinefelter syndrome: A guide for XXY males and their families. Washington, DC: National Institutes of Health.

Bogdan, R. (1986). The sociology of special education. In R. J. Morris & B. Blatt (Eds.), *Special education: Research and trends* (pp. 344–359). New York: Pergamon.

Bogdan, R., & Biklen, D. (1977). Handicapism. *Social Policy, 7*(5), 59–63.

Bolger, M. (1992, May). *Stress, coping and psychological well-being in mothers and fathers of young children with a handicapping condition and typically developing children.* Paper presented at the annual meeting of the American Association on Mental Retardation, New Orleans.

Bondurant-Utz, J., & Luciano, L. B. (1994). *A practical guide to infant and preschool assessment in special education.* Boston: Allyn & Bacon.

Bondy, A. S., & Frost, L. A. (1994). The picture exchange communication system. *Focus on Autistic Behavior, 9*(3), 1–20.

Bookman, J. (2000a, March 26). Wearable computers: We'll strap them on just like wristwatches. *Atlanta Journal-Constitution,* pp. A1, A14.

Bookman, J. (2000b, April 2). Building a computer from brain cells. *Atlanta Journal-Constitution,* p. A14.

Borkowski, J. G., Peck, V. A., & Damberg, P. R. (1983). Attention, memory, and cognition. In J. L. Matson & J. A. Mulick (Eds.), *Handbook of mental retardation* (pp. 479–497). New York: Pergamon.

Borthwick-Duffy, S. A. (1994). Epidemiology and prevalence of psychopathology in people with mental retardation. *Journal of Counseling and Clinical Psychology, 62,* 17–27.

Borthwick-Duffy, S. A., & Eyman, R. K. (1990). Who are the dually diagnosed? *American Journal on Mental Retardation, 94,* 586–595.

Bottge, B. A., & Hasselbring, T. S. (1993). A comparison of two approaches for teaching complex, authentic mathematics problems to adolescents in remedial math classes. *Exceptional Children, 59,* 556–566.

Bouchard, T. J., Lykken, D. T., McGue, M., Segal, N. L., & Tellegen, A. (1990). Sources of human psychological differences: The Minnesota study of twins reared apart. *Science, 250,* 223–228.

Boyle, J. R., & Weishaar, M. (2001). The effects of a strategic note-taking technique on the comprehension and long term recall of lecture information for high school students with LD. *LD Research and Practice, 16*(3), 125–133.

Bracken, B. A., & McCallum, R. S. (1998). *Universal Nonverbal Intelligence Test.* Chicago: Riverside.

Braddock, D. (1999). Aging and developmental disabilities; Demographic and policy issues affecting American families. *Mental Retardation, 37*(2), 155–161.

Braddock, D., Kemp, R., Parish, S., & Westrich, J. (1998). *The state of the states in developmental disabilities.* Washington, DC: American Association on Mental Retardation.

Bradley, V. J. & Knoll, J. (1995). Shifting paradigms in services to people with developmental disabilities. In O. C. Karan & S. Greenspan (Eds.), *The community revolution in rehabilitation services* (pp. 5–37). Boston: Butterworth-Heinemann.

Bramlett, M. D., & Mosher. W. D. (2002). Cohabitation, marriage, divorce, and remarriage in the United States. *Vital Health Stat, 23*(22). Washington, DC: National Center for Health Statistics.

Brandon, R. N. (1990). *Adaptation and environment* (2nd ed.). Princeton, NJ: Princeton University Press.

Bredekamp, S., & Copple, C. (Eds.). (1997). *Developmentally appropriate practice in early education programs.* Washington, DC: National Association for the Education of Young Children.

Bricker, D. D. (1996). Assessment for IFSP development and intervention planning. In S. J. Meisels & E. Fenichel (Eds.), *New visions for the developmental assessment of infants and young children* (pp. 169–192). Washington, DC: Zero to Three National Center for Infants, Toddlers, and Families.

Bricker, D. D., & Cripe, J. J. (1992). *An activity-based approach to early intervention.* Baltimore: Brookes.

Bricker, D. D., Pretti-Frontczak, K., & McComas, N. (1998). *An activity-based approach to early intervention* (2nd ed.). Baltimore: Brookes.

Bricker, D. D., & Veltman, M. (1990). Early intervention programs: Child-focused approaches. In S. Meisels & J. Shonkoff (Eds.), *Handbook of early childhood intervention* (pp. 373–399). New York: Cambridge University Press.

Brinker, R. P. (1985). Interactions between severely mentally retarded students and other students in integrated and segregated public school settings. *American Journal of Mental Deficiency, 89,* 587–594.

Brinker, R. P., Seifer, R., & Sameroff, A. J. (1994). Relations among maternal stress, cognitive development, and early intervention in middle- and low-SES infants with developmental disabilities. *American Journal on Mental Retardation, 98,* 463–480.

Brolin, D. E. (1982). *Vocational preparation of persons with handicaps* (2nd ed.). Upper Saddle River, NJ: Merrill/Prentice Hall.

Brolin, D. E. (1986). *Life-centered career education: A competency-based approach* (Rev. ed.). Reston, VA: Council for Exceptional Children.

Brolin, D. E. (1997). *Life-centered career education: A competency-based approach* (5th ed.) Reston, VA: Council for Exceptional Children.

Brolin, J. C., & Brolin, D. E. (1979). Vocational education for special students. In D. Cullinan & M. Epstein (Eds.), *Special education for adolescents: Issues and perspectives.* Upper Saddle River, NJ: Merrill/Prentice Hall.

Bromley, B. E., & Blacher, J. (1989). Factors delaying out-of-home placement of children with severe handicaps. *American Journal on Mental Retardation, 94*(3), 284–291.

Bromley, B. E., & Blacher, J. (1991). Parental reasons for out-of-home placement of children with severe handicaps. *Mental Retardation, 29*(5), 275–280.

Brooks, P. H., & McCauley, C. (1984). Cognitive research in mental retardation. *American Journal of Mental Deficiency, 88,* 479–486.

Brown, A. L. (1974). The role of strategic behavior in retardate memory. *International Journal of Research in Mental Retardation, 7,* 55–111.

Brown, A. L., Campione, J. C., & Murphy, M. D. (1974). Keeping track of changing variables: Long-term retention of a trained rehearsal strategy by retarded adolescents. *American Journal of Mental Deficiency, 78,* 453–466.

Brown, L., Sherbenou, R., & Johnsen, S. K. (1997). *Test of Nonverbal Intelligence* (3rd ed.). Austin, TX: PRO-ED.

Brown v. Board of Education of Topeka, Kansas, 347 U.S. 483 (1954).

Bruininks, R. H. (1974). Physical and motor development of retarded persons. *International Review of Research in Mental Retardation, 7,* 209–261.

Bruininks, R. H., & McGrew, K. S. (1987). *Exploring the structure of adaptive behavior* (Report No. 87-1). Minneapolis: University of Minnesota, Department of Educational Psychology.

Bruininks, R. H., Morreau, L. E., Gilman, C. J., & Anderson, J. L. (1992). *Adaptive living skills curriculum.* Chicago: Riverside.

Bruininks, R. H., Thurlow, M. L., & Gilman, C. J. (1987). Adaptive behavior and mental retardation. *Journal of Special Education, 21*(1), 69–88.

Bruininks, R. H., Woodcock, R. W., Weatherman, R. F., & Hill, B. K. (1996). *Scales of Independent Behavior—Revised (SIB-R).* Chicago: Riverside.

Bryant, B. R. (1997). Intelligence testing. In R. L. Taylor (Ed.), *Assessment of individuals with mental retardation* (pp. 13–32). San Diego: Singular.

Bryant, D. P., & Bryant B. R. (1998a). Using assistive technology adaptations to include students with learning disabilities in cooperative learning activities. *Journal of Learning Disabilities, 31,* 41–54.

Bryant, D. P., & Bryant, B. R. (1998b). Using assistive technology to enhance the skills of students with learning disabilities. *Intervention in School and Clinic, 34*(1), 53.

Bryant, D. P. & Bryant, B. R. (2003). *Assistive technology for people with disabilities.* Boston: Allyn & Bacon.

Bryant, D. P., Erin, J., Lock, R., Allan, J. M., & Resta P. E. (1998). Infusing a teacher preparation program in learning disabilities with assistive technology. *Journal of Learning Disabilities, 31,* 55–66.

Buck v. Bell, 274 U.S. 200 (1927).

Buscemi, L., Bennett, T., Thomas, D., & Deluca, D. (1996). Head Start: Challenges and training needs. *Journal of Early Intervention, 20*(1), 1–13.

Butler, C. (1988). High-tech tots: Technology for mobility, manipulation, communication, and learning in early childhood. *Infants and Young Children, 1,* 66–73.

Buyse, M. L., (1990). *Birth defects encyclopedia.* Dover, MA: Center for Birth Defects Information Services.

Bybee, J., & Zigler, E. (1992). Is outerdirectedness employed in a harmful or beneficial manner by students with and without mental retardation? *American Journal on Mental Retardation, 96,* 512–521.

California Assistive Technology System. (1999). *AT network.* Retrieved December 8, 1999, from the Web site of California Assistive Technology System (http://www.catsca.org/).

Calvez, M. (1993). Social interactions in the neighborhood: A cultural approach to social integration of individuals with mental retardation. *Mental Retardation, 31*(6), 418–423.

Campbell, F. A., & Ramey, C. T. (1994). Effects of early intervention on intellectual and academic achievement: A follow-up study of children from low-income families. *Child Development, 65,* 684–698.

Campbell, V. A., & Fedeyko, H. J. (2001). The healthy people 2010 process: Difficulties related to surveillance and data collection. In A. J. Tymchuk, K. C. Lakin, & R. Luckasson (Eds.), *The forgotten generation: The status and challenges of adults with mild cognitive limitations* (pp. 221–240). Baltimore: Brookes.

Cantu, E. S., Stone, J. W., Wing, A. A., Langee, H. R., & Williams, C. A. (1990). Cytogenetic survey for autistic fragile X carriers in a mental retardation center. *American Journal of Mental Retardation, 94,* 442–447.

Carlson, B. E. (1997). Mental retardation and domestic violence: An ecological approach to intervention. *Social Work, 42*(1), 79–89.

Carr, E. G., & Durand, V. M. (1985). Reducing behavior problems through functional communication training. *Journal of Applied Behavior Analysis, 18*(2), 111–126.

Carroll, J. B. (1993). *Human cognitive abilities: A survey of factor analytic studies.* New York: Cambridge University Press.

Carta, J. J. (1994). Developmentally appropriate practices: Shifting the emphasis to individual appropriateness. *Journal of Early Intervention, 18*(4), 342–343.

Carter, B., & McGoldrick, M. (1999). Overview: The expanded family life cycle: Individual, family, and social perspectives. In B. Carter & M. McGoldrick (Eds.), *The expanded family life cycle: Individual, family, and social perspectives* (3rd ed., pp. 1–26). Needham Heights, MA: Allyn & Bacon.

Carter, J. L. (1975). Intelligence and reading achievement of EMR in three educational settings. *Mental Retardation, 13*(5), 26–27.

Cavallaro, C. C., Haney, M., & Cabello, B. (1993). Developmentally appropriate strategies for promoting full participation in early childhood settings. *Topics in Early Childhood Special Education, 13*(3), 292–307.

Cedar Rapids Community School District v. Garret F., 106 F.3d 822 (8th Cir. 1997).

Cedar Rapids Community School District v. Garret F., 119 S. Ct. 992 (1999).

Cha, K. H. (1992). The effect of flanking context and its time course in focused attention of mentally retarded and nonretarded persons. *Dissertations Abstracts International, 53,* 2087.

Cha, K. H., & Merrill, E. C. (1994). Facilitation and inhibition in visual selective attention processes of individuals with and without mental retardation. *American Journal on Mental Retardation, 98,* 594–600.

Chalfant, J. C., & Pysh, M. V. (1989). Teacher assistance teams: Five descriptive studies of 96 teams. *Remedial and Special Education, 19*(6), 49–58.

Chamberlain, M. A. (1988). Employer's rankings of factors judged critical to job success for individuals with severe disabilities. *Career Development for Exceptional Individuals, 11*(2), 141–147.

Chapman, D. A., Scott, K. G., & Mason, C. A. (2002). Early risk factors for mental retardation: Role of maternal age and maternal education. *American Journal on Mental Retardation, 107,* 46–59.

Charlot, L. R. (1998). Developmental effects on mental health disorders in persons with developmental disabilities. *Mental Health Aspects of Developmental Disabilities, 1,* 29–38.

Chinn, P. C., Drew, C. J., & Logan, D. R. (1979). *Mental retardation: A life cycle approach* (2nd ed.). St Louis: Mosby.

Christenson, S. L., Ysseldyke, J. E., & Thurlow, M. L. (1989). Critical instructional factors for students with mild handicaps: An integrative review. *Remedial and Special Education, 10*(5), 21–31.

Christian, L., & Poling, A. (1997). Drug abuse in persons with mental retardation: A review. *American Journal on Mental Retardation, 102*(2), 126–136.

Clark, G. M. (1998). *Assessment for transitional planning.* Austin, TX: PRO-ED.

Clark, G. M., Carlson, B. C., Fisher, S., Cook, I. D., & D'Alonzo, B. J. (1991). Career development for students with disabilities in elementary schools: A position statement of the Division on Career Development. *Career Development for Exceptional Individuals, 14,* 109–120.

Clark, G. M., & Kolstoe, O. P. (1990). *Career development and transition education for adolescents with disabilities.* Boston: Allyn & Bacon.

Clark, G. M., & Patton, J. R. (2006). *Transition planning inventory (updated version).* Austin, TX: PRO-ED.

Clarke, J. T., Gates, R. D., Hogan, S. E., Barrett, M., & MacDonald, G. W. (1987). Neuropsychological studies on adolescents with phenylketonuria returned to phenylalanine-restricted diets. *American Journal on Mental Retardation, 92,* 255–262.

Clausen, J. A. (1967). Mental deficiency: Development of a concept. *American Journal of Mental Deficiency, 71,* 727–745.

Clausen, J. A. (1972a). The continuing problem of defining mental deficiency. *Journal of Special Education, 6,* 97–106.

Clausen, J. A. (1972b). Quo vadis, AAMD? *Journal of Special Education, 6,* 52–60.

Clayman, C. B. (Ed.). (1989). *The AMA encyclopedia of medicine.* New York: Random House.

Cleburne Living Center, Inc. v. City of Cleburne, Texas, 735 F.2d 832 (5th Cir. 1984).

Clinton, J. (1995). *Taming the technology.* Materials distributed at the Florida Assistive Technology Impact Conference, Orlando.

Cnaan, R. A., Adler, I., & Ramot, A. (1986). Public reaction to establishment of community residential facilities for mentally retarded persons in Israel. *American Journal of Mental Deficiency, 90*(6), 677–685.

Cohen, D. E. (2000). Health promotion and disability prevention: The case for personal responsibility and independence. In M. L. Wehmyer & J. R. Patton (Eds.), *Mental retardation in the 21st century* (pp. 251–264). Austin, TX: PRO-ED.

Coleman, J. (1966). *Equality of educational opportunity.* Washington, DC: U.S. Government Printing Office.

Condeluci, A. (1995). *Interdependence: The route to community* (2nd ed.). Winter Park, FL: GR Press.

Conway, R. N. (1994). Abuse and intellectual disability: A potential link or an inescapable reality? *Australia and New Zealand Journal of Intellectual Disabilities, 19,* 165–171.

Cook, R. E., Tessier, A., & Klein, M. D. (2000). *Adapting early childhood curricula for children in inclusive settings* (5th ed.). Upper Saddle River, NJ: Merrill/Prentice Hall.

Cooley, E. (1989). Community support. In G. H. Singer & L. K. Irvin (Eds.), *Support for caregiving families: Enabling positive adaptation to disability* (pp.143–157). Baltimore: Brookes.

Craig, E. M., & Tassé, M. J. (1999). Cultural and demographic group comparisons of adaptive behavior. In R. L. Schalock (Ed.), *Adaptive behavior and its measurement: Implications for the field of mental retardation* (pp. 419–439). Washington, DC: American Association on Mental Retardation.

Cravioto, J., DeLicardie, E. R., & Birch, H. G. (1966). Nutrition, growth, and neurointegrative development: An experimental and ecological study. *Pediatrics, 38*(Suppl. 2), 319.

Crawford v. Honig, 37 F.2d 485 (9th Cir. 1994).

Crocker, A. C. (1992). Data collection for the evaluation of mental retardation prevention activities: The fateful 43. *Mental Retardation, 30,* 303–317.

Crocker, A. C. (2000). Community-based and managed health care. In M. L. Wehmeyer & J. R. Patton (Eds.), *Mental retardation in the 21st century* (pp. 265–279). Austin, TX: PRO-ED.

Cromwell, R. L. (1963). A social learning approach to mental retardation. In N. R. Ellis (Ed.), *Handbook of mental deficiency: Psychological theory and research* (pp. 41–91). New York: McGraw-Hill.

Cronin, M. E., & Patton, J. R. (1993). *Life skills instructions for all students with special needs: A practical guide for integrating real life content into the curriculum.* Austin, TX: PRO-ED.

Cronin, M. E., Patton, J. R., & Wood, S. J. (2006). *Life skills instruction: A practical guide for integrating real-life content into the curriculum at the elementary and secondary levels for students with special needs or who are placed at risk.* Austin, TX: PRO-ED.

Cummins, J. P., & Das, J. P. (1980). Cognitive processing, academic achievement, and WISC-R performance in EMR children. *Journal of Consulting and Clinical Psychology, 46,* 777–779.

Cuskelly, M., & Gunn, P. (2003). Sibling relationships of children with Down syndrome: Perspectives of mothers, fathers, and siblings. *American Journal on Mental Retardation, 108,* 234–244.

Daniel R. R. v. State Board of Education, 874 F.2d 1036 (5th Cir. 1989).

Das, J. P., Naglieri, J. A., & Kirby, J. R. (1994). *Assessment of cognitive processes: The PASS theory of intelligence.* Boston: Allyn & Bacon.

Davis, L. A. (2000). More common than we think: Recognizing and responding to signs of violence. *Impact, 13*(3), 8–9.

Davis, S. (Ed.) (2003). *A family handbook on future planning.* Chicago: Rehabilitation Research and Training Center on Aging with Developmental Disabilities, Department of Disability and Human Development, University of Illinois at Chicago.

deFur, S. & Williams, B. T. (2002). Cultural considerations in the transition process and standards-based education. In C. A. Kochhar-Bryant & D. Bassett (Eds.), *Aligning transition and standards-based education: Issues and strategies* (pp. 105–123). Arlington, VA: Council for Exceptional Children.

Delaney, D., & Poling, A. (1990). Drug abuse among mentally retarded people: An overlooked problem? *Journal of Alcohol and Drug Education, 35,* 48–54.

Demark, J. L., Feldman, M. A., & Holden, J. A. (2003). Behavioral relationship between autism and fragile X syndrome. *American Journal on Mental Retardation, 108,* 314–326.

DeMitchell, T. A., & Kerns, G. M. (1997). Where to educate Rachel Holland? Does least restrictive environment mean no restrictions in the environment? *Clearinghouse, 70*(3), 161–166.

Denning, C. B., Chamberlain, J. A., & Polloway, E. A. (2000). An evaluation of state guidelines for mental retardation: Focus on definition and classification practices. *Education and Training in Mental Retardation and Developmental Disabilities, 35,* 226–232.

Deno, S. L., & Mirkin, P. K. (1980). Data-based IEP development: An approach to substantive compliance. *Teaching Exceptional Children, 12,* 92–97.

Developmental Disabilities Assistance and Bill of Rights Act. 45 U.S.C. 6000 (1994).

Dewey, J. (1966). *Democracy and education.* New York: Macmillan.

Diana v. State Board of Education, C-70-37 R.F.P. (N.D. Cal. January 7, 1970, and June 18, 1972).

Dimitropoulos, A., Feurer, I. D., Butler, M. G., & Thompson, T. (2001). Emergence of compulsive behavior and tantrums in children with Prader-Willi syndrome. *American Journal on Mental Retardation, 106,* 39–51.

Division for Early Childhood (DEC) Task Force. (1993). *DEC recommended practices: Indicators of quality in programs for infants and young children with special needs and their families.* Pittsburgh: Council for Exceptional Children, Division for Early Childhood.

Division for Early Childhood (DEC) Task Force. (2000). *DEC recommended practices in early intervention, early childhood special education.* Longmont, CO: Council for Exceptional Children, Division for Early Childhood.

Dix, D. (1976). Memorial to the legislature of Massachusetts, 1843. Reprinted in M. Rosen, G. R. Clark, & M. S. Kivitz (Eds.), *The history of mental retardation: Collected papers* (Vol. 1, pp. 3–30). Baltimore: University Park Press. (Original work published 1843)

Doll, E. A. (1935). A genetic scale of social maturity. *American Journal of Orthopsychiatry, 5,* 180–188.

Doll, E. A. (1941). The essentials of an inclusive concept of mental deficiency. *American Journal of Mental Deficiency, 46,* 214–229.

Doll, E. A. (1947). *Social Maturity Scale.* Circle Pines, MN: American Guidance Service.

Doll, E. A. (1953). *Measurement of social competence: A manual for the Vineland Social Maturity Scale.* Circle Pines, MN: American Guidance Service.

Doll, E. A. (1962). Historical survey of research and management of mental retardation in the United States. In E. P. Trapp & P. Hinestein (Eds.), *Readings on the exceptional child* (pp. 21–68). New York: Appleton-Century-Crofts.

Doll, E. A. (1965). *Vineland Social Maturity Scale: Condensed manual of directions* (1965 ed.). Circle Pines, MN: American Guidance Service.

Donaldson, M. D. C., Chu, C. E., Cooke, A., Wilson, A., Greene, S. A., & Stephenson, J. B. P. (1994). The Prader-Willi syndrome. *Archives of Disease in Childhood, 70,* 58–63.

Dosen, A., & Day, K. (Eds.). (2001). *Treating mental illness and behavior disorders in children and adults with mental retardation.* Washington, DC: American Psychiatric Press.

Downey, J., Elkin, E. J., Ehrhardt, A. A., Meyer-Bahlburg, H. F., Bell, J. J., & Morishima, A. (1991). Cognitive ability and everyday functioning in women with Turner syndrome. *Journal of Learning Disabilities, 24,* 32–39.

Downing, J. E., & Eichinger, J. (2002). The important role of peers in the inclusion process. In J. E. Downing (Ed.), *Including students with severe and multiple disabilities in typical classrooms* (pp. 129–146). Baltimore: Brookes.

Drew, C. J., Hardman, M. L., & Hart, A. W. (1996). *Designing and conducting research in education and social science.* Needham Heights, MA: Allyn & Bacon.

Drew, C. J., Hardman, M. L., & Logan, D. R. (1996). *Mental retardation: A lifecycle approach* (6th ed.). Upper Saddle River, NJ: Merrill/Prentice Hall.

Drew, C. J., Logan, D. R., & Hardman, M. L. (1992). *Mental retardation: A life cycle approach*

(5th ed.). Upper Saddle River, NJ: Merrill/Prentice Hall.

Drinkwater, S., & Demchak, M. (1995). The preschool checklist: Integration of children with severe disabilities. *Teaching Exceptional Children, 28*(1), 4–8.

Driscoll, A., & Nagel, N. G. (2001). *Early childhood education, birth–8.* Boston: Allyn & Bacon.

DuBow, S., & Greer, S. (1984). Special education law since *Rowley. Clearinghouse Review, 17,* 1001–1007.

Dudley, J., Calhoun, M., Ahlgrim-Delzell, L., & Conroy, J. (1998). Measuring the consumer satisfaction of class members of a lawsuit. *International Journal of Disability Research, 42*(3), 199–207.

Dugdale, R. L. (1877). *The Jukes: A study in crime, pauperism, disease, and heredity.* New York: Putnam.

Dunn, L. M. (1968). Special education for the mildly retarded: Is much of it justifiable? *Exceptional Children, 35,* 5–22.

Dunn, L. M. (1973). *Exceptional children in the schools: Special education in transition.* New York: Holt, Rinehart & Winston.

Dunst, C., Trivette, C., & Deal, A. (1998). *Enabling and empowering families.* Cambridge, MA: Brookline Books.

Dykens, E. M. (2000). Contaminated and unusual food combinations: What do people with Prader-Willi syndrome choose? *Mental Retardation, 138,* 163–171.

Dykens, E. M. (2001). Introduction to the special issue on behavioral phenotypes. *American Journal on Mental Retardation, 106,* 1–3.

Dykens, E. M., Cassidy, S. D., & King, B. H. (1999). Maladaptive behavior differences in Prader-Willi syndrome due to maternal deletion versus maternal uniparental disomy. *American Journal on Mental Retardation, 104,* 67–77.

Dykens, E. M., Hodapp, R. M., & Finucane, B. M. (2000). *Genetics and mental retardation syndromes.* Baltimore: Brookes.

Dykens, E. M. & Rosner, B. A. (1999). Refining behavioral phenotypes: Personality-motivation in Williams and Prader-Willi syndromes. *American Journal on Mental Retardation, 104,* 158–169.

Dykens, E. M., Rosner, B. A., & Ly, T. M. (2001). Drawings by individuals with Williams syndrome: Are people different from shapes? *American Journal on Mental Retardation, 106,* 94–107.

Edgar, E. (1987). Secondary programs in education: Are many of them justifiable? *Exceptional Children, 53,* 555–561.

Edgerton, R. B. (1967). *The cloak of competence: Stigma in the lives of the mentally retarded.* Berkeley: University of California Press.

Edgerton, R. B. (1981). Another look at culture and mental retardation. In M. J. Begab, H. C. Haywood, & H. L. Garber (Eds.), *Psychosocial influences in retarded performance* (Vol. 1, pp. 309–324). Baltimore: University Park Press.

Edgerton, R. B. (1990). Quality of life from a longitudinal research perspective. In R. L. Schalock (Ed.), *Quality of life: Perspectives and issues* (pp. 149–160). Washington, DC: American Association on Mental Retardation.

Edgerton, R. B., & Sabagh, G. (1962). From mortification to aggrandizement: Changing self-conceptions in the careers of the mentally retarded. *Psychiatry, 25,* 263–272.

Edwards, W. J., & Reynolds, L. A. (1997). Defending and advocating on behalf of individuals with "mild" mental retardation in the criminal justice system. *Impact 10*(2), 12–13. (ERIC Document Reproduction Service No. ED411627)

Einfeld, S. L., Tonge, B. J., & Rees, V. W. (2001). Longitudinal course of behavioral and emotional problems in Williams syndrome. *American Journal on Mental Retardation, 106,* 73–81.

Eisenhower, D. D. (1954). Special message to the Congress on health needs of the American people. January 8, 1954. Retrieved February 14, 2005, from www.presidency.ucsb.edu/index.php

Elliott, C. D. (1990). *Differential Ability Scales.* San Antonio, TX: Psychological Corporation.

Ellis, N. R. (1963). The stimulus trace and behavioral inadequacy. In N. R. Ellis (Ed.), *Handbook of mental deficiency: Psychological theory and research* (pp. 134–158). New York: McGraw-Hill.

Ellis, N. R., & Dulaney, C. L. (1991). Further evidence for the cognitive inertia of persons with mental retardation. *American Journal on Mental Retardation, 95,* 613–621.

Epstein, C. J. (1988). New approaches to the study of Down syndrome. In F. J. Menolascino & J. A. Stark (Eds.), *Preventive and curative intervention in mental retardation* (pp. 35–36). Baltimore: Brookes.

Epstein, M. H., Cullinan, D., & Polloway, E. A. (1986). Patterns of maladjustment among mentally retarded children and youth. *American Journal of Mental Deficiency, 91,* 127–134.

Epstein, M. H., Cullinan, D., Quinn, K. P., & Cumblad, C. (1994). Characteristics of children with emotional and behavioral disorders in community-based programs designed to prevent placement in residential facilities. *Journal of Emotional and Behavioral Disorders, 2*(1), 51–71.

Epstein, M. H., Polloway, E. A., Patton, J. R., & Foley, R. (1989). Mild retardation: Student characteristics and services. *Education and Training of the Mentally Retarded, 24,* 7–16.

Eriksen, C. W., & Yeh, Y. (1985). Allocation of attention in the visual field. *Human Perception and Performance, 11,* 583–597.

Essex, L. E. (2002). Mothers and fathers of adults with mental retardation: Feelings of intergenerational closeness. *Family Relations, 51,* 156–165.

Essex, L. E., Seltzer, M. M., & Krauss, M. W. (1999). Differences in coping effectiveness and well-being among aging mothers and fathers of adults with mental retardation. *American Journal on Mental Retardation, 104*(6), 545–563.

Estes, W. K. (1970). *Learning theory and mental development.* New York: Academic Press.

Evans, D. W., & Gray, F. L. (2000). Compulsive-like behavior in individuals with Down syndrome: Its relation to mental age level, adaptive and maladaptive behavior. *Child Development, 71,* 288–300.

Everington, C., & Fulero, S. (1999). Competence to confess: Measuring understanding and suggestibility of defendants with mental retardation. *Mental Retardation, 37,* 212–220.

Everington, C., & Luckasson, R. (1992). *Competence Assessment for Standing Trial for Defendants with Mental Retardation (CAST*MR).* Worthington, OH: IDS.

Everington, C., Olley, G., & Patton, J. (in press). Implications of *Atkins v. Virginia:* Issues in defining and diagnosing mental retardation.

Everson, J. M., & Zhang, D. (2000). Person-centered planning: Characteristics, inhibitors, and supports. *Education and Training in Mental Retardation and Developmental Disabilities, 35*(1), 36–43.

Eyman, R. K., & Borthwick-Duffy, S. A. (1994). Trends in mortality rates and predictors of mortality. In M. M. Seltzer, M. W. Krauss, & M. P. Janicki (Eds.), *Life course perspectives on adulthood and old age* (pp. 93–105). Washington, DC: American Association on Mental Retardation.

Eyman, R. K., Call, T. E., & White, J. F. (1991). Life expectancy of persons with Down syndrome. *American Journal on Mental Retardation, 95,* 603–612.

Ferrara, M. L. (1992). *Substance abuse treatment program for persons with mental retardation.* Austin: Texas Commission on Alcohol and Drug Abuse.

Fewell, R. R. (2000). Assessment of young children with special needs: Foundations for tomorrow. *Topics in Early Childhood Special Education, 20*(1), 38–42.

Fewell, R. R., & Kelly, J. F. (1983). Curriculum for young handicapped children. In S. G. Garwood (Ed.), *Educating handicapped children* (pp. 407–433). Rockville, MD: Aspen.

Fidler, D. J., Hodapp, R. M., & Dykens, E. M. (2002). Behavioral phenotypes and special education. *Journal of Special Education, 36*(2), 80–88.

Fiedler, C. R. (2000). *Making a difference: Advocacy competencies for special education professionals.* Austin, TX: PRO-ED.

Field, S., & Hoffman, A. (1996). *Steps to self-determination.* Austin, TX: PRO-ED.

Field, S., Martin, J., Miller, R., Ward, M., & Wehmeyer, M. (1998). *A practical guide to teaching self-determination.* Reston, VA: Council for Exceptional Children.

Fishler, K., Azen, C. G., Henderson, R., Friedman, E. G., & Koch, R. (1987). Psychoeducational findings among children treated for phenylketonuria. *American Journal on Mental Retardation, 92,* 65–73.

Flynn, J. R. (1998). WAIS-III and WISC-III IQ gains in the United States from 1972 to 1995: How to compensate for obsolete norms. *Perceptual and Motor Skills, 86,* 1231–1239.

Forest, M., & Pearpoint, J. (1992). MAPS: Action planning. In J. Pearpoint, M. Forest, & J. Snow (Eds.), *The inclusion papers: Strategies to make inclusion work* (pp. 52–56). Toronto: Inclusion Press.

Foxx, R. M., Faw, G. D., Taylor, S. D., Davis, P. K., & Fulia, R. (1993). "Would I be able to . . . ?" Teaching clients to assess the availability of their living style preferences. *American Journal on Mental Retardation, 98*(2), 235–248.

Frankenburg, W. K. (1984). A survey of state guidelines for identification of mental retardation. *Mental Retardation, 22*(1), 17–20.

Fraser, W. I., & Rao, J. M. (1991). Recent studies of mentally handicapped young people's behavior. *Journal of Child Psychology and Psychiatry, 32,* 79–108.

Frederick, R. I. (2003). *Validity Indicator Profile* (2nd ed.). Bloomington, MN: Pearson Assessments.

Freeman, J. M., Vining, E. P. G., & Pillas, D. J. (1997). *Seizures and epilepsy in childhood: A guide for parents* (2nd ed.). Baltimore: Johns Hopkins University Press.

Freeman, R. (1968, July 8). Schools and the elusive "average children" concept. *Wall Street Journal,* p. 10.

Freeman, S. F. N., & Kasari, C. (2002). Characteristics and quality of the play dates of children with Down syndrome: Emerging or true friendships? *American Journal on Mental Retardation, 107,* 16–31.

Fuchs, D., Fuchs, L. S., & Bahr, M. W. (1990). Mainstream assistance teams: A scientific basis for the art of consultation. *Exceptional Children, 57,* 128–139.

Fulton, F. (1997). Challenging stereotypes and ignorance: The San Francisco Police Department. *Impact 10*(2), 18. (ERIC Document Reproduction Service No. ED411627)

Furey, E. M. (1994). Sexual abuse of adults with mental retardation: Who and where. *Mental Retardation, 32,* 173–180.

Furlong, M. J., & LeDrew, L. (1985). IQ = 68 = mildly retarded? Factors influencing multidisciplinary team recommendations on children with FS IQs between 63 and 75. *Psychology in the Schools, 22,* 5–9.

Garber, H. L. (1988). *The Milwaukee project: Preventing mental retardation in children at risk.* Washington, DC: American Association on Mental Retardation.

García, S. B., Mendez-Pérez, A., & Ortiz, A. A. (2000). Interpreting Mexican-American mother's beliefs about language disabilities from a sociocultural perspective. *Remedial and Special Education, 21,* 90–102.

Gardner, H. (1993). *Frames of mind: The theory of multiple intelligences.* New York: Basic Books.

Gardner, H. (2000). *Intelligence reframed: Multiple intelligences for the 21st century.* New York: Basic Books.

Gardner, J. F., & Chapman, M. S. (1985). *Staff development in mental retardation services: A practical handbook.* Baltimore: Brookes.

Garnett, R. (2003). *In opposition to a name change.* Retrieved May 30, 2003, from the Web site of the American Association on Mental Retardation (www.aamr.org/Reading Room/con memo.shtml).

Garrison, M., & Hammill, D. D. (1971). Who are the retarded? *Exceptional Children, 38,* 13–20.

Gaudet, L., Pulos, S., Crethar, H., & Burger, S. (2002). Psychosocial concerns of adults with developmental disabilities: Perspectives of the self, family member, and provider. *Education and Training in Mental Retardation and Developmental Disabilities, 37,* 23–26.

Gaylord, V., Abery, B., & Schoeller, K. (Eds.). (1997). Feature issue on the social inclusion of adults with developmental disabilities. *Impact, 10*(3).

Gaylord-Ross, R., & Chadsey-Rusch, J. (1991). Measurement of work-related outcomes for students with severe disabilities. *Journal of Special Education, 25*(3), 291–304.

Geisthardt, C. L., Brotherson, M. J., & Cook, C. C. (2002). Friendships of children with disabilities in the home environment. *Education and Training in Mental Retardation and Developmental Disabilities, 37,* 235–252.

Gesell, A. (1941). *Wolf child and human child.* New York: Harper Brothers.

Giangreco, M. F., Cloninger, C. J., & Iverson, V. S. (1998). *Choosing outcomes and accommodations for children: A guide to planning inclusive education* (2nd ed.). Baltimore: Brookes.

Ginzberg, E., & Bray, D. W. (1953). *The uneducated.* New York: Columbia University Press.

Glass, G. V. (1983). Effectiveness of special education. *Policy Studies Review, 2* (Special No. 1), 65–78.

Glidden, L. M., & Johnson, V. E. (1999). Twelve years later: Adjustment in families who adopted children with developmental disabilities. *Mental Retardation, 37*(1), 16–24.

Goddard, H. H. (1907). Psychological work among the feeble-minded. *Journal of Psycho-Asthetics, 12*(1–4), 22.

Goddard, H. H. (1912). *The Kallikak family.* New York: Macmillan.

Goddard, H. H. (1917). Mental tests and the immigrant. *Journal of Delinquency, 2,* 243–277.

Goddard, H. H. (1920). *Feeble-mindedness: Its causes and consequences.* New York: Macmillan.

Goddard, H. H. (1973). *The Kallikak family.* New York: Arno Press. (Original work published 1912)

Gold, M. W. (1980). *"Did I say that?" Articles and commentary on the Try Another Way system.* Champaign, IL: Research Press.

Goldberg, R. T., McLean, M. M., LaVigne, R., Fratolilli, J., & Sullivan, F. T. (1990). Transition of persons with developmental disabilities from extended sheltered employment to competitive employment. *Mental Retardation, 28,* 299–304.

Goldenberg, I., & Goldenberg, H. (2000). *Family therapy: An overview* (5th ed.). Pacific Grove, CA: Brooks/Cole.

Goldman, J. J. (1988). Prader-Willi syndrome in two institutionalized older adults. *Mental Retardation, 26,* 97–102.

Gordon, J. R. (1991). *A diagnostic approach to organizational behavior* (3rd ed.). Boston: Allyn & Bacon.

Gould, S. J. (1981). *The mismeasure of man.* New York: Norton.

Grabe, M., & Grabe, C. (2000). *Integrating the Internet for meaningful learning.* Boston: Houghton Mifflin.

Graham, F. K., Ernhart, C. B., Thurston, D., & Craft, M. (1962). Development three years after perinatal anoxia and other potentially damaging experiences. *Psychological Monographs, 76*(Whole No. 522).

Graham, M., & Scott, K. G. (1988). The impact of definitions of higher risks on services to infants and toddlers. *Topics in Early Childhood Special Education, 8,* 23–28.

Gray, G. (1975). Educational service delivery. In W. J. Cegelka (Chair), *Educating the 24-hour retarded child.* Symposium conducted at the National Training Meeting on Education of the Severely and Profoundly Retarded. Arlington, TX: National Association for Retarded Citizens.

Graziano, A. M. (2002). *Developmental disabilities: Introduction to a diverse field.* Boston: Allyn & Bacon.

Greenspan, S. (1994). Review of the 1992 AAMR manual. *American Journal on Mental Retardation, 98,* 544–549.

Greenspan, S. (1997). Dead manual walking? Why the 1992 AAMR definition needs redoing. *Education and Training in Mental Retardation and Developmental Disabilities, 32,* 179–190.

Greenspan, S. (2003). Perceived risk status as a key to defining mental retardation. In H. N. Switzky & S. Greenspan (Eds.), *What is mental retardation: Ideas for an evolving disability* (pp. 202–218). Washington, DC: American Association on Mental Retardation.

Greenspan, S., & Driscoll, J. (1997). The role of intelligence in a broad model of personal competence. In D. P. Flanagan, J. L. Genshaft, & P. L. Harrison (Eds.), *Contemporary intelligent assessment: Theories, tests, and issues* (p. 133). New York: Guilford.

Greenspan, S., & Switzky, H. N. (2003). Forty years of American Association on Mental Retardation manuals. In H. N. Switzky & S. Greenspan (Eds.), *What is mental retardation: Ideas for an evolving disability* (pp. 38–63). Washington, DC: American Association on Mental Retardation.

Gresham, F. M. (1982). Misguided mainstreaming: The case for social skills training with handicapped children. *Exceptional Children, 48,* 422–433.

Gresham, F. M., MacMillan, D. L., & Siperstein, G. N. (1995). Critical analysis of the 1992 AAMR definition: Implications for school psychology. *School Psychology Quarterly, 10,* 1–19.

Griesbach, L. S., & Polloway, E. A. (1991). *Fetal alcohol syndrome.* (ERIC Document Reproduction Service No. 326 035)

Griffiths, P., Smith, C., & Harvie, A. (1997). Transitory hyperphenylalanineaemia in children with continuously treated phenylketonuria. *American Journal on Mental Retardation, 102,* 27–36.

Grigal, M., Neubert, D. A., & Moon, M. S. (2005). *Transition services for students with significant disabilities in college and community settings: Strategies for planning, implementation, and evaluation.* Austin, TX: PRO-ED.

Grossman, H. J. (Ed.). (1973). *Manual on terminology and classification in mental retardation* (1973 rev.). Washington, DC: American Association on Mental Retardation.

Grossman, H. J. (Ed.). (1977). *Manual on terminology and classification in mental retardation* (1977 rev.). Washington, DC: American Association on Mental Retardation.

Grossman, H. J. (Ed.). (1983). *Manual on terminology and classification in mental retardation* (3rd ed. rev.). Washington, DC: American Association on Mental Retardation.

Grossman, H. J., & Tarjan, G. (1987). *AMA handbook on mental retardation.* Chicago: American Medical Association, Division of Clinical Science.

Guilford, J. P. (1967). *The nature of human intelligence.* New York: McGraw-Hill.

Gumpel, T. (1994). Social skills competence and social skills training for persons with mental retardation: An expansion of a behavioral paradigm. *Education and Training in Mental Retardation and Developmental Disabilities, 29*(3), 194–201.

Guralnick, M. J. (1998). Effectiveness of early intervention for vulnerable children: A developmental perspective. *American Journal on Mental Retardation, 102*(4), 319–345.

Guralnick, M. J. (2000). Early childhood intervention: Evolution of a system. In M. L. Wehmeyer & J. R. Patton (Eds.), *intellectual disabilities in the 21st century* (pp. 37–58). Austin, TX: PRO-ED.

Guralnick, M. J., & Weinhouse, E. (1984). Peer-related social interactions of developmentally delayed young children: Their development and characteristics. *Developmental Psychology, 20,* 815–827.

Guterman, B. R. (1995). The validity of categorical learning disabilities services: The consumer's view. *Exceptional Children, 62,* 112–124.

Guttmacher, M., & Weihofen, H. (1952). *Psychiatry and the law.* New York: Norton.

Haggard, H. W., & Jellinek, E. M. (1942). *Alcohol explained.* Garden City, NY: Doubleday.

Halderman v. Pennhurst State School and Hospital, 446 F. Supp. 1295 (E.D. Pa. 1977), *aff'd* in part, remand in part. Nos. 84-1490, 78-1564, 78-1602 (3rd Cir. December 13, 1979).

Hall, J. G. (2000). Molecular and clinical genetics for the practicing pediatrician. *Advances in Children's Health 2000: Pediatric Academic Societies and the American Academy of Pediatrics Year 2000 Joint Meeting.* N.p.: Pediatric Academic Societies and the American Academy of Pediatrics.

Hallahan, D. P., & Kauffman, J. M. (1997). *Exceptional learners.* Boston: Allyn & Bacon.

Hallahan, D. P., Keller, C. E., McKinney, J. D., Lloyd, J. W., & Bryan, T. (1988). Examining the research base of the regular education initiative: Efficacy studies and the adaptive learning environment model. *Journal of Learning Disabilities, 21,* 29–35.

Halle, J., Alpert, C. L., & Anderson, S. R. (1984). Natural environment language assessment and intervention with severely impaired preschoolers. *Topics in Early Childhood Special Education, 4,* 35–56.

Halle, J. W., Silverman, N. A., & Regan, L. (1983). The effects of a data-based exercise program on physical fitness of retarded children. *Education and Training of the Mentally Retarded, 18*(3), 221–225.

Halpern, A. S. (1992). Transition: Old wine in new bottles. *Exceptional Children, 58,* 202–212.

Halpern, A. S. (1994). The transition of youth with disabilities to adult life: A position statement of the Division on Career Development and Transition, Council for Exceptional Children. *Career Development for Exceptional Individuals, 17,* 115–124.

Halpern, A. S., Herr, C. M., Doren, M., & Wolf, N. K. (2001). *Next S.T.E.P.: Student transition and evaluation planning* (2nd ed.). Austin, TX: PRO-ED.

Hammill, D. D., Pearson, N. A., & Wiederholt, J. L. (1997). *Comprehensive Test of Nonverbal Intelligence.* Austin, TX: PRO-ED.

Hannah, M. E., & Midlarsky, E. (1999). Competence and adjustment of siblings of children with mental retardation. *American Journal on Mental Retardation, 104*(1), 22–37.

Hanneman, R., & Blacher, J. (1998). Predicting placement in families who have children with severe handicaps: A longitudinal analysis. *American Journal on Mental Retardation, 102*(4), 392–408.

Hanson, M. J. (1999). *Early transition for children and families: Transitions from infant/toddler services to preschool education.* Reston, VA: ERIC Clearinghouse on Disabilities and Gifted Education, Council for Exceptional Children. (ERIC Document Reproduction Service No. ED434436)

Hanson, M. J., & Lynch, E. W. (1995). *Early intervention: Implementing child and family services for infants and toddlers who are at-risk or disabled.* Austin, TX: PRO-ED.

Hardie, A. (2000, April 9). *Atlanta Journal-Constitution,* pp. H1, H8.

Hardman, M. L., Drew, C. J., & Egan, M. W. (1996). *Human exceptionality: Society, school, and family* (5th ed.). Boston: Allyn & Bacon.

Hardman, M. L., Drew, C. J., Egan, M. W., & Wolf, B. (1993). *Human exceptionality: Society, school, and family* (4th ed.). Boston: Allyn & Bacon.

Harlan-Simmons, J. E., Holtz, P., Todd, J., & Mooney, M. F. (2001). Building social relationships through valued roles: Three older adults and the community membership project. *Mental Retardation, 39,* 171–180.

Harrington, T. F., & O'Shea, A. J. (1992). *The Harrington-O'Shea Career Decision-Making System.* Circle Pines, MN: American Guidance Service.

Harrison, P. L. (1987). Research with adaptive behavior scales. *Journal of Special Education, 21*(1), 37–68.

Harrison, P. L., & Boney, T. L. (2002). Best practices in the assessment of adaptive behavior. In A. Thomas & J. Grimes (Eds.), *Best practices in school psychology IV* (pp. 1167–1179). Washington, DC: National Association of School Psychologists.

Harrison, P. L., & Oakland, T. (2000). *Adaptive behavior assessment system.* San Antonio, TX: Psychological Corporation.

Harry, B. (1992). *Cultural diversity, families, and the special education system.* New York: Teachers College Press.

Hartmann v. Loudoun County Board of Education (4th Cir. 1997).

Hasselbring, T. S., & Peabody College of Vanderbilt University (1998). *The future of special education and the role of technology.* Available on the Web site of Peabody College of Vanderbilt University (http://peabody.vanderbilt.edu/ltc/hasselbringt/future.html).

Hatton, C. (1998). Whose quality of life is it anyway? Some problems with the emerging quality of life consensus. *Mental Retardation, 36*(2), 104–115.

Hatton, D. D., Wheeler, A. C., Skinner, M. L., Bailey, D. B., Sullivan, K. M., Roberts, J. E., et al. (2003). Adaptive behavior in children with fragile X syndrome. *American Journal on Mental Retardation, 108,* 373–390.

Hayden, A. H., & Pious, C. G. (1979). The case for early intervention. In R. York & E. Edgar (Eds.), *Teaching the severely handicapped* (Vol. 4). Seattle: American Association for the Education of the Severely/Profoundly Handicapped.

Hayden, M. F. (1998). Civil rights litigation for institutionalized persons with mental retardation: A summary. *Mental Retardation, 36,* 75–83.

Haywood, H. C., & Paour, J. (1992). Alfred Binet (1857–1922): Multifactored pioneer. *Psychology in Mental Retardation and Developmental Disabilities, 18,* 1–4.

Haywood, H. C., & Stedman, J. D. (1969). Poverty and mental retardation: Staff position paper prepared for President's Committee on Mental Retardation. Washington, DC: President's Committee on Mental Retardation.

Heal, L. W., Borthwick-Duffy, S. A., & Saunders, R. R. (1996). In J. W. Jacobson & J. A. Mulick (Eds.), *Manual of diagnosis and professional practice in mental retardation* (pp. 199–209). Washington, DC: American Psychological Association.

Healey, K. N., & Masterpasqua, F. (1992). Interpersonal cognitive problem-solving among children with mild mental retardation. *American Journal on Mental Retardation, 96,* 367–372.

Heber, R. F. (1959). A manual on terminology and classification in mental retardation. *Monograph Supplement to the American Journal of Mental Deficiency, 62.*

Heber, R. F. (1961). A manual on terminology and classification in mental retardation (Rev. ed.). *Monograph Supplement to the American Journal of Mental Deficiency, 64.*

Heber, R. F. (1964). Personality. In H. A. Stevens & R. F. Heber (Eds.), *Mental retardation: A review of research* (pp. 143–174). Chicago: University of Chicago Press.

Heiman, T. (2000). Quality and quantity of friendships: Students' and teachers' perceptions. *School Psychology International, 21,* 265–280.

Heller, T., Janicki, M., Hammel, J., & Factor, A. (2002). *Promoting healthy aging, family support, and age-friendly communities for persons aging with developmental disabilities: Report of the 2001 Invitational Research Symposium on Aging with Developmental Disabilities.* Chicago: Rehabilitation Research and Training Center on Aging with Developmental Disabilities, Department of Disability and Human Development, University of Illinois at Chicago.

Henderson, R. A., & Vitello, S. J. (1988). Litigation related to community integration. In L. W. Heal, J. I. Haney, & A. R. Novak Amado (Eds.), *Integration of developmentally disabled individuals into the community* (2nd ed., pp. 272–282). Baltimore: Brookes.

Heward, W. L. (2000). *Exceptional children: An introduction to special education* (6th ed.). Upper Saddle River, NJ: Merrill/Prentice Hall.

Heward, W. L. (2002). *Exceptional children: An introduction to special education* (7th ed.). Upper Saddle River, NJ: Merrill/Prentice Hall.

Hewett, F. M., & Forness, S. (1977). *Education of exceptional learners* (2nd ed.). Boston: Allyn & Bacon.

Hill, B. K., & Bruininks, R. H. (1984). Maladaptive behavior of mentally retarded people in residential facilities. *American Journal of Mental Deficiency, 88*(4), 380–387.

Hill, B. K., Lakin, K. C., Bruininks, R. H., Amado, A. N., Anderson, D. J., & Copher, J. I. (1989). *Living in the community: A comparative study of foster homes and small group homes for people with mental retardation* (Report No. 28). Minneapolis: University of Minnesota, Center for Residential and Community Integration.

Hill, B. K., Lakin, K. C., Sigford, B. B., Hauber, F. A., & Bruininks, R. H. (1982). *Programs and services for mentally retarded people in residential facilities* (Report No. 16). Minneapolis: University of Minnesota, Center for Residential and Community Integration.

Hilliard, L. T., & Kirman, B. H. (1965). *Mental deficiency* (2nd ed.). London: Churchill.

Hobfall, S. E. (1998). *Stress, culture, and community: The psychology and philosophy of stress.* New York: Plenum.

Hobson v. Hansen, 269 F. Supp. 401 (D.D.C. 1967, *aff'd* sub nom).

Hodapp, R. M. (1997). Direct and indirect behavioral effects of different genetic disorders of mental retardation. *American Journal on Mental Retardation, 102,* 67–79.

Hodapp, R. M., & Dykens, E. M. (2001). Strengthening behavioral research on genetic mental retardation syndromes. *American Journal on Mental Retardation, 106,* 4–15.

Hodapp, R. M., & Krasner, D. V. (1995). Families of children with disabilities: Findings from a national sample of eighth-grade students. *Exceptionality, 5*(2), 71–81.

Hoefnagel, D., Andrew, E. D., Mireault, N. G., & Berndt, W. O. (1965). Hereditary choreoathetosis, self-mutilation, and hyperuricemia in young males. *New England Journal of Medicine, 273,* 130–135.

Hoelke, G. M. (1966). *Effectiveness of special class placement for educable mentally retarded children.* Lincoln: University of Nebraska.

Holm, V. A., Cassidy, S. B., Butler, M. G., Hanchett, J. M., Greenswag, L. R. Whitman, B. Y., & Greenberg, F. (1993). Prader-Willi syndrome: Consensus diagnostic criteria. *Pediatrics, 182,* 398–402.

Holsen, L., & Thompson, T. (2004). Compulsive behavior and eye blink in Prader-Willi syndrome: Neurochemical implications. *American Journal on Mental Retardation, 109,* 197–207.

Honig v. Doe, 108 S. Ct. 592 (1988).

Hoover, J. J., & Patton, J. R. (1997). *Curriculum adaptations for students with learning and behavior problems: Principles and practices.* Austin, TX: PRO-ED.

Hope, L. N. (1997). "I look out for them, they look out for me"—Finding home in a gang. *Impact, 10*(3), 1, 26.

Horn, E., & Fuchs, D. (1987). Using adaptive behavior in assessment and intervention: An overview. *Journal of Special Education, 21*(1), 11–26.

Horn, J. L., & Cattell, R. B. (1966). Refinement of the theory of fluid and crystallized general intelligence. *Journal of Educational Psychology, 57,* 253–270.

Horner, R. D. (1980). The effects of an environmental "enrichment" program on the behavior of institutionalized profoundly retarded children. *Journal of Applied Behavior Analysis, 13*(3), 473–491.

Horner, R. H., & Carr, E. G. (1997). Behavioral support for students with severe disabilities: Functional assessment and comprehensive intervention. *Journal of Special Education, 31*(1), 84–109.

Houchins, J. (1997). Breaking the cycle: "Justice now!" *Impact, 10*(2), 10. (ERIC Document Reproduction Service No. ED411627)

Huberty, T. J., Koller, J. R., & Ten Brink, T. D. (1980). Adaptive behavior in the definition of mental retardation. *Exceptional Children, 46,* 256–261.

Hume, R. (1999, November/December). Learning disabilities and child sexual abuse. *LDA Newsbriefs, 34,* 8–9, 15, 18.

Humphrey, G., & Humphrey, M. (Eds. & Trans.). (1962). *Wild boy of Aveyron.* New York: Appleton-Century-Crofts.

Hungerford, R. H., DeProspo, C. J., & Rosenzweig, I. E. (1948). The non-academic pupil. In *Philosophy of occupational education* New York: Association of New York City Teachers of Special Education.

Hunt, N. (1967). *Nigel Hunt; The diary of a mongoloid youth.* New York: Garrett.

Hurry v. Jones, 734 F.2d 829 (1st Cir. 1984).

Ianacone, R. N., & Leconte, P. J. (1986). Curriculum-based vocational assessment: A viable response to a school-based service delivery issue. *Career Development for Exceptional Individuals, 9,* 113–120.

Idol, L., Nevin, A., & Paolucci-Whitcomb, P. (1999). *Models of curriculum-based assessment: A blueprint for learning* (3rd ed.). Austin: PRO-ED.

Individuals with Disabilities Education Act (IDEA). 20 U.S.C. 1400 *et seg.* (1997).

Individuals with Disabilities Education Act Amendments. 20 U.S.C.A. 1414 *et seq.* (1997).

Inhelder, B. (1968). *The diagnosis of reasoning in the mentally retarded.* New York: Day.

International Society for Technology in Education (ITSE). (2003). *National educational technology standards for teachers.* Retrieved July 22, 2004, from the Web site of the ISTE NETS Project (http://cnets.iste.org/docs/NETS_T.doc).

Irving Independent School District v. Tatro, 104 S. Ct. 3371 (1984).

Itard, J. M. (1962). *Wild boy of Aveyron* (G. Humphrey & M. Humphrey, Eds. & Trans.). New York: Appleton-Century-Croft. (Original work published 1801)

Itard, J. M. (1972). *The wild boy of Aveyron.* New York: Monthly Review Press. (Original work published 1801)

Ittenbach, R. F., Abery, B. H., Larson, S. A., Spiegel, A. N., & Prouty, R. W. (1994). Community adjustment of young adults with mental retardation: Overcoming barriers to inclusion. *Palaestra, 10*(2), 32–42.

Ittenbach, R. F., Esters, I. G., & Wainer, H. (1997). The history of test development. In D. P. Flanagan, J. L. Genshaft, & P. L. Harrison (Eds.), *Contemporary intellectual assessment: Theories, tests, and issues* (pp. 17–31). New York: Guilford.

Ittenbach, R. F., Larson, S. A., Spiegel, A. N., Abery, B. H., & Prouty, R. W. (1993). Community adjustment of young adults with mental retardation: A developmental perspective. *Palaestra, 9*(4), 19–24.

Ittenbach, R. F., & Lawhead, W. F. (1997). Historical and philosophical foundations of single-case research. In R. D. Franklin, D. B. Allison, & B. S. Gorman (Eds.), *Design and analysis of single-case research* (pp. 13–39). Hillsdale, NJ: Erlbaum.

Ittenbach, R. F., Spiegel, A. N., McGrew, K. S., & Bruininks, R. H. (1992). Confirmatory factor analysis of early childhood ability measures within a model of personal competence. *Journal of School Psychology, 30,* 307–323.

Iwata, B. A., Dorsey, M. F., Slifer, K. J., Bauman, K. E., & Richman, G. S. (1994). Toward a functional analysis of self-injury. *Journal of Applied Behavior Analysis, 27*(2), 197–209.

Iwata, B. A., Pace, G. M., Dorsey, M. F., Zarcone, J. R., Vollmer, T. R., Smith, R. G., Rodgers, T. A., Lerman, D. C., Shore, B. A., Mazalesli, J. L., Goh, H., Cowdery, G. E.,

Kalsher, M. J., McCosh, K. C., & Willis, K. D. (1994). The functions of self-injurious behavior: An experimental-epidemiological analysis. *Journal of Applied Behavior Analysis, 27*(2), 215–240.

Jacobson, J. W., & Mulick, J. A. (1996). *Manual of diagnosis and professional practice in mental retardation.* Washington, DC: American Psychological Association.

Janicki, M. (2001). *Coordinating systems serving carers of children and adults with developmental disabilities.* Chicago: Rehabilitation Research and Training Center on Aging with Developmental Disabilities, Department of Disability and Human Development, University of Illinois at Chicago.

Janicki, M., Dalton, A., Henderson, C., & Davidson, P. (1999). Mortality and morbidity among older adults with intellectual disability: Health services considerations. *Disability and Rehabilitation, 21,* 284–294.

Jaquish, C., & Stella, M. A. (1986). Helping special needs students move from elementary to secondary school. *Counterpoint, 7*(1), 1.

J.B. v. Independent School District, 21 IDELR 1157 (D. Minn. 1995).

Jenkins, M. W. (1987). Effect of a computerized individual education program (IEP) writer on time savings and quality. *Journal of Special Education, 8*(3), 55–66.

Jensen, A. R. (1969). How much can we boost IQ and scholastic achievement? *Harvard Educational Review, 39,* 1–23.

Jensen, A. R. (1998). *The g factor: The science of mental ability.* Westport, CT: Praeger.

Johns, B. H. (2004). NCLB and IDEA: Never the twain should meet. *Learning Disabilities, 12*(3), 89–91.

Johnson, A. (2004). *Williams syndrome.* Unpublished manuscript, Lynchburg College.

Johnson, C. F., Koch, R., Peterson, R. M., & Friedman, E. G. (1978). Congenital and neurological abnormalities in infants with phenylketonuria. *American Journal of Mental Deficiency, 82,* 375–379.

Johnson, D. R., & Lewis, D. R. (1994). Supported employment: Program models, strategies, and evaluation perspectives. In M. F. Hayden & B. H. Abery (Eds.), *Challenges for a service system in transition* (pp. 449–482). Baltimore: Brookes.

Johnson, G. O. (1959). Here and there in the Onandaga census: Fact or artifact? *Exceptional Children, 25,* 226–231.

Jones, K. L., Smith, D. W., Ulleland, C. N., & Streissguth, A. P. (1973). Patterns of malformation in offspring of chronic alcoholic mothers. *Lancet, 1*(1267), 1271.

Jordan, T. E. (1976). *The mentally retarded* (4th ed.). Upper Saddle River, NJ: Merrill/Prentice Hall.

Jordan, T. E. (2000). Down's (1866) essay and its sociomedical context. *Mental Retardation, 38,* 322–329.

Joseph, B., Egli, M., Koppekin, A., & Thompson, T. (2002). Food choice in people with Prader-Willi syndrome: Quantity and relative preference. *American Journal on Mental Retardation, 107,* 128–135.

Kail, R. (1992). General information processing by persons with mental retardation. *American Journal on Mental Retardation, 97,* 333–341.

Kaiser, A. P. (1993a). Introduction: Enhancing children's social communication. In A. P. Kaiser & D. B. Gray (Eds.), *Enhancing children's communication: Research foundations for intervention* (Vol. 2, pp. 3–10). Baltimore: Brookes.

Kaiser, A. P. (1993b). Parent-implemented language intervention: An environmental system perspective. In A. P. Kaiser & D. B. Gray (Eds.), *Enhancing children's communication: Research foundations for intervention* (Vol. 2, pp. 63–84). Baltimore: Brookes.

Kaiser, A. P., Yoder, P. J., & Keetz, A. (1992). Evaluating milieu teaching. In S. F. Warren & J. Reichle (Eds.), *Causes and effects in communication and language intervention* (Vol. 1, pp. 9–47). Baltimore: Brookes.

Kalyanpur, M., & Harry, B. (1999). *Culture in special education: Building reciprocal family-professional relationships.* Baltimore: Brookes.

Kamin, L. J. (1974). *The science and politics of IQ.* Hillsdale, NJ: Erlbaum.

Kamphaus, R. W. (1987). Conceptual and psychometric issues in the assessment of adaptive behavior. *Journal of Special Education, 21*(1), 27–36.

Kanaya, T., Scullin, M., & Ceci, S. (2003). The Flynn effect and U.S. policies. *American Psychologist, 58,* 778–790.

Kanner, L. A. (1964). *A history of the care and study of the mentally retarded.* Springfield, IL: Thomas.

Kapp-Simon, K., & Simon, D. J. (1991). Social skills training for teens with special needs. *Connections, 2*(2), 2–5.

Karp, N. (1996). Individualized wrap-around services for children with emotional, behavior, and mental disorders. In E. H. Singer, L. E. Powers, & A. L. Olson (Eds.), *Redefining family support: Innovations in public–private partnerships* (pp. 291–310). Baltimore: Brookes.

Kasari, B. C., Freeman, S. E. N., & Hughes, M. A. (2001). Emotion recognition by children with Down syndrome. *American Journal on Mental Retardation, 106,* 59–72.

Katims, D. S. (2001), Literacy assessment of students with mental retardation. *Education and Training in Mental Retardation and Developmental Disabilities, 36*(4), 363–372.

Kauffman, J. M. (1987). Research in special education: A commentary. *Remedial and Special Education, 85*(6), 57–62.

Kauffman, J. M., & Krouse, J. (1981). The cult of educability: Searching for the substance of things hoped for, the evidence of things not seen. *Analysis and Intervention in Developmental Disabilities, 1,* 53–60.

Kaufman, A. S. (1994). *Intelligent testing with the WISC-III.* New York: Wiley.

Kaufman, A. S., & Kaufman, N. L. (1983). *Kaufman Assessment Battery for Children (K-ABC).* Circle Pines, MN: American Guidance Service.

Kaye, H. S. (1997). Disability watch: The status of people with disabilities in the United States. (ERIC Document Reproduction Service No. ED417540)

Kaye, H. S. (2003). *Improved employment opportunities for people with disabilities* (Disability statistics report 17). Washington, DC: U.S. Department of Education.

Keith, T. Z., Fehrman, P. G., Harrison, P. L., & Pottebaum, S. M. (1987). The relation between adaptive behavior and intelligence: Testing alternative explanations. *Journal of School Psychology, 24,* 31–43.

Kennedy, C. H., Horner, R. H., & Newton, J. S. (1989). Social contacts of adults with severe disabilities living in the community: A descriptive analysis of relationship patterns. *Journal of the Association for Persons with Severe Handicaps, 14,* 190–196.

Kennedy, C. H., & Itkonen, T. (1994). Some effects of regular class participation on the social contacts and social networks of high school students with severe disabilities. *Journal of the Association for Persons with Severe Handicaps, 19*(1), 1–10.

Keogh, B. K. (1988). Improving services for problem learners: Rethinking and restructuring. *Journal of Learning Disabilities, 21,* 19–22.

Keogh, B. K. (1990). Narrowing the gap between policy and practice. *Exceptional Children, 57,* 186–190.

Kerns, K. A., Don, A., Mateer, C. A., & Streissguth, A. (1997). Cognitive deficits in nonretarded adults with fetal alcohol syndrome. *Journal of Learning Disabilities, 30,* 685–693.

Keyes, D. W. (1997). The expert witness: Issues of competence, criminal justice, mental retardation. *Impact, 10*(2), 14–16. (ERIC Document Reproduction Service No. ED411627)

Keyes, D. W., & Edwards, W. J. (1996). Competence assessment: Questions and (some) answers. *Champion,* 10–21.

Keyes, D. W., Edwards, W., & Perske, R. (1997). People with mental retardation are dying, legally. *Mental Retardation, 35*(1), 59–63.

Khemka, I., & Hickson, L. (2000). Decision-making by adults with mental retardation in simulated situations of abuse. *Mental Retardation, 38,* 15–26.

Kidd, J. (1979). An open letter to the Committee on Terminology and Classification of AAMD from the Committee on Definition and Terminology of CEC-MR. *Education and Training of the Mentally Retarded, 14,* 74–76.

Kim, S. H., Larson, S. A., & Lakin, K. C. (2001). Behavioral outcomes of deinstitutionalization for people with intellectual disability: A review of U. S. studies conducted between 1980 and 1999. *Journal of Intellectual and Developmental Disability, 26,* 35–50.

Kincaid, C. (1999). Alternative keyboards. *Exceptional Parent, 29*(2), 34–37.

King, B. H., DeAntonio, C., McCracken, J. T., & Forness, S. R. (1994). Psychiatric consultation in severe and profound mental retardation. *American Journal of Psychiatry, 151*(12), 1802–1808.

King, M. (2004). Effects of prenatal drug exposure. Unpublished manuscript, Lynchburg College.

Kirk, S. A. (1964). Research in education. In H. A. Stevens & R. Heber (Eds.), *Mental Retardation.* Chicago: University of Chicago Press.

Knackendofel, E. A., Robinson, S. M., Deshler, D. D., & Schumaker, J. B. (1992). *Collaborative problem solving.* Lawrence, KS: Edge Enterprises.

Knight, T. (2003). Academic access and the family. In P. Kluth, D. M. Straught, & D. P. Biklen (Eds.), *Access to academics for all students: Critical approaches to inclusive curriculum, instruction, and policy* (pp. 49–68). Mahwah, NJ: Erlbaum.

Knox, M., & Hickson, F. (2001). The meanings of close friendship: The views of four people with intellectual disabilities. *Journal of Applied Research in Intellectual Disabilities, 14,* 276–291.

Kobe, F. H., Rojahn, J., & Schroeder, S. R. (1991). Predictors of urgency of out-of-home placement needs. *Mental Retardation, 29*(6), 323–328.

Koch, J. H. (1997). *Robert Guthrie: The PKU story.* Pasadena, CA: Hope.

Koch, R., Friedman, E. C., Azen, C. G., Wenz, E., Parton, P., Ledue, X., & Fishler, K. (1988). Inborn errors of metabolism and the prevention of mental retardation. In F. J. Menolascino & J. A. Stark (Eds.), *Preventive and curative intervention in mental retardation* (pp. 61–90). Baltimore: Brookes.

Koegel, L. K., Koegel, R. L., & Dunlap, G. (Eds.). (1996). *Positive behavioral support: Including people with difficult behavior in the community.* Baltimore: Brookes.

Kolstoe, O. P. (1972). *Mental retardation; An educational viewpoint.* New York: Holt, Rinehart & Winston.

Kolstoe, O. P., & Frey, R. M. (1965). *A high school work study program for mentally subnormal students.* Carbondale, IL: Southern Illinois University Press.

Kopp, C. B., Baker, B. L., & Brown, K. W. (1992). Social skills and their correlates: Preschoolers with developmental disabilities. *American Journal on Mental Retardation, 96,* 357–366.

Kostelnik, M. J., Soderman, A. K., & Whiren, A. P. (1999). *Developmentally appropriate curriculum: Best practices in early childhood education.* Upper Saddle River, NJ: Merrill/Prentice Hall.

Krauss, M. W., Seltzer, M. M., Gordon, R., & Friedman, D. H. (1996). Binding ties: The roles of adult siblings of persons with mental retardation. *Mental Retardation, 34*(2), 83–93.

Kregel, J. (2004). Designing instructional programs. In P. Wehman and J. Kregel (Eds.), *Functional curriculum for elementary, middle, and secondary age students with special needs* (2nd ed., pp. 37–66). Austin, TX: PRO-ED.

Krupski, A. (1986). Attentional problems in youngsters with learning handicaps. In J. K. Torgeson & B. Y. L. Wong (Eds.), *Psychological and educational perspectives on learning disabilities* (pp. 161–192). Orlando, FL: Academic Press.

Krupski, A. (1987). Attention: The verbal phantom strikes again—A response to Samuels. *Exceptional Children, 54*(1), 62–65.

Kubiszyn, T., & Borich, G. (2002). *Educational testing and measurement: Classroom application and practice* (7th ed.). New York: HarperCollins.

Kübler-Ross, E. (1969). *On death and dying.* New York: Macmillan.

Lachiewicz, A., Harrison, C., Spiridigliozzi, G. A., Callanan, N. P., & Livermore, J. (1988). What is the fragile X syndrome? *North Carolina Medical Journal, 49,* 203–208.

LaDue, R., & Dunne, T. (1997). Legal issues and FAS. In A. Streissguth & J. Kanter (Eds.), *The challenge of fetal alcohol syndrome: Overcoming secondary disabilities* (pp. 146–161). Seattle: University of Washington Press.

Lahm, E. A., & Nickels, B. L. (1999). Assistive technology competencies for special educators. *Teaching Exceptional Children, 32*(1), 56–63.

Lakin, K. C., & Bruininks, R. H. (1985). Challenges to advocates of social integration of developmentally disabled persons. In K. C. Lakin & R. H. Bruininks (Eds.), *Strategies for achieving community integration of developmentally disabled citizens* (pp. 313–330). Baltimore: Brookes.

Lakin, K. C., Bruininks, R. H., & Larson, S.A. (1992). The changing face of residential services. In L. Rowitz (Ed.), *Mental retardation in the year 2000* (pp. 197–250). New York: Springer-Verlag.

Lakin, K. C., Larson, S. A., Prouty, R. W., & Coucouvanis, K. (2003). Characteristics and movement of residents of large state facilities. In R. W. Prouty, G. Smith, & K. C. Lakin (Eds.), *Residential services for persons with developmental disabilities: Status and trends through 2002.* Minneapolis: University of Minnesota, Institute on Community Integration, Research and Training Center on Community Living.

Lambert, N., Nihira, K., & Leland, H. (1993a). *AAMR Adaptive Behavior Scale—School* (2nd ed.). Austin, TX: PRO-ED.

Lambert, N., Nihira, K., & Leland, H. (1993b). *AAMR Adaptive Behavior Scale—School (2nd ed.): Technical manual.* Austin, TX: PRO-ED.

Larry P. v. Riles, No. C-71-2270 R.F.P., 1992 Lexis 13677 (N.D. Cal. 1992).

Larson, S. A. (1991). Quality of life for people with challenging behavior living in community settings. *Impact, 4*(1), 4–5.

Larson, S. A., & Lakin, K. C. (1989). Deinstitutionalization of persons with mental retardation: Behavioral outcomes. *Journal of the Association for Persons with Severe Handicaps, 14*(4), 324–332.

Larson, S. A., Lakin, K. C., Anderson, L., Kwak, N., Lee, J. H., & Anderson, D. (2000a). *Final report: Center on emergent disability.* Minneapolis: University of Minnesota, Institute on Community Integration.

Larson, S. A., Lakin, K. C., Anderson, L., Kwak, N., Lee, J. H., & Anderson, D. (2000b). Prevalence of mental retardation and/or developmental disabilities: Analysis of the 1994–1995 NHIS-D. *MR/DD Data Brief, 1*(2). Minneapolis: University of Minnesota, Institute on Community Integration, Research and Training Center on Community Living.

Larson, S. A., Lakin, K. C., & Huang, J. (2003). *DD data brief: Service use by and needs of adults with functional limitations or ID/DD in the NHIS-D: Difference by age, gender, and disability.* Minneapolis: University of Minnesota, Institute on Community Integration, Research and Training Center on Community Integration.

Laski, F., & Keefe, K. (1997). The ADA in the justice system. *Impact, 10*(2), 2–3. (ERIC Document Reproduction Service No. ED411627)

Laurent, J., Swerdlik, M., & Ryburn, M. (1992). Review of validity research on the Stanford-Binet Intelligence Scale: Fourth Edition. *Psychological Assessment, 4*(1), 102–112.

Lavor, M.L. (1977). Federal legislation for exceptional children: Implications and a view of the field. In R. D. Kneedler & S. G. Tarver (Eds.), *Changing perspectives in special education* (pp. 245–270). Upper Saddle River, NJ: Merrill/Macmillan.

Lazar, I., Darlington, R., Murray, H., Royce, J., & Snipper, A. (1982). Lasting effects of early education: A report from the consortium for longitudinal studies. *Monographs of the Society for Research in Child Development, 47,* 2–3 (Serial No. 195).

Leal, L. (1999). *A family centered approach to people with mental retardation.* Washington, DC: American Association on Mental Retardation.

Lee, T. (1998, March–April). You probably won't like James Watson's ideas about us. *Ragged Edge,* p. 16.

Leffert, J. S., & Siperstein, G. N. (1996). Assessment of social-cognitive processes in children with mental retardation. *American Journal on Mental Retardation, 100*(5), 441–445.

Lehr, D. M., & Brown, F. (1984). Perspectives on the severely handicapped. In E. L. Meyden (Ed.), *Mental retardation: Topics of today and issues of tomorrow* (pp. 41–65). Reston, VA: Council for Exceptional Children.

Lejeune, J., Gautier, M., & Turpin, R. (1959). Etudes des chromosomes somatiques de neuf enfants mongoliers. *Academie de Science, 248,* 1721–1722.

Leland, H. W. (1978). Theoretical considerations of adaptive behavior. In W. A. Coulter & H. W. Morrow (Eds.), *Adaptive behavior: Concepts and measurements* (pp. 21–44). Orlando, FL: Grune & Stratton.

Lemperle, G. (1985). Plastic surgery. In D. Lane & B. Stratford (Eds.), *Current approaches to Down's syndrome* (pp. 131–145). New York: Holt, Rinehart & Winston.

Lemperle, G., & Rada, D. (1980). Facial plastic surgery in children with Down's syndrome. *Plastic and Reconstructive Surgery, 66,* 337–342.

Lerner, J. W. (2000). *Learning disabilities: Theories, diagnoses, and teaching strategies.* Boston: Houghton Mifflin.

Lerner, J. W., Lowenthal, B., & Egan, R. W. (2003). *Preschool children with special needs: Children at-risk and children with disabilities* (2nd ed.). Boston: Pearson Education.

Lesar, S. (1998). Use of assistive technology with young children with disabilities: Current status and training needs. *Journal of Early Intervention, 21*(2), 146–159.

Lesch, M., & Nyhan, W. L. (1964). A familial disorder of uric acid metabolism and central nervous system function. *American Journal of Medicine, 36,* 561–570.

Levesque, R. J. (1996). Regulating the private relations of adults with mental disabilities: Old laws, new policies, hollow hopes. *Behavioral Sciences and the Law, 14*(1), 83–106.

Levitas, A. S. (1998). MR syndromes: Phenylketonuria (PKU) and the hyperphenylalanineisma II. *Mental Health Aspects of Developmental Disabilities, 1,* 113–118.

Levitas, A. S., & Gilson, S. F. (2001). Predictable crises in the lives of people with mental retardation. *Mental Health Aspects of Mental Retardation, 4,* 89–100.

Lewis, R. B. (1993). *Special education technology: Classroom applications.* Pacific Grove, CA: Brooks/Cole.

Lewis, R. B. (1998). Assistive technology and learning disabilities: Today's realities and tomorrow's promises. *Journal of Learning Disabilities, 31*(1), 16–26.

Libby, J. D., Polloway, E. A., & Smith, J. D. (1983). Lesch-Nyhan syndrome: A review. *Education and Training of the Mentally Retarded, 18,* 226–231.

Lilly, S. M. (1986). The relationship between good general and special education: A new face on an old issue. *Counterpoint, 10,* 1.

Linder, T. W. (1990). *Transdisciplinary play-based assessment.* Baltimore: Brookes.

Lindley, L. (1990). Defining TASH: A mission statement. *TASH Newsletter, 16*(8), 1.

Llewellyn, G., Dunn, P., Fante, M., Turnbull, L., & Grace, R. (1999). Family factors influencing out-of-home placement decisions. *Journal of Intellectual Disability Research, 43*(3), 219–233.

Lohrmann-O'Rourke, S., & Browder, D. M. (1998). Empirically based methods to assess the preferences of individuals with severe disabilities. *American Journal on Mental Retardation, 103*(92), 146–161.

Losardo, A., & Notari-Syverson, A. (2001). *Alternative approaches to assessing young children.* Baltimore: Brookes.

Lovell, R. W., & Reiss, A. L. (1993). Dual diagnosis: Psychiatric disorders in developmental disabilities. *Pediatric Clinics of North America, 40,* 579–592.

Lower, T. A. (1999). Intellectual disabilities: Have we lost our senses? *Mental Retardation, 37,* 498–503.

Lubin, R. A., Schwartz, A. A., Zigmond, W. B., & Janicki, M. P. (1982). Community acceptance of residential programs for developmentally disabled persons. *Applied Research in Mental Retardation, 3,* 191–200.

Luckasson, R., Borthwick-Duffy, S., Buntinx, W. H. E., Coulter, D., Ellis, E. M., Reeve, A., Schalock, R., Snell, M., Spitalnik, D., Spreate, S., & Tassé, M. J. (2002). *Mental retardation: Definition, classification, and systems of support.* Washington, DC: American Association on Mental Retardation.

Luckasson, R., Coulter, D. L., Polloway, E. A., Reiss, S., Schalock, R. L., Snell, M. E., Spitalnik, D. M., & Stark, J. A. (1992a). *Mental retardation: Definition, classification, and systems of support* (9th ed.). Washington, DC: American Association on Mental Retardation.

Luckasson, R., Coulter, D., Polloway, E. A., Reiss, S., Schalock, R., Snell, M., Spitalnik, D., & Stark, J. (1992b). *Mental retardation: Definition, diagnosis, and systems of support.* Washington, DC: American Association on Mental Retardation.

Luckasson, R., & Reeve, A. (2001). Naming, defining, and classifying in mental retardation. *Mental Retardation, 39*(1), 47–52.

Lue, M. S., & Green, C. E. (2000). No easy walk: African American educators coping with their own children with special needs. *Multiple Voices, 4*(1), 30–40.

Luiselli, J. K. & Cameron, M. J. (Eds.). (1998). *Antecedent control: Positive approaches to behavioral support.* Baltimore: Brookes.

Lumsden, C. J., & Wilson, E. O. (1985). The relation between biological and cultural evolution. *Journal of Social Biology Structures, 8,* 343–359.

Lund, K. A., & Bos, C. S. (1981). Orchestrating the preschool classroom: The early schedule. *Teaching Exceptional Children, 14,* 121–125.

Luria, A. R. (1980). *Higher cortical functions in man* (2nd ed., revised and expanded) (B. Haigh, Trans.). New York: Basic Books.

Lustig, D. (2002). Family coping in families with a child with a disability. *Education and Training in Mental Retardation and Developmental Disabilities, 37*(1), 14–21.

MacArthur, C. A. (1996). Using technology to enhance the writing processes of students with learning disabilities. *Journal of Learning Disabilities, 29*(4), 344–354.

MacArthur, C. A., Graham, S., & Schwartz, S. (1991). Knowledge of revision and revising behavior among students with learning disabilities. *Learning Disability Quarterly, 14,* 61–73.

Mackintosh, N. J. (1998). *IQ and human intelligence.* New York: Oxford University Press.

MacMillan, D. L. (1971). Special education for the mildly retarded: Servant or savant. *Focus on Exceptional Children, 2*(9), 1–11.

MacMillan, D. L. (1982). *Mental retardation in school and society* (2nd ed.). Boston: Little, Brown.

MacMillan, D. L. (1989). "New" EMRs. In G. A. Robinson, J. R. Patton, E. A. Polloway, & L. R. Sargent (Eds.), *Best practices in mental retardation* (pp. 1–20). Reston, VA: Council for Exceptional Children, Division on Mental Retardation and Developmental Disabilities.

MacMillan, D. L., & Balow, I. H. (1991). Impact of *Larry P.* on education programs and assessment practices in California. *Diagnostique, 17,* 57–69.

MacMillan, D. L., & Borthwick, S. (1980). The new educable mentally retarded population: Can they be mainstreamed? *Mental Retardation, 18,* 155–158.

MacMillan, D. L., Gresham, F. M., & Siperstein, G. N. (1993). Conceptual and psychometric concerns over the 1992 AAMR definition of mental retardation. *American Journal on Mental Retardation, 98,* 325–335.

MacMillan, D. L., Gresham, F. M., & Siperstein, G. N. (1996). A challenge to the viability of mild mental retardation as a diagnostic category. *Exceptional Children, 62,* 356–371.

MacMillan, D. L., & Reschly, D. J. (1998). Overrepresentation of minority students: The case for greater specificity or reconsideration of the variables examined. *Journal of Special Education, 32,* 15–24.

Maes, B., Fryns, J. P., Ghesquiere, Q., & Borghgraef, M. (2000). Phenotypic checklist to screen for fragile X syndrome in people with mental retardation. *Mental Retardation, 38,* 207–215.

Male, M. (2003). *Technology for inclusion: Meeting the special needs of all students* (4th ed.). Boston: Allyn & Bacon.

Maloney, M. P., & Ward, M. P. (1978). *Mental retardation and modern society.* New York: Oxford University Press.

Malson, L. (1972). *Wolf children.* New York: Monthly Review Press.

Mamlin, N., Harris, K. R., & Case, L. P. (2001). A methodological analysis of research on locus of control and learning disabilities: Rethinking a common assumption. *Journal of Special Education, 34,* 214–225.

Mandlawitz, M. (2006). *What every teacher should know about IDEA 2004.* Boston: Allyn & Bacon.

Mann, B. (2003). Fetal alcohol syndrome. Unpublished manuscript, Lynchburg College, Lynchburg, VA.

Manni, J. L., Winikur, D. W., & Keller, M. (1980). *The status of minority group representation special education programs in the state of New Jersey.* Trenton: New Jersey State Department of Education. (ERIC Document Reproduction Service No. ED203575)

Mansell, J., & Ericsson, K. (Eds.). (1996). *Deinstitutionalization and community living: Intellectual disability services in Britain, Scandinavia, and the USA.* London: Chapman & Hall.

Mar, H. H., & Sall, N. (1999). Profiles of the expressive communication skills of children and adolescents with severe cognitive disabilities. *Education and Training in Mental Retardation and Developmental Disabilities, 34*(1), 77–89.

Marchetti, A. G. (1987). *Wyatt v. Stickney:* A consent decree. *Research in Developmental Disabilities, 8,* 249–259.

Marino, P. E., Landrigan, P. J., Graef, J., Nussbaum, A., Bayan, G., Boch, K., & Boch, S. (1990). A case report of lead poisoning during renovation of a Victorian farmhouse. *American Journal of Public Health, 80,* 1183.

Martin, J. E., & Huber Marshall, L. H. (1996). *Choicemaker self-determination transition assessment.* Longmont, CO: Sopris West.

Masland, R., Sarason, S., & Gladwin, T. (1958). *Mental subnormality.* New York: Basic Books.

Massie, R. K. (1967). *Nicholas and Alexandra.* New York: Atheneum.

Matthews, W. S., Barabas, G., Cusack, E., & Ferrari, M. (1986). Social quotients of children with phenylketonuria before and after discontinuation of dietary therapy. *American Journal of Mental Deficiency, 91,* 92–94.

Mauer, S. (1997). Struggling with the definition issue: A state level perspective. *Education and Training in Mental Retardation and Developmental Disabilities, 32,* 191–193.

Max M. v. Thompson, 566 F. Supp. 1330, 592 F. Supp. 1437, 592 F. Supp. 1450 (N.D. Ill. 1984).

May, D. C. (1988). Plastic surgery for children with Down syndrome: Normalization or extremism? *Mental Retardation, 26,* 17–19.

May, D. C., & Turnbull, N. (1992). Plastic surgeons' opinions of facial surgery for individuals with Down syndrome. *Mental Retardation, 30,* 29–33.

Mayo, L. W. (1962). *A proposed program for national action to combat mental retardation.* Report to the President's Committee on Mental Retardation. Washington, DC: U.S. Government Printing Office.

McBride, J. W., & Forgnone, C. (1985). Emphasis of instruction provided LD, EH, and EMR students in categorized and cross-categorical programming. *Journal of Research and Development in Education, 18*(4), 50–54.

McCabe, M. P., & Cummins, R. A. (1996). The sexual knowledge, experience, feelings, and needs of people with mild intellectual disability. *Education and Training in Mental Retardation and Developmental Disabilities, 31,* 13–21.

McCarney, S. B. (1995). *Adaptive Behavior Evaluation Scale: Revised.* Columbia, MO: Hawthorne Educational Services.

McCarthy, M. M. (1983). The *Pennhurst and Rowley* decisions: Issues and implications. *Exceptional Children, 49,* 517–522.

McClean, M., Bailey, D. B., & Wolery, M. (1996). *Assessing infants and preschoolers with special needs.* Upper Saddle River, NJ: Merrill/Prentice Hall.

McConnell, S. R. (2000). Assessment in early intervention and early childhood special education: Building on the past to project into our future. *Topics in Early Childhood Special Education, 20*(1), 43–48.

McDaniel, G. (1977). Successful programs for young handicapped children. *Educational Horizons, 56*(1), 26–27, 30–33.

McGrew, K. S., & Bruininks, R. H. (1990). The factor structure of adaptive behavior. *School Psychology Review, 18,* 64–81.

McGrew, K. S., Bruininks, R. H., & Johnson, D. R. (1996). Confirmatory factor analytic investigation of Greenspan's model of personal competence. *American Journal on Mental Retardation, 100*(5), 533–545.

McHale, J. (1980). Mental retardation and the future: A conceptual approach. In S. C. Plog & M. B. Santamour (Eds.), *The year 2000 and mental retardation* (pp. 19–70). New York: Plenum.

McKenzie v. Jefferson, 566 F. Supp 43 (D.D.C. 1983).

McKinney, J. D., & Hocutt, A. M. (1988). Policy issues in the evaluation of the Regular Education Initiative. *Learning Disabilities Focus, 4*(1), 15–23.

McLaren, J., & Bryson, S. E. (1987). Review of recent epidemiological studies of mental retardation: Prevalence, associated disorders, and etiology. *American Journal on Mental Retardation, 92,* 243–254.

McLaughlin, M. J., & Warren, S. H. (1994). *Performance assessment and students with disabilities: Usage in outcomes-based accountability systems.* Reston, VA: Council for Exceptional Children.

McLaughlin, P. J., & Wehman, P. (1996). *Mental retardation and developmental disabilities* (2nd ed.). Austin, TX: PRO-ED.

McLean, J. E., & Snyder-McLean, L. (1991). Communicative intent and its realizations among persons with severe intellectual deficits. In N. Krasnegor, D. Rumbaugh, R. Schiefelbusch, & M. Studdert-Kennedy (Eds.), *Biological and behavioral determinants of language development* (pp. 481–508). Hillsdale, NJ: Erlbaum.

McLean, L. K., Brady, N. C., McLean, J. E., & Behrens, G. A. (1999). Communication forms and functions of children and adults with severe mental retardation in community and institutional settings. *Journal of Speech, Language, and Hearing Research, 42*(1), 231–240.

McLean, M., Bailey, D. B., & Wolery, M. (1996). *Assessing infants and preschoolers with special needs.* Upper Saddle River, NJ: Merrill/Prentice Hall.

McNab, T. C., & Blackman, J. A. (1998). When medical complications of the critically ill newborn: Review for early intervention professionals. *Topics in Early Childhood Special Education, 18,* 197–205.

Meisels, S. J. (1996). Charting the continum of assessment and intervention. In S. J. Meisels & E. Fenichel (Eds.), *New visions for the developmental assessment of infants and young children* (pp. 27–52). Washington, DC: Zero to Three National Center for Infants, Toddlers, and Families.

Menolascino, F. J., & Egger, M. L. (1978). *Medical dimensions of mental retardation.* Lincoln: University of Nebraska Press.

Merbler, J. B., Hadadian, A., & Ulman, J. (1999). Using assistive technology in the inclusive classroom. *Preventing School Failure, 43*(3), 113–118. Retrieved February 14, 2000, from Academic Search Elite on the Web site of EBSCO Publishing (http://www.epnet.com/ehost/login.html).

Mercer, C. D., & Snell, M. E. (1977). *Learning theory research in mental retardation: Implications for teaching.* Upper Saddle River, NJ: Merrill/Prentice Hall.

Mercer, J. R. (1973a). *Labeling the mentally retarded.* Berkeley: University of California Press.

Mercer, J. R. (1973b). The myth of 3% prevalence. In G. Tarjan, R. K. Eyman, & C. E. Meyers (Eds.), *Sociobehavioral studies in mental retardation: Monographs of the American Association on Mental Deficiency, 1,* 1–8. Washington, DC: American Association on Mental Deficiency.

Mercer, J. R. (1978). *System of Multicultural Pluralistic Assessment: Parent interview manual.* San Antonio, TX: Psychological Corporation.

Mercer, J. R., & Lewis, J. F. (1982). *Adaptive Behavior Inventory for Children.* San Antonio, TX: Psychological Corporation.

Merrill, E. C. (1990). Attentional resource allocation and mental retardation. In N. W. Bray (Ed.), *International review of research in mental retardation* (Vol. 16, pp. 51–88). San Diego: Academic Press.

Mervis, C. B., Klein-Tasman, B. P., & Mastin, M. E. (2001). Adaptive behavior of 4- through 8-year-old children with Williams syndrome. *American Journal on Mental Retardation, 106,* 82–93.

Messick, S. (1988). The once and future issues of validity: Assessing the meaning and consequences of measurement. In H. Wainer & H. I. Braun (Eds.), *Test validity* (pp. 33–45). Hillsdale, NJ: Erlbaum.

Meyer, D. J., & Vadasy, P. F. (1996). *Living with a brother or sister with special needs* (2nd ed.). Seattle: University of Washington Press.

Meyerowitz, J. H. (1965). Family background of educable mentally retarded children. In H. Goldstein, J. W. Moss, & L. J. Jordan, *The efficacy of special education training on the development of mentally retarded children* (pp. 152–182). Urbana, IL: University of Illinois Institute for Research on Exceptional Children.

Meyers, C. E., & MacMillan, D. L. (1976). Utilization of learning principles in retardation. In R. Koch & J. Dobson (Eds.), *The mentally retarded child and his family: A multidisciplinary handbook* (2nd ed., pp. 323–348). New York: Brunner/Mazel.

Meyers, R., Nihira, K., & Zetlin, A. (1979). The measurement of adaptive behavior. In N. R. Ellis (Ed.), *Handbook of mental deficiency: Psychological theory and research* (2nd ed., pp. 431–481). Hillsdale, NJ: Erlbaum.

Miller, D., Brown, A., & Robinson, L. (2002). Widgets on the Web: Using computer-based learning tools. *Teaching Exceptional Children, 35*(2), 24–28.

Miller, L. K. (1997). *Principles of everyday behavior analysis* (3rd ed.). Pacific Grove, CA: Brooks/Cole.

Mills v. Board of Education of the District of Columbia, 348 F. Supp. 866 (D.D.C. 1972).

Minder, B., Das-Smaal, E. A., & Orlebeke, J. F. (1998). Cognition in children does not suffer from very low lead exposure. *Journal of Learning Disabilities, 31,* 495–502.

Mirfin-Veitch, B., Bray, A., & Ross, N. (2003). It was the hardest and most painful decision of my life! Seeing permanent out-of-home placement for sons and daughters with intellectual disabilities. *Journal of Intellectual and Developmental Disability, 28*(2), 99–111.

Moon, M. S., Inge, K. J., Wehman, P., Brooke, V., & Barcus, J. M. (1990). *Helping persons with severe mental retardation get and keep employment: Supported employment issues and strategies.* Baltimore: Brookes.

Morgan, C. L., Baxter, H., & Kerr, M. P. (2003). Prevalence of epilepsy and associated health service utilization and mortality among patients with intellectual disability. *American Journal on Mental Retardation, 108,* 293–300.

Morgan, D. P., & Rhode, G. (1983). Teachers' attitudes toward IEPs: A two-year follow-up. *Exceptional Children, 50,* 64–67.

Morris, R. J., & Blatt, B. (1986). *Special education: Research and trends.* New York: Pergamon.

Moser, H. W. (2000). Genetics and gene therapies. In M. L. Wehmeyer & J. R. Patton (Eds.), *Mental retardation in the 21st century* (pp. 235–250). Austin, TX: PRO-ED.

Mosier, H. D., Grossman, H. J., & Dingman, H. F. (1965). Physical growth in mental defectiveness. *Pediatrics, 36,* 465–519.

Murphy, C. (1999, June 14). Gay parents find more acceptance. *Washington Post,* p. A1. Retrieved June 16, 2004, from the Washington Post Web site (http://www.washingtonpost.com/wp-srv/local/daily/june99/gays14.htm).

Murphy, S. T., Rogan, P. M., Handley, M., Kincaid, C., & Royce-Davis, J. (2002). People's situations and perspectives eight years after workshop conversion. *Mental Retardation, 40,* 30–40.

Murphy, W. D., Coleman, E. M., & Abel, G. G. (1983). Human sexuality in the mentally retarded. In J. L. Matson & F. Andrasnik (Eds.), *Treatment issues and innovations in mental retardation.* New York: Platinum Press.

Naglieri, J. A. (1985). *Matrix Analogies Test—Expanded Form.* San Antonio, TX: Psychological Corporation.

National Association of Parents and Friends of Mentally Retarded Children. (1950). *Constitution and bylaws.* Minneapolis: Author.

National Center for Education Statistics. (2003). Teachers in public and private elementary and secondary schools, by selected characteristics: 1999–2000. *Digest of Education Statistics, 2002.* Retrieved June 1, 2004, from the NCES Web site (http://nces.ed.gov/programs/digest/d02/tables/dt068.asp).

National Center for Education Statistics. (n.d.). *Enrollment by race/ethnicity for 2001–2002 school year.* Retrieved May 7, 2004, from the NCES Web site (http://nces.ed.gov/ccd/bat/Result.asp?id=493532019&CurPage=2&view=State).

National Council on Disability (NCD). (1993). *Study on the financing of assistive technology devices and services for individuals with disabilities.* A report to the president and the Congress of the United States. Washington, DC: Author.

National Council on Disability (NCD). (2000). *Federal policy barriers to assistive technology.* Retrieved August 8, 2004, from the Web site of the National Council on Disability (http://www.ncd.gov).

National Information Center for Children and Youth with Disabilities (NICHCY). (1988). Children with disabilities: Understanding sibling issues. *NICHCY News Digest, 11.* Retrieved January 15, 2004, from LD OnLine (http://www.Ldonline.org/ld_indepth/family/family-sib1.html).

National Institute of Neurological Disorders and Stroke. (1988). *Developmental speech and language disorders: Hope through research* (NIH Publications Pamphlet No. 88-2757). Bethesda, MD: Author.

National Telecommunications and Information Administration (NTIA). (1999). *Falling through the net: Defining the digital divide.* Retrieved August 8, 2004, from the NTIA Web site (http://www.ntia.doc.gov/ntiahome/fttn99/contents.html).

National Telecommunications and Information Administration (NTIA). (2000). *Falling through the net: Toward digital inclusion.* Retrieved August 8, 2004, from the NTIA Web site (http://www.ntia.doc.gov/ntiahome/fttn99/contents.html).

Nativio, D. G., & Belz, C. (1990). Childhood neurofibromatosis. *Pediatric Nursing, 16,* 575–580.

Neely, C. W. (1991). Family bonds: A mother's story about fragile X syndrome. *LDA/Newsbriefs, 24*(4), 3, 6, 8.

Newcomer, J. R., & Zirkel, P. A. (1999). An analysis of judicial outcomes of special education cases. *Exceptional Children, 65,* 469–480.

New York Association for Retarded Children v. Rockefeller, 357 F. Supp. 752 (E.D. N.Y. 1973). Final consent judgment entered, Civil Nos. 72C 356, 72C 357 (E.D. N.Y. entered May 5, 1975).

Nihira, K. (1999). Adaptive behavior: A historical overview. In R. L. Schalock (Ed.), *Adaptive behavior and its measurement: Implications for the field of mental retardation* (pp. 7–14). Washington, DC: American Association on Mental Retardation.

Nihira, K., Leland, H., & Lambert, N. (1993a). *AAMR Adaptive Behavior Scale—Residential and Community* (2nd ed.). Austin, TX: PRO-ED.

Nihira, K., Leland, H., & Lambert, N. (1993b). *AAMR Adaptive Behavior Scale—Residential and Community (2nd ed.): Technical manual.* Austin, TX: PRO-ED.

Nirje, B. (1969). The normalization principle and its human management implications. In R. B. Krugel & W. Wolfensberger (Eds.), *Changing patterns in residential services for the mentally retarded* (pp. 179–195). Washington, DC: U.S. Government Printing Office.

Nolley, D., & Nolley, B. (1984). Microcomputer data analysis at a clinical mental retardation site. *Mental Retardation, 22,* 85–89.

Noonan, M. J., Brown, F., Mulligan, M., & Rettig, M. A. (1982). Educability of severely handicapped persons: Both sides of the issue. *Journal of the Association for Persons with Severe Handicaps, 7,* 3–12.

Nyhan, W. L. (1976). Behavior in the Lesch-Nyhan syndrome. *Journal of Autism and Childhood Schizophrenia, 6,* 235–252.

Nyhan, W. L., Johnson, H. G., Kaufman, I. A., & Jones, K. (1980). Serotonergic approaches to the modification of behavior in the Lesch-Nyhan syndrome. *Applied Behavior in Mental Retardation, 1,* 25–40.

O'Connor, N. (1975). Imbecility and color blindness. *American Journal of Mental Deficiency, 62,* 83–87.

O'Connor v. Donaldson, 493 F.2d 507 (5th Cir. 1974), vacated and remanded on the issues of immunity, 95 S. Ct. 258b (1975).

Olbrisch, R. R. (1982). Plastic surgical management of children with Down's syndrome: Indications and results. *British Journal of Plastic Surgery, 35,* 195–200.

Olmstead v. L.C. 526 U.S. 1037 (1999).

Olson, J. L., & Platt, J. M. (2000). *Teaching children and adolescents with special needs.* Upper Saddle River, NJ: Merrill/Prentice Hall.

O'Neill, R. E., Horner, R. H., Albin, R. W., Storey, K., & Sprague, J. R. (1990). *Functional analysis of problem behavior: A practical assessment guide.* Sycamore, IL: Sycamore.

Orelove, F. P., & Malatchi, A. (1996). Curriculum and instruction. In F. P. Orelove & D. Sobsey (Eds.), *Educating children with multiple disabilities* (3rd ed.), pp. 377–410. Baltimore: Brookes.

Orelove, F. P., & Sobsey, D. (1996). *Educating children with multiple disabilities: A transdisciplinary approach* (3rd ed., p. 380). Baltimore: Brookes.

Orelove, F. P., & Sobsey, R. (1987). *Multiple disabilities: A transdisciplinary approach.* Baltimore: Brookes.

Osborne, A. G. (1996). *Legal issues in special education.* Boston: Allyn & Bacon.

Parents in Action on Special Education (PASE) v. Hannon, 506 F. Supp. 831. (N.D. Ill. 1980).

Parette, H. P., Brotherson, M. J., Hourcade, J. J., & Bradley, R. H. (1996). Family-centered assistive technology assessment. *Intervention in School and Clinic, 32,* 104–112.

Parette, H. P., Jr., Brotherson, M. J., & Huer, M. B. (2000). Giving families a voice in augmentative and alternative communication decision-making. *Education and Training in Mental Retardation and Developmental Disabilities, 35,* 177–190.

Parette, H. P., & Murdick, N. L. (1998). Assistive technology and IEPs for young children with disabilities. *Early Childhood Education Journal, 25*(3), 193–197.

Parish, S. L., Pomeranz-Essley, A., & Braddock, D. (2003). Family support in the United States: Financing trends and emerging initiatives. *Mental Retardation, 41,* 174–187.

Park, J., & Turnbull, A. P. (2001). Cross-cultural competency and special education: Perceptions and experiences of Korean parents of children with special needs. *Education and Training in Mental Retardation and Developmental Disabilities, 36,* 133–147.

Parker, R. (2001a). *OASIS-3 Aptitude Survey.* Austin, TX: PRO-ED.

Parker, R. (2001b). *OASIS-3 Interest Schedule.* Austin, TX: PRO-ED.

Parsons, C. L., Iacone, T. A., & Rozner, L. (1987). Effect of tongue reduction on articulation in children with Down's syndrome. *American Journal of Mental Deficiency, 91,* 328–332.

Patrick, J. L., & Reschly, D. L. (1982). Relationship of state educational criteria and demographic variables to school-system prevalence of mental retardation. *American Journal of Mental Deficiency, 86,* 351–360.

Patton, J. R. (2003). *Mental retardation and developmental disabilities: An international perspective on terminology.* Presentation at the annual convention of the Council for Exceptional Children, Seattle.

Patton, J. R., Blackbourn, J. M., & Fad, K. S. (1996). *Exceptional individuals in focus* (6th ed.). Upper Saddle River, NJ: Merrill/Prentice Hall.

Patton, J. R., & Dunn, C. (1998). *Transition from school to young adulthood: Basic concepts and recommended practices.* Austin, TX: PRO-ED.

Patton, J. R., Polloway, E. A., & Smith, T. E. C. (2000). Educating students with mild mental retardation. *Focus on Autism and Other Developmental Disorders, 15*(2), 80–89.

Patton, J. R., & Trainor, A. (2003). Using applied academics to enhance curricular reform in secondary education. In C. Kochhar-Bryant, & D. S. Bassett (Eds.), *Aligning transition and standards-based education: Issues and strategies* (pp. 55–76). Arlington, VA: Council for Exceptional Children.

Paul-Brown, D., & Diggs, C. C. (1993). Recognizing and treating speech and language disabilities. *American Rehabilitation, 19*(4), 30–37.

Peck, C. A., Donaldson, J., & Pezzoli, M. (1990). Some benefits nonhandicapped adolescents perceive for themselves from their social relationships with peers who have severe handicaps. *Journal of the Association for Persons with Severe Handicaps, 15*(4), 241–249.

Pedersen, N. L., Plomin, R., Nesselroade, J. R., & McClearn, G. E. (1992). A quantitative genetic analysis of cognitive abilities during the second half of the life span. *Psychological Science, 3,* 346–353.

Pellegrino, L. (1997). Cerebral palsy. In M. L. Batshaw (Ed.), *Children with disabilities* (4th ed., pp. 499–528). Baltimore: Brookes.

Pennsylvania Association for Retarded Children (PARC) v. Commonwealth of Pennsylvania, 334 F. Supp. 1257 (E.D. Pa. 1971), 343 F. Supp. 279 (E.D. Pa. 1972).

Penrose, L. S. (1966). *The biology of mental defect* (Rev. ed.). Orlando, FL: Grune & Stratton.

Petersilia, J. (1998, January). *Persons with developmental disabilities in the criminal justice system: Victims, defendants, and inmates.* Statement prepared for the California Senate Public Safety Committee. Available on the Web site of the University of California at Irvine (http://mrrc.bio.uci.edu/members/peters/testimony/html).

Peterson, K. (2004, March). Supporting the dynamic development of youth with disabilities during transition: A guide for families. *Addressing Trends and Developments in Secondary Education and Transition, 3*(2) retrieved June 30, 2004, from the Web site of NCSET, the National Center on Secondary Education and Transition (http://www.ncset.org/publications/viewdesc.asp?id=1432).

Peterson, K. S. (2004, March 9). Looking straight at gay parents. *USA Today.* Retrieved from the USA Today Web site (http://www.usatoday.com/life/lifestyle/2004-03-09-gay-parents_x.htm).

Philofsky, R., Hepburn, S. L., Hayes, A., Hagerman, R., & Rogers, S. J. (2004). Linguistic and cognitive functioning and autism symptoms in young children with fragile X syndrome. *American Journal on Mental Retardation, 109,* 208–218.

Piaget, J. (1952). *The origins of intelligence in children.* New York: International Universities Press.

Piaget, J. (1969). *The theory of stages in cognitive development.* New York: McGraw-Hill.

Pipitone, P. (1992). Acquired pediatric brain damage: Diverse causes. *Headlines, 3*(5), 5.

Plomin, R. (1994). *Genetics and experience: The interplay between nature and nurture.* Thousand Oaks, CA: Sage.

Plomin, R., & Petrill, S. A. (1997). Genetics and intelligence: What's new? *Intelligence, 24*(1), 53–77.

Polloway, E. A., Epstein, M. H., & Cullinan, D. (1985). Prevalence of behavior problems among mentally retarded students. *Education and Training of the Mentally Retarded, 20,* 3–13.

Polloway, E. A., Epstein, M. H., Patton, J. R., Cullinan, D., & Luebke, J. (1986). Demographic, social, and behavioral characteristics of students with educable mental retardation. *Education and Training of the Mentally Retarded, 21,* 27–34.

Polloway, E. A., Miller, L., & Smith, T. E. C. (2003). *Language instruction for students with disabilities* (3rd ed.). Denver: Love.

Polloway, E. A., & Patton, J. R. (1997). *Strategies for teaching learners with special needs* (6th ed.). Upper Saddle River, NJ: Merrill/Prentice Hall.

Polloway, E. A., Patton, J. R., Epstein, M. H., & Smith, T. E. C. (1989). Comprehensive curriculum for students with mild handicaps. *Focus on Exceptional Children, 21*(8), 8.

Polloway, E. A., & Rucker, H. (1997). Etiology: Biological and environmental considerations. In T. E. C. Smith, C. A. Dowdy, E. A. Polloway, & G. E. Blalock (Eds.), *Children and adults with learning disabilities.* (pp. 160–187). Boston: Allyn & Bacon.

Polloway, E. A., Patton, J. R., & Serna, L. (2001). *Strategies for teaching learners with special needs* (7th ed.). Upper Saddle River, NJ: Merrill/Prentice Hall.

Polloway, E. A., Patton, J. R., & Serna, L. (2005). *Strategies for teaching learners with special needs* (8th ed.). Upper Saddle River, NJ: Merrill/Prentice Hall.

Polloway, E. A., & Smith, J. D. (1983). Changes in mild mental retardation: Population, programs, and perspectives. *Exceptional Children, 50,* 149–159.

Polloway, E. A., & Smith, J. D. (1987). Current status of the mild mental retardation construct: Identification, placement, and programs. In M. C. Wang, M. C. Reynolds, & H. J. Wahlberg (Eds.), *The handbook of special education: Research and practice* (pp. 1–22). New York: Pergamon.

Polloway, E. A., Smith, J. D., Patton, J. R., & Smith, T. E. C. (1996). Historical changes in mental retardation and developmental disabilities. *Education and Training in Mental Retardation and Developmental Disabilities, 31,* 3–12.

Porter, M. E., & Stodden, R. A. (1986). A curriculum-based vocational assessment procedure: Addressing the school-to-work transition needs of secondary schools. *Career Development for Exceptional Individuals, 9,* 121–128.

Powell, L., Houghton, S., & Douglas, J. (1997). Comparison of etiology-specific cognitive functioning profiles for individuals with fragile X and individuals with Down syndrome. *Journal of Special Education, 31,* 362–376.

President's Committee on Mental Retardation. (1969). *The six-hour retarded child.* Washington, DC: U.S. Government Printing Office.

President's Committee on Mental Retardation (PCMR). (1970). *The six-hour retarded child.* Washington, DC: U.S. Government Printing Office.

President's Committee on Mental Retardation (PCMR). (1976). *Mental retardation: The known and the unknown.* Washington, DC: U.S. Government Printing Office.

Prosser, C. L. (1986). *Adaptational biology: Molecules to organisms.* New York: Wiley.

Prouty, R. W., Smith, G., & Lakin, K. C. (2003). *Residential services for persons with developmental disabilities: Status and trends through 2002.* Minneapolis: University of Minnesota, Institute on Community Integration, Research and Training Center on Community Living.

Pueschel, S. M. (1991). Ethical considerations relating to prenatal diagnosis of fetuses with Down syndrome. *Mental Retardation, 29,* 185–190.

Pueschel, S. M. (1997). *Down syndrome.* Available online from the Arc of the United States (http://www.thearc.org/faqs/downsyndrome.doc).

Pugach, M. C., & Johnson, L. J. (1989). Preferral interventions: Progress, problems, and challenges. *Exceptional Challenges, 56,* 217–226.

Quinn, J. M., Sherman, J. A., Sheldon, J. B., Quinn, L. M., & Harchik, A. E. (1992). Social validation of component behaviors of following instructions, accepting criticism, and negotiating. *Journal of Applied Behavior Analysis, 25*(2), 401–413.

Rabasca, L. (1999, November). Knocking down societal barriers for people with disabilities. *APA Monitor, 30*(10), 1, 29.

Rainforth, B., & York, J. (1991). Handling and positioning. In F. Orelove & D. Sobsey (Eds.), *Educating children with multiple disabilities: A transdisciplinary approach* (pp. 79–118). Baltimore: Brookes.

Ramey, C. T., & Campbell, F. A. (1984). Preventive education for high-risk children: Cognitive consequences of the Carolina Abecedarian Project. *American Journal of Mental Deficiency, 88,* 515–523.

Ramey, C. T., & Ramey, S. L. (1992). Effective early intervention. *Mental Retardation, 30,* 337–345.

Ramey, C. T., & Ramey, S. L. (1996). Early intervention: Optimizing development for children with disabilities and risk conditions. In M. L. Wolraich (Ed.), *Disorders of development and learning: A practical guide to assessment and measurement* (2nd ed., p. 147). St. Louis: Mosby.

Rasmussen, S. A., & Friedman, J. M. (1999). NF1 gene and neurofibromatosis type 1. *American Journal of Epidemiology, 151,* 33–40.

Raver, S. A. (1999). *Intervention strategies for infants with special needs: A team approach.* Upper Saddle River, NJ: Merrill/Prentice Hall.

Raymond, E. B. (2000). *Learners with mild disabilities: A characteristic approach.* Boston: Allyn & Bacon.

Rea, P. J., & Davis-Dorsey, J. (2004). ADA in the public school setting. *Journal of Disability Policy Studies, 15*(2), 66–69.

Reber, M., & Borcherding, B. G. (1997). Dual diagnosis: Mental retardation and psychiatric disorders. In M. L. Batshaw (Ed.), *Children with disabilities* (4th ed., pp. 405–424). Baltimore: Brookes.

Reichle, J., & Light, C. (1992). *Positive approaches to managing challenging behavior among persons with developmental disabilities living in the community.* Minneapolis: University of Minnesota, Institute on Community Integration, Research and Training Center on Community Living.

Reichle, J., & Wacker, D. P. (Eds.). (1993). *Communicative alternatives to challenging behavior: Integrating functional assessment and intervention strategies.* Baltimore: Brookes.

Reiss, D. (1981). *The family's construction of reality.* Cambridge, MA: Harvard University Press.

Report gives unbalanced impression of special education practices. (2000, March). *CEC Today, 6,* 1, 9, 15.

Reschly, D. (1985). Best practices: Adaptive behavior. In A. Thomas & J. Grimes (Eds.), *Best practices in school psychology* (pp. 353–368). Kent, OH: National Association of School Psychologists.

Reschly, D. (1988). Incorporating adaptive behavior deficits into instructional programs. In G. A. Robinson, J. R. Patton, E. A. Polloway, & L. R. Sargent (Eds.), *Best practices in mental disabilities* (Vol. 2, pp. 53–80). Des Moines: Iowa State Department of Education.

Reschly, D., Robinson, G., Volmer, L., & Wilson, L. (1988). *Iowa mental disabilities research report: Final report and executive summary.* Des Moines: Iowa State Department of Education.

Reschly, D. J., Myers, T. G., & Hartel, C. R. (Eds.). (2002). *Mental retardation: Determining eligibility for Social Security benefits.* Washington, DC: National Academies Press.

RESNA Technical Assistance Project. (2000). *Tools for 2000: Assistive technology.* Arlington, VA: Author.

Resnick, O. (1988). Nutrition, neurotransmitter regulation, and developmental pharmacology. In F. J. Menolascino & J. A. Stark (Eds.), *Preventive and curative intervention in mental retardation* (pp. 161–176). Baltimore: Brookes.

Resource Center on Substance Abuse Prevention and Disabilities. (1992). *Mental retardation: A look at alcohol and other drug abuse prevention.* Washington, DC: U.S. Department of Health and Human Services, Office for Substance Abuse Prevention.

Reynolds, L. A., & Berkobien, R. (1997). The ARC: Tackling criminal justice issues at national, state, and local levels. *Impact, 10*(2), 8–9. (ERIC Document Reproduction Service No. ED411627)

Reynolds, M. C. (1989). A historical perspective: The delivery of special education to mildly disabled and at-risk students. *Remedial and Special Education, 19*(6), 7–11.

Richardson, S. A., & Koller, H. (1996). *Twenty-two years: Causes and consequences of mental retardation.* Cambridge, MA: Harvard University Press.

Richey, D. D., & Wheeler, J. J. (2000). *Inclusive early childhood education.* Albany, NY: Delmar.

Ridley, M. (2000). *Genome: The autobiography of a species in 23 chapters.* New York: HarperCollins.

Ridley, M. (2003). *Nature via nurture: Genes, experience, and what makes us human.* New York: HarperCollins.

Riordan, J., & Vasa, S. F. (1991). Accommodations for and participation of persons with disabilities in religious practice. *Education and Training in Mental Retardation, 26*(2), 151–155.

Rizzo, A. A., Buckwalter, J. G., McGee, J. S., Bowerly, T., van der Zaag, C., Neumann, U., et al. (2001). Virtual environments for assessing and rehabilitating cognitive/functional performance: A review of projects at the USC Integrated Media Systems Center. *Teleoperators and Virtual Environments, 10*(4), 359–374. Retrieved October 10, 2003, from Academic Search Elite on the Web site of EBSCO Publishing (http://web18.epnet.com/citation.asp?tb=1&ug=dbs+1!ln+en%2DU).

Roach, M. A., Orsmond, G. I., & Barratt, M. S. (1999). Mothers and fathers of children with Down syndrome: Parental stress and involvement in childcare. *American Journal on Mental Retardation, 104*(5), 422–436.

Roberts, C. D., Strough, L. M., & Parrish, L. H. (2002). The role of genetic counseling in the elective termination of pregnancies involving fetuses with disabilities. *Journal of Special Education, 36,* 48–54.

Robinson, N. K., & Robinson, H. B. (1976). *The mentally retarded child* (2nd ed.). New York: McGraw-Hill.

Roblyer, M. D., & Edwards, J. E. (2000). *Integrating educational technology into teaching.* Upper Saddle River, NJ: Merrill/Prentice Hall.

Roblyer, M. D., & Erlanger, W. (1998). Preparing Internet-ready teachers. *Learning and Leading with Technology, 26*(4), 58–61.

Rocklage, L. A., & Lake, M. E. (1998). *Inclusion through infusion: A technology/curriculum partnership for all children.* Retrieved from the Web site of Closing the Gap (http://www.closingthegap.com/cgibin/lib/libDsply.pl?a=1049&b=3).

Rogers, R. C., & Simensen, R. J. (1987). Fragile X syndrome: A common etiology of mental retardation. *American Journal of Mental Deficiency, 91,* 445–449.

Roid, G. H. (2003). *Stanford Binet Intelligence Test* (5th ed.). Itasca, IL: Riverside.

Roid, G. H., & Miller, L. J. (1997). *Leiter International Performance Scale—Revised.* Wood Dale, IL: Stoelting.

Roistacher, R. C., Holstrom, E. I., Cantrill, A. H., & Chase, J. T. (1982). *Toward a comprehensive data system on the demographic and epidemiological characteristics of the handicapped population: Final report.* Washington, DC: National Institute of Handicapped Research. (ERIC Document Reproduction Service No. ED182465)

Romski, M. A., & Sevcik, R. A. (1993). Language learning through augmented means: The process and its products. In A. P. Kaiser & D. B. Gray (Eds.), *Enhancing children's communication: Research foundations for intervention* (Vol. 2, pp. 85–104). Baltimore: Brookes.

Roncker v. Walter, 700 F.2d 1058 (6th Cir. 1983).

Rosen, J. W., & Burchard, S. N. (1990). Community activities and social support networks: A social comparison of adults with and adults without mental retardation. *Education and Training in Mental Retardation, 25,* 193–203.

Rothstein, L. F. (1995). *Special education law.* New York: Longman.

Rotter, J. B. (1954). *Social learning and clinical psychology.* Upper Saddle River, NJ: Merrill/Prentice Hall.

Rovet, J. (1993). The psychoeducational characteristics of children with Turner syndrome and adolescents with insulin-dependent diabetes mellitus. *Journal of Learning Disabilities, 26,* 333–341.

Rowe, D. C. (1995). *The limits of family influence.* New York: Guilford.

Rusch, F. R., Enchelmaier, J. F., & Kohler, P. D. (1994). Employment outcomes and activities for youths in transition. *Career Development for Exceptional Individuals, 17*(1), 1–15.

Rusch, F. R., & Phelps, L. A. (1987). Secondary special education and transition from school to work: A national priority. *Exceptional Children, 53,* 487–492.

Russell, A. T., & Forness, S. R. (1985). Behavioral disturbance in mentally retarded children in TMR and EMR classrooms. *American Journal of Mental Deficiency, 89,* 338–344.

Russo, C. J., Morse, T. E., & Glancy, M. C. (1998). Special education: A legal history and overview. *School Business Affairs, 64*(8), 8–12.

Ryan, C. S., & Coyne, A. (1985). Effects of group homes on neighborhood property values. *Mental Retardation, 23,* 241–245.

Rynders, J. E., & Horrobin, J. M. (1990). Always trainable? Never educable? Updating educational expectations concerning children with Down syndrome. *American Journal on Mental Retardation, 95,* 77–83.

Rynders, J. E., Spiker, D., & Horrobin, J. M. (1978). Underestimating the educability of Down syndrome children: Examination of methodological problems in recent literature. *American Journal of Mental Deficiency, 82,* 440–448.

Sacramento City Unified School District v. Rachel H., 14 F.3d 1398 (9th Cir. 1994).

Safford, P. L., & Safford, E. J. (1996). *A history of childhood and disability.* New York: Teachers College Press.

Salkind, N. J. (1994). *Child development* (7th ed.). Fort Worth, TX: Harcourt Brace.

San Antonio Independent School District v. Rodriguez, 411 U.S. 1 (1973).

Sarason, S. B. (1985). *Psychology and mental retardation: Perspectives in change.* Austin, TX: PRO-ED.

Sattler, J. M. (2001). *Assessment of children: Cognitive applications* (4th ed.). San Diego: Sattler.

Sax, C. L., & Thoma, C. A. (2002). *Transition assessment: Wise practices for quality lives.* Baltimore: Brookes.

Scarr, S., & Carter-Saltzman, L. (1982). Genetics and intelligence. In R. J. Sternberg (Ed.), *Handbook of human intelligence* (pp. 798–896). Cambridge, UK: Cambridge University Press.

Schalock, R. L. (1996). *Quality of life: Vol. 1. Conceptualization and measurement.* Washington, DC: American Association on Mental Retardation.

Schalock, R. L. (Ed.). (1999). *Adaptive behavior and its measurement: Implications for the field of mental retardation.* Washington, DC: American Association on Mental Retardation.

Schalock, R. L., Keith, K. D., Hoffman, K., & Karan, O. C. (1989). Quality of life: Its measurement and use in human service programs. *Mental Retardation, 27,* 25–31.

Schalock, R. L., & Kiernan, W. E. (1990). *Habilitation planning for adults with developmental disabilities.* New York: Springer.

Scheerenberger, R. C. (1983). *A history of mental retardation.* Baltimore: Brookes.

Scheerenberger, R. C. (1987). *A history of mental retardation: A quarter century of promise.* Baltimore: Brookes.

Schleien, S. J., Meyer, L. H., Heyne, L. A., & Brandt, B. B. (1995). *Lifelong leisure skills and lifestyles for persons with developmental disabilities.* Baltimore: Brookes.

Schleien, S. J., Ray, M. T., & Green, F. P. (1996). *Community recreation and people with disabilities: Strategies for inclusion* (2nd ed.). Baltimore: Brookes.

Schloss, P. J., Alper, S., & Jayne, D. (1994). Self-determination for persons with disabilities: Choice, risk, and dignity. *Exceptional Children, 60,* 215–225.

Schoeller, K. (1997). Overcoming barriers to social inclusion. *Impact, 10*(3), 4–5.

Schroeder, S. R. (1999). A review of "Robert Guthrie: The PKU Story" by J. H. Koch. *American Journal on Mental Retardation, 104,* 392–393.

Schultz, D. P., & Schultz, S. E. (1996). *A history of modern psychology* (6th ed.). San Diego: Harcourt Brace.

Schultz, F. R. (1983). Phenylketonuria and other metabolic diseases. In J. A. Blackman (Ed.), *Medical aspects of developmental disabilities in children birth to three* (pp. 197–201). Iowa City: University of Iowa Press.

Schultz, J. B., & Carpenter, C. D. (1995). *Mainstreaming exceptional students* (4th ed.). Needham Heights, MA: Allyn & Bacon.

Schumaker, J. B., & Deshler, D. D. (1988). Implementing the regular education initiative in secondary schools: A different ball game. *Journal of Learning Disabilities, 21,* 36–42.

Schwier, K. M., & Hingsburger, D. (2000). *Sexuality: Your sons and daughters with mental disabilities.* Baltimore: Brookes.

Scott, E., Smith, T. E. C., Hendricks, M. C., & Polloway, E. A. (1999). Prader-Willi syndrome: A review and implications for educational intervention. *Education and Training in Mental Retardation and Developmental Disabilities, 34,* 110–116.

Scudder, R. R., & Tremain, D. H. (1992). Repair behaviors of children with and without mental retardation. *Mental Retardation, 30,* 277–282.

Searcy, Y. M., Lincoln, A. J., Rose, F. E., Bavar, N., Korenberg, J. R., & Klima, E. (2004). The relationship between age and IQ in Williams syndrome. *American Journal on Mental Retardation, 109,* 231–236.

Seguin, E. O. (1846). *Traitement moral, hygiene et education des idiots et des autres enfants arrières.* Paris: Baillier.

Seligman, M. E. (1975). *Helplessness: On depression, development, and death.* San Francisco: Freeman.

Seltzer, M. M. (1984). Correlates of community opposition to community residences for mentally retarded persons. *American Journal of Mental Deficiency, 89*(1), 1–8.

Semmel, M. A., Abernathy, T. V., Butera, G., & Lesar, S. (1991). Teacher perceptions of the regular education initiatives. *Exceptional Children, 58,* 9–24.

Sewall, A. M., & Balkman, K. (2002). DNR orders and school responsibility. *Remedial and Special Education, 23,* 7–14.

Sherman, J. A., Sheldon, J. B., Harchik, A. E., Edwards, K., & Quinn, J. M. (1992). Social evaluation of behaviors comprising three social skills and a comparison of the performance of people with and without mental retardation. *American Journal on Mental Retardation, 96,* 419–431.

Showers, B. (1985). Teachers coaching teachers. *Educational Leadership, 42*(7), 789–797.

Simeonsson, R. J., Granlund, M., & Bjorck-Akesson, E. (2003). Classifying mental retardation: Impairment, disability, handicap, limitations, or restrictions. In H. N. Switzky & S. Greenspan (Eds.), *What is mental retardation: Ideas for an evolving disability* (pp. 309–329). Washington, DC: American Association on Mental Retardation.

Simmerman, S., Blacher, J., & Baker, B. L. (2001). Fathers' and mothers' perceptions of father involvement in families with young children with a disability. *Journal of Intellectual and Developmental Disability, 26,* 325–338.

Sinsheimer, R. (1969). The prospect of designed genetic change. *Engineering and Science, 32,* 7, 8–13.

Sitlington, P. L., & Clark, G. M. (2006). *Transition education and services for students with disabilities* (4th ed.). Boston: Allyn & Bacon.

Sitlington, P. L., Clark, G. M., & Kolstoe, O. P. (2000). *Transition education and services for adolescents with disabilities* (3rd ed.). Boston: Allyn & Bacon.

Skeels, H. M. (1942). A study of the effects of differential stimulation on mentally retarded children: A follow-up report. *American Journal of Mental Deficiency, 46,* 340–350.

Skeels, H. M., & Dye, H. B. (1939). A study of the effects of differential stimulation on mentally retarded children. *Convention Proceedings of the American Association on Mental Deficiency, 44,* 114–136.

Skeels, H. M., & Skodak, M. (1966). Adult status of children with contrasting early life experiences: A follow-up study. *Monographs of the Society for Research in Child Development, 31,*(3, Serial No. 105).

Skinner, B. F. (1953). *Science and human behavior.* New York: Macmillan.

Skinner, D., Bailey, D. B., Correa, V., & Rodriguez, P. (1999). Narrating self and disability: Latino mothers' construction of identities vis-à-vis their child with special needs. *Exceptional Children, 65,* 481–495.

Skrtic, T. M. (1991). The special education paradox: Equity as a way to excellence. *Harvard Educational Review, 61*(2), 148–206.

Smith, B. J., & Strain, P. S. (1984). *The argument for early intervention* [Fact sheet]. Reston, VA: Council for Exceptional Children.

Smith, D. W., & Wells, M. W. (1983). Use of a microcomputer to assist staff in documenting resident progress. *Mental Retardation, 21,* 111–115.

Smith, H. W., & Kennedy, W. A. (1967). Effects of three educational programs on mentally retarded children. *Perceptual and Motor Skills, 24,* 174.

Smith, J. D. (1981). Down's syndrome, amniocentesis, and abortion: Prevention or elimination? *Mental Retardation, 19,* 8–11.

Smith, J. D. (1985). *Minds made feeble: The myth and legacy of the Kallikaks.* Rockville, MD: Aspen Systems.

Smith, J. D. (1987). *The other voices: Profiles of women in the history of special education.* Seattle: Special Child.

Smith, J. D. (1988, September). CEC-MR position statement on the right of children with mental retardation to life sustaining medical care and treatment. *CEC-MReport, 2.*

Smith, J. D. (1989). On the right of children with mental retardation to life-sustaining medical care and treatment: A position statement. *Education and Training in Mental Retardation, 24,* 3–6.

Smith, J. D. (1995). *Pieces of purgatory: Mental retardation in and out of institutions.* Pacific Grove, CA: Brooks-Cole.

Smith, J. D. (1997). Mental retardation as an educational construct: Time for a new shared view? *Education and Training in Mental Retardation and Developmental Disabilities, 32,* 167–173.

Smith, J. D. (2002). The myth of mental retardation: Paradigm shifts, disaggregation, and developmental disabilities. *Mental Retardation, 40,* 62–64.

Smith, J. D. (2003). Constructing and deconstructing mental retardation. In H. N. Switzky & S. Greenspan (Eds.), *What is mental retardation: Ideas for an evolving disability* (pp. 87–96). Washington, DC: American Association on Mental Retardation.

Smith, J. D., & Mitchell, A. L. (2001). "Me? I'm not a drooler. I'm the assistant": Is it time to abandon mental retardation as a classification? *Mental Retardation, 39,* 144–146.

Smith, J. E., & Payne, J. S. (1980). *Teaching exceptional adolescents.* Upper Saddle River, NJ: Merrill/Prentice Hall.

Smith, S. W. (1990). Individualized education programs (IEPs) in special education—From intent to acquiescence. *Exceptional Children, 57,* 6–14.

Smith, T. E. C., Polloway, E. A., Patton, J. R., & Dowdy, C. A. (2001). *Teaching students with special needs in inclusive settings* (3rd ed.). Needham Heights, MA: Allyn & Bacon.

Smith, T. E. C., Polloway, E. A., Patton, J. R., & Dowdy, C. (2004). *Teaching students with special needs in inclusive settings* (4th ed.). Boston: Allyn & Bacon.

Snell, M. E. (1993). *Instruction of students with severe disabilities.* Upper Saddle River, NJ: Merrill/Prentice Hall.

Snell, M. E. (2000). *Instruction of students with severe disabilities* (5th ed.). Upper Saddle River, NJ: Merrill/Prentice Hall.

Sobsey, D. (1997). Equal protection of the law for crime victims with developmental disabilities. *Impact, 10*(2), 6–7. (ERIC Document Reproduction No. ED411627)

Sobsey, D., & Doe, T. (1991). Patterns of sexual abuse and assault. *Sexuality and Disability, 9,* 243–259.

Sorenson, D. D. (1997). The invisible victims. *Impact, 10*(2), 1, 26. (ERIC Document Reproduction No. ED411627)

Soto, G., Belfiore, P. J., Schlosser, R. W., & Haynes, C. (1993). Teaching specific requests: A comparative analysis on skill acquisition and preference using two augmentative and alternative communication aids. *Education and Training in Mental Retardation, 28*(2), 169–178.

Sparrow, S. S., Cicchetti, D. V., & Balla, D. A. (2005). *Vineland Adaptive Behavior Scales* (2nd ed.). Circle Pines, MN: American Guidance Service.

Spearman, C. E. (1927). *The abilities of man.* New York: Macmillan.

Spinath, F. M., Harlaar, N., Ronald, A., & Plomin, R. (2004). Substantial genetic influence on mild mental impairment in early childhood. *American Journal on Mental Retardation, 109,* 34–43.

Spitz, H. H. (1966). The role of input organization in the learning and memory of mental retardates. *International Review of Research in Mental Retardation, 2,* 29–56.

Spitz, H. H. (1973). Consolidating facts into the schematized learning and memory of mental retardates. *International Review of Research in Mental Retardation, 6,* 149–168.

Spitz, H. H. (1979). Beyond field theory in the study of mental deficiency. In N. R. Ellis (Ed.), *Handbook of mental deficiency: Psychological theory and research* (2nd ed., pp. 121–141). Hillsdale, NJ: Erlbaum.

Spradlin, J. E. (1968). Environmental factors and the language development of retarded children. In S. Rosenberg & J. H. Koplin (Eds.), *Developments in applied psycholinguistic research* (pp. 261–290). New York: Macmillan.

Spring, J. H. (1986). *The American school 1642–1985.* New York: Longman.

Staddon, J. E. (1983). *Adaptive behavior and learning.* New York: Cambridge University Press.

Stark, J. A., & Goldsbury, T. L. (1990). Quality of life from childhood to adulthood. In R. L. Schalock (Ed.), *Quality of life: Perspectives and issues* (pp. 71–83). Washington, DC: American Association on Mental Retardation.

Stark, J. A., Menolascino, F. J., & Goldsbury, T. L. (1988). An updated search for the prevention of mental retardation. In F. J. Menolascino & J. A. Stark (Eds.), *Preventive and curative intervention in mental retardation* (pp. 3–25). Baltimore: Brookes.

State of Connecticut, Department of Education. (2000). *Guidelines for identifying children with intellectual disability/mental retardation.* Hartford: Author.

Steere, D. E., & Burcoff, T. L. (2004). Living at home: Skills for independence. In P. Wehman & J. Kregel (Eds.), *Functional curriculum for elementary, middle, and secondary age students with special needs* (2nd ed., p. 297). Austin, TX: PRO-ED.

Stephens, W. E. (1966). Category usage of normal and subnormal children on three types of categories. *American Journal of Mental Deficiency, 71,* 266–273.

Stephens, W. E. (1972). Equivalence formation by retarded and nonretarded children at different mental ages. *American Journal of Mental Deficiency, 77,* 311–313.

Stephenson, J. R., & Dowrick, M. (2000). Parent priorities in communication intervention for young students with severe disabilities. *Education and Training in Mental Retardation and Developmental Disabilities, 35,* 25–35.

Sternberg, R. J. (1985). *Beyond IQ: A triarchic theory of intelligence.* New York: Cambridge University Press.

Sternberg, R. J. (1988). *The triarchic mind: A new theory of intelligence.* New York: Viking.

Sternberg, R. J. (1997). The triarchic theory of intelligence. In D. P. Flanagan, J. Genshaft, & P. L. Harrison (Eds.), *Contemporary intellectual assessment: Theories, tests, and issues* (pp. 92–104). New York: Guilford.

Sternberg, R. J., & Spear, L. C. (1985). A triarchic theory of mental retardation. *International Review of Research in Mental Retardation, 13,* 301–326.

Stevens, H. A. (1964). Overview of mental retardation. In H. A. Stevens & R. Heber (Eds.), *Mental retardation* (pp. 3–15). Chicago: University of Chicago Press.

Stinnett, T. A., Havey, J. M., & Oehler-Stinnett, J. (1994). Current test usage by practicing school psychologists: A national study. *Journal of Psychoeducational Assessment, 12,* 331–350.

Stipek, D. J. (1993). *Motivation to learn: From theory to practice* (2nd ed.). Boston: Allyn & Bacon.

Stoddard, K. (1992). The changing role of teachers: Refocus on the family. *LD Forum, 17*(1), 15–17.

Stoneman, Z. (1997). Mental retardation and family adaptation. In W. E. MacLean, Jr. (Ed.), *Ellis' handbook of mental deficiency, psychological theory and research* (3rd ed., pp. 405–437). Mahwah, NJ: Erlbaum.

Streissguth, A. (1997). *Fetal alcohol syndrome: A guide to families and communities.* Baltimore: Brookes.

Strully, J. L., & Strully, C. F. (1989). Friendships as an educational goal. In S. Stainback, W. Stainback, & M. Forest (Eds.), *Educating all students in the mainstream of regular education* (pp. 59–68). Baltimore: Brookes.

Study points to unmet technology needs among those with mental retardation. (1999). *Assistive Technology Messenger Newsletter.* Retrieved September 27, 1999, from the Web site of Applied Science and Engineering Laboratories (http://www.asel.udel.edu/dati/Atmessenger/julaugsep98/study.html).

Sugai, G. (1985). Case study: Designing instruction from IEPs. *Teaching Exceptional Children, 17,* 239.

Sundram, C. J. (2004). *Wyatt v. Stickney:* A long odyssey reaches an end. Retrieved September 19, 2004, from the Web site of the American Association on Mental Retardation (http://www.aamr.org/Reading_Room/pdf/wyatt.shtml).

Sundram, C. J., & Stavis, P. F. (1994). Sexuality and mental retardation: Unmet challenges. *Mental Retardation, 32*(4), 255–264.

Swanson, H. L., & Cooney, J. B. (1991). Learning disabilities and memory. In B. Y. L. Wong (Ed.), *Learning about learning disabilities* (pp. 103–127). San Diego: Academic Press.

Symons, F. J., Butler, M. G., Sanders, M. D., Feurer, I. D., & Thompson, T. (1999). Self-injurious behavior and Prader-Willi syndrome: Behavioral forms and body location. *American Journal on Mental Retardation, 104,* 260–269.

Symons, F. J., Clark, R. D., Roberts, J. P., & Bailey, D. B. (2001). Classroom behavior of elementary school-age boys with fragile X syndrome. *Journal of Special Education, 34,* 194–202.

Szasz, T. (1974). *The myth of mental illness: Foundations of a theory of personal conduct.* New York: HarperCollins.

Taylor, A. R., Asher, S. R., & Williams, G. A. (1987). The social adaptation of mainstreamed mildly retarded children. *Child Development, 58,* 1321–1334.

Taylor, H. (1999). Overwhelming majority of Americans continue to support the Americans with Disabilities Act [Harris Poll #50]. Retrieved May 12, 1999, from the Web site of Harris Interactive (http://www.harrisinteractive.com/harris_poll/index.asp?PID=63).

Taylor, R. L. (1990). The *Larry P.* decision a decade later: Problems and future directions. *Mental Retardation, 28*(1), iii–vi.

Taylor, S. J. (1988). Caught in the continuum: A critical analysis of the principle of the least restrictive environment. *Journal of the Association for Persons with Severe Handicaps, 13,* 41–53.

Technology in school and at home. (2000, April). *CEC Today Online, 5*(8). Available on the Web site of the Council for Exceptional Children (http://www.cec.sped.org/bk/cectoday/archives/2000/hometech_april2000.html).

Temple University Developmental Disabilities Center. (1990). *The final report on the 1990 National Consumer Survey of people with developmental disabilities and their families.* Philadelphia: Author.

Terman, L. M. (1916). *The measurement of intelligence.* Boston: Houghton Mifflin.

Terman, L. M., & Merrill, M. A. (1937). *Measuring intelligence: A guide to the administration and scoring of the new revised Stanford-Binet tests of intelligence.* Boston: Houghton Mifflin.

Terman, L. M., & Merrill, M. A. (1960). *The Stanford-Binet Intelligence Scale: Manual for the third revision, Form L-M.* Boston: Houghton Mifflin.

T.G. v. Board of Education of Piscataway, 576 F. Supp. 420 (D.N.J. 1983).

Thomas, R. M. (2001). *Recent theories of human development.* Thousand Oaks, CA: Sage.

Thompson, J. R., Bryant, B., Campbell, E. M., Craig, E. M., Hughes, C., Rotholz, D. A., Schalock, R. L., Silverman, W., & Tassé, M. J. (2004). *Supports Intensity Scale (SIS): User's manual.* Washington, DC: American Association on Mental Retardation.

Thompson, J. R., Hughes, C., Schalock, R. L., Silverman, W., Tassé, M. J., Bryant, B., et al. (2002). Integrating supports in assessment and planning. *Mental Retardation, 40,* 390–405.

Thompson, J. R., McGrew, K. S., & Bruininks, R. H. (1999). Adaptive and maladaptive behavior: Functional and structural characteristics. In R. L. Schalock (Ed.), *Adaptive behavior and its measurement: Implications for the field of mental retardation* (pp. 15–42). Washington, DC: American Association on Mental Retardation.

Thorin, E., Yovanoff, P., & Irvin, L. (1996). Dilemmas faced by families during their young adults' transitions to adulthood: A brief report. *Mental Retardation, 34*(2), 117–120.

Thorndike, E. L. (1927). *The measurement of intelligence.* New York: Columbia University, Teacher's College Press.

Thorndike, R. L., Hagen, E. P., & Sattler, J. P. (1986). *Stanford-Binet Intelligence Scale, 4th Edition.* Chicago: Riverside.

Thorp, E. K. (1997). Increasing opportunities for partnerships with culturally and linguistically diverse families. *Intervention in School and Clinic, 32*(5), 261–269.

Thurstone, L. L. (1938). Primary mental abilities. *Psychometric Monographs,* No. 1.

Tilson, G. P., Luecking, R. G., & Donovan, M. R. (1994). Involving employers in transition: The Bridges model. *Career Development for Exceptional Individuals, 17*(1), 77–89.

Timothy W. v. Rochester School District, 875 F.2d 954 (1st Cir. 1988).

Tomporowski, P. D., & Hager, L. D. (1992). Sustained attention in mentally retarded individuals. In N. W. Bray (Ed.), *International review of research on mental retardation* (Vol. 18, pp. 111–136). New York: Academic Press.

Tomporowski, P. D., & Simpson, R. G. (1990). Sustained attention and intelligence. *Intelligence, 14,* 27–38.

Tomporowski, P. D., & Tinsley, V. (1994). Effects of target probability and memory demands on the vigilance of adults with and without mental retardation. *American Journal on Mental Retardation, 96,* 525–530.

Trainor, A., Patton, J., & Clark, G. (2005). *Case studies in transition.* Austin, TX: PRO-ED.

Tredgold, A. F. (1937). *A textbook of mental deficiency.* Baltimore: Wood.

Trent, J. W. (1994). *Inventing the feeble mind: A history of mental retardation in the United States.* Berkeley: University of California Press.

Turkington, C. (1987). Special talents. *Psychology Today, 20,* 42–46.

Turnbull, A. P. (1982). Preschool mainstreaming: A policy and implementation analysis. *Education, Evaluation, and Policy Analysis, 4*(3), 281–291.

Turnbull, A. P., & Turnbull, H. R. (2001). *Families, professionals, and exceptionality: A special partnership* (4th ed.). Upper Saddle River, NJ: Merrill/Prentice Hall.

Turnbull, A. P., Turnbull, H. R., III, Shank, M., & Leal, D. (1995). *Exceptional lives: Special education in today's schools.* Upper Saddle River, NJ: Merrill/Prentice Hall.

Turnbull, H. R. (1998). *Free appropriate public education: The law and children with disabilities.* Denver: Love.

Turnbull, H. R., III, & Turnbull, A. P. (2000). *Free appropriate public education: The law and children with disabilities* (6th ed.). Denver: Love.

Turnbull, H. R., III, & Turnbull, A. P. (2001). *Families, professionals, and exceptionality: Collaborating for empowerment* (4th ed.). Upper Saddle River, NJ: Merrill/Prentice Hall.

Turnure, J., & Zigler, E. (1964). Outer-directedness in the problem solving of normal and retarded children. *Journal of Abnormal and Social Psychology, 69,* 427–436.

Umansky, W., & Hooper, S. R. (1998). *Young children with special needs.* Upper Saddle River, NJ: Merrill/Prentice-Hall.

Underwood, J. K., & Mead, J. F. (1995). *Legal aspects of special education and pupil services.* Boston: Allyn & Bacon.

University of Minnesota, Research and Training Center on Community Integration. (1999). *Questions to ask providers when making decisions about residential supports for family members with disabilities.* Minneapolis: Author.

U.S. Census Bureau. (1998). U.S. Government Printing Office.

U.S. Census Bureau. (2003a, October). Language use and English speaking ability: 2000. *Census 2000 Brief.* Retrieved May 25, 2004, from the Web site of the U. S. Census Bureau (http://www.census.gov/population/www/cen2000/briefs.html).

U.S. Census Bureau. (2003b, October). Marital status: 2000. *Census 2000 Brief.* Retrieved May 25, 2004, from the Web site of the U.S. Census Bureau (http://www.census.gov/population/www/cen2000/briefs.html).

U.S. Congress, Office of Technology Assessment. (1988). *Power on! New tools for teaching and learning,* OTA-SET-379. Washington, DC: U.S. Government Printing Office.

U.S. Department of Education. (2002). *To assure the free appropriate education of all children with disabilities: Twenty-fourth annual report to Congress on the implementation of the Individuals with Disabilities Education Act.* Washington, DC: Author.

U.S. Department of Education. (2003). IDEA Part B Child Count (2002). In *Data Tables for OSEP State Reported Data.* Retrieved March 1, 2005, from www.ideadata.org/tables26th/ar_aa15.htm

U.S. Department of Education. (2004). *The Individuals with Disabilities Education Improvement Act.* Washington, DC: Author.

U.S. Department of Education, Office of Special Education Programs. (1996). *Eighteenth annual report to Congress on the implementation of the Individuals with Disabilities Education Act.* Washington, DC: U.S. Government Printing Office.

U.S. Department of Education, Office of Special Education Programs. (1999). *Twenty-first annual report to Congress on the implementation of the Individual with Disabilities Education Act.* Washington, DC: U.S. Government Printing Office.

U.S. Department of Education, Office of Special Education Programs. (2002). *Twenty-fourth annual report to Congress on the implementation of the Individuals with Disabilities Education Act.* Washington, DC: U.S. Government Printing Office.

U.S. Department of Education, Office of Special Education Programs. (2003). *Twenty-fourth annual report to Congress on the implementation of the Individual with Disabilities Education Act.* Washington, DC: U.S. Government Printing Office.

U.S. Department of Health and Human Services. (1990). *Task II: Federal programs for persons with disabilities.* Washington, DC: U.S. Government Printing Office.

Utley, C. A., Lowitzer, A. C., & Baumeister, A. A. (1987). A comparison of the AAMD's definition, eligibility criteria, and classification schemes with state departments of education guidelines. *Education and Training in Mental Retardation, 22,* 35–43.

Valdez, G., McNabb, M., Foertsch, M., Anderson, M., Hawkes, M., & Raack, L. (2000). *Computer-based technology and learning: Evolving uses and expectations.* Retrieved August 8, 2004, from the Web site of North Central Regional Educational Library (http://www.ncrel.org/).

Valenzuela, A. (1999). *Subtractive schooling: U.S. Mexican youth and the politics of caring.* New York: SUNY Press.

Van Houten, R., & Axelrod, S. (Eds.). (1993). *Behavior analysis and treatment.* New York: Plenum.

Vernon, P. E. (1950). *The structure of human abilities.* New York: Wiley.

Vernon-Levett, P. (1991). Head injuries in children. *Pediatric Trauma, 3,* 411–421.

Vincent, L. J., Poulsen, M. K., Cole, C. K., Woodruff, G., & Griffith, D. R. (1991). *Born substance abused, educationally vulnerable.* Reston, VA: Council for Exceptional Children.

Vollmer, T. R., Iwata, B. A., Zarcone, J. R., Smith, R. G., & Mazaleski, J. L. (1993). The role of attention in the treatment of attention-maintained self-injurious behavior: Noncontingent reinforcement and differential reinforcement of other behavior. *Journal of Applied Behavior Analysis, 26*(1), 9–21.

Voorhees, P. J. (1996). Travel training for persons with cognitive or physical disabilities: An overview. *NICHCY Transition Summary, 9,* 7–9.

Wagner, M., Newman, L., & Shaver, D. (1989). Report on procedures for the first wave of data collection (1987). *The National Longitudinal Transition Study of Special Education Students.* Menlo Park, CA: SRI International.

Walsh, F. (2002). A family resilience framework: Innovative practice applications. *Family Relations, 51,* 130–137.

Walther-Thomas, C., & Brownell, M. T. (1998). An interview with Dr. Mitchell Yell: Changes in IDEA regarding suspension and expulsion. *Intervention in School and Clinic, 34*(1), 46–49.

Warren, K. R., & Bast, R. J. (1988). Alcohol-related birth defects: An update. *Public Health Reports, 103,* 638–642.

Warren, S. F. (2003). *In favor of a name change.* Retrieved May 30, 2003, from the Web site of the American Association on Mental Retardation (www.aamr.org/Reading Room/con memo.shtml).

Warren, S. F., & Abbeduto, L. (1992). The relation of communication and language development to mental retardation. *American Journal on Mental Retardation, 97,* 125–130.

Watson, A. L., Franklin, M. E., Ingram, M. A., & Ellenberg, L. B. (1998). Alcohol and other drug abuse among persons with disabilities. *Journal of Applied Rehabilitation Counseling, 29*(2), 22–29.

Watson, J. (1993). Looking forward. *Gene, 135,* 309–315.

Watson v. City of Cambridge, 32 N.E. 864 (Mass. 1893).

W.B. v. Matula, 67 F. 3d 484 (3rd. Cir. 1995).

Webb, K. (2000). Sex chromosomal abnormalities in mental retardation. Unpublished manuscript, Lynchburg College.

Webb, S., Hochberg, M. S., & Sher, M. R. (1988). Fetal alcohol syndrome: Report of a case. *Journal of the American Dental Association, 116,* 196–198.

Wechsler, D. (1939). *The measurement of adult intelligence.* Baltimore: Williams & Wilkins.

Wechsler, D. (1949). *Wechsler intelligence scale for children.* San Antonio, TX: Psychological Corporation.

Wechsler, D. (1955). *Wechsler Adult Intelligence Scale.* San Antonio, TX: Psychological Corporation.

Wechsler, D. (1958). *The measurement and appraisal of adult intelligence* (4th ed.). Baltimore: Williams & Wilkins.

Wechsler, D. (1967). *Wechsler Preschool and Primary Scale of Intelligence.* San Antonio, TX: Psychological Corporation.

Wechsler, D. (1974). *Wechsler Intelligence Scale for Children, Revised.* San Antonio, TX: Psychological Corporation.

Wechsler, D. (1981). *Wechsler Adult Intelligence Scale, Revised.* San Antonio, TX: Psychological Corporation.

Wechsler, D. (1989). *Wechsler Preschool and Primary Scale of Intelligence, Revised.* San Antonio, TX: Psychological Corporation.

Wechsler, D. (1991a). *Wechsler Intelligence Scale for Children, 3rd Edition.* San Antonio, TX: Psychological Corporation.

Wechsler, D. (1991b). *Wechsler Intelligence Scale for Children, 3rd Edition: Manual.* San Antonio, TX: Psychological Corporation.

Wechsler, D. (1997). *Wechsler Adult Intelligence Scale, 3rd Edition.* San Antonio, TX: Psychological Corporation.

Wechsler, D. (2002). *Wechsler Preschool and Primary Scale of Intelligence, 3rd Edition.* San Antonio, TX: Psychological Corporation.

Wechsler, D. (2003). *Wechsler Intelligence Scale for Children, 4th Edition: Manual.* San Antonio, TX: Psychological Corporation.

Wehman, P. (1990). School-to-work: Elements of successful programs. *Teaching Exceptional Children, 23*(1), 40–43.

Wehman, P., Bricout, J., & Kregel, J. (2000). Supported employment in 2000: Changing the locus of control from agency to consumer. In M. L. Wehmeyer & J. R. Patton (Eds.), *Mental retardation in the 21st century* (pp. 115–150). Austin, TX: PRO-ED.

Wehman, P., Brooke, V., West, M., Targett, P., Green, H., Inge, K. J., & Kregel, J. (1998). Barriers to competitive employment for persons with disabilities. In P. Wehman (Ed.), *Developing transition plans* (pp. 5–23), Austin, TX: PRO-ED.

Wehman, P., & Kregel, J. (1985). A supported work approach to competitive employment of individuals with moderate and severe handicaps. *Journal of the Association for Persons with Severe Handicaps, 10,* 3–11.

Wehman, P., & Kregel, J. (1995). At the crossroads: Supported employment a decade later. *Journal of the Association for Persons with Severe Handicaps, 20,* 286–299.

Wehman, P., & Kregel, J. (Eds.). (2004). *Functional curriculum for elementary, middle, and secondary age students with special needs* (2nd ed.). Austin, TX: PRO-ED.

Wehman, P., Parent, W., Wood, W., Talbert, C. M., Jasper, C., Miller, et al. (1989). From school to competitive employment for young adults with mental retardation: Transition in practice. *Career Development for Exceptional Individuals, 12,* 97–105.

Wehman, P., Revell, W. G., & Brooke, V. (2003). Competitive employment: Has it become the "first choice" yet? *Journal of Disability Policy Studies, 14,* 163–173.

Wehman, P., Revell, W. G., & Kregel, J. (1997). Supported employment: A decade of rapid growth and impact. In P. Wehman, J. Kregel, & M. West (Eds.), *Supported employment research: Expanding competitive employment opportunities for persons with significant disabilities.* Richmond: Virginia Commonwealth University, Rehabilitation Research and Training Center.

Wehman, P., Revell, W. G., & Kregel, J. (1998). Supported employment: A decade of rapid growth and impact. *American Rehabilitation, 24,* 31–43.

Wehmeyer, M. (1993). Self-determination as an educational outcome. *Impact, 6*(4), 6–7, 16–17, 26.

Wehmeyer, M., & Metzler, C. (1995). How self-determined are people with mental retardation? The National Consumer Survey. *Mental Retardation, 33,* 111–119.

Wehmeyer, M. L. (1994). Perceptions of self-determination and psychological empowerment of adolescents with mental retardation. *Education and Training in Mental Retardation, 29,* 9–21.

Wehmeyer, M. L. (1998). National survey of the use of assistive technology by adults who are retarded. *Mental Retardation, 36*(1), 44–51.

Wehmeyer, M. L., Field, S., Doren, B., Jones, B., & Mason, C. (2004). Self-determination and student involvement in standards-based reform. *Exceptional Children, 70,* 413–425.

Wehmeyer, M. L., Morningstar, M., & Husted, D. (1999). *Family involvement in transition planning and implementation.* Austin, TX: PRO-ED.

Wehmeyer, M. L., Palmer, S. B., Agran, M., Mithaug, D. E., & Martin, J. E. (2000). Promoting causal agency: The self-determined learning model of instruction. *Exceptional Children, 66,* 439–453.

Weissman, R. A., & Littman, D. C. (1996). Early intervention. In P. J. McLaughlin & P. Wehman (Eds.), *Mental retardation and developmental disabilities* (pp. 29–48). Austin, TX: PRO-ED.

West, J. F., Idol, L., & Cannon, G. (1989). *Collaboration in the schools.* Austin, TX: PRO-ED.

Westling, D. L. (1986). *Introduction to mental retardation.* Upper Saddle River, NJ: Merrill/Prentice Hall.

Westling, D. L., & Fox, L. (2000). *Teaching students with severe disabilities.* Upper Saddle River, NJ: Merrill/Prentice Hall.

White, B. L. (1975). *The first three years.* Upper Saddle River, NJ: Merrill/Prentice Hall.

White, K. R., Bush, D., & Casto, G. (1986). Let the past be prologue: Learning from previous reviews of early intervention efficacy research. *Journal of Special Education, 19*(4), 417–428.

Whitman, T. L. (1990). Self-regulation and mental retardation. *American Journal on Mental Retardation, 94,* 347–362.

Widaman, K. F., & McGrew, K. S. (1996). The structure of adaptive behavior. In J. W. Jacobson & J. A. Mulick (Eds.), *Manual of diagnosis and professional practice in mental retardation* (pp. 97–110). Washington, DC: American Psychological Association.

Widaman, K. F., Reise, S. P., & Clatfelter, D. L. (1994). *Assessing the measurement structure of adaptive behavior: Factor analytic versus item response theory approaches.* Paper presented at the Gatlinburg Conference on Research and Theory in Mental Retardation and Developmental Disabilities, Gatlinburg, TN.

Widaman, K. F., Stacy, A. W., & Borthwick-Duffy, S. A. (1993). Construct validity of dimensions of adaptive behavior: A multitrait-multimethod evaluation. *American Journal on Mental Retardation, 98,* 219–234.

Widerstrom, A. H., Mowder, B. A., & Sandall, S. R. (1991). *At-risk and handicapped newborns and infants.* Upper Saddle River, NJ: Prentice Hall.

Wilbur, H. (1976). Eulogy to Edouard Seguin: Remarks made at Seguin's funeral, Clamecy, France, 1880. Reprinted in M. Rosen, G. R. Clark, & M. S. Kivitz (Eds.), *The history of mental retardation: Collected papers* (Vol. 1, pp. 181–187). Baltimore: University Park Press. (Original work published 1880)

Wilcox, B., & Bellamy, G. T. (1982). *Design of high school programs for severely handicapped students.* Baltimore: Brookes.

Will, M. C. (1984). *OSERS programming for the transition of youth with disabilities: Bridges from school to working life.* Washington, DC: U.S. Department of Education, Office of Special Education and Rehabilitative Services.

Williams, C. (1993). Vulerable victims? A current awareness of the victimization of people with learning disabilities. *Disability, Handicap, and Society, 8,* 161–172.

Winking, D. L., DeStefano, L., & Rusch, F. R. (1988). *Supported employment in Illinois: Job coach issues.* Champaign: University of Illinois, Secondary Transition Intervention Effectiveness Institute. (ERIC Document Reproduction Service No. ED295407)

Wolery, M., Bailey, D. B., & Sugai, G. (1988). *Effective teaching: Principles and procedures of applied behavior analysis with exceptional students.* Boston: Allyn & Bacon.

Wolery, M., & Fleming, L. A. (1993). Implementing individualized curricula in integrated settings. In C. A. Peck, S. L. Odom, & D. D. Bricker (Eds.), *Integrating young children with disabilities into community programs: Ecological perspectives on research and implementation* (pp. 109–132). Baltimore: Brookes.

Wolfe, P. S., & Kubina, R. M. (2004). Functional academics. In P. Wehman & J. Kregel (Eds.), *Functional curriculum for elementary, middle, and secondary age students with special needs* (2nd ed., p. 118). Austin, TX: PRO-ED.

Wolfensberger, W. (1972). *The principle of normalization in human services.* Toronto: National Institute on Mental Retardation.

Wolfensberger, W. (1985). An overview of social role valorization and some reflections on elderly mentally retarded persons. In M. P. Janicki & H. M. Wisniewski (Eds.), *Expanding systems of service delivery for persons with developmental disabilities* (pp. 127–148). Baltimore: Brookes.

Wolraich, M. L. (Ed.). (1996). *Disorders of development and learning: A practical guide to assessment and management* (2nd ed.). St. Louis: Mosby.

Woodcock, R., McGrew, K., & Mather, N. (2001). *Woodcock-Johnson III.* Itasca, IL: Riverside Publishing.

Woodward, W. M. (1963). The application of Piaget's theory to research in mental deficiency. In N. R. Ellis (Ed.), *Handbook of mental deficiency: Psychological theory and research* (pp. 297–324). New York: McGraw-Hill.

Woodward, W. M. (1979). Piaget's theory and the study of mental retardation. In N. R. Ellis (Ed.), *Handbook of mental deficiency: Psychological theory and research* (2nd ed., pp. 169–195). Hillsdale, NJ: Erlbaum.

World Health Organization. (1978). *International classification of diseases* (9th ed.). Washington, DC: Author.

World Health Organization. (1993). *International statistical classification of diseases and related health problems* (10th ed.). Geneva: Author.

World Health Organization. (2001). *International classification of functioning, disability, and health (ICF).* Geneva: Author.

Wright, B., King, M. P., & National Conference of State Legislatures Task Force on Developmental Disabilities. (1991). *Americans with developmental disabilities.* Washington, DC: National Conference of State Legislatures Task Force on Developmental Disabilities.

Wyatt v. Hardin, Civil Action No. 3195-N (M.D. Ala. 1975).

Wyatt v. Ireland, Civil Action No. 3195-N (M.D. Ala. 1979).

Wyatt v. Stickney, 344 F. Supp. 387, 344 F. Supp. 373 (M.D. Ala. 1972), 334 F. Supp. 1341, 325 F. Supp. 781 (M.D. Ala. 1971), 772 *aff'd* sub nom. *Wyatt v. Aderholt,* 503 F.2d, 1305 (5th Cir. 1974).

Yell, M. L. (1998). *The law and special education.* Upper Saddle River, NJ: Merrill/Prentice Hall.

Yell, M. L., Rogers, D., & Rogers, E. L. (1998). The legal history of special education: What a long strange trip it's been! *Remedial and Special Education, 19,* 219–228.

Yell M. L., & Shriner, J. G. (1997). The IDEA amendments of 1997: Implications for special and general education teachers, administrators, and teacher trainers. *Focus on Exceptional Children, 30,* 1–20.

Youngberg v. Romeo, 102 S. Ct. 2452 (1982).

Ysseldyke, J. E., & Algozzine, B. (1990). *Introduction to special education.* Boston: Houghton Mifflin.

Yuan, S. (2003). Seeing with new eyes: Metaphors of family experience. *Mental Retardation, 3,* 207–211.

Zantal-Weiner, K. (1987). *Child abuse and handicapped children.* Reston, VA: ERIC Clearinghouse on Handicapped and Gifted Children.

Zeaman, D., & House, B. J. (1963). The role of attention in retardate discrimination learning. In N. R. Ellis (Ed.), *Handbook of mental deficiency: Psychological theory and research* (pp. 159–223). Hillsdale, NJ: Erlbaum.

Zeaman, D., & House, B. J. (1979). A review of attention theory. In N. R. Ellis (Ed.), *Handbook of mental deficiency: Psychological theory and research* (2nd ed., pp. 63–120). Hillsdale, NJ: Erlbaum.

Zervigon-Hakes, A. (1995). Translating research findings into large-scale public programs and policies. *The Future of Children: Long-Term Outcomes of Early Childhood Programs, 6*(3), 175–191.

Zetlin, A. G., & Turner, J. L. (1985). Transition from adolescence to adulthood: Perspectives of mentally retarded individuals and their families. *American Journal of Mental Deficiency, 89*(6), 570–579.

Zhang, D. (2001). Self-determination and inclusion: Are students with mild mental retardation more self-determined in regular classrooms? *Education and Training in Mental Retardation and Developmental Disabilities, 36*(4), 357–362.

Zigler, E. (1973). The retarded child as a whole person. In D. K. Routh (Ed.), *The experimental psychology of mental retardation* (pp. 231–322). Chicago: Aldine.

Zigler, E. (1999). The individual with mental retardation as a whole person. In E. Zigler & D. Bennett-Gates (Eds.), *Personality development in individuals with mental retardation* (pp. 1–16). Cambridge, UK: Cambridge University Press.

Zigler, E., Balla, D. A., & Hodapp, R. (1984). On the definition and classification of mental retardation. *American Journal of Mental Deficiency, 89*, 215–230.

Zigman, W. S., Schupf, N., Lubin, R. A., & Silverman, W. P. (1987). Premature regression of adults with Down syndrome. *American Journal on Mental Retardation, 92*, 161–168.

Zirpoli, T. (1986). Child abuse and children with handicaps. *Remedial and Special Education, 7*(2), 39–48.

Zucker, S. H., & Polloway, E. A. (1987). Issues in identification and assessment in mental retardation. *Education and Training in Mental Retardation, 22*, 69–76.

Name Index